CHRONOLOGY OF AMERICAN INDIAN HISTORY

THE TRAIL OF THE WIND

LIZ SONNEBORN

Facts On File, Inc.

Chronology of American Indian History: The Trail of the Wind

Facts On File, Inc.
11 Penn Plaza
New York, NY 10001

Library of Congress Cataloging-in-Publication Data

Sonneborn, Liz.
   Chronology of American Indian history : the trail of the wind / Liz Sonneborn.
      p.   cm.
   Includes bibliographical references and index.
   ISBN 0-8160-3977-1 (hardcover)
   1. Indians of North America—History—Chronology. I. Title.
E77.S72   2001
973.04'97'00202—dc21   00-062255

Facts On File books are available at special discounts when purchased in bulk quantities for businesses, associations, institutions, or sales promotions. Please call our Special Sales Department in New York at 212/967-8800 or 800/322-8755.

You can find Facts On File on the World Wide Web at http://www.factsonfile.com

Cover design by Cathy Rincon
Text design by Joan M. Toro
Map on page viii by Dale Williams

Printed in the United States of America.

MP FOF 10 9 8 7 6 5 4 3 2 1

This book is printed on acid-free paper.

It was the wind
That gave them life.
It was the wind
That comes our of our mouths
Now that gives us life.
When this ceases to blow we die.
In the skin at the tips of our fingers
We see the trail of the wind;
It shows us the wind blew
where our ancestors were created.

—A Navajo song recorded in Washington
Matthews's *Navajo Legends* (1897)

Contents

TRADITIONAL TRIBAL LOCATIONS

BEFORE 1492
EMERGENCE

According to oral tradition, the Navajo (Dineh) came into being by emerging through three worlds—the Black World, the Blue-Green World, and the Yellow World—before finally reaching the Glittering World, the one they still inhabit in the American Southwest. This story, told from generation to generation for hundreds of years, is believed by some scholars to confirm their own theories of how the Navajo came to live in their homeland. According to archaeological evidence, the early Navajo traveled through the Arctic to central Canada and on to the Rocky Mountain region before settling in the lands they occupy today. In their creation story, the Black World seems to correspond to the cold, harsh environment of the Arctic, the Blue-Green World to the Canadian forests, and the Yellow World to the mountains and plains on the Rockies' eastern slope.

Like the Navajo's, the ancestors of all Indians experienced a southward migration in the distant past, according to the Bering Strait Theory. The theory holds that during the last ice age, the waters of the strait separating Siberia from Alaska withdrew, exposing between Asia and North America a land bridge that ancient hunters unwittingly crossed while following herds of large game. (The ancestors of the Inuit and Aleut are believed to have arrived in North America during a much later migration, perhaps navigating the strait in skin boats.) Although generally accepted by archaeologists and other scholars, some Indians contest the Bering Strait Theory, observing that their creation stories hold that their people were created in their traditional homelands.

Once in North America, early Indians fanned across the continent, following herds of large game they hunted for food. Beginning in about 11,000 B.C., a warming climate forced changes in their way of life. With rising temperatures, game animals such as the mammoth and mastodon began to die out. At the same time, new plants and animals emerged that were better equipped to survive in the changing environment. Indians themselves adapted by taking advantage of these new food sources. Living as gatherers and small-game hunters, they were able to inhabit all reaches of North America by about 9000 B.C.

About two thousand years later, Indians in Mexico developed still another means of increasing their food stores. At that time, they started cultivating wild plants, such as beans and pumpkins. Their early farming experiments began to reap greater benefits when they started growing an early variety of maize, or Indian corn, in about 5000 B.C. After several thousand years of experimentation, Mexican Indians created a hearty hybrid corn plant that produced large enough crops to change significantly their way of life. Coming to rely increasingly on farmed foods, they gradually shifted away from hunting and gathering and toward a settled agricultural lifestyle. As farmers, the Indians had a more reliable source of food; their populations could grow larger, with less chance of famine. The cultivation of maize thus made possible the great ancient civilizations of Mesoamerica, including the Olmec (ca. 1500 B.C. to A.D. 300), the Maya (ca. A.D. 300 to A.D. 1500), the Toltec (ca. A.D. 900 to A.D. 1200), and the Aztec (ca. A.D. 1430 to A.D. 1517).

As the knowledge of farming spread northward, it had an equally significant impact on Indians in what is now the United States and Canada. In areas where farming was difficult or where other food sources were extremely plentiful (for instance, fish in the Pacific Northwest and wild plant foods in present-day California), people continued to live in small tribal groups. In the Midwest and Southwest, however, agriculture allowed Indians to develop urban areas as large and sophisticated as those in Mexico.

In the Midwest emerged the Adena (ca. 1000 B.C. to A.D. 200), the Hopewell (ca. 200 B.C. to A.D. 400), and the Mississippian cultural traditions (ca. A.D. 700 to A.D. 1550). The early peoples of these cultures are now commonly known as the Mound Builders, for the massive burial mounds they constructed in their ceremonial and trade centers. For instance, Cahokia, the largest Mississippi urban center, had a population of more than 20,000 and featured the enormous Monk's Mound, which was larger than the Great Pyramid of Giza, in Egypt. The presence of such massive structures puzzled non-Indian archaeologists of the nineteenth century. Regarding the Indians of the Mississippi valley as too primitive

to have constructed the great mounds, they developed a succession of bizarre theories, attributing the structures to Phoenicians, Egyptians, Aztec, Danes, and Hindus.

In the Southwest, farming allowed for the development of the Mogollon (ca. A.D. 200 to A.D. 1400), the Hohokam (ca. A.D. 400 to A.D. 1500), and the Anasazi (200 B.C. to A.D. 1400) cultures. These early peoples constructed large adobe houses in villages whose burgeoning populations were sustained by agricultural products and items obtained through trade with other Indians—sometimes groups living more than a thousand miles away. The greatest trade network was established by the Anasazi, who are also known as cliff dwellers, because of their large adobe structures they built in the sides of mountains. At their height, the Anasazi lived in large pueblo settlements along Chaco Canyon, an area that served as their trade and administrative center. More than 250 miles of road connected outlying pueblos to the canyon, allowing for an easy flow of food and trade goods between Anasazi communities.

By the late 15th century, the great southwestern civilizations had largely disappeared. Possibly due to climactic changes, it seems to have become impossible for the Indians of these cultures to farm enough food to feed their growing settlements. Over time, they abandoned their urban centers to live in smaller tribal groups, like those of most other Indians in North America. Despite their small size, these groups over thousands of years had created highly sophisticated methods of surviving and even thriving in the wide variety of environments the continent offered—from the forbidding deserts of the Great Basin to the lush forests of the Eastern Woodlands to the frozen tundra of the Arctic. As Christopher Columbus set his sights westward, however, the Indian peoples of North America were about to face a new and possibly even greater challenge—protecting the ways of life they had so laboriously developed from an enemy often intent on destroying them.

ca. 25,000 to 12,000 B.C.

Ancient humans migrate from Asia to North America.

According to archaeologists, during the ice ages, Beringia—a 60-mile land bridge between Siberia and Alaska—is periodically exposed as the formation of glaciers lowers the waters of the Bering Sea. Ancient Asian hunters following herds of mammoths, bison, and reindeer easily transverse Beringia in a series of migrations and become the first residents of the North American continent. The ancestors of modern Indians, these people head south over time, eventually populating areas throughout the Americas.

Archaeologists disagree about when the first of these migrations took place. While some hold they began as long as 40,000 years ago, most place the earliest date of human habitation in North America between 27,000 and 14,000 years ago, with the majority favoring the later dates.

Many Indians dispute the Bering Strait Theory as a whole. Although it is supported by geological and biological evidence, the theory contradicts the creation stories of many Indian tribes maintaining that the first humans were created in their homelands.

"There are immense contemporary political implications to [the Bering Strait] theory which makes it difficult for many people to surrender. Considerable residual guilt remains over the manner in which the Western Hemisphere was invaded and settled by Europeans.... People want to believe that the Western Hemisphere ... was a vacant, unexploited, fertile land.... [and] that American Indians were not original inhabitants of the Western Hemisphere but latecomers who had barely unpacked before Columbus came knocking on the door. If Indians had arrived only a few centuries earlier, they had no *real* claim to land that could not be swept away by European discovery."

—Vine Deloria Jr. in *Red Earth, White Lies* (1995)

ca. 17,600 or 10,000 B.C.

Early Indians begin occupying the Meadowcroft site.

Meadowcroft, south of what is now Pittsburgh, Pennsylvania, is one of the earliest known settlements of ancient humans in North America. Meadowcroft features an enormous rock shelter that covers nearly one thousand square feet of land. The natural structure provides protection for its inhabitants, while the large animal population in the area offers ample food sources. Archaeologists agree that the site was definitely occupied by 10,000 B.C. Radiocarbon dates for some objects excavated from the site in the 1970s lead some scientists to believe humans lived at Meadowcroft as early as 17,600 B.C.—a theory that challenges the consensus view that the first Indians arrived in North Americans about 14,000 years ago (see entry for CA. 25,000 TO 12,000 B.C.).

ca. 12,000 B.C.

The Bering land bridge is engulfed in water.

As the last ice age draws to an end, warming global temperatures begin to melt the great glaciers that cover much of the earth. The melting ice unleashes torrents of water over the earth's surface, causing sea levels to rise. As water pours over the Bering land bridge (see entry for CA. 25,000 TO 12,000 B.C.), the land route between Asia and North America disappears. Some immigrants who crossed over the bridge retreat back to Siberia before the process is complete. Others are trapped in their new homeland. These people and their descendants will gradually move south to more hospitable environments and eventually populate the entire North and South American continents.

ca. 10,900 to 9000 B.C.

Large wild game species become extinct.

The mammoth, mastodon, giant sloth, and other big game species begin to die out throughout North America. Their extinction leads to the end of the Clovis cultural tradition (see entry for CA. 9200 TO 8900 B.C.), in which early Indians relied on hunting large game animals for their survival. The reason these game species disappeared is unclear. One prominent theory holds that they were overhunted, while another contends that changing climate conditions as the last ice age came to an end, killed off the animals' food supply, and dried up their watering areas.

ca. 9500 to 5000 B.C.

The Paleo-Indian tradition emerges in eastern and central North America.

The first people in North America develop the Paleo-Indian tradition. The Paleo-Indians are hunters of large wild mammals, such as mammoths, mastodons, and giant sloths. Within the tradition emerges several cultures, including the Clovis (see entry for CA. 9200 TO 8900 B.C.) and Folsom (see entry for CA. 8500 TO 8000 B.C.) cultures, which are characterized by innovations in the crafting of projectile points—the stone tips

on Paleo-Indian hunting tools. The Paleo-Indian tradition will slowly fade as the climate of North America grows warmer. The rising temperatures will lead to the demise of many large game animals (see entry for CA. 10,900 TO 9000 B.C.) and at the same time offer early Indians new species of flora and fauna to use as food sources (see entry for CA. 8000 TO 4000 B.C.).

ca. 9200 to 8900 B.C.

The Clovis culture emerges in central North America.

Named after an excavation site near present-day Clovis, New Mexico, the Clovis culture of early Indian people develops throughout central North America. These people are identified by three-to-four-inch projectile points crafted from chipped flint and fluted at the lower end. (These are now known as Clovis points.) The fluting makes it easy for Clovis hunters to create simple spears by attaching points to wooden poles. Mammoths are the preferred prey, but these roving hunters also stalk caribou, bison, antelopes, and sloths. The Clovis tradition disappears with the dying out of the mammoths and other prehistoric big-game species (see entry for CA. 10,900 TO 9000 B.C.).

ca. 9000 B.C.

Humans settle all of North America.

Only several thousands of years after humans began migrating from Asia over the Bering land bridge (see entry for CA. 25,000 TO 12,000 B.C.), their descendants are found in all regions of North America, as they have learned to adapt to a wide variety of environments. These Paleo-Indians live in small, isolated bands of about 15 to 50 people. They survive by gathering wild plant foods and hunting game, using simple tools.

> "For a long time everyone spoke the same language, but suddenly people began to speak in different tongues. [The Creator] Kulsu, however, could speak all of the languages, so he called his people together and told them the names of the animals in their own language, taught them to get food, and gave them their laws and rituals. Then he sent each tribe to a different place to live."
> —from a Maidu Indian creation myth

ca. 9000 to 5000 B.C.

Early Indians in the Northwest develop the Old Cordilleran culture.

The Old Cordilleran cultures emerges among the Indians in the Columbia River valley of what are now Washington and Oregon. The culture is characterized by varied strategies for obtaining food. Old Cordilleran Indians use projectile points in the shape of willow leaves for hunting small animals, make fishhooks, and craft other simple tools to prepare wild plants for eating. These peoples are most likely the ancestors of modern Indian groups, such as the Cayuse, Chinook, and Klamath.

ca. 8500 to 8000 B.C.

The Folsom culture develops in the Great Plains region.

In the Great Plains and portions of the Southwest, Paleo-Indians create a cultural tradition based on bison hunting. Unlike many other large game animals (see entry for CA. 10,900 TO 9000 B.C.), the

Folsom Indians' prey survived changing weather conditions in North America by becoming grass-eaters who feed on the grasslands that grew up on the Great Plains. Folsom hunters develop shorter, narrower projectile points than did their Clovis predecessors (see entry for CA. 9200 TO 8900 B.C.). With fluting on both sides, these delicate points are also much more carefully crafted, making the Folsom peoples perhaps the most skilled stone workers in all of ancient North America. In addition to stalking bison on foot, small bands of Folsom hunters often come together to join in communal hunts, in which they drive herds into natural enclosures, then slaughter the trapped animals with their spears.

ca. 8000 B.C.

Paleo-Indians occupy the Lindermeier site.

Early Indians of the Folsom tradition (see entry for CA. 8500 TO 8000 B.C.) settle in what is now Lindermeier, Colorado, which will become one of the first Paleo-Indian sites to be excavated. The people of Lindermeier spend much of their time in small groups moving from place to place hunting wild bison herds. These roaming bands range hundreds of miles from the Lindermeier, but they regularly return to the well-watered site and join in bison drives, in which, working together, they can kill large numbers of animals at one time. In addition to the distinctive Folsom projectile points, the inhabitants of Lindermeier make thin knives, drills for punching holes in wood and stone, and scrapers for preparing animal hides. Some of these are made from obsidian, a volcanic rock found more than three hundred miles away. These objects testify to the Lindermeier Indians' participation in a large network of trade.

ca. 8000 to 4000 B.C.

The ecology of North America is transformed by a warming climate.

The end of the last ice age causes dramatic changes in the North American continent. As the atmosphere of the earth becomes warmer, runoff from melting glaciers creates the Great Lakes, the Mississippi River, and other waterways. Trees blanket the East, grasslands sprout up in the Plains, and dry deserts cover much of the West. This transformation provides early Indians with more comfortable environments as well as new plant and animal food sources.

ca. 8000 to 1000 B.C.

The Archaic tradition replaces Paleo-Indian ways.

With rising temperatures, the ecology of North America changes dramatically (see entry for CA. 8000 TO 4000 B.C.), prompting equally significant changes in the way ancient Indians live. Throughout the continent, the hunting way of life of the Paleo-Indians (see entry for CA. 9500 TO 5000 B.C.) is replaced by the Archaic tradition, characterized by a greater variation in strategies for getting food. The Archaic Indians adapt to a wide variety of the new environments and learn to exploit the food sources available in each. Depending on their surroundings, some come to rely on wild plant foods, some on fishing, some on hunting, and some on a combination of these activities. These varied food-getting methods allow the Archaic Indians to protect themselves from food shortages more effectively than their Paleo-Indian ancestors could.

In the east, the Archaic tradition will be replaced by the Woodland tradition (see entry for CA. 1000 B.C. TO 1600 A.D.), which is distinguished by a reliance on farming, the crafting of pottery, and the construction of funerary mounds. In other areas, such as California and the Pacific Northwest, where agriculture will play a less important role, the Archaic way of life will survive up to the period of first contact with non-Indians.

ca. 7000 B.C.

Farming begins in Mesoamerica.

At sites in Tamaulipas, Tehuacan, and the Valley of Oaxaca in present-day Mexico, early Indians begin to experiment with cultivating plants found in the wild, such as beans, pumpkins, peppers, and gourds. At this stage, the Indians' primitive farming methods produce only a small amount of food—possibly representing as little as 5 percent of their diet. Their primary food sources remain hunting wild game and gathering wild plants. (See also entry for CA. 5000 B.C.)

ca. 7000 B.C. to A.D. 1

Cochise Desert culture emerges in the American Southwest.

Early Indians in what is now Arizona and western New Mexico develop the Cochise Desert culture. These people travel in small bands, moving from place to place and living in caves and rock shelters. Unlike the people of the Clovis (see entry for CA. 9200 TO 8900 B.C.) and Folsom (see entry for CA. 8500 TO 8000 B.C.) cultures to the east, the Cochise people rely on gathering wild plant foods rather than on hunting. The earliest Cochise sites include such tools as scrapers and milling stones for grinding seeds. In later settlements, projectile points indicate that the Cochise Indians will become more interested in hunting. Early forms of maize at these sites also suggest that they will make attempts at farming. The Cochise Desert culture may provide a base for later, more sophisticated southwestern farming cultures, such as the Mogollon (see entry for CA. 200 TO 1400) and Hohokam (see entry for CA. 400 TO 1500).

ca. 6800 B.C.

Anangula becomes the first settlement on the Aleutian Islands.

The village of Anangula is settled on an islet off Umnak Island in the eastern Aleutians. Its inhabitants are the first known occupants of the Aleutian Islands. Most likely a permanent settlement for fishermen and hunters of sea mammals, Anangula features large oval-shaped dwellings about 15 feet in length. Artifacts uncovered at Anangula include several sizes of simple blade tools.

ca. 6400 B.C. to A.D. 1200

The Koster site is occupied.

One of the best studied archaeological sites in the American Midwest, Koster (located in Greene County, Illinois) is originally a temporary camp occupied by people of the Early Archaic tradition (see entry for CA. 8000 TO 1000 B.C.). These first occupants hunted deer and harvested mussels and wild seeds. By 5600 B.C., the site is used year-round. A permanent village established there in about 3900 B.C. has a population of as many as 150 people, who subsist on a wide variety of wild game, fish, and plants. The largest Koster village, occupied from A.D. 800 to 1000, has about one thousand inhabitants and covers 25 acres.

ca. 5000 B.C.

Mexico Indians begin growing maize as a food crop.

In present-day Mexico, Indians begin selecting and planting seeds of a primitive species of maize (Indian corn). This early domestic corn may have been developed from a wild corn plant or from *teosinte,* a related wild grass. Each plant yields only one inch-long ear with some fifty small, edible kernels. The presence of grinding stones at ancient sites suggests that most of this maize is eaten in the form of meal. (See also entry for CA. 1500 B.C.)

ca. 4000 B.C.

Northwest Indians learn to preserve fish.

The peoples living along the Pacific coast of what is now the northwestern United States and southwestern Canada develop methods of drying and storing fish. This capability allows them to preserve the thousands of salmon and other fish caught in the spring runs for use at other times of the year. An example of early North Americans' increasing skill at taking advantage of the natural resources in their lands, the Northwest Indians' fish-preservation technique leads them to become more reliant on fishing than on hunting.

ca. 4000 B.C. to A.D. 300

Hunters use Head-Smashed-In as a buffalo jump.

At the Head-Smashed-In site in what is now western Alberta, Canada, bands of early Indians come together for communal hunts, now called buffalo jumps. Popular buffalo jump sites such as Head-Smashed-In feature high cliffs. Groups of hunters initiate a buffalo stampede by screaming and chasing a frightened herd down a long drive toward the cliff and force the animals to run off the edge. Possibly annual events, successful jumps could provide hunters with hundreds of killed animals at one time. Near Head-Smashed-In is a designated area where people gather to strip the carcasses, remove the meat, and process the hides so that they can be used for clothing and shelter.

"At a signal, the hunters rose from their concealment, shouting and yelling, and waving robes to frighten the herd. Spears began to fall among the animals, and at once the bison began a wild stampede toward the south. . . . Animal after animal pressed from behind, spurred on by the shower of spears and the shouts of the Indians now in full pursuit. . . . In a matter of seconds, the arroyo was filled to overflowing with a writhing, bellowing mass of bison, forming a living bridge over which a few animals escaped."

—archaeologist Joe Ben Wheat, describing a buffalo jump kill

A diorama depicting a buffalo jump on the northern Great Plains. By inciting a buffalo stampede and steering the rampaging animals over a cliff, early hunters could kill hundreds of buffalo at one time. *(Courtesy of Montana Historical Society, Helena)*

ca. 3000 to 2500 B.C.

The Old Copper culture emerges in the Great Lakes region.

Archaic Indians (see entry for CA. 8000 TO 1000 B.C.) in the Great Lakes region develop the Old Copper culture after discovering deposits of copper on the shore of Lake Superior. Using simple tools, these people are able to dig out the copper easily in chunks and sheets. They learn to shape the metal, first by chipping and hammering, later by heating the copper to make it more malleable. From this raw material the Indians create tools and weapons, such as projectile points and ax blades, as well as shiny bracelets, beads, and other ornaments. These items will become valued as luxury goods in a trade network that will develop throughout the Eastern Woodlands (see entry for CA. 1000 B.C. TO A.D. 200).

ca. 3000 to 1000 B.C.

The ancestors of the Aleut and Inuit arrive in North America.

Thousands of years after early peoples traveled from Asia to North America across the Bering land bridge (see entry for CA. 25,000 TO 12,000 B.C.), the ancestors of the Aleut and Inuit arrive in the continent. These people probably used small skin or wooden boats to cross the Bering Strait (the waterway that covered the Bering land bridge once the polar ice caps melted at the end of the last ice age). These newcomers will eventually settle throughout the Arctic and on the Aleutian Islands off the southwest coast of present-day Alaska. Because their ancestors arrived in North America far later, the modern Aleut and Inuit are more closely related to Asians than Indians are.

ca. 2500 B.C.

Eastern Archaic Indians begin growing crops.

Early Indians of the Eastern Woodlands begin farming gourds and squash. Seeds and knowledge of how to grow these plants were probably brought north from Mexico (see entry for CA. 7000 B.C.). With the ability to grow and store foods, eastern Indians no longer have to rely exclusively on hunting and gathering for their survival. Farming also marks the beginnings of tribal life, as groups band together to plant and harvest the crops, store their yields, and protect their stores from theft by other peoples.

ca. 2000 B.C.

The cultures of the early Aleut and Inuit begin to diverge.

About 1,000 years after they arrive in North America (see entry CA. 3000 TO 1000 B.C.), the ancestors of the modern Aleut and Inuit develop distinct culture. The early Aleut settle the 1,400-mile Aleutian Island chain off the coast of what is now Alaska. The Aleutian environment is warmer, windier, and wetter than that of the frozen Arctic of the Inuit. The Aleut share with Inuit an expertise in hunting, but their village life, in which people are ranked by social position and wealth, more closely resembles that of the Indians of the northwest coast of the present-day United States.

ca. 2000 to 1000 B.C.

Southwestern Indians begin growing maize.

Early Indians in the southwest begin to plant fields of maize, which was first domesticated in Mexico at least three millennia earlier (see entry for CA. 5000 B.C.). Initially, maize supplements food obtained by hunting and gathering. Southwestern Indians soon become more dependent on the crop as they start growing a hybrid species, crossed with wild grass (see entry for CA. 1500 B.C.). The new species, which produces far larger ears with more rows of kernels, spreads quickly through the region.

Over time the southwestern Indians develop newer, even hardier breeds that grow well with little moisture. They also learn to divert streams to water their crops. By about A.D. 1, an expanding population makes agriculture a more attractive food strategy than hunting and gathering. Maize farming, therefore, transforms the Indians' way of life. Instead of living in small, mobile bands, they begin to settle in larger, more permanent villages.

ca. 1800 to 500 B.C.

Poverty Point is settled in Louisiana.

Indians begin building a massive settlement at Poverty Point, overlooking the floodplain of the Mississippi River, in what is now northeastern Louisiana. The habitation area covers nearly 500 acres and includes, at its height, as many as 600 dwellings occupied by some 5,000 people. Located near the confluence of six rivers, the Poverty Point site serves as a major trading center for three hundred years. Exotic materials such as copper, argillite, and quartz—some from as far away as the Great Lakes region—are traded there.

Poverty Point also features great earthworks. Most prominent are mounds about 82 feet wide and nine feet tall that form six concentric semicircles. The massive construction will be the largest in North American for the next thousand years. Why the mounds were built and how they were used remains a mystery.

ca. 1500 B.C.

Mexican farmers develop an improved species of maize.

By crossing primitive species of maize (see entry for CA. 5000 B.C.) with wild grass plants, Mexican Indians create a hybrid plant that is far superior as a food source. The new species offers larger ears, covered with protective husks, and with many more kernels than earlier forms of maize. Exported from Mexico, this heartier and more productive plant will allow Indian groups to the north to adopt settled, largely agricultural ways of life (see entry for CA. 2000 TO 1000 B.C.).

1500 B.C. to A.D. 300

The Olmec establish the first great civilization in Mesoamerica.

Called the "mother civilization" because of its great influence on the cultures of later Mesoamerican people, the Olmec civilization emerges in the humid lands along the Gulf coast in what is now southern Mexico. The rich wild-plant resources in the region allow the Olmec population to grow and eventually spread throughout Mesoamerica.

The Olmec build large urban areas such as San Lorenzo and La Venta, where people gather to trade and attend religious ceremonies. These centers feature large public buildings and pyramids, constructed by great teams of workers. Commoners also farm nearby fields, and craftsworkers produce

A plaster reproduction of one of the gigantic stone heads found at the Olmec site of San Lorenzo *(Neg. no. 321216, Photo by Rota, Courtesy Dept. of Library Services, American Museum of Natural History)*

figurines, ceremonial paraphernalia, and ornaments for the elite. Artisans create monumental sculptures, such as the gigantic human heads excavated at the San Lorenzo site. Measuring as tall as five feet and weighing as much as 20 tons, these basalt sculptures may be portraits of the Olmec's rulers.

The Olmec culture largely disappears by A.D. 300, but through the Maya (see entry for CA. 300 TO 1500), Toltec (see entry for CA. 900 TO 1200), and Aztec (see entry for CA. 1430 TO 1517) civilizations many elements of its social, religious, military, and artistic traditions will survive for more than a millennium.

ca. 1000 B.C. to A.D. 200

Adena culture evolves in the Ohio River valley.
The Adena culture emerges in small settlements in what is now southern Ohio and parts of present-day West Virginia, Pennsylvania, Kentucky, and Indiana. The inhabitants farm a few crops—including pumpkins, gourds, and tobacco—but they are primarily hunters and gatherers. In their plentiful environment, they can rely on wild plants and animals for food and still maintain a relatively sedentary existence.

The most distinctive characteristic of Adena sites are clusters of burial mounds. Early mounds include ridges formed along natural hills and free-standing earthworks in the shapes of circles, squares, and pentagons. The Adena people construct between 300 to 500 mounds. The largest, such as the Great Serpent Mound (see entry for 200 B.C. TO A.D. 400), require the cooperative labor of many people. That some burial mounds are much larger than others also indicates that some Adena have higher status than others.

The contents of the mounds provide evidence that the structures were built for religious rather than defensive purposes. Used for burials of corpses or cremated remains, many contain luxury goods for the dead to take with them to the afterlife. These goods include neck ornaments, slate pipes for smoking tobacco, and stone tablets carved with

designs and animal shapes that may have been used as stamps for body tattooing. Some goods also suggest that the Adena are participants in a long-distance trade network. A number of mounds, for instance, hold bracelets, rings, and axes that Adena artisans craft from copper imported from present-day Michigan (see entry for CA. 3000 TO 2500 B.C.). The Adena culture will begin to disappear in the first century A.D. and will gradually be displaced by the people of the Hopewell tradition (see entry for CA. 200 B.C. TO A.D. 400).

"All preconceived notions were abandoned ... respecting the singular remains of antiquity scattered so profusely around us. It was concluded that, either the field should be entirely abandoned to the poet and the romancer, or, if these monuments were capable of reflecting any thing upon the grand archaeological [problem] connected with the primitive history of the American continent, the origin, migration, and early state of the American race, that then they should be carefully and minutely, and above all, systematically investigated."
—archaeologists E. G. Squier and E. H. Davis on their excavation of ancient Indian mounds

ca. 1000 B.C. to A.D. 1600

The Woodland tradition spreads through eastern North America.
With the domestication of wild plants native to eastern North America, the Woodland cultural

tradition grows up among the Indians of the region. Accompanying the development of agriculture is the manufacture of pottery and the construction of funerary mounds. The Woodland tradition encompasses several distinct cultures, including the Adena (see entry for CA. 1000 B.C. TO A.D. 200), Hopewell (see entry for CA. 200 B.C. TO A.D. 400), and Mississippian (see entry for CA. 700 TO 1550).

ca. 800 B.C. TO A.D. 1300

Eastern Canada sees the rise of Dorset culture.

The peoples of present-day eastern Canada and Greenland develop the Dorset culture, which is based on the hunting of marine mammals, such as seals and walruses, using bows and arrows. Their settlements feature subterranean houses, and the Dorset people may also construct igloo-like dwellings from blocks of ice. They also make small stone lamps, construct kayaks, and craft unique animal and human figures from bone and ivory, which they may use as charms to bring them luck on the hunt.

The Dorset culture begins to fade in importance in the 11th century with the arrival of people of the Thule culture in the region (see entry for CA. 900 TO 1600). The Thule's tools and weapons are more sophisticated and better suited to helping humans survive in this challenging environment.

ca. 500 B.C.

Southwestern farmers begin growing beans.

Agricultural communities in what is now the American Southwest learn to farm beans, which soon become staples. Beans prove to be a particularly healthful food, because they contain an amino acid that allows early Indians to digest more effectively the protein found in maize, their earlier staple crop (see entry for CA. 2000 TO 1000 B.C.). Beans also help farmers by returning nitrogen to soil that corn plants deplete, thus keeping their fields fertile year after year.

ca. 500 B.C. TO A.D. 900

The Zapotec culture emerges at Monte Albán.

From the mountaintop urban center of Monte Albán, the Zapotec people extend influence over much of the present-day state of Oaxaca. The Zapotec are ruled by divine kings. Their military conquests are recorded in carvings known as the Danzante ("dancers") on stone tablets, depicting the naked bodies of slain and mutilated captives. Like other Mesoamerican political and ceremonial centers, Monte Albán features temples and ball courts arranged around a great plaza. Perhaps as a result of the decline of Teotihuacán (see entry for CA. 200 B.C. TO A.D. 750), whose leaders may have paid tribute to those of Monte Albán, the Zapotec ruler loses control of the surrounding area in about A.D. 900. As centralized control diminishes, the Zapotec people begin living in small independent settlements until they fall prey to, first, invading Aztec (see entry for CA. 1430 TO 1521) in the late 1400s, then Spanish armies in the early 1500s.

ca. 200 B.C. TO A.D. 400

The Great Serpent Mound is constructed.

The largest effigy mound in North America, the Great Serpent Mound, is constructed in what is now Adams County, Ohio, by Indians of the Adena (see entry CA. 1000 B.C. TO A.D. 200) or Hopewell (see entry for CA. 200 B.C. TO A.D. 400) tradition. The serpent is about five feet tall, 20 feet wide, and nearly a mile long. From the air, it looks like a gigantic uncoiling snake with its mouth open, holding an oval shape that may represent an egg or a celestial body. Although the meaning the serpent mound held for its builders is unclear, the serpent is common in the oral traditions of the Indians of the region.

The Hopewell culture develops throughout the Midwest.

The Hopewell cultural tradition emerges in the Ohio River valley and gradually spreads throughout the Midwest, stretching south to the Gulf of Mexico and north to the Great Lakes. This culture has much in common with the Adena tradition (see entry for CA. 1000 B.C. TO A.D. 200), which predated it in what is now Ohio. Like the Adena, the Hopewell obtain food by hunting and gathering, supplemented with farming. Hopewell farmers, however, eventually add a new crop—maize (Indian corn)—that give them a more secure food supply and allow their population to grow.

The Hopewell live in small villages, often clustered around large ceremonial centers. The settlements feature burial mounds that are far larger than those constructed by the Adena. These mounds cover crypts that serve as burial chambers for the social and political elite. Buried with corpses or their cremated remains are elaborate goods, such as copper breastplates and ear ornaments, pipes carved in animal shapes, pearl bead necklaces, painted fabrics, and

"Reclining on one of the huge folds of this gigantic serpent, as the last rays of the sun, glancing from distant hilltops, cast their long shadows over the valley, I mused on the probabilities of the past; and there seemed to come to me a picture as of a distant time, and with it came a demand for an interpretation of this mystery. The unknown must become known."
—Fredric Ward Putnam, director of the Peabody Museum, on the Great Serpent Mound

The Great Serpent Mound, constructed by Adena or Hopewell Indians in present-day Ohio, is one of the largest mounds in the world. *(Library of Congress, Neg. no. USZ62-049402)*

By 900, the Maya civilization in the southern lowlands declines, possibly because of epidemic disease, exhaustion of natural resources, or a change in climate that adversely affects agricultural yields. The Maya continue to flourish in Yucatán until the beginning of the 16th century. Already weakened by smallpox, ecological changes, or civil war, the Yucatán Maya are subjugated by the Spanish after a series of invasions (see entries for 1523 and for 1546). Although most of their culture has disappeared, Maya dialects are still spoken by more than 3 million descendants of the Classic and Postclassic Maya. (See also entry for 987.)

"On that day, dust possesses
    the earth;
On that day, a blight is on the
    face of the earth;
On that day, a cloud rises,
On that day, a mountain rises,
On that day, a strong man
    seizes the land,
On that day, things fall to ruin,
On that day, the tender leaf is
    destroyed,
On that day, the dying eyes are
    closed,
On that day, three signs are on
    the tree,
On that day, three generations
    hang there,
On that day, the battle flag is
    raised,
And they are scattered afar in
    the forests."
    —The *Chilam Balam* on the
        decline of the Maya

ca. 400 to 1300

The Fremont tradition develops in present-day Utah.

In what is now Utah and portions of Nevada, Colorado, and Idaho, the Fremont culture emerges. The Fremont peoples live in scattered villages, where they adopt several traits of Anasazi culture (see entries for CA. 200 B.C., A.D. 750, and for CA. 750 TO 1400), such as building subterranean pit houses, making pottery, and cultivating maize. The ways of life among these people vary widely according to the natural resources available. Some live in sedentary farming communities; others travel in small groups in search of wild game and plants; still others alternate between these food-getting strategies. The Fremont culture is also characterized by anthropomorphic clay figurines and rock paintings that suggest shared religious beliefs. The tradition fades in the 13th century, probably because of drought conditions that make farming difficult and because of competition from other groups who have moved onto their lands.

ca. 400 to 1500

The Hohokam culture develops in present-day Arizona.

In the desert area of what is now southern Arizona and northern Mexico, the Hohokam tradition evolves and dominates the region for more than one thousand years. In the culture's earliest years, villages are no more than clusters of several dwellings. Over time, at such sites as Snaketown (see entry for CA. 975 TO 1150), larger settlements grow up with populations exceeding five hundred. Unlike the contemporaneous Anasazi settlements in Chaco Canyon (see entry for CA. 900 TO 1150), however, these villages are probably economically and politically independent of one another.

Hohokam villages are characterized by platform mounds and large ball courts, both of which may be used for rituals. The ball courts may also function as open-air markets, where traders from surrounding settlements gather. Parrot bones, shells, turquoise, and other exotic items from faraway areas later found at Hohokam sites are evidence that the Hohokam people are part of a vast trade network.

The Hohokam obtain most of their food by farming corn, beans, and squash. To grow these crops in their dry lands, the Hohokam become pioneers in irrigation technology. Beginning in about 800, they build an enormous network of canals to carry water from nearby rivers into their fields. As their farming methods improve, they start to grow tobacco and cotton, in addition to their staple food crops. The Hohokam also supplement their food supply by gathering mesquite beans and cactus fruit and by hunting deer and rabbits.

After 1100, the Hohokam tradition begins to decline, possibly because of a series of floods or invasions by outsiders. By 1500, the culture has disappeared, although the present-day Akimel O'odham (formerly known as the Pima) may be the Hohokam's direct descendants.

ca. 500

The bow and arrow are used throughout North America.

Possibly used by Arctic people as early as 2000 B.C., the bow and arrow become widely adopted by Indians across the North American continent. The innovation proves to be a much more effective hunting tool than the atlatl, or spear thrower. In addition to being easier to make and lighter to carry, arrows shot from bows allow hunters to fell their prey at a greater distance. Bows can also be reloaded quickly, so that a skilled hunter can shoot several arrows at a single target.

ca. 600 to 1500

The Mixtec culture emerges in Mesoamerica.

Living in the present-day Mexican states of Oaxaca, Guerrero, and Puebla, the Mixtec people develop a distinct culture. Unlike such later Mesoamerican

peoples as the Aztec (see entry for CA. 1430 TO 1521), they do not establish a united empire administered from a capital city but instead occupy many separate states, each with its own political leaders. These states, ruled by local dynasties, are socially stratified, with commoners laboring for the benefit of the noble and royal classes. They build the temples, ball courts, and royal residences that characterize Mixtec urban centers. Artisans produce a wide array of luxury goods—such as gold and silver necklaces and ear and nose ornaments—for the Mixtec elite and for trade with Indians in other areas. The Mixtec also develop a picture writing system, which they use to make genealogical records and take down historical and religious information.

In the late 15th and early 16th centuries, most of the Mixtec states are overrun by either Aztec invaders or Spanish conquistadors. Approximately a quarter of a million direct descendants of the ancient Mixtec still live in Mexico.

ca. 700

Southwestern Indians begin building houses from adobe.

Indians in the Southwest abandon their pithouses and begin constructing multiroomed, above-ground dwellings from adobe (sun-dried clay, often mixed with straw). The shift is a response to their increasing dependence on corn and bean crops to feed a growing population; the pithouses are too small for storing and preparing these foods. Their new adobe houses are not only larger but also can easily be increased in size by adding more rooms as needed. The clay also provides excellent insulation, making these dwelling comfortable during both hot summers and cool winters.

ca. 700 to 1550

The Mississippian culture extends over the central United States.

The Mississippian Indian culture evolves in what is now the central United States, stretching north to south from Minnesota to the Gulf of Mexico and east to west from the Appalachians to the eastern Plains. The largest Mississippian settlements are centered along the Mississippi River and its major tributaries. At the culture's greatest extent, the Mississippian population numbers in the millions.

The Mississippians construct urban areas that serve as ceremonial and trade centers. The largest is Cahokia (see entry for CA. 800 TO 1400), which at its height has at least 20,000 residents. In these centers the Mississippian construct enormous platform mounds. These mounds are rectangular at the base and topped with a series of flat tiers. On their flat tops rest houses for hereditary leaders. These houses are lavishly furnished with walls covered with deer skins, and their roofs are decorated with precious shells and pearls. When a leader dies, his house is destroyed and in its place is built a new tier of earth, which becomes the foundation of the next leader's dwelling.

The Mississippian urban centers rely on goods obtained by traders who travel area rivers by canoe to outlying settlements. This far-reaching trade network brings to the centers such exotic items as copper from the Great Lakes region, silver from present-day Ontario, mica from the Appalachian Mountains, obsidian from the Rocky Mountains, and sharks' teeth and barracuda jaws from the Gulf of Mexico.

The Mississippians depend on corn, beans, and squash, which are farmed mostly by women. Unlike earlier mound-building cultures (see entries for CA. 200 TO 1400 and for CA. 400 TO 1500), they use a new tool—the stone-bladed hoe—to make their

The Mississippian urban center of Cahokia, as it looked ca. 1100 to 1150. A log palisade surrounds the grand plaza, which is dominated by the massive Monk's Mound. *(Cahokia Mounds State Historic Site, painting by William R. Iseminger)*

fieldwork easier. Mississippian men employ another innovation—the bow and arrow (see entry for CA. 500)—to hunt deer and other animals for meat.

Although some sites are abandoned earlier, the Mississippian culture survives into the historic area. Soldiers under Hernando de Soto (see entry for 1539) will leave records of their large urban centers in the Mississippi River valley. Contact with non-Indians, however, destroys the remaining centers, whose populations thereafter fall victim to repeated epidemics of infectious European diseases to which the Indians have no natural immunity.

"There is hardly a rising town, or a farm of an eligible situation, in whose vicinity some of these remains may not be found. . . . What a stupendous pile of earth [is the greatest mound]! To heap up such a mass must have required years, and the labor of thousands."

—a visitor to St. Louis on seeing the remains of the Cahokia mounds in 1811

ca. 750

Teotihuacán is destroyed.
Teotihuacán, the greatest pre-Aztec urban center in Mesoamerica (see entry for CA. 200 B.C. TO A.D. 750), is looted and burned. Its ravagers are either invaders from outside of the city (perhaps the Toltec; see entry for CA. 900 TO 1200) or city residents in revolt. Many of the pyramids that rose above Teotihuacán's central plaza are destroyed in the attack. The ruins of the city will be revered by the Aztec (see entry for CA. 1430 TO 1521) who enter the region in the 14th century. They will give

Teotihuacán its name, which means "the City of the Gods" in Nahuatl, the Aztec language.

ca. 750 to 1400

Anasazi culture enters the Pueblo Period.
The Anasazi move from the Basketmaker Period (see entry for CA. 200 B.C. TO A.D. 750) to the Pueblo Period with the introduction of an innovation in architecture—the widespread use of aboveground dwellings made from adobe (clay) bricks or from stone mortared with adobe (see entry for CA. 500). The new housing style gives the Anasazi more space for storing and milling corn, a food source that becomes more important as their population increases. They retain a form of their old underground pithouses but use these structures—known as kivas—exclusively for ceremonies.

Starting in about 1000, Anasazi villages grow far larger. Some Anasazi settlements house as many as 10,000 people, and their total population numbers as high as one hundred thousand. The many roads connecting the villages allow the Anasazi to enjoy a vast trade network centered on the Chaco Canyon (see entry for CA. 900 TO 1150).

These large villages are abandoned by the Anasazi beginning in the 14th century. They may have relocated to smaller settlements after suffering droughts that made farming enough food for their large populations impossible. The Anasazi may also have been driven from their lands by less sophisticated peoples, who then adopted some of their ways. The remnants of the Anasazi will become the ancestors of modern Pueblos groups, such as the Hopi and the Zuni. (See also entry for CA. 1100 TO 1200.)

ca. 875 to 1500

The Patayan culture develops in western Arizona.
South of the Grand Canyon, the Patayan culture (also known as the Hakataya culture) emerges along the Colorado River in what is now western Arizona.

ca. 1100 to 1300

The Southern Cult emerges among the Mississippians.

The people of the Mississippian tradition (see entry for CA. 700 TO 1550) in the modern southeastern United States create artifacts that reflect a set of religious beliefs later termed the Southern Cult. Common motifs of Southern Cult artifacts include skulls, warriors holding axes, severed heads, weeping eyes, and hands with eyes in their palms. These are most often engraved into shell but also carved into wood and stone and embossed on sheets of copper. The gruesome imagery suggests that the Southern Cult is related to war and possibly human sacrifice. Many of the materials used to craft these objects also indicate that the Southern Cult Mississippian are involved in a far-reaching trade network. Copper axes, for instance, are made from metal mined in the Great Lakes region.

ca. 1150

The Anasazi establish Oraibi.

In what is now northeastern Arizona, the Anasazi (see entry for CA. 750 TO 1400) found the village of Oraibi. By the late 13th century, the settlement will have a population of as many as 1,000. It will later be occupied by the Hopi, descendants of the Anasazi, and become the longest continually occupied settlement in the present-day United States. (See also entry for SEPTEMBER 9, 1906.)

ca. 1300 to 1400

Migrants to Hohokam territory develop the Salado culture.

As the Sinagua culture (see entry for CA. 1100) comes to an end, a group of Sinagua people travel south and settle among the Hohokam (see entry for CA. 400 TO 1500) in the Gila River valley. The culture that evolves among these migrants as they take on Hohokam traits will become known as the Salado tradition.

The Salado people are probably responsible for introducing a new form of architecture among the Hohokam. One example is the four-story Great House at Casa Grande. Accustomed to building structures from stone, the Salado Indians have difficulty working with the adobe bricks used by the Hohokam. Perhaps unsure about the stability of the material, they fill the centers of the bottom floors with bricks to ensure the buildings will not collapse.

ca. 1325

The early Aztec found Tenochtitlán.

The Mexica, a tribe of nomadic hunters who will later become known as the Aztec (see entry for CA. 1430 TO 1521), arrive in Central Mexico, where they encounter more powerful groups that demand tribute. To escape these groups, the early Aztec found a settlement on a muddy island in the center of what is now Lake Texcoco. According to Aztec legend, the god Huitzilopochtli leads them to this place (today the site of Mexico City), where they find an eagle seated on cactus with a serpent in its beak. This image now appears on the flag of Mexico. The legend also survives in the name Tenochtitlán, meaning "place of the cactus" in Nahuatl, the Aztec language.

ca. 1400

The Peacemaker and Hiawatha form the Iroquois Confederacy.

According to Iroquois oral tradition, a Huron prophet known as the Peacemaker advocates the end of warfare associated with the blood feud—a custom that requires the family of a victim of violence to avenge the crime by attacking members of the perpetrator's family. The message of peace is embraced by Hiawatha, an Onondaga leader who communicates the Peacemaker's words to his own tribe and four others—the Cayuga, Mohawk,

Seneca, and Oneida—living in what is now New York State and southeastern Canada. All are receptive except for a powerful Onondaga war leader, Tadadaho, whose evil character is symbolized the snakes woven in his hair. Hiawatha finally secures Tadadaho's cooperation by offering him the chairmanship of the Grand Council, an assembly of 50 leaders representing each tribe the Peacemaker has conceived to resolve disputes amicably. The council is to meet in the centrally located territory of the Onondaga, gathering at what the Peacemaker calls the Great Tree of Peace.

"Roots have spread out to form the Tree of Great Peace, one to the north, one to the east, one to the south, and one to the west. These are the Great White Roots and their nature is Peace and Strength.

"If any man or any nation of the Five Nations shall obey the laws of the Great Peace and shall make known to the statesmen of the League, they may trace back the roots to the Tree. If their minds are clean, and if they are obedient and promise to obey the wishes of the Council of the League, they shall be welcomed to take shelter beneath the Great Evergreen Tree."

—from the Iroquois Confederacy's Law of Great Peace

The people of the confederacy organized by the Peacemaker and Hiawatha call themselves Haudenosaunee, meaning the "people of the longhouse." Several families live in harmony in this traditional dwelling, just as the tribes vow to live in peace within the same realm. Non-Indians will begin referring to the Haudenosaunee as the Iroquois and their powerful confederacy as the Iroquois League, or the Five Nations. (A sixth tribe, the Tuscarora, will later join the league; see entry for 1722.)

ca. 1430 to 1521

The Aztec become the primary power in Mesoamerica.

Clustered on a muddy island in Lake Texcoco—the site of present-day Mexico City (see entry for CA. 1325)—the Aztec people stage a series of wars on neighboring Indian groups in what is now the Valley of Mexico. By about 1440, they emerge as the dominant people of the region. In a long succession of military conquests, the ambitious, despotic Aztec rulers build up a vast empire. At its height, it comprises some 500 small states, spreading over 80,000 square miles throughout much of present-day Mexico.

Although absolute power rests with the ruler, the Aztec observe several layers of social rank—ranging from high-ranking nobles to middleranking merchants and artisans to low-ranking commoners. Individuals can rise or fall in position; warriors who distinguish themselves in battle are most frequently able to better their social positions.

The enormous empire is administered through a bureaucracy centered in Tenochtitlán, which is also the home of the Aztec ruler. The advanced Aztec farming technology, which employs manmade irrigation canals, helps sustain the population of this huge urban center. The residents of Tenochtitlán also rely on tributes of food and goods from conquered people in outlying areas. In addition, the conquests of Aztec warriors bring captives to the capital, who are killed in ever-growing numbers during religious ceremonies. The Aztec believe the sacrifices are necessary to nourish Huitzilopochtli, the god of the sun and of war (see entry for CA. 1325). Without the shedding of blood through these human sacrifices and ritual bloodletting, they fear that their world will come to an end. Their dire prophesies will come true with the arrival of Spanish conquistadores in their realm (see entries for 1502, 1519, and 1521).

ca. 1450 to 1500

The Navajo (Dineh) and Apache arrive in the Southwest.

Originally living in what is now southwestern Canada, the ancestors of the Navajo (Dineh) and Apache tribes migrate for reasons unknown to what is now the American Southwest. There, initially they remain hunters and gatherers who move from place to place in search of wild ani-

mals and plants. Their way of life contrasts with that of their new Pueblo neighbors—the descendants of the Anasazi (see entry for CA. 750 TO 1400)—who live in villages and obtain most of their food through farming. The first contacts between the newcomers and the Pueblo were likely hostile, with the Navajo and Apache raiding Pueblo villages for food and supplies. Some groups, however, may have developed a peaceful relationship based on trade.

By the 17th century, increased contact and intermarriage with the Pueblo will create a hybrid culture among the Navajo that blends their old ways with Pueblo farming techniques, ceremonies, and customs. The Apache, in contrast, will remain a mobile people with a culture focused on hunting, gathering, and raiding.

1492 TO 1606
STRANGERS ARRIVE

When Christopher Columbus "discovered" North America, the continent had been the home of Indian peoples for thousands and maybe even tens of thousands of years. Although population estimates vary, by 1492 as many as 18 million people were living north of present-day Mexico. Still, what Columbus and the early European explorers who followed him saw was not a settled continent but a new world rich with resources to exploit. Among these resources were the Indians themselves. While some Europeans imagined the Indians' primary worth as potential slave labor, others quickly recognized their enormous value as sources of information on how to survive in an unfamiliar land.

Inspired by Columbus's voyages, England financed the explorations of John Cabot in 1497, while France sent Giovanni da Verrazano in 1524 and Jacques Cartier in 1534 to stake out claims in the so-called New World. But in the 16th century, Spain launched the most extensive expeditions in North America. Conquistadores made inroads into the West Indies, Mesoamerica, and the American Southeast and Southwest. The brutality of these invaders was typified by Hernán Cortés's conquest of the Aztec Empire. In 1521, with the help of the Aztec's Indian enemies, he and his men looted and destroyed the Aztec's capital of Tenochtitlán, enslaved its people, and forced them to mine precious metals that would make their conquerors rich.

The lure of gold also led to the 1539 expedition headed by Hernando de Soto, whom the Spanish Crown granted the right to conquer and colonize lands north of Cuba. For two years, his 600 men terrorized Indians, pillaging their villages and taking captives to use as slaves, throughout what is now the southeastern United States. In 1541, during Francisco Vásquez de Coronado's search for the fabled gold-filled Seven Cities of Cibola, Spaniards similarly abused the Indians of the Southwest and western Plains. To their relief, Coronado's failure to find the riches he hoped for dissuaded other Spaniards from following in his path for nearly 40 years.

Reports of the conquistadores' mistreatment of Indians sparked a debate among Spanish intellectuals on the Indians' humanity. The consensus held that Indians were in fact human beings. This determination placed on the Spanish Crown a responsibility not only to rein in the conquistadores' violent tendencies but also to save the souls of the heathen Indians they sought to conquer. Thus along with warfare and chaos the Spaniards brought the Indians they encountered Christianity. Although missionary priests often declared impressive numbers of converts, the Indians who were said to have embraced Christianity more likely did not understand foreign rituals such as baptism or went along with them only to placate the invaders, all the while continuing to observe their own religious traditions.

Much more welcome than Christianity were the goods non-Indians brought with them from Europe. Items manufactured from metal were particularly treasured. Aside from their novelty, these objects were much more durable than those Indians made themselves from clay or stone. In the Southwest, Indians also almost immediately integrated into their culture the strange, new animals introduced to them by the Spanish. Sheep and hogs were important new food sources, but most influential was the horse. The horse allowed a rider to travel long distances in a far shorter period than Indians previously could have imagined. The animal's introduction would change the lives of Indians throughout the continent, but its greatest effect would be felt on the Great Plains. The horse would redefine Indian cultures in the region by turning settled farmers and gatherers into mounted hunters whose days were spent following the great buffalo herds.

Yet overwhelmingly the most important and tragic consequence of early contact was the spread of epidemic disease. Everyday European diseases such as smallpox, measles, and influenza had previously been unknown in the Americas; therefore, the native population had no natural immunities to them. When exposed to these germs for the first time, Indian villages were devastated as illness decimated their populations. In addition to the diseases themselves, survivors were often faced with famine as the epidemics disrupted their ability to replenish their food supplies. Among some Indian groups as many as 90 percent died within years of exposure to foreign germs.

The horrors of epidemic disease perhaps played the greatest role in determining the future of Indian peoples. Non-Indian germs spread to many Indian groups even before they first encountered whites. By the time of first contact, their populations and societies therefore had already suffered the impact of epidemics. Had Indians not been so weakened by disease, they perhaps would have been better able and more inclined to drive away non-Indian invaders by force. Instead, though initially low in numbers, non-Indians were able to use their biological advantage and their superior weaponry to compel Indians to accept their presence, whether welcome or not.

1492

October 12

The Arawak encounter Christopher Columbus and his men.

The Arawak of what is now the island of San Salvador sight three ships off the coast. The ships carry crews led by Christopher Columbus, an Italian explorer who had convinced the Spanish Crown to finance an expedition to reach Asia by sailing west from Europe. Upon landing, Columbus erroneously concludes that he has reached the Indies—a term then used to describe much of Asia—and dubs the indigenous peoples he encounters Indians.

Determined to find China, the Europeans explore the islands in the area, including Hispaniola (now comprising Haiti and the Dominican Republic). From their ships anchored off its coast, the men conduct an active trade with the Arawak. One night as many as 1,500 Indians visit the ships. The trading continues until December 24, when one of their ships, the *Santa Maria,* runs aground. With the Indian's help, Columbus's men are able to save the supplies on the sinking ship. The *Santa Maria* destroyed, Columbus decides to return to Spain in his two remaining ships but leaves 39 men behind at a fort built from wood salvaged from the wreckage (see entry for NOVEMBER 28, 1493).

1493

March

The Santángel-Sánchez letters announce Columbus's "discovery" of the Indies.

Anchored off the coast of Portugal, Christopher Columbus sends overland two nearly identical letters to court officials Luis de Santángel and Rafael Sánchez, in which he describes his successful voyage to the Indies (see entry for OCTOBER 12, 1492). Within weeks, the letters are published in three languages and widely circulated around Europe. The Santángel-Sánchez letters provide Europeans their first impression of the "new world" Columbus has found and of the peoples he calls Indians.

April

Christopher Columbus presents captive Indians to the Spanish court.

At the request of Queen Isabella and King Ferdinand of Spain, a triumphant Christopher Columbus appears before the Spanish court and tells of the exotic land he visited during his exploration the previous year (see entry for OCTOBER 12, 1492). In addition to gold items and parrots he obtained through trade with the Arawak Indians, he brings before the monarchs several Indians wearing plumed headdresses, whom he had captured and brought back to Spain. The impressive presentation helps convince Isabella to fund a second voyage.

May 3

A papal bull confirms Spanish claims to North American lands.

As news of Columbus's journey spreads (see entry for OCTOBER 12, 1492), the Portuguese king prepares to challenge the claims of the explorer's Spanish sponsors to the lands he has found. To establish the legitimacy of its claims, the Spanish Crown appeals to Pope Alexander VI, who issues the first of a series of papal bulls on the matter. Establishing a line of demarcation bisecting the Atlantic Ocean and stretching from the North to South Pole, the pope declares that all lands west of the line not already ruled by a Christian are under the rule of Spain. He also places all indigenous peoples on these lands under Spanish guardianship and encourages the Spanish to spread the Catholic faith among them.

November 28

Thirty-nine Spaniards are found murdered by Arawak Indians.

On his second journey to Hispaniola, Christopher Columbus and a crew of 1,200 men arrive to find upon the death of his uncle Ahitzotl. Generous and benevolent, Ahitzotl is well loved by his subjects but weak in battle. His successor will chose to be a far more stern and militaristic leader. Before the arrival of the Spanish in his realm (see entries for 1519 and for 1521), he will add some 40 communities to the powerful Aztec Empire, inciting the wrath of those conquered and fending off several rivals' attempts to subvert his authority.

1503

Fall

Eighty-five Arawak leaders are executed by the Spanish.

Soon after being appointed the Spanish governor, Nicolás de Ovando sets about destroying the traditional political structure among the Arawak. He targets the leaders of Jaraguá, who have paid tribute to his rivals for control over Spanish claims. Ovando's troops invade Jaraguá, round up 84 chiefs, and sentence them to death by fire. The Spaniards also capture Anacaona, a woman who is the paramount leader of Jaraguá. She is killed by hanging, which the Spanish considered a more appropriate way of executing a person of her high rank.

1511

Antonio de Montesinos preaches about the humanity of Indians.

In a sermon to the Spanish leaders of Hispaniola, Dominican friar Antonio de Montesino protests the hideous mistreatment of the Indians of the West Indies at the hands of the Spanish. Condemning forced Indian labor, he insists that Indians are human beings who have a right to freedom. The issue of Indian humanity will be fiercely debated by Spanish clerics and intellectuals for decades to come (see entry for 1550).

1512

The Catholic Church decrees that Indians have souls.

Responding to the continuing debate on Indian humanity (see entries for 1502 and for 1511), Pope Julius II declares that Indians are descended from Adam and Eve. At the Fifth Lateran Council, which the pope assembles in Rome, Indians are found to have souls. These declarations reinforce the obligation of Spanish conquistadores and colonists in North America to attempt to convert Indians to Catholicism. (See also entry for 1550.)

Spanish intellectuals approve holy wars against non-Christian Indians.

As the Spanish Crown prepares to create a legal code to govern Spaniards relations to Indians, it seeks advice from legal scholars and the clergy. The most significant contributors confirm that Spain has a legitimate claim to title to its lands in North America and to authority over the Indians living there. They also agree that wars waged against Indians in order to force them to convert to Catholicism are just.

The Spanish Laws of Burgos formalizes the encomienda system.

The Spanish Crown issues the Laws of Burgos, a code of laws to govern Spanish-Indian relations. The laws focus on the *encomienda* system, through which the nobles who had helped drive the Muslims from Spain were rewarded with land grants. The Laws of Burgos are intended to regulate the granting of *encomiendas* in North America, where conquistadores have already begun to institute the system to reward their most valued men (see entry for 1498). Many of these early *encomienda* owners have made great fortunes by enslaving the Indians on their lands and forcing them to farm, build houses, and mine for gold and silver. The Indians have been worked so hard and so ill treated that they have died in large numbers.

The Laws of Burgos require that landowners provide food for Indians on the *encomiendas* and improve their working conditions. One provision, for instance, stipulates that Indian miners be given 40 days of rest after every five months of labor. The *encomienda* owners' most important obligation, however, is to instruct the Indians in Catholicism and encourage their conversion.

out of their territory. The Spaniards continue on, in search of both gold and a fountain that, according to Indian tales, can restore a person's health and youth. Ponce de León finds neither, and he returns to Spain the following year. (See also entry for 1521.)

1531

Juan Ponce de León arrives in Florida.

Juan Ponce de León, the Spanish governor of Puerto Rico, leads three ships to the coast of present-day Florida near what is now the city of St. Augustine. He and his men thus become the first Europeans to travel to the area. While traveling along the coast of the Florida peninsula, the Spanish expedition meets, near present-day Fort Myers, a force of Calusa warriors, who chase the invaders

1519

Spaniards led by Hernán Cortés attack the Aztec capital of Tenochtitlán.

Diego Velásquez, the Spanish governor of Cuba, appoints Hernán Cortés to lead a company of soldiers to the eastern coast of what is now Mexico, where Indians are said to have amassed a huge store of gold and other treasures. Before Cortés sets sail, Velásquez has second thoughts about the appointment and places another officer in charge of the expedition. Cortés ignores Velásquez's change in

A 20th-century drawing of Tenochtitlán, based on Spanish descriptions of the Aztec capital. The tallest pyramid is the Great Temple of Huitzilopochtli, the god who was said to have led the Aztec to their homeland. *(Neg. no. 326597, Photo by Rota, Courtesy Dept. of Library Services, American Museum of Natural History)*

plans and heads west with approximately 600 men in 11 ships.

When the Spaniards reach the coast, they make alliances with several Indian peoples, who have been subjugated by the powerful Aztec empire (see entry for ca. 1430 TO 1521). Embittered by their treatment from the Aztec, they welcome the chance to help the Spanish conquer them. Of particular importance is the aid provided by Malintzin, a native woman whom Cortés takes as a mistress. She informs him of the political atmosphere of Tenochtitlán, the Aztec capital, and identifies the enemies of the Aztec ruler Montezuma (see entry for 1502).

Supported by his Indian allies, Cortés and his men march on Tenochtitlán, where they are initially welcomed by Montezuma. Responding to a legend propagated by Cortés, Montezuma takes the Spanish leader to be the Aztec god Quetzalcóatl (see entry for ca. 900 TO 1200), who had left the earth but promised to come back one day. Cortés returns his hospitality by taking Montezuma hostage and pillaging a massive amount of gold that had belonged to the ruler's father. The Spanish also begin slaughtering the Aztec people. During a religious ceremony, they massacre approximately 600 unarmed Indians.

> "When we saw so many cities and villages built in the water and other great towns on dry land and that straight and level Causeway going towards [Tenochtitlán], we were amazed.... And some of our soldiers even asked whether the things that we saw were not a dream.... I do not know how to describe it, seeing things as we did that had never been heard of or seen before, not even dreamed about."
>
> —Cortés expedition leader Bernal Díaz del Castillo, on the Spaniards' first view of Tenochtitlán

The furious Aztec finally rise up against the invaders. During the fighting, Montezuma dies. Cortés and his men frantically try to escape Tenochtitlán, but weighed down by their golden loot, as many as two-thirds of them are killed before they can find refuge with their Indian allies in the nearby city-state of Tlaxcala.

1520

Guayocuya leads an Arawak revolt.

Rebel Arawak escape Spanish control by fleeing into the mountains of Hispaniola. From there, under the leadership of Guayocuya (known to the Spanish as Enrique), they stage raids on Spanish settlements for the next 14 years. The Spanish will finally yield to the rebels in 1534 by offering a land grant and exempting them from paying tribute to Spanish authorities.

1521

A Calusa warrior fells Juan Ponce de León.

Appointed governor of Florida after his exploration of its coast (see entry for 1513), Juan Ponce de León organizes a party of 200 to establish a Spanish colony in the area. The men land on what is now Sanibel Island, where they are attacked by Calusa Indians. Ponce de León orders his men to retreat to Cuba, but before they can, he is hit in the thigh by a warrior's arrow. Later, in Havana, the Spanish leader dies from the wound.

May to July

Hernán Cortés and his men conquer the Aztec.

With the help of their Indian allies in Tlaxcala, Spanish conquistador Hernán Cortés and about 200 soldiers stage a second attack on the Aztec capital of Tenochtitlán (see entry for 1519). They surround the city, cutting off the supply of food and water to an already beleaguered population. Since their initial encounter with the Spanish two years before, the

Aztec have been decimated by epidemics of non-Indian diseases. One Aztec survivor will later remember, "Almost the whole population suffered from wracking coughs and painful, burning sores."

Armed with cannons, the Spanish begin a long siege of Tenochtitlán. They methodically destroy building after building, effectively leveling what Cortés himself will call the "most beautiful city in the world." After three months the Aztec surrender, and Cortés names himself the new leader of the region. On the ruins of Tenochtitlán, the Spanish will begin to build Mexico City as the capital of New Spain.

> "Worms are swarming in the
>   streets and plazas,
> and the walls are splattered
>   with gore.
> The water has turned red, as if
>   it were dyed,
> and when we drink it,
> it has the taste of brine."
>
> "We have pounded our hands
>   in despair
> against the adobe walls,
> for our inheritance, our city, is
>   lost and dead.
> The shields of our warriors
>   were its defense,
> but they could not save it."
>   —an Aztec account of the
>   destruction of Tenochtitlán

1523

Soldiers led by Pedro de Alvarado attack the Maya.

After conquering the Aztec (see entry for 1521), Hernán Cortés sends his lieutenant Pedro de Alvarado to take over the lands of the Maya (see entry for ca. 300 TO 1500) in present-day Guatemala. Alvarado leads his soldiers in a bloody campaign, leaving in its wake a path of carnage and destruction. The invasion is the first in a series of brutal attacks on the Maya, many of whom fight to the death to defend their land and independence. (See also entry for 1546.)

1524

Atlantic coast Indians encounter Giovanni da Verrazano's exploratory party.

Hired by the French king Francis I, the Italian navigator Giovanni da Verrazano explores the Atlantic coast from what is now North Carolina to Newfoundland. At several locations, Verrazano meets coastal Indians, including members of the Wampanoag, Narragansett, and Lenni Lenape (Delaware) tribes. The encounters are generally friendly, with the exception of a meeting in present-day Maine with Indians who are openly hostile to Verrazano and his men, possibly because they have been attacked by previous European visitors to their shores.

1528

Karankawan Indians come to the rescue of shipwrecked Spaniard Alvar Núñez Cabeza de Vaca.

Intent on colonizing Florida for Spain, an expedition of 600 led by Pánfilo de Narváez sails to the Gulf of Mexico. When the Spaniards go ashore and leave the coast to explore inland areas, their ships are destroyed in a storm, leaving the expedition stranded. As disease and Timucua Indian attacks begin to decimate their ranks, they craft their own rafts and attempt to sail them to Cuba, but a second storm nearly wipes them out. The four survivors include Alvar Núñez Cabeza de Vaca and Esteban, a black Moorish slave.

Karankawan Indians of the Gulf coast find the starving men and take them to live in their villages.

Cabeza de Vaca's party enjoys their hospitality for six years before deciding to embark on foot toward Spanish-held lands in what is now Mexico. Their 6,000-mile journey will take them across present-day Texas and northern Mexico, making them the first non-Indians to travel through the region. (See also entry for 1536.)

"At sunset the Indians, thinking that we had not gone, looked for us again and brought us food.... I let them know through sign language that one of our boats had sunk and that three of our men had drowned....The Indians, seeing the disaster that had come upon us and brought so much misfortune and misery, sat down with us. They felt such great pain and pity at seeing us in such a state that they all began to cry so loudly and sincerely that they could be heard from afar."

—Alvar Núñez Cabeza de Vaca, on his Indian friends' reaction to finding him shipwrecked

1531

The Yaqui repel Spanish slavers.

Soldiers led by Nuño de Guzman trek through what is now the American Southwest on the first Spanish expedition to capture Indian slaves. When they reach Yaqui territory in what is now southern Arizona, the Indians draw a line in the sand and tell the Spaniards they will be attacked if they cross it. Guzman's men ignore the threat but are soon forced to retreat by Yaqui warriors in the fighting that follows.

1534

Jacques Cartier explores the St. Lawrence River region for France.

French king Francis I sends explorer Jacques Cartier to North America to claim lands for France and to search for the Northwest Passage—a water route between the Atlantic and Pacific Oceans. When he arrives, he kidnaps two Iroquoian men to serve as guides for the expedition. The Indians tell the Frenchmen about great Indian settlements close by, which excites the Europeans with visions of enormous riches like those confiscated by Spanish conquistadores in Mexico (see entries for 1519 and for 1521). Eager to find the settlements, Cartier explores what is now the Gulf of St. Lawrence and the mouth of the St. Lawrence River before the approach of winter compels him to return to France with his Indian captives. (See also entries for 1535 and for 1541.)

1535

French explorer Jacques Cartier makes a second voyage to North America.

The French explorer Jacques Cartier returns to the St. Lawrence River region in search of the Northwest Passage and Indian settlements full of riches (see entry for 1534). He and his men visit the villages Stadacona and Hochelaga and establish a base at the site of present-day Quebec City. There, the Frenchmen are nursed by nearby Huron Indians when they fall prey to scurvy.

In 1536 Cartier, eager to convert the Indians to Catholicism, takes Indian leader Donnaconna and nine of his followers captive and returns with them to France. The captives are baptized and soon after die from non-Indian diseases. Before his death, however, Donnaconna entices the French king Francis I with stories of the "many mines of gold and silver" in his native land. (See also entry for 1541.)

"[W]ee caused a faire high Crosse to be made of the height of thirty foot.... So soon as it was up, we altogether kneeled down before them, with our hands toward Heaven, yielding God thanks: and we made signs unto [the Indians], showing them the Heavens.... [T]heir Captain clad with an old Bear's skin ... came unto us.... [T]here he made ... a cross with two fingers, then did he show us all the Country about us, as if he would say that all was his, and that wee should not set up any cross without his leave."

—Jacques Cartier on introducing the Indians to Christianity

1536

Alvar Núñez Cabeza de Vaca tells the Spanish of the Seven Cities of Cibola.

Eight years after being stranded on the Gulf of Mexico, Spanish explorer Alvar Núñez Cabeza de Vaca, a Moorish slave named Esteban, and two companions reach Spanish-held lands in what is now western Mexico (see entry for 1528). They tell the Spaniards they meet of their years of living among Indians and their 6,000-mile trek across western North America. Cabeza de Vaca will publish these tales in 1555 in *Naufagios* (Shipwrecks), one of the earliest works to provide information about the region's Indian groups, geography, and animal and plant life.

The Spanish are particularly entranced by one of the survivors' stories—the tale told by some Indians of seven cities full of fabulous riches located north of Mexico. The rumors will help convince New Spain to send the Coronado expedition (see entry for 1540) to find and conquer the fabled cities, which become known as the Seven Cities of Cibola. (See also entry for MARCH 1539.)

1539

Hernando de Soto begins exploring the American Southeast.

Charles I of Spain (Holy Roman Emperor Charles V) grants Hernando de Soto, the governor of Cuba, the right to conquer and colonize "La Florida," a region then defined by the Spanish as all lands north of Cuba. Hoping to find riches as he had as a conquistador in Peru several years earlier, de Soto leads an ambitious expedition into the area. Sailing on nine ships, his crew of 600 men, with 200 horses, lands on the west coast of present-day Florida. Over the next

"I am king in my land, and it is unnecessary for me to become the subject of a person who has no more vassals than I. I regard those men as vile and contemptible who subject them-selves to the yoke of someone else when they can live as free men. Accordingly, I and all my people have vowed to die a hundred deaths to maintain the freedom of our land. This is our answer, both the present and forevermore."

—Timucua leader Acuera in a message to Spanish conquistador Hernando de Soto two years, de Soto's soldiers will travel north through present-day Georgia, South Carolina, and North Carolina before turning west. They will then journey through the Appalachian Mountains and finally cross the Mississippi River into modern Arkansas and Louisiana.

Along their 4,000-mile trek they spread terror through the Indian groups they meet. The Spaniards attack Indians whether they are friendly or not. In addition to plundering the Indians' villages, the invaders take captives and force them to carry their baggage. Unknowingly, the Spanish also introduce the Indians they encounter to non-Indian diseases, such as smallpox, that will soon decimate their populations. (See also entries for 1540 and for MAY 21, 1542.)

Dominican intellectual Francisco de Victoria defends Indian rights.

One of the first European intellectuals to examine the rights of Indians, Dominican priest Francisco de Victoria argues in *On the Indians Lately Discovered* that the Spanish have no moral grounds to force Christianity on Indians or to take their lands if they refuse to convert. Victoria, however, does defend warring with Indians if they break natural law, an idea that the Spanish use to justify their violence against Indians.

March

Explorer Marcos de Niza claims a Zuni pueblo is one of the Seven Cities of Cibola.

Picturing the great wealth plundered from the Aztec (see entries for 1519 and for 1521) and the Inca, Antonio de Mendoza, the viceroy of New Spain, sends a small party in search of the Seven Cities of Cibola. According to Spanish explorer Alvar Núñez Cabeza de Vaca (see entry for 1536), several Indians have told of seven cities full of riches located somewhere to the north of present-day Mexico.

Friar Marcos de Niza is chosen to head the expedition, and Esteban, a black slave, is hired as its guide. Having spent six years living among Gulf Coast Indians (see entry for 1528), Esteban is valued for his diplomatic skills and experience in dealing with Indian peoples. De Niza sends the guide ahead to scout the route, while he follows with the rest of the exploratory party. As De Niza's men travel through present-day Arizona and New Mexico, an Indian messenger tells them that Esteban is dead at the hands of the Zuni Indians. De Niza proceeds far enough to see the Indians' village and then returns to Mexico. He claims he has found one of the great seven cities, fueling the viceroy's growing thirst for fortune.

1540

The Coronado expedition begins its exploration of the American West.

Encouraged by a reported sighting of one of the Seven Cities of Cibola (see entry for 1539), Antonio de Mendoza, the viceroy of New Mexico, sends an expedition of 300 Spanish soldiers and one thousand Indians lead by Francisco Vásquez de Coronado north in search of riches. On July 7 Coronado arrives in the Zuni pueblo of Hawikuh near what is now Albuquerque, New Mexico. The army has to battle the Zuni to gain entrance. Inside, they are disappointed when they cannot find any great stores of gold.

Coronado's troops remain among the Zuni for four months. They enrage the Indians by their brutality and constant demands for food and supplies. Still intent on finding wealth, Coronado, who has invested most of his own money in the expedition, sends a small party under Garcia López de Cárdenas to the lands of the Hopi. The Hopi tell them of a great river to the west; during an expedition to find it, the men become the first whites to see the Grand Canyon. Another exploratory party travels through the Rio Grande Valley. Its members are impressed by the enormous herds of buffalo they see on the Great Plains.

Coronado decides to lead the entire expedition into the Plains when a Zuni assures them that there the Spaniards will find the gold they are looking for. During the trek, Coronado's men make contact with many Indian groups, who are repelled by the Spaniards' violence but intrigued by the horses, cattle, and other European livestock they have brought with them. The Spanish travel as far east as present-day Wichita, Kansas, before turning back empty-handed. In 1542, Coronado arrives in Mexico, where the expedition is considered such a disaster that no Spanish parties will be sent into the American West for the next 40 years.

The Choctaw nearly destroy the de Soto expedition.

While traveling through the lands of the Choctaw, Spanish soldiers led by Hernando de Soto (see entry for 1539) threaten tribal leader Tuskaloosa and demand that he give over several tribe members for the Spaniards to use as slaves. Tuskaloosa agrees and tells the invaders to meet him at the village of Moma Bina near what is now Mobile, Alabama, to collect the captives. When de Soto and his men arrive, they are met by a huge army of Choctaw warriors. The Spaniards manage to escape only by setting fire to the village and, in the process, many of their own possessions. Many Spaniards are killed, and more, including de Soto, are wounded by the Choctaw's arrows. (See also entry for MAY 21, 1542.)

1541

The French king orders Jacques Cartier to return to North America.

Francis I commands French explorer Jacques Cartier to make a third voyage to North America (see entries for 1534 and for 1535), officially to create a permanent French settlement and to "establish the Christian Religion in a country of savages." Unofficially, the exploratory party, which includes two goldsmiths, is also to search for fabled Indian villages with vast stores of gold and other precious metals.

Cartier and several hundred men settle near what is now Quebec City, but they are plagued by harsh weather and Indian attacks. In the spring, they give up on establishing a colony and sail home with a hoard of what Cartier takes to be gold and

diamonds. When they are found to be merely rocks, the French Crown loses interest in further exploration of North America for nearly 50 years.

1542

The Spanish Crown issues the New Laws of the Indies.

Dominican friar Bartolomé de Las Casas travels from Cuba to Spain to persuade King Charles I to adopt a more humane policy toward the Indians native to lands in the Americas claimed by Spain. During the meeting, passages are read from Las Casas's *A Very Brief Recital of the Devastation of the Indies* (see entry for 1502), which details the gruesome torture and murder of thousands of Indian men, women, and children at the hands of their Spanish conquerors.

As a result of Las Casas's testimony, the king adopts the New Laws of the Indians. These laws ban Indian slavery and call for an end to the *encomienda* system (see entry for 1512). When Spanish colonists outraged by these reforms begin to revolt, the Crown modifies the laws to minimize their impact. The incident, however, demonstrates to Spain that the *encomienda* owners are becoming dangerous to its authority in the colonies. In the future, Spain's rulers will avoid granting new *encomiendas* and make inheriting existing ones increasingly difficult.

> "We order and command that henceforth, for no reason of war or any other, even though it be by reason of rebellion or purchase, may any Indian be made a slave, and we wish them to be treated as our vassals of the Crown of Castile, which they are. No person may make use of any Indian . . . against his will."
> —from the New Laws of the Indies

Juan Rodriguez Cabrillo explores the Pacific coast.

A Spanish exploration headed by Juan Rodriguez Cabrillo travels up the coast of the Pacific Ocean and claims the region for the Spanish crown. Cabrillo later writes that the tribes he encounters have become hostile toward Spaniards after hearing about atrocities committed by the Coronado expedition (see entry for 1540). The Ipai Indians, for instance, knew that "men like us were traveling about, bearded, clothed and armed . . . killing many native Indians, and . . . for this reason they were afraid."

May 21

Hernando de Soto dies en route to Spanish territory.

After two years of exploring the American Southeast, the Spanish soldiers under Hernando de Soto (see entries for 1539 and for 1540) are exhausted from constant fighting with Indians and disappointed by their inability to find gold and other riches. De Soto decides to end the expensive expedition and begins to lead his men back to their camp on the coast of present-day Florida. As the Spaniards reach the Mississippi River, de Soto falls ill and dies. Afraid that Indians will attack them if they know their leader is dead, the soldiers wrap the corpse in chains and drop it in the river. Without de Soto, the men decide to continue their quest for gold for six more months. With no success, they take rafts down the Mississippi and along the Gulf Coast until they reach Spanish settlements in present-day Mexico.

1546

The Yucatán Maya are defeated by the Spanish.

In their last united effort to defend themselves from Spanish soldiers (see entry for 1523), the Maya of the Yucatán wage a guerrilla war for four months before being subdued. Their defeat marks the end of more than 20 years of the Maya's armed resistance to Spanish rule.

1550

The humanity of Indians is debated in Spain.

Following decades of debate, the question of whether Indians are human beings is argued before the Spanish court by Juan Gine Sepulveda and Bartolomé de Las Casas (see entries for 1502 and for 1542). Sepulveda supports wars of conquest against the Indians because they are "inferior" to the Spanish "just as children are to adults, women to men, and, indeed, one may even say, as apes are to men." Las Casas, a Dominican missionary, maintains that Indians have souls and therefore deserve to be treated humanely while the Spanish try to convert them to Christianity.

As a result of the discussion, the court, appearing to accept Las Casas's point of view, issues a directive to its subjects calling for better treatment of Indian peoples. The order will be largely ignored by the Spaniards in the Americas. The arguments of Sepulveda and Las Casas, however, will have a great deal of influence over future colonizers from England, France, and the Netherlands. They will help persuade some that Indians are inferior savages who should be exterminated, and others that they are human beings, whose liberty must be protected and whose immortal souls must be saved.

1554

The Chichimec raid silver from a Spanish wagon train.

The Chichimec, tribes of roving Indians north of Mexico City, are infuriated by the increased presence of Spaniards in their lands. Since the late 1540s, when the Spanish discovered silver in the area, a constant traffic of wagon trains has been traveling back and forth through Chichimec territory. Even more galling to the Chichimec are Spanish efforts to enslave them and force them to work in their mines. The fierce Chichimec tribes respond with a series of guerrilla raids on Spanish settlements and mines. In their most successful raid, the Chichimec take 30,000 pesos' worth of silver and supplies.

The Maya's *Popul Vuh* is written.

Using Spanish characters, the Maya (see entry for ca. 300 TO 1500) begin to write the *Popul Vuh* in the Quiché language of the Guatemalan Maya. The *Popul Vuh* is a sacred Maya text that preserves ancient stories of the Maya's creation, the actions of their gods, and the history of the Maya people and their kings. In the 18th century, the text will be found by Spanish priests, who will translate it into Spanish. The *Popul Vuh* remains a primary source of information about the Maya's history, religion, and worldview.

"Truly now,
double thanks, triple thanks
that we've been formed, we've
been given
our mouths, our faces,
we speak, we listen,
we wonder, we move,
our knowledge is good, we've
understood
what is far and near
and we've seen what is great
and small
under the sky, on the earth.
Thanks to you we've been
formed,
we've come to be made and
modeled.
our grandmother, our
grandfather."
—the first people's expression of
thanks to their creator, from the
Maya's *Popul Vuh*

1562

Jacques Le Moyne creates the first European images of Indians from life.

To escape persecution, a group of French Huguenots travel to North America and establish settlements in what is now South Carolina and Florida. Among them is Jacques Le Moyne, an artist whose paintings of the Timucua will be the first European images of Indians created by an eyewitness. Although painted from life, Le Moyne's Indians are often positioned in poses and given proportions of classical sculpture, a convention that later European artists will adopt in their depictions of Indians. Although only one of his pictures will survive, they will be popularized in a 1591 publication of engravings by Theodor de Bry.

July 12

Diego de Landa destroys sacred books of the Maya.

Diego de Landa, a Spanish official in the Yucatán, initiates an inquisition to end the native religious practices of the Maya Indians (see entry for ca. 300 TO 1500). Over a three-month period, he oversees the torture of more than 4,500 Maya, about 150 of whom die of their injuries. Landa burns 27 Maya books written in hieroglyphs, thus destroying many of the most important chronicles of the Maya world. Ironically, the Spaniard will later write *Relacion de las cosas de Yucatán*—now one of the best sources on Maya culture, history, and religion.

1565

September 8

The Spanish found St. Augustine.

Appointed governor of Spanish Florida by King Philip II, Pedro Menéndez de Avilés and 3,000 Spanish colonists arrive on the coast of present-day northern Florida. To eliminate French presence from the area, they attack Fort Carolina, near what is now Jacksonville, and kill all of its male

A Theodore de Bry engraving of Timucua women weeping for their dead after the Spanish conquest. The work is based on a painting by Jacques Le Moyne, the first European artist to depict Indians from life. *(Neg. no. 324285, Photo by Rota, Courtesy Dept. of Library Services, American Museum of Natural History)*

inhabitants. The expedition then establishes a military post to the south, St. Augustine. The first permanent European settlement in North America, St. Augustine will become a base for Spanish Jesuit missionaries working among area Indians.

1568

Jesuit missionaries establish an Indian school in Havana, Cuba.

To bolster their efforts to establish a chain of missions along the Atlantic coast, Spanish Jesuits open a school for the sons of Indian leaders. Located in Havana, Cuba, the school teaches Spanish and the Catholic faith in order to train the boys to assist mission priests. The Jesuits take some of their best students to Spain to impress them with the country's grandeur and population. The priests hope that after returning home the boys will share stories about Spain's power and thus help intimidate their people into submission.

1571

Indian convert Don Luis leads a revolt against Jesuit missionaries.

An early convert, baptized Don Luis, leads a revolt against Spanish Jesuits. The missionaries were brought to his people, an Algonquian tribe on the

York River in present-day Virginia, a year earlier by Don Luis himself. He had been picked up by a Spanish ship traveling the river in about 1560 and had spent the next decade receiving instruction in Cuba and Spain. A retaliatory force will invade the homeland of Don Luis's tribe in 1572 and kill some 40 Indians.

1576

English mariner Martin Frobisher kidnaps Baffin Island Inuit.

With a license from Elizabeth I of England, explorer Martin Frobisher sails west on the first of three expeditions to the Canadian Arctic in search of the Northwest Passage between the Atlantic and Pacific Oceans. Frobisher captures several of the Inuit he meets on the coast of Baffin Island. The explorer takes them to London, where they become objects of fascination among the English public. Probably due to exposure to non-Indian disease, all of the captives soon die in the foreign city.

1577

The Florentine Codex escapes destruction by the Spanish Inquisition.

Enforcing a 1559 order from the Inquisition, the Spanish Crown issues a decree that all books in New Spain about Indian people must be sent to Spain. Franciscan missionary Bernardino de Sahagún is excommunicated when he refuses to give up his 13-volume *General History of the Things of New Mexico,* a history of traditional Aztec life (see entry for ca. 1430 TO 1521) and the Spanish invasion of their empire (see entries for 1519 and for 1521), based on the Indians' remembrances. Convinced that the Inquisition will destroy his work, which is highly critical of the Spanish conquest, Sahagún gives a copy to a Franciscan who is supposed to transport it to Seville. The book instead is taken to Florence, Italy, where it becomes known as the Florentine Codex. The history will become an important source of information on the Aztec and their early contact with the Spanish.

> "[The Aztec] were all prudence, industry, and craftsmanship. [They were] feather workers, painters, masons, gold workers, metal casters, carpenters, stone cutters, lapidaries, grinders, stone polishers, weavers, spinners; they were adroit in speech, distinctive in food preparation, elegant with capes, with clothes, offers of incense. They were brave, able in war, takers of captives, conquerors."
>
> —Bernardino de Sahagún in the *General History of the Things of New Mexico*

1579

Francis Drake meets California Indians.

English adventurer Francis Drake explores the Pacific coast in an unsuccessful search for the Northwest Passage—a water route connecting the Pacific and Atlantic Oceans. During the voyage, Drake anchors off the coast of what is now northern California, where he and his crew encounter the Miwok. The English spend five weeks among the tribe, exchanging gifts. The Miwok treat the sailors with reverence. The Englishmen assume that the Indians consider them gods. More likely, the Miwok are awed by the visitors because they sailed to their lands from the west, where the tribe believes the land of the dead is located.

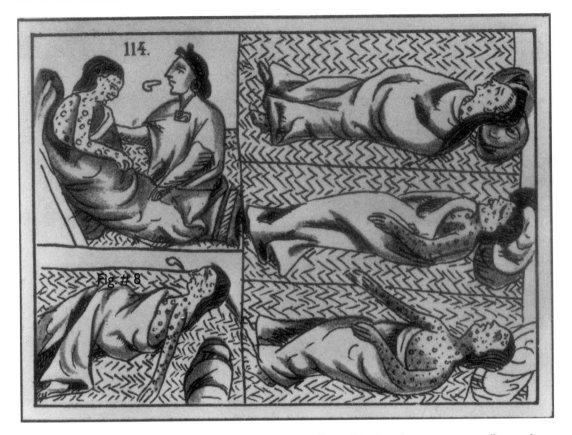

An image from the Florentine Codex showing the devastating effects of the Aztec's exposure to smallpox, a disease introduced to them by the Spanish *(Neg. no. 286821, Photo by Bierwers, Courtesy Dept. of Library Services, American Museum of Natural History)*

1584

The English found a colony on Roanoke Island.

At the encouragement of Sir Walter Raleigh, Queen Elizabeth I of England sends a company of soldiers to North America to establish a colony. The men settle in what is now North Carolina, on Roanoke Island. The Indians in the area welcome them as trading partners, and the English, neglecting to plant their own crops, come to rely on them for food. The dependent colonists soon earn the Indians' ill will. When a silver cup is missed from their supplies, the settlers accuse the Indians of theft and burn one of their villages to the ground. Afraid that an Indian attack is imminent, many of the English return home in late 1585. The colony is kept alive by a new group of 110 settlers, who arrive at Roanoke in 1587. (See also entry for 1590.)

John White uses drawings and paintings to document Indian life.

Soon after the founding of Roanoke in present-day North Carolina, English settler John White begins work on a collections of drawings and watercolors illustrating the customs of Indians living nearby. The images record the Indians' fishing

A watercolor by John White depicting the various fishing methods used in the 16th century by Indians in present-day North Carolina *(National Archives, Neg. no. 208-LU-251-4)*

and farming methods, clothing, ceremonial dances, and family life. Intended to promote further English colonization, White's works show Indians to be odd but industrious, dignified, and joyous people and their land to be fertile and rich with game and fish. His drawings and paintings will become well known through engravings by Theodore de Bry that will be printed in Thomas Hariot's *Briefe and True Report of the New Found Land of Virginia* (1590).

"We found the people most gentle, loving, and faithful, void of all guile and treason, and such as live after the manner of the golden age. The people only care how to defend themselves from the cold in their short winter, and to fed themselves with such meat as the soil affordeth. . . . The earth bringeth forth all things in abundance, as at the first creation, without toil or labor."

—colonist Arthur Barlowe after returning to England from Roanoke in 1584

1589

José de Acosta proposes Asian origins for Indians.

Jesuit missionary José de Acosta theorizes that North America was originally populated before the birth of Christ by humans who crossed a land bridge between Asia and the continent. De Acosta's speculation is the first version of the Bering Strait Theory (see entry for CA. 25,000 TO 12,000 B.C.) to appear in print.

1590

Virginia governor John White finds Roanoke deserted.

After bringing 110 settlers to the struggling English settlement of Roanoke in present-day North Carolina (see entries for 1584), John White returns to England in 1587 to obtain more supplies. His voyage back to North America is delayed when all available English ships are sent to fight the invading Spanish Armada in 1588.

By 1590, when White is finally able to return to Roanoke, the settlement has been deserted. The only evidence of the colonists are some books and armor and the word "CROATOAN" carved into a tree. The settlers' disappearance marks the failure of England's first attempt to establish a permanent colony in North America. Although the fate of the Roanoke colonists will never be known for certain, some scholars will theorize that they were absorbed into the nearby Lumbee tribe or killed by the Powhatan Indians of present-day Virginia.

1598

Pueblo territory is invaded by Don Juan de Oñate.

With the permission of the viceroy of New Spain, Don Juan de Oñate organizes an expedition to found a new Spanish colony, to be called New Mexico, north of the Rio Grande. Funding the enterprise with his own fortune, Oñate travels with approximately 130 soldiers and their families, eight wagons of supplies, and nearly 7,000 head of cattle. Like Coronado before him (see entry for 1540), Oñate hopes to find large gold and silver mines in the American Southwest. Although he will not find the riches he dreams of, Oñate will succeed in establishing the first permanent European colony in the region.

North of what is now Santa Fe, the Spaniards invade a Pueblo village and declare it a Spanish town, San Juan. Oñate sends messengers to other pueblos to inform the Indians that they are now subjects of Spain and must obey Spanish law. He tells the Pueblo

Indians that through their submission they will obtain such benefits as new trade goods and the Catholic religion, which promises them "an eternal life of great bliss." (See also entry for JANUARY 1599.)

1599

January

Pueblo at Acoma are massacred by the Spanish.

Angered by their constant demands for food and clothing, the Indians of Acoma Pueblo rebel against the Spanish soldiers and settlers led by Don Juan de Oñate (see entry for 1598) who have invaded their lands. Acoma warriors kill 13 men, including several officers. Oñate immediately organizes a swift and brutal retaliation. A well-armed Spanish army sets upon Acoma, destroys the pueblo, and massacres approximately 800 residents. Eighty men and 500 woman and children are taken captive.

Oñate punishes the survivors by sentencing women older than 12 and men between 12 and 25 to 20 years of servitude. Men older than 25 are to serve an equal number of years as slaves, but in addition they are to have one foot cut off in a public ceremony. The Spanish also amputate one hand of two Hopi who had been at Acoma at the time of the rebellion. They are set free to tell the people of other pueblos of the hideous consequences of the quelled revolt. The punishments will have the effect Oñate hopes for: the Spanish will not have to contend with another well-organized Pueblo revolt for 80 years (see entry for AUGUST 10, 1680).

1602

The Company of New France is given a trading monopoly.

The French Crown grants the Company of New France a monopoly on trade in its lands in North America. Modeled after the English and Dutch trading companies in the East Indies, the firm is instructed to settle 4,000 colonists within 15 years and to support missionaries in their efforts to convert Indians to Catholicism. Although the company will succeed in bringing France into the lucrative Indian fur trade, it will do little to encourage colonization or missionary work.

1603

Samuel de Champlain begins exploring the Northeast.

Sailing for France, Samuel de Champlain starts his extensive travels along the Atlantic coast of what is now southern Canada and northern United States—explorations that will solidify his country's land claims in the region. During his journeys, Champlain encounters many different Indian groups and tries to establish friendly relationships. In part because he meets the most hostility from southern Indians, the French will focus on settling less fertile areas to the north, making them more dependent on trade with Indians for food and supplies than are other European colonizers. (See also entries for 1608, SUMMER 1609, JUNE 1610, and AUGUST 1615.)

1604

The Micmac establish a trade relationship with the French at Port Royal.

At Port Royal, a trading post on the Bay of Fundy, the French court the nearby Micmac as trading partners. French traders offer the Micmac an array of European goods, such as metalware and clothing. Even more interesting to the Indians are muskets and steel arrow points, which help them defeat their Indian enemies. Several traders, including Charles Biencourt de Saint-Just and Robert Gravé du Pont, also please the Micmac by learning their language and adopting many of their ways. The Micmac and French at the post will develop such a close friendship that both groups will routinely offer to share provisions whenever the other's food stores run low.

3

1607 TO 1775
NATIVES AND NEWCOMERS

In 1607 the English founded Jamestown; in 1608 the French built Quebec; and in 1609 the Spanish established Santa Fe. Non-Indians had been arriving in North America for more than 100 years, and by the beginning of the 17th century, as Europeans established these and other permanent settlements, the signs were clear that they intended to stay.

Indian reactions to these invaders in their lands varied according to the foreigners' aims and behavior. Overall, the French were given the highest regard. They primarily came to North America as businessmen intent on amassing fortunes in the fur trade, in which they gave European goods to Indians in exchange for the pelts of fur-bearing animals, most often the beaver. The French sought to create strong friendships with their Indian trading partners, because their livelihoods depended on it. Traders often adopted Indian customs, particularly the ritual of giving gifts to express goodwill, and they sometimes married Indian women to strengthen these crucial business relationships.

The Spanish incursions in the Southwest and Southeast were far more disruptive to the Indian groups there. Using methods of conquest pioneered by the Spanish in Mexico, soldiers swept into Indian villages and compelled the inhabitants to perform labor for them. In exchange, the Spanish promised protection from their Indian and non-Indian enemies. Responding to the Spanish Crown's insistence on the conversion of its Indian subjects, Catholic priests established missions among the Indians.

Groups under Spanish control generally tried to keep the peace by accommodating—or seeming to accommodate—the demands of soldiers and missionaries. Indians such as the Pueblo, for instance, worked for the Spanish and agreed to become Christian converts, all the while retaining much of their autonomy and their traditional culture and religion. Only when conditions became intolerably oppressive did the Indians respond with violence. The 17th century saw a series of Pueblo revolts, the most effective being the rebellion led by Popé in 1680, which forced the Spanish to abandon the Pueblos' territory for 12 years.

Despite the frequent brutality of the Spanish, the English posed perhaps an even greater threat to their Indian neighbors. Relatively uninterested in the Indians' souls or animal furs, they instead had their eyes on tribal lands. As their population and number of settlements grew, the English showed little regard for the Indian populations they displaced. With the exception of a few enlightened colonial leaders such as Roger Williams and William Penn, British settlers generally viewed Indians with contempt. They took whatever land they wanted without its inhabitants' consent and without offering any sort of compensation. When met with Indian resistance, they fought back with unequaled ferocity. Their aim in such conflicts as the Pequot War and King Philip's War was not just victory but the total annihilation of their Indian enemies.

Increased contact with whites did not just bring Indians into conflict with the newcomers. It also created new rivalries or inflamed old ones between Indian groups. The Pueblo and the Apache had long had a contentious relationship. But when the Spanish refused to provide the Apache with the Pueblo corn they needed, the Apache had to resort to attacking and raiding Pueblo villages to steal the food they previously had obtained through trade. Competition in the fur trade similarly pitted the Huron tribes against the mighty Iroquois Confederacy. As allies of the French, the Huron grew wealthy as middlemen, trading food to interior tribes for furs, which they in turn traded to their French partners. Armed by the Dutch, the jealous Iroquois set out to destroy their Huron rivals. In a brutal 1649 attack, they killed huge numbers of Huron and drove the survivors from their lands, forever destroying the unity of the tribe.

By the beginning of the 18th century, Indians were increasingly drawn into the conflicts between the English and French, who had emerged as the primary non-Indian competitors for lands in the east. A series of wars fought on European and North American soil culminated in what was called in North America the French and Indian War (1754–63)—so named because most Indian groups involved in the conflict chose to fight on the side of the French. England's victory in the war proved disastrous for all eastern Indians. In the peace treaty, France was forced to relinquish nearly all its land claims in North America. Indians were stunned by these concessions: accustomed to playing the two European powers against one another, they now had to deal with the British only, leaving them in a far more vulnerable position than ever before.

The Indians' fears about the English were quickly borne out. General Jeffrey Amherst, the commander of British troops in North America, abandoned the European practice of distributing gifts to ingratiate Indians and solidify allegiances with them. Many groups had come to rely on the goods they had routinely received from the French, so Amherst's policy posed a dire threat to their well-being. Indian fury at the British exploded in a series of attacks on Detroit and other English forts. The conflict became known as Pontiac's Rebellion, after the Ottawa leader who helped instigate the attacks by translating the anti-British religious movement of the popular Lenni Lenape (Delaware) prophet Neolin into military action.

Although the rebellion was short-lived, it impressed upon the English government the need to court Indian favor. The Crown responded by establishing the Proclamation Line of 1763, a boundary stretching along the crest of the Appalachian Mountains. The king declared that all land west of the line was for Indian use and forbade all colonists from entering it. The declaration, however, did little except fuel the growing anger of the colonists, who resented royals an ocean away dictating where the colonists could and could not settle. These tensions would only become more intense and would eventually draw Indians into still another non-Indian war.

1607

May

English colonists establish Jamestown on Powhatan land.

In three ships, approximately 100 English arrive on the coast of what is now Virginia. They are financed by the Virginia Company, which was chartered by James I to found a colony there. The crew establishes Jamestown, named after the English king, on a site along what is now called the James River, in the lands of the Powhatan Indians—a confederacy of some 32 tribes, united by conquest under the powerful leader Wahunsunacock, also known as Powhatan.

Although Jamestown will become the first permanent English settlement in North America, the settlement will be nearly abandoned after about two-thirds of the colonists die during the first winter. The undisciplined settlers will be so distracted by the discovery of iron pyrite—fool's gold, which they take to be the real thing—that they neglect to plant the crops needed for their survival. The survivors are saved only by the arrival of ships carrying more settlers and supplies in January 1608.

December

Pocahontas "rescues" John Smith.

While exploring the Chickahominy River, Jamestown leader John Smith is taken captive by a band of warriors. According to Smith's 1624 account of the incident, the Indians take him to their village and treat him to a great feast in the presence of the warriors' chief, Powhatan. Powhatan then tells his men to place two large blocks of stone before him and force Smith to kneel down with his head on the stone. As the warriors lift their clubs, Powhatan's 11-year-old daughter hurls herself over the Englishman and pleads for his life. Powhatan stops the execution and frees Smith.

Smith's story will become one of the most popular anecdotes in American history. If not a complete fabrication, the tale is likely colored by Smith's lack of knowledge of Indian culture. Rather than an execution, the event is most likely an initiation ceremony, during which Pocahontas symbolically saves Smith so he can be reborn as a member of the Powhatan Confederacy. (See also entries for APRIL 6, 1808, and for JUNE 1995.)

> "[I was] taken prisoner by the power of *Powhatan*, their chief King. . . . After some six weeks fatting amongst those Saluage Courtiers, at the minute of my execution, [Pocahontas] hazarded the beating out of her own brains to saue mine, and not only that, but so prevailed with her father, that I was safely conducted to *Jamestowne*."
>
> —John Smith on his "rescue" in *General Historie of Virginia* (1624)

1608

July 3

Samuel de Champlain founds Quebec.

Samuel de Champlain (see entry for 1603) and a crew of 28 Frenchmen sail up the St. Lawrence River and found a settlement at Stadacona, the site of present-day Quebec City. The future capital of New France, the tiny settlement will rely on trade with area Indians for its survival. Under Champlain, the French learn to develop relationships with Indians based on mutual need. In exchange for food, supplies, and knowledge of how to thrive in their new environment, the French offer the Indians coveted European goods such as metal tools and guns. (See also entries for SUMMER 1609, JUNE 1610, AUGUST 1615, and 1629.)

1609

English explorer Henry Hudson travels up the Hudson River.

Hired by the Dutch East India Company, Englishman Henry Hudson and a crew of 24 sails to North America in search of the fabled Northwest Passage connecting the Atlantic and Pacific Oceans. Hudson explores the New England coast and Delaware Bay before traveling up the river that now bears his name to the site of present-day Albany. His explorations will allow the Dutch to claim the area and for a time dominate the Indian fur trade in the region.

The Spanish found Santa Fe.

On the site of ancient Indian ruins, Spaniards establish the settlement of Santa Fe. The site will become the capital of the Spanish province of New Mexico and serve as the most important trading center for the Spanish and Indians in the American Southwest for more than 200 years.

Summer

Indians and the French join forces against the Mohawk.

Huron, Algonkin, and Montagnais warriors and Frenchmen led by Samuel de Champlain (see entry for 1603) attack a large party of Mohawk on what is now Lake Champlain. Although outmanned, the Huron-French force—well armed with muskets—quickly repels the Mohawk, who are stunned when Champlain shoots and kills two of their leaders in the initial volley. The encounter greatly impresses the French-allied Indians, who come to see maintaining a friendship with the French (and thus access to European weapons) as the key to protecting themselves from their traditional Iroquois enemies. It also seals the Iroquois hatred of the French, which will lead them into alliances with the Dutch and English during the early years of contact.

1610

The Powhatan and the English go to war.

On the brink of starvation, the colonists at Jamestown (see entry for MAY 1607) are ready to abandon their settlement when ships from England arrive with provisions and 300 more settlers. Bolstered by the newcomers, the English begin expanding their colony into the lands of the tribes ruled by the Indian leader Powhatan. As the Indians defend their territory, war breaks out between the Powhatan Confederacy and the Virginians. In response to the Indians' guerrilla attacks, the English launch vicious retaliatory campaigns, in which they set entire villages ablaze and slaughter Indian women and children. The fighting will continue for four bloody years until a peace is solidified through the marriage of Pocahontas, the daughter of Powhatan, to the wealthy colonist John Rolfe (see entry for APRIL 5, 1614).

> "Why should you take by force that from us which you can have by love? Why should you destroy us, who have provided you with food? What can you get by war? We can hide our provisions, and fly into the woods; and then you must consequently famish by wronging your friends. What is the cause of your jealousy? You see us unarmed, and willing to supply your wants, if you come in a friendly manner, and not with swords and guns as to invade an enemy."
>
> —Powhatan to the Jamestown colonists in 1609, as recorded by Captain John Smith

The French clergy begins ministering to Indians in New France.

Jessé Fléché, a secular priest, starts preaching Catholicism to the Micmac Indians and succeeds in baptizing more than 100. The ceremonies, however, violate Church law, since the Micmac do not understand the meaning of baptism. Fléché's errors will motivate later French missionaries to make an effort to learn Indian languages.

June

Samuel de Champlain organizes a cultural exchange with France's Indian allies.

At the urging of French explorer Samuel de Champlain (see entry for 1603), the Algonkin tribe takes in a young Frenchman named Étienne Brûlé. Champlain also agrees to send to France a young Huron Indian, called Sauvignon by the French. The exchange is meant to help the French and their Indian allies understand each other's culture. Champlain specifically hopes that Brûlé will master the Algonkin language and that Sauvignon, upon returning home, will impress his people with stories of France's greatness and power.

1612

The English colonists begin to cultivate tobacco.

Through a series of experiments, Virginia planter John Rolfe develops a strain of tobacco for export to Europe. American Indians have long cultivated tobacco for ceremonial use, but their variety, which is strong enough to produce hallucinations, is deemed too harsh to sell to Europeans for recreational use. By 1620, tobacco will become Virginia's largest cash crop. The income the crop generates will help allow the colony to grow quickly, causing increasing threats to Indian peoples in the region. (See also entry for APRIL 5, 1614.)

1613

The Beothuk are exterminated by the French and their Micmac allies.

In present-day Newfoundland, Canada, the Beothuk kill 37 French fishermen after a Frenchman guns down a tribe member. The French retaliate by arming the Micmac, the Beothuk's enemies, and offering bounties for Beothuk scalps. With French assistance, the Micmac nearly wipe out the Beothuk tribe. (See also entry for 1829.)

Smallpox strikes the Timucua tribe.

The Timucua Indians of present-day northern Florida are hard hit by an epidemic of smallpox, a disease introduced to North America by non-Indians. With no natural immunities to fight the illness, more than half of the Timucua will die of smallpox over the next four years.

Spring

Pocahontas is captured by the English.

While visiting relatives in a neighboring village, Pocahontas, the teenage daughter of the Indian leader Powhatan (see entry for DECEMBER 1607), encounters an English captain named Samuel Argall. Argall offers her gifts and leads her onto his ship, where she is taken hostage. The English refuse to release Pocahontas until Powhatan's people surrender their guns.

When Powhatan declines to meet their demands, Pocahontas is taken to Jamestown (see entry for MAY 1607), where she is schooled in English and white customs. Claiming that she is a willing convert, the English baptize Pocahontas and rename her Rebecca. The settlers use her conversion to convince their English patrons of their success in bringing Christianity to the Indian "heathens."

1614

Squanto is kidnapped and taken to Europe.

Englishmen under the command of Thomas Hunt kidnap about 20 Wampanoag Indians along the coast of what is now Massachusetts and sail to Spain. There Hunt begins to sell his captives, until priests stop him and take over the care of the Indians, whom they try to convert to Catholicism. Among those taken in by the priests is a young man named Squanto. During the next five years Squanto will travel to London, where he will become fluent in English and knowledgeable in British ways. After his return to North America in 1619, his experiences will allow him to help colonists of Plymouth adapt to their new environment (see entry for MARCH 1621).

Dutch traders arrive in what is now New York State.

Four Dutch firms merge to form the United New Netherlands Trading Company. The company receives a royal charter that grants the firm a monopoly on lands claimed by the Dutch crown in what is now New York State. The charter allows Dutch traders to begin taking advantage of the lucrative Indian fur trade in northeastern North America.

"[M]y chiefest intent and purpose [is] to strive with all my power and body and mind, in the undertaking of so mighty a matter, no way led (so far forth as mans weakness may permit) with the unbridled desire of carnal affection: but for the good of this plantation, for the honour of our country, for the glory of God, for my owne salvation, and for the converting to the true knowledge of God and Jesus Christ, an unbelieving creature, namely Pocahontas."

—John Rolfe in a letter to Virginia deputy governor Thomas Dale on his reasons for marrying Pocahontas

April 5

Pocahontas marries John Rolfe.

With the permission of the powerful Indian leader Powhatan, John Rolfe, a wealthy Jamestown settler (see entry for 1612), marries Powhatan's daughter Pocahontas (see entries for DECEMBER 1607 and SPRING 1613) in a Christian ceremony. The wedding is primarily an act of diplomacy, symbolizing a truce between the Powhatan Indians and the English. While it is unknown whether Pocahontas entered the union voluntarily, the marriage produces one child, Thomas Rolfe. For many generations, prominent families in Virginia will trace their ancestries back to Thomas Rolfe and proudly claim Pocahontas as an ancestor (see entry for 1924).

1615

August

Samuel de Champlain goes to live among the Huron.

To solidify the allegiance between France and the Huron, Samuel de Champlain (see entry for 1603) travels to the Huron villages, where he lives until the following spring. The Huron welcome Champlain, who has earned their friendship by helping them fight their Iroquois enemies (see entry for 1609). While staying with the Huron, the French leader joins them in another successful raid on the Iroquois near present-day Lake Ontario.

1616

Smallpox strikes New England.

Tribes throughout what is now New England fall victim to a massive smallpox epidemic. The non-Indian disease may have been spread to them by whites fishing in coastal waters or by English slave traders who raided Indian villages in present-day Massachusetts two years earlier. Over the next three years, Indians, who have no natural immunity to the disease, die in huge numbers. The total Indian population of the region falls by perhaps as much as 90 percent. Some tribes virtually cease to exist.

June

Pocahontas begins touring England.

To raise funds for the fledgling colony of Jamestown, the Virginia Company sends Pocahontas and her family (see entry for APRIL 5, 1614) to England. There she is welcomed as an Indian "princess" by the English elite and granted an audience with King James I. During her English tour she is nicknamed *"la belle sauvage"* ("the beautiful savage"). According to one eyewitness, she "carr[ied] herself as the daughter of a King, and was accordingly respected . . . [by] persons of Honor."

Pocahontas in an engraving made during her 1616–17 tour of England. It is most likely the only image of Pocahontas for which she posed. (*Virginia Historical Society*)

1617

March 21

Pocahontas dies in England.

As Pocahontas, accompanied by her husband John Rolfe and her infant Thomas, sets sail for Virginia, she falls ill in Gravesend, England. There, at the age of 21, she dies of a disease that she contracted during her tour of England (see entry for JUNE 1616). Pocahontas is one of millions of Indians who will lose their lives to European diseases.

March 24

King James endorses the establishment of Indian churches and schools.

In James I's royal charter to the Virginia Company (see entry MAY 1607), he charged the firm to bring Christianity to Indians who "as yet live in darkness and miserable ignorance of the true knowledge and worship of God." Disappointed by the colonists' slow progress in creating Indian converts, King James orders the archbishops of Canterbury and York to collect funds for the building of Indian churches and schools in Virginia. Even with these efforts, few Indians will show much enthusiasm for the whites' religion. Parents will be especially resistant to the idea of sending their children to English-run schools intent on indoctrinating pupils in the Christian religion and other white beliefs and customs.

1618

April

Opechancanough becomes the leader of the Powhatan tribes.

At the age of about 70, Powhatan, the powerful leader of a confederacy of tribes in present-day Virginia (see entry for MAY 1607), dies of natural causes. With his demise, the hope for a lasting peace between the English and the Powhatan dies as well. He is succeeded by his brother Opechancanough, who is faced with leading his people through a time of crisis. As the Powhatan population is ravaged by a smallpox epidemic, land-hungry colonists take advantage of the Indians' vulnerability by demanding more and more of their territory. Opechancanough's rage at the English will soon erupt into open warfare (see entry for MARCH 22, 1622). (See also entries for APRIL 18, 1644, and OCTOBER 1646.)

1620

A royal order regulates the use of Indian labor in Spanish New Mexico.

Amid growing tensions between Spanish authorities and clergy in Pueblo territory, the viceroy of New Mexico issues the Royal Order of 1620. The measure is meant to prevent the New Mexico governor, Juan de Eulate, and his supporters from exploiting Indian labor, as priests ministering to the Pueblo have accused them of doing. According to the order, only 2 percent of the Pueblo can be pressed into working for the Spanish as herders and tillers, and these laborers are to be paid for their work. The order also prevents Spanish livestock from grazing on or near the Pueblo's fields.

December 21

The Pilgrims establish the Plymouth colony on Indian lands.

Approximately 100 Puritan separatists from the Church of England (now known as the Pilgrims) arrive on the coast of what is now Cape Cod, in Massachusetts. The area is occupied by several Indian groups, including the Wampanoag, Massachuset, Pawtucket, and Nipmuck. The Pilgrims immediately begin staking out farming plots on the Indians' land.

1621

The Dutch West India Company is formed.

The Netherlands grants a charter to the Dutch West India Company, which is to have a monopoly on Dutch trade in North America and Africa. The firm quickly makes impressive inroads in the fur trade with northeastern Indian groups, such as the Mahican and the Mohawk. By the end of the decade it will have more than 15,000 employees and will actively encourage colonization by offering large estates in North America to Dutchmen who bring 50 settlers to the Dutch colony of New Netherlands.

The English kill Powhatan prophet Nenmattanaw.

The Powhatan Indians, exhausted by skirmishes with the English and decimated by non-Indian diseases (see entry for APRIL 1618), turn to new religious leaders who promise the return of the Indian world as it existed before contact with Europeans. Prominent among them is Nenmattanaw, who tells his followers that he has an ointment that will make them invulnerable to the colonists' bullets. Amidst rumors that he is planning a rebellion, Nenmattanaw kills an Englishman and walks into the dead man's village. The colonists shoot him dead. Many of the prophet's followers will avenge his murder the following year by joining Powhatan leader Opechancanough's surprise attack against the English villages (see entry for MARCH 1622).

March

Samoset and Squanto offer help to the starving Pilgrims.

During a harsh winter with little food, half of the Plymouth Pilgrims died from disease (see entry for DECEMBER 21, 1620). Wampanoag leader Massasoit takes pity on the survivors and sends Samoset, an Abenaki who learned a little English from coastal fishermen, to their settlement. The English colonists are stunned to see the Indian man approach them calling out, "Welcome Englishmen." The Pilgrims feed Samoset, who returns home the next day.

Several days later, Samoset comes back to Plymouth with a Pawtucket Indian named Squanto. Squanto learned to speak English fluently in London after he was captured and taken to Europe as a slave seven years before (see entry for 1614). Squanto shows the Pilgrims how to build shelters, how to fish in area rivers, and even more important, how to grow corn, squash, and pumpkins.

Squanto also acts as an interpreter for the Pilgrims in their early dealings with Indians. On March 22, he helps Massasoit and the Pilgrim leaders negotiate a treaty that promises friendly relations between the Wampanoag and the English. Massasoit's overtures are probably motivated by his desire for the Pilgrims' assistance in battling his people's enemies, the Narragansett.

> "[Squanto] was their interpreter, and was a spetiall instrument sent of God for their good beyond their expectation. He directed them how to set their corn, where to take fish, and to procure other commodities, and was also their pilot to bring them to unknown places for their profit, and never left them till he dyed."
>
> —Plymouth leader William Bradford on Squanto's aid to the colonists

Autumn

The Pilgrims and their Wampanoag guests celebrate the first Thanksgiving.

The English of the Plymouth settlement invite Wampanoag leader Massasoit (see entry for MARCH 1621) to a feast in appreciation for his people's help in teaching the Europeans how to farm in their new homeland. Massasoit arrives accompanied by 90 warriors. When it becomes clear that the colonists do not have enough food for all, Massasoit orders his people to contribute to the feast. The event follows the Indian tradition of thanking the Creator for a plentiful harvest. An annual commemoration of the thanksgiving feast will be declared a national holiday by U.S. president Abraham Lincoln in 1863.

1622

March 22

Opechancanough's warriors attack Virginia colonists.

While professing peace and friendship with the English colonists, Powhatan leader Opechancanough (see entry for APRIL 1618) makes careful plans to drive them from their lands forever. His warriors strike on the morning of Good Friday. Gathering in the English villages ostensibly to trade, they suddenly seize the colonists' weapons and set upon the Europeans. In the battle, more than 300 whites—nearly one-fourth of Virginia's population—are killed. The casualties would have been higher had not several Indians friendly with the colonists alerted a few settlements to Opechancanough's plot at the last minute.

The slaughter prompts the colonists' to organize a campaign to exterminate their Indian neighbors. With plenty of supplies and provisions from Europe, they devote themselves to battling area tribes. The colonists are directed by the Virginia Company (see entry for MAY 1607) to "pursue and follow [the Indians], surprising them in the habitation, intercepting them in their hunting, burning their towns, [and] demolishing their temples."

1623

The Plymouth militia kills eight Massachuset Indians.

Angered by the insulting behavior of several Massachuset leaders, Miles Standish leads the Plymouth militia against the tribe on the false pretext that the Indians are plotting an attack on English settlements. Eight of the formerly friendly Massachuset are killed. Among them is Wituwamet, a sachem whose severed head the colonists' display atop the fort at Plymouth.

May 22

The English murder Powhatan leaders at a peace conference.

Beaten down by the Virginia colonists' relentless military campaign against the Powhatan people (see entry for MARCH 1622), Opechancanough and several other Powhatan leaders agree to release a few English prisoners and discuss terms of a truce. At the end of the meeting, the colonists offer the Indians wine tainted with poison. As the drug takes effect, the English open fire on the groggy Powhatan. Opechancanough is shot, but he survives the attack and manages to escape.

1624

The Dutch found the trading post at Fort Orange.

The Dutch establish their first trading post in North America at what is now Albany, New York. From the post, named Fort Orange, the Dutch will develop prosperous trading relationships with several area Indian groups, including the Mahican and the Mohawk.

1626

The Dutch and the Mahicans are defeated by the Mohawk.

Although the Dutch generally follow a policy of neutrality in intertribal warfare, four Dutch traders join the Mahicans in a raid against their Mohawk enemies. The Dutch-Mahican force is soundly defeated by the powerful Mohawk, and the traders are killed.

May 6

The Canarsee sell Manhattan to the Dutch.

Peter Minuit, the governor of New Netherlands, purchases the island now known as Manhattan from the Canarsee Indians for 60 Dutch guilders' worth of goods. Minuit is following the instructions of the charter of the United New Netherlands Company, which stipulates that the company cannot take control of Indian land without their consent and must be fair and honest in all negotiations with Indian groups. After discovering that the island they bought is not part of Canarsee territory, the Dutch will later make another payment for the land to the Manhattan Indians, who claim Manhattan as their hunting grounds.

1628

The Merry Mount colony is destroyed.

Thomas Morton, the leader of the small English colony of Merry Mount, infuriates the leaders of nearby Plymouth by trading gunpowder and liquor to area Indians and abandoning Puritan reserve to stage dances around a maypole. A force of Plymouth colonists led by Miles Standish (see entry for 1623) attacks Merry Mount and arrests Morton, who is sent back to England in order to remove his immoral influence from the colonies.

1629

July

The Montagnais aid David Kirke in taking over New France.

An English crew led by adventurer David Kirke compels Samuel de Champlain to surrender Quebec (see entry for JULY 3, 1608). In this bold move, Kirke is probably supported by the Montagnais, who have grown disenchanted with the French as trading partners. Quebec will be restored to French control in 1632 by the Treaty of Saint Germain-en-Laye.

1631

The Lenni Lenape (Delaware) attack Swanendael.

A band of Lenni Lenape (Delaware) Indians attack the Dutch settlement of Swanendael (the site of present-day Lewes, Delaware). The Indians destroy the town and massacre 32 settlers. Eager to maintain peace, the Dutch West India Company (see entry for 1621) chooses to negotiate with the Lenni Lenape rather than retaliate. To ingratiate the rebel Indians, the Dutch offer them gifts and increased avenues for trade.

1632

The Pequot attack a Dutch trading post.

Pequot warriors attack Indians gathered to trade at House of Hope, a Dutch trading post established at present-day Hartford, Connecticut. The Pequot are angered that the Dutch are trading directly with area tribes, bypassing Pequot middlemen. In retaliation, the Dutch kill Pequot leader Tatotem.

"[O]our lives depend upon a single thread.... [T]he malice of the Savages gives especial cause for almost perpetual fear; a malcontent may burn you down, or cleave your head open in some lonely spot. And then you are responsible for the sterility or fecundity of the earth, under penalty of your life; you are the cause of droughts; if you cannot make rain, they speak of nothing less than making away with you."

—Father Paul le Jeune
in *Jesuit Relations*

Jesuit Relations begins publication.

Jesuit missionaries record their efforts to convert Indians in New France in the first volume of *Jesuit Relations*. The publication will appear annually until 1674. Although largely a propaganda tool to promote Jesuit missions, *Jesuit Relations* will become a source of extensive information on the earliest relationships between Indians and the French.

Bernal Díaz del Castillo's *True Story of the Conquest of New Spain* is published.

Fifty-one years after his death, Bernal Díaz del Castillo's account of the Spanish conquest of the Aztec Empire (see entry for CA. 1430 TO 1521) is published. Díaz del Castillo was a conquistador who participated in both of Hernán Cortés's brutal campaigns against the Aztec capital of Tenochtitlán (see entries for 1519 and for 1521). *New Spain* is the first history of these events written by an eyewitness.

1633

The Zuni kill Spanish priests and soldiers.

To convert the Zuni, in 1629 the Spanish sent four priests under the protection of a group of soldiers into the Indians' territory. After four years, the Zuni become so angered by the presence of foreigners in their midst that they rise up against the Spanish, killing all of the soldiers and two of the missionaries.

Smallpox spreads through eastern Indian groups.

An epidemic of smallpox, a disease brought to North America by non-Indians, strikes Indian populations throughout what is now the northeastern United States and southeastern Canada. For two years the disease will spread quickly from Indian group to Indian group. With no natural immunity to the disease, Indians die in huge numbers. The Huron alone lose more than 10,000 tribe members.

The English colonists celebrate the horrendous epidemic as proof of God's approval of their efforts to expand into Indian territory. Charleston town records state, "[W]ithout this remarkable and terrible stroke of God upon the natives, [we] would with much more difficulty have found room, and at far greater charge have obtained and purchased Indian land."

1634

Jean Nicolet encounters Indians of the Great Lakes.

Jean Nicolet, a French explorer living among the Huron, heads west into the Lake Michigan region to find new sources of furs. The first white man to arrive in the area, Nicolet comes into contact with many large Great Lakes tribes, such as the Menomonee and the Winnebago. At present-day Green Bay, Wisconsin—the future site of an important French trading center—Nicolet concludes a treaty with area Indians.

The Jesuits found a mission on Huron lands.

Three French Jesuit priests, accompanied by six servants, establish the mission of Saint Joseph in the Huron village of Ihonatiria. The Jesuits, who have been active in New France since 1626, target the Huron for conversion because they are France's most loyal Indian allies and because their settled agricultural way of life makes them appear good candidates for "civilization." Despite some tension, the Huron tolerate the Jesuits in their lands, although few are eager to adopt Catholicism. Nevertheless, the Jesuit mission system will grow steadily until the Huron tribe is decimated by Iroquois warfare (see entry for MARCH 1649).

November 1

The Pequot ally themselves to the Massachusetts colonists.

Desperate after a smallpox epidemic (see entry for 1633), the Pequot sign a treaty with the colonists of Massachusetts. The colonists offer to help the Pequot battle their Narragansett enemies. In return, the Pequot are required to pay the colony an enormous tribute of wampum (shell beads). The Pequot are also to surrender the murderers of a white trader, John Sloan, who most likely was killed by Indians of another tribe. The English add this provision possibly knowing that the Pequot will have difficulty fulfilling it, therefore giving the English an excuse to break the treaty when it proves convenient. (See also entry for AUGUST 25, 1636.)

1636

Roger Williams establishes Providence on Narragansett land.

After being expelled from the colony of Massachusetts for advocating a separation of church and state, minister Roger Williams heads south and establishes the settlement of Providence on lands he purchases from the Narragansett Indians. Williams promotes the idea that the English should negotiate fairly with Indians tribes for all lands they claim and occupy. (See also entry for 1643.)

August 25

Massachusetts troops attack Block Island Pequot.

On the order of Massachusetts leaders, Captain John Endicott leads an expedition against the Pequot of Block Island, off the coast of present-day Rhode Island. The expedition is supposedly to avenge the murder of a white trader, but the man was most likely killed by Indians of another tribe (see entry for 1634). Endicott is told to kill all Pequot men at the Block Island, but he finds their village nearly deserted, so his soldiers set it ablaze.

After the attack, the Pequot attempt to organize a pan-Indian alliance to drive the whites out of their lands. When they are unable to persuade the Narragansett, Mohegan, and Massachuset to join their cause, the Pequot resolve to battle the English alone (see entry for MAY 25, 1637).

1637

May 25

The English destroy the Pequot's village at Mystic.

In a vicious campaign against the Pequot, whom the English regard as their greatest Indian enemies (see entry for AUGUST 25, 1636), about 250 well-armed militiamen set ablaze the tribe's principal village at present-day Mystic, Connecticut. The soldiers slaughter everyone who flees the flames. In the massacre, between 400 and one thousand Indians, mostly women and children, are brutally killed. The English are aided by Mohegan and Narragansett warriors, who later express their horror at the ferocity of the white militia.

After the attack, the English hunt down the Pequot who have escaped. Many are slaughtered; others are taken captive. About 50 captives are made slaves to serve the colonists, but those deemed the most hostile are sold into slavery in the West Indies in exchange for Africans, who become the first black slaves in New England.

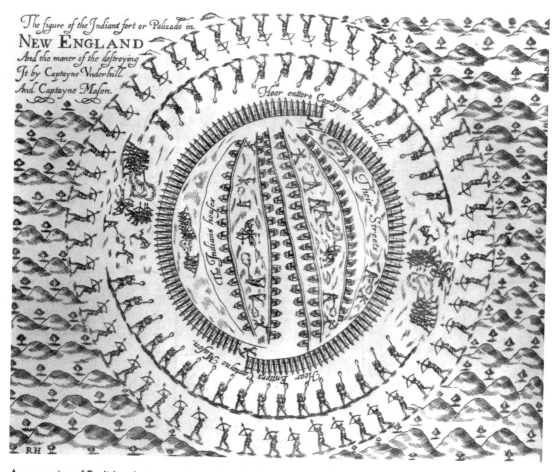

An engraving of English colonists attacking a fortified Pequot village during their 1636–37 war against the tribe (*Library of Congress, Neg. no. USZ62-32055*)

The Pequot massacre has enormous ramifications for Indian-white relations in the colonies. In addition to nearly destroying the Pequot as tribe, the slaughter sends a message to other area Indians that resistance to the English is futile. It also helps unite the Massachusetts colonists, who have been struggling with dissension within their leadership. By demonizing the Pequot, the English come to see the massacre as a shared victory in a holy war. Puritan minister Cotton Mather celebrates the killings by writing, "No less than six hundred souls were brought down to hell that day." (See also entry for 1638.)

> "It was a fearful sight to see them thus frying in the fire and the streams of blood quenching the same, and horrible was the stink and scent thereof; but the victory seemed a sweet sacrifice, and they gave the praise thereof to God, who had wrought so wonderfully for them, thus to enclose their enemies in their hands and give them so speedy a victory over so proud and insulting an enemy."
>
> —Plymouth leader William Bradford on the slaughter of the Pequot Indians

1638

The Treaty of Hartford ends the Pequot War.

The hostilities between the Massachusetts colonists and the Pequot Indians are officially concluded with the Treaty of Hartford. Decimated by the colonists' attack on their principal village (see entry for MAY 25, 1637), the now-powerless Pequot are offered nothing in the treaty. It holds that any Pequot who escaped massacre will be forced to live as a slave with an English-allied tribe. It also forbids the Pequot from ever again living in their former lands.

March

The Swedish buy Indian land in the Delaware Valley.

With the help of Dutch envoy Peter Minuit, Swedish colonists purchase land along what is now Delaware Bay from the Indians of the region. The settlement they establish at the site of present-day Wilmington, Delaware, is the first in New Sweden. Although the Swedish presence in North America remains limited, the Swedes will become important trading partners of the Susquehannock (see entry for 1643), Lenni Lenape (Delaware), and Mingo until the colony is dissolved in the 1650s.

November 14

The English establish the first Indian reservation.

The English compel the Wappinger Indians of present-day Connecticut to cede most of their territory. The agreement reserves only 1,200 acres for the tribe's use. The Indians are forbidden from leaving or selling this land, and their activities are to be monitored by an English agent. The arrangement represents the earliest enforcement of many elements of later reservation policy.

1639

The Dutch tax their Indian neighbors.

The governor of the Dutch West India Company, Willem Kieft, attempts to help finance the struggling colony of New Netherlands by imposing a tax on nearby tribes. The tax—payable in furs, wampum, or corn—is greatly resented by the

Indians, most of whom are unwilling to pay it. Their refusal increases the animosity of the New Netherlands colonists toward surrounding Indian groups.

The Huron begin embroidering in moose hair.

In Quebec, five French nuns establish a seminary for Huron girls, whom they teach to embroider floral designs using needle and thread. When their supplies run out, the young women improvise, using individual strands of moose hair colored with vegetable dyes in place of thread. Dyed moose hair had long been used by the tribal craftspeople to decorate items made from birch bark. By the 19th century, the Huron of Quebec will create a sizable industry selling clothing embroidered in moose hair to non-Indians.

1641

The Dutch offer bounties for Indian scalps.

A group of Hackensack Indians kill two Dutch farmers who allowed their cattle to trample the Indians' corn fields. Following tribal tradition, the Hackensack tribe offers their widows wampum to atone for the murders, but Dutch officials demand that the tribe give up the killers. When the Indians refuse, New Netherlands governor Willem Kieft offers bounties for Hackensack scalps.

1643

Roger Williams's *Key into the Language of America* is published.

A student of Narragansett language and culture, Providence's founder Roger Williams (see entry for 1636) compiles *A Key into the Language of America.* The book is among the earliest works on Indian language written by a non-Indian. As well as recording Narragansett words such as *succotash* and *squash,* which have entered the colonists' language, Williams also notes that the Narragansett have adopted versions of English words, including *moneash* for *money* and *pigsuck* for *pig.*

The Susquehannock drive off Maryland settlers.

Frustrated by the movement of Maryland settlers onto their lands, the Susquehannock ask their Swedish trading partners (see entry for 1638) living along Delaware Bay for help. The Swedes give the Indians advice as well as guns and ammunition, which the Susquehannock use to force the whites off their territory.

The Iroquois become Dutch allies.

The powerful tribes of the Iroquois Confederacy negotiate a treaty of alliance with the Dutch. In the agreement, the Indians promise to give the Dutch furs in exchange for guns—an arrangement that will spell doom for many of the Iroquois' enemies. In the next decade, the Iroquois wage war against the Huron, Petunia, Neutral, and Erie (see entries for MARCH 1649, 1650, and 1654).

Mohegan leader Uncas kills Narragansett chief Miantonomo.

Colonial leaders grow tired of dealing with Miantonomo, a Narragansett Indian leader who resists the whites' constant demands for land and their increasing efforts to subjugate his people. On the instructions of English officials, the troublesome chief is assassinated by Mohegan leader Uncas. Born a Pequot, Uncas formed the Mohegan tribe and supported the English in their brutal war against his people (see entry for MAY 25, 1637). (See also entry for 1847.)

February 26

The Dutch massacre 100 Indians at Pavonia.

Just after midnight, 80 Dutch soldiers set upon a camp of Wecquaesgeek Indians seeking refuge from Mohawk raiders at the Dutch settlement of Pavonia in present-day New Jersey. The Dutch had ignored the Wecquaesgeek's pleas for help and allow the Mohawk to attack their camp. Although the surviving Wecquaesgeek pose no threat to Pavonia, Governor Willem Kieft orders a Dutch force to kill all of the Wecquaesgeek men and take the women and children prisoner. The soldiers instead brutally murder every Indian they can. The Dutch bring 30 prisoners back to New Amsterdam and publicly torture them to death.

In addition to avenging the murder of two Pavonia settlers who were murdered by Hackensack Indians two years before (see entry for 1641), the horrible slaughter is intended to frighten other tribes into submission. Instead, it motivates the Indians to exact their own revenge for the Wecquaesgeek massacre in a series of bloody attacks against Dutch settlements.

> "When it was day, the soldiers returned to the fort, having massacred or murdered eighty Indians, and considering they had done a deed of Roman valor, in murdering so many in their sleep; where infants were torn from their mother's breasts, and hacked to pieces in the presence of their parents, and the pieces thrown into the fire and in the water, and other sucklings were bound to small boards, and then cut, stuck, and pierced, and miserably massacred in a manner to move a heart to stone."
>
> —Dutchman Willem DeVries on the Pavonia Massacre

1644

The Dutch and English kill 500 Indians at Pound Ridge.

The Dutch hire Captain John Underhill, one of the English leaders of the Pequot massacre (see entry for MAY 25, 1637), to lead a combined Dutch and English force against Indian settlements in present-day New York and Connecticut. Underhill's men stage a relentless and bloody campaign, culminating in a brutal attack on an Indian settlement at Pound Ridge. With fire and guns, the colonists kill more than 500 Tankiteke, Wiwanoy, and Wappinger. Worn down by the attacks, the Indians negotiate a peace with the Dutch.

Spring

The Narragansett ask the English Crown for protection.

Fearing attack from English colonists, the Narragansett leaders appeal directly to Charles I for help. They promise to submit themselves to the king "upon condition of His Majesties royal protection." They maintain, however, that they will not bow to the demands of the colonists "having ourselves been the chief Sachems, or Princes successively, of the country, time out of mind." (See also entry for 1645.)

April 18

Opechancanough leads a Powhatan uprising.

Twenty-two years after masterminding a devastating surprise attack on the Virginia colonists (see entry for MARCH 22, 1622), the elderly Powhatan leader Opechancanough plans a second uprising. His warriors stage a series of assaults on English villages and kill about 500 colonists. Troops led by colonial governor William Berkeley quickly move in to retaliate. The fighting will continue for two years (see entry for 1646).

1645

August 28

The Narragansett negotiate a treaty with New England.

The Narragansett, faced with the threat of war with the colonists of New England (see entry for spring 1644), reluctantly agree to a punishing treaty. In addition to taking the blame for various acts of misconduct, they cede land, promise to pay a tribute for every Pequot living among them, and give up several tribe members to the English as a guarantee that they will obey the colonists in the future.

1646

October

The Powhatan make peace with the English.

Exhausted after two years of fighting (see entry for APRIL 18, 1646), the Powhatan negotiate a truce with the Virginia colonists. In the peace treaty, a boundary is drawn between their lands, but the English soon routinely ignore the border, and the Indians are too weak to enforce it.

The agreement comes on the heels of the death of Opechancanough, the organizer of the most sustained Powhatan uprising (see entry for MARCH 22, 1622). More than 80 years old, he was taken prisoner by the English. Unable to walk unaided, Openchancanough was carried by his captors to Jamestown, where he was shot by a militiaman.

1649

The Society for the Propagation of the Gospel in New England is founded.

The English parliament establishes the Society for the Propagation of the Gospel in New England. The first organization to promote Protestant conversion efforts in North America, the society will sponsor most of the missionary work in the English colonies before the American Revolution, including that of the influential clergymen John Eliot (see entries for 1651 and 1663) and Thomas Mayhew (see entry for AUGUST 22, 1670).

March

The Iroquois nearly annihilate the Huron.

With the expansion of the fur trade, old rivalries between the Iroquois and Huron (see entries for SUMMER 1609 and AUGUST 1615) grow increasingly intense. The powerful Iroquois particularly resent the Huron's success as middlemen. The Huron have amassed great wealth by trading corn to tribes in the north for beaver pelts, which they then trade to their French allies for European manufactured goods.

Armed with guns obtained from the Dutch (see entry for 1643), warriors from the Mohawk and Seneca tribes of the Iroquois Confederacy storm the Huron villages, attacking with a ferocity scarcely seen before in Indian warfare. The Huron population, already ravaged by smallpox (see entry for 1633), is decimated by the Iroquois assault. The few survivors are forced to flee their homeland forever. Some escape to what is now Quebec, Canada, while others, later called the Wyandot, head west to lands in present-day Michigan and Ohio. A number of Huron are also adopted by their Iroquois enemies, to replace warriors killed in battle.

1650

The Iroquois begin expanding into the Great Lakes region.

As fur-bearing animals near extinction in the Iroquois' territory in present-day New York State, the powerful confederacy of tribes moves westward toward the rich hunting grounds of the Great Lakes area. The Iroquois forcibly expel many of the tribes native to the region. In this expansion, the Iroquois will nearly exterminate some tribes, such as the Petun and Erie (see entry for 1654). Other larger groups, such as the Chippewa, Shawnee, and Cheyenne, will be forced to abandon their homelands and move elsewhere.

May 30

New Netherlands outlaws counterfeit wampum.

The Council of New Netherlands declares the manufacture of wampum by Dutch traders to be illegal. Wampum are white and purple shell beads prized by many Indian groups, especially the Iroquois. Traditionally, they have strung the beads into strings held during condolence rituals and into belts commemorating events, particularly diplomatic missions. Since the early 1600s, however, non-Indians have used wampum as a currency in their trade with eastern Indians. Whites quickly discovered that they could make wampum with metal awls far more easily than Indians could with their stone tools. Many unscrupulous traders have reaped huge profits by selling Indians counterfeit wampum produced by non-Indians.

1651

John Eliot establishes the first "praying town."

With funds from the Society for the Propagation of the Gospel in New England (see entry for 1649), John Eliot—the minister of the church at Roxbury,

"For many years together when the Indians resorted to the houses of godly people, they saw their manner of life and worship in families and in public also ... but liked not of it—yea, so disliked, that if any began to speak of God and heaven and hell and religion unto them they would presently be gone. So that it was a received and known thing to all English that if [Indians] were burdensome, speak of religion and you were presently rid of them."

—Missionary John Eliot in 1657 on English colonists' failed efforts to convert Indians

Massachusetts—founds Natick, a settlement for Indian converts, who come to be known as Praying Indians. Over the next 25 years, Eliot will establish 13 more "praying towns," whose populations will grow to nearly 2,500. The towns are created to separate converts from the corrupting influence of their non-Christian kin and to help further "civilize" Indian Christians by teaching them to adopt other white customs and beliefs.

1654

The Iroquois begin attacking the Erie.

Seeking access to the rich hunting grounds in the Ohio River valley, the Iroquois launch a war against the Erie, whose territory stands between the westernmost Iroquois villages and the lands they covet. With guns obtained from Dutch traders (see entry for 1633), the Iroquois have little difficulty fighting the largely unarmed Erie. Within three years, the tribe will be forced to abandon its homeland. Some of the surviving Erie will escape to Carolina, where they become known as the Westo; others will be absorbed into the Seneca tribe.

1655

The Lenni Lenape (Delaware) attack Dutch settlements in the Peach Wars.

Dutch farmer Hendrick Van Dyck kills a Lenni Lenape (Delaware) woman whom he finds picking peaches on his property. The victim's family then murders Van Dyck, and several bands of Lenni Lenape, eager for revenge, begin attacking Dutch settlements throughout New Netherlands. In New Amsterdam, the Indians kill about 50 Dutch settlers and take another one hundred prisoner. The violence will continue until the English wrest control over New Netherlands from the Dutch (see entry for 1664).

The Timucua rebel against the Spanish.

Weakened by a devastating smallpox epidemic (see entry for 1613), the Timucua of what is now northern Florida are subjugated by the Spanish, who compel them to labor in their missions. Just as a second wave of smallpox hits the tribe, Spanish officials trade away supplies intended for their Timucua laborers. Angry and desperate, the Timucua, led by Lucas Menendez, rise up against their oppressors. The rebels are armed with guns given to them by the Spanish to fight the English in the event of an invasion. The Timucua kill several Spaniards at the San Pedro mission, but the rebellion is quickly quashed by a Spanish retaliatory force. Menendez and 10 others are publicly hanged. The Timucua are destroyed as a tribe, as many of the rebellion's survivors are sold into slavery by the Spanish. Others escape and join the Seminole tribe.

A Spanish priest murders a Hopi man for idolatry.

In the Hopi village of Shongopovi, Spanish priest Salvador de Guerra discovers an Indian named Juan Cuna with a kachina doll—a figurine representing a supernatural being. Guerra accuses Juan Cuna of idolatry and publicly whips him in the village plaza. The priest carries the bludgeoned Indian, by then close to death, into the church at Shongopovi, where Guerra covers him with turpentine and sets him on fire. His body in flames, Juan Cuna rushes from the church, with Guerra in pursuit. The priest mounts a horse, knocks over the Indian, and tramples his burning body until he dies. A Hopi delegation reports the grisly event to Santa Fe authorities, who recall Guerra to the Spanish colonial capital.

1656

Massachusetts appoints a superintendent of Indian affairs.

The Massachusetts legislature establishes the office of superintendent of Indian affairs, the first such post created by the English. Appointed as the first superintendent, Daniel Gookin is responsible for selecting Native leaders, distributing gifts to friendly Indians, encouraging Indians to attend church, and "promoting and practicing morality, civility, industry, and diligence."

Powhatan warriors join the English in fighting hostile Indians.

The English convince two Powhatan tribes, the Pamunkey and Chickahominy, to help them fight the Iroquois, who are moving into Virginia from the north. During the conflict, Totopotomoy, the husband of Pamunkey leader Cockacoeske (see entry for 1676), and most of his men are killed. The Indian-English force is defeated, largely because of the incompetence of the English commander.

1659

Dutch soldiers murder Esopus leaders at a peace council.

Intent on driving Dutch settlers out of their lands, the Esopus Indians launch attacks on their farms and settlements, including the town of Wiltwyck. A militia organized by Governor Peter Stuyvesant pressures Esopus leaders to meet in council at Wiltwyck to negotiate a peace. While the Esopus delegates are asleep, the soldiers murder them. In retaliation, the Esopus capture eight Dutchmen and burn them alive.

1660

The Dutch take Indian children as hostages.

To force Indians to comply with Dutch demands, Governor Peter Stuyvesant inaugurates a policy of taking hostage several children from area tribes. Many tribes, weakened by warfare with the Dutch, have no choice but to offer them up. The Esopus, however, resist. They have harbored an especially strong hatred and distrust of the Dutch since their leaders were murdered at peace council by Dutch soldiers the year before (see entry for 1659). When the Esopus refuse to give them hostages, the Dutch take several Esopus women and children captive and sell them into slavery in the West Indies.

1661

The Spanish destroy Pueblo religious paraphernalia.

Angered by the Pueblo's unwillingness to become Catholic converts, Spanish officials order soldiers to stage a series of raids on kivas, underground structures in which the Pueblo perform religious ceremonies. The raiders loot and burn ceremonial items, including 1,600 masks representing kachinas, the spirit beings that control the Pueblo world.

"[The Pueblo] are totally lost, without faith, without law, and without devotion to the church; they neither respect nor obey their ministers, and it makes one weep to see that in such a short time they have lost and forgotten what they have been taught in all these years."
—Fray Francisco de Salazar in 1660 on the difficulty of converting the Pueblo

March

Virginia issues identification medals to Indian travelers.

The Virginia General Assembly passes an act that requires all Indians leaving their villages and entering white settlements to wear medals made by the colonists, as forms of identification. These medal passports are only given to Indians who are considered friends of the colony.

1662

Metacom becomes chief of the Wampanoag.

The Massachusetts authorities call Wamsutta to Plymouth after hearing rumors of a planned Indian uprising. Wamsutta became the leader of the Wampanoag two years before on the death of his father, Massasoit, who had long worked to maintain a peaceful relationship with the English (see entries for MARCH 1621 and AUTUMN 1621). When the new Wampanoag chief refuses, a force of Englishmen comes to his village to compel him at gunpoint to honor the colonists' order. The English berate and interrogate Wamsutta, who repeatedly complains of feeling ill. The Massachusetts officials finally agree to release him, but Wamsutta, on his way home, suddenly dies. Like many other Wampanoag, his younger brother and successor Metacom comes to suspect that Wamsutta was poisoned while in Plymouth.

1663

John Eliot's Massachuset Bible is published.

Missionary John Eliot (see also entry for 1651) translates the Bible for use by Massachuset Indians near the settlements of Roxbury and Boston. The translation is the fruit of Eliot's 15-year effort to learn the Massachuset language and invent an orthography so that it can be written down. He is aided by several Massachuset translators and a Nipmuck Indian known as James Printer, who helps set the Bible into type. Described by Eliot as "a sacred and holy work, to be regarded with fear, care, and reverence," the Massachuset Bible is the first Bible in any language to be printed in the Americas.

New France becomes a colony.

The Company of New France, a trading company that initiated French colonization in North America (see entry for 1602), disbands as New France is placed under a royal governor. At the time of the transition the colony is in disarray, because Iroquois raiders, allies of the English, have been disrupting the French fur trade. To control the Iroquois, King Louis XIV sends to New France 1,500 soldiers (see entry for OCTOBER 1666), most of whom will later settle there.

1664

The Spanish issue laws to restrict Pueblo trade.

Suspecting that the Apache are obtaining horses and other supplies through trade with the Pueblo, New Mexico's governor forbids non-Pueblo Indians from entering the Pueblo villages except during specified times. The order is an attempt to end Apache raids against Spanish outposts.

September 8

English troops take over New Netherlands.

Three hundred British soldiers march into New Netherlands and wrest control of the colony from the Dutch. Severely weakened by its continuing wars with Indians (see entry for 1655), the colony no longer has the military strength to resist the invasion. The colony of New Netherlands and the city of New Amsterdam are both renamed New York by the British.

1666

October

Mohawk villages are attacked by the French.

In an attempt to intimidate their trading rivals, French troops sent to North American by Louis XIV (see entry for 1663) invade Mohawk territory and burn several villages to the ground. The incident panics the Iroquois, who agree to make peace with the French the following July. The peace will stay in effect for nearly 15 years.

1670

The Hudson's Bay Company is established to promote British trade.

At the suggestion of French traders Pierre Esprit Radisson and Médard Chouart, sieur des Groselliers, the British Crown grants a royal charter to the Hudson's Bay Company, a fur-trading firm based in the Hudson Bay region of what is now central Canada. Radisson and Chouart began obtaining rich furs from the Indians in the area during an expedition in 1668–69. They approached the French with the idea of establishing posts on Hudson Bay but were rebuffed and subsequently fined for trading without the proper license.

The Hudson's Bay Company soon builds trading posts along water routes frequented by Indian traders and hunters. Although the Indians are accustomed to dealing with the French, many welcome the English, because they offer quality goods at lower prices. In the years to come, many Indian groups will be drawn into violent conflicts arising from the growing rivalry between English and French traders.

August 22

Hiacoomes becomes the first Indian ordained as a minister.

The first ordained Indian minister, Hiacoomes of the Wampanoag tribe, takes the position of pastor at an Indian church on what is now Martha's Vineyard, in Massachusetts. He was converted to Protestantism in 1642, by a Congregational minister, Thomas Mayhew (see entry for 1649), and served as Mayhew's interpreter and assistant until the clergyman's death in 1657.

1671

April 10

Metacom surrenders Wampanoag weapons to the English.

Angered by the rapid growth of English settlements on their lands, Wampanoag leader Metacom (see entry for 1662) allows some of his warriors to parade fully armed through the town of Swansea as a warning to the Massachusetts colonists. English officials react by summoning Metacom and demanding that he relinquish his tribe's weapons. Left with no choice, Metacom agrees and turns over 70 guns at the meeting as a show of faith, although later he refuses to give up any more. The incident humiliates Metacom and convinces him of the impossibility of solving the Wampanoag's disagreements with the English through peaceful means. Soon after, the leader will begin gathering support for large-scale Indian resistance (see entry for June 1675).

1675

The Spanish put four Pueblo leaders to death.

Spanish authorities in Santa Fe order the arrest of 47 Pueblo leaders. The men are charged with sorcery, but the Spanish are actually intent on punishing their failure to recruit an adequate number of Christian converts from their followers. Following their trial, four Pueblos are sentenced to death by hanging, and the rest are whipped. Among those whipped are Popé, who five years later will lead the Pueblo in a successful rebellion against their Spanish tormentors (see entry for AUGUST 10, 1680).

June 8

The English execute three Wampanoag for murder.

In December 1674, John Sassamon, a Christian Indian who was educated at Harvard, informs English officials at Plymouth that the Wampanoag leader Metacom (see entry for 1671) is planning to attack their settlements. A month later Sassamon's body, with its neck snapped, is discovered in a frozen pond.

Acting on the information from a supposed Indian witness, the English arrest and try three Wampanoag for the crime. Aside from the testimony of the witness, who may owe a gambling debt to one of the accused, there is no real evidence of their guilt. Nevertheless, the English court sentences them to death by hanging.

Their execution infuriates the Wampanoag. In the past, crimes committed by Indians against Indians were dealt with by tribes. The interference of the English in what the Wampanoag see as a tribal matter brings the tension between the colonists and Indians to the boiling point.

Late June

King Philip's War breaks out in New England.

Terrified that an Indian uprising is imminent, Massachusetts settlers in the town of Swansea flee to safety in Plymouth. Wampanoag warriors, enraged by the execution of three Indian men by the English (see entry for JUNE 8, 1675), surround the town and begin looting the abandoned homes. After one of the frightened colonists kills a Wampanoag, the warriors attack the town. The assault marks the beginning of King Philip's War, the bloodiest conflict between Indians and settlers in the 17th century.

"The English who came first to this country were but a handful of people, forlorn, poor and distressed. . . . [They] flourished and increased. By various means they got possession of a great part of [my father's] territory. But he still remained their friend till he died. . . . Soon after I became sachem they disarmed my people . . . [and] their land was taken. But a small part of the domination of my ancestors remains. I am determined not to live until I have no country."

—Metacom in a speech to English authorities at the beginning of King Philip's War

Immediately after the attack, an army led by Benjamin Church marches from Plymouth to the Mount Hope Peninsula, where the Wampanoag leader Metacom lives. Metacom (known to the English as King Philip) manages to escape and rallies other tribes to join the growing uprising. The rebellion quickly spreads throughout the region, especially after colonial troops begin attacking Indians formerly friendly to the English.

July

The Virginia militia attacks the Nanticoke and Susquehannock.

Several Nanticoke steal hogs from the farm of Thomas Mathew, a Virginia planter who, the Indians maintain, refused to pay a debt to them. Neighboring whites seize the thieves and kill at least one of them. To avenge his death, the Nanticoke murder Mathew's overseer. Virginia authorities respond by sending the militia into the villages of not only the Nanticoke but also the Susquehannock, who had formerly had friendly relations with the colonists.

September

Colonists slaughter Susquehannock leaders.

When the government of Virginia will not make reparations for the deaths of 14 Susquehannock murdered by colonists several months earlier (see entry for JULY 1675), tribe members begin raiding the colonists' settlements. In revenge, a thousand-man militia surrounds a Susquehannock village on the Potomac River and calls its leaders to a meeting to discuss a peace. When five leaders emerge, the militiamen murder them. The brutal act sparks the short-lived Susquehannock War, during which the tribe's warriors will launch a series of retaliatory attacks on nearby white settlements. The violence increases tension between colonists and Indians, which will explode the following year in Bacon's Rebellion (see entry for SPRING 1676).

December 18

The English battle the Narragansett in the Great Swamp Fight.

Led by Benjamin Church, approximately 1,000 soldiers from Massachusetts, Connecticut, and Plymouth travel east into Narragansett territory. As the army advances, the Narragansett seek refuge in an unfinished fort on the Great Swamp near present-day Kingston, Rhode Island. The troops rush into the garrison and kill more than 600 Narragansett men, women, and children. The battle later becomes known as the Great Swamp Fight. With their tribe nearly exterminated by the horrendous slaughter, the survivors, including Narragansett leader Canonchet, eagerly join King Philip's War against the English (see entry for LATE JUNE 1675).

1676

February 10

Mary Rowlandson is taken captive.

While fighting in King Philip's War (see entry for LATE JUNE 1675), Wampanoag and Narragansett warriors capture Mary Rowlandson, the wife of a Puritan minister, during an attack on the small white settlement of Lancaster, Massachusetts. For 12 weeks she is held captive before the Indians return her in exchange for a ransom. Her account of her experiences among the Indians will become one of America's first bestsellers (see entry for 1682).

Spring

Indian support for Metacom's rebellion dwindles.

Early in the year, Indian warriors in King Philip's War (see entry for LATE JUNE 1675) attack more than 20 towns in Plymouth and Massachusetts. Despite these successes, the Indian uprising suffers a series of setbacks. Its leader, Metacom, attempts to persuade the powerful Mohawk to join his cause, but they remain loyal to the British and, more alarming to Metacom, fight alongside the colonists. With the help of the Mohawk, the English are victorious in a number of decisive battles, during one of which they capture and later execute Narragansett chief Canonchet, one of the Indians' most important leaders. The English also destroy much of the rebels' food stores, leading to mass starvation. By the summer, Metacom's followers are forced to surrender en masse.

Spring

Virginia colonists attack Indians in Bacon's Rebellion.

Hoping to calm tension between colonists and Indians, William Berkeley, the governor of Virginia, forbids colonists from launching unauthorized attacks on Indian villages. Berkeley's policy infuriates many of Virginia's poor and landless, who are already angry at officials for hoarding the colony's wealth. Organized by Nathaniel Bacon, a wealthy planter, these Virginians rebel against the colonial government and begin attacking Indian settlements without regard to whether their residents are the colonists' allies or enemies. The movement loses much of its momentum after Bacon dies of dysentery in October, but colonists will continue to terrorize Virginia's Indians until the rebels are finally defeated by Berkeley's troops the following January.

Summer

Pamunkey leader Cockacoeske confronts the Virginia General Assembly.

Dubbed the "queen of the Pamunkey" by the English, Cockacoeske is summoned by the General Assembly, the governing body of Virginia. The assemblymen ask for the help of the 150 warriors at her command in putting down the colonists fighting the assembly's authority in Bacon's Rebellion. Cockacoeske answers their request first with an angry silence, then with a tirade against the English. Speaking through an interpreter, she demands to know why she should help them when

in the past the English had never compensated her for warriors killed while fighting on their behalf, including her own husband Totopotomoy (see entry for 1656). The meeting ends with a disgusted Cockacoeske agreeing to supply the English with only 12 fighting men, far fewer than had been expected.

August 12

King Philip War's ends with Metacom's death.

An Indian informer tells colonial militiamen the location of Metacom's camp on the Mount Hope Peninsula. They surround the Wampanoag rebellion leader and his small band of followers, and in the ensuring battle Metacom is shot and killed by an Indian fighting on the side of the English. The soldiers mutilate his corpse and take his severed head to Plymouth, where it will be displayed for the next 25 years. According to Wampanoag legend, Metacom kinsmen will one day steal the head and bury it at his home village of Mount Hope.

Metacom's death effectively ends King Philip's War (see entries for LATE JUNE 1675 and for SPRING 1676). The conflict proves devastating to the Indians of southern New England. In addition to spelling the end of their political independence, the fighting has decimated their populations. Approximately 3,000 people—about 40 percent of the total Indian population of the region—have been killed in battle or have died from starvation. Five hundred more Wampanoag have been captured by the militia and sold into slavery to help offset English war debts. Among them are Metacom's widow and children.

The war has also been costly to the English. Approximately 600 colonists have been killed during the conflict. Fifty-two of their 90 settlements have been attacked, and at least 12 completely destroyed. With some 1,800 houses burned to the ground, most of these town sites will be abandoned for decades.

1677

May 29

The Powhatan tribes negotiate a peace treaty with Virginia.

As Bacon's Rebellion is quelled (see entry for SPRING 1676), the Treaty of Middle Plantation is signed by Virginia authorities and leaders of the Pamunkey, Weanock, Appamatuck, and Nansemond tribes. Unlike most treaties of the time, the agreement attempts to be fair to both sides. It names the Indians as subjects of the British Crown but grants each tribe a reservation surrounded by a three-mile buffer area in which whites are prohibited from settling. It also declares that Cockacoeske, the leader of the Pamunkey (see entry for SUMMER 1676), will rule over "several scattered Indians," a clause she vigorously lobbied the English to include. These "scattered Indians" included the Chickahominy, who resent and resist Cockacoeske's leadership. Until her death in 1686, she will try (with little success) to bully the Chickahominy into paying her tribute.

1680

April 17

Kateri Tekakwitha dies at the Kahnawake mission.

After years of severe fasting and self-flagellation, Mohawk nun Kateri Tekakwitha dies during Holy Week, at the age of 24. Against the wishes of her relatives, Tekakwitha converted to Catholicism in 1676. Her devotion to her new religion bred such contempt in her people that, fearing for her life, she soon had to flee from her home village and seek refuge at the mission in Kahnawake, a settlement of Christian Mohawk. During her lifetime, the Jesuits at the mission were disturbed by Tekakwitha's penchant for self-torture, but after her death they will celebrate her devoutness as a model for other Indian converts. Through the lobbying of the Jesuits, in the 20th century Tekakwitha will be declared venerable and blessed by the Roman Catholic Church (see entries for 1939; MAY 19, 1939; and JUNE 22, 1980).

August 10 to 21

Popé leads the Pueblo Revolt.

A war leader named Popé unifies the Pueblo in a carefully planned rebellion against the Spaniards in their territory. Before attacking the Europeans, the rebels tell the Spanish to leave. The Pueblo allow settlers who do so voluntarily to escape with their lives, but the Indians seize all of their property. As the northern Pueblo attack the Spanish capital of Santa Fe, the Hopi, Acoma, and Zuni set upon the settlers and missionaries near their villages. During the conflict, about 400 Spaniards are killed. The rebels also set the Spaniards' churches and houses on fire and destroy every object the Pueblo identify as Spanish.

"[Popé proclaimed] that we should burn all the images and temples, rosaries and cross and that all the people should discard the names given them in holy baptism.... [We] were not to mention in any manner the name of God, of the ...Virgin, or of the Saints ... [and were] not to teach the Castilian language in any pueblo and to burn the seeds which the Spaniards sowed and to plant only [corn] and beans, which are the crops of our ancestors."

—Tesuque Indian Juan on the Pueblo Revolt of 1680

Although Popé's revolt is the most successful Indian uprising ever staged, the Pueblo's unification does not last long. Popé alienates many of his followers by his tyrannical prohibition against all things Spanish, including new crops that the Pueblo have come to rely upon. The Pueblo soon divide into pro-Popé and anti-Popé factions.

1682

Mary Rowlandson's captivity narrative is published.

Four years after her death, Mary Rowlandson's account of her 12 weeks as a captive of the Wampanoag and Narragansett during King Philip's War (see entry for FEBRUARY 10, 1676) is published by a firm in Cambridge, England. Titled *The Sovereignty & Goodness of God, Together with the Faithfulness of His Promises Displayed; Being a Narrative of the Captivity and Restoration of Mrs. Mary Rowlandson,* it will become, after the Bible, the most popular book in colonial America and will establish the conventions of a new publishing genre, the captivity narrative. Such narratives deal with the travails of whites (usually women) taken as captives during Indian wars. (See also entries for 1824, 1830, and 1851.)

April 9

France claims Indian lands in the Mississippi Valley.

French explorer René-Robert Cavelier, sieur de La Salle, descends the Mississippi River to the Gulf of Mexico and claims the entire river valley for France. He names the region Louisiana after the French king Louis XIV. At the beginning of the 18th century, France will begin exploiting La Salle's claim by sending colonists and traders into the region.

July 15

William Penn concludes a treaty with the Lenni Lenape (Delaware).

William Penn, the wealthy Quaker founder of the colony of Pennsylvania, negotiates a treaty with the Lenni Lenape (Delaware) Indians in which they cede lands along the Delaware River in exchange

for a wide array of trade goods, including wampum, blankets, clothing, knives, and guns. The event will become a popular metaphor for peace in American art, most notably in famous representations by painters Benjamin West and Edward Hicks.

Penn's treaty reflects the Quaker belief that Indians are owners of their land and that therefore it cannot be taken from them without their consent and proper compensation. This idea runs counter to the prevailing European view that Christians have a natural right to lands occupied by non-Christians. Penn also advocates non-violence in whites' relations with Indians and respect for Indian culture among non-Indians. (See also entry for SEPTEMBER 19, 1737.)

"They do speak but little, but fervently, and with elegance. I have never seen more natural sagacity, considering them with the help (I was going to say spoil) of tradition; and he will deserve the name wise who outwits them in any treaty about a thing they understand. ... Do not abuse them but let them have justice and you will win them."

—Pennsylvania governor William Penn on negotiating a 1682 treaty with the Lenni Lenape (Delaware)

1689

King William's War breaks out.

Emerging out of the War of the League of Augsburg between England and France, King William's War is the first European conflict to spread to North America. This development will have an enormous impact on Indians, whose European allies will call

Penn's Treaty with the Indians, a romanticized depiction of William Penn's 1682 negotiations with the Lenni Lenape (Delaware), painted by American master Benjamin West in 1771–72 *(The Pennsylvania Academy of the Fine Arts, Philadelphia. Gift of Mrs. Sarah Harrison. The Joseph Harrison, Jr. Collection)*

upon them to supply military support in this and three other major wars during the next 74 years. The eight-year King William's War (see entry for 1697) will be particularly destructive to the Iroquois. Long the allies of the English, the Iroquois and their villages are targeted by French soldiers and pro-French Indian warriors, who want to break the Iroquois' dominance in the fur trade.

1691

Virginia outlaws interracial marriage.

Eighty-seven years after Virginia officials celebrated the wedding of Pocahontas and John Rolfe (see entry for APRIL 5, 1614), the colony's legislature bans from Virginia any English person who marries someone of Indian or African descent. Reflecting whites' growing sense of superiority over Indian and African "savages," similar laws will soon be passed in Massachusetts, Maryland, Delaware, Pennsylvania, Georgia, North Carolina, and South Carolina.

1692

The Spanish return to the lands of the Pueblo.

Spanish soldiers led by Diego de Vargas march into the southwestern lands of the Pueblo Indians. Their arrival marks the first extended Spanish presence among the Pueblo Indians since they revolted against Spanish rule 12 years before (see entry for AUGUST 10–12, 1680). Seeing the population weakened by droughts and Navajo (Dineh) and Apache raiders, Vargas sets about recolonizing the region. Over the next four years, he will succeed in reclaiming all of the Pueblo villages for New Spain. Aside from one unsuccessful rebellion (see entry for JUNE 4, 1696), the Pueblo offer little resistance to renewed Spanish rule. The Spanish offer the Pueblo protection from their Indian enemies, and, learning from the 1680 revolt, they are now less intolerant of Indian religious practices.

1695

The Akimel O'odham (Pima) destroy Spanish missions.

After establishing missions among the Akimel O'odham (Pima) of present-day Arizona, the Spanish incur the Indians' wrath by their ill-treatment of their leaders. When the enraged Akimel O'odham kill three Christian Indians and a missionary, the Spanish retaliate by murdering some 50 Akimel O'odham, most of whom had nothing to do with the initial attack. The Akimel O'odham respond by destroying the missions at Tubutama and Caborca. The violence continues until several Akimel O'odham leaders, fearing further Spanish reprisals, surrender the uprising's instigators. The brief rebellion deepens the Akimel O'odham distrust and hatred of the Spanish, which 56 years later will result in a second Akimel O'odham revolt (see entry for 1751).

1696

June 4

Pueblo Indians revolt against Spanish rule.

Resentment over the Spanish reconquest of Pueblo lands after Popé's revolt (see entries for AUGUST 10–12, 1680, and for 1692) erupts in a second Pueblo rebellion. The Pueblo Indians of Pi-

curis, Taos, and Jemez kill five missionaries and 21 soldiers. The rebels, however, fail to take over the Spanish capital of Santa Fe. Attacking several pueblos and destroying the inhabitants' food stores, the Spanish are able to quell the uprising in a few months' time.

1697

King William's War ends inconclusively.

The Treaty of Ryswick ends King William's War (see entry for 1689). The war, fought between the English and the French, does little to resolve the growing tension between these European powers in North America. The Indian allies of both sides were drawn into the conflict, but it has the greatest effect on the Iroquois. The French and pro-French Indian groups battled the pro-English relentlessly in an effort to stop their interference in the French fur trade. During the fighting, about 500 Iroquois warriors were killed, while their overall population

> "You stet us on daily to fight & destroy your Enemies, & bid us geo on with Courage, but we See not that you doe anything to it yourselves, neither doe wee See any great Strength you have to oppose them if the Enemy should break out upon you; . . . The war must also be hotly Pursued on your Sides. . . . England and the Rest of the English that are in Covenant with us doe, they all Stay at home & Set us on to doe the work."
>
> —an Iroquois orator, complaining in 1692 of the English insistence that the Iroquois fight the French

declined by nearly 20 percent. The unwillingness of the English to provide the Iroquois with support and protection disappoints the Indians and will help persuade them to declare neutrality in later European conflicts (see entry for SUMMER 1701).

March 15–30

Hannah Duston (Dustin) is held captive by the Abenaki.

During a raid on Haverhill, Massachusetts, Abenaki warriors capture a white woman named Hannah Duston, her nurse (Mary Neff), and her infant child, whom the Indians later murder. To avenge the baby's death, Duston and a fellow captive, ten-year-old Samuel Lennardson, attack their sleeping captors on the night of March 30. With hatchets in hand, they kill and scalp 10 Indians, including several children; only one boy and an elderly woman escape with their lives. Duston, Neff, and Lennardson then flee. After Duston's arrival in Haverhill, her husband, on her behalf, collects 25 pounds from the Massachusetts government, which has placed a bounty on Indian scalps. The story of Hannah Duston's captivity and escape will be celebrated in Cotton Mather's *Humiliations Followed with Deliverances* (1697). In the 19th century, it will also be retold in works by Nathaniel Hawthorne and Henry David Thoreau.

1700

The College of William and Mary enrolls its first Indian students.

Established in Williamsburg, Virginia, in 1693, the College of William and Mary begins admitting Indians despite the resistance of local tribal leaders, who fear the students will be enslaved by the English. The school supplies an elementary education in reading and writing English. Increasingly, however, Virginia officials will value the school primarily as a means of holding Indian youths to help ensure that nearby tribes will not attack

Williamsburg. Due to a lack of funds, the Indian school at the college will close in 1777.

"[O]ur ideas of this kind of Education happen not to be the same as yours. We have had some Experience of it. Several of our young People were formerly brought up at the Colleges of the Northern Provinces ... but, when they came back to us, they were bad Runners, ignorant of every means of living in the woods.... [N]either fit for Hunters, Warriors, nor Counselors, they were totally good for nothing."

—an Iroquois delegation declining an offer to educate their youths at the College of William and Mary in 1744

The San Xavier del Bac mission is founded in Akimel O'odham (Pima) territory.

Jesuit missionary Eusebio Kino establishes San Xavier del Bac near what is now Tucson, Arizona. From this mission, Kino preaches to area Indians and is particularly active among the Akimel O'odham (Pima). Generally respectful of the Indians he encounters, Kino will convert as many as 4,500 Indians to Christianity, while also teaching them non-Indian methods of farming and ranching. He will also explore and chart much of the region, thus expanding the boundaries of New Spain.

1701

The Hopi slaughter the men of Awatovi.

Amidst rumors that the Awatovi Hopi have agreed to allow the Spanish to settle on their lands, Hopi from other villages stage a violent attack on Awatovi. When the invasion begins, most of the men of Awatovi are in kivas, underground ceremonial structures, where they are preparing for a religious ritual. The attacking Hopi pull away the ladders at their entrances and set the kivas ablaze. After they kill all of the village's male residents, they capture the women and children, whom they send to live in other Hopi villages. Through the destruction of Awatovi, the Hopi express their passionate hatred of the Spanish and their allies.

Summer

The Iroquois adopt a policy of neutrality.

In Montreal, Iroquois diplomats meet with the French and declare that their tribes will remain neutral in any future wars between France and England. The promise is heartening to the French: The powerful Iroquois' traditional loyalty to the English has long posed a threat to their settlements and trading posts in North America.

At the same time, in Albany Iroquois leaders enter negotiations with the English. To maintain friendly relations with their old military ally, the Iroquois cede to England western hunting territory that they obtained through their defeat of their Huron enemies (see entry for MARCH 1649).

Summer

Detroit is founded as a French fur trading post.

With the backing of the French Crown, explorer Antoine de la Mothe, sieur de Cadillac, establishes on what is now the Detroit River a large trading post, which he names Fort Pontchartrain du Detroit (of the Strait). Detroit is occupied by about 100 settlers and soldiers as a means of keeping English traders out of the area. Although the post does not immediately live up to Cadillac's claim that it is "the Paris of New France," Detroit soon attracts many area Indians interested in trading with the French.

1702

Indians are drawn into Queen Anne's War.

The War of the Spanish Succession breaks out in Europe, with England and France on one side and Spain on the other. The conflict soon extends to North America, where it is called Queen Anne's War, after the English queen. As with King William's War (see entry for 1689), the Indian allies of both these European powers will be called upon to help them battle their enemies. (See also entry for 1713.)

The English and the Creek begin attacking Florida missions.

Under the command of James Moore, governor of Carolina, an army of English soldiers and Creek warriors launch the first of three military campaigns against Franciscan missions in Spanish Florida. The troops hope to eliminate the Spanish and their Apalachee Indian allies as competitors in the deerskin trade. During the next five years, many unarmed mission Indians will be killed in these attacks, and a large number of survivors will be taken as slaves. The missions will continue in operation, but their Indian populations will be drastically reduced.

1704

Virginia officials destroy the Nansatico tribe.

After receiving no help from the Virginia authorities, warriors from the small Nansatico tribe in northern Virginia attack whites who have been illegally moving onto their lands. When the Indians kill a white family, Virginia arrests all 49 Nansatico. Four men are hanged for the murders, and although the others are not found guilty of any crime, they are sent to the West Indies to live as slaves. Officials then sell the Nansatico's homeland, thus erasing any trace of the tribe's existence.

February

An Indian and French force attacks Deerfield, Massachusetts.

As part of the continuing fighting in Queen Anne's War (see entry for 1702), the English town of Deerfield, Massachusetts, is set upon by Abenaki and Caughnawaga warriors with the assistance of French soldiers. About 50 of the inhabitants are killed as they sleep, and another hundred are taken prisoner. The town suffered previous attacks during King Philip's War (see entry for LATE JUNE 1675) and King William's War (see entry for 1689).

1705

Virginia restricts the legal rights of off-reservation Indians.

In a series of laws, the Virginia General Assembly establishes rules for "free persons of color," defined as Indians living outside a reservation as well as free blacks and people of black and white ancestry. Passed as a response to the recent uprising of the Nansatico (see entry for 1704), the laws bar these people from holding political office, appearing as witnesses in court, and hunting on lands claimed by whites. These restrictions violate the rights guaranteed to Virginia Indians in an earlier treaty (see entry for MAY 29, 1677). They also divide Indians in Virginia into two classes, reservation Indians (who retain many of the same legal rights as colonists) and off-reservation Indians (who now suffer the low social and legal status of freed slaves).

1710

April 19

Mohawk and Mahican leaders have an audience with Queen Anne.

Four Indian ambassadors—three Mohawk and one Mahican—accompany two English officials to London. At the request of British colonists, the Indian

Mohawk leader Hendrick holding a wampum belt similar to one he gave to Queen Anne during his 1710 visit to London *(Verelst, John/National Archives of Canada/C-092414)*

leaders agree to meet with Queen Anne to request increased military protection from the French. Exalted as "Indian kings," the visitors are treated as celebrities by the English public. During their trip, they have their portraits painted, hunt a deer in an outdoor park, and draw a crowd when they attend the theater. (See also entry for SEPTEMBER 8, 1755.)

"We have undertaken a long and tedious voyage, which none of our predecessors could ever be prevailed upon to undertake. The motive that induced us, was that we might see our great

> Queen, and relate to her those things we thought absolutely necessary, for the good of her, and us, heralies on the other side of the great water.... [A]s a token of the sincerity of the Six Nations, we do here, in the name of all, present our great Queen with the belts of wampum."
>
> —four Indian ambassadors addressing Queen Anne during their 1710 trip to London

1711

September

The Tuscarora War breaks out.

The Tuscarora of present-day North Carolina attack non-Indian settlements, killing as many as 200 whites. The Tuscarora are infuriated by the whites' encroachment on their territory, as well as by the arrogance and dishonesty of British traders and their practice of selling Indian captives into slavery.

Carolina officials counter the attack by sending troops to destroy the Tuscarora's villages. The troops are provided military assistance by England's Indian allies, including the Yamasee (see entries for APRIL 15, 1715, and for 1717). (See also entry for MARCH 1713.)

1712

The Fox (Mesquaki) begin warring with the French.

When the Fox (Mesquaki) Indians of what are now western Wisconsin and Illinois begin demanding tribute from foreigners in their lands, the French arm the Ojibway, who are the allies of the French and the traditional enemies of the Fox. The Fox respond by raiding French and Ojibway (Anishinabe) settlements. Their assaults create a problem for the French by effectively cutting off trade routes between New France and Louisiana. Attacks and counterattacks will continue for more than two decades (see entry for 1730).

1713

March

The Tuscarora are defeated in the Tuscarora War.

A brutal three-day attack on the Tuscarora fort of Nooherooka near present-day Snow Hill, North Carolina, seals England's victory in the Tuscarora War (see entry for SEPTEMBER 1711). During the war, the Tuscarora have suffered as many as 1,000 casualties, and several hundred tribe members have been sold into slavery by their enemies. The defeat is devastating to the tribe, which is left with only a small reservation in what is now North Carolina. Soon after the war, the demoralized Tuscarora will begin moving north to New York to find refuge with their Iroquois kin. (See also entry for 1722.)

July 13

France cedes Hudson Bay to England in the Treaty of Utrecht.

Queen Anne's War (see entry for 1702) ends with the signing of the Treaty of Utrecht. In the treaty, France cedes to England its claims to what is now Nova Scotia and the Hudson Bay region. Unwilling to trade with the British, whose treatment of Indian traders is far less generous than that of the French, the Micmac and several other Indian groups in the region refuse to recognize British rule.

While the land cession is a boon to the English colonists, the long and exhausting war impresses upon them their military weakness in battle against the French and their many Indian allies. Because both sides are hesitant to enter another drawn-out conflict, the peace established by the treaty will last for more than 30 years (see entry for MAY 1744).

1715

April 15

The Yamasee attack English settlements.

At dawn the Yamasee attack English settlements near Savannah and kill more than a hundred traders and settlers. They are enraged by their treatment by the English, particularly traders. As white settlers have taken over the Yamasee's hunting grounds in preset-day South Carolina, many hunters have found themselves unable to pay debts owed to English traders. In lieu of payment, many traders have taken Yamasee women and children captive and sold them into the slavery.

Soon the Yamasee are joined by their Indian allies, including Creek warriors, who perhaps have been encouraged to fight against the English by rival French traders. Alarmed by the growing threat, the English send out a militia to initiate a full-scale war against the Yamasee (see entry for 1717).

1717

The Cherokee join the Yamasee War on the side of the British.

The English coax the powerful Cherokee tribe into helping them fight against the Yamasee and their Creek allies (see entry for APRIL 15, 1715). The Cherokee are willing to join the conflict largely because they want to battle their traditional Creek enemies. By November, the combined English-Cherokee force has so overwhelmed the Creek that they agree to sign a peace treaty. The Yamasee are so reduced in numbers as to be nearly extinct as a tribe. The survivors retreat to Spanish Florida, where they continue to stage small raids on Carolina settlements for more than a decade.

1720

The French and Choctaw begin waging war against the Chickasaw.

Attracted by low prices, the Chickasaw develop a trade relationship with the English. To protect their control of the Mississippi Valley, the French, aided by their Choctaw allies, try to discourage the Chickasaw from becoming English allies by attacking their lands. The Chickasaw take revenge by raiding Choctaw villages and blocking the movement of French trade ships. The raids quickly prove costly to French traders, who try to end the Chickasaw attacks by offering the Choctaw guns and ammunition for their enemies' scalps. The bloody war continues until four years later the exhausted Chickasaw are ready to sue for peace with the French.

August 13

Pawnee and Kaw (Kansas) warriors drive the Spanish from the southern Plains.

Led by Pedro de Villasur, an army of 42 Spanish soldiers and 70 Pueblo warriors travel to the southern Plains to prevent the French from establishing trade inroads with the tribes there. They are met by a force of Pawnee and Kaw (Kansas) Indians who, using guns supplied by the French, kill 45 of the invaders and drive the survivors back to the Spanish capital of Santa Fe.

1721

Spain abolishes the *encomienda* system.

Instituted in the Americas more than 200 years earlier, the *encomienda* system (see entry for 1512) is formally ended by Spain. The system gave conquistadores land grants in the Spanish colonies as rewards for service. Indians on the *encomienda* were forced into brutal servitude by their Spanish owners. Fearing that the *encomienda* owners were becoming too independent of the Crown, Spain had been trying to end the system since the mid-16th century (see entry for 1542).

September 8

The English Board of Trade recommends intermarriage between Indians and whites.

In correspondence with the British Crown, the English Board of Trade suggests that the intermarriage between Indians and colonists be encouraged. Marriages between Indian women and French men are common, but they are practically unheard of in the English colonies, largely because of the colonists' sense of superiority over Indians and their societies. The board, however, sees intermarriage as the easiest way of securing a meaningful peace between the English and their Indian allies.

1722

The Tuscarora join the Iroquois Confederacy.

For the first time since its founding, the Iroquois Confederacy (see entry for CA. 1400) invites a new tribe, the Tuscarora, to join its ranks. The Tuscarora, who share cultural traits with the other Iroquois tribes, probably lived in Iroquois territory before migrating southward to what is now North Carolina in about 500 B.C. The tribe began moving north to live with their Iroquois relatives following the Tuscarora War (see entries for SEPTEMBER 1711 and for MARCH 1713), during which the English decimated their population and took most of their southern lands.

June

Dummer's War breaks out.

Possibly incited by the French, a group of Eastern Abenaki attack English settlements near present-day Brunswick, Maine. The warriors burn several houses and take several of the inhabitants captive. Dummer, the acting governor of Massachusetts, sends in troops to battle the tribe (see entry for AUGUST 1724). The conflict will continue until

1727, when the Eastern Abenaki, receiving little support from their French allies, can no longer afford to fight the English.

1724

August

English colonists destroy an Eastern Abenaki village.

The Massachusetts colonial government orders troops to attack Norridgewock, a village of the Eastern Abenaki. The troops are also instructed to arrest Sébastien Râle, a French Jesuit priest who founded a mission in Norridgewock. Massachusetts officials believe Râle has encouraged the Abenaki to attack colonial settlements in the larger conflict known as Dummer's War (see entry for JUNE 1722). As the soldiers storm Norridgewock, Râle joins the Indian residents in battling the intruders. The troops kill the missionary and at least 80 Indians before setting the village ablaze. They later parade through the streets of Boston, displaying 26 Indian scalps (including 14 from slaughtered children) as trophies of victory.

1726

Gulliver's Travels lampoons European notions of civilization.

In Jonathan Swift's satire *Gulliver's Travels* (subtitled *Travels into Several Remote Nations of the World*), the title character's final journey is to the land of the Houyhnhnms, horselike creatures who live in peace and harmony. Gulliver describes England's "civilized" society to them; the Houyhnhnms are baffled by its violence and its social and economic inequities. Many scholars, seeing the Houyhnhnms as representing American Indians, interpret this section of Swift's book as a satire on the arrogance of the English in considering themselves superior to North America's indigenous peoples.

1729

November 28

The Natchez attack Fort Rosalie.

The Natchez Indians of Louisiana storm Fort Rosalie, a French outpost, and kill more than 200 settlers and soldiers. They also take captive several hundred women, children, and African-American slaves. The French governor of Louisiana had enraged the Natchez by ordering that their largest village, which Fort Rosalie overlooks, be turned into a plantation. Although the Yazoo lend support for the Natchez uprising, the revolt is swiftly put down by the French and their Choctaw allies. The war against the Natchez nearly destroys the tribe. Many are killed, and nearly 500 are taken as prisoners and sent to Santo Domingo, where they are sold into slavery. The few survivors scatter and join nearby tribes, such as the Chickasaw, Creek, and Cherokee.

1730

A French attack ends the Fox (Mesquaki) resistance.

Trying to escape French raiders, a large group of Fox Indians travel east to seek protection in Seneca lands. Along the way they are set upon by French troops. In the attack, 400 Fox are killed, and another 500 are sold into slavery. Although isolated violence between the Fox and the French will continue for several more years, the massacre effectively ends decades of warfare (see entry for 1712). The surviving Fox find refuge among the Sac, who together escape from the French by relocating to lands in what is now Iowa.

September 30

Cherokee leaders sign the Articles of Agreement in London.

Alarmed that their Cherokee allies are being courted by the French, the English send Sir Alexander Cummings to Cherokee territory to confirm the tribe's loyalty to the British Crown. Cherokee leaders again pledge their allegiance to the English but request that they be allowed to meet with the king. Seven chiefs are selected to accompany Cummings to London, where they are presented to King George II. During their audience, the Cherokee sign the Articles of Agreement, a document that sets out the terms of their alliance with the British. Both groups promise to live in peace. In addition, the English agree not to occupy Cherokee lands, and the Cherokee pledge to trade exclusively with the English and to help them fight their European and Indian enemies.

1736

Benjamin Franklin begins publishing Indian treaties.

Philadelphia printer Benjamin Franklin begins issuing Indian treaties in small booklets, a publishing enterprise he will continue for nearly 30 years. Franklin's popular booklets will familiarize many non-Indians with Indian oratory. They will also teach Franklin about the organization and philosophy of the Iroquois Confederacy (see entry for CA. 1400), which will later influence his own ideas about the formation of the United States (see entry for JUNE TO JULY 1754).

1737

September 19

Pennsylvania enforces the Walking Purchase treaty.

Thomas Penn, son of Pennsylvania's founder William Penn, finds a treaty that his father negotiated with three Lenni Lenape (Delaware) chiefs regarding lands along the Delaware River. The treaty granted Penn the woods extending from the river "as far as a man can go in one day and a half."

Eager to take over Lenni Lenape land north of the river, Pennsylvania officials insist that the colony's boundaries be redrawn according to the terms of the treaty. They hire the colony's three best athletes to measure the maximum distance a person can transverse in one and a half days. The athletes train for nine days, while colonists clear trees and brush to make their path easier to travel. As the athletes set off, Lenni Lenape witnesses shout at them to walk, not run. Ignoring the Indians, the men race at full speed. The fastest runs 65 miles in the allotted time. Based on his feat, Pennsylvania claims 1,200 square miles of Lenni Lenape territory, outraging its Indian inhabitants. (See also entry for 1742.)

> "This very ground that is under me was my land and inheritance, and is taken from me by fraud. ...When I have sold lands fairly, I look upon them to be really sold. A bargain is a bargain. Tho' I have sometimes had nothing for the lands I have sold but broken pipes or such triffles, yet when I have sold them. . . . I look upon the bargain to be good. Yet I think that I should not be ill used on this account by those very people who have had such an advantage in their purchases no be called a fool for it. Indians are not such fools."
> —Lenni Lenape (Delaware) leader Teedyuscung on the Walking Purchase

1740

January

An Indian force attacks Spanish Florida.

Georgia governor James Oglethorpe leads Creek, Chickasaw, and Cherokee warriors in an invasion of Spanish-held Florida. The battle is part of a larger conflict known as the War of Jenkins's Ear (1740–43), which involves disagreements between England and Spain over treaty violations. Oglethorpe's force twice attempts unsuccessfully to capture St. Augustine (see entry for 1565) before retreating to Georgia.

1741

Alaska Natives make contact with Russian explorers.

A Russian exploring party led by Danish navigator Vitus Bering sails to the region of present-day Alaska, becoming the first non-Indians to encounter the indigenous peoples of Alaska and the Aleutian Islands. From them the Russians receive sea otter furs, which create a sensation among their countrymen when they return home. Hoping to make their fortunes, Russian traders flock to the region to obtain more furs.

The sea otter fur trade proves a disaster for the Aleutians. With no regulation of their conduct, the foreign traders—known as *promyshlenniki*—often sail to a village, take women and children hostage, and refuse to release the prisoners until the village's men hunt for them. Many of these brutal traders rape their captives and kill men if they are unsuccessful on the hunt.

1742

The Iroquois use the Walking Purchase to challenge Lenni Lenape (Delaware) land claims.

At a conference in Philadelphia, the Iroquois mediate the land dispute between Pennsylvania and the Lenni Lenape (Delaware) resulting from the fraudulent Walking Purchase treaty (see entry for SEPTEMBER 19, 1737). The Iroquois support Pennsylvania's dubious claim and order the Lenni Lenape off the land. Possibly bribed by Pennsylvania officials, Iroquois leader Canasatego insults the Lenni Lenape, calling their men "lewd women" and insisting they "take the advice of a Wise Man and remove immediately."

> "Let this Belt of Wampum serve to Chastise You; You ought to be taken by the Hair of the Head and shaked severely till you recover your Senses and become Sober; you don't know what Ground you stand on, nor what you are doing. . . . This land that you Claim is gone through Your Guts. You have been furnished with Clothes and Meat and Drink by the Goods paid you for it, and now You want it again Children as you are. . . . For all these reasons we charge You to remove instantly."
>
> —Iroquois orator Canasatego to the Lenni Lenape at their 1742 council

1744

May

King George's War breaks out.

King George's War—known in Europe as the War of the Austrian Succession—ends the 30 years of peace between England and France inaugurated by the Treaty of Utrecht (see entry for JULY 13, 1713). The fighting begins in present-day Nova Scotia, when French soldiers from the fort at Louisbourg attack English villages in the area. In retaliation, English troops descend on Louisbourg and capture it the following year. Sporadic raids are made by both the English and French, aided by the Indian allies, until 1748. The peace treaty requires England to return Louisbourg to French control but does little to resolve the underlying conflicts between the two powers.

Within six years, they and their Indian supporters will again be at war (see entry for JULY 4, 1754).

1745

Russian traders slaughter 15 Aleut at Attu.

Using a standard Russian trading practice (see entry for 1741), a trade expedition kidnaps women and children from an Aleut village on the island of Attu and forces Attu's men to hunt for their ransom. When the number of sea otter furs the Aleut deliver is not great enough, the traders murder 15 of the hunters as a warning to other villages of the consequences of not meeting the Russians' demands.

1746

Trade rivalries drive the Choctaw to civil war.

For more than a decade, the Choctaw have been divided between those to the east who prefer to deal with French traders and those to the west who favor the British as trading partners. The contentiousness grows into warfare when Red Shoes, a pro-English leader, is murdered by a pro-French tribe member for a bounty placed on Red Shoes's head by the governor of Louisiana. In the resulting civil war, both sides rely on their European allies for weapons. Because the British are less willing to trade guns, the pro-English faction is defeated. Once peace is restored in 1750, three new divisions in the tribe develop: a southern and a western distinct that support the French, and a northeastern district that sides with the British.

1747

July

Mary Bosomworth (Coosaponakeesa) declares herself queen of the Creek.

A member of a powerful Creek family, Coosaponakeesa (known to whites as Mary Bosomworth) meets with authorities in the colony of Georgia and requests payment for her past assistance to the colony. In the past, she had served as an interpreter for the colony's founder, James Oglethorpe, and used her influence among the Creek to help him establish white settlements on tribal lands.

When the authorities ignore her demands, Bosomworth, now calling herself the Creek's queen, leads a small force of Creek warriors into the town of Savannah and threatens to destroy it. Town officials treat her gingerly until they discover that her warriors feel no allegiance to Bosomworth. Becoming hysterical when her authority is questioned, Bosomworth is placed in a guardhouse, but she is soon released. The incident earns her the enmity of both the Georgia colonists and her fellow Creek.

1751

November 20

The Akimel O'odham (Pima) rebel against the Spanish.

Angered by their brutal oppression at the hands of the Spanish military, Akimel O'odham (Pima) Indians led by Luis Oacpicagigua rise up against the Spanish in their territory. The Indians kill more than one hundred Spaniards and burn their churches. The rebels, however, are soon overtaken by the Spanish, largely because the Tohono O'odham (Pagago) and Apache refuse to join in the rebellion as they earlier had pledged to do. Oacpicagigua is imprisoned but escapes execution by agreeing to rebuild the churches—a promise he later refuses to keep. (See also entry for 1695.)

1752

The Treaty of Logstown gives whites control of prime Ohio lands.

At a Mingo village at Logstown in Pennsylvania, leaders of the Mingo, Lenni Lenape (Delaware), Shawnee, and other Ohio Valley tribes meet with representatives of the British government and the Ohio Company of Virginia. Offering the Indians a huge gift of trade goods, the company negotiates a treaty that gives it title to rich lands surrounding the forks of the Ohio River. The English treaty commissioners also use the occasion to berate the French and solidify their friendship with the Indian groups present, particularly the mighty Iroquois.

June 21

French troops destroy a Miami trading center.

Angered by the high prices and scarcity of French goods, Miami trader Memeskia (known to whites as Old Briton) persuades his band to establish the village of Pickawilany in present-day western Ohio. At Pickawilany, the Miami welcome English traders, infuriating their former French allies. After Pickawilany emerges as a major trading center, the French with the help of their Ottawa and Ojibway allies storm the village in a surprise attack. Outnumbered 10 to one, the Miami are quickly defeated, and Pickawilany is destroyed. The French commander, Charles Langlade, orders Memeskia's execution. In a demonstration of their contempt for the British-allied Indian trader, some of Langlade's fighters boil Memeskia's body and eat his remains.

1753

George Washington demands that the French abandon their forts in the Ohio River valley.

The Virginia government sends George Washington, a 21-year-old surveyor, to negotiate with the French who are building forts in the Ohio River valley. The forts are intended to solidify French control over the area, which is also claimed by Virginia, Pennsylvania, the Iroquois Confederacy, and the Indians who live in the region. On behalf of Virginia, Washington insists that the French abandon their forts. When they refuse, he recommends that the Virginia militia be sent to remove them (see entry for JULY 4, 1754).

1754

Moor's Indian Charity School is founded.

Congregational minister Eleazer Wheelock establishes Moor's Indian Charity School in Lebanon, Connecticut, with the support of the Society in Scotland for Propagating Christian Knowledge. The school will educate approximately 45 Indian boys and 15 Indian girls. The boys will receive a classical education, including lessons in Greek, Latin, and Hebrew. The girls will be trained in sewing and housekeeping, so they will be able to assist the male students in future missionary work. The school will later be moved to Hanover, New Hampshire, and become part of Dartmouth College (see entry for 1769).

July 4

A Virginia militia attack initiates the French and Indian War.

Following a failed attempt to persuade the French to leave the Ohio River valley (see entry for 1753), George Washington leads the Virginia militia to the region, where the English have begun building forts to protect their land claims. With the help of the Mingo Indians under Chief Half-King, the soldiers attack a patrol of Frenchmen, killing 10 and capturing 24. In response to the attack, the French force the militia to retreat and drive off the Englishmen constructing the forts.

The incident leads the French to amass a huge army of Indian warriors and helps initiate the French and Indian War. Although this conflict, pitting the English against the French for control over North America, begins with Washington's attack, war will not be formally declared until two years later. (See also entries for JULY 9, 1755; SEPTEMBER 8, 1755; SEPTEMBER 9, 1760; and FEBRUARY 10, 1763.)

June to July

The Albany Congress is held.

Preparing for war with France, representatives from seven British colonies gather in Albany, New York, to organize a united military offensive. Also in attendance are Iroquois leaders, whom the colonists want to impress with their resolve to band together to battle the French. The colonial leaders hope to coax the Iroquois into abandoning their policy of neutrality in European wars (see entry for SUMMER 1701) and joining the British cause.

"It would be a very strange thing if *Six Nations* of ignorant savages should be capable of forming a scheme for such a union, and be able to execute it in such a manner, as that it has subsisted for ages, and appears indissoluble; and yet that a like union should be impracticable for ten or a dozen *English* colonies, to whom it is more necessary and must be more advantageous, and whom cannot be supposed to want an equal understanding of their interests."

—Benjamin Franklin in 1751 on the Iroquois League as a model for a confederacy of colonies

The British fail miserably in these aims. The meetings are contentious, and leaders from Pennsylvania and Connecticut scramble to make secret, illegal deals with the Iroquois for Indian land that both colonies claim as their own. Disgusted by the colonists' behavior and unconvinced of their military preparedness, the Iroquois declare that the

English are "like women: bare and open and without fortifications."

The congress does, however, succeed in approving the Albany Plan of Union. This document, based on the ideas of Benjamin Franklin, proposes a centralized colonial government modeled after the Grand Council of the Iroquois Confederacy (see entry for CA. 1400). The plan, however, is later rejected by the colonial legislatures and is never even examined by the British government.

1755

William Johnson is appointed Indian superintendent.

The British government chooses William Johnson, an experienced trader and merchant, to oversee its dealings with Indians in North America. Johnson quickly embraces Mohawk ways. Often dressing in Indian garb and participating in Mohawk ceremonies, Johnson becomes fluent in the Mohawk language and fathers many children with his Mohawk wife Molly Brant. His enthusiasm for Indian life earns the respect of the Iroquois. Largely because of Johnson's influence, they will become England's most loyal Indian allies and provide the English with valuable military support during the French and Indian War (see entry for JULY 4, 1754). Johnson will also lend important support to Molly Brant's brother Joseph, who will emerge as one of the most powerful Iroquois leaders during the Revolutionary War era (see entries for NOVEMBER 1775; JULY 1777; NOVEMBER 11, 1778; and FALL 1781).

The "noble savage" stereotype is advanced by Jean-Jacques Rousseau.

French philosopher Jean-Jacques Rousseau popularizes the idea of Indians as "noble savages" in *Discourse upon the Origin and Foundation of the*

Iroquois Indians gathering at Johnson Hall, the mansion of British superintendent of Indian affairs William Johnson *(Collection of the Albany Institute of History & Art)*

Inequality among Mankind. Rousseau holds that Indians, largely ignorant of the ways of European civilization, live in a more "pure state of nature," where their innocence gives them greater happiness than Europeans, corrupted by their societies, can ever achieve. For centuries, non-Indians will employ the stereotype of the noble savage to diminish the achievements and sophistication of Indian societies.

May

The Cherokee become British allies.

Representatives from the colony of South Carolina negotiate an alliance with the powerful Cherokee. The Indians agree to become subjects of the English king and cede some of their territory. In return, the English promise to build a fort in their territory to help protect the Cherokee from their French and Creek enemies and to supply them with trade goods at low prices. The allegiance will be short-lived: English abuses will soon lead the Cherokee to turn against their new allies (see entries for SUMMER 1760 and SUMMER 1761).

June 12

Massachusetts Bay offers bounties on Indian scalps.

William Shirley, the captain-general of the Massachusetts Bay Colony, issues a proclamation that offers colonists cash bounties for the scalps of Indians of French-allied tribes. The scalps of male adults are to be rewarded with 40 pounds; those of female adults and males under 12 are to bring the scalper half that amount.

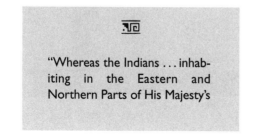

"Whereas the Indians . . . inhabiting in the Eastern and Northern Parts of His Majesty's territories of *New-England,* . . . [have] been guilty of the most perfidious, barbarous and inhuman Murders of . . . his Majesty's *English* Subjects; and have abstained from all Commerce and Correspondence with His Majesty's said Subjects for many Months past; and the said *Indians* have fully discovered an inimical, traitorous and rebellious intention and Disposition; . . . I do hereby require His Majesty's subjects of this Province to embrace all Opportunities of pursuing, captivating, killing and destroying all and any of the aforesaid Indians."

—from a poster announcing the Massachusetts Bay Colony's Indian scalp bounties

July 9

A French and Indian force defeat the British at Fort Duquesne.

English soldiers led by General Edward Braddock and Virginia militiamen under George Washington advance on the French Fort Duquesne, on the Allegheny River. They are ambushed by French soldiers and Indian warriors, soundly trounced, and forced to retreat. During the foray, the first major battle of the French and Indian War (see entry for JULY 4, 1754), more than 900 Englishmen and Virginians, including Braddock, are killed.

The British debacle sets the tone for the war for the rest of the year. Eager to drive the British from their lands, Indian raiders will effectively harass English settlements in Virginia, Pennsylvania, and Maryland, and the French will repel attacks on their forts at Niagara and Crown Point.

September 8

The Iroquois and the British force are victorious in the Battle of Lake George.

French soldiers, joined by a group of Mohawk and Abenaki warriors, lay in wait as a British-Iroquois force led by William Johnson (see entry for 1755) approaches Lake George in New York. Before the French are ready to engage the enemy, one of their Indian allies begins shooting, alerting the English and Iroquois to the trap set for them. The battle that follows ends in a British victory, but their Iroquois allies mourn the loss of Hendrick, an aged Mohawk leader who was fiercely loyal to the British. One of the battle's first casualties, Hendrick was part of an Indian delegation presented to English queen Anne 65 years earlier (see entry for APRIL 19, 1710).

1758

October

Ohio River tribes become British allies through the Treaty of Easton.

Five hundred representatives from the Iroquois, Lenni Lenape (Delaware) and other smaller Indian groups from the Ohio River valley gather at Easton, Pennsylvania, to negotiate with the British. In 18 days of discussion, the Indians agree to withdraw their support of the French in exchange for the return of some of the lands taken from them illegally by the British. The treaty is a turning point in the French and Indian War (see entry for JULY 1754). After losing their Indian allies, the French suffer a series of devastating defeats, including the loss of Fort Duquesne (see entry for JULY 9, 1755) and Fort Niagara to an invading British and Indian force.

Winter

The Cherokee begin attacking British posts and settlements.

Several Cherokee, returning home from aiding the English in an attack on Fort Duquesne, round up a herd of wild horses that a group of Virginia settlers claim as their own. The Virginians kill 12 of the Cherokee and take the horses; the tribe retaliates by murdering some 20 settlers. United in their fury over this incident and their past mistreatment by the British, the Cherokee announce that they are no longer allies of the English. Their raids on the British and the British counterraids will lead to the Cherokee War (see entries for SUMMER 1760 and for SUMMER 1761).

1760

Summer

The Cherokee War breaks out.

A force of 1,300 colonial troops, augmented by Catawba warriors, advances on the Cherokee of South Carolina to put down an Indian uprising there (see entry WINTER 1759). The Cherokee quickly repel the invading army, force it to retreat to Charleston, and lay siege to Fort Loudoun, an important British post in their territory. The troops at the fort surrender on the condition that they will be allowed to leave unharmed. The Cherokee, eager to avenge previous attacks, break their pledge and ambush the soldiers, killing many and taking others prisoner. (See also entry for SUMMER 1761.)

September 9

The British win the French and Indian War.

With the fall of Montreal to the British, the French are forced to surrender, and the French and Indian War (see entry for JULY 4, 1754) effectively comes to an end, although the official peace will not be concluded until three years later (see entry for FEBRUARY 10, 1763). In the terms of surrender, the English will agree to respect France's previous reservation of certain lands exclusively for Indian use.

1761

The Aleut attack Russians at Umnak.

On the Aleutian island of Umnak, the Aleut attack a party of Russian traders who have tried to force Aleut men to hunt for them by taking women and children hostage (see entry for 1741). The assault sets off a highly effective series of raids and attacks on traders and trading ships over the next five years (see entry for 1766).

February

British general Jeffrey Amherst refuses to give gifts to Indians.

General Jeffrey Amherst, the commander of British forces in North America, issues a decree that ends the practice of giving gifts—such as metal goods, guns, and ammunition—to England's Indian allies. Amherst condemns gift-giving as too expensive and overindulgent. Indians, however, have come to rely on gifts from Europeans for many of their basic necessities. Their outrage over Amherst's policy will lead many Indians to join Pontiac's Rebellion (see entry for MAY 9, 1763). (See also entry for JUNE 1763.)

Summer

An English army crushes the Cherokee uprising.

After an unsuccessful attempt to put down the revolting Cherokee the previous year (see entry for SUMMER 1760), the English send a massive army of 1,800 regular soldiers and 700 militiamen into the tribe's territory. In a relentless campaign, the troops destroy more than 15 villages and burn the inhabitants' stores of food. Unable to obtain supplies from the French, the Cherokee are forced to agree to a peace treaty, in which they formally recognize British rule and promise to release prisoners taken during the war.

1762

Neolin urges his Lenni Lenape (Delaware) followers to reject non-Indian ways.

Neolin, a Lenni Lenape (Delaware) holy man (also known as the Delaware Prophet), begins preaching a new Indian religion from his home in present-day Ohio. He maintains that two years earlier he visited the Creator's realm in a vision. Through the experience, he learned of the Creator's disappointment with Indians for adopting the corrupting ways of whites. Neolin tells his followers that they must now purify themselves by abandoning white customs, restoring Indian traditions, and driving the English from their lands. If Indians do not follow these reforms, Neolin holds, after death their souls will be punished by an evil spirit—a concept of hell possibly borrowed from Christianity.

> "Hear what the Great Spirit has ordered me to tell you! You are to make sacrifices, in the manner that I shall direct; to put off entirely from yourselves the customs which you have adopted since the white people came among us; you are to return to that former happy state, in which we lived in peace and plenty, before these strangers came to disturb us."
>
> —Lenni Lenape (Delaware) prophet Neolin's instructions to his followers

Neolin's beliefs spread quickly and are embraced by such Indian groups as the Ottawa, Potawatomi, Wyandot, and Ojibway throughout what is now Ohio and Michigan. They will have a great influence over the Indians involved in the rebellions led by Pontiac (see entry for MAY 9, 1763) and Tecumseh (see entry for 1808).

1763

Lenni Lenape (Delaware) chief Teedyuscung dies in a fire.

Teedyuscung, an influential leader of the Lenni Lenape (Delaware), dies when unidentified arsons set fire to his cabin in the Wyoming Valley of Pennsylvania. A champion of Indian rights, Teedyuscung had been a highly vocal opponent of Pennsylvania colonial officials, whom he accused of committing fraud in their land deals with the Lenni Lenape (see entry for SEPTEMBER 19, 1737).

February 10

The Treaty of Paris is signed.

The Treaty of Paris marks the conclusion of the nine-year French and Indian War (see entry for JULY 4, 1754), which ends with a British victory. In the agreement, France cedes New France to England and Louisiana (except for New Orleans) to Spain. All lands from Canada to Florida and from the Atlantic Ocean to the Mississippi River fall under British control.

The war's outcome is a blow to the Indians in the Northeast and Midwest. Most of those who took sides allied themselves to the French, whose policies were generally much more benevolent to Indians than those of the British.

May 9

Pontiac's War begins.

With their lands now under British control, the tribes of the Ohio River valley and Great Lakes region—including the Lenni Lenape (Delaware), Ottawa, Wyandot, Potawatomi, Ojibway, and Seneca—unite and rise up against the English colonists invading their territory. Their confederacy is led by an Ottawa warrior named Pontiac. He is inspired by the Lenni Lenape prophet Neolin (see entry for 1762), who preaches that Indians should resist the corrupting influence of the English and their efforts to move onto Indian land.

Pontiac's war begins with an attack on Fort Detroit, to which he will lay siege for more than six months. During May and June, his forces will battle and capture most of the British forts to the west of the Appalachian Mountains. In one of the most notorious events of the war, Ojibway Indians stage a surprise attack on Fort Michilimackinac, in present-day Michigan, while playing lacrosse with Sac Indian visitors. During the game, a player tosses the ball into the fort. Several Ojibway rush into the stockade, ostensibly to retrieve the ball, but they pull guns on the British once they are inside. The warriors kill the commander and take several soldiers hostage. (See also entries for AUGUST 4–5, 1763; SEPTEMBER 14, 1763; AUGUST 17, 1765; and JULY 23, 1766.)

June

The British initiate an Indian smallpox epidemic.

British soldiers at Fort Pitt (now Pittsburgh) give Indians seeking asylum gifts of blankets that had

> "You will do well to try to inoculate the Indians by means of blankets, as well as to try every other method that can serve to extirpate this execrable race. I should be very glad your scheme for hunting them down by dogs could take effect, but England is at too great a distance to think of that at present."
>
> —Sir Jeffrey Amherst, recommending that Indians be given smallpox-infested blankets

belonged to smallpox victims. The disease-infected blankets spread smallpox through the Lenni Lenape (Delaware) and Shawnee villages, killing much of their population. This early example of biological warfare is masterminded by Sir Jeffrey Amherst, the commander in chief of the British colonies. He suggested the idea in a letter to an officer at the fort, adding "We must on this occasion use every stratagem in our power to reduce [the Indian population]."

August 4–5

Indian rebels are defeated at the Battle of Bushy Run.

About 500 British troops meet a force of Lenni Lenape (Delaware), Shawnee, Wyandot, and Iroquois near Fort Pitt, a British stronghold that has been taken over by warriors under Pontiac's command (see entry for MAY 9, 1763). The Indians surround the small British army, but the soldiers, by inciting overexcited warriors to attack them, manage to inflict heavy casualties, which included two Lenni Lenape chiefs. To the surprise of Pontiac's men, the conflict, later known as the Battle of Bushy Run, ends with an English victory. Already weary of war and now convinced that the English cannot be defeated, warriors from the Lenni Lenape and Shawnee tribes start to abandon Pontiac's cause in large numbers.

September 14

Pontiac's warriors ambush an English wagon train.

A wagon train equipped with supplies for the British Fort Niagara is attacked by hundreds of Indian followers of Pontiac (see entry for MAY 9, 1763) in a heavily wooded area just below Niagara Falls known as Devil's Hole. Most of the English accompanying the supply train are killed in the attack. The Indians inflict more casualties in an ensuing battle with a British regiment that rushes to rescue the beleaguered train crew. The conflict, which will become known as the Battle of Devil's

Hole Road, is the greatest Indian victory of Pontiac's War. The triumph, however, will not prevent increasing numbers of warriors from giving up on the rebellion as unwinnable.

October 7

The Proclamation Line of 1763 is established.

King George III of England issues the Royal Proclamation of 1763, which creates the Proclamation Line. This boundary, roughly following the crest of the Appalachian Mountains, separates the lands to the east, where the king sanctions white settlement, from those to the west, which are to be occupied only by Indians. The Proclamation Line is meant to placate the tribes involved in Pontiac's War (see entry for MAY 9, 1763), by promising that their lands will no longer be encroached upon by English settlers. The colonists, however, will be angered by the proclamation and will ignore the king's demands that they keep off Indian territory in the Midwest.

December

The Paxton Boys murder Conestoga Indians.

A mob of 57 armed frontiersmen from Paxton, Pennsylvania, attack a nearby village of peaceful Conestoga Indians. Known as the Paxton Boys, the vigilantes murder three men, two women, and one child. Colonial officials place the 14 Indians who manage to escape in protective custody in the Lancaster, Pennsylvania, jail. Two weeks later, the Paxton Boys storm the jail and slaughter the Conestoga held there.

John Penn, the governor of Pennsylvania, issues a proclamation calling for the arrest of the killers. Although their identities are known by many colonists in the region, no one comes forward, and no arrests are made.

The Paxton Boys' vigilante violence had been inspired by increased fears of Indian attack following Pontiac's successful raids on British forts (see entry for MAY 9, 1763). Their Indian victims, however, are scapegoats for the colonial government—the true target of the Paxton Boys' wrath. Dominated by pacifist Quakers, the government has been reluctant to build up the colony's military, leaving settlers on Pennsylvania's western frontier feeling vulnerable as Indians began to wage war against the English in their lands.

"What could old Shehaes, so old he had been present at Penn's Treaty in 1701, done that he should have been cut to pieces in bed? What could he or the other poor old men and women do? What had the little boys and girls done? What could children of a year old, babes at the breast, what could they do that they must be shot and hatched? And in their parents' arms! This is done by no civilized nation in Europe. Do we come to America to learn and practice the manners of barbarians?"

—Benjamin Franklin on the Paxton Boys' massacre of the Conestoga Indians

1765

August 17

Pontiac makes peace with the English.

Seeing support for his Indian confederacy dwindle in the face of continued English attacks,

Pontiac meets with an Indian agent sent by English officials. The Indian leader agrees to end his war against the English (see entry for MAY 9, 1763). He also accepts a pension from his former enemies—an action that will embitter many of the warriors who had followed him into battle. (See also JULY 23, 1766.)

1766

Russians attack Aleut villages.

To stop a rash of Aleut attacks (see entry for 1761), Russian trader Ivan Solovief launches an assault against the Aleut's villages. Traveling on ships armed with cannons, Russian mercenaries shell the Aleut homes, then enslave or execute all of the survivors they can capture. The brutal massacres so reduce the Aleut population that they will no longer be able to sustain their rebellion against the Russians.

Alaska Natives are made subjects of Russia.

Catherine the Great of Russia declares that the indigenous peoples of the Aleutian Islands and Alaska Peninsula are Russian subjects, who can be taxed by the Russian government. The czarina also decrees that, as subjects, they should be treated well, a demand that will have little influence on the behavior of Russian traders and explorers.

July 23

Pontiac's War officially ends.

The informal peace made between Pontiac and the English (see entry for AUGUST 17, 1765) is made official with a peace agreement signed by 40 Indian leaders and William Johnson (see entry for 1755), the British superintendent of Indian affairs, at Oswego, New York. The treaty ends the organized resistance to English settlement in the Ohio River valley.

1768

The Iroquois cede Shawnee land in the Treaty of Fort Stanwix.

The British compel the Iroquois to grant them a large tract of land stretching from the Ohio River to what is now northern Kentucky. The treaty represents the first major cession of land west of the Appalachians since the Proclamation of 1763 (see entry for OCTOBER 7, 1763), which reserved the region exclusively for Indian use. The area sold by the Iroquois encompasses much of the traditional homeland of the Shawnee. Furious that the Iroquois have dared to cede their territory, the Shawnee will soon band together with their Lenni Lenape (Delaware) and Miami allies to resist English efforts to take over their land.

1769

Dartmouth College is established as a school for Indians.

Through a charter granted to Congregational minister Eleazer Wheelock, Dartmouth College is founded in Hanover, New Hampshire, "for the education and instruction of Youth of the Indian Tribes in this Land in reading, writing and all parts of Learning." Wheelock moves Moor's Indian Charity School (see entry for 1754) to Dartmouth and uses funds collected in England by his protégé, Mohegan minister Samson Occom (see entries for 1772 and for NOVEMBER 1785), to finance several of the college's first buildings. Despite its early commitment to Indian education, Dartmouth will soon concentrate on teaching English students. Only nine Indians will graduate from the college over the following 200 years.

Junípero Serra founds the first California mission.

A Spanish expedition of soldiers headed by Gaspar de Portolá and Franciscan missionaries led by Junípero Serra travels north into Alta California, where Serra establishes San Diego de Alcalá—a Catholic mission at the site of present-day San Diego. The mission is intended to be a military base, from which the Spaniards can protect their land claims from other Europeans, and a center for the conversion of Indians. Over the next 55 years, 17 more missions will be founded in California on the model of San Diego.

The missions will have a devastating effect on the Indians of California. Indians brought to the missions as neophytes—the mission priests' term for converts—are subjected to Spanish rule and routinely punished with beatings for any infraction. Such brutal punishments, coupled with widespread starvation and disease caused by bad sanitation, will lead to the deaths of thousands of Mission Indians. (See also entry for 1834.)

"The following day after my baptism, they took me to work with other Indians, and they put me to cleaning a [field] of maize. . . . I cut my foot and could not continue working. . . . Every day they lashed me . . . because I could not finish. . . . I found a way to escape; but I was tracked and they caught me like a fox. . . . They lashed me until I lost consciousness. . . . For several days I could not raise myself from the floor where they had laid me."

—Kamia Indian Janitin on his treatment at the San Diego mission

April 20

Pontiac is killed by a Peoria assassin.

The great Ottawa rebellion leader Pontiac (see entry for MAY 9, 1763) is living among the Illinois Indians when Makatchinga, the nephew of the chief of the Peoria, kills him in the village of Cahokia. Rumors fly that the British paid the assassin, to eliminate any possibility that Pontiac might instigate a second revolt. Since the end of his rebellion, however, Pontiac has made many Indian enemies through his arrogance and assumption of political powers that his followers have not conferred on him.

1770

The first cigar store Indian is displayed.

A large sculpture of an Indian in a tobacco shop in Pennsylvania becomes the first documented appearance of a "cigar store Indian" in North America. For more than 100 years, such figures have been displayed in European cigar stores to advertise their wares to a largely illiterate public. Most of the sculptures are categorized as chiefs or squaws and depict stereotyped features and clothing, modeled on early European figures made by carvers with no firsthand knowledge of Indian appearance. Until the early 20th century, cigar store Indians will be among the best known and most widely seen representations of North American Indians.

March 5

Massachuset Indian Crispus Attucks dies in the Boston Massacre.

During a protest against taxation, Boston residents attack a troop of British soldiers outside the city's custom house. The soldiers retaliate by shooting into the crowd. The first of five casualties is Crispus Attucks, the son of a Massachuset Indian mother and African-American father. In 1888 Attucks will be honored with a monument on the Boston Common.

1772

Samson Occom's *Sermon Preached at the Execution of Moses Paul* is published.

Mohegan minister Samson Occom (see entries for 1767 and NOVEMBER 1785) preaches a sermon on

Mohegan minister Samson Occom, whose *Sermon Preached at the Execution of Moses Paul* was the first work written by an American Indian to be published in English *(Courtesy of the Boston Public Library, Print Dept.)*

the dangers of alcohol abuse at the funeral of Moses Paul, a fellow tribesman who was executed after killing another man in a drunken rampage. Appearing in 19 editions, Occom's sermon, the first published work written in English by an American Indian, will become a highly popular temperance tract. Occom will also later write *A Choice Selection of Hymns* (1774) and the posthumously published *An Account of the Montauk Indians on Long Island* (1809).

1773

December 16

Rebel colonists dress as Mohawk Indians during the Boston Tea Party.

To protest England's manipulation of the tea market in the American colonies, about 50 men board three ships in Boston Harbor and dump 10,000 pounds worth of tea into the water below. The protesters are dressed as Mohawk Indians and sing "Rally Mohawks, and bring your axes/and tell King George we'll pay no taxes on his foreign tea." Their costume is only one of many instances of colonists using American Indian imagery to express a new American identity that distinguishes them from their European forebears.

1774

The Quebec Act creates borders between Indian and non-Indian territory.

The British parliament passes the Quebec Act, which establishes a border between lands held by the English colonists in Canada and British territory reserved for Indians. It extends the boundaries of the province of Quebec south to the Ohio River and west to the Mississippi. This provision outrages colonists in Massachusetts, Connecticut, and Virginia, who claim much of the land assigned to Quebec. This challenge to colonial land claims will become one of the primary causes of the American Revolution.

The First Continental Congress allocates funds to Indian affairs.

Representatives to the First Continental Congress vote to put aside 40,000 pounds to finance its dealings with Indian groups. It also establishes the post of commissioner of Indian affairs to negotiate with Indians. As the colonies move closer toward war with England, the commissioner's most important responsibility is to try to persuade tribes to declare neutrality in the coming conflict.

April 30

An attack on Mingo Indians incites Lord Dunmore's War.

In 1773 Lord Dunmore, the governor of Virginia, declares that lands in what is now western Pennsylvania are part of his own colony, even though the area was guaranteed to the Shawnee by the Treaty of Fort Stanwix (see entry for 1768). Ignoring this treaty and the Proclamation of 1763 (see entry for OCTOBER 7, 1763), in which the British king forbade white settlement west of the Appalachians, English squatters flood into the area claimed by Virginia, infuriating the Indians of the region.

> "Such was my love for the whites, that my countrymen pointed as they passed, and said, 'Logan is the friend of white men.' I had even thought to have lived with you but for the injuries of one man, Colonel Cresap, in cold blood and unprovoked, murdered all the relations of Logan, not even sparing my women and children. There runs not a drop of my blood in the veins of any living creature. This called on me for revenge. I have sought it; I have killed many; I have glutted my vengeance."
>
> —Mingo rebel John Logan in a 1774 letter to Lord Dunmore

Growing tensions between the Indians and the squatters erupts into violence when a group of settlers kill five Mingo warriors and the sister of Mingo leader John Logan. Logan, who had been an advocate for maintaining peace with whites, vows revenge. He tells of his change of heart in an impassioned speech he submits in writing to a peace council he refuses to attend. The speech, later included in *McGuffy's Reader,* will be taught to millions of non-Indian school children in the 19th century.

A total of 13 of Logan's relatives have been murdered by the English; he sets about killing an equal number of whites. John Connelly, the commander of Fort Pitt (now Pittsburgh), sends out a warning to area whites suggesting that a large-scale Indian war is in the offing. Responding to Connelly's alarm, Lord Dunmore sends two columns of troops out of Virginia to battle Indians in the contested region, inciting what will become known as Lord Dunmore's War. (See also entries for OCTOBER 9, 1774, and for SEPTEMBER 12 TO OCTOBER 12, 1775.)

October 9

The Shawnee fight Virginia troops in the Battle of Point Pleasant.

A force of about 1,000 Shawnee led by Cornstalk meet 300 soldiers from Virginia at Point Pleasant on the Ohio River's southern bank. In the day-long battle, the Indians are close to defeating the Virginians when, mistakenly believing English reinforcements have arrived, the Shawnee decide to retreat. The casualties are heavy on both sides. Among those killed is the Shawnee war chief Pucksinwah, who is the father of the future rebellion leader Tecumseh (see entry for 1808).

The Battle of Point Pleasant is the largest engagement of Lord Dunmore's War (see entry for APRIL 30, 1774). Soon after, a force of more than 1,000 troops led by Lord Dunmore approaches the Shawnee's villages at the site of present-day Chillicothe, Ohio. Fearing for the lives of their wives and children, Shawnee leaders agree to a truce on October 26, although another year will pass before the peace is formally concluded (see entry for SEPTEMBER 12 TO OCTOBER 12, 1775).

1775

James Adair's *History of the American Indians* is published.

A Scotch-Irish trader who spent many years living among the Chickasaw, James Adair writes *History of the American Indians,* which will later become an important source of information for anthropological research on the tribes of the Southeast. Adair also takes the opportunity to praise the character of the Indians he had come to admire and to condemn colonial officials whose incompetence Adair believed often incited violence between Indians and the English.

March 10

Daniel Boone begins staking out the Wilderness Road.

Employed by the Transylvania Land Company, frontiersman Daniel Boone leads a party of 30 west from North Carolina. The group blazes the 300-mile Wilderness Road across the Appalachians, through the Cumberland Gap, and into Cherokee lands. There Boone finds the Cherokee chiefs most susceptible to bribery and at Sycamore Shoals on the Tennessee River buys from them 20,000,000 acres in what is now Kentucky and central Tennessee on behalf of Transylvania. Over the next 15 years, approximately 100,000 whites will travel along the Wilderness Road and settle in this region in defiance of the Proclamation of 1763 (see entry for OCTOBER 7, 1763). (See also entries for SPRING 1778 and for AUGUST 19, 1782.)

May 1

The Tammany Society meets in Philadelphia.

Thomas Jefferson, James Madison, Benjamin Franklin, and other influential colonists join the Sons of King Tammany, also known as the Tammany Society. Based in Philadelphia, the organization celebrates American culture as the blending of the best ideas and traditions of Indian and European societies. The society is named after Tamanend, a Lenni Lenape (Delaware) chief who developed friendly relations with William Penn (see entry for 1682). Its members' disillusionment with the king is expressed through Tammany Day celebrations, during which the monarchy is parodied in a mock crowning of King Tammany.

July 12

The Second Continental Congress establishes three Indian departments.

The Second Continental Congress establishes three departments to oversee the colonies' dealings with Indian tribes. The Northern Department is to oversee the Iroquois Confederacy and the Indians living to the north of their lands; the Southern Department is to deal with the Cherokee and all tribes living to the south of them; and the Middle Department is responsible for all Indian groups in between. The Congress appoints three commissioners to the Northern and Middle Departments and five to the Southern Department.

The commissioners are charged with identifying any British agents who try to turn Indians against the colonies and also with attempting to persuade tribes to ally themselves with colonists. Initially, the American officials will be leery of fighting alongside Indians, whom they considered to be undisciplined in war. But there are more than 35,000 Indian warriors in the East, and the American officials come to see the wisdom in attempting to tap this vast fighting force. Despite their efforts, however, the commissioners will largely be unsuccessful at forging alliances, because most Indian groups view the colonists as the greatest threat to their lands and societies. The officials also lack supplies, hindering their ability to earn the favor of Indian leaders through traditional gift giving.

August

The Iroquois meet with U.S. commissioners at German Flats.

Fearing that the six Iroquois tribes will fight on the side of the English in the American Revolution, representatives of the colonial government meet with Iroquois leaders at German Flats, New York. The Americans, explaining that they will fight a war against England to protect their civil rights, succeed in persuading the Iroquois to declare neutrality in the upcoming war. During the meeting, Benjamin Franklin presents the Pine Tree Flag as the first flag of the United States. The imagery is similar to that of the Great Tree of Peace, an Iroquois symbol used to represent the confederacy (see entry for CA. 1400).

September 12 to October 12

The Shawnee negotiate the Treaty of Camp Charlotte.

At a conference at Camp Charlotte, Shawnee leaders agree to a peace treaty that formally ends Lord Dunmore's War (see entries for APRIL 30, 1774, and for OCTOBER 9, 1774). The Shawnee promise to remain north of the Ohio River, effectively ceding their hunting territory in Kentucky. Soon, however, tribal hunters will violate the treaty terms by returning to their old hunting grounds. The tribe will also break a provision guaranteeing their neutrality in the American Revolution when the Shawnee ally themselves to the British cause in 1777.

November

Mohawk leader Joseph Brant meets with King George III.

With the American colonists threatening to rebel, Joseph Brant, a Mohawk leader and secretary to Superintendent of Indian affairs Guy Johnson, travels to London, England. There he meets with King George III, who assures Brant that the British can win a war with the Americans. He also promises that if the Iroquois help them fight the rebels, the Indians will be allowed to stay in their homelands. Brant returns home convinced that the Iroquois should give the English their support.

Mohawk leader Joseph Brant, in a portrait commissioned by the earl of Warwick in 1776. His costume, a combination of Indian and English clothing, suggests his staunch support for the British. *(Library of Congress, Neg. no. USZ62-20488)*

"This dispute was solely occasioned by some people, who notwithstanding a law of the King and his wise Men, would not let some Tea land, but destroyed it, on which he was angry, and sent some Troops with the General, whom you have long known, to see the Laws executed and bring the people to their senses [*sic*], and as he is proceeding with great wisdom, to show them their great mistake, I expect it will soon be over."

—British superintendent of Indian affairs Guy Johnson to the Iroquois on the cause of the American Revolution

4

1776 TO 1829
SURVIVING IN EARLY AMERICA

When the American Revolution erupted, both the English and the colonists initially sought guarantees of neutrality from Indian tribes. Neither side wanted Indians to join their ranks; given their history of abuses against Indian peoples, they did not trust armed warriors to attack only the enemy.

Yet the thousands of fighting men Indian groups could recruit proved too attractive not to exploit. As in the French and Indian War, Indian tribes were soon pressured to become involved in a non-Indian conflict. Although the colonists and the English made active efforts to woo powerful Indian groups, tribes generally chose sides less on the basis of their promises of friendship than on the Indians' own sense of which group posed them the smaller threat.

The tribes most affected by the revolution were those of the Iroquois Confederacy. Most Iroquois, including notably the Mohawk led by Joseph Brant, sided with the English, with whom they had a long-standing trade relationship. When factions of the Oneida and Tuscarora broke ranks and became allies of the colonists, the unity of the centuries-old Iroquois Confederacy was endangered. Ironically, the American Revolution nearly destroyed the very political organization that Benjamin Franklin had proposed as a model for the union of states the colonial rebels hoped to establish.

At the end of the war, the new United States made no distinction between their Indian allies and those of the English. All tribes were treated as defeated enemies, and their lands were increasingly seen by Americans as part of the fruits of their victory. Immediately threatened were the tribes of the Northwest Territory (now Ohio, Indiana, Illinois, Michigan, Wisconsin, and portions of Minnesota).

Despite the swarm of settlers into their lands, the Shawnee, Miami, Potawatomi, Ojibway, and other tribes living north of the Ohio River continued to resist encroachment. To drive the Indians out, President George Washington launched three full-scale military campaigns. A massive number of troops led by "Mad" Anthony Wayne finally defeated the Indian forces in 1794. As a result, the following year the Indian combatants were compelled by the Treaty of Greenville to sign away 25,000 square miles of land in the Ohio country.

The new U.S. government had finally won its battle for Ohio, but victory had come at an enormous price. Facing a possible conflict with the English, who refused to abandon American lands completely, the Washington administration was hesitant to expend any more of its meager resources on fighting long-term and costly Indian wars. Instead, it sought to extinguish Indian land claims through treaties. Toward the same end, the government also launched an effort to end collective Indian resistance by assimilating individual Indians into American society. Its so-called civilization programs focused on creating Indian schools and encouraging Indians to adopt the settled way of life of the non-Indian farmer. Except for among some large southeastern tribes, these programs were largely unsuccessful. Just as Indians did not want to relinquish their lands, they had little interest in giving up their own cultures in exchange for "civilization."

In the Jeffersonian era, an alternative solution to end Indian resistance to white encroachment emerged. In 1803, President Thomas Jefferson purchased from France the Louisiana Territory—an 828,000-square-mile tract stretching from the Mississippi River to the Rocky Mountains. One of Jefferson's reasons for making the purchase was to provide an area to which tribes living east of the Mississippi could be relocated. In his mind, tribes pressured by increasing white settlement would voluntarily elect to leave their homelands for new territory to the west. Soon, however, Americans eager for Indian land would insist that tribes be expelled from the East by force.

Fear of forced relocation and anger at the government's misguided assimilation efforts rekindled the spirit of rebellion in the Northwest Territory. There, among the Shawnee, a spiritual leader named Tenskwatawa drew a devoted following by preaching that Americans were evil. He told the faithful that they should preserve their traditional ways and shun any contact with whites.

As Tenskwatawa's influence spread, his brother Tecumseh began to transform the religious movement into a political alliance dedicated to preserving the Indians' control over their remaining lands. Tecumseh traveled throughout the East for three years, garnering increasing support for his Indian confederacy. His dream faded, however, after Tenskwatawa initiated an ill-fated attack on American forces sent out to subdue his supporters. The defeat of Tenskwatawa's warriors disillusioned many of the prophet's followers, irrevocably dampening enthusiasm for a united Indian front. By 1813, when Tecumseh was killed by American troops, his vision of an Indian confederacy was also dead.

Tecumseh's influence was still felt, however, among a faction of the Creek Indians known as the Upper Creeks of the Red Sticks, who were particularly inspired by the Shawnee leader's message. They launched a year-long military campaign against the Americans in their midst, but in the 1814 Battle of Horseshoe Bend their warriors were crushed by a much larger force of American soldiers led by Andrew Jackson.

Jackson's victory over the Red Sticks had ramifications not only in Creek territory but throughout Indian country. Now revered as an intrepid Indian fighter, Jackson began to draw broad political support from land-hungry settlers impatient with the federal government's attempts to eliminate Indian presence in the East by peaceful means. In the light of Tecumseh's demise, these whites believed that the era of armed Indian resistance had come to an end. Rallying behind Jackson, they would demand that eastern Indians—weakened and demoralized by war, disease, and their ever-shrinking territory—be banished once and for all from the lands the settlers had come to see as their own.

1776

July

Indians discuss white settlement of the Ohio River valley at the Muscle Shoals Council.

Large numbers of Lenni Lenape (Delaware), Ottawa, Cherokee, Wyandot, and Shawnee gather at Muscle Shoals in present-day Alabama to discuss the increasing tide of white settlers onto their lands. During the council, many, including the influential Shawnee chief Cornstalk (see entry for OCTOBER 9, 1774), decide to become allies of the British and to help them fight their war against the American colonists. Although the Indians feel no great loyalty to the British, they share with them the desire to keep Americans out of the Ohio River valley.

July

Dragging Canoe attacks white settlers on Cherokee land.

Cherokee leader Dragging Canoe, angered by the whites moving onto his tribe's lands, plans to lead an attack against several settlements. His cousin Nanye'hi, known to whites as Nancy Ward, tries to avert bloodshed by sending the settlers word of the impending raid. Because of Ward's warning most of the whites are able to escape before Dragging Canoe's men arrive, and those that remain are well prepared. During the conflict, 13 warriors, including Dragging Canoe's brother Little Owl, are killed. Dragging Canoe himself is shot through the hips, but he recovers from the injury. (See also entry for APRIL 1778.)

July 4

The Declaration of Independence accuses England of inciting Indian attacks.

In the Declaration of Independence, the newly formed United States lists among its grievances that George III of England has "endeavored to bring on the inhabitants of our frontiers the merciless Indian savages, whose known rule of warfare is an undistinguished destruction of all ages, sexes, and conditions." The document does not mention the rights of natives within its borders.

1777

July

The Iroquois tribes choose sides in the American Revolution.

At a great council held in Oswego, New York, the British bring together leaders of the six Iroquois tribes to try to secure their help in fighting the American Revolution. Maintaining that the war is essentially a conflict between whites, Seneca leaders Cornplanter and Red Jacket initially recommend neutrality. Their stance is vigorously challenged by the Mohawk Joseph Brant (see entry for NOVEMBER 1775). Brant has long been a supporter of the British, largely because of his close association with the British superintendents of Indian affairs William Johnson (see entry for 1755) and Guy Johnson. His fiery rhetoric accuses those who refuse to join the fight of cowardice.

Largely because of Brant's persuasive powers, the majority of the Mohawk, Onondaga, Cayuga, and Seneca pledge allegiance to the English. Most of the Tuscarora and Oneida, however, are influenced by trade ties to ally themselves to the Americans. The disagreement among the tribes creates a deep rift within the Iroquois Confederacy (see entry for CA. 1400).

August 6

Iroquois fight Iroquois at the Battle of Oriskany.

After an unsuccessful attempt to take over Fort Stanwix, near present-day Rome, New York, a combined Indian and British army ambush American militiamen and Indian warriors led by General Nicholas Herkimer near the village of Oriskany. The battle pits British-allied Mohawk against American-allied Tuscarora and Oneida. Casualties are high on both sides, making it one of the most gruesome battles of the American Revolution.

November

Shawnee war leader Cornstalk is killed.

After leading Wyandot, Cayuga, Cherokee, and Shawnee warriors in a summer raid against white settlements in present-day Wheeling, West Virginia, the Shawnee chief Cornstalk (see entries for OCTOBER 9, 1774, and for JULY 1776) is invited to Fort Randolph in Pennsylvania to discuss terms for a peace. Although Cornstalk enters the fort under a flag of truce, he and four other Shawnee are taken captive by whites and murdered.

"I desire it may be remembered, that if the frontier people will not submit to the Laws, but thus set them at Defiance, they will not be considered as entitled to the protection of the Government. ... For where is this wretched business to end? The Cherokees, the Delawares and every other Tribe may be set on us in this manner this Spring for what I know. Is not this the work of Tories? No Man but an Enemy of American Independence will do it."

—Virginia governor Patrick Henry, expressing his outrage over the murder of Shawnee chief Cornstalk

1778

The Cook Expedition arrives in the Pacific Northwest.

An expedition led by British captain James Cook anchors off the coast of Vancouver Island while searching for the Northwest Passage—a presumed water route between the Atlantic and Pacific Oceans. On the basis of Cook's exploration, England will claim lands in what are now Oregon, Washington, Idaho, and parts of present-day Montana and Wyoming.

Cook's sailors obtain 1,500 sea otter pelts through trade with Indians on the island. The Englishmen intend to use the furs to make clothing for themselves, but when they travel on to China they discover that they can sell them to their Chinese trading partners for an enormous profit. As the Chinese clamor for furs for use as hats and trim, large numbers of Englishmen, Russians, and Americans will rush to the Pacific Northwest to trade with Indian trappers.

Spring

Daniel Boone is held captive by the Shawnee.

A series of Indian raids drive settlers out of most of Kentucky, except for the settlements at Harrodsburg and Boonesboro. During one attack, Boonesboro's founder Daniel Boone (see entry for MARCH 10, 1775) is captured and taken to the Shawnee village of Chillicothe. There he learns that the Shawnee leader Black Fish is planning an attack on the Boonesboro fort. After three months in the village, Boone manages to escape and rushes to the fort to warn the inhabitants that the Shawnee are en route. He reaches Boonesboro in time to help in the successful defense of the settlement. (See also entry for AUGUST 19, 1782.)

April

Army troops destroy Chickamauga Cherokee villages.

After the wounding of Dragging Canoe (see entry for JULY 1776), his Cherokee followers leave tribal territory and resettle in abandoned Creek sites along the Chickamauga Creek, in present-day eastern Tennessee. To avenge the Indians' past raids against whites, 600 troops led by Colonel Evan

Shelby invade the Chickamauga Cherokee's new homeland and destroy the villages.

Summer

Seneca and Cayuga Indians aid in raids on Wyoming Valley settlements.

British soldiers and Seneca and Cayuga warriors under an English officer, John Butler, launch a series of brutal attacks in the Wyoming Valley of Pennsylvania. The force captures eight stockades. At most forts, the inhabitants surrender quickly and are allowed to escape unharmed, though many later die of starvation. At one stockade called Forty Fort, however, the Americans take on Butler's men. More than 200 militiamen are killed in the battle.

September 17

The United States negotiates its first Indian treaty.

At Fort Pitt (now Pittsburgh, Pennsylvania), representatives of the United States and the Lenni Lenape (Delaware) sign the first of the 370 treaties the U.S. government will negotiate with Indian nations. In return for the Lenni Lenape's allegiance during the American Revolution, the treaty offers the possibility that Lenni Lenape territory could enter the Union as the 14th state. This provision will not be acted upon.

November 11

Iroquois warriors massacre Americans at Cherry Valley.

Mohawk leader Joseph Brant (see entry for JULY 1777) and British captain Walter Butler lead a combined Iroquois-British force in an attack on Cherry Valley, a town about 40 miles west of Albany, New York. Brant instructs his warriors to destroy the town, loot the inhabitants' possessions, and take captives. Many Seneca in Brant's force, however, are eager for revenge against the Americans for previous raids on their villages. They ignore their leader's orders and slaughter and mutilate some 30 women and children. One eyewitness account holds that Brant "turned

round & wept" when he saw what his warriors had done. News of the Cherry Valley Massacre will terrify colonists throughout New York. Many will abandon their homes and flee south to escape further attacks.

Winter

Skenandoah delivers food to soldiers at Valley Forge.

As General George Washington's troops suffer through a harsh winter at the American army's headquarters at Valley Forge, Pennsylvania, Oneida leader Skenandoah provides relief by bringing them 300 bushels of corn. Washington will later honor Skenandoah by naming Virginia's Shenandoah Valley after him.

1779

The remains of Cahokia are discovered.

During his military campaign in the Northwest Territory, General George Rogers Clark comes upon the remains of the ancient Indian city of Cahokia (see entry for CA. 700 TO 1550) near the confluence of the Missouri and Mississippi Rivers. With a population of at least 20,000 Cahokia was the largest urban center north of present-day Mexico before non-Indians arrived in North America. The city contained more than about 100 mounds, including the enormous Monks Mound, whose base was larger than that of the Great Pyramid of Egypt. Unable to believe that Indians of the region could create such monumental structures, many whites conclude that Cahokia's mounds were built by either the Aztec of Mesoamerica (see entry for CA. 1430 TO 1521) or by the biblical lost tribes of Israel.

July 10

American troops destroy the Shawnee village of Chillicothe.

While most of its warriors are out raiding, an American force of 250 men under Colonel John Bowman attack Chillicothe, one of the Shawnee's most important villages. After looting the inhabitants' homes, the troops set the village ablaze. The next year, what little remains of Chillicothe will be destroyed in a second attack by soldiers led by George Rogers Clark.

1780

A smallpox epidemic breaks out on the Great Plains.

Smallpox spreading north from Mexico causes the death of thousands of Indians on the Great Plains. During the next two years many Plains groups—including the Cree, Assiniboine, Chipewyan, Gros Ventre (Atsina), and Shoshone—will lose as much as half of their populations.

An Indian is used to represent Massachusetts on its state seal.

Expecting victory in the American Revolution, Massachusetts commissions Paul Revere to create a state seal. The government instructs him to depict "an Indian dressed in his shirt, moggosins [sic], belted proper—in his right hand a bow—in his left, an arrow, its point toward the base." Through the image of an Indian, Massachusetts officials identify themselves as North Americans, free of and independent from the English government they are rebelling against.

1781

The Articles of Confederation treat Indian tribes as sovereign nations.

Based on the Albany Plan of Union (see entry for JUNE TO JULY 1754), the Articles of Confederation establish the first national government of the United States. In the articles, Congress continues the British practice of assuming that Indian tribes are sovereign nations, whose claims to their land can be extinguished only by treaty. The document also grants Congress the responsibility for "regulating trade and managing all affairs with Indians, not members of any of the states, provided that the legislative right of any state within its own limits be not infringed or violated."

July

The Quechan revolt against the Spanish.

Angered by the dominating Spaniards in their lands, the Quechan of present-day Arizona rise up against them, killing about 75 soldiers, settlers, and priests and destroying two missions near the Indians' villages. Although skirmishes between the Quechan and Spanish continue for several years, the revolt succeeds in effectively driving the Spanish out of the Quechan lands along the lower Colorado River. The rebellion will therefore greatly hinder Spanish colonization, by cutting off the only convenient land route between Spanish settlements in Alta California and Mexico.

"[W]hite men would be always telling us of their great Book which God had given them. They would persuade us that every man was bad who did not believe in it. They told us a great many things which they said was written in the Book; and wanted us to believe it. We would likely have done so, if we had seen them practice what they pretended to believe—and acted according to the good words which they told us. But no! While they held the Big Book in one hand, in the other they held murderous weapons—guns and swords—wherewith to kill us poor Indians."

—Lenni Lenape (Delaware) leader David Heckewelder on the Gnaddenhutten Massacre

Autumn

Ninety Moravian Christian Lenni Lenape (Delaware) are murdered in the Gnaddenhutten Massacre.

Mohawk war leader Joseph Brant (see entry for NOVEMBER 11, 1778) tries to persuade a group of Lenni Lenape (Delaware) converts to the Moravian sect to help his warriors raid white settlements in western Pennsylvania. When the Moravian Indians refuse, they are advised to leave the area if they want to stay out of the warfare. Harsh winter weather, however, forces them to stay. In their villages, they are set upon by American troops led by Colonel David Williamson. He orders his soldiers to execute 90 Moravian Indian women and men by striking them in the head with mallets. The governor of Pennsylvania condemns the mass execution, known as the Gnaddenhutten Massacre, but no action is taken against Williamson and his men.

1782

Thomas Jefferson excavates an Indian mound.

An enthusiastic student of American Indian life, Virginia statesman Thomas Jefferson systematically excavates a small mound along the Rivanna River in Virginia. He unearths several layers of human bones and artifacts sandwiched between layers of earth. In his detailed records of his excavation, possibly the first in archaeological history to observe the strata of rock with great care, Jefferson writes, "That [Indian mounds] were repositories of the dead, has been obvious to all; but on what occasion constructed, was a matter of doubt."

August 19

Indian raiders meet the Kentucky militia in the Battle of Blue Licks.

The Kentucky militia follows a group of Indian raiders to Blue Licks Springs. The troops pursue the Indians against the advice of Daniel Boone (see entries for MARCH 10, 1775, and for SPRING 1778),

who recommends that they call for reinforcements before proceeding. Lying in wait, the Indians ambush the militiamen as they approach. Approximately 100 soldiers are killed, in one of the worst defeats of the militia's campaign in Kentucky.

1783

England cedes land to the United States in the Treaty of Paris.

In the treaty of Paris, which ends the American Revolution, England cedes its lands from the Appalachian Mountains to the Mississippi River to the new United States. The provision spells disaster for the Indians in the region. By the Proclamation of 1763 (see entry for OCTOBER 7, 1763), the British government had prohibited white settlement in the area. The U.S. government, however, will ignore this edict and soon open the ceded region to a flood of land-hungry whites.

1784

Russians establish a settlement in Alaska.

On Kodiak Island, Russian fur trader Gregory Shelikov founds Three Saints, the first permanent non-Indian settlement in Alaska. Through the efforts of Shelikov and his employee Alexander Baranov, the Russians will dominate the fur trade in the region. They will brutally exploit the indigenous populations, compelling entire villages through threats and force to hunt and prepare pelts for them. (See also entry for 1799.)

Iroquois led by Joseph Brant begin moving to Canada.

At the insistence of Mohawk leader and British loyalist Joseph Brant (see entries for NOVEMBER 11, 1778; JULY 1777; and NOVEMBER 1775), the English government grants a tract of land on the Grand River in Ontario to Indians who fought on their side during the American Revolution. Brant and his followers will found the present-day town of Brantford. Eventually, more than 2,000 Indians, most of whom are from the Iroquois tribes, will move to the Grand River settlement.

The North West Company joins the fur trade.

English, Scottish, and American merchants and traders based in Montreal join to form the North West Company. In addition to dominating Montreal's fur trade, the new firm will challenge its greatest competitor, the Hudson's Bay Company (see entry for 1670), by exploring previously uncharted areas in western Canada and establishing posts and trading relationships with the Indians there. Until the two companies merge (see entry for 1821), Indians will be drawn into numerous conflicts sparked by the firms' heated rivalry.

June 1

The Creek sign the Treaty of Pensacola with Spain.

Under the leadership of Alexander McGillivray, Creek negotiators agree to the Treaty of Pensacola, in which Spain pledges to protect Creek lands in Spanish Florida. The treaty also allows the Creek to import goods, particularly guns and other military gear they need to defend their nation. McGillivray's first great diplomatic victory, the agreement will help persuade the U.S. government to respect the Creek's borders out of fear of attack by combined Creek and Spanish forces.

October 22

The Treaty of Fort Stanwix is signed.

At Fort Stanwix, near present-day Rome, New York, U.S. treaty negotiators meet with a small group of Iroquois. The negotiators are eager to punish the four Iroquois tribes that sided with the British during the American Revolution (see entry for JULY 1777) and to gain control of their western lands. Using intimidation and violence, they force the Iroquois into signing the Treaty of Fort Stanwix. In exchange for peace with the United States,

the Indians cede their lands west of Pennsylvania and New York. The treaty infuriates many Iroquois, who maintain that the signers had no authority to speak for all of their people.

1785

Indians of African-American ancestry lose Indian status in Virginia.

The Assembly of Virginia defines any person with one-quarter African-American ancestry as a mulatto. Indians with at least one African-American grandparent, therefore, are no longer legally considered Indians and are denied all rights and privileges conferred with Indian status.

Toypurina leads a mission uprising.

Under the leadership of a Gabrielino medicine woman named Toypurina, six villages of Indians rise up against the priests and soldiers at the San Gabriel mission, near what is now Los Angeles. Toypurina's followers are convinced that her supernatural powers will lead them to victory. The Spanish, however, are warned about the attack; their forces quickly quash the uprising and arrest Toypurina. At her trial, the medicine woman is permitted to speak, an opportunity she uses to eloquently condemn the Spanish for their harsh treatment of her people. Toypurina's life is spared, but she is exiled to the San Carlos mission to prevent her from further influencing the Gabrielino.

May 20

The Land Ordinance is passed.

The Confederation Congress establishes a means of distributing public domain land in the Old Northwest (today the states of Ohio, Indiana, Illinois, Michigan, and Wisconsin) through the passage of the Land Ordinance. This law calls for a federal survey to divide the land into six-square-mile townships each containing 36 lots. Each lot is then to be sold by auction for a minimum of $640 (one dollar per acre). By making this land readily available to whites, the ordinance will accelerate the flow of non-Indians into Indian land in the West.

November

Mohegan missionary Samson Occom establishes Brothertown.

During a weeklong ceremony, the Christian Indian settlement of Eeayam Quittoowauconnuck, also known as Brothertown, is opened as a home for recent converts. The community is founded by Samson Occom, a Mohegan who has ministered to Indians throughout New England for 25 years (see entries for 1769 and 1772). Built on Oneida land in central New York, Brothertown is conceived by Occom as a haven where Christian Indians can retreat from the corrupting influence of white settlers. He will devote himself to promoting Brothertown and raising funds for the community until his death in 1792.

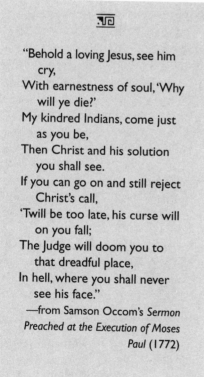

"Behold a loving Jesus, see him cry,
With earnestness of soul, 'Why will ye die?'
My kindred Indians, come just as you be,
Then Christ and his solution you shall see.
If you can go on and still reject Christ's call,
'Twill be too late, his curse will on you fall;
The Judge will doom you to that dreadful place,
In hell, where you shall never see his face."

—from Samson Occom's *Sermon Preached at the Execution of Moses Paul* (1772)

November 18

The Cherokee sign the Treaty of Hopewell.

At Hopewell, South Carolina, Cherokee leaders sign a treaty that places them "under the protection of the United States of America and of no other sovereign whatsoever." The United States promises to order Americans who have settled in their territory to leave and to protect the tribe's lands from further white encroachment. Despite this guarantee, the new nation will do little to stem the tide of white settlement in the Cherokee's lands.

1787

May to September

The merits of Indian governments are debated at the Constitutional Convention.

To strengthen the weak central government established by the Articles of Confederation (see entry for 1781), state representatives gather in Philadelphia to draft a constitution for the United States. Benjamin Franklin proposes a unicameral legislature following the model of the Grand Council of Iroquois Confederacy (see entry for CA. 1400), whose egalitarian approach to government Franklin has long admired. John Adams resists Franklin's efforts with "Defence of the Constitutions of Government in the United States of America," an essay sent to the convention from Europe, where Adams is serving as an ambassador. Adams maintains that Franklin and other students of Indian political life want to "set up governments of . . . modern Indians." Although he promotes the British constitution as a better model for the new U.S. government, Adams does recommend further study into Indian governments as examples of political systems in which "real sovereignty resided in the body of the people."

July 13

The Confederation Congress passes the Northwest Ordinance.

With the Northwest Ordinance, the Congress established by the Articles of Confederation (see entry for 1781) creates a plan for governing the Old Northwest (now Ohio, Indiana, Illinois, Michigan, Wisconsin, and portions of Minnesota). The ordinance calls for the lands to be organized first as a territory managed by a governor appointed by Congress. As its population grows, the territory is eventually to be divided into the three to five states that will join the Union with the same rights and privileges as the original 13.

In its third article, the ordinance attempts to clarify the rights of Indians in the Old Northwest. It promises that the government will deal with Indians in good faith and guarantees that their lands will not be taken from them without their consent. In practice, however, non-Indian settlers will largely ignore this congressional pledge, as will most future administrations.

"The utmost good faith shall always be observed towards the Indians, their lands and property shall never be taken from them without their consent; and in their property, rights and liberty, they never shall be invaded or disturbed, unless in just and lawful wars authorized by Congress; but laws founded in justice and humanity shall from time to time be made, for preventing wrongs being done to them, and for preserving peace and friendship with them."

—from the Northwest Ordinance of 1787

June 21

The U.S. Constitution is ratified.

With its ratification, the U.S. Constitution supersedes the Articles of Confederation (see entry for 1781) as the blueprint for the government of the United States. The document includes only two references to Indians. In Article 1, Section 2, "Indians not taxed" are excluded from the population figures used to determine how many representatives each state can send to Congress. The clause will be interpreted to mean that these Indians are not U.S. citizens. In Article 1, Section 8, Congress is given the exclusive right to "regulate Commerce with foreign nations, and among the several states, and with the Indian Tribes." This section will lead to the passage of a series of Indian Trade and Intercourse Acts (see entry for 1790).

1789

January 9

The United States takes control of Ohio country with the Treaty of Fort Harmar.

At Fort Harmar, near the present-day town of Marietta, Ohio, Iroquois leaders meet with representatives of the U.S. government. There they negotiate a treaty in which the Iroquois cede most of what is now Ohio, even though the region is primarily the territory of other tribes, including the Shawnee and Miami. The movement of white settlers into the Ohio country following the treaty will outrage these Indians, leading to a series of violent confrontations with the U.S. Army (see entries for OCTOBER 1790; NOVEMBER 4, 1791; and AUGUST 20, 1794).

July 7

Congress authorizes funds for the purchase of Indian lands.

On the recommendation of Secretary of War Henry Knox, Congress allocates $20,000 for the negotiation of Indian land cessions. Knox is concerned that more warfare will break out on the frontier if whites are permitted to overrun Indian territory before the U.S. government can agree on proper compensation by treaty with the Indian tribes involved. Knox is less motivated by fairness than by fear. The new U.S. government can ill afford the resources needed to fight drawn-out wars with western Indians.

"That the civilization of the Indians would be an operation of complicated difficulty; that it would require the highest knowledge of the human character, and a steady perseverance in a wise system for a series of years, cannot be doubted. . . . Were it possible to introduce among the Indian tribes a love for exclusive property, it would be a happy commencement of the business."

—Secretary of War Henry Knox to President George Washington in 1789

August 7

Indian affairs becomes the responsibility of the new War Department.

By an act of Congress, the War Department is created to oversee U.S. military operations. Largely because many Indian groups maintain allegiance to the British or the Spanish, the new department is also charged with the responsibility for the government's dealings with Indian tribes. A separate bureau for administering Indian affairs will be established within the department 35 years later (see entry for 1824).

September 17

President George Washington calls for Senate ratification of Indian treaties.

The new U.S. Constitution gives the executive branch the responsibility for negotiating treaties with foreign nations, but they must also be ratified by the Senate. These stipulations do not, however, explicitly state that Indian tribes are to be considered foreign nations in this context. President George Washington addresses this issue by advising the Senate to insist on ratifying all Indian treaties "as a check on the mistakes and indiscretions of ministers or commissioners." Following an extended debate, the Senate agrees to Washington's request.

1790

Congress passes the first Indian Trade and Intercourse Act.

Congress fears that greedy traders are threatening national security by antagonizing the Indians they do business with. To help maintain peace between Indians and traders, it passes the Trade and Intercourse Act, the first of a series of laws intended to regulate the fur trade. The act outlined means of licensing traders and sets out punishments for trading without a license and for committing crimes against Indians.

Spain grants England trading rights in the Pacific Northwest.

As the sea otter fur trade (see entry for 1778) became more profitable, a Spanish expedition set out for Nootka Sound near Vancouver Island in 1789 and seized three trading ships of their British rivals. The incident brought Spain and England close to war. To avoid more conflict, Spain agrees to the Nootka Convention, in which it gives England the right to trade along the coast of the Pacific Northwest. As a result, England and the United States will come to dominate trade with Northwest Indians and will become the main foreign competitors for control of the region.

Seneca chief Cornplanter meets with George Washington.

Cornplanter and several other Seneca leaders travel to Philadelphia to see President George Washington. During their meeting, Cornplanter complains of the dubious tactics used to obtain Seneca land cessions during the negotiation of the Treaty of Fort Stanwix (see entry for OCTOBER 22, 1784). He claims that negotiators acted "as if our want of strength had destroyed our rights" and asks rhetorically, "Were the terms dictated to us by your commissioners reasonable and just?" The encounter likely influenced Washington to urge future negotiators to deal with Indians honestly.

August 7

Creek leaders sign the Treaty of New York.

At the invitation of George Washington, a delegation of 26 Creek leaders led by Alexander McGillivray (see entry for JUNE 1, 1784) travels to New York, where they negotiate a treaty with the United States. In the agreement, the Creek representatives cede about 3 million acres of hunting territory and promise that the Creek and their Seminole relatives will turn over to federal officials any runaway slaves in their villages. In exchange, the United States guarantees to protect Creek land from invasion and gives the Creek the right to punish white trespassers as they see fit. During the meeting, McGillivray also persuades the American negotiators to make him a brigadier general in the U.S. Army and permit him to import goods without paying duties on them.

The Treaty of New York is the greatest triumph of McGillivray's career as a diplomat. The federal government's treaty promise to protect the Creek from white encroachment at least for the time being blocks Georgia's efforts to take over Creek territory. It allows McGillivray to control Creek trade, which helps solidify his authority within the tribe. (See also entry for FEBRUARY 27, 1793.)

October

Little Turtle's force defeats troops led by Josiah Harmar.

The Shawnee, Miami, Potawatomi, and Ojibway living north of the Ohio River continue to resist American settlement in their lands, which the United States has supposedly purchased by the terms of the Treaty of Fort Harmer (see entry for JANUARY 9, 1789). To force the Indians to abide by the treaty, President George Washington sends Brigadier General Josiah Harmar and 1,400 troops to the region.

When Harmar's troops reach the Indians' territory, they are lured into thick forests by fires, believing that the Indians have set their villages ablaze before fleeing. The fires, however, were purposely set by the Indians as a trick. In the forests, the warriors set upon the unsuspecting soldiers and surround them. Nearly 200 are killed before the Indians' leader, the Miami war chief Little Turtle, allows the others to escape. Because of the defeat, Washington removes Harmar from his command and replaces him with General Arthur St. Clair (see entry for NOVEMBER 4, 1791). (See also entry for AUGUST 20, 1794.)

1791

November 4

Little Turtle's warriors are victorious at the Battle of the Wabash.

After Brigadier General Josiah Harmar's defeat by Little Turtle's warriors (see entry for OCTOBER 1790), approximately 2,000 American troops, many badly trained and ill equipped, are sent out to attack the Indians. They are led by General Arthur St. Clair, the governor of the Northwest Territories. By the time St. Clair's forces approach the Indians encampments on

Opposite page: A broadside commemorating the 600 soldiers under General Arthur St. Clair who were killed in battle by Little Turtle's rebel warriors on November 4, 1791 *(The Connecticut Historical Society, Hartford)*

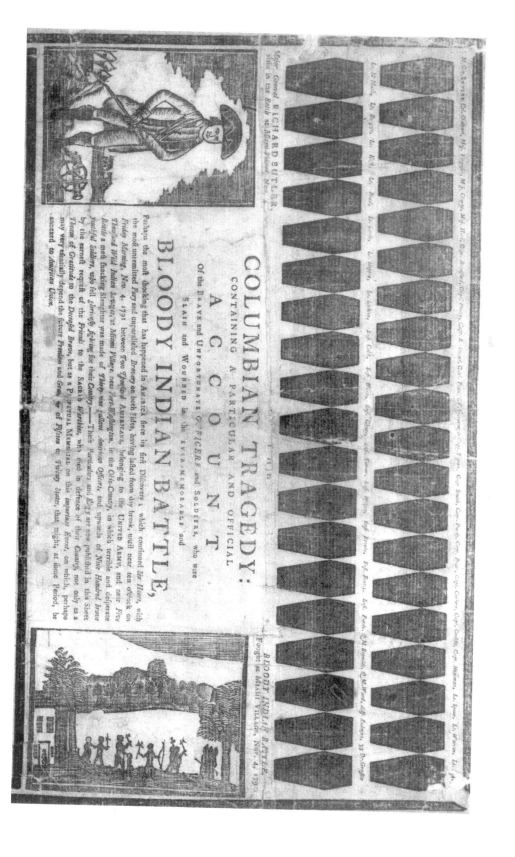

THE

COLUMBIAN TRAGEDY:

CONTAINING A PARTICULAR AND OFFICIAL

ACCOUNT

Of the BRAVE and UNFORTUNATE OFFICERS and SOLDIERS, who were

SLAIN and WOUNDED in the EVER-MEMORABLE and

BLOODY INDIAN BATTLE,

Perhaps the most shocking that has happened in America, since its first Discovery; which continued Six Hours, with the most unremitted Fury and unparalleled Bravery on both Sides, having lasted from day break, until near ten o'clock on Friday Morning, Nov. 4. 1791. between Two Thousand American Savages, belonging to the United States Army, and near Four Thousand Wild Indian Savages at Miami Village, near Fort-Washington, in the Ohio-Country, in which terrible and desperate battle a most shocking Slaughter was made of Thirty-nine gallant American Officers, and upwards of Nine Hundred brave, but unfortunate Soldiers, who fell gloriously fighting for their Country.——Their Particulars and Elegy are now published in this Sheet, by the earnest request of the Friends to the Sacred Militia, who died in defence of their Country, not only as a Token of Gratitude to the Deranged Brave, but as a Perpetual Memorial on this important Event, on which, perhaps may very essentially depend the future Freedom and Greatness of Elysium to Unborn States, that might, at some Period, be annexed to American Union.

Major-General RICHARD BUTLER, slain in the Battle at Miami-Village, Nov. 4.

BLOODY INDIAN BATTLE, fought at MIAMI VILLAGE, Nov. 4. 1791.

the Wabash River, many of his men have deserted because of lack of supplies and rations.

The Indian warriors strike first, in a dawn attack. In the three-hour battle, they kill 600 soldiers—almost half of St. Clair's men—and wound more than 300 more. The Indians, in contrast, have only 21 casualties. St. Clair's disastrous campaign is one of the worst defeats ever suffered by American soldiers in an Indian war. St. Clair is compelled to resign his commission the following March. (See also entry for AUGUST 20, 1794.)

1792

October

Six tribes meet in council on the Auglaize River.

Members of the Sac, Fox, Shawnee, Cherokee, Creek, and Ottawa tribes gather at the "Glaize," a popular area for Indian councils located along the Auglaize River, in what is now northwestern Ohio. The meeting is called to discuss how to stem the tide of whites arriving in their lands. Intertribal rivalries, however, color the discussion. When the Glaize council breaks up, the Indians have failed to create a plan for a unified course of action.

1793

February 27

Creek leader Alexander McGillivray dies.

Long ill from rheumatism and syphilis, Alexander McGillivray dies suddenly at the age of 34. The great Creek diplomat and war leader had spent his life attempting to ward off white settlers intend on taking over Creek lands (see entries for JUNE 1, 1784, and for AUGUST 7, 1790). McGillivray worked toward establishing a more centralized Creek government so that the tribe could develop a coherent strategy for dealing with foreign states. He also skillfully played the governments of the United States, Georgia, and Spain against each other to achieve his ends. With McGillivray's untimely death, the Creek lose an effective leader and negotiator, who, had he lived, may have been able to protect them from later efforts to relocate the tribe to western lands.

Summer

Explorer Alexander MacKenzie arrives at the Pacific Ocean.

With the help of Indian guides, a party led by Alexander MacKenzie, a Scottish fur trader and explorer, reaches the Pacific Ocean. MacKenzie and his men thereby become the first Europeans to cross the continent of North America. An employee of the North West Company (see entry for 1784), MacKenzie is the first non-Indian to have contact with many western tribes. His explorations will hasten the spread of the fur trade in the West.

1794

Russian Orthodox missionaries arrive in Alaska.

Ten Russian Orthodox monks come to southwestern Alaska, inaugurating decades of missionary work among the indigenous peoples there. Russian Orthodox priests will help protect them from abusive traders and establish a network of schools where children are instructed in the Russian language and academic subjects.

August 20

Indian rebels are defeated at the Battle of Fallen Timbers.

Approximately 4,000 regular soldiers and militiamen led by General Anthony Wayne are sent out to the Ohio River valley to put an end to the confederacy of Indians headed by Shawnee leader Blue Jacket. He took over leadership of the confederacy after its Miami founder, Little Turtle (see entries for OCTOBER 1790 and for NOVEMBER 4, 1791), recommended that the rebels sue for peace but was unable to persuade his warriors.

The army destroys the fields at the Indians' abandoned stronghold at the confluence of the Maumee and Auglaize Rivers. The Americans continue on to a swampy area known as Fallen Timbers, filled with trees ripped from the ground by a tornado the year before. There an advance unit is set upon by a group of Ottawa, whose impulsive attack alerts Wayne's men to the larger Indian force lying in wait. Without the element of surprise, the Indians are at a loss against the Americans, who outnumber them by more than two to one. The warriors flee the battlefield, many to nearby Fort Miami. They expect their British allies at the fort to protect them, but the Englishmen refuse to open the gates to let them in.

In the Battle of Fallen Timbers, hundreds of warriors are killed, while the Americans suffer only 38 casualties. As the Indians retreat, Wayne's soldiers set their villages and crops ablaze. The Americans' decisive victory destroys Little Turtle's confederacy and ends organized Indian resistance to white settlement north of the Ohio River.

> "[T]he Eastern fires [United States] . . . did not take Lowinaki [Canada], but became free of Dolojo [King George]. We went to Wapahani [the White River region of Indiana] to be farther from them; but they followed us everywhere, and we made war on them, till they sent Makhiakho [General Anthony Wayne], who made strong war. We next made peace and settled limits."
> —an account of the Battle of Fallen Timbers from the Lenni Lenape (Delaware) tribal history known as the *Walam Olum*

November 19

Jay's Treaty allows Indians to move freely over the Canadian-U.S. border.

The United States and Great Britain sign the Treaty of Amity, Commerce, and Navigation—popularly known as Jay's Treaty—in which Britain agrees to abandon its trade and military posts on U.S. land between the Great Lakes and the Ohio River. Britain earlier consented to vacate the posts in the Treaty of Paris (see entry for 1783) but refused to make good on its promise—a situation that had contributed to the growing tension between the two countries.

Jay's Treaty is a blow to British-allied Indians who were displaced during the American Revolution and flocked to the English posts for aid. Over the long term, the end of British military presence in the Northwest Territory (now Ohio, Indiana, Illinois, Michigan, Wisconsin, and portions of Minnesota) will also encourage American settlers to encroach on Indian lands in the region. The treaty, however, does grant Indians the right to travel over the international boundary without interference. This provision will become important to Indian activists in the 20th century as they fight both countries' attempt to regulate their movement over the border (see entries for 1926 and for NOVEMBER 18, 1968).

December 2

The United States promises educational aid in an Indian treaty.

In appreciation of their support during the American Revolution, the United States signs a treaty that provides compensation to the Oneida, Tuscarora, and Stockbridge (a group of Christian Mohegan) for property destroyed during the war. The federal government offers them $5,000 for their lost property and $1,000 for a church that was torched by the British, and it promises to build a gristmill and a sawmill for their use. The treaty also stipulates that the United States will hire teachers to "instruct some young men of these three nations in the arts of the miller and the sawer." The agreement thereby becomes the first treaty to provide for educational assistance to an Indian tribe. In the 19th century, such provisions will become commonplace as the United States increasingly uses federally employed teachers to aid its efforts to assimilate Indians into white society.

1795

August 3

Ohio tribes sign the Treaty of Greenville.

Nearly a year after the end of Little Turtle's War (see entry for AUGUST 20, 1794), more than 1,000 representatives from the Shawnee, Lenni Lenape

"Elder Brother [the United States] . . . You have told your younger brothers [the Indians] that the British imposed falsehoods on us when they said the United States wished to take our lands from us, and that the United States had no such designs. You pointed out to us the [proposed] boundary line . . . [which] takes in the great and best part of your brothers' hunting ground. Therefore, your younger brothers are of [the] opinion you take too much of their land away and confine the hunting of our young men within the limits too contracted."

—Miami rebel leader Little Turtle during the negotiation of the Treaty of Greenville

(Delaware), Ottawa, Wyandot, Ojibway, Kickapoo, Potawatomi, Miami, and several smaller tribes come together for a treaty council at Fort Greenville, in what is now Ohio. The Indians recognize the need to negotiate with the United States as their British allies began to withdraw from their lands by the terms of Jay's Treaty (see entry for NOVEMBER 19, 1794).

In the treaty negotiated at Greenville, the tribes cede 25,000 square miles constituting much of present-day Ohio. In return, the United States sets boundaries of a large territory for the tribes and guarantees that it will not allow white settlers to cross its borders. The Indians, however, are compelled to allow federal soldiers to occupy 16 posts throughout these lands. Most of the important leaders of the groups in attendance (including Little Turtle) sign the Treaty of Greenville. Among the few who refuse is a young Shawnee man named Tecumseh, who soon will take Little Turtle's place as the most powerful Indian confederacy leader (see entry for 1808).

October 27

Pinckney's Treaty gives Americans unrestricted access to the Mississippi River.

The United States and Spain sign the Treaty of San Lorenzo, also known as Pinckney's Treaty, after U.S. negotiator Thomas Pinckney. The treaty gives the United States the right to navigate the Mississippi freely, which will allow whites to travel more easily into the Indian lands to the west of the river. The agreement also sets the U.S. southern border at the 31st parallel. This provision brings the majority of the territory of the Creek, Cherokee, Chickasaw, and Choctaw under the control of the United States.

1796

The United States establishes the factory system.

To regulate trade with Indians, Congress creates the factory system, by which the U.S. government operates its own trading houses (known as "factories"). These trading houses are to be staffed by federal employees and are authorized to provide Indians with non-Indian goods on credit. The factory system is meant to end tension between Indians and independent traders, who often earned the enmity of their Indian trading partners by offering shoddy goods, selling alcohol, and negotiating unfair deals.

The Land Act permits the sale of land in the Northwest Territory.

To encourage white settlement in the Northwest Territory (what is now Ohio, Indiana, Illinois, Michigan, Wisconsin, and portions of Minnesota), Congress passes the Land Act. The act allows Americans to buy tracts of public domain land in the territory for a minimum of two cents per acre. The law will quickly accelerate the displacement of the Indians native to the region.

1799

The Russian American Company is chartered.

After years of lobbying by Russian trader Gregory Shelikov (see entry for 1784), the czar grants a royal charter that authorizes the establishment of the Russian American Company, which will monopolize Russian fur trading in Alaska. Shelikov, who died four years earlier, had convinced the Russian government that by backing a fur-trading firm it could better oversee the traders' treatment of native peoples and organize efforts to convert them to the Russian Orthodox Church (see entry for 1794).

June 15

Handsome Lake founds the Longhouse Religion.

Living in the house of his half-brother, the Seneca leader Cornplanter (see entry for 1789), an ailing alcoholic named Handsome Lake becomes unconscious and wakes up hours later claiming that he

has seen three visions. In the first, three messengers offered him berries to heal him and told him that the Creator has chosen him for a mission. In the second, a man with nail holes in his hands shows him the paths to Heaven and Hell. In the third, he is given instructions from the Creator, instructions that will become known as the Code of Handsome Lake.

Handsome Lake's visions provide the basis of the Longhouse Religion, which spreads quickly among the Seneca. By the prophet's code, his followers are instructed to shun alcohol, witchcraft, gambling, sexual promiscuity, selfishness, and vanity. They are encouraged to value marriage and children, seek harmonious relationships with family members, and perform the Great Feather Dance, the Drum Dance, and other rituals of thanksgiving. Handsome Lake also advocates the adoption of many non-Indian ways, including white clothing, house styles, and farming methods.

"The Creator forbids
unkindness to the Old.
We, the Four Messengers, say
this.

The Creator made it to be this
way.
An old woman shall be
as a child again
and her grandchildren
shall care for her.
For only because she is,
they are.

So they said and he said.
It was that way."
—Handsome Lake on the
Creator's prescribed treatment
of the elderly

1800

January 18

Congress passes the Peace Preservation Act.

Intended to stop European settlers from encouraging Indians to war against Americans, the Peace Preservation Act imposes high fines on anyone who incites Indian attacks on the western frontier. It also allows for the imprisonment of people convicted of eroding an Indian tribe's loyalty to the U.S. government.

1802

The United States agrees to remove Indians from Georgia.

Georgia cedes to the United States its claims to lands to the west of the present-day state. In exchange, the United States promises to relocate all Indians living within the state's borders. The agreement will lead to the Trail of Tears—the removal of the Cherokee tribe to Indian Territory—34 years later (see entry for MAY 1838).

The Tlingit raid a Russian trading post.

Angered by their treatment by Russian traders (see entry for 1784), the Tlingit capture a Russian post near present-day Sitka, Alaska. In their surprise attack they kill about 20 Russians and 130 Aleut working for them and make off with more than a thousand furs. The Tlingit will hold the fort until two years later, when they will be routed by shells from a fleet of Russian ships. The Indians, however, will continue to stage periodic attacks on the Russians for the next 65 years.

March 30

Congress restricts Indian liquor sales.

With the passage of the second Trade and Intercourse Act (see entry for 1790), Congress gives the president the right to regulate the sale of liquor to Indians. The law, which will remain in place for nearly 150 years (see entry for 1953), will do little to discourage non-Indian traders from dealing in alcohol.

1803

March 22

The Nootka attack an American ship.

A group of Nootka Indians led by Maquinna sets upon the U.S. merchant ship *Boston* anchored off Vancouver Island and kills all the crew except for two men. The Nootka are angry that American traders have begun to trade directly with inland tribes, thus cutting out the middleman role that the Nootka have played in the sea otter fur trade (see entry for 1778).

April 30

The United States buys Louisiana from France.

In exchange for approximately $15 million, France signs a treaty to sell the United States the area known as Louisiana in exchange for approximately $15 million. Although the boundaries are not precisely set, the region purchased encompasses some 828,000 square miles bordered on the east by the Mississippi River, on the west by the Rocky Mountains, on the north by the Canadian boundary, and on the south by the Gulf of Mexico.

With the Louisiana Purchase, the size of the United States doubles. The acquisition also gives the United States control of the Mississippi River. Perhaps even more important to President Thomas Jefferson, the purchase offers a solution to conflicts between Indians and whites in the East. One of the first supporters of what would later become known as the Removal policy (see entry for MAY 28, 1830), Jefferson sees Louisiana as a place where eastern Indians can be relocated, allowing their former lands to be opened to white settlement.

The Louisiana Purchase also has great significance for the Indians who live in the acquired region. When France claimed the land, it did not have the resources to settle it. The United States, however, will soon begin encouraging its citizens to move into area and onto lands the Indian residents consider their own. The Indians' view is upheld by international law. Technically, the United States purchased from France only the right to negotiate with the Indians of Louisiana for their lands. In practice, however, Americans will often act as though they purchased the land itself, by seizing Indian territory without consultation or compensation.

1804

May 14

The Lewis and Clark Expedition begins to explore the Louisiana Territory.

Organized by President Thomas Jefferson and funded by $2,500 appropriated by Congress, an expedition of 35 men sets off from St. Louis to explore the recently acquired Louisiana Purchase (see entry for APRIL 30, 1803). The explorers are led by Meriwether Lewis and William Clark. Among the expedition's goals are finding a land route to the Pacific Ocean, strengthening American claims to the Oregon Territory, and gathering information about the American Indian tribes living between the Mississippi River and the Pacific coast. (See also entries for APRIL 1805 and for SEPTEMBER 23, 1806.)

November 3

The Sac and Fox sign the Treaty of St. Louis.

Following the deaths of several settlers at the hands of Sac and Fox warriors, federal officials invite the Indians' leaders to travel to St. Louis for a treaty conference. There they sign a treaty that they believe allows whites to hunt in their territory. In fact it cedes 50 million acres of land to the United States. Many Sac and Fox leaders, including Black Hawk, later denounce the treaty, as will a number of Sac and Fox bands who had no representatives at the conference. The U.S. refusal to address their complaints will help lead to Black Hawk's War (see entry for APRIL TO AUGUST 1832).

1805

The Munsee Prophetess reforms the Big House religion.

As the United States takes control of the Lenni Lenape (Delaware)'s homeland, a woman known as the Munsee Prophetess has a vision indicating that the Lenni Lenape's Big House religion must be reformed. She preaches that the Lenni Lenape should maintain their traditional ways and resist adopting non-Indian customs and Christianity. She also gives women a more prominent role in the rites of the Big House and encourages young men to take on positions of leadership. Largely owing to the prophetess's teachings, the Lenni Lenape will execute several tribe members for supporting Americans and practicing the Christian religion. (See also entry for AUTUMN 1924.)

April

The Shawnee prophet Tenskwatawa founds an Indian religion.

A Shawnee named Lalawethika (meaning "noisemaker"), known for his laziness and fondness for alcohol, falls into a trance from which he emerges advocating a new Indian religion taught to him by the Master of Life. He preaches that all Indians should unite in preserving their traditional cultures and shunning the ways of non-Indians. He is especially adamant that Indians should not drink liquor or intermarry with whites. Called the Prophet by some, Lalawethika gives himself the name Tenskwatawa, which means "The Open Door"—a reference to Jesus' statement, "I am the Open Door."

Tenskwatawa attracts followers from many tribes who are drawn to his promise that if Indians heed his words, "all the white people will be covered, and you alone shall inhabit the land." Among those inspired by Tenskwatawa is his brother Tecumseh, who will organize an Indian confederacy to halt white encroachment in the Ohio River valley (see entry for 1808).

April

Sacagawea (Sacajawea) joins the Lewis and Clark Expedition.

Spending the winter near the villages of the Hidatsa on the Knife River, in present-day North Dakota, Meriwether Lewis and William Clark (see entry for MAY 14, 1804) meet a young Shoshone woman named Sacagawea (Sacajawea) and her French-Canadian husband Toussaint Charbonneau. When the weather breaks, the explorers hire the couple to serve as interpreters for the expedition as it continues west to the Pacific Ocean. Traveling with Sacagawea is her two-month-old son Jean-Baptiste, whom the explorers give the nickname "Pomp."

In later accounts of the expedition, Sacagawea will be hailed for guiding the expedition through the Rocky Mountains. In fact, she plays only a small role as a guide. She does, however, help the explorers survive by finding and cooking wild roots and berries. Even more important, she persuades her Shoshone relatives to help the expedition cross the Rocky Mountains. Without their assistance, it is unlikely the Lewis and Clark Expedition would have survived. (See also entries for 1823, 1902, and MAY 4, 1999.)

> "The Indians who visit us behave with the greatest decorum.... We have again to admire the perfect decency and propriety of their conduct, for although so numerous, they do not attempt to crowd round our camp or take anything which they see lying about, and whenever they borrow knives or kettles or any other article from the men, they return them with great fidelity."
>
> —explorer Meriwether Lewis on his admiration for the Shoshone

Office of Indian Trade is established.

The secretary of war creates the Office of Indian Trade within the War Department. The new bureau is charged with regulating the fur trade and overseeing the federal employees of the government-run trading houses (see entry for 1796) that dominate trade between Indians and whites. (See also entry for 1822.)

September 23

The Lewis and Clark Expedition returns to St. Louis.

After nearly 28 months of exploration, the Lewis and Clark Expedition (see entries for MAY 14, 1804, and for APRIL 1805) makes its way back to its original starting point, St. Louis. The public, which had given up the explorers as dead, widely celebrates the event. Lewis and Clark's maps, notes, and specimens document a huge amount of information about Indian lands west of the Mississippi. As a result of their expedition, non-Indian traders and trappers almost immediately begin moving into this territory to take advantage of the large beaver population the explorers found along western waterways.

1808

April 6

The Indian Princess premieres.

The first American play about an Indian subject, James Nelson Barker's *The Indian Princess; or, La Belle Sauvage,* is performed at the Chestnut Theatre in Philadelphia. Billed as "an operatic melodrama," the play tells the story of Pocahontas as presented in John Smith's *General History of Virginia* (see entry for DECEMBER 1607). Its success helps propagate the myth of Pocahontas as the savior of Jamestown.

Tenskwatawa and Tecumseh establish Prophet's Town.

As a headquarters for their growing Indian confederacy, Shawnee brothers Tenskwatawa and Tecumseh found the village of Prophet's Town near the confluence of the Wabash River and Tippecanoe Creek in western Ohio. Thousands of Indians from the Ohio River valley and the Great Lakes region move to Prophet's Town. They are drawn by the prophet Tenskwatawa's teachings (see entry for SPRING 1805) and by Tecumseh's efforts to form a confederacy of Indian tribes to stop the sale of Indian land and to present a united resistance to American settlement in their lands. The growing population of Prophet's Town frightens neighboring settlers and increases tension between Indians and whites in the area.

John Jacob Astor founds the American Fur Company.

With the encouragement of President Thomas Jefferson, entrepreneur John Jacob Astor forms the American Fur Company. The firm plans on founding trading posts all along the route Lewis and Clark took to the Pacific Ocean (see entries for MAY 14, 1804, and for SEPTEMBER 23, 1806). His traders will become the first whites to encounter many Indian groups in the West. The company will also become the most successful fur-trading operation in the United States and will help make Astor the richest man in the country by the time of his death in 1848.

1809

September 30

William Henry Harrison negotiates the Treaty of Fort Wayne.

At Fort Wayne, Indiana, territorial governor William Henry Harrison assembles leaders of the Lenni Lenape (Delaware), Potawatomi, Kickapoo, and Miami. Plying the chiefs with whiskey, he persuades them to sign the Treaty of Fort Wayne, in which they cede approximately a million acres of land along the Wabash River in what is now Indiana and Illinois. The price paid for the territory is only about two cents per acre.

The treaty outrages Shawnee leader Tecumseh (see entry for 1808), whose homeland was ceded by a Potawatomi with no power to speak for the Shawnee. Tecumseh travels to the territorial capital, where he confronts Harrison and tells him that his tribe will not abide by the fraudulent treaty. The Shawnee is quoted as saying, "Sell a country! Why not sell the air, the great sea, as well as the earth? Did not the Great Spirit make them all for the use of his children?"

"The implicit obedience and respect which the followers of Tecumseh pay him are really astonishing and more than any other circumstance bespeak him one of those uncommon geniuses which spring up occasionally to produce revolutions and overturn the existing order of things. If it were not for the vicinity of the United States, he would be the founder of an empire that would rival in glory Mexico or Peru."

—William Henry Harrison, governor of Indiana Territory, on Shawnee rebel leader Tecumseh

1810

Fletcher v. Peck allows states to sell Indian land without their permission.

In 1795 the Georgia legislature approved the sale of 35 million acres of land in present-day Alabama and Mississippi for only $500,000. The deal was questioned by the next legislature, because some of the buyers likely to profit from the sale included legislature members who approved it. When the new legislature canceled the deal, the buyers took their case to court, claiming that their contract for the sale had been violated.

After 15 years of litigation, the Supreme Court decides for the buyers, ruling that the original contract is valid and binding. In its ruling, the Court also determines that legally a state can sell land occupied by Indians, whether or not the Indians approve of the sale. The decision will encourage states to seize and sell Indian land without consulting the Indians who live on it.

1811

Summer

Tecumseh seeks the support of southeastern tribes.

After years of traveling through Ohio, Michigan, Indiana, and Illinois trying to recruit Indians to

"Accursed be the race that has seized on our country and made women of our warriors. Our fathers from their tombs reproach us as slaves and cowards. I hear them now in the wailing winds.... the spirits of the mighty dead complain. Their tears drop from the wailing skies. Let the white race perish. They seize your land, they corrupt your women, they trample on the ashes of your dead! Back whence they came, upon a trial of blood, they must be driven."

—Tecumseh to an Indian council in present-day Alabama

join his confederacy, the Shawnee leader Tecumseh (see entries for 1808 and for SEPTEMBER 30, 1809) heads south in the hope of convincing more warriors to join his cause. He wins the support of the Creek but is unable to convince the Cherokee and Choctaw, who are afraid of being drawn into a war with the United States.

November 7

Tenskwatawa's followers are defeated in the Battle of Tippecanoe.

While Tecumseh travels through the South, Indiana Territory governor William Henry Harrison (see entry for SEPTEMBER 30, 1809) leads a 1,000-man force of regular soldiers and militiamen toward his Indian confederacy's stronghold at Prophet's Town (see entry for 1808). Against the prior instructions of Tecumseh, his brother, the prophet Tenskwatawa, tells his people to make the first strike against the advancing army at the Tippecanoe Creek. Tenskwatawa's decision proves to be a mistake; the Indians are soundly defeated in the battle, and Prophet's Town is destroyed. The disaster discredits Tenskwatawa in the eyes of many of his followers. In the aftermath of the battle, Tecumseh finds support for his confederacy waning, leading him to rely more heavily on support from his British allies. (See also entry for 1840.)

December 5

An earthquake shakes the lower Mississippi Valley.

A massive earthquake strikes the Mississippi Valley in what is now southeastern Missouri. One of the most violent earthquakes in the history of North America, the disaster destroys the city of New Madrid, Missouri, and its aftershocks are felt as far away as Baltimore.

The earthquake also solidifies the Creek's support of Tecumseh (see entry for SUMMER 1811). When he left Creek territory in November, he told the tribespeople that he would stomp the ground when he had safely returned to

Prophet's Town (see entry for 1808). Believing Tecumseh's foot caused the quake, many Creek become fanatical in their faith in his confederacy.

1812

New Jersey v. Wilson affirms nontaxable status of Lenni Lenape (Delaware) land.

Deciding to move west, the Lenni Lenape (Delaware) sell their lands in New Jersey to non-Indians, including a man named John Wilson. The state tries to collect taxes from Wilson, who refuses, because New Jersey declared the land nontaxable when it granted it to the Lenni Lenape. The Supreme Court rules in favor of Wilson. It holds that according to New Jersey's contract with the Lenni Lenape the land is not taxable, whether or not it is owned and occupied by tribe members.

Russians establish a post in California.

Russian traders found Fort Ross, near what is now California's Bodega Bay, in Pomo Indian territory. As they have been in Alaska, the Russians in California are brutal in their treatment of the indigenous population. Through threats and violence, they force the Pomo to labor for them. For the next 30 years the Pomo will resist their enslavement with periodic attacks on the Russians.

June 19

The War of 1812 breaks out.

After continued clashes between American and English frontiersmen, the United States declares war against England. The conflict, known as the War of 1812, forces the Shawnee rebellion leader Tecumseh to abandon his efforts to build an Indian confederacy to help his British allies fight American troops. Tecumseh and his followers will fight alongside the British in a series of engagements, including the Battle of Monguagon (1812) and the siege of Fort Meigs (1813). (See also entries for OCTOBER 5, 1813, and for DECEMBER 24, 1814.)

December

An earthquake kills 40 Indians at San Juan Capistrano.

The great stone church at the San Juan Capistrano mission is destroyed during a mass by an enormous earthquake. In the rubble, the bodies of 40 Indian neophytes are discovered. The remains of the building, the most elaborate of all California mission churches, are abandoned by the mission fathers.

1813

July 27

The Red Stick Creek are attacked at Burnt Corn Creek.

Led by Peter McQueen, a faction of Creek Indians known as the Upper Creek or Red Sticks travel to Pensacola to meet with Spanish officials and try to convince them to give the Indians weapons and ammunition to battle American settlers and their opponents among the Creek (also known as the White Sticks). On their way back to Creek territory, the Red Sticks are attacked by militia troops at Burnt Corn Creek, a tributary of the Alabama River. Though surprised by the assault, the Creek are soon able to drive off the Americans, with few casualties on both sides. The Battle of Burnt Corn Creek signals that the civil conflicts among the Creek have escalated into a war between the Red Stick Creek and the United States. (See also entries for AUGUST 30, 1813, and for MARCH 27, 1814.)

August 30

Fort Mims is attacked by Creek rebels.

Fearing a retaliatory attack by the Red Stick Creek (see entry for JULY 27, 1813), hundreds of White Stick Creek, American settlers, and their African-American slaves take refuge at Fort Mims on the Alabama River. On August 29, several slaves warn

A melodramatic depiction of the 1813 attack on Fort Mims, which left more than 500 non-Indians dead at the hands of the Red Stick Creek *(Library of Congress, Neg. no. USZ62-36279)*

the fort commander, Major Daniel Beasley, that they have seen Indians hiding in the tall grass outside the post, but Beasley ignores their warnings and orders them flogged.

At noon the next day, 700 Red Sticks led by Red Eagle (also known as William Weatherford) enter the fort, whose gates have been left open. The warriors kill more than 500 whites and White Stick Creek, but they spare the lives of most of the slaves, taking them as war prisoners. The Red Sticks suffer about one hundred casualties.

The Fort Mims attack creates a panic among settlers on the southern frontier. Militia forces from Georgia and Tennessee, augmented by federal troops, are immediately sent out to subdue the Creek rebels. (See also entry for MARCH 27, 1814.)

October 5

Tecumseh is killed at the Battle of the Thames.

Shawnee war leader Tecumseh, fighting alongside British troops led by Colonel Henry Procter (see entry for JUNE 19, 1812), is angered by British plans to retreat before American forces invading Canada. Accused of cowardice, Procter acquiesces to Tecumseh's demand that their British-Indian force turn back and fight. They encounter the American army on the Thames River near what is now Moraviantown, Ontario. The British troops soon flee the battlefield, while Tecumseh's warriors continue to fight. During the battle, Tecumseh is killed, and his corpse is mutilated and skinned. Later, Colonel Richard M. Johnson will claim that he shot the great Shawnee leader. In 1836 Johnson will lead a successful vice-presidential campaign with the slogan "Rumsey Dumsey/Rumsey Dumsey/Colonel Johnson killed Tecumsey."

After Tecumseh's death, the confederacy he built will quickly crumble. With it will end all hope for any continued large-scale Indian resistance to white settlement east of the Mississippi River.

1814

March 27

The Creek War ends with the Battle of Horseshoe Bend.

After a series of skirmishes with the Red Stick Creek (see entries for JULY 17, 1813, and for AUGUST 30, 1813), some 5,000 regular and volunteer troops led by Andrew Jackson descend on the village of To-hopeka, on a peninsula in a horseshoe-shaped bend in the Tallapossa River in present-day eastern Alabama. As the troops surrounded the Red Stick stronghold, Cherokee scouts fighting with the Americans steal canoes the Red Sticks have left on the riverbank to help them flee in case of attack.

"I am in your power: do with me what you please. I am a soldier. I have done the white people all the harm I could. I have fought them, and fought them bravely. If I had an army, I would yet fight, and contend to the last. But I am done—my people are all gone—I can do no more than weep over the misfortunes of my nation."

—Red Stick Creek leader Red Eagle on surrendering to Andrew Jackson

Aided by White Stick Creek, Choctaw, and Cherokee warriors, Jackson's men kill nearly 800 Red Sticks, while the survivors retreat to the villages of their Seminole relatives in Spanish Florida. The defeat effectively ends the Red Sticks' war against the United States and earns Jackson acclaim as an Indian fighter. (See also entry for AUGUST 9, 1814.)

August 9

The Treaty of Fort Jackson forces Creek land cession.

With their defeat at the Battle of Horseshoe Bend (see entry for MARCH 27, 1814), the Creek are compelled to sign a peace treaty with the U.S. government at Fort Jackson, in what is now Alabama. The terms of peace are punishing: the Creek sign away more than 22 million acres in present-day southern Georgia and central Alabama. The ceded tract includes lands of both the Red Stick Creek, who had battled against the U.S. Army, and the White Stick Creek, who were allies of the United States during the conflict.

December 24

The Treaty of Ghent ends the War of 1812.

In the Treaty of Ghent, the British acknowledge that the United States owns all lands south of the Great Lakes and promises not to aid its former Indian allies in the region. The treaty ends the War of 1812 (see entry for JUNE 19, 1812) and spells disaster for the Indians in the East. With the defeat of the British, they lose the military support and supplies they would need to continue to resist American settlement of their lands.

1815

January 8

Andrew Jackson emerges a hero from the Battle of New Orleans.

Unaware that the War of 1812 ended two weeks earlier with the signing of the Treaty of Ghent (see entry for DECEMBER 24, 1814), a British army commanded by General Sir Edward Pakenham attacks American forces led by General Andrew Jackson at New Orleans. Jackson scores a major defeat: more than 2,000 British soldiers (including Pakenham) are killed, while the American casualties number only 13. The battle makes a war hero of Jackson, already revered as an Indian fighter (see entry for MARCH 27, 1814), thus easing his path to the White House. After his election to the presidency, Jackson will become the foremost advocate of removing eastern tribes to western lands (see entry for MAY 28, 1830).

1816

The Society of Red Men is founded.

Non-Indians veterans of the War of 1812 (see entry for JUNE 19, 1812) establish the Society of Red Men, a benevolent society that offers relief to widows and orphans of men killed in battle. Modeled on the Freemasons, the organization features secret rituals referred to as "Indian mysteries." Among them is an elaborate initiation rite, after which new members are given "Indian" names, such as Black Wampum and Split Log.

William Clark opens his Indian Museum.

The governor of the Missouri Territory, William Clark, builds a wing onto his house in St. Louis to display his collection of more than 200 objects made and used by western Indians. He obtained these items from the Indians he encountered while heading the Lewis and Clark Expedition (see entry for MAY 14, 1804) and from Indian delegations and fur traders he met when serving as superintendent of Indian affairs. Intended to inform the public about Indian life, Clark's museum will become a popular tourist attraction hailed by a St. Louis visitor's guide as "the most complete Museum of Indian curiosities to be met with anywhere in the United States."

June 19

The Métis declare victory in the Battle of Seven Oaks.

In 1812 the Hudson's Bay Company provided a small land grant to a group of Scottish farmers in Canada's Red River Colony. Ever since, the Métis—a group of people of mixed Indian and European ancestry with a distinct culture—have resented the presence of these settlers. The escalating tension between the groups is encouraged by Hudson's Bay's rival, the North West Company (see entry for 1784), which provides arms to the Red River Métis.

Violence breaks out when 60 starving Métis, led by North West Company employee Cuthbert Grant, attack a Hudson's Bay Company brigade carrying a supply of pemmican (cakes made of dried meat and fruit) and ransack a Hudson's Bay post. At an area called Seven Oaks, the marauding Métis confront the governor of Red River and an army of 21 settlers. In the ensuing battle, all but three of the whites are killed; the Métis suffer only one casualty. Their success in the battle increases the Métis's sense of themselves as a separate, sovereign nation and establishes Grant as an important Métis leader.

Summer

American troops attack the Seminole settlement at Prospect Bluff.

Led by Andrew Jackson, volunteer troops attack an old British fort at Prospect Bluff in Spanish Florida. The United States wants the fort sacked because it has become a refuge for runaway African-American slaves from Georgia and from North and South Carolina. The community centered around the fort is also the home of many Seminole, including Chief Neamathla, whom the soldiers execute. Many other Indians and slaves are killed, and all of the surrounding farms are destroyed. The attack, illegal under international law, will spark a series of Seminole retaliatory raids on American settlements, sparking in turn what will become known as the First Seminole War.

1817

The "Old Settler" Cherokee begin relocating to the West.

Frustrated by the harassment of white settlers, thousands of Cherokee cede lands in Georgia in exchange for lands west of the Mississippi River. These Cherokee, later known as the Old Settlers, are the first to leave their homeland. Unlike the Cherokee, who will be forcibly removed to Indian Territory (now Oklahoma) on the Trail of Tears (see entry for MAY 1838), the Old Settlers are allowed to take their possessions with them. Many conflicts will later arise out of tension between the relatively prosperous Old Settlers and the ill and impoverished Cherokee who arrive in the West decades later.

1818

March

Creek leader Josiah Francis is executed.

A military leader during the Creek War (see entry for JULY 17, 1813), Josiah Francis is lured onto a ship flying a British flag docked near the post at St. Mark's, in present-day northern Florida. It is, in fact, an American gunboat under General Andrew Jackson. He orders Francis's execution in retaliation for his warriors' attacks against soldiers under Jackson during the war (see entry for MARCH 17, 1814).

1819

Two Kickapoo bands resist removal.

The treaties of Edwardsville and Fort Harrison call for the relocation of the Kickapoo from their Illinois homeland to lands in the West. Two bands, one led by Chief Mecina and another headed by Kennekuk, refuse to obey the treaty terms. Some of Mecina's people will join Black Hawk's rebel troops (see entry for APRIL TO AUGUST 1832), while the rest, after years of looting white settlements, will

finally be convinced to leave by military threats and diplomatic persuasion. By trying to maintain peaceful relations with whites, Kennekuk's band will be able to resist removal for four more years (see entry for 1833).

Spain cedes Florida to the United States.

Fearing that Spanish Florida (what is now Florida and portions of Alabama and Georgia) will suffer increased attacks by U.S. forces (see entry for SUMMER 1816), Spain reluctantly agrees to sell it to the United States. The cession threatens Indians in Florida, whom the U.S. government wants to move to lands in the West.

March 3

Congress establishes the "civilization fund."

Congress passes a law allocating $10,000 to employ whites to teach Indian adults to farm using non-Indian methods and to establish schools to instruct Indian children to read and write in English.

> "[F]or the purpose of providing against the further decline and final extinction of the Indian tribes, . . . the President of the United States shall be [authorized] . . . to employ capable persons of good moral character, to instruct them in the mode of agriculture suited to their situation; and for teaching their children in reading, writing, and arithmetic."
>
> —from the Civilization Fund Act

Known as the "civilization fund," the money is primarily used to finance schools overseen by missionaries already working to convert Indian groups. Initially, there are few complaints about this violation of the First Amendment's separation of church and state, perhaps because of the fund's early success. Over the next five years, the fund will contribute to 32 schools for Indian children. (See also entry for 1873.)

1820

October 18

The Choctaw cede 5 million acres to the United States.

By the Treaty of Doak's Stand, the Choctaw tribe is compelled to relinquish its claim to more than 5 million acres, much of its southeastern homeland. The agreement sets the boundaries for a reduced Choctaw Nation but stipulates that they will be dissolved when the Choctaw have become "so civilized and enlightened as to be made citizens." At that time, the lands are to be divided into farming plots owned by individual Indians. The Doak's Stand treaty also threatens any Choctaw "who live[s] by hunting and will not work" with being forced to move to western lands.

1821

Sequoyah creates a Cherokee syllabary.

After 12 years of work, Cherokee scholar Sequoyah develops a system of 85 symbols that can be used to write the Cherokee language. He is the first person ever to create a written language entirely by himself.

Initially, Sequoyah attempted to assign a unique symbol to represent each Cherokee word, but this system proved too complicated. In his final syllabary, each symbol stands for a discrete sound. The writing system's simplicity allows a Cherokee speaker to learn to read and write in only a few days.

Seeking the endorsement of the Cherokee tribal government, Sequoyah and his daughter Ahyokeh give a public demonstration, during which they take turns deciphering messages written using Sequoyah's symbols. Soon after the government sanctions the use of syllabary, the Cherokee become a literate people. The writing system becomes invaluable for recording laws, business transactions, and healing techniques and for staying in contact with relatives who have left their traditional homeland (see entry for 1817). In part because of the Cherokee's use of a written language, they earn the reputation among non-Indians as the most "civilized" of eastern Indian tribes. (See also entry for FEBRUARY 21, 1828.)

The Hudson's Bay Company and North West Company merge.

After nearly 40 years of rivalry and conflict, the two most powerful North American trading companies—the Hudson's Bay Company and the North West Company (see entry for 1784)—merge to create one large firm, which retains the Hudson's Bay name. The merger will take away much of the bargaining power of Indian fur trappers, who in the past had been able to play off the competing companies against one another to make deals more advantageous to them.

Charles Bird King is commissioned to paint Indian portraits.

The superintendent of Indian trade under President James Monroe, Thomas McKenney, hires artist Charles Bird King to paint portraits of Indian leaders who come to Washington to meet with the president. King will make more than one hundred paintings. Hung in the superintendent's office, they will become known as McKenney's "Indian Gallery."

Mexico grants Indians citizenship.

After declaring its independence from Spain, Mexico confers full citizenship on Indians living within the new country's borders. In the Plan of Iguala, the government states, "All the inhabitants of New Spain, without any distinction of Europeans, Africans or Indians are citizens of this monarchy with choice of all employment according to merit and disposition." Indians' citizenship rights will be upheld in the Mexican constitution adopted in 1824.

1822

The United States ends the factory system.

Congress abolishes the Office of Indian Trade (see entry for 1806) and the factory system, through which the United States operated its own trading houses. The trading houses proved too inefficient to accommodate the growing demands for furs. In place of the factory system, the government authorizes independent traders to deal with Indian trappers and hunters.

1823

Johnson v. M'Intosh restricts Indian land sales.

In *Johnson v. M'Intosh*, a non-Indian who purchased a tract of land from the Piankasaw Indians sues a non-Indian who claimed he was granted the same plot by the U.S. government. The Supreme Court finds that the man who obtained the tract through the government land grant had the superior claim. In the decision, the Court maintains that when tribal territory is incorporated into the United States, the tribes' "rights of complete sovereignty, as independent nations, [are] necessarily diminished." In addition to further undermining Indian tribes' sovereign status, the ruling determines that Indian tribes have no authority to negotiate land cessions with anyone except the U.S. government.

Sacagawea's (Sacajawea's) son, Jean-Baptiste Charbonneau, travels to Europe.

Under the sponsorship of Prince Paul Wilhelm, Shoshone Indian Jean-Baptiste Charbonneau travels to Germany, where he sets up residence in a castle outside of Stuttgart. Over the following six years, Charbonneau will study languages and tour lands throughout Africa and Europe. The son of Sacagawea (Sacajawea), as an infant he accompanied his famous mother on the Lewis and Clark Expedition (see entry for APRIL 1804). (See also entry for MAY 4, 1999.)

1824

Mission Indians at La Purísima Concepción revolt.

Indians at La Purísima Concepción, a mission near present-day Lompoc, California, rebel against their Spanish overlords after two Indians are killed in a dispute. With the aid of Indians from the nearby Mission Santa Ines, they take over La Purísima and hold it for a month. The rebels are finally subdued by Spanish troops in a three-hour battle. During the conflict, 16 Indians are killed, and many more are injured. Spanish officials come down hard on the uprising's instigators, executing seven and imprisoning 18 others.

The *Life of Mary Jemison* is published.

The highly popular *Life of Mary Jemison* recounts the 70 years Jemison spent among the Seneca after

"Not long after the Delawares came to live with us, my [Iroquois] sisters told me that I must go and live with one of them, whose name was Sheninjee. Not daring to cross them, or disobey their commands, with a great degree of reluctance I went; and Sheninjee and I were married according to Indian custom. . . . The idea of spending my days with him, at first seemed perfectly irreconcilable to my feelings: but his good nature, generosity, tenderness, and friendship towards me, soon gained my affection; and, strange as it may seem, I loved him!"

—Mary Jemison, captive of the Seneca, in her 1824 autobiography being taken as a captive in southwestern Pennsylvania during the French and Indian War (see entry for JULY 4, 1754). Adopted into the tribe, Jemison had two Seneca husbands and chose not to return to white society when she later had the opportunity.

The Bureau of Indian Affairs is created.

Secretary of War John C. Calhoun establishes the Bureau of Indian Affairs within the War Department. The bureau is charged with administering the United States's various dealings with the Indian tribes within its borders. Calhoun chooses Thomas McKenney (see entry for 1821) as the bureau's first head and instructs him to manage funds allocated for Indians, regulate Indian trade, and oversee Indian schools.

1825

The Choctaw Academy is established.

The Choctaw Academy, a boarding school for Choctaw boys, is founded in Kentucky using tribal funds from earlier land cessions. The first manual labor school for Indians, the institution offers students both academic and religious instruction and training in farming and shop work.

The Treaty of Prairie du Chien attempts to settle Dakota-Ojibway land disputes.

For more than 100 years, the Dakota and the Ojibway have fought for control over lands to the west of the Great Plains. To try to establish a peace between the two groups, Indian agent Lawrence Taliaferro calls Indian leaders to a council at Prairie du Chien, in present-day Wisconsin. In addition to the Dakota and Ojibway, the Sac, Fox, Menominee, Iowa, Winnebago, Ottawa, and Potawatomi send representatives. The treaty negotiated at Prairie du Chien fixes the Red River as the boundary between the Dakota and Ojibway territory. Both tribes, however, will ignore this border. The conflict between them will continue more than 30 years until the groups are confined on reservations.

Alexis de Tocqueville analyzes white Americans' treatment of Indians.

Following a nine-month tour of the United States and Canada, French nobleman Alexis de Tocqueville writes *Democracy in America*. In this classic commentary on American behavior and values, he writes that Americans "kindly take the Indian by the hand and lead them to a grave far from the lands of their fathers." He predicts that even after eastern Indians are removed to western land "the most grasping nation of the globe" will continue to displace tribes by eventually taking over their new homelands.

February 12

William McIntosh signs away Creek land in the Treaty of Indian Springs.

A leader of the Lower Creek (also called the White Sticks), William McIntosh signs the Treaty of Indian Springs, in which he cedes most of the Creek's remaining land in the Southeast. Long a supporter of the United States, McIntosh served as a general in the U.S. army during the Creek War (see entry for JULY 27, 1813). He has since become an advocate for the Creek's removal to the West. Believing their relocation is inevitable. McIntosh and fifty other Lower Creek agree to sell the territory to obtain money to fund the removal. (See also entry for MAY 31, 1825.)

May 31

The Creek execute William McIntosh.

On the orders of the Creek council, a force of 170 men is sent to the home of Lower Creek leader William McIntosh. They are led by Menawa, an Upper Creek political opponent of McIntosh. The warriors capture McIntosh and hang him for violating the council's prohibition on further land cessions by negotiating the Treaty of Indian Springs with the United States (see entry for FEBRUARY 12, 1825). Congress will later nullify the treaty, maintaining that McIntosh and the other signers did not have the authority to speak for the Creek Nation as a whole.

1826

James Fenimore Cooper's *The Last of the Mohicans* is published.

Based on the Battle of Lake George in the French and Indian War (see entry for SEPTEMBER 8, 1755), *The Last of the Mohicans* proves to be the most popular work by American novelist James Fenimore Cooper. The book is the second novel in his five-book "Leatherstocking Tales" series, which is widely read in the United States and Europe. In addition to being the first works of American fiction to depict Indian characters, the series also helps to establish several of the most persistent stereotypes of Americans Indians. Most of Cooper's Indians are either vicious killers or noble savages—with an innate sense of honor but without the benefits of "civilization." (See also entry for 1847.)

1827

California and Oregon Indians encounter the Jedidiah Smith expedition.

Fur trapper and adventurer Jedidiah Smith leads the first non-Indian expedition from present-day southern California to what is now southern Oregon. Several Indians groups they come upon react to the newcomers with violence. Along the Colorado River, the Mojave attack Smith and his men, killing 10 of them. The survivors continue north, but they are set upon a second time along Oregon's Umpqua River after one of Smith's men rapes an Indian woman. Only four of the whites, including Smith, escape with their lives.

David Cusick's *Sketches of Ancient History of the Six Nations* is published.

Tuscarora artist and doctor David Cusick publishes *Sketches of Ancient History of the Six Nations,* an account of Iroquois mythology and history. Finding a wide readership, the book will be reprinted in 1828 and 1848. These later editions will include four woodcuts made by Cusick—the first images of

Iroquois myths produced by an Indian artist using non-Indian techniques.

"I have been long waiting in hopes that some of my people, who have received an English education, would have undertaken [a history of the Iroquois]; but found no one seemed to concur in the matter, after some hesitation I determined to commence the work....I have taken much [*sic*] pains procuring the materials, and translating it into English language. I have endeavored to throw some light on the history of the original population of the country, which I believe never have been recorded."

—David Cusick on the difficulty of writing *Sketches of Ancient History of the Six Nations*

June 26 to September 27

The Winnebago strike out against whites in their territory.

Since the early 1820s, white settlers and miners have been moving into the lands of the Winnebago in present-day Wisconsin. Tension between these whites and the tribe explodes when two Winnebago men are arrested for killing a white family. The Winnebago are outraged when they hear a rumor that non-Indian authorities have turned over the accused to the Ojibway, the Winnebago's traditional enemies, who have supposedly beat the alleged murderers to death. The Winnebago leaders call on Red Bird, a respected warrior, to avenge the deaths. His men kill three whites—two men and a child—near the town of Prairie du Chien on June 26. Three days later, the warriors strike a boat crew on the Mississippi and murder two more men.

After the U.S. government threatens to conduct an all-out war against the Winnebago, Red Bird decides on September 27 to surrender to protect his tribe. Initially, Red Bird is sentenced to death, but largely because whites are impressed by his personal dignity, he is sent to jail instead.

July

The Cherokee adopt a written constitution.

With the encouragement of federal officials, the members of the Cherokee Council draft a constitution modeled on that of the United States. The document maintains that the Cherokee Nation is "sovereign and independent," a phrase that alarms authorities in Georgia, who are trying to strip the Cherokee of their autonomy and thus pave the way for their tribe's removal from the state (see entry for 1828).

1828

John Ross becomes the principal chief of the Cherokee.

Following the death of conservative Cherokee leader Pathkiller, tribe members elect John Ross as their new principal chief. He is the first person to hold this position chosen under the terms of the Cherokee's new constitution (see entry for JULY 1827). A prosperous merchant and a slave owner, Ross is committed to continuing Pathkiller's efforts to maintain Cherokee sovereignty. Serving as principal chief for more than 40 years, he will serve as an influential leader during the most tumultuous period of Cherokee history.

Georgia extends legal jurisdiction over the Cherokee.

The legislature of Georgia passes a series of laws that places the Cherokee under its legal jurisdiction, abolishes the powers of their tribal

government, and bans Cherokee from testifying against citizens of Georgia in court. The action, which completely disregards the Cherokee's status as a sovereign nation, is meant to intimidate the tribe and increase the pressure on it to relocate to the West. The legality of the legislature's measures will be tested in several landmark Supreme Court cases (see entries for 1831 and 1832).

Stanislaus leads a revolt at the Santa Clara and San Jose missions.

Seemingly a model Indian convert, Stanislaus escapes from San Jose Mission, where he has lived since childhood. With Cipriano, another disgruntled neophyte, he organizes a rebellion against the Spanish priests at San Jose and Santa Clara. Responding to the priests' appeal for help, a small Mexican army is sent out to fight the Indians but is defeated by the rebels in battle. Two more military campaigns are launched against Stanislaus's followers before they are finally subdued the following year. Stanislaus escapes to the San Jose mission, where he is given sanctuary. Later, after returning to his life as a mission Indian, he will be pardoned by Spanish authorities.

February 21

The *Cherokee Phoenix* begins publication.

With $1,500 authorized by the Cherokee government to buy a press and type fonts, a young northern-educated Cherokee, Elias Boudinot, begins publishing the *Cherokee Phoenix*—the first newspaper published by Indians. The articles are printed in English and in Cherokee using Sequoyah's syllabary (see entry for 1821). The first issue features an editorial by Boudinot criticizing whites for coveting Cherokee land, and an appreciation of the Cherokee syllabary by Samuel Worcester, a missionary who had lent considerable support to the establishment of the newspaper.

The *Phoenix* will become the Cherokee's most powerful tool for presenting to the world their opposition to white encroachment on their lands. As whites become more aggressive in their

EDITED BY ELIAS BOUDINOTT.

PRINTED WEEKLY BY

ISAAC H. HARRIS,

FOR THE CHEROKEE NATION.

At $2 50 if paid in advance, $3 in six months, or $3 50 if paid at the end of the year.

To subscribers who can read only the Cherokee language the price will be $2,00 in advance, or $2,50 to be paid within the year.

Every subscription will be considered as continued unless subscribers give notice to the contrary before the commencement of a new year.

The Phoenix will be printed on a Super-royal sheet, with type entirely new procured for the purpose. Any person procuring 6 subscribers, and becoming responsible for the payment, shall receive a seventh gratis.

Advertisements will be inserted at seventy-five cents per square for the first insertion, and thirty-seven and a half cents for each continuance; longer ones in proportion.

☞ All letters addressed to the Editor, post paid, will receive due attention.

ᏟᏪ ᏕᎦᎤᎤᎠ ᎠᏗ ᏂᏓᎨᎣᎢ. ᏥᎤᎠᏢᎤᎠ ᏔᎠᏉ ᎤᎢ ᎢᎭᏆᎠᎢ ᎦᏌᎢ. ᎨᎾᎩᏌᎤᏦᎠᎤᎢ ᏕᎢᎠ ᎠᏣᏈ ᎣᎤᏈᎢ ᎢᎠᎢ. ᏔᎨ ᏔᎾᎢᎤᏈ ᏕᎤᎠᎢᏉ.Ꭲ. ᎨᎿ ᏪᎤ ᏔᎤᎪᎢ ᎭᎤᏈᎤᎿᏈ.Ꭲ. ᏔᎢ ᏪᎤᏈ ᏔᎤᎪᎢ Ꮦ Ꮎ Ꭴ ᎢᏈᏣᏈ.Ꭲ. ᏔᎾᎠᏈ ᎢᏉᎾᏈᏂ.Ꭲ. ᎣᎾᎿᏈ ᎤᏈ ᏙᎳᏉᏈᏉᏙ, ᏪᎤᏈ ᏕᏈ ᎾᏈ.Ꭲ ᏔᎠᎢᏉ ᎣᏈ ᎤᏈᏈᏈᏈᏈ-ᏈᎢ. ᏔᎢᎠ ᏕᏈ ᏪᏐ ᎤᏈ ᏔᎾᎤᏈᏈ.Ꭲ ᏕᎤᏈᏉᎿ.Ꭲ.

A GOOD CONSCIENCE.

WHAT is there, in all the pomp of a world, the enjoyments of luxury, the gratification of passion, comparable to the tranquil delight of a good conscience? It is the health of the mind, is a sweet perfume, that diffuses fragrance over every thing near it without exhausting its store. Unacquainted with this, the gay pleasures of the world are like brilliants to a diseased eye, music to a deaf ear, wine in an ardent fever, or dainties in the languor of an ague. To lie down on the pillow, after a day spent in temperance, beneficence, and piety, how sweet it is! How different from the state of him, who reclines, at an unnatural hour, with his blood inflamed, his head throbbing with wine and gluttony, his heart aching with rancorous malice, his thoughts totally estranged from him who has protected him in the day, and will watch over him, ungrateful as he is, in the night season! A good conscience is, indeed, the peace of God. Passions lulled to sleep, clear

CONSTITUTION OF THE CHE-ROKEE NATION,

Formed by a Convention of Delegates from the several Districts, at New Echota, July 1827.

WE, THE REPRESENTATIVES of the people of the CHEROKEE NATION in Convention assembled, in order to establish justice, ensure tranquility, promote our common welfare, and secure to ourselves and our posterity the blessings of liberty; acknowledging with humility and gratitude the goodness of the sovereign Ruler of the Universe, in offering us an opportunity so favorable to the design, and imploring his aid and direction in its accomplishment, do ordain and establish this Constitution for the Government of the Cherokee Nation.

ARTICLE I.

SEC. 1. THE BOUNDARIES of this nation, embracing the lands solemnly guarantied and reserved forever to the Cherokee Nation by the Treaties concluded with the United States, are as follows; and shall forever hereafter remain unalterably the same—to wit—Beginning on the North Bank of Tennessee River at the upper part of the Chickasaw old fields; thence along the main channel of said river, including all the islands therein, to the mouth of the Hiwassee river, thence up the main channel of said river, including Islands, to the first hill which closes in on said river, about two miles above Hiwassee old Town; thence along the ridge which divides the waters of the Hiwassee and little Tellico, to the Tennessee river at Tallassee; thence along the main channel, including Islands, to the junction of the Cowee and Nanteyalee; thence along the ridge in the fork of said river, to the top of the blue ridge; thence along the blue ridge to the Unicoy Turnpike road; thence by a straight line to the main source of the Chestatee; thence along its main channel, including Islands, to the Chattahoochy; and thence down the same to the Creek boundary at Buzzard Roost; thence along the boundary line which separates this and the Creek Nation, to a point on the Coosa river opposite the mouth of Wills Creek; thence down along the South bank of the same to a point opposite to Fort Strother; thence up the river to the mouth of Wills Creek; thence up along the East bank of said creek, to the West branch thereof, and up the same to its source; and thence along the ridge

[Cherokee syllabary text]

I.

[Cherokee syllabary text columns]

readmission. Moreover, the Legislature shall have power to adopt such laws and regulations, as its wisdom may deem expedient and proper, to prevent the citizens from monopolizing improvements with the view of speculation.

ARTICLE II.

SEC. 1. THE POWER of this Government shall be divided into three distinct departments;—the Legislative, the Executive, and the Judicial.

SEC. 2. No person or persons, belonging to one of these Departments, shall exercise any of the powers properly belonging to either of the others, except in the cases hereinafter expressly directed or permitted.

ARTICLE III.

SEC. 1. THE LEGISLATIVE POWER shall be vested in two distinct branches; a Committee, and a Council; each to have a negative on the other, and both to be styled, the General Council of the Cherokee Nation; and the style of their acts and laws shall be,

"RESOLVED by the Committee and Council in General Council convened."

SEC. 2. The Cherokee Nation, as laid off into eight Districts, shall so remain.

SEC. 3. The Committee shall consist of two members from each District, and the Council shall consist of three members from each District, to be chosen by the qualified electors of their respective Districts for two years; and the elections to be held in every District on the first Monday in August for the year 1828, and every succeeding two years thereafter; and the General Council shall be held once a year, to be convened on the second Monday of October in each year, at New Echota.

SEC. 4. No person shall be eligible to a seat in the General Council, but a free Cherokee Male citizen, who shall have attained to the age of twenty-five years. The descendants of Cherokee men by all free women, except the African race, whose parents may be or have been living together as man and wife, according to the customs and laws of this Nation, shall be entitled to all the rights and privileges of this Nation, as well as the posterity of Cherokee women by all free men. No person who is of negro or mulatto parentage, either by the father or mother side, shall be eligible to hold any office of profit, honor or trust, under this Government.

[Cherokee syllabary text column]

The front page of the initial issue of the *Cherokee Phoenix,* the first newspaper published by an Indian tribe. The articles are printed in English and in Cherokee, using the syllabary developed by Sequoyah. *(Courtesy American Antiquarian Society)* demands for the Cherokee's removal to the West, Boudinot and the rest of the *Phoenix* staff will be targets of harassment by Georgia officials.

1829

The last Beothuk Indian dies.

With the death of Shanawdithit, the Beothuk tribe of present-day Newfoundland becomes extinct. Shanawdithit had been taken captive by whites in 1823. She was one of the few survivors of the century of war, disease, and starvation suffered by the Beothuk after French traders began arriving in their homeland (see entry for 1613). While living as a captive, Shanawdithit helped James P. Hawley compile a list of 400 Beothuk words, one of the few primary sources of information about Beothuk culture.

William Apess's *A Son of the Forest* is published.

The first autobiography written by an Indian, *A Son of the Forest* tells the story of the abuses suffered by Pequot William Apess as an indentured servant to whites. Writing for white readers, Apess uses his experiences to criticize whites' treatment of Indians and to challenge Indian stereotypes. Falling into the popular genre of spiritual confessions, the book describes Apess's ultimate redemption through his conversion to Christianity. Apess is ordained as a Methodist minister soon after writing his autobiography and will become renowned for his sermons throughout New England during the 1830s (see entry for 1836).

July

Gold is discovered in Cherokee territory.

News of gold in Cherokee lands sends thousands of miners into the tribe's territory. Although in treaties with the Cherokee the United States has guaranteed that it will protect their lands from white encroachment, President Andrew Jackson removes all federal troops from the area, signaling to whites that no effort will be made to keep them out.

December 15

Metamora; or the Last of the Wampanoags premieres.

Loosely based on the life of the 17th-century Wampanoag leader Metacom (Philip) (see entry for LATE JUNE 1675), John Augustus Stone's play *Metamora; or the Last of the Wampanoags* is first performed in New York City. The tragedy is the winner of a contest held by actor Edwin Forrest for the best play with a hero who is "an aboriginal of this country." Performed, with Forrest in the title role, for more than 40 years, *Metamora* is an enormous popular success, ushering in an era in which the American theater is inundated with "Indian dramas." Like many of the plays that followed, *Metamora* presents its Indian protagonist as noble and brave but also implies that the subjugation of his people is the inevitable consequence of contact with white civilization.

Oceana: Teach him, Walter; make him like us.
Walter: 'Twould cost him half his native virtues. Is justice goodly? Metamora's just. Is bravery virtue? Metamora's brave. If love of country, child and wife and home, be to deserve them all—he merits them.
Oceana: Yet he is a heathen.
Walter: True, Oceana, but his worship though untaught and rude flows from his heart, and Heaven alone must judge of it.
—two white characters discussing the Indian hero of *Metamora; or the Last of the Wampanoags*

1830 TO 1865
THE REMOVAL ERA

With overwhelming support in the South, war hero and renowned Indian fighter Andrew Jackson was elected to the presidency in 1828. He wasted little time setting forth the Indian policy his administration would follow. In his first address to Congress, Jackson called for federal legislation to formalize Removal—the relocation of eastern Indians to lands west of the Mississippi River. After much discussion, Congress responded with the Indian Removal Act of 1830, which allowed Jackson to put his plan in motion.

During the decade that followed, many tribes were compelled to abandon their homelands by intimidation and sometimes by force. Victims of Removal included the Sac and Fox, the Potawatomi, and the large southeastern groups popularly known as the Five Civilized Tribes (the Cherokee, Creek, Choctaw, Chickasaw, and Seminole). Many Indians resisted their relocation. The Sac and Fox, led by Black Hawk, for instance, launched a full-scale rebellion in the summer of 1832. A more successful resistance effort was staged by the Seminole of Florida. In a conflict known as the Second Seminole War, a tribal faction retreated to the Everglades and waged a guerrilla war on U.S. troops for seven years.

After spending $20 million on the campaign against the Seminole renegades, the United States declared the war unwinnable and allowed the rebels to remain in Florida.

The Cherokee took another tactic in the battle against Removal. Believing their legal right to their land was clear, they took their cause to court to force the state of Georgia from imposing its laws on the tribe. In the landmark case *Worcester v. Georgia,* the Supreme Court determined that the Cherokee constituted a "domestic dependent nation" that was entitled to federal protection from Georgia. The decision, however, had little impact. Jackson flatly declared that he would ignore the Court's mandate and allowed Georgia free reign in its efforts to expel the Cherokee from the state.

Despite the Court's finding, the Cherokee and the other Five Civilized Tribes were all eventually forced to relocate to Indian Territory, in what is now Oklahoma. Many officials in charge of organizing their removals were corrupt or incompetent. Their mismanagement left the Indians without adequate food and supplies. As a result, the journeys west were difficult for all relocatees and fatal for some. On the Cherokee's removal, known today as the Trail of

Tears, as many as one in four tribe members did not survive. Ill, starving, and stripped of their possessions, those who did had to take on the nearly impossible job of reestablishing their society in a foreign land.

Adding to their problems, the Five Civilized Tribes were also faced with the resentment of Plains tribes, such as the Pawnee and the Lakota, who did not appreciate having to compete with these newcomers for the resources of Indian Territory. At the same time, the Plains Indians had to cope with the ever-increasing traffic of settlers traveling across their territory. Through its acquisition of Oregon Territory in 1846 and victory in the Mexican-American War in 1848, the United States extended its borders to the Pacific coast. The fertile farmlands of Oregon and the gold fields of California themselves were enough to lure thousands of Americans west. But the concept of Manifest Destiny, first set forth by journalist John O'Sullivan in 1846, added a sense of moral obligation to their quest. "Our manifest destiny [is] to overspread and to possess the whole of the continent which Providence has given us," O'Sullivan wrote, implying it was God's will that Americans settle the West without regard to Indian claims to this land.

As western expansion continued, it became clear that Removal was no longer a viable policy. With fewer and fewer unsettled lands left in which to relocate Indians, the Bureau of Indian Affairs (BIA) sought to confine tribes in smaller and smaller portions of their aboriginal lands. Through treaties, BIA officials chipped away at tribal territories in order to open up more lands for white settlement and to make way for railroad lines. All too often, the Indian leaders who signed the treaties did not understand their provisions, and corrupt Indian agents pocketed the goods and money the agreements intended as compensation for the lost lands.

Alarmed by the flood of whites into their territories, western Indians increasingly raided westward-bound wagon trains and attacked non-Indian settlements. The continual atmosphere of fear exploded into terror during such highly publicized revolts as the Whitman massacre of 1847 and the Dakota Sioux uprising of 1862, during which Indians murdered white families, including women

and children. Incidents such as these allowed whites to demonize Indians (fighting to protect their lands) as subhuman savages who, for the sake of God and progress, non-Indians had an obligation to exterminate.

This fury helped fuel the western military campaigns launched against Indians during the Civil War. Troops led by Kit Carson mercilessly pursued the Navajo (Dineh) and Mescalero Apache to stop their raiding. Once subdued, the groups were forced to relocate under military guard to Bosque Redondo, a barren area in what is now east-central New Mexico. During the Navajo's journey to Bosque Redondo—now known as the Long Walk—and their four-year confinement there, more than 10 percent of the tribal population died of disease and starvation.

In Colorado Territory, the Third Colorado Cavalry, a group of undisciplined volunteers, was formed by the territorial government to protect whites from Indian attack. When after three months the soldiers had not fired a shot, they were branded the "Bloodless Third" by local journalists. Humiliated by this nickname, the volunteers set upon a group of Southern Cheyenne and Arapaho peacefully camped along Sand Creek. Nearly 200 men, women, and children were slaughtered by the soldiers, who were then celebrated as heroes by Colorado settlers.

In Indian Territory, the Five Civilized Tribes were drawn into the Civil War itself. At the start of the war, representatives of the Confederacy pressured these tribes to ally themselves to the South. Left with little choice, the tribes joined the Confederate cause—a decision that would cost them dearly. During the war, their lands became a battlefield, and their peoples were plagued with death, disease, and hunger. Despite the extent of their suffering, they were shown no mercy by the Union following their surrender. In their punishing peace treaties with the United States, the Indians were forced to give up their lands in western Indian Territory—lands that their Removal treaties had guaranteed to them for all time. Their villages and fields destroyed and their populations decimated, the Indians were then faced for the second time in only 30 years with the daunting task of rebuilding their nations.

1830

John Tanner's *Narrative* is published.

In his autobiography, non-Indian John Tanner tells the story of his 30 years spent among the Ojibway. In 1789, when Tanner was about nine years old, he was taken captive by a raiding party. He eventually became a member of the Ojibway tribe and married an Indian woman, with whom he raised a family. His book also recounts his desire in later life to reconnect with white society, only to find himself distrusted among both Indians and non-Indians. In addition to its vivid presentations of the conflicts between the white and Indian worlds on the frontier, *Narrative of the Captivity and Adventures of John Tanner* will later be recognized as an important ethnographic source on traditional Ojibway life.

Georgia ignores the Supreme Court ruling in *Georgia v. Tassel.*

In *Georgia v. Tassel,* an Indian man named George Tassel challenges his conviction for murder in a Georgia state court. Tassel maintains that because the crime was committed on Indian land, his case is outside of the state's jurisdiction. John Marshall, chief justice of the Supreme Court, agrees and holds that Tassel's case should be reconsidered by a federal court. The state of Georgia, believing the Court is infringing on its rights, ignores Marshall's order and hangs Tassel before he can be retried. The incident alarms the Cherokee of Georgia and moves them to launch a lawsuit to stop the state from interfering in their affairs (see entry for 1831).

May 28

Congress passes the Indian Removal Act.

With the passage of the Indian Removal Act, the federal government formalizes its Removal policy. Through this policy, the United States seeks to relocate, or remove, eastern Indian groups (particularly the large tribes of the Southeast) to Indian Territory, a vaguely defined area west of the Mississippi River. The act is pushed forward by President Andrew Jackson. He sympathizes with the demands of Georgia officials who several decades earlier had ceded to the United States land to the west of their state's present border in exchange for the federal government's guarantee that it would extinguish Cherokee land claims in Georgia (see entry for 1802). The act is also supported by government officials who want to open eastern Indian lands for white settlement, and by reformers, who believe Removal will protect Indians from the corrupting influence of white homesteaders.

September 27

The Choctaw sign the Treaty of Dancing Rabbit Creek.

At a treaty council called by Bureau of Indian Affairs officials, Choctaw leaders reject the government's proposal that the tribe leave their Mississippi homeland

> "Amid the gloom and honors of our present separation, we are cheered with the hope that ere long we shall reach our destined home, and that nothing short of the basest acts of treachery will ever be able to wrest it from us, and that we may live free.... I ask you in the name of justice for repose, for myself, and my injured people. Let us alone—we will not harm you, we want rest. We hope, in the name of justice that another outrage may never be committed against us."
>
> —Choctaw leader George W. Harkins on his tribe's impending removal to Indian Territory

and move to lands west of the Mississippi River designated as Indian Territory. After all but a few pro-Choctaw walk away from the negotiations, the officials persuade those who remain to sign the Treaty of Dancing Rabbit Creek. The first Removal treaty negotiated by the U.S. government, it violates earlier agreements in which the United States guaranteed that the tribe would not be forced to leave its ancestral lands. The Dancing Rabbit Creek treaty also stipulates that Choctaw who opt to claim individually owned homesteads can remain in the Southeast. In practice, however, the U.S. government will do little to prevent settlers and state officials from taking over these Indians' plots.

1831

The Supreme Court refuses to hear *Cherokee Nation v. State of Georgia.*

In *Cherokee Nation v. State of Georgia,* the Cherokee bring suit against Georgia to stop the state from applying its laws to tribe members. The suit is prompted by a series of abuses. In the most recent, Georgia executed a Cherokee convicted of murder before his case could be appealed (see entry for 1830).

The Cherokee's case relies on the argument that they are a foreign nation and that therefore, according to the U.S. Constitution, the federal government must protect them from Georgia's attempt to exert authority over them. However, John Marshall, the chief justice of the Supreme Court, disagrees. He holds that Indian tribes are "domestic dependent nations." Because he does not consider the Cherokee tribe a sovereign foreign power, Marshall refuses to hear their case. Redefining Indian tribes relationship with the United States to that of "a ward to his guardian," Marshall's decision will have enormous implications for future federal Indian policy.

June

The Illinois militia destroys Black Hawk's village.

The followers of Sac leader Black Hawk refuse to leave their village of Saukenuk near present-day Rock Island, Illinois. Their stance defies the Treaty

of St. Louis (see entry for NOVEMBER 3, 1804), in which some Sac and Fox leaders relinquished their people's claims to all lands east of the Mississippi River. The governor of Illinois sends in the militia to destroy the Indian village. Before escaping to the west bank of the Mississippi, Black Hawk is compelled to sign a pledge never to return to Saukenuk. (See also entry for APRIL TO AUGUST 1832.)

1832

Worcester v. Georgia denies states the right to regulate Indian affairs.

In *Worcester v. Georgia,* Samuel Worcester and several other missionaries sue Georgia after they are sentenced to four years of hard labor. Their crime was violating a state statute that prohibits whites from living on the Cherokee Reservation within Georgia's borders without the state's permission. They lost their case in state court but appeal the decision to the Supreme Court. There the missionaries argue that Georgia does not have the authority to regulate the reservation population.

In a landmark ruling, the Supreme Court finds for the missionaries. It holds that Georgia has no right to pass laws concerning the Cherokee Reservation, because Indian affairs are the sole responsibility of the federal government. The decision will serve as the foundation for many future laws governing Indians. However, it will have little effect on the Cherokee's efforts to block Georgia from applying its laws to the tribe (see entry for 1831). Largely because of President Andrew Jackson's sympathy for Georgia's position, the Court's decision will not be enforced in the state.

Ralph Waldo Emerson protests the Cherokee's removal.

In a letter to President Andrew Jackson, the eminent poet and essayist Ralph Waldo Emerson speaks out against Georgia's efforts to remove the Cherokee from the state. He describes Cherokee removal as "a crime . . . that confounds our understandings by its magnitude" and warns that if the president supports

Georgia "the name of this nation, hitherto the sweet omen of religion and liberty, will stink to the world." Emerson's angry words will do nothing to dissuade Jackson from his commitment to the Removal policy.

Artist George Catlin begins painting western Indians.

Perhaps inspired by McKenney's "Indian Gallery" (see entry for 1821), George Catlin, a 34-year-old Pennsylvania artist, travels west to make a pictorial record of Indian life. Over the next seven years, Catlin will travel more than 1,800 miles and visit scores of tribes living along the Missouri River, on southern Plains, and in the Great Lakes region. In thousands of sketches and hundreds of paintings, he will document the ceremonies and customs of the Indians he meets. Among his most famous works will be his portraits of noted Indian leaders, including Black Hawk (see entry for APRIL TO AUGUST 1832) and Tenskwatawa (see entry for APRIL 1805). (See also entry for 1841.)

April to August

The Black Hawk War breaks out in Illinois.

After being forced from Saukenuk, his old village in Illinois (see entry for JUNE 1831), the Sac leader Black Hawk attempts to create an Indian alliance to fight the settlers who have moved into his homeland. He is inspired by the teachings of Winnebago prophet White Cloud and his own experience fighting alongside Tecumseh (see entry for JUNE 19, 1812). With 600 warriors, he returns to the site of Saukenuk. Almost immediately, a force of regular army troops and fresh militia recruits (including the young Abraham Lincoln) are sent out to repel the Indians.

For fifteen weeks, Black Hawk's followers try to elude the American army. On May 12, at the Battle of Stillman's Run, the warriors turn on the untrained militiamen and cause them to retreat in a panic. Despite this early victory, the Indians are quickly worn down. On August 1, they are desperately trying to cross the Mississippi River to safety

when they are attacked by soldiers led by General Henry Atkinson. The Indians attempt to surrender, but the troops open fire. During the Battle of Bad Axe about 150 Indians are killed. Black Hawk flees to the Winnebago village of Prairie du Chien to the north, where he surrenders and is led to prison in chains. In the treaty that ends the Black Hawk War, the Sac, Fox, and Winnebago are forced to cede 6 million acres of land in what is now eastern Iowa. (See also entry for 1833.)

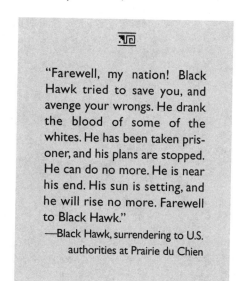

"Farewell, my nation! Black Hawk tried to save you, and avenge your wrongs. He drank the blood of some of the whites. He has been taken prisoner, and his plans are stopped. He can do no more. He is near his end. His sun is setting, and he will rise no more. Farewell to Black Hawk."

—Black Hawk, surrendering to U.S. authorities at Prairie du Chien

May 9

Seminole leaders sign the Treaty of Paynes Landing.

Pressured by U.S. officials, several Seminole leaders sign a treaty at Paynes Landing, in present-day Florida, in which they agree to consider relocating to Creek lands in Indian Territory. Most Seminole are opposed to the treaty terms. Though they once had been part of the Creek tribe, few want to settle among the Creek, because the Seminole now regard them as their enemies. The document also grants the Seminole only about $15,000 for their Florida territory and requires them to pay $7,000 in compensation for runaway slaves who have joined the tribe.

A portrait of the Winnebago Prophet White Cloud, Black Hawk (center), and Whirling Thunder (Black Hawk's son), painted from life while they were held prisoner at Fort Monroe following their defeat in Black Hawk's War. *(The Library of Virginia)*

1833

The Maximilian expedition begins exploring the American interior.

Alexander Philipp Maximilian, a German prince and an amateur anthropologist, leads a two-year expedition up the Missouri River. Among the explorers is Karl Bodmer, a Swiss artist hired to document the expedition. His detailed drawings and paintings will provide a meticulous record of western Indian life before extended contact with whites.

The Kickapoo under Kennekuk relocate to Kansas.

Following the terms of earlier treaties (see entry for 1819), a band of about 300 Kickapoo living in Illinois moves to present-day Kansas. For more than a decade, these Kickapoo resisted removal, largely through the efforts of their spiritual leader Kennekuk (also known as the Kickapoo Prophet). Kennekuk was able to delay their relocation by seeming to be willing to cooperate with U.S. officials while coming up with excuse after excuse for why his people could not leave their settlements just yet. The holy man's skill at dealing with whites will also help his people cope with life in their western territory. Kennekuk will instruct his followers in a new religion that teaches them to live peacefully with non-Indians while refusing to relinquish any more of their lands to whites.

Black Hawk's autobiography is published.

Sac rebellion leader Black Hawk (see entry for APRIL TO AUGUST 1832) tells his life story, in one of the first as-told-to Indian autobiographies. The book is dictated to French interpreter Antoine LeClair, who claims Black Hawk approached him to write the manuscript so "that the people of the United States . . . might know the *causes* that impelled him to act as he had done, and the *principles* by which he was governed." White interest in Black Hawk was aroused during his government-sponsored tour of eastern cities after he was released from prison in late 1832.

January

Elias Boudinot resigns as the *Cherokee Phoenix* editor.

Editor of the Cherokee's tribal newspaper, the *Cherokee Phoenix* (see entry for FEBRUARY 21, 1828), Elias Boudinot begins reporting on the dissension within the Cherokee Tribal Council regarding Removal to lands to the west. Once a vocal opponent of Removal, Boudinot has begun to reverse his stance, largely because the aftermath of *Worcester v. Georgia* (see entry for 1832). The Supreme Court's decision in this case held that Georgia law could not be applied to the Cherokee. This legal victory meant little in practice, however, because the federal government refused to protect the Cherokee from Georgia's efforts to control their lands.

When Boudinot writes about some council members' doubts about whether the Cherokee, without federal support, will be able to win the fight against Removal, Principal Chief John Ross (see entry for 1828) orders him to stop. Boudinot refuses and resigns in protest. Ross appoints his brother-in-law Elijah Hicks as Boudinot's successor, but publication

becomes increasingly erratic as Georgia officials pressure the newspaper to close its doors. On May 31, 1834, the last issue of the *Phoenix* is published. The next year, the Cherokee's printing press will be confiscated by Georgia authorities. (See also entries for DECEMBER 25, 1835, and for JUNE 22, 1839.)

"I could not consent to be the conductor of the [*Cherokee Phoenix*] without having the right and privilege of discussing these important matters; and from what I have seen and heard, were I to assume that privilege, my usefulness would be paralyzed by being considered, as I have already been, an enemy to the interests of my country and my people."

—from Elias Boudinot's letter of resignation as editor of the *Cherokee Phoenix*

March

Nez Perce and Flathead are reported to be eager for conversion.

Published in the *Christian Advocate and Journal,* a letter written by William Walker, a Wyandot convert to Christianity, provides an account of a Nez Perce and Flathead delegation's 1831 trip to St. Louis. According to Walker, the delegates traveled more than 1,000 miles to ask that missionaries be sent to their tribal territories. Although the delegation most likely made the trip for another reason, the story will persuade many missionaries to set out for the West to work among the Indians there. Among them are Marcus and Narcissa Whitman, who will establish an ill-fated mission among the Cayuse (see entries for 1836 and for NOVEMBER 29, 1847).

1834

The Mashpee "revolt" against Massachusetts authorities.

In the 18th century, the colony of Massachusetts declared that the Mashpee tribe's settlement on Cape Cod was an Indian "plantation" and appointed white overseers to manage it. Long angered by this interference in their affairs, the Mashpee are encouraged by William Apess, a Pequot minister and writer (see entries for 1829 and 1836), to expel a white minister, take over their council house, and block non-Indians from chopping wood in their forests. Although the Mashpee commit no acts of violence, Apess convinces the Massachusetts governor that bloodshed will follow if the Mashpee's demands for self-government are not met. In response to the so-called Mashpee Revolt, the governor recognizes the tribe's right to control their own land.

Mexico secularizes the California missions.

The Mission period (see entry for 1769) ends in California as the Mexican government orders civil authorities to replace priests as administrators of the area's missions. Many of the 30,000 Mission Indians cheer as officials allow them to leave the missions. The government, however, refuses to grant the newly freed Indians legal equality or, except in rare cases, legal title to any of their former lands. Some Mission Indians move inland to live with Indian tribes there. Others remain in California, working as laborers for minuscule wages on Mexican-owned farms and ranches.

The Western Territory Bill proposes the establishment of Indian Territory.

With the support of President Andrew Jackson, the Western Territory Bill is introduced in Congress, but it fails to pass. The bill proposes formal boundaries for an unorganized territory reserved for Indians. By its terms, Indian Territory would cover much of what is now Oklahoma, Kansas, southern Nebraska, and eastern Colorado.

Congress passes the Indian Country Crimes Act.

The Indian Country Crimes Act establishes that federal courts have the responsibility of trying Indians accused of committing most criminal acts. The exceptions cited are crimes committed by an Indian against another Indian, which are to be tried by tribes. This provision will stay in place until the passage of the Major Crimes Act (see entry for MARCH 3, 1885).

June 30

Congress passes the Intercourse Act of 1834.

Intended to protect Indians from ruthless traders, a new intercourse act gives Indian agents greater power in determining who will be licensed to trade with Indian tribes. It also prohibits the use of alcohol during trade negotiations.

To help officials enforce regulations on Indian trade, the law also defines the borders of "Indian Country." According to its terms, Indian Country includes all U.S. lands west of the Mississippi and any area east of the river that is not part of a state and has not been officially ceded to the U.S. government.

In another important provision, the act gives the War Department the authority to use military force to end wars between Indian groups. This measure effectively reverses the previous U.S. policy of noninterference in conflicts among Indians.

1835

The Shawnee begin publishing the *Shawnee Sun.*

The second Indian-operated newspaper (see entry for FEBRUARY 21, 1828), the *Shawnee Sun,* also called *Siwinowe Kesibi,* is published in what is now Kansas. Under the editorship of Johnston Lykins, the monthly periodical is printed in Shawnee using the English alphabet, making it the first newspaper published entirely in an Indian language.

December 28

The Second Seminole War breaks out.

Incensed over their pending relocation to Indian Territory, a Seminole war party sets upon 108 troops led by Major Francis L. Dade near Tampa, Florida. In the surprise attack, the Seminole kill all but two of the soldiers. Nearby, the war leader Osceola fights and kills Indian agent Wiley Thompson.

The conflicts spark the Second Seminole War. The war will last for seven years and cost the United States more than $20 million, making it the most expensive U.S. military campaign ever waged on an Indian tribe. (See also entries for OCTOBER 23, 1837, and for AUGUST 14, 1842.)

December 29

The United States negotiates the Treaty of New Echota.

Impatient with the Cherokee's efforts to prevent their removal to Indian Territory, President Andrew Jackson authorizes John F. Schermerhorn to negotiate a Removal treaty with the small number of tribal leaders willing to move west. These leaders, most of whom are of mixed white-Indian ancestry, believe that Removal is inevitable and that further resistance is self-defeating. Led by the Cherokee leader Major Ridge, the signers of the resulting document, the Treaty of New Echota, include his son John and nephews Elias Boudinot and Stand Watie. The treaty cedes all of the Cherokee's lands in the Southeast for a large tract in Indian Territory and a one-time payment of $5 million.

Vehemently opposed to leaving their southeastern homeland, the majority of the Cherokee are outraged by the treaty. As the New Echota signers set off for Indian Territory, most tribespeople vow to stay and continue to defy the government's efforts to displace them. Their fury over the betrayal of Major Ridge and his followers will lead to a near civil war within the tribe during the late 1830s and 1840s. (See also entry for JUNE 22, 1839.)

"The Georgians have shown a grasping spirit lately; they have extended their laws, to which we are unaccustomed, which harass our braves and make the children suffer and cry; but I can do them justice in my heart. . . . They are willing to buy these lands on which to build houses and clear fields. I know the Indians have an older title than theirs. We obtained the land from the living God above. They got their title from the British. Yet they are strong and we are weak. They are many. We cannot remain here in safety and comfort."

—Cherokee leader Major Ridge
at the negotiation of the
Treaty of New Echota

1836

William Apess delivers his "Eulogy on King Philip."

In his last known public appearance, William Apess, an influential Pequot minister and writer (see entries for 1829 and 1834), delivers a passionate sermon about the death of Metacom (see entry for AUGUST 12, 1679), the Wampanoag rebellion leader of the 17th century who was known to non-Indians as King Philip. Claiming to be a direct descendant of Metacom, Apess questions the Christianity of the Puritans because of their brutal treatment of the Indians they encountered. The controversial sermon will become Apess's last published work.

> "During the bloody contest, the pious fathers wrestled hard and long with their God, in prayer, that he would prosper their arms, and deliver their enemies into their hands.... Nor could they, the Pilgrims, cease crying to the Lord against Philip, until they had prayed the bullet through his heart.... If this is the way they pray, that is bullets through people's hearts, I hope they will not pray for me; I should rather be excused."
>
> —from William Apess's "Eulogy on King Philip"

The Lenni Lenape (Delaware)'s *Walam Olum* is published.

French biologist Constantine Samuel Rafinesque publishes a translation of a portion of the *Walam Olum,* a sacred pictographic record of Lenni Lenape (Delaware) creation and history. Rafinesque's book also includes information about the Lenni Lenape he has collected from Indian informants. A complete translation of the *Walam Olum* will be published by anthropologist Daniel Brinton in 1885.

Marcus Whitman establishes a mission among the Cayuse.

Presbyterian missionary Marcus Whitman of New York arrives at Fort Walla Walla on the Columbia River, in present-day Oregon. There he establishes an Indian mission and school at the Cayuse village of Waiilatpu. With Whitman are his associate Henry Spaulding and their wives, Narcissa Whitman and Eliza Spaulding, who are the first white women ever to cross the Great Plains. (See also entry for NOVEMBER 29, 1847.)

May 19

Cynthia Ann Parker is taken captive by the Comanche.

Angered by white settlers encroaching on their lands, a party of several hundred warriors from the Comanche, Caddo, and Kiowa tribes attack Fort Parker, a white settlement in what is now Texas. During the assault, five members of the Parker family are killed, and five others are captured. Among the captives is nine-year-old Cynthia Parker.

During the next six years, all of the captives except for Cynthia are ransomed and returned to their families. Although the Parkers negotiate for Cynthia, the Comanche refuse their offers. They claim that she wants to stay with the tribe, which has adopted her as one of their own. Taking the Comanche name Preloch, Cynthia Parker will marry Peco Nocoma, a respected Comanche warrior who participated in the raid on Fort Parker. One of their three children, Quanah Parker, will become the most important Comanche leader of the reservation era. (See also entry for DECEMBER 1860.)

1837

Smallpox decimates the Mandan and Hidatsa tribes.

A smallpox epidemic sweeps through the villages of the Mandan and Hidatsa in present-day North Dakota. Nearly half of the Hidatsa fall victim to the disease. The Mandan suffer even greater losses: Only about 125 out of 1,600 survive. After this disaster, the remaining Hidatsa and Mandan band together to protect themselves from their Indian enemies, particularly the Dakota Sioux.

October 23

Seminole war leader Osceola is taken captive.

Leader of the rebelling Seminole (see entry for DECEMBER 28, 1835), Osceola agrees to a temporary peace in order to negotiate with General Joseph M. Hernandez for the release of a Seminole chief captured

A winter village of the Mandan, painted by Karl Bodmer several years before an 1837 smallpox epidemic devastated the tribe *(National Archives, Neg. no. 111-SC-92845)*

by the army in September. Although Osceola carries a white flag, he is betrayed and taken captive along with 80 Seminole warriors. The following January, Osceola dies of malaria while held prisoner at Fort Moultrie near Charlestown, South Carolina.

1838

The Texas Rangers go to war with the Texas Cherokee.

Beginning in 1818, Cherokee led by Chief Philip Bowles moved to what is now eastern Texas as whites took over their homeland. Although Sam Houston, the first president of the Republic of Texas, promised the Texas Cherokee that they could stay in the region, his successor Mirabeau B. Lamar responds to pressure from Texas whites to remove Bowles's people. Lamar offers to pay for their removal, but the Cherokee refuse to leave. The president then declares war "without mitigation and compassion" on the Indians.

Five hundred Texas Rangers march on the Cherokee's village, mercilessly attacking the inhabitants and burning their houses and possessions. Among those killed are Chief Bowles, whose body is flayed and scalped. Some of the Cherokee, led by Bowles's son John, try to flee to Mexico, but they are intercepted by soldiers. Most of the other survivors head north into Arkansas and eventually join their kin in Indian Territory.

The U.S. government dissolves the Seneca's reservations.

By the terms of the Treaty of Buffalo Creek, the land of the four Seneca reservations in western New York State—Allegany, Buffalo Creek, Cattaraugus, and Tonawanda—is sold to the Ogden Land Company, and arrangements are made to force the Seneca to relocate to Kansas. Most Seneca oppose the treaty and accuse the leaders who signed it of taking bribes. The protests of tribe members and sympathetic whites will lead to the restoration of the Allegany and Cattaraugus Reservations in 1842. (See also entries for 1848 and for 1857.)

> "The fact that the whites want our land imposes no obligation on us to sell it, nor does it hold forth an inducement to do so, unless it leads them to offer a price equal in value to us. We neither know nor feel any debt of gratitude which we owe to them, in consequence of their 'loving kindness or tender mercies' toward us, that should cause us to make a sacrifice of our property or our interest, to their wonted avarice and which, like the mother of the horse leech, cries give, give, and is never sated."
>
> —Seneca Maris Bryant Pierce in a speech protesting tribal land sales

April

The Cherokee ask the United States to invalidate their Removal treaty.

Principal Cherokee chief John Ross (see entry for 1828) submits a petition to Congress requesting it to void the Treaty of New Echota (see entry for DECEMBER 29, 1835). In the treaty, a small pro-Removal faction of Cherokee agreed to cede the tribe's eastern homeland for a tract in Indian Territory. Signed by more than 15,000 Cherokee, the petition maintains that the treaty is invalid. The government ignores the document and continues to make plans for the tribe's removal.

May

The forced Removal of the Cherokee begins.

The Treaty of New Echota (see entry for DECEMBER 29, 1835) required the Cherokee to relocate to Indian Territory within two years. As the deadline passes, most of the Cherokee remain in the Southeast. Authorized to force them to move, U.S. troops storm their villages and destroy their crops, property, and homes. They also round up the Cherokee, placing them in concentration camps while the government makes arrangements for their relocation. In the camps, large numbers fall ill because of unsanitary conditions. That summer, under armed guard, the Cherokee are ordered to begin the long march to their new homeland. (See also entry for MARCH 1839.)

1839

British Parliament passes the Crown Lands Protection Act.

With the Crown Lands Protection Act, the British parliament declares that all Indian lands are under the guardianship of the British Crown. An attempt to regulate white encroachment on Indian territory, the measure also denies individual Indians all political rights based on land ownership.

March

The Cherokee arrive in Indian Territory.

After months of travel (see entry for MAY 1838), the majority of the Cherokee reach Indian Territory. Although estimates vary, about 4,000 Cherokee—one out of every four who traveled west—did not survive the trip. Corrupt officials stole much of the food and supplies allocated for Indians, causing many to fall victim to disease and starvation. Because of the misery they suffered on the long journey, the Cherokees refer to it as *Nunna Daul Tsunyi,* "the trail where they cried." Among non-Indians, the tragedy becomes known as the Trail of Tears. Although other southeastern Indian tribes, such as the Choctaw and Creek, have similarly horrendous experiences during their relocation to the west, the Cherokee's Trail of Tears becomes the most infamous example of the abusive treatment of Indians during the Removal era.

June 22

Three Cherokee leaders are assassinated.

At daybreak, the house of John Ridge, the leader of the Cherokee's Treaty faction, is surrounded by 25 members of the opposing National faction. The men storm the house, drag Ridge out of his bed, and stab him repeatedly while his family looks on in horror. The assassins then march in single file by the body, each taking the opportunity to stomp on it. At the same time, two more assassination parties fall on Ridge's father, Major Ridge, and his cousin Elias Boudinot. Another target for assassination, Ridge's cousin Stand Watie, manages to escape.

The brutal murders are a result of the enormous political schism between the Cherokee of the National party—traditionalists who had opposed the Treaty of New Echota (see entry for DECEMBER 25, 1835)—and those of the Treaty party—reformists, many of mixed Indian-white ancestry, who had supported it. John Ross, the National leader and principal chief of the tribe (see entry for 1828), claims he had no prior knowledge

of the attacks, but he stymies the efforts of federal authorities to find and prosecute the assassins.

> ᏠᎥ
>
> "I may yet die some day at the hand of some poor, infatuated Indian deluded by the counsels of [John] Ross and his minions. . . . I am resigned to my fate, whatever it may be."
>
> —John Ridge, predicting his assassination, at signing of the Treaty of New Echota

1840

A campaign slogan celebrates William Henry Harrison as an Indian fighter.

In the presidential campaign of 1840, the Whig Party sells its candidates, former Indiana Territory governor William Henry Harrison and his running mate John Tyler, as friends of the frontiersman. Using the slogan "Tippecanoe and Tyler, Too," the party reminds voters of Harrison's defeat of Tecumseh's Indian forces at the Battle of Tippicanoe (see entry for NOVEMBER 7, 1811).

1841

A hymnal in Cree syllabics is published.

James Evans, a Methodist missionary working among the northern Cree in Canada, develops a syllabic system to represent the Cree language. A hymnal Evans publishes introduces this writing system throughout Cree territory. Largely because many of Evans's symbols are adapted from those already used by the Cree, the Indians quickly embrace the syllabary. By the late 19th century, the Cree will have one of the world's highest literacy rates. Evans's writing system will also be adapted by other groups, including the Ojibway, Montagnais, and Inuit.

Major Ethan Allen Hitchcock investigates fraud in Indian Removals.

The U.S. government appoints Major Ethan Allen Hitchcock to look into widespread allegations that officials misappropriated money and supplies intended for southeastern tribes during their Removal to Indian Territory (see entry for MARCH 1839). Hitchcock finds that "bribery, perjury, and forgery . . . and every conceivable subterfuge was employed by designing white men." The government declines to make Hitchcock's devastating report public. (See also entry for 1844.)

George Catlin's *North American Indians* is published.

Painter George Catlin chronicles his eight-year journey through Indian country (see entry for 1832) in *The Manner, Customs, and Condition of*

> "I have been reproachfully designated the 'Indian-loving Catlin.' What of this? What have I to answer? . . . I love a people who have always made me welcome to the best they had[,] . . . who are honest without laws, who have no jails and no poorhouses[,] . . . who are free from religious animosities[,] . . . who never fought a battle with white men except on their own ground. . . . [A]nd Oh, how I love a people who don't live for their love of money."
>
> —artist George Catlin on his reputation as an "Indian lover"

the North American Indians. The popular work contains stories of his travels and approximately 300 engravings based on paintings and drawings of Indians he made from life.

1842

The Bagot Commission reviews Canadian Indian policy.

The Bagot Commission begins its two-year investigation of Canada's dealings with Indian peoples. The commission will recommend that the government develop programs to teach Indians to farm using non-Indian methods, create schools for Indian children, and support religious instruction as a means of assimilating Indians into white society.

August 14

The Second Seminole War ends.

After almost seven years of fighting, the United States negotiates a peace that ends the U.S. Army's campaign against the Seminole (see entry for DECEMBER 28, 1835). The army has compelled more than 4,000 tribe members to move to western lands; some 500, however, have eluded the troops by hiding in the swamps of southern Florida. Because this land is unattractive to whites, the United States allows these Seminole to stay in the region rather than continue its costly and seemingly unwinnable war against them.

1844

The *Cherokee Telegraph* begins publication.

Established by the Cherokee Tribal Council, the *Cherokee Telegraph* becomes the first Indian newspaper in Indian Territory. Like its predecessor, the *Cherokee Phoenix* (see entry for FEBRUARY 21, 1828), the newspaper publishes articles in Cherokee and in English. Its first editor, William Potter Ross, envisions the *Telegraph* as a tool for encouraging tolerance among the tribe's white neighbors by presenting the Cherokee as "civilized" Indians willing to adopt white customs. The newspaper will continue publication until 1911, when the United States sells the printing office following the dissolution of the Cherokee Nation.

Milly Francis receives the Congressional Medal of Honor.

In 1817, a Creek teenager named Milly Francis pled for the life of Georgia captain Duncan McKrimmon, saving him from execution by a Creek war party. Twenty-four years later, she is found living in desperate poverty in Indian Territory by Major Ethan Allen Hitchcock, who is investigating charges of ill-treatment of the Creek and other southeastern tribes during their Removal to western lands (see entry for 1841). Due to Hitchcock's lobbying, Congress awards Francis the Congressional Medal of Honor and an annual pension of $96. She will die four years later of tuberculosis without having received the medal or any pension money.

George Henry forms an Indian acting troupe.

George Henry, an Ojibway also known as Maungwudaus, creates a show featuring "wild Indians." His players spend the next two years touring the United States, England, France, and Belgium. The first acting troupe of Indians organized and managed by an Indian, Henry's actors are criticized for promoting negative stereotypes by his half-brother Peter Jones, an important Ojibway leader and a Methodist minister.

1845

"Manifest Destiny" becomes the justification for the seizure of Indian land.

In *The United States Magazine and Democratic Review,* New York journalist John O'Sullivan writes that it is the United States's "manifest destiny to overspread and to possess the whole of the continent which Providence has given us for the development of the great experiment of liberty and

federated self-government entrusted to us." The term *Manifest Destiny* comes to be popularly used to describe the belief that God intends for the United States to extend from the Atlantic to the Pacific Ocean. Politicians immediately use this concept to garner popular support for the Mexican-American War (1846–48). Throughout the rest of the 19th century, Manifest Destiny will also provide the justification for ignoring western Indians' rights and claims to their land.

1846

Historian Francis Parkman travels west to study Indians.

Beginning his career as one of the United States's foremost historians, Francis Parkman begins a six-month journey along the Oregon Trail to learn about Indians, whom he regards as the "living representatives of the 'stone age.'" Parkman emerges from his travels convinced that all Indians are childlike creatures ruled entirely by emotions and an "utter intolerance of restraint." This attitude toward Indian people will later inform his studies of the early conflicts between France and England in North America.

> "An impassable gulf lies between … [the white man] and his red brethren. Nay, so alien to himself do they appear, that, after breathing the air of the prairie for a few months or weeks, he begins to look upon them as a troublesome and dangerous species of wild beasts."
>
> —historian Francis Parkman on his impression of western Indians

1847

A statue of the Mohegan leader Uncas is dedicated.

In Norwich, Connecticut, a statue of Mohegan chief Uncas (see entry for 1643) is erected. It is the first monument dedicated to an Indian by whites. Uncas supported the colonists during the Pequot War (see entry for MAY 25, 1637) and King Philip's War (see entry for LATE JUNE 1675) during the 17th century. Although celebrated in James Fenimore Cooper's *The Last of the Mohicans* (see entry for 1826), Uncas was condemned among his own people for selfishness and dishonesty.

November 29

The Cayuse attack the Whitman mission.

For more than 10 years, the Cayuse of Oregon Territory have abided the presence of Presbyterian missionaries in the village of Waiilatpu. The mission there was founded by Marcus Whitman (see entry for 1836), whose fanatical efforts to convert the Cayuse earns the Indians' disdain.

When several children attending the mission school contract measles, starting an epidemic within the tribe, the Cayuse blame Whitman. Warriors attack the mission, killing Whitman, his wife Narcissa, and 10 others. A volunteer militia sent to punish the killers stages attacks on Cayuse who had nothing to do with the mission murders. As a result, the Cayuse wage their own campaign against the whites and attempt, largely unsuccessfully, to bring other tribes into the fray. Skirmishes between the Cayuse forces and the militia will continue throughout the next two years. (See also entry for JUNE 8, 1850.)

1848

Ancient Monuments of the Mississippi Valley is published.

The newly founded Smithsonian Institution publishes *Ancient Monuments of the Mississippi Valley*, by Ephraim G. Squier and Edwin H. Davis. The first major work on the archaeology of North America, the monograph provides an account of Squier and Davis's study of burial mounds made by ancient Indians in Ohio (see entries for CA. 1000 B.C. TO A.D. 200; CA. 200 B.C. TO A.D. 400; and CA. 700 TO 1550). Some of the mounds they discuss will later be destroyed by looters, thereby making the writers' description the only surviving record of the mounds' existence.

The Commissioner of Indian Affairs proposes Indian "colonies."

In his annual report to the president, Commissioner of Indian Affairs William Merrill proposes the creation of "colonies"—lands with specific borders in which Indians could be contained. Merrill's concept is an early articulation of the Reservation policy that will dominate U.S. Indian affairs by 1860. The policy will seek to move Indians to well-defined reservations, where they can be compelled to give up Indian ways and be trained to live as settled, Christian farmers.

The Allegany and Cattaraugus Seneca adopt a written constitution.

Since several hereditary chiefs sold Seneca land against the wishes of the tribe (see entry for 1838), the Seneca's confidence in their traditional form of government has been shaken. To ensure their chiefs will not make any more unauthorized land sales, the Seneca on the Allegany and Cattaraugus Reservations draft a written constitution that allows them to elect their leaders.

The Qualla Cherokee receive a settlement from the U.S. government.

The state of North Carolina petitions the federal government for monies owed to the Qualla Cherokee. These Cherokee, who live near Quallatown, North Carolina, avoided traveling west on the Trail of Tears (see entries for MAY 1838 and for MARCH 1839) because they owned their own land outside of tribal territory. Due to the persistence of William H. Thomas, a white man who was adopted by a Qualla chief as a boy, North Carolina convinces the United States to give every Qualla the

$53.33 payment appropriated to remove each Cherokee. The payments are used to purchase the mountain land that will later become the reservation of the Eastern Band of Cherokee Indians.

January 24

Gold is discovered on Nisenan land.

James Marshall, an associate of Swiss settler John A. Sutter, accidentally discovers gold while a sawmill is being constructed near a ranch and trading center known as Sutter's Fort. Sutter's estate, which was built by local Indian labor, is located near the village of Culloma in the lands of the Nisenan Indians. To gain exclusive mineral rights to the area,

"The majority of tribes are kept in constant fear on account of the indiscriminate and inhuman massacre of their people for real or supposed injuries. . . . I have seldom heard of a single difficulty between the whites and the Indians in which the original cause could not readily be traced to some rash or reckless act of the former. In some instances it has happened that innocent Indians have been shot down for imaginary offenses which did not in fact exist."

—Indian agent Adam Johnston on miners' treatment of Indians during the California Gold Rush

Sutter negotiates an agreement with the Nisenan in which they consent to lease to Sutter for three years the land he occupies in exchange for food and some manufactured items. Sutter forwards the agreement to the military governor of California, who refuses to approve it, maintaining that Indians have no rights to their lands and therefore cannot enter into lease agreements.

Sutter also fails in his efforts to keep his discovery secret. Word of his gold find spreads quickly, first in the West and then throughout the East, sparking the California Gold Rush. Initially, California Indians will be little affected by the influx of miners, some of whom will employ Indian men as prospectors. But as the trickle of whites seeking riches grows into a flood, many California tribes will lose their land and even face extinction.

February 2

The Treaty of Guadalupe Hidalgo ends the Mexican-American War.

The Mexican-American War concludes with the signing of the Treaty of Guadalupe Hidalgo. In the document, Mexico agrees to cede to the United States about half of its territory, including lands in present-day California, Nevada, Utah, Colorado, Wyoming, Arizona, New Mexico, and Texas. Without their consent, millions of Indians in the ceded region are brought under the control of the U.S. government. The treaty also includes a promise by the United States to punish any Indians who cross the international boundary to raid Mexican settlements. This provision will lead to extended conflicts between U.S. troops and the Apache and Navajo.

1849

March 3

The Bureau of Indian Affairs becomes part of the Department of the Interior.

Signaling a new emphasis in federal Indian policy, Congress moves the Bureau of Indian Affairs from the Department of War to the new Department of the Interior. In the 1850s, the number of Indians in the United States will double with the organization of the territories of Texas, Oregon, California, Arizona, and New Mexico. With the huge growth in its responsibilities, the BIA will focus on controlling Indians by "civilizing" them, through the adoption of white ways and containing them on reservations, thereby allowing more of their homelands to be opened to white settlement.

August

The Quechan attack ferryman at Yuma Crossing.

After the discovery of gold in California (see entry for JANUARY 24, 1848), the Quechan developed a business of helping westward-bound whites cross the Colorado River below its confluence with the Gila, an area known as Yuma Crossing. The travelers load their supplies and livestock onto rafts that Quechan swimmers pull across the river in exchange for clothing, blankets, and other goods. When members of the Duval party attempt to carry their own possessions by wagon, the Quechan attack them, killing several and stealing their animals, baggage, and food.

The incident convinces the U.S. Army to build a fort at Yuma Crossing the following year to ensure safe passage for whites. The troops mark the first permanent non-Indian presence in the land of the Quechan since they revolted against Spanish settlers 70 years earlier (see entry for JULY 1781). (See also SEPTEMBER 29, 1852.)

August 31

American soldiers murder Navajo (Dineh) leader Narbona.

A group of Navajo (Dineh) led by Narbona meet with Colonel John Washington and his men in the Chuska Mountains of New Mexico. As the meeting ends, a Mexican traveling with the Americans claims that one of the Navajo's horses has been stolen from him. Washington demands that the Navajo return the horse, but they refuse and turn to leave. The soldiers then open fire on the Indian

party, killing Narbona and six other Navajo men. The murder of Narbona outrages the Navajo and deepens their growing mistrust of the U.S. Army.

1850

Mexican soldiers attack an Apache camp at Janos.

Angered by repeated Apache raids on Mexican settlements, 400 Mexican troops led by José Carrasco attack a group of Apache camping near Janos, a town in Chihuahua. When the Mexicans set on the camp, nearly all of the Apache men are away on a trading expedition. The troops kill 19 women and children, taking captive 62 more to be sold as slaves. Among the slain are the mother, wife, and three small children of Geronimo, an influential young warrior. Later one of the Apaches' greatest military leaders, Geronimo will spend his life trying to exact revenge against Mexicans for the murder of his family.

The Mariposa Indian War breaks out.

The Miwok and Yokuts of California's San Joaquin Valley rise up against miners flooding into their lands. Led by Chief Tenaya, warriors attack prospectors and destroy trading posts operated by James D. Savage. To subdue the Indians, Savage organizes the Mariposa Battalion, a force of state militia. The battalion fights minor clashes with the Indians throughout the next year before the Indian rebellion dies down.

The U.S. Army attacks a Pomo Indian encampment.

A group of Pomo in northern California kill two white ranchers—Andrew Kelsey and Charles Stone—who have been abusing them. Through whippings, Kelsey and Stone forced the Indians to dig for gold. The ranchers then used the gold to buy a herd of cattle that in turn drove off the native animals the Pomo depended on for their survival.

To avenge the murders, a force of regular army troops and civilian volunteers attack a Pomo camp on Clear Lake. There, they kill approximately 60 people. At a nearby village on Russian River, the soldiers slaughter another 75 Pomo.

California legalizes Indian indenture.

The legislature of California passes the Act for the Government and Protection of Indians. Despite its benevolent name, the law allows whites to declare any Indian a vagrant; the vagrant must then perform up to four months of unpaid labor for whatever party offers the highest bid at a public auction. The act also states that parents can legally bind Indian children to work for whites for food only for a period of several years. Non-Indians in California soon take advantage of this law to obtain free Indian labor. Routinely, groups of Indians are rounded up, forced to work for whites throughout the summer, then released, physically broken and starving, at the onset of winter. The kidnapping and sale of Indian children, particularly older girls, also becomes widespread. Before the act is repealed in 1863, about 10,000 California Indians will have been indentured or sold into slavery.

Dreamer Religion leader Smohalla is forced from his village.

A Wanapam shaman named Smohalla ("Dreamer") attracts followers among Plateau Indians with a message of passive resistance to white encroachment and influence. He opposes land sales and counsels his followers to practice traditional ways while awaiting a future day when the Creator will drive all the non-Indians from their lands. His teachings anger Homily, another leader in his village, who welcomes whites and their goods. In a confrontation between the two men, Homily declares, "Look at you, you are a poor man. . . . You always talk of the old customs while . . . others accept the new ways and they grow rich." Driven from the village by Homily's followers, Smohalla and his people form a new village near what is now Vernita, Washington, on lands that will be ceded to the United States only five years later (see entry for MAY 24 TO JUNE 11, 1855). Among future adherents to Smohalla's Dreamer Religion will be Chief Joseph (Heinmot Tooyalaket) of the Nez Perce (see entry for JUNE 15, 1877).

"You ask me to plow the ground. Shall I take a knife and tear my mother's breast? Then when I die she will not take me to her bosom to rest.

You ask me to dig for stone. Shall I dig under her skin for her bones? Then when I die I cannot enter her body to be born again.

You ask me to cut grass and make hay and sell it and be rich like white men. But how dare I cut off my mother's hair?"

—Wanapam prophet Smohalla, rejecting whites' demands that Indians take up farming

June 8

Five Cayuse are executed for the Whitman mission murders.

Since Cayuse warriors murdered missionary Marcus Whitman and 11 other whites (see entry for NOVEMBER 29, 1847), the Oregon Territory militia has been attacking any Cayuse, whether involved in the killings or not. Exhausted by continual skirmishes with white soldiers, the tribe turns in five of the attackers to the authorities. With little understanding of the white legal system, the men stand trial, defended by a lawyer provided by the Oregon territorial government. The accused are found guilty, sentenced to death, and hanged.

September 29

Congress passes the Donation Land Act.

A year after Oregon is organized as a territory, the United States offers American settlers flooding into areas on the Oregon Trail an opportunity to claim free land. Through the Donation Land Act, each male settler is entitled to 320 acres. Soon more than 2 million acres of fertile farmland in western Oregon Territory will be granted to these homesteaders.

None of this land, however, has been ceded to the U.S. government by the Indian peoples who occupy it. As the settlers move onto their territory, they will force the Indians to leave, often through violence. Tribes such as the Tillamook and Luckiamute will be left both landless and impoverished.

1851

Henry Rowe Schoolcraft begins publishing *Indian Tribes of the United States.*

Ethnologist and former Indian agent Henry Rowe Schoolcraft publishes the first volume of his *Historical and Statistical Information Respecting the History, Condition, and Prospects of the Indian Tribes of the United States* (1851–57). The six-volume work will be the first major ethnological study of the American Indian tribes. Since 1822 Schoolcraft has traveled extensively among Indian groups, with his most important research conducted among the Ojibway. His work will provide source material for Henry Wadsworth Longfellow's narrative poem *Song of Hiawatha* (see entry for 1855).

The Dakota Sioux cede 24 million acres in the Treaty of Traverse des Sioux.

After decades of conflict with the Ojibway (see entry for 1825), the Dakota Sioux surrender 24 million acres of contested land during treaty negotiations at Traverse des Sioux. In return, they are granted two reservations along the Upper Missouri River. To encourage the Dakota's assimilation, the government also promises to build mills, blacksmith shops, and manual labor schools for the tribe. The treaty plants the seeds of disaster; as the Dakota's displeasure with reservation conditions and resistance to assimilation will erupt into violence 12 years later during the Minnesota Uprising (see entry for AUGUST 18 TO SEPTEMBER 23, 1862).

Lewis Henry Morgan's *League of the Ho-de-no-sau-nee* is published.

Lewis Henry Morgan compiles the results of years of research as a manuscript titled *League of the Ho-de-no-sau-nee, or Iroquois*. A lawyer born near Aurora, New York, Morgan, long fascinated with the Iroquois Indians of the region, is the founder of the Grand Order of the Iroquois, a men's social club of elite white men with similar interests. Morgan's participation in the group led to a cursory study of the Iroquois tribes, but a chance meeting with Ely S. Parker (see entry for 1869), a young Seneca man who served as translator for his tribe, brought a new sophistication to Morgan's efforts. Parker introduced Morgan to Seneca leaders and elders, who in time came so to trust the white man that in 1846 they adopted him as a tribal member.

Although Morgan's history romanticizes precontact Iroquois life, the book is the first account of a tribe's culture that attempts to present the Indians' beliefs and ways in their own terms. It also represents one of the earliest close collaborations between a white researcher and an Indian informant. Morgan himself acknowledges Parker's vital contribution by dedicating the book to his Seneca friend and identifying the work as the "fruit of our joint researches."

The Oatman family is attacked by Yavapai Indians.

Traveling by covered wagon from Illinois to California, Royce and Mary Ann Oatman and their seven children are set upon by Yavapai Indians about 80 miles west of Fort Yuma in present-day Arizona. The parents and four children are killed. Two girls, Olive and Mary Ann, are taken captive, and one boy, Lorenzo, is wounded and left for dead. The Yavapai sell the girls to the Mojave as slaves, and Mary Ann soon dies.

Olive Oatman will remain with the Mojave for five years before she is rescued and reunited with Lorenzo. The story of her ordeal, published as *Life among the Indians* (1857), will become the most popular captivity narrative since Mary Rowlandson's account of her capture by the Wampanoag (see entry for 1682).

>
>
> "A large company of Americans, Indians and Mexicans, were present and witnessed the meeting of Lorenzo and his sister. . . . [N]ot an unmoved heart, nor a dry eye witnessed it. Even the rude and untutored Indian, raised his brawny hand to wipe away the unbidden tear, that stole upon his cheek as he stood speechless and wonder struck!"
>
> —from Lorenzo and Olive Oatman's *Life among the Indians*

January

Treaty commissioners begin negotiating treaties with California tribes.

Setting off from San Francisco, a three-person commission travels throughout California to negotiate peace treaties with all of the Indians within its borders. The commission was formed by Congress to bring an end to a recent rash of skirmishes between Indians and miners in the new state. None of the three men appointed to the commission by President Millard Fillmore is familiar with the culture and ways of California Indians.

The group carries out its mission haphazardly, attempting to negotiate agreements with any group of Indians it comes upon. The commissioners make no effort to distinguish Indian tribes from local bands or villages, and they fail to meet with many large groups altogether. The treaties they conclude call for the cession of the Indians' land to the United States in exchange for a small reservation and a range of goods and services. Although an interpreter accompanies the commission, he most likely does not know the languages of most of the groups the commissioners encounter. Probably most Indians signing the treaties have no under-

Olive Oatman, who became a celebrity after surviving five years as a captive among the Mojave. Her chin is marked with tattoes in the style worn by Mojave women. *(Courtesy of the Douglas County Museum)*

standing of their provisions. (See also entry for JULY 8, 1852.)

February

Congress appropriates $100,000 for the "Concentration" policy.

In the Indian Appropriation Act, Congress earmarks $100,000 to implement a policy of "Concentration" endorsed by Commissioner of Indian Affairs Luke Lea. He recommends that each tribe should be assigned to an area of "limited extent and well-defined boundaries" within which they "should be compelled constantly to remain until such time as their general improvement and good conduct may supersede the necessity of such restrictions."

September 8

Indian leaders of the northern Plains sign the Treaty of Fort Laramie.

Indian agent Thomas Fitzpatrick calls a treaty conference at Fort Laramie, in what is now Wyoming. His goal is to end both intertribal warfare and Indian raids on settlers moving through the northern Plains on their way to Oregon Territory and California. More than 10,000 Indians—including Lakota Sioux, Cheyenne, Arapaho, Crow, Shoshone, Mandan, and Hidatsa—come to the meeting, making it the largest gathering of Indians ever assembled. Some groups, such as the Pawnee, Kiowa, and Comanche, refuse to attend, largely because of their ill-will toward the Lakota.

Following several days of pageants, during which warriors in full war regalia try to impress other tribes with their power and strength, Indian and army leaders come together to discuss treaty terms. In the final treaty, the Indians agree to live in peace with one another, stop their attacks on whites on the Oregon Trail, and allow the government to build forts and roads in their lands. In return, they receive a great store of goods and promises of more.

The peace established by the Treaty of Fort Laramie will be short-lived. As the number of whites arriving in the Plains increases and the threat to Indian land and ways grows, the promises made in the treaty will have little meaning to either Indians or whites.

November

Antonio Garra leads a California Indian uprising.

Organized by Cupeño Indian leader Antonio Garra, the Cupeño and a small number of Cahuilla, Quechan, and Cocopa join together to resist the illegal attempts of the new state of California to compel the Indians to pay property taxes. When the state will not relent, the Indians soon resolve to expel all non-Indians from their lands. When the rebelling Indians kill two whites and two Mexicans, the Cupeño rise up against Juan José Warner, a white man who was granted ownership of their homeland by the governor of California and has since held the Cupeño living there in virtual slavery. The Cupeño burn down Warner's house and kill four whites before the state militia and U.S. troops attack and destroy the Indians' village of Cupa.

The uprising is quelled when a Cahuilla leader betrays Garra and turns him over to the U.S. Army. In a military court, Garra is tried for treason, but because he declares that he has never pledged allegiance to the United States, he is convicted of murder instead. Garra and four other rebel leaders are executed. Although fewer than 50 Indians ever joined Garra, news of the uprising, with exaggerated accounts of white deaths, spreads through California. The reports create a panic and inflame anti-Indian sentiment throughout the white population.

1852

July 8

Congress rejects treaties made with California Indians.

Succumbing to pressure from non-Indians in California, the Senate withholds its ratification of 18 treaties made with the Indians of the state (see entry for JANUARY 1851). In these treaties, commissioners appointed by the president guaranteed Indians exclusive use of about 7.5 million acres. Although this amounts to only about 7.5 percent of the land in California, many white Californians loudly object to the creation of these reserved areas, insisting instead that the government should force Indians to leave the state completely.

September 29

Fort Yuma troops attack the Quechan.

Amidst rumors of a large-scale Indian rebellion, troops stationed at Fort Yuma in Quechan territory (see entry for AUGUST 1849) march on an Indian encampment. Taken by surprise, possibly because they believe an earlier truce with the army is still in effect, the Quechan flee their homes. Although angered by the soldiers' presence in their lands, the Quechan soon sue for peace, out of fear that a confrontation with the army will disrupt their planting season and leave them starving in the upcoming winter.

1853

The last surviving Chumash is found on San Nicolas Island.

A crew of hunters on San Nicolas Island off the California coast come upon an Indian woman sitting with her dog outside a house she constructed from whale bones. The woman has lived alone on the island for 18 years. She was accidentally left behind when the rest of her people, the San Nicolas Chumash, were moved to the mainland by mission priests. All have since died of non-Indian diseases.

The hunters take the woman to Santa Barbara, where she is baptized as Juana Maria and dies of disease seven weeks later. Her story will be told in several works of fiction, most notably Scott O'Dell's *Island of the Blue Dolphins,* a young-adult novel that will win the 1960 Newbery Award.

Fall

The United States compels land cessions from northern Indian Territory tribes.

In order to clear land for the construction of a transcontinental railroad through the Great Plains, Commissioner of Indian Affairs George W. Manypenny negotiates land cessions from tribes relocated to lands in Indian Territory above 37 degrees latitude. The Indian groups affected include the Lenni Lenape (Delaware), Kickapoo, Miami, Omaha, and Shawnee. Reporting that their leaders have dealt with him "without enthusiasm," Manypenny notes that many of their tribes "have been removed, step by step, from mountain to valley, and from river to plain, until they have been pushed halfway across the continent."

December 30

United States makes the Gadsden Purchase.

Diplomat James Gadsden negotiates the Gadsden Purchase, in which Mexico agrees to sell for $10 million a 45,000-square-mile tract south of the Gila River in what is now southern New Mexico and Arizona. The agreement settles boundary disputes left unresolved by the Treaty of Guadalupe Hidalgo (see entry for FEBRUARY 2, 1848). It also provides the United States with lands needed to construct a railroad route through the Southwest. Indian groups living in the area, including the Chiricahua Apache and the Papago (now known as the Tohono O'odham), are not consulted in the negotiations and will refuse to acknowledge the new international boundary.

1854

John Rollin Ridge's *Life and Adventures of Joaquin Murieta* is published.

The grandson of Cherokee leader Major Ridge (see entries for DECEMBER 29, 1835, and for JUNE 22, 1839), John Rollin Ridge becomes the first American Indian novelist, with the publication of *Life and Adventures of Joaquin Murieta.* Ridge's book tells the story of a man of mixed Spanish and Indian ancestry who is forced from his land by whites. When whites kill his brother, Joaquin Murieta vows revenge and becomes a noble outlaw in the tradition of Robin Hood. The character's romantic adventures will inspire many

Mexican-American authors to write their own stories featuring Joaquin Murieta for the popular press.

> "He dashed along that fearful trail as he had been mounted upon a spirit-steed, shouting as he passed:
> 'I am Joaquin! Kill me if you can!'
> Shot after shot came clanging around his head, and bullet after bullet flattened on the wall of salt at his right. In the midst of the first firing, his hat was knocked from his head, and left his long black hair streaming behind him."
> —from John Rollin Ridge's novel
> *The Life and Adventures of Joaquin Murieta*

A figure in Indian headgear appears on American coins.

A female figure representing liberty is depicted wearing a plumed Indian headdress on one-dollar and three-dollar coins issued by the United States. "Liberty" previously had worn a turbanlike cap associated with Roman slaves who had been given their freedom. The change was possibly made to address complaints of southern slaveholders, who were discomforted by the image of a freed slave on American coinage.

Congress passes the Kansas-Nebraska Act.

The Kansas-Nebraska Act creates the Kansas and Nebraska territories out of the northern portion of Indian Territory (see entry for AUTUMN 1853). With its new northern boundary, Indian Territory covers roughly the same area as present-day Oklahoma. During the next decade, more than 100,000 white settlers will move onto these former Indian lands.

August 19

The Brulé Sioux kill 30 soldiers in the Grattan Massacre.

As a party of Mormons travel west along the Oregon Trail, one of their cows wanders into the territory of the Brulé band of the Lakota Sioux. Afraid of confronting the Indians, the Mormons tell army officers at Fort Laramie that the cow was stolen. Meanwhile, a Brulé named High Forehead kills the cow with an arrow.

Acting on the Mormons' complaint, Lieutenant John L. Grattan leads a force of 30 men into High Forehead's village and orders his arrest. When High Forehead resists, Grattan tells his men to open fire. As the influential Chief Conquering Bear falls dead, the Brulé attack the soldiers, killing them all. The incident ends any hope that the peace established between the Lakota Sioux and U.S. Army in the Treaty of Fort Laramie (see entry for SEPTEMBER 8, 1851) will last. (See also entry for SEPTEMBER 2, 1855.)

December

Chief Seattle delivers a speech at the Point Elliot Treaty negotiations.

In council with Washington territorial governor Isaac Stevens at Point Elliot, Chief Seattle of the Suquamish speaks about the trials of his people. Eyewitnesses describe the speech as eloquent and moving. Among those present is poet Henry A. Smith, who claims he took notes in English as Seattle spoke. Thirty-three years later, a version of the speech written by Smith appears in print for the first time in the *Seattle Sunday Star.* Although this version will become one of the most famous examples of Indian oratory, the history of its transcription casts doubts about how accurately it represents Seattle's actual words. (See also entry for APRIL 1992.)

1855

Henry Wadsworth Longfellow's *Song of Hiawatha* is published.

Among the United States's most popular writers Henry Wadsworth Longfellow creates a romantic legend of an Ojibway chief in his narrative poem *The Song of Hiawatha*. Longfellow relies largely on Henry Rowe Schoolcraft's research (see entry for 1851) for information on Ojibway culture, but for the eponymous character he borrows the name of Hiawatha, one of the founders of the Iroquois Confederacy (see entry for CA. 1400). Because of the popularity of Longfellow's poem, many non-Indians will come to confuse the historical Hiawatha with Longfellow's fictional creation.

The Chickasaw reestablish their independence.

After the Chickasaw's removal from their southeastern homeland, the tribe is forced to make a new home in Indian Territory on lands owned by the Choctaw. The Chickasaw grow frustrated living among the Choctaw and believe they are discriminated against under Choctaw law. With funds saved from annuities paid by the U.S. government, the tribe purchases land to the west of the Choctaw's, where they re-create an independent Chickasaw nation.

May 24 to June 11

The Walla Walla Council reduces the land base of Washington Territory Indians.

As whites flood into the Northwest, Washington Territory governor Isaac Stevens is charged with extinguishing the land claims of area Indians, including the Cayuse, Nez Perce, Walla Walla, and Yakama. In addition to clearing rich farmland for settlement by whites, Stevens wants to free land for the construction of the northern route of the Pacific Railroad.

To negotiate the necessary treaties, the governor organizes the Walla Walla Council, one of the largest gatherings of Indians ever held. The meetings are tense, as mistrustful Indians plot against

Stevens, his men, and sometimes against other Indians. Three treaties are finally signed, under duress, during the final days of the conference. Many of those who agree to the treaties have little understanding of their provisions. In the documents, the tribes cede approximately 30,000 square miles of land in exchange for two small reservations.

Within days of the conference, much of the Indians' former territory is opened to white settlement, despite a treaty promise that the tribes will not be displaced for two years. Fury over Stevens's treachery creates unrest throughout the Northwest and leads directly to the Yakama War (see entry for SEPTEMBER 1855).

> "After everybody had talked and Pu-Pu-Mox-Mox had talked, General Stevens wanted to hear from the head Chief of the Yakimas. He said, 'Kamiaken, the great Chief of the Yakimas, has not spoken at all. His people have had no voice here today. He is not afraid to speak—let him speak out.' . . . Then Chief Kamiaken said, 'I am afraid that the white men are not speaking straight; that their children will not do what is right by our children; that they will not do what you have promised for them.'"
>
> —Chief Weninock of the Yakama on the negotiations at the Walla Walla Council

September

The Yakama War breaks out.

Following the Walla Walla Council (see entry for MAY 24 TO JUNE 11, 1855), tensions between the

Yakama and whites intensify as a stream of miners begins passing through the Indians' lands en route to gold fields north of the Spokane River. When miners rape several Yakama women and steal horses from the tribe, Qualchin, the nephew of Yakama leader Kamiaken, murders the criminals. Despite warnings that his life is in danger, Indian agent Andrew Bolon comes to investigate the murders and himself is killed at Yakama hands.

Bolon's murder sets into motion the Yakama War of 1855–56. To avenge Bolon's death, a 102-soldier expedition headed by Major Granville O. Haller is sent to Yakama territory. In their first battle, at Toppenish Creek, Yakama warriors defeat Haller's troops. Other tribes then join the Yakama to launch a full-scale war on the American force, with skirmishes continuing for the next 10 months. (See also entry for DECEMBER 1855.)

September 2

The U.S. Army avenges the Grattan Massacre at the Battle of Blue Water Creek.

In search of the Indians responsible for the Grattan Massacre (see entry for AUGUST 19, 1854), a force of 700 men led by Brigadier General William S. Harney marches on a Brulé Sioux (Lakota) village on Blue Water Creek, in present-day Nebraska. Although the village leader, Little Thunder, tries to negotiate a surrender, Harney's soldiers attack the Indians, killing nearly 100 Brulé. The bloody encounter further deteriorates the supposed peace between the Lakota Sioux and the United States established by the Fort Laramie Treaty only four years earlier. (See entry for SEPTEMBER 8, 1851.)

October

The Rogue River War erupts.

In the mountainous Rogue River valley of southern Oregon, Captain Andrew Jackson Smith attempts to protect area Indians from white settlers by encouraging young Indian warriors to settle near Fort Lane. Before he can resettle their relatives, the Indians' camps are attacked by volunteer soldiers, who slaughter 23 women, children, and elderly men. In retaliation, warriors kill 27 white settlers. Throughout the winter, vengeful volunteers seek out and attack Indians camping in the mountains. (See also entry for MAY 27 TO 28, 1856.)

November

The Third Seminole War begins.

A crew surveying the Everglades in Florida trample and raid the garden of Seminole leader Billy Bowlegs. When his outraged followers attack and wound several of the surveyors in retaliation, the army sends in troops to fight the Seminole, igniting the Third Seminole War. These soldiers will continue to skirmish with the tribe's warriors for more than two years. (See also entry for JANUARY 19, 1858.)

December

Oregon volunteers murder Chief Pu-Pu-Mox-Mox.

Oregon volunteers recruited to fight the Yakama War (see entry for SEPTEMBER 1855) capture Chief Pu-Pu-Mox-Mox, a respected leader of the Walla Walla, during a peace council. The soldiers shoot the chief to death, cut off his ears and scalp, and display them before the area's white settlers as trophies. The Walla Walla, outraged by the murder of Chief Pu-Pu-Mox-Mox and the defilement of his corpse, raid settlements with renewed ferocity.

1856

Indians are used to represent America's "savage" past in a Capitol Building sculpture.

Commissioned to design a bas-relief sculpture for the pediment of the U.S. Capitol in Washington, D.C., Thomas Crawford chooses the theme of the progress of civilization. To the right of a figure representing America, Crawford depicts an Indian man and woman watching as a frontiersman clears their land. The relief also shows a forlorn Indian chief, holding his head in his hand, sitting next to an empty grave.

According to Crawford, the chief is meant to embody "all the despair and profound grief resulting from the conviction of the white's triumph."

May 27 to 28

The Rogue River War ends with the Battle of Big Meadows.

As the army sends reinforcements to southern Oregon to battle the warriors involved in the Rogue River War (see entry for OCTOBER 1855), the Indians' leaders agree to surrender, all the while planning a surprise attack. At Big Meadows in the Rogue River valley, the warriors set upon the soldiers. On the second day of fighting, the soldiers have almost run out of ammunition when another company of troops arrives. Together, they drive off the Indian forces. The last-minute defeat demoralizes the Indians, most of whom will surrender within a month after the battle.

1857

The Seneca buy back the Tonawanda Reservation.

The Seneca are authorized to use U.S. funds set aside for their removal to the West to buy back their Tonawanda Reservation. The land was sold by the U.S. government by the terms of the Treaty of Buffalo Creek (see entry for 1838), which some chiefs were bribed to sign. The sale was upheld in an 1842 agreement, which the Seneca successfully claim cannot be applied to them since none of their chiefs were present during its negotiation.

March 8 to 9

Dakota Sioux murder white settlers in the Spirit Lake Massacre.

Unwilling to settle on a reservation by the terms of the Treaty of Traverse des Sioux (see entry for 1851), a Dakota named Inkpaduta and 14 followers rise up against neighboring whites near Spirit Lake, in northwestern Iowa. The Indian renegades kill about 40 settlers. The massacre foreshadows the larger Minnesota Uprising, which will occur five years later (see entry for AUGUST 18 TO SEPTEMBER 23, 1862).

August 29

U.S. troops attack Cheyenne Indians at Solomon Fork.

Soldiers under the command of Colonel Edwin Sumner are sent out to punish a group of Cheyenne in western Kansas for raiding mining camps. At a fork of the Solomon River, Sumner's 300 troops meet approximately the same number of Cheyenne warriors. Although the Indians have been warned of the attack, most withdraw as the soldiers rush toward them with sabers. The Battle of Solomon Fork results in few casualties but ushers in the era of armed combat between the Cheyenne and the U.S. Army.

September 11

The Ute and Mormons kill California-bound settlers in the Mountain Meadows Massacre.

In an area known as Mountain Meadows, about 300 miles south of Salt Lake City, a force of Ute sets upon a wagon train carrying some 150 settlers, mostly Methodists, headed for California. The warriors believe the settlers have poisoned their local water and ask their Mormon allies for help. When one of the Methodists manages to escape the onslaught, several Mormons shoot him dead.

After holding off their attackers for several days, John D. Lee, a young associate of Mormon leader Brigham Young, persuades the settlers to lay down their weapons. In return, he promises that the Ute will allow the settlers to continue on their journey. Once the travelers pile their arms into a wagon, however, the Mormons and the Indians attack, slaughtering everyone except for 17 children, whom the Mormons later adopt. The massacre is intended to protect the Mormons from federal troops en route to Utah to suppress an alleged rebellion; the Mormons fear the soldiers will annihilate them if any of the adult Methodists live to tell of the attack. The Mormons' later attempt to blame the carnage wholly on the Ute fails, but Young succeeds in averting a war, by negotiating with the U.S. government. Twenty years later, Lee will later be executed for his part in the Mountain Meadows Massacre.

> "[T]he original plan was for the Indians to do all the work, and the whites to do nothing, only to stay back and plan for them, and encourage them to do the work. Now we knew the Indians could not do the work, and we were in a sad fix."
>
> —John D. Lee on the Mormons' role in the Mountain Meadows Massacre

1858

The Mojave battle whites in their territory.

Mojave warriors attack a wagon train of California-bound settlers crossing the Colorado River and force them to turn back to Albuquerque, in present-day New Mexico. To protect white travelers, troops from California establish an outpost at the crossing. Their arrival sets off a series of skirmishes later called the Mojave War. The fighting largely comes to an end when 700 more troops are sent to the area, where they construct Fort Mojave.

January 19

The Third Seminole War ends.

Exhausted by constant fighting, the Florida Seminole bring an end to the Third Seminole War (see entry for NOVEMBER 1855) by surrendering to the United States. Seminole leader Billy Bowlegs and 162 of his followers agree to join their kin in Indian

Territory. The majority, however, continue to refuse to leave Florida and retreat to the swamplands of the Everglades.

May 17

An intertribal force drives troops off the Colville Indian Reservation.

A force of 158 troops led by Lieutenant Colonel Edward J. Steptoe descends on the Colville Indian Reservation, in what is now Washington State, to intimidate Indians angered by plans to build a road through their lands. Encountering about 100,000 Palouse, Spokane, and Coeur d'Alene warriors, Steptoe's soldiers begin to leave when the Indians attack, killing two officers. That night the troops flee and return to Fort Walla Walla. (See also entry for SEPTEMBER 1 TO 5, 1858.)

July to October

The Navajo (Dineh) clash with soldiers at Fort Defiance.

Manuelito, a wealthy Navajo (Dineh) leader, is outraged when American soldiers kill 60 of his cattle as they graze on lands claimed by the U.S. Army. The troops are stationed at Fort Defiance, a fort established in Navajo territory in 1851 to protect the tribe from Mexican slave raiding parties.

To retaliate, the Navajo shoot arrows at the fort, and a warrior kills the African-American servant of the fort's commander. When the Navajo refuse to surrender the guilty party, the soldiers burn the village of leader Zarcillas Largos, which they mistake for Manuelito's. The incident increases the growing animosity between the Navajo and the army, which will soon lead the Indians to attack their fort (see entry for APRIL 30, 1860).

September 1 to 5

The army defeats an Indian force at Battles of Spokane Plains and Four Lakes.

Troops under Colonel George Wright are sent to punish the Colville Reservation Indians responsible for humiliating Lieutenant Colonel Edward J. Steptoe's men (see entry for MAY 17, 1858). At Spokane Plains on September 1 and Four Lakes on September 5, battles end in the defeat of the Indians, whose arms cannot match the howitzers and long-range rifles of Wright's men. The victorious Wright travels through the countryside, rounding up and hanging leaders he deems responsible for the conflict.

1859

The Cherokee found the Keetoowah Society.

Led by white Baptist missionary Evan Jones, conservative Cherokee Indians form the secret Keetoowah Society to restore the traditional values of the tribe, which they believe have been under threat ever since the tribe's relocation to Indian Territory (see entries for MAY 1838 and MARCH 1839). Naming themselves after one of the towns in the original Cherokee Nation, the Keetoowah are primarily interested in social and political, rather than religious, reform. Among their early goals are ending slavery and resisting attempts to assimilate the Cherokee into white society.

1860

February 26

White vigilantes massacre Indians camped on Humboldt Bay.

In the middle of the night, a party of about 40 white men set upon several Indian villages along Humboldt Bay near the town of Eureka, California. They slaughter approximately 80 people, most of whom are women and children. The whites stage the attack because the Indians have been harboring members of mountain tribes suspected of killing the men's cattle.

April 30

The Navajo (Dineh) attack Fort Defiance.

After years of conflict between the Navajo (Dineh) and soldiers in New Mexico Territory (see entry for JULY TO OCTOBER 1858), Navajo warriors attack Fort Defiance, a U.S. Army post in the center of their territory. The Navajo nearly take the fort, but the soldiers are able eventually to repulse them.

The attack leads the secretary of war to launch a full-scale military campaign against the tribe. Led by Major Edward R. S. Canby, about 600 soldiers aided by Ute scouts harass the Navajo through the winter and following spring. Navajo casualties are low, but the troops kill more than 1,000 of the tribe's horses and even more of their sheep. Accompanied by a severe drought, this loss of livestock causes the Navajo extreme hardship. (See entry for SEPTEMBER 22, 1861.)

"After the soldiers had killed all but some little children and babies still tied up in their baskets, the soldiers took them also, and set the camp on fire and threw them into the flames to see them burn alive. I had one baby brother killed there. ...They went after my people all over Nevada. Reports were made everywhere throughout the whole country by the white settlers, that the red devils were killing their cattle, and by this lying of the white settlers the trail began which is marked by the blood of my people."

—Paiute author Sarah Winnemucca on the Paiute War

May

The Paiute battle miners in the Paiute War.

Traveling through present-day Nevada, white traders kidnap and rape two Paiute girls. After rescuing the girls, the Paiute in retaliation set fire to a mail station along the trail, killing five whites. To avenge the attack, about 100 white miners join the ranks of a volunteer army led by Major William Ormsby. As the army approaches the Big Bend of the Truckee River on May 12, they are ambushed by warriors, who kill 46 soldiers. The governor of California sends out a second army, about 800 men, which attacks the Paiute near Pinnacle Mountain. About 25 Paiute are killed before the outnumbered Indian forces ask for peace, thus ending the brief Paiute War.

December

Cynthia Ann Parker is "rescued" by the U.S. Army.

During an attack on a Comanche camp along the Pease River, U.S. troops encounter a woman holding up a baby and shouting "Americanos" to dissuade them from shooting her and her child. The soldiers take the woman, and she is soon identified as Cynthia Ann Parker, who had been taken captive by the Comanche when she was nine years old (see entry for MAY 19, 1836). Parker, accompanied by her infant daughter Topsannah, is taken to live with her white family after her well-publicized "rescue." Although newspaper accounts celebrate the reunion, she is terrified of her white relatives and despondent at being separated from her Comanche husband and sons—one of whom, Quanah, will later emerge as a great tribal leader. Cynthia Ann Parker attempts to end her misery by starving herself to death before finally succumbing to influenza in 1870.

Cynthia Ann Parker with her daughter Topsannah, photographed after Parker was taken from her Comanche family. Her short hairstyle is a traditional Comanche symbol of mourning. *(Joseph Taulman Collection, CN 805, The Center for American History, The University of Texas at Austin)*

1861

The Southern Cheyenne and Arapaho cede lands in the Treaty of Fort Wise.

In preparation for Colorado statehood, U.S. negotiators compel the Southern Cheyenne and Arapaho to give up claim to nearly all their lands in Colorado Territory, in the Treaty of Fort Wise. The Indians retain only a small tract of land along the Arkansas River at Sand Creek, in what is now southeastern Colorado. Although the government intends for the Indians to abandon buffalo hunting and become settled farmers, the lands at Sand Creek are too infertile to sustain the tribes. Starving and suffering from an epidemic of smallpox, Southern Cheyenne and Arapaho hunters will soon ignore orders to stay within the reservation boundaries as they go off in search of buffalo herds.

February 4

Cochise escapes from U.S. soldiers in the Cut-the-Tent Affair.

At the request of U.S. Army lieutenant George Bascom, Chiricahua Apache leader Cochise agrees to meet with Bascom and his men. Unbeknownst to Cochise, Bascom is convinced that he is responsible for raiding a ranch of a local white man and abducting his children. When confronted by Bascom, Cochise denies any involvement in the raid. Sensing his life is in danger, the Apache slips out a knife and cuts a hole in the meeting tent, through which he escapes from the soldiers. The Cut-the-Tent affair confirms to the Chiricahua that the U.S. Army is not to be trusted.

April

Soldiers leave the western frontier with the outbreak of the Civil War.

With the beginning of the Civil War, the U.S. Army recalls soldiers in the West to help fight the Confederate rebels. Troops policing the western frontier are replaced by volunteers recruited by state and territorial governments. From 1860 to 1865, these volunteer armies will grow from 11 to 20,000 troops. The recruitment of these zealous volunteers will result in increasing tension and violence as they lead brutal attacks against Indian raiders on the Plains and in the Southwest.

Summer

The Confederacy negotiates treaties with Indian Territory tribes.

As the federal troops withdraw from Indian Territory (see entry for APRIL 1861), Confederate agents arrive and begin meeting with leaders of the tribes there to persuade them to become their allies. Many of the largest groups—including the so-called Five Civilized Tribes—had originally lived in the South and therefore already had close ties to the Confederates.

The agents are able to secure treaties with four of the Five Civilized Tribes (the Choctaw, Chickasaw, Creek, and Seminole) as well as with Quapaw, Seneca, Caddo, Wichita, Osage, and Shawnee. The only major holdout is the Cherokee tribe, whose principal chief, John Ross, advocates neutrality (see entry for OCTOBER 1861). In the treaties, the Confederacy pledges to protect the Indians' land from invasions by Union troops. It also promises to let the Indians participate in the Confederate government in the event of a southern victory. The tribes in return agree to organize troops for Indian Territory's defense.

September 22

Seventeen Navajo (Dineh) are killed in the Fort Fauntleroy Massacre.

According to the terms of a treaty made with Major Edward R. S. Canby (see entry for APRIL 30, 1860) in February, a group of Navajo (Dineh) arrive at Fort Fauntleroy in present-day New Mexico to collect food rations. As usual on ration day, the Navajo and soldiers at the fort hold a series of horse races. During one race, a Navajo rider loses control of his horse because the rein on its bridle had been cut with a knife. The Navajo accuse the soldiers of cheating, and in the confusion that follows soldiers fire into the crowd, shooting 12 women and children. The fort commander, Colonel Marcus Chaves, orders his men to shoot howitzers at the fleeing Indians.

Chaves, who in the past had raided Navajo settlements to capture Indians to sell as slaves, maintains that the Navajo had tried to rush the fort. Even though an investigation proves Chaves's claim false, efforts to court-martial the officer fail.

October

Cherokee leader John Ross decides to side with the Confederacy.

Despite pressure from Confederate authorities and their Cherokee sympathizers, John Ross, principal chief of the Cherokee, adopts a policy of neutrality in the American Civil War (see entry for SUMMER 1861). He, however, reconsiders his position when Confederacy supporter Stand Watie threatens to incite a civil war within the tribe over the issue. Also fearing that southern troops might invade a neutral Cherokee Nation, Ross signs a treaty declaring the Cherokee's allegiance to the Confederate cause. (See also entry for SUMMER 1862.)

> "In years long since past, our ancestors met undaunted those who would invade their mountain homes beyond the Mississippi; let not their descendants of the present day be found unworthy of them, or unable to stand by the chivalrous men of the South by whose side they may be called to fight in self defense
>
> The Cherokee people do not desire to be involved in war, but self-preservation fully justifies them in the course they have adopted, and they will be recreant to themselves if they do not sustain it to the utmost of their humble abilities."
>
> —Cherokee principal chief John Ross on his tribe's allegiance to the Confederacy

December 26

Creek led by Opothle Yoholo are defeated in the Battle of Round Mountain.

The wealthiest Creek in Indian Territory, Opothle Yoholo, speaks out against the Creek's support of the Confederacy (see entry for SUMMER 1861). He asks why the Creek would become allies of the same southerners who had forced them out of their homelands less than 25 years before. Declaring that the Creek should stay neutral, Opothle Yoholo attracts several thousand followers.

Fearing attack, Opothle Yoholo and his people flee to Kansas. On the way, they are confronted by Confederate troops several times before they are finally defeated in the Battle of Round Mountain. Opothle Yoholo's followers scatter after the battle, but they do not give up their opposition to the South. Instead, many join the Union army and help invade the lands of the Confederate-allied Cherokee (see entry for SUMMER 1862).

1862

Whites begin traveling on the Bozeman Trail.

The Bozeman Trail is established to carry whites from the Oregon Trail to goldfields in what is now southwestern Montana. The trail runs directly through prime hunting grounds of the Lakota Sioux, who are soon enraged by the growing traffic of non-Indians in their lands. These invasions will lead to the conflict known as Red Cloud's War (see entry for 1866).

Congress passes the Morrill Act.

Through the Morrill Act, Congress approves land grants for the establishment of colleges for agricultural research across the United States. The act will have an enormous impact on Indians in the West, particularly those whose lands have been unattractive to whites because they are difficult to farm. The research resulting from the Morrill Act will so improve agricultural techniques that in coming decades even these previously unwanted lands will be flooded by white farmers.

March 7 to 8

Indian troops fight the Battle of Pea Ridge.

By the treaties of allegiance the Confederacy negotiated with the Five Civilized Tribes (see entry for SUMMER 1861), these tribes are entitled to establish military regiments to protect Indian Territory in case of attack by Union troops. The treaties also hold that these forces will not be required to fight outside of Indian Territory. Ignoring these provisions, Confederate general Earl Van Dorn orders 25 Indian soldiers to join his campaign against Union forces in Missouri.

Van Dorn's army confronts Union troops in northwest Arkansas at the Battle of Pea Ridge, the only Civil War battle in which a large number of Indian soldiers will fight. They and their Confederate allies are forced to retreat when they run out of ammunition. Despite the defeat, Cherokee leader Stand Watie (see entries for OCTOBER 1861 and SUMMER 1862) distinguishes himself in the battle. He will later become the only Indian to rise to the rank of general in the Confederate army (see entry for JUNE 23, 1865).

May 20

Congress passes the Homestead Act.

The Homestead Act allows U.S. citizens to apply for title to 160 acres of land in present-day Kansas and Nebraska. Aside from a $10 registration fee, the land is free to homesteaders who agree to make certain improvements and live on their tract for five years. Over the next 18 years, the act will grant more than 100,000 whites title to land formerly held by Indians. It will also influence the allotment of Indian land (see entry for FEBRUARY 8, 1887), by establishing 160 acres as a suitable amount of land for individual homesteads.

Summer

Union troops invade the Cherokee capital.

Federal soldiers, bolstered by pro-Union Indians, march south from Kansas into northeastern Indian Territory. When they reach the Cherokee capital of Tahelquah, they arrest Principal Chief John Ross, who hesitantly agreed to sign a treaty of allegiance with the Confederacy in order to avert a civil war within his tribe (see entry for OCTOBER 1861). Ross is sent first to Fort Leavenworth in Kansas, then to Philadelphia, where he declares a pro-Union stance. During his exile in the East, his political rival Stand Watie will be elected the new principal chief.

July 1

The Pacific Railroad Act is passed.

The Pacific Railroad Act gives 174 million acres of public land to transcontinental railroad companies. Aside from making these companies the largest landowners in the West, these land grants will allow construction of nine major rail routes through the region. These railroads will threaten Indian societies by bringing a flood of whites into their territory and disrupting the buffalo herds on which the Plains Indians rely for their survival.

July 15

Apache warriors attack U.S. troops at Apache Pass.

In late 1861, troops led by Brigadier General James H. Carleton were sent into the Southwest to guard the southern route to California from Indian raiding parties. To drive off the intruders, Mimbreno Apaches led by Mangas Coloradas and Chiricahua Apaches led by Cochise stage a surprise attack on an advance party at Apache Pass, an abandoned mail station in southern Arizona. Armed with howitzers and rifles, the soldiers successfully defend themselves. Before the Apaches' retreat, Mangas Coloradas suffers a serious, but not fatal, bullet wound in the chest.

August 18 to September 23

The Dakota Sioux wage war on white settlers.

Pressured by whites moving onto their land, the Dakota Sioux of Minnesota agreed to settle on a reservation (see entry for MARCH 8 TO 9, 1857). The U.S. government, however, has not honored its promise to protect their lands from further encroachment. Adding to the Dakota's desperation, it also refuses to give them the rations guaranteed to them by the treaty.

As the Dakota face starvation, four warriors murder five white settlers. Although earlier an advocate of making peace with the government, Dakota leader Little Crow decides to escalate the violence and organize a full-scale war against their white neighbors. On August 18, the first day of warfare, Little Crow's men attack non-Indian settlements and trading posts and kill approximately 400 whites. As the Indians continue their raids, an army of 1,500 troops led by General Henry Hastings Sibley arrive in Minnesota to repulse them. After several encounters, Little Crow's force is defeated on September 23, causing the Dakota warriors to scatter. Little Crow flees to Canada but soon returns to Minnesota. (See also entries for JULY 3, 1863; DECEMBER 26, 1863; and JULY 28, 1864.)

September 12

Cherokee leader John Ross meets with Abraham Lincoln.

To seek aid and protection for his people, John Ross, the former principal chief of the Cherokee Nation, visits the White House to speak with President Abraham Lincoln. Lincoln is cold to Ross, who signed, but later repudiated, a treaty of allegiance with the Confederacy (see entries for OCTOBER 1861 and SUMMER 1861). Ross tells the president that the tribe sided with the South only after the United States failed to live up to its treaty obligations to them. To his disappointment, Lincoln offers little assurance that in the event of a Union victory the United States will do anything to protect the Cherokee—even those, like Ross, who have sided with the Union. (See also entry for SEPTEMBER 1866.)

1863

January 17 to 18

Mangas Coloradas is killed in custody.

Nearing 70 and still suffering from wounds he received during the Apache Pass conflict (see entry for JULY 15, 1862), a weakened Mangas Coloradas agrees to meet American soldiers at a peace conference. The meeting, scheduled for January 17, proves to be merely a ruse to capture the elderly

Apache military leader. According to an eyewitness, for the next two days Mangas Coloradas is tortured with heated bayonets. When he resists, he is shot dead. The official army report holds that he was accidentally killed while trying to escape.

January 27

The Shoshone suffer the Bear River campaign.

Led by California businessman Patrick Edward Connor, the Utah state militia attacks a Shoshone camp along the Bear River in Idaho. The assault is in retaliation for raids on whites traveling along the Overland Mail Route. With 300 men, Connor sets upon the village at sunrise, closing off all escape routes. The Shoshone fight for their lives, but most are killed either in their encampment or while frantically trying to escape by swimming across the river. The militia estimates Indian casualties at 224 and takes 164 women and children captive. For his leadership during the bloody slaughter, the War Department gives Connor the title of brigadier general.

Spring

Kit Carson's troops battle the Mescalero Apache.

To stop the raids of Mescalero Apache, Brigadier General James H. Carleton assigns former Indian agent and trader Christopher "Kit" Carson to lead a campaign against them. Exhausted by Carson's constant attacks, the Mescalero surrender and agree to resettle on Bosque Redondo, an area in what is now east-central New Mexico that Carleton has reserved as a place to confine renegade Apache and Navajo (Dineh). (See also entry for NOVEMBER 1865.)

Summer

Union troops make a second expedition into Indian Territory.

With the aid of pro-Union Indians, federal troops invade Indian Territory from the north for a second time (see entry for SUMMER 1862). They drive off Confederate-allied Indians, who scatter to the south and west. The invading army pushes through the Cherokee and Creek Nations to the Canadian River before the soldiers are called back East following the Union's decisive victory at Gettysburg.

July 3

Rebellion leader Little Crow is murdered.

Near Acton, Minnesota, a white farmer comes upon Little Crow, the Dakota leader of the Minnesota Uprising (see entry for AUGUST 18 TO SEPTEMBER 23, 1862), picking berries with his son. The farmer shoots the Indian dead and disposes of his body at a local slaughterhouse. Reflecting the hatred whites of the area feel for Little Crow, the Minnesota legislature votes to award $500 to his murderer.

"Another shot was heard, and another and another. The firing gradually picked up, and soon it sounded like frying, with bullets hitting all over the cave. This went on nearly all afternoon. Then the firing ceased, but, by that time, nearly all of the Navajos were killed. Men, women, children, young men and girls were all killed on the cliffs. Some just slid off the cliffs. . . . At the bottom were piles of dead Diné [Navajo]; only a few survived. Blood could be seen from the top of the cliffs all the way down to the bottom."

—Navajo Eli Gorman, on the invasion of Canyon de Chelly by Kit Carson's troops

July 22

The U.S. Army launches a military campaign against the Navajo (Dineh).

After subjugating the Mescalero Apache (see entry for SPRING 1863), Brigadier General James H. Carleton prepares to war against the Navajo (Dineh) tribe. In June, he declares that any Navajo who has not surrendered by July 20 "will be considered as hostile, and treated accordingly." He makes little attempt to let the Navajo people know of his order, however. Two days after his deadline, the army begins its military campaign against the tribe. By September, field troops under the command of Kit Carson are waging a full-scale operation. In addition to capturing "hostiles," they set about destroying the Navajo's fields, houses, and livestock herds. (See also FEBRUARY TO MARCH 1864.)

December 26

Dakota rebels are hanged in a public execution.

Following the Minnesota Uprising (see entry for AUGUST 18 TO SEPTEMBER 23, 1862), many of the Indian rebels fled their homeland for what is now Dakota Territory and Canada. Of those who stayed behind, about 1,300 people, mostly women and children, are exiled to the desolate Crow Creek region of the Dakota Territory, while more than 300 are arrested. Although those arrested deny any involvement in the killing of whites during the rebellion, all are sentenced to death. Most of the condemned are saved by President Abraham Lincoln, who, ignoring the protests of Minnesota authorities, commutes the sentence of all but 38. Before a crowd of angry whites, these Indians are hanged in Mankato, Minnesota, in the largest mass execution in U.S. history.

1864

February to March

The Navajo (Dineh) endure the Long Walk.

During the early weeks of 1864, thousands of cold and hungry Navajo (Dineh) surrender to the U.S.

The hanging of 38 Dakota Sioux convicted of participating in the Minnesota Uprising of 1862. The event was the largest public execution in the history of the United States. *(Library of Congress, USZ62-37940)*

Army after soldiers laid waste their homes and lands (see entry for JULY 22, 1863). The defeated Indians are ordered by Brigadier General James H. Carleton to relocate to Bosque Redondo, an area in what is now east-central New Mexico that the army established as the new home of the Navajo and Mescalero Apache (see entry for SPRING 1863). Although a few wagons are available to carry their belongings, the Navajo are forced to make the grueling 300-mile journey on foot. Anyone who complains or falls behind is shot and left for dead. More than 10 percent of the Navajo sent to Bosque Redondo die en route.

Their troubles continue after they reach the fort. The water supplies are inadequate, little wood is available, and the land is so infertile that it is virtually unfarmable. Homesick and demoralized, hundreds of Navajo run away to escape the horrendous living conditions. Hundreds of others fall victim to starvation and disease.

July 28

The U.S. Army battles Dakota rebels at Killdeer Mountain.

Brigadier General Alfred Sully leads a force of 2,000 to Killdeer Mountain (also known as Tahkahokuty Mountain), in what is now northwestern North Dakota. There, Dakota Sioux who participated in the Minnesota Uprising (see entry for AUGUST 18

TO SEPTEMBER 23, 1862) have come to live with their Lakota Sioux relatives. The Indians, numbering as many as 6,000, initially hold off Sully's men but are eventually forced to flee. In addition to about 100 casualties, the Sioux suffer the loss of supplies and weapons destroyed by the army after the Indians retreat.

August 13

The Third Colorado Cavalry is formed to fight Indians.

After petitioning the federal government, Colorado Territory governor John Evans is granted permission to recruit the Third Colorado Cavalry, a special military unit whose sole purpose is to subdue area Indians. The cavalrymen are nicknamed the "Hundred Dazers," because they are to serve for only 100 days. Coming only a month before Coloradans will be asked to vote for or against statehood, Evans's insistence on forming the group is largely meant to placate voters calling for a military solution to outbreaks of Indian violence in the territory.

September 28

Southern Cheyenne leader Black Kettle asks for peace.

Following a successful peace council with Edward W. Wynkoop, the commander of Fort Lyon in southeastern Colorado Territory, Black Kettle of the

Navajo laborers working under the watch of armed U.S. Army soldiers at Bosque Redondo *(Courtesy Museum of New Mexico, Neg. no. 1816)*

Southern Cheyenne accompanies Wynkoop to Camp Weld in Denver. There he meets with Colonel John M. Chivington and John Evans, the territory's military commander and governor. After hours of debate, Chivington tells Black Kettle that the only way his followers can live in peace is by surrendering to Wynkoop at Fort Lyon.

Black Kettle leaves the meeting believing that the territorial officials have promised not to attack his people as long as they camp close to the fort. Neither Chivington nor Evans, however, are interested in a peaceful coexistence between Colorado whites and the Southern Cheyenne. Politically ambitious, both are sensitive to public pressure to drive the Indians from the territory (see entry for AUGUST 13, 1864). On the very day of his meeting with Black Kettle, Evans writes General Samuel R. Curtis, "I want no peace til the Indians suffer more."

November 25

Kit Carson's troops attack Comanche and Kiowa at Adobe Walls.

The First New Mexico Cavalry, led by Colonel Christopher "Kit" Carson, descends on a winter camp of Kiowa, who have been threatening forts in present-day New Mexico. Hearing of the attack, several thousand Kiowa and Comanche in the area rush to join the battle. Armed with two howitzers, the soldiers hold off the Indian forces and manage to kill some 100 warriors before retreating the next day. (See also entry for JUNE 17, 1874.)

November 29

The Colorado cavalry murders hundreds of Indians in the Sand Creek Massacre.

At dawn, led by Colonel John M. Chivington, the 700 soldiers of the Third Colorado Cavalry (see entry for AUGUST 13, 1864) ride into the camp of Black Kettle's Southern Cheyenne followers on the Sand Creek near Fort Lyon. Based on conversations with the territorial governor two months

earlier, Black Kettle believes he has established a peace with the United States (see entry for SEPTEMBER 28, 1864). Accordingly, an American flag and a white flag of surrender are raised on a pole outside his tipi.

Angry that they have been castigated in the press as the "Bloodless Third" for not battling the Colorado Indians, the cavalrymen ignore the promises made to Black Kettle and open fire on the camp, determined to take no prisoners. As the Southern Cheyenne and visiting Southern Arapaho emerge from their tipis, the troops mow them down. Southern Cheyenne leader White Antelope, wearing a peace medal given to him by President Abraham Lincoln, is among the first to be killed. Those who survive the cavalry's initial attack rush toward the sandy creekbed, where they frantically try to cover themselves with sand to evade the relentless killers. Hours later, when the cavalry rides away, approximately 200 Indians, two-thirds of them women and children, lie dead. Many of the corpses are scalped or otherwise grotesquely mutilated.

> "That night will never be forgotten as long as any of us who went through it are alive.... Many who had lost wives, husbands, and children, or friends, went back down the creek and crept over the battleground among the naked and mutilated bodies of the dead. Few were found alive, for the soldiers had done their work thoroughly."
> —Southern Cheyenne George Bent on the Sand Creek Massacre

When news of the massacre is reported, non-Indians in the area—terrified by the violent raids of the Dog Soldiers, the war society of the Southern Cheyenne—hail Chivington and his men as heroes. They are cheered as they parade through the streets of Denver, and whites flock to see Indian scalps displayed as war trophies in the city's opera house. (See entries for JANUARY 10, 1864, and for JANUARY TO FEBRUARY 1864.)

1865

Cherokee Jesse Chisholm blazes the Chisholm Trail.

Cherokee interpreter and businessman Jesse Chisholm drives a wagon from Texas to his trading post in Kansas. Following his wagon ruts, others begin to take this route north. Popularly known as the Chisholm Trail, the path will become the primary route Texas cattlemen use to drive their herds to Kansas railroad terminals, from which the cattle can be transported to eastern markets.

The Winnebago receive a reservation in Nebraska.

The federal government establishes the Nebraska Winnebago Reservation, an act that ends their 25-year "trail of tears." After the United States forced the Winnebago to cede the last of their original homeland, the tribe, beginning in 1840, was removed five times to lands in present-day Iowa, Minnesota, South Dakota, and Nebraska. During the Removal period, more than 700 Winnebago died.

January 1

A Texas Ranger attack brings on the Kickapoo Uprising.

In the early 1850s, 700 Kickapoo left what is now Kansas to escape reservation life and relocated to Mexico. About 15 years later, they are set upon at Dove Creek by the Texas Rangers, who crossed the international border to fight the Indians. Although the Kickapoo win the battle, they are enraged by the unprovoked attack. Their fury unleashes almost 10 years of violence, during which

the Kickapoo launch a vicious and effective military campaign against Texas ranches and settlements along the Rio Grande. (See also entry for MAY 18, 1873.)

January 10

A congressional committee issues a report on the Sand Creek Massacre.

The rumored horrors of the Sand Creek Massacre (see entry for NOVEMBER 29, 1864) prompt Congress's

"As to Colonel Chivington, your committee can hardly find fitting terms to describe his conduct. Wearing the uniform of the United States, which should be the emblem of justice and humanity[,] . . . he deliberately planned and executed a foul and dastardly massacre which would have disgraced the veriest savage among those who were the victims of his cruelty.... [T]he truth is that he surprised and murdered, in cold blood, the unsuspecting men, women, and children on Sand Creek . . . and then returned to Denver and boasted of the brave deeds he and the men under his command had performed."

—from an 1865 report on the Sand Creek Massacre by a Joint Special Committe of the United States Congress

Joint Committee on the Conduct of the War to hold hearings to determine the facts of the event. The committee's final report is a scathing indictment of the conduct of the soldiers responsible, reserving particularly harsh words for their commander, Colonel John M. Chivington. Although the committee recommends that Chivington and his troops be punished, no action will ever be taken against them.

January to February

Plains Indians avenge the Sand Creek Massacre.

News of the Sand Creek Massacre (see entry for NOVEMBER 29, 1864) spreads through the Plains, leading to a new rash of violence. Lakota Sioux, Cheyenne, and Arapaho warriors attack whites along the South Platte River, raiding livestock herds, charring wagon trains, and sacking the Colorado town of Julesburg twice. Despite their ferocity, most of the Indians soon decide to abandon the confrontations with whites and move to live with northern kin.

Spring

Thousands of U.S. troops are sent to the Plains.

Prompted by the violent attacks by Plains Indians early in the year (see entry for JANUARY TO FEBRUARY 1864), the United States launches a massive offensive led by General John Pope, one of the most ardent supporters of a military solution to unrest on the Plains. Under his command, more than 6,000 troops are sent into the area to protect trade and travel routes from Indian warriors. The campaign will later be deemed a failure: The soldiers prove difficult to manage, their provisions are hugely expensive to purchase and transport, and many troops, exhausted from fighting the Civil War, desert their posts.

Spring

Henry Berry Lowry heads a band of Lumbee outlaws.

As the Confederacy faces defeat, the already tense relationship between whites and Lumbee Indians in Robeson County, North Carolina, turns violent. After a group of whites kills his father and brother, a Lumbee named Henry Berry Lowry leads a small band of relatives and friends in looting and killing to avenge their deaths. Lowry's spree will continue for 10 years, during which he will kill or drive from the county all of his kinsmen's murderers. Never captured or killed by his pursuers, Lowry will become a revered folk hero among the Lumbee.

April 9

Seneca Ely S. Parker records the Appomattox surrender.

As the military secretary to General Ulysses S. Grant, Ely S. Parker, a Seneca lawyer and engineer, is present at the Appomattox Court House when the Confederate Army of Northern Virginia, represented by General Robert E. Lee, surrenders to the Union, thus ending the Civil War. Parker is entrusted with writing out the final copies of the surrender terms. Introduced to Parker, Lee quips, "I'm glad to see one real American." Parker replies, "We are all Americans." (See also entries for 1869 and 1871.)

June 23

Cherokee general Stand Watie surrenders.

Two months after the surrender of Robert E. Lee, Cherokee leader Stand Watie becomes the last Confederate general to surrender to the United States. The only Indian to attain the rank of general in the Confederate army, Watie had been in charge of protecting the Cherokee Nation from invasion by Union troops (see entry for SUMMER 1862).

July 14

The Civil War ends in Indian Territory.

With the surrender of the Cherokee and Caddo, the Civil War ends in Indian Territory. The war has taken a tremendous toll on the Indians of the region. Among the Confederate-allied tribes, as many as 10,000 people have been killed. Hardest hit have been the Cherokee, Creek, and Seminole, whose populations have dropped as much as 25 percent because of war-related deaths.

The world of the survivors is dominated by scarcity and chaos. Many buildings and fields have been burned or otherwise destroyed during the war. Indian Territory residents are further terrorized in the final days of the war by Indian and non-Indian deserters, who roam through the countryside in gangs, looting and killing. (See also entry for SEPTEMBER 1866.)

July 26

The Cheyenne and Lakota attack troops at the Platte Bridge.

In response to rumors of an impending Indian attack, a detachment of soldiers is sent from Platte Bridge Station, near present-day Casper, Wyoming, to protect a wagon train approaching from the West. As the soldiers cross the bridge, they are surrounded by a force of as many as 3,000 Cheyenne and Lakota warriors. Repelling the Indians with their howitzer, most of the soldiers are able to escape to the station's stockade.

October

The Edmunds Commission signs a peace treaty with Lakota Sioux leaders.

Organized by Dakota territorial governor Newton Edmunds, a delegation solicits the signatures on a peace treaty of several Lakota Sioux chiefs already friendly with whites. The event is the governor's attempt to reshape public opinion about Dakota. Many settlers avoid the territory because of its reputation for violence between Indians and whites.

October 18

The Kiowa and Comanche sign the Little Arkansas Treaty.

Wanting to open lands for the construction of railroads through Kansas, U.S. treaty commissioners meet in council with Kiowa and Comanche leaders by the Little Arkansas River, near what is now Wichita, Kansas. The resulting treaty requires the tribes to stay in a designated area south of the Kansas border, stop attacking frontier settlements, and release white prisoners held by the Indians.

November

The Mescalero Apache escape from Bosque Redondo.

Confined at Bosque Redondo for more than two years (see entry for SPRING 1863), the Mescalero Apache are driven to desperation by hunger and disease. In addition, they are forced to share their area with the Navajo (Dineh), their traditional enemies. Unable to stand these living conditions any longer, the Mescalero flee Bosque Redondo and return to their homeland, holing up in the mountains there to evade recapture by U.S. troops.

6

1866 TO 1890
FROM RESISTANCE TO RESERVATIONS

In 1869, while touring Indian Territory, General Philip M. Sheridan was introduced to a Comanche man who was described to him as a "good Indian." According to later reports, Sheridan replied, "The only good Indians I ever saw were dead," a statement eventually rephrased in the popular mind as "The only good Indian is a dead Indian." Even though Sheridan denied ever saying these words, they were to become a favorite quotation in discussions of the so-called Indian Problem—that is, what should be done about the Indians blocking the western expansion of the United States. Those seeking to annihilate the Indians found a rallying cry in Sheridan's pithy phrase, whereas those hoping to assimilate tribal peoples quoted the words in horror.

Official Indian policy after the Civil War reflected both attitudes. Exhausted from warfare, the government under the Grant administration in 1869 adopted the Peace Policy, which proposed to end the Indian Problem without further bloodshed and without the expense of protracted military campaigns. Two years earlier, a commission had been sent west to negotiate with troublesome Indians treaties that would require them to stay within specified reservation boundaries, thus opening up vast areas of hunting grounds for white settlement. Treaties were negotiated with nearly all major Plains Indian tribes. Yet these agreements meant little. Most Indians neither understood nor accepted their provisions, and those few who did hardly felt bound to uphold them.

The treaties, however, were far from useless from the government's perspective. Now if Indians left their reservations, it had justification for using the military to force their return. Non-Indian settlers fearful of "renegade" Indians often demanded this military protection, while unemployed Civil War veterans were eager to sign up to fight. As a result, the Peace Policy helped to usher in a new era of brutal and bloody Indian wars.

During the Indian Wars, many brilliant Indian leaders of great bravery and cunning emerged. There were Red Cloud, Crazy Horse, and Sitting Bull of the Lakota; Quanah Parker of the Comanche; Geronimo and Cochise of the Apache; and Chief Joseph of the Nez Perce, to name only a few. But despite their leadership, Indian forces, already weakened by disease and inadequate rations, were ultimately outarmed and outmanned when pitted against U.S. soldiers and state militiamen.

Military campaigns were only one means used to destroy traditional Plains Indian society. The railroads joining East and West disturbed the migrations of buffalo herds, thus threatening the animals on which Plains Indians relied for every necessity—from food to building materials to fuel. The buffalo's doom was further sealed when eastern tanneries began to make leather from their hides in the 1870s. To cash in on the demand for this new product, white hunters flocked to the West and littered the Plains with bloody carcasses. Recognizing that Plains Indian culture could not exist without the buffalo, the military encouraged this mass killing, which in a matter of decades resulted in the near extinction of the once-great herds.

The ways of western Indians were under siege also by reformers, who hoped to see the Indians assimilated into mainstream, non-Indian society. Calling themselves the "Friends of the Indians," they mounted missionary efforts to convert Indians to Christianity and supported legislation that would help transform Indian hunters into settled farmers. One of the Assimilationists' most effective tools were Indian boarding schools. These institutions separated Indian children from traditional communities, then indoctrinated them in non-Indian customs. The value of this education was not always clear. Rather than assimilating into white society, many boarding-school students upon graduation found themselves adrift, alienated from both the Indian and non-Indian worlds.

Even more devastating to Indian society was the Friends of the Indian's trumpeting of the Allotment policy. As the government whittled away at reservation lands, these reformers rightly feared that Indians were in danger of losing the small portions of their ancestral lands they still retained. Allotment supporters believed that the best means of protecting Indian lands was to divide reservations into small plots known as *allotments*. These tracts would be held as private property and thus would be legally protected from white encroachment. In part through reformers' lobbying efforts, the U.S. Congress passed the General Allotment Act of 1887, which provided for the large-scale allotment of Indian lands, as well as the sale of "surplus land" left over after all qualified allottees received their tracts. The policy ultimately had the opposite effect from what its most benevolent supporters had envisioned: In a matter of decades, nearly 100 million acres of Indian land would pass into non-Indian hands as a direct result of Allotment.

Amid the many assaults on their traditional ways, reservation Indians in the late 19th century increasing looked to new religions for comfort. The messages preached by Indian prophets such as Wodziwob, Nakaidoklini, and John Slocum varied in their particulars, but all promised adherents a return to the traditional world Indians had known before the arrival of non-Indians in their lands.

The most influential of these visionaries was the Northern Paiute (Numu) Wovoka. He told followers that if they lived in peace with whites and danced the Paiute's traditional Round Dance, their dead ancestors would come back to life. Wovoka's message spread quickly from his people to tribes of the Plains. Their version of his teachings, which became known as the Ghost Dance, prophesied that non-Indians would die as their ancestors were revived. To demoralized reservation populations, the appeal of the Ghost Dance was obvious. For reasons just as clear, it also greatly unnerved their non-Indian neighbors.

However understandable, white panic over the Ghost Dance led to tragedy. Army troops sent to subdue the "rebelling" Indians set upon a group of Ghost Dancers preparing to settle near the Pine Ridge Agency to show their desire to keep the peace. In the ensuing melee, more than 300 Lakota women, men, and children were slaughtered. Often cited as the end of Indian resistance in the West, the massacre at Wounded Knee created a wound in Indian and white relations that more than a century later has yet to heal fully.

1866

The Indian Scouting Service is established.

Amidst military budget cuts following the Civil War, the army asks Congress to form the Indian Scouting Service as a permanent branch of the military. Indian scouts are hired to provide the military with information about the geography of the West and the ways of tribes in the Plains and the Southwest. Generally, scouts are recruited from Indian groups that are the traditional enemies of tribes at war with the United States. (See also entry for 1943.)

The Hopi ask the New Mexico governor for famine relief.

Because of a severe drought in the Southwest in 1864, the Hopi people face famine. They dispatch a delegation to request help from the governor of New Mexico, which was organized as a territory in 1850. Assuming the Indians are hostile, white authorities put the group in prison. They are released soon afterward, but the incident embitters the Hopi, whose population will plummet due to starvation and epidemic disease throughout the late 1860s.

The Supreme Court rules in the Kansas Indians case.

Following Kansas's admittance into the Union in 1861, the state has attempted to collect property taxes from tribes living within its borders. Ten tribes join together to bring suit against the state, claiming that they do not owe Kansas taxes because they are not bound by its laws. In an important legal victory for tribal sovereignty, the Supreme Court finds that as long as the tribes function as legal entities separate from Kansas, they are not obligated to pay state taxes.

The U.S. Army launches a campaign against the Snake Indians.

The Yahuskin and Walpapi bands of the Northern Paiute (Numu), known to whites as the Snake Indians, make a series of raids on mines in what is now southern Oregon and Idaho. General George Crook and the men under his command set out to punish the raiders, initiating one of the longest campaigns fought against an Indian group. Crook's troops and the Snake will fight nearly 50 battles over the next two years (see entry for July 1868).

January 1

U.S. officials define freedmen's status in Indian Territory.

The government appoints Major General John B. Sanborn to regulate the absorption of former African-American slaves into the tribes of Indian Territory. In a series of documents, Sanborn instructs Indian agents to explain to the slaves that they are now free. He also directs that freedmen should be allowed to sign up for Indian rations and be offered 160 acres of Indian land to farm.

Although some tribes, such as the Creek and Seminole, largely comply, others resist taking freedmen into their nations. The Choctaw, for instance, refuse to give their freedmen citizenship and push the U.S. government to remove their former slaves from their lands. The Choctaw will not accept freedmen as citizens until the end of the 19th century.

June

The United States calls a peace council at Fort Laramie.

U.S. Army officials meet with Red Cloud, Man-Afraid-of-His-Horses, Spotted Tail, and other Indian leaders at Fort Laramie in present-day Wyoming. Their aim is to end the Indians' sporadic attacks on whites traveling through the Powder River area on the Bozeman Trail en route to Montana gold mines (see entry for 1862). The Indians are even more agitated by the growing military presence in their lands.

During the meeting, the officers, while trying to placate the Indians with gifts, reveal the army's plans to build forts along the Bozeman. With the announcement, Red Cloud storms out of the fort, with his followers in tow. The army concludes a treaty with Spotted Tail and several other Lakota Sioux, but with Red Cloud's opposition, the council ends with little hope for long-term peace. (See also entry for JULY 1866.)

July

The U.S. Army establishes forts on the Bozeman Trail.

To protect the whites traveling along the Bozeman Trail, the army constructs three military posts— Fort Reno, Fort Phil Kearny, and Fort C. F. Smith (see entry for JUNE 1866). The presence of the forts outrages the Lakota Sioux, Led by war chief Red Cloud, Lakota warriors vow to battle the troops stationed at the forts in order to maintain their control over the region. The series of attacks they stage will become known as Red Cloud's War.

September

U.S. officials meet with Confederate-allied tribes at Fort Smith.

To make a formal peace with the United States, leaders from the Five Civilized Tribes and other groups that sided with the Confederacy (see entry for SUMMER 1861) are called to a conference at Fort Smith, Arkansas. Called the "Great Father's [President's] erring children" by the commissioner of Indian affairs, the Indian leaders, even those who supported the Union during the Civil War, are treated as conquered peoples.

The U.S. officials demand harsh concessions from the rebel tribes. They are to sell their lands in western Indian Territory to the United States, allow railroads to be build throughout their nations, free their slaves and make them full tribal members, and accept a territorial government organized by the United States. Although most of the leaders passively accept these terms, some, particularly John Ross of the Cherokee (see entry for SUMMER 1861 and SEPTEMBER 12, 1862), object vigorously to the threat the provisions pose to tribal sovereignty.

September 1

Navajo (Dineh) leader Manuelito surrenders.

When the U.S. Army waged its campaign against the Navajo (Dineh) (see entry for JULY 22, 1863), tribal leader Manuelito and his followers evaded capture by moving constantly and hiding in mountains and canyons. To the Navajo who surrendered and were forced to move to Bosque Redondo (see entry for FEBRUARY TO MARCH 1864), Manuelito became a potent symbol of resistance.

After three years, unable to fight any longer, Manuelito and 23 followers are finally forced to surrender. En route to Bosque Redondo, they are marched down the streets of Santa Fe as evidence to area whites of the army's success in its war against the Navajo.

December 21

Eighty soldiers are killed in the Fetterman Fight.

Eighty U.S. troops led by Captain William J. Fetterman are stationed at Fort Phil Kearny, located near present-day Sheridan, Wyoming, to protect whites traveling on the Bozeman Trail (see entry for JULY 1866). Disobeying orders, Fetterman leads

"I do not understand how the massacre of Colonel Fetterman's party could have been so complete. We must act with vindictive earnestness against the Sioux, even to their extermination, men, women and children. Nothing less will ever reach the root of the case."

—General William Tecumseh Sherman in a letter to his friend General Ulysses S. Grant his men far from the fort to guard a train carrying wood. As they pass over Lodge Trail Ridge, they are ambushed by some 2,000 Lakota, Arapaho, and Cheyenne warriors. In the bloody fight that follows, all of the soldiers are killed. Indian casualties number between 10 and 100.

Reports of the Fetterman Fight, known to the Indians as the Battle of the Hundred Slain, horrifies U.S. officials. The turning point in Red Cloud's War, the slaughter reveals the army's inability to police the Bozeman Trail in the face of Indian resistance.

1867

January

The Doolittle Report advocates the reservation system.

In 1865, in the wake of the Sand Creek Massacre (see entry for NOVEMBER 29, 1864), three congressional committees were charged with evaluating the condition of Indian tribes in the West. The fact-finding mission was headed by Wisconsin senator James R. Doolittle, the chairman of the Senate Committee on Indian Affairs.

The findings of the commission are published in the Doolittle Report, which challenges the wisdom of a military solution to Indian-white conflicts on the Plains. Concluding that the declining buffalo population and increasing incursions by whites have left Indians desperate, the report recommends that Indians be placed on reservations where they can be taught to farm and adopt white values and customs. The document holds the germ of the Peace Policy (see entry for JANUARY 25, 1869), which will soon dominate the United States's dealings with western tribes.

April to July

The Lakota and Cheyenne are attacked during the Hancock campaign.

A military expedition headed by Major General Winfield Scott Hancock is sent to frighten the Indians of the central Plains into compliance. Following a tense conference with Indian leaders at Fort Larned in Kansas, Hancock's troops move toward a nearby village, but the Lakota and Cheyenne there escape without incident. They are followed by soldiers led by Lieutenant George Armstrong Custer for months throughout Kansas, Nebraska, and Colorado Territory. During the chase, the Lakota and Cheyenne evade the troops, all the while raiding wagon trains and stagecoaches carrying whites across the Plains.

July

The U.S. Peace Commission is formed to end Plains conflicts.

Alarmed by the Fetterman Fight (see entry for DECEMBER 21, 1866), Congress establishes a commission, headed by Civil War general William Tecumseh Sherman, to negotiate peace settlements with the Indians of the Plains. By creating the commission, the U.S. government implicitly acknowledges the military's failure to subdue the warriors led by Red Cloud, who have been waging war against troops stationed along the Bozeman Trail (see entry for JULY 1866). Some members of Congress, particularly those from the West, denounce the decision, favoring a stronger military presence over negotiation with the Indians. (See also entries for JANUARY 1868 and OCTOBER 7 TO 8, 1868.)

July 1

The Dominion of Canada is established.

The British North America Act establishes the four Canadian colonies (Nova Scotia, New Brunswick, Quebec, and Ontario) as the Dominion of Canada. In Canada's new constitution, the federal government in Ottawa is charged with all negotiations with the 23,000 indigenous people within the dominion's borders. The government is also responsible for administering reserves, lands set aside for Indian use.

August 1 to 2

The Cheyenne and Lakota battle U.S. troops in the Hayfield and Wagon Box Fights.

On August 1, a Cheyenne and Lakota Sioux war party falls on a group of whites cutting hay near Fort C. F. Smith on the Bozeman Trail (see entry for JULY 1866). The haycutters and about 20 troops guarding them retreat into a small log corral they built for protection in case of Indian attack. Armed with new breech-loading rifles, the soldiers are able to hold off the warriors until reinforcements arrive.

The following day, Lakota warriors led by Red Cloud attack about 30 soldiers near Fort Phil Kearny, the target of the Fetterman Fight a year before (see entry for DECEMBER 21, 1866). The troops are guarding whites loading logs into wagon boxes on an open plain at the foot of the Bighorn Mountains. Barricading themselves behind the wagon boxes, the soldiers, like those in the previous day's fight, suffer few casualties, largely because of their superior weaponry. Popularly known as the Hayfield Fight and the Wagon Box Fight, these two encounters will be the last major conflicts of Red Cloud's War.

October 18

Alaska becomes part of the United States.

By the terms of the Treaty of Cession with Russia, Alaska becomes the property of the United States. In return, the United States agrees to pay Russia $7.2 million. Russia's right to sell the territory is questionable, however, because it has never entered negotiations with Alaskan Natives for the cession of their territory. The United States similarly makes no effort to compensate the natives for their land. Also without their consultation or knowledge, the treaty stipulates that the "uncivilized tribes" of Alaska will be subject to whatever laws the United States chooses to apply to them.

October 21 to 28

U.S. Peace Commission meets with Plains tribes at Medicine Lodge Creek.

Five thousand Kiowa, Comanche, Southern Arapaho, and Southern Cheyenne Indians meet near

Fort Larned in Kansas at the invitation of the U.S. Peace Commission (see entry for JULY 1867). Accompanied by some 600 soldiers, the commissioners hope to reach a settlement that will end the conflicts with these tribes and guarantee that railroads can be built through their lands without interference.

> "All the chiefs of the Kiowas, Comanches, and Arapahos are here today; they have come to listen to good words. We have been waiting here a long time to see you and are getting tired. All the land south of Arkansas belongs to the Kiowas and Comanches, and I don't want to give away any of it. I love the land and the buffalo and will not part with it. I want you to understand well what I say. Write it on paper. Let the Great Father [U.S. president] see it, and let me hear what he has to say."
> —Kiowa leader Satanta during the negotiation of the Treaty of Medicine Lodge Creek

Under a shaded arbor, the commissioners deliver speeches in which they insist that the Indians cede the majority of their hunting lands in exchange for reservations. The Indians are resistant, but Kiowa and Comanche leaders, offered many gifts and eager to end the conference, sign the commissioners' treaty. The agreement relinquishes the tribes' claim to 90 million acres for firm title to nearly 3 million acres of land in Indian Territory, which was forfeited by the Five Civilized Tribes in their peace treaty with the

United States after the Civil War (see entry for JULY 14, 1865). In the Treaty of Medicine Lodge Creek, both sides also promise to live in peace with one another. However, because many Kiowa and Comanche do not consider the treaty binding, sporadic fighting will continue between the tribes and Americans throughout the next decade.

1868

The surgeon general calls for the collection of Indian skulls.

To research Indian intelligence, the surgeon general of the United States orders that Indian skulls be collected from grave sites and battlefields. As a result, more than 4,000 Native American skulls will be sent to the Army Medical Hospital for study. By measuring the size and shape of the skulls, scientists attempt to prove that Indians are inherently the intellectual inferiors of whites.

January 7

The U.S. Peace Commission reveals corruption in Indian agencies.

The U.S. Peace Commission, formed by Congress the previous year (see entry for JULY 1867), issues its first report on the living conditions in western Indian communities. The report maintains that corruption abounds among Indian agents, the Bureau of Indian Affairs employees charged with administering reservations. The commission also cites the need for a Christian influence on reservation populations, a need that is not being met by the current agents.

Spring

Navajo (Dineh) leaders petition for their return to their homeland.

Manuelito, Baboncito, and other Navajo (Dineh) leaders travel to Washington, D.C., to discuss the tribe's confinement at Bosque Redondo (see entry

for FEBRUARY TO MARCH 1864). In a meeting with President Andrew Johnson, they describe the horrendous living conditions at the site, which does not have enough farmable land or drinkable water to sustain their population. Their claims and pleas to return to their homeland persuade the government to send peace commissioners to investigate the Navajo's complaints. After visiting Bosque Redondo, the commissioners report that the Navajo are living in "absolute poverty and despair."

April to August

Lakota Sioux leaders meet with the U.S. Peace Commission at Fort Laramie.

Eager to end Red Cloud's War, the U.S. Peace Commission (see entry for JULY 1867) asks Lakota Sioux leaders to a meeting at Fort Laramie in present-day Wyoming. Some friendly Lakota, including Spotted Tail, agree to sign a treaty, largely in order to obtain the gifts the commissioners are offering in exchange for compliance. Red Cloud, however, steadfastly refuses to speak with the Americans until they abandon their three forts along the Bozeman Trail (see entry for JULY 1866).

Worn down by his resistance, the U.S. Army finally withdraws from the posts, two of which are promptly burned to the ground by the Lakota. Even after the commissioners have satisfied Red Cloud's demands, the leader ignores the commissions' continued overtures, while his people prepare their store of meat for the winter. (See also entry for NOVEMBER 7, 1868.)

June 1

The Navajo (Dineh) sign the Treaty of 1868.

Declaring peace between the U.S. government and the Navajo (Dineh), the Treaty of 1868 creates a 3.5-million acre reservation for the tribe in the heart of their ancestral territory in northern Arizona and New Mexico. Although the reservation is the largest in the United States, it includes

Lakota leaders with U.S. peace commissioners during the negotiation of the 1868 Treaty of Fort Laramie *(South Dakota State Historical Society/State Archives)*

"The nights and days were long before it came time for us to go to our homes. The day before we were to start we went a little way towards home, because we were so anxious to start. . . . We told the drivers to whip the mules, we were in such a hurry. When we saw the top of the mountain from Albuquerque we wondered if it was our mountain, and we felt like talking to the ground, we loved it so, and some of the old men and women cried with joy when they reached their homes."

—Navajo leader Manuelito, describing his tribe's 1868 return to their homeland

only about one-fifth of the Navajo's original homeland.

The treaty also ends the tribe's four-year incarceration at Bosque Redondo in eastern New Mexico, where the Navajo had been forcibly removed by the U.S. Army (see entry for FEBRUARY TO MARCH 1864). The tribe's return to their homeland and subsequent efforts to rebuild their lives and traditions there marks the beginning of the modern Navajo Nation.

July

The Snake Indians surrender to the U.S. Army.

Ending a two-year military campaign against them (see entry for 1866), 800 Northern Paiute (Numu) known as the Snake surrender at Fort Harney in Oregon. The Snake Indians fought nearly 50 battles with troops led by General George Crook. During these conflicts, approximately 500 Snake were killed, including the influential Chief Pauline.

July 8

The Fourteenth Amendment denies the vote to Indians.

Congress ratifies the Fourteenth Amendment, which grants citizenship rights to African-American males. The amendment also specifies that "Indians not taxed" will not be counted in determining the number of a state's representatives in Congress. This provision will later be cited in the Supreme Court decision of *Elk v. Wilkins* (see entry for 1884), which determines that the guarantees of citizenship in the Fourteenth Amendment do not apply to Indians.

September 17

Indian warriors attack U.S. troops on Beecher Island.

After several months of skirmishes between Indians and whites in Kansas, a company of soldiers led by Major George A. Forsyth follow a group of Indian raiders to the Arikara River. Camped on an island, the 50 troops are set upon by a war party of 600 Cheyenne, Lakota Sioux, and Arapaho. The siege continues for more than a week, during which the soldiers suffer many casualties and are forced to eat the flesh of their fallen horses to survive. After nine days, reinforcements finally arrive to drive the Indians away. The island will become known as Beecher Island after Lieutenant Frederick Beecher (nephew of the abolitionist Henry Ward Beecher), who is killed in the conflict.

October 7 to 8

The U.S. Peace Commission meets for the last time.

In the wake of the Battle of Beecher Island (see entry for SEPTEMBER 17, 1868), the mission of the U.S. Peace Commission (see entry for JULY 1867) is reexamined during a meeting in Chicago. Rallying around General William T. Sherman, the majority of those in attendance maintain that Indian tribes should no longer be recognized as sovereign nations, therefore eliminating the need for the United States to make peace treaties with them. When the meeting disbands, so does the commission.

November 7

Red Cloud approves the Fort Laramie treaty.

Red Cloud and his followers are the last Lakota Sioux to agree to the Treaty of Fort Laramie (see entry for APRIL TO AUGUST 1868). In the final treaty, the Lakota promise to end their attacks on U.S. forts. In exchange, the United States agrees to abandon its forts on the Bozeman Trail (see entry for JULY 1866), prevent non-Indians from settling along the trail, and establish the Great Sioux Reservation between the Missouri River and the Rocky Mountains for the Lakota's "absolute and undisturbed" use. The federal government also promises to provide the Indians with schools and agencies from which the government will distribute supplies, such as clothing and seeds. The treaty includes a provision stating that it cannot be amended unless three-fourths of Lakota males approve the change. (See also entries for APRIL TO JUNE 1870 and for 1877.)

November 27

Black Kettle's band is slaughtered in the Washita River Massacre.

The Southern Cheyenne led by Black Kettle are camped along the Washita River on the reservation established for them by the Medicine Lodge Creek Treaty (see entry for OCTOBER 21 TO 28, 1867), when a war party of young Cheyenne men approach the camp. The warriors, who have been raiding white settlements in Kansas, are followed by the Seventh Cavalry, headed by Lieutenant Colonel George Armstrong Custer.

Blaming Black Kettle's people erroneously for the recent attacks, Custer's men attack the Washita camp at dawn. Eerily reminiscent of the Sand Creek Massacre (see entry for November 29, 1864)—which occurred four years before almost to the day—the soldiers rush to slaughter men, women, and children who have been living peacefully on their reservation. Before nearby bands of warriors are able to come to their rescue and chase off the Americans, more than 100 people are killed, including Black Kettle—a Sand Creek survivor who out of fear for his followers' safety consistently urged them to capitulate to the United States.

"[I]n his native village, on the war path, and when raiding our frontier settlements and lines of travel, the Indian forfeits his claim to the appellation of the '*noble* red man.' We see him as he is, and, so far as all knowledge goes, as he ever has been, a savage in every sense of the word; . . . one whose cruel and ferocious nature far exceeds that of any wild beast of the desert."

—George Armstrong Custer
in his autobiography
My Life on the Plains

1869

Ely S. Parker becomes the commissioner of Indian affairs.

The former military secretary of Ulysses S. Grant, Seneca Ely S. Parker (see entry for APRIL 9, 1865) is appointed commissioner of Indian affairs. Parker, the first Native American to hold this position, supports Grant's efforts to "civilize" Indians by compelling them to give up traditional ways and join the non-Indian mainstream both culturally and economically. (See also entry for 1871.)

"The Indian tribes of the United States are not sovereign nations, capable of making treaties. . . . But because treaties have been made with them, generally for the extinguishment of their supposed absolute title to the land inhabited by them, or over which they roam, they have become falsely impressed with the notion of national independence. It is time that this idea should be dispelled, and the government cease the cruel farce of dealing with its helpless and ignorant wards."

—Commissioner of Indian affairs
Ely S. Parker in his annual report
in 1869

Northern Paiute (Numu) prophet Wodziwob founds a new Indian religion.

Also known as Fish Lake Joe, Wodziwob attracts devoted followers on the Northern Paiute's (Numu) Walker River Reservation with his religious teachings. Wodziwob predicts that in the future all whites will die, dead Indians will come back to life, and the traditional Indian ways of life will be revived. His inspirational message resembles that preached by Wovoka, founder of the Ghost Dance movement, nearly 20 years later (see entry for JANUARY 1, 1889).

Sitting Bull is chosen head chief of the Lakota Sioux.

A council of Lakota Sioux leaders elects 36-year-old Sitting Bull as the head chief of the seven Lakota groups. Traditionally, the position had not existed. As the Lakota are increasingly pressured to live on reservations, however, they recognize the need for a single leader to guide them in their dealings with whites. Although still a young man, Sitting Bull impresses the Lakota elders with his success in battle, his courage, and his generosity to people in need.

Philip M. Sheridan praises "dead Indians."

When introduced to a Comanche chief in Indian Territory, veteran Indian fighter General Philip M. Sheridan is told the man is a "good Indian." Sheridan replies, "The only good Indians I ever saw were dead." Although Sheridan will later deny ever making the statement, his words will become famous and be frequently quoted as evidence of the U.S. Army's vicious attitude toward all Indians.

United States v. Lucero dissolves Pueblo land title.

According to the terms of the Treaty of Guadelupe Hidalgo (see entry for FEBRUARY 2, 1848), the Pueblo, as Indians, received legal title to their lands in New Mexico Territory. With whites clamoring for access to these rich landholdings, the Pueblo's claims are challenged before the New Mexico Supreme Court in *United States v. Lucero*. The judge finds that the Pueblo are in fact not Indians at all but Mexicans and therefore do not hold title to the lands they occupy according to the previous treaty. The legality of the decision will be questioned more than 40 years later in *United States v. Sandoval* (see entry for 1913).

January 25

Quakers meet with Ulysses S. Grant to discuss an Indian "Peace Policy."

Following a convention of Quakers, a delegation travels to Washington, D.C., for an audience with the President-elect Ulysses S. Grant. The group asks Grant to attempt a peaceful resolution to Indian-white conflicts and recommends that military personnel be replaced by people of strong Christian convictions as the government's liaisons with Indian groups.

In the months following the meeting, Grant puts into motion a "Peace Policy" much like that suggested by the Quakers. For the president, the primary goal of the policy is to reduce hostilities between Indians and whites in the West as quickly and inexpensively as possible. The policy's major tool is Assimilation. It aims to place Indians on reservations, where they can be watched and controlled; to replace Indian traditions with Christian values; and to force Indians to give up their traditional livelihoods and take up the lives of settled farmers. Toward these ends, Protestant clergy and lay people active in Protestant churches are hired as Indian agents and reservation schoolteachers.

Ironically, the so-called Peace Policy will usher in an era of increased Indian-white warfare in the West. By moving Indians off their traditional lands to reservations with inadequate rations and few means of making a living, the policy will often force Indians, in order to survive, to defy the government and return to their native lands—a violation of the government's Assimilation campaign that will usually elicit swift and brutal military responses.

March

Cheyenne Indians surrender to U.S. forces at Sweetwater Creek.

Searching for renegade Cheyenne, forces led by Lieutenant Colonel George Armstrong Custer discover two Indian villages along the Sweetwater Creek on the Texas Panhandle. Instead of attacking the Cheyenne, Custer asks to negotiate with their leaders for the release of two white women whom the Indians are holding as captives. The colonel then takes four of the leaders hostage and threatens to hang them if the women are not released. Exhausted and war-weary, the Cheyenne meet his demands, and most agree to return to their reservation.

April 10

Congress creates the Board of Indian Commissioners.

As part of President Grant's Peace Policy (see entry for JANUARY 25, 1869), Congress passes the

Indian Appropriations Act, which calls for the formation of the Board of Indian Commissioners. The group is made up of non-Indian businessmen and philanthropists appointed by the president and charged with overseeing the expenditures of the Bureau of Indian Affairs (BIA). The board is established primarily to root out corrupt Indian agents (see entry for JANUARY 7, 1868) and BIA officials and to advance the Grant administration's Assimilationist agenda in Indian affairs. The organization will remain in place until 1933, when it will be disbanded by President Franklin D. Roosevelt.

May 10

The first transcontinental railroad is completed.

At Promontory Point, Utah, a ceremony is held to celebrate the driving of the last spike joining the Union Pacific and Central Pacific Railroads to create the first transcontinental railroad. For most Americans, the event is great moment for their country. For Indians of the West, however, the transcontinental railroad spells disaster: It will bring many more whites into their lands, including buffalo hunters, who will decimate the great herds on which Plains Indians depend for their survival (see entries for 1871, 1875, and 1876).

October 11

The Métis drive government surveyors from their lands.

Beginning in the early 19th century, Manitoba, Canada, was settled by Métis—a culturally distinct people of Indian and European (primarily French and Scottish) ancestry. The Hudson's Bay Company, a fur-trading operation, held a grant to the land of the Red River Métis, but it gave the Métis permission to live there (see entry for JULY 19, 1816). After confederation in 1867, the new Canadian government bought the Hudson's Bay Company's land, including the Red River territory. Fearing that Canada will allow their lands to be overrun by non-Métis migrating from the East, the Métis drive off government surveyors, who arrived in their lands unannounced. For leadership, the rebel Métis turn to Louis Riel Jr., a former law student who is the son of a prominent Métis man and the first French-Canadian woman to live in Canada's western provinces. (See also entries for NOVEMBER 2, 1869; JUNE 23, 1870; and AUGUST 24, 1870.)

November 2

The First Northwest Rebellion erupts in Canada.

Maintaining that the Métis occupation of Manitoba's Red River region is ordained by God, Louis Riel Jr. (see entry for OCTOBER 11, 1869) leads a group of armed Métis in taking Fort Garry, in the center of their territory. The rebels seize the fort without any bloodshed.

In what will become known as the First Northwest Rebellion, Riel's followers establish a provisional government, with Riel as its president, and declare the Métis's independence from Canada. The rebels arrest several people in the area for violating Métis law and execute one non-Métis man for plotting an attack on the Métis-held fort. The execution alarms non-Indian Canadians and turns public opinion against Riel. (See also entries for JUNE 23, 1870, and for AUGUST 24, 1870.)

1870

McKay v. Campbell denies citizenship to Indians born with a "tribal allegiance."

In *McKay v. Campbell,* the Supreme Court finds that the Fourteenth Amendment's granting of citizenship to "all persons born or naturalized in the United States" does not apply to Indians with a "tribal allegiance." The Court reasons that such Indians are not technically born in the United States but in "distinct and independent political communities, retaining the right to self-government."

January 23

U.S. troops massacre a Piegan village.

Two squadrons of the Second Cavalry led by Major Eugene Baker attack a village of Piegan Indians (a subtribe of the Blackfeet) in what is now northern Montana to punish the Indians for past raids. Baker follows the orders of his superior General Philip H. Sheridan to "strike them hard." His men slaughter 173 Piegan, including 50 women and children, and take another 140 prisoner. The public denounces the massacre and pressures Congress to defeat a bill that would transfer the Bureau of Indian Affairs back to the Department of War (see entry for MARCH 3, 1849).

April to June

Red Cloud visits Washington, D.C., and New York City.

With the support of reformers from the East, Red Cloud, the Lakota Sioux leader, known for his war on army forts along the Bozeman Trail (see entry for JULY 1866), lobbies to meet with President Ulysses S. Grant to discuss the United States's insistence that the Lakota move to the Great Sioux Reservation. The federal government agrees to send him and a delegation of 20 followers to Washington, D.C., to negotiate with President Grant and other officials.

The talks between the two parties quickly become heated. After a brief visit with the president, Red Cloud meets with the secretary of the interior, who reads the text of the 1868 Treaty of Fort Laramie signed by Red Cloud (see entry for NOVEMBER 7, 1868) in order to remind the chief of his promise to relocate to a reservation. He angrily counters, "This is the first time I have heard of such a treaty," and declares he will not obey its terms. When offered a copy of the document, he refuses it, claiming, "It is all lies."

After leaving Washington, D.C., Red Cloud travels to New York City, at the invitation of reformers sympathetic to his anger at the government. There he gives an impassioned address at Cooper Union, in which he outlines his people's long history

of mistreatment. In the speech, Red Cloud asks for his audience's help in obtaining justice.

> "In 1868 men came to our land and brought papers. We could not read them, and they did not tell us truly what was in them.... When I reached Washington the Great Father [the president] explained to me what the treaty was, and showed me that the interpreters had deceived me. All I want is right and justice. I have tried to get from the Great Father what is right and just. I have not altogether succeeded."
>
> —Lakota chief Red Cloud in a speech at New York City's Cooper Union

June 23

Canada passes the Manitoba Act to placate rebelling Métis.

In response to the First Northwest Rebellion (see entry for NOVEMBER 2, 1869), the Canadian parliament agrees to several Métis demands in the Manitoba Act. Among its provisions is a land grant of 1.4 million acres for the Métis, which is to be divided into plots and allotted to individuals. Although the act is passed into law, this plan will never be implemented. (See also entry for AUGUST 24, 1870.)

August 24

Troops put down the First Northwest Rebellion.

Alarmed by the Red River Métis's declaration of independence from Canada (see entry for NOVEMBER 2, 1869), the Canadian government sends more than

1,000 British and Canadian soldiers to the Red River area of Manitoba to end the uprising. Outmanned, the rebellion is quashed. Rebel leader Louis Riel Jr. flees south to Montana, while most of his followers move to Canadian lands to the west. (See also entries for MARCH 19, 1885, and for MAY 12 TO 15, 1885.)

1871

Commissioner Ely S. Parker is investigated by Congress.

Responding to charges of corruption leveled by William Welch, the former chairman of the Board of Indian Commissioners (see entry for APRIL 10, 1869), Congress launches an investigation into the activities of Commissioner of Indian Affairs Ely S. Parker. Parker, the first Indian to serve in this post (see entry for 1869), is cleared of the charges, but his judgment in many matters is questioned, prompting Congress to pass a law that limits the commissioner's powers. As a result of the investigation, Parker resigns and retires to his home in Fairfield, Connecticut.

Whites begin slaughtering buffalo on the southern Plains.

When eastern tanneries start using buffalo hides as a source for cheap leather for machine belts, whites flock to the southern Plains to hunt the great buffalo herds there. They are aided by improved firearms and the new western railroads, which allow professional hunters to ship hides inexpensively to markets in the East. (See also entry for 1875.)

March 3

The United States ends the negotiation of Indian treaties.

At the urging of Commissioner of Indian Affairs Ely S. Parker, Congress, with the passage of the Indian Appropriations Act, votes to prohibit the United States from negotiating treaties with Indian groups. Advocates of the decision hold that Indian nations are no longer sovereign entities capable of entering into treaties because their leaders have too little authority to ensure that their people abide by treaty provisions. Although the legislation will end treaty making, in the years to come Congress will continue to negotiate "agreements" with Indian tribes, most often to reduce the size of their reservations.

April 30

Tucson vigilantes massacre the Camp Grant Apache.

Seeking revenge for an Apache raid, residents of Tucson in Arizona Territory attack a camp of peaceful Apache near Camp Grant. While the Indians' agent looks on, the vigilantes slaughter as many as 100 people—nearly all women, children, and elders—and capture 29 children to be sold as slaves.

"That evening they began to come in from all directions, singly and in small parties, so changed in forty-eight hours as to be hardly recognizable. . . . Many of the men, whose families had all been killed, when I spoke to them and expressed sympathy for them, were obliged to turn away, unable to speak. . . . The women whose children had been killed or stolen were convulsed with grief, and looked to me appealingly, as though I was their last hope on earth. Children who two days before had been full of fun and frolic kept at a distance, expressing wondering horror."

—U.S. Army lieutenant Royal E. Whitman on encountering the survivors of the Camp Grant Massacre

The eastern press reports the murders as an outrage, but local whites largely support the killers. In the aftermath, only one of the vigilantes is brought to trial; he is found not guilty by a jury of whites after 19 minutes of deliberation.

May

The Kiowa raid a Texas wagon train in the Salt Creek Massacre.

Although the Kiowa have settled on the reservation laid out for them by the Treaty of Medicine Lodge Creek (see entry for October 21 to 28, 1867), they display open contempt for their Quaker agent and refuse to stop attacking whites in Texas. On one such raid, Kiowa leader Satanta and 100 warriors fall on a train of 10 wagons traveling through the Salt Creek Prairie. The Indians kill seven men and mutilate their corpses before riding off with 41 mules.

News of the massacre quickly spreads to General in Chief William Tecumseh Sherman, who is visiting Texas to investigate Kiowa raids there. At Fort Sill on the Kiowa reservation, Sherman confronts the Kiowa's leaders, including Satanta, who boasts of his participation in the raid. As Sherman orders his arrest, Satanta reaches for his revolver but stops when he realizes the building they are in is surrounded by troops. Satanta and two other Kiowa, Satank and Big Tree, are arrested and transported to Texas. Satank is killed in an escape attempt, while Satanta and Big Tree are tried, found guilty of murder, and sentenced to hang. Due to Quaker lobbying, the Indians are later pardoned.

May 1

The decision in the Cherokee Tobacco Case erodes tribal sovereignty.

In *Boudinot v. United States,* Cherokee businessmen Elias Cornelius Boudinot and Stand Watie bring suit against the United States for imposing a tax on tobacco produced in their factory in the Cherokee Nation. The tax, instituted in 1868, was levied on all tobacco and liquor products sold within U.S. borders. The Cherokees claim, however, the tax cannot legally be applied to them because it violates an 1866 treaty that guaranteed tribe members the right to sell any product without having to pay tax to the federal government.

The Supreme Court finds that because the 1868 tax law and the 1866 treaty contradict one another only the one made last is legally enforceable. This "last-in-time" rule is devastating to Indian tribes. It allows Congress to create new laws that completely override treaty promises. It also erodes tribal sovereignty by establishing that general laws can be applied to sovereign Indian nations if these nations are not explicitly excluded.

October

Creek traditionalists join the Sands Rebellion.

Accompanied by 300 armed men, Sands, a leader of the traditionalist faction of the Creek tribe, storms the annual meeting of the Creek National Council. Sands and his followers oppose the new Creek constitution and government, which was founded after the tribe made peace with the United States at the end of the Civil War (see entry for JULY 14, 1865). Samuel Checote, principal chief of the Creek, sends in the tribal militia, which quickly quells the Sands Rebellion. The anger of the traditionalists, however, will continue to drive a wedge into Creek politics for many years to come.

1872

October 1 to 11

Apache leader Cochise and General Oliver O. Howard meet.

Frontiersman Thomas Jeffords agrees to take peace commissioner and general Oliver O. Howard into the Dragoon Mountains, where Jefford's friend Cochise, the Chiricahua Apache war leader (see entries for FEBRUARY 4, 1861, and for JULY 15, 1862), and his followers are hiding out. For nearly two weeks, Cochise and Howard discuss the Chiricahua's settlement on a reservation. During the negotiations, Cochise holds out for a reservation in the Chiricahua homeland in present-day southeastern Arizona. He also insists that Jeffords be assigned as the reservation's agent.

November 14

An earthquake rocks Indian lands in Washington State.

A large earthquake strikes north-central Washington State, east of the Cascade Mountains. Its epicenter is in the lands of the Chelan Indians. Catholic missionaries take advantage of the natural disaster by using it to frighten would-be-Chelan converts into giving up their traditional religion and adopting Christianity. Furious at the missionaries' efforts, Chelan leader Nmosize burns the priests' mission to the ground.

The quake has an even more dire effect on the Entiat, who were relocated to Lake Chelan by the terms of the Yakima Treaty of 1855. When rocks dislodged by the quake dam the Columbia River, the Entiat's new lands are flooded, forcing them to uproot their villages for the second time in two decades.

November 29

U.S. troops attack renegade Modoc led by Kintpuash.

Responding to complaints by whites in the Lost River Valley of California, the U.S. Army sends out troops to expel a group of Modoc Indians led by Kintpuash (known to whites as Captain Jack) from the region and take them back to the Klamath Indian Reservation in Oregon. The Modoc, who traditionally lived in northern California and southern Oregon, had been assigned to the Klamath's reservation by an 1864 treaty. The Klamath, however, refused to let the Modoc hunt or fish in the area. Unhappy and desperate, Kintpuash's followers soon escaped the reservation and returned to their ancestral territory near Lost River.

When the soldiers arrive, they immediately attack Kintpuash's camp, killing several Indians before the Modoc are able to retreat to the lava beds on the shore of Tule Lake. The lava beds are a natural stronghold, with caves in which the Modoc can easily hide from the troops.

The renegade Modoc will remain holed up in the caves for six months, while more than 1,000 soldiers lie in wait. The cost of siege to the U.S. Army will be great. Some 400 troops will be killed, and nearly $500,000 will be spent on their efforts to root out the Indians. (See also entries for APRIL 11, 1873, and for OCTOBER 3, 1873.)

1873

Congress repeals the "civilization fund."

Early in the 19th century, Congress established the "civilization fund" (see entry for 1819) to finance Indian education at schools run by missionaries. Repeatedly challenged as unconstitutional for violating the separation of church and state, the fund is repealed. The measure moves the Bureau of Indian Affairs to establish a system of government-operated Indian day and boarding schools.

April 11

U.S. negotiators are attacked by renegade Modoc.

Attempting to end the six-month standoff with Modoc hiding in the lava beds near Tule Lake (see entry for NOVEMBER 29, 1872), the federal government sends four peace commissioners to meet with the Modoc and negotiate a settlement. Led by Kintpuash (Captain Jack), the Modoc attack the commissioners, murdering two, including Edward Canby, the only regular army general killed during the Indian Wars. A third commissioner, Alfred Meacham, is shot and almost fatally knifed, but Kintpuash's cousin Winema (also known as Toby Riddle) scatters his attackers by screaming that more U.S. troops are en route.

News of the Modoc attack is widely reported, making frightened whites thirsty for revenge. The army sends a huge number of troops to track down Kintpuash and followers. In May, they defeat a Modoc band, which then agrees to join the manhunt. With the band's help, soldiers find and capture Kintpuash on June 1. (See also entry for OCTOBER 3, 1873.)

"I have got but a few men and I don't see how I can give them up. Will they give up their people who murdered my people while they were asleep? I never asked for the people who murdered my people.... I can see how I could give up my horse to be hanged; but I can't see how I could give up my men to be hanged. I could give up my horse to be hanged, and wouldn't cry about it, but if I gave up my men I would have to cry about it."
—Modoc rebel leader Kintpuash (Captain Jack) on his refusal to surrender

May 18

U.S. cavalry slaughters Kickapoo at Nacimiento.

Without the permission of the Mexican government, the Fourth U.S. Cavalry crosses the international boundary to attack the Kickapoo's settlement at Nacimiento. Most of the Indian casualties are women and children. Eight years earlier (see entry for 1865), these Kickapoo were among several hundred who left Kansas for Mexico to escape confinement on a reservation. Exhausted by years of warfare with nearby Texans, 317 Kickapoos agree to relocate to Indian Territory, while more than 200 opt to remain in Mexico.

June 1

Assiniboine Indians are killed in the Cypress Hills Massacre.

Near the Cypress Hills in what is now southwestern Canada, 10 American and Canadian traders attack a camp of Assiniboine Indians whom they believe stole some of their horses. Between 20 and 30 Indians are slaughtered. The incident brings attention to the need for stricter law enforcement on the Canadian frontier.

October 3

Kintpuash (Captain Jack) and three other Modoc assassins are executed.

Vilified in the press, four Modoc leaders (including Kintpuash [Captain Jack]) are hanged after being found guilty of murdering two peace commission-

Modoc rebellion leader Kintpuash, known to whites as Captain Jack, photographed after his capture (National Archives, Neg. no. 165-MH-404)

ers six months earlier (see entry for APRIL 11, 1873). The heads of the executed men are cut off and sent to the Army Medical Hospital in Washington, D.C., for study (see entry for 1868). Two other Modoc are sentenced to life imprisonment at Alcatraz for their involvement, and about 150 of Kintpuash's followers are sent to live at Fort Quapaw in Indian Territory.

While awaiting his execution, Kintpuash asks Alfred Meacham, who was injured in the Modoc's attack, to take down the Modoc leaders's version of events. Meachem will include this material in his book *Wi-Ne-Ma (The Woman-Chief) and Her People* (1876), which will make a folk hero out of Kintpuash's cousin Winema (Toby Riddle), the would-be peacemaker of the Modoc War.

1874

Summer

George Armstrong Custer leads soldiers into the Black Hills.

In violation of the Treaty of Fort Laramie (see entries for APRIL TO AUGUST, 1868, and for NOVEMBER 7, 1868), Lieutenant Colonel George Armstrong Custer leads an expedition of U.S. troops through the Great Sioux Reservation. In the Black Hills, an area sacred to the Lakota Sioux and other Indian groups, the soldiers find gold. Their discovery inspires white miners to flock to the region. Despite its treaty promises, the federal government does little to keep the whites out of the reservation (see entry for 1876).

June 27

Indian warriors attack buffalo hunters at the Battle of Adobe Walls.

In the first attack of a planned campaign against non-Indian buffalo hunters (see entry for 1871), a war party of 250 Cheyenne, Comanche, and Kiowa led by Quanah Parker and Lone Wolf descend on 28 men and one woman camping near the trading post of Adobe Walls on the Texas Panhandle. The area has symbolic importance to the Indians as the site of a battle between a Kiowa-Comanche force and U.S. Army troops 10 years earlier (see entry for NOVEMBER 25, 1864).

One member of the war party, Eschiti, claims to have the power to make warriors bulletproof. The Indians are, therefore, stunned at their vulnerability to the hunters' breechloading guns, which are much faster to reload than traditional muzzle-loading guns. In the face of withering gunfire, the warriors retreat after several hours of fighting. The inconclusive battle is demoralizing to the Indian forces, which as a result of their attack will become the target of the massive military retaliation later known as the Red River War (see entry for SEPTEMBER 28, 1874).

September 28

U.S. soldiers attack a Kiowa-Comanche camp at Palo Duro Canyon.

Troops led by Ranald S. Mackenzie set upon Kiowa, Comanche, and Cheyenne in their stronghold in Palo Duro Canyon. Although only three Indians are killed, the entire camp is destroyed, including the Indians' herd of 1,500 ponies. The attack is so demoralizing to the exhausted Indians that many soon decide to give themselves up to soldiers at reservation agencies. By the following spring, the Red River War (see entry for JUNE 27, 1874) ends with the surrender of nearly all off-reservation Kiowa and Comanche. (See also entries for MAY 1875 and for MAY 3, 1875.)

1875

Congress passes the Indian Homestead Act.

Modeled after the Homestead Act (see entry for MAY 20, 1862), the Indian Homestead Act offers 160-acre homesteads to western Indians willing to leave their reservations and become private landowners. These Indians are to receive title to their homesteads if they occupy them for five years and make certain improvements to the land. Intended to encourage Indians to assimilate into white society, the act will have little impact because few Indians will opt to take up homesteads under its terms.

White hunters exterminate the southern buffalo herds.

In a matter of years, professional buffalo hunters have killed so many buffalo on the southern Plains that the once-great herds native to the region are nearly extinct (see entry for 1871). Between 1872 and 1874, the height of the buffalo hunt, whites slaughter more than 5 million of the animals. (By comparison, the Plains Indians who depend on the buffalo for their survival hunt just over 1 million during the same period.) Some hunters shoot more than they can skin, infuriating Indians by leaving the animals' bloody carcasses to rot. Even those who skin them often leave the rest to rot. The Indians traditionally used every part of the buffalo. The extermination of the buffalo has been supported by some officials, including the secretary of the interior, as a means of destroying traditional Plains Indian culture.

"Twelve hundred men were employed in the construction of the [Kansas Pacific Railroad]. The Indians were very troublesome, and it was difficult to obtain fresh meat for the hands. The company therefore concluded to engage expert hunters to kill buffaloes. . . . During my engagement as hunter for the company, which covered a period of eighteen months, I killed 4,280 buffaloes."

—William "Buffalo Bill" Cody on his career as a professional buffalo hunter

May 3

Kiowa chief Kicking Bird dies under mysterious circumstances.

Kicking Bird, who is considered the principal chief of the Kiowa by the United States, is found dead, possibly poisoned by his political enemies. Long an advocate of peaceful relations with the U.S. government, Kicking Bird had been asked by federal officials to identify Kiowa war leaders who had participated in the Red River War (see entries for JUNE 27, 1874, and for SEPTEMBER 28, 1874). These men are soon exiled to Florida, where they are imprisoned for three years at Fort Marion (see entry for MAY 21, 1875).

May

The Comanche under Quanah Parker surrender.

Comanche leader Quanah Parker, after four years of fighting and weeks of negotiation, leads his 400 men to Fort Sill in Indian Territory and surrenders to U.S. Army colonel Ranald Mackenzie. The meeting between the former adversaries is cordial. Perhaps in an attempt to ingratiate himself to Mackenzie, Parker, whose followers long terrorized Texas settlers with their raiding, reminds the colonel that his white mother had been a Texan (see entries for MAY 19, 1836, and for DECEMBER 1860). Throughout the encounter, the Comanche displays his considerable talents as a diplomat— skills that will make him an extremely effective leader as his people adjust to reservation life and to dealing with Indian agents and other white authorities.

May 21

Plains Indian prisoners arrive at Fort Marion.

After surrendering to the U.S. Army, 72 Kiowa, Cheyenne, and Arapaho warriors are sent to Fort Marion, a prison in St. Augustine, Florida. Considered the most dangerous Indians of the southern

Plains, they are imprisoned thousands of miles from their homelands to keep them from further influencing other members of their tribes.

During their three years in prison, the Fort Marion inmates are overseen by Richard Pratt, a former army officer. Sympathetic to the Indians' plight, he teaches his charges English and educates them about non-Indian customs. Pratt also gives the Indians pencils and paper to draw pictures, which he sells to non-Indian tourists to raise funds for his school. Using simple lines and figures reminiscent of hide paintings, the inmates, such as Howling Wolf and Zotom, use their pictures to tell the story of their imprisonment and to record their memories of living as hunters and fighters on the Plains. (See also entry for MAY 3, 1875.)

December

The commissioner of Indian affairs orders Plains Indians to settle on reservations.

The commissioner of Indian affairs announces that any Indians on the northern plains who do not report to their reservation agencies by January 31, 1876, will be considered "hostiles" at war with the United States. The declaration helps justify a military solution to the problem presented by Americans clamoring for access to lands and goldfields in the Black Hills (see entry for SUMMER 1874), an area assigned to the Lakota Sioux by the 1868 Treaty of Fort Laramie.

1876

The U.S. Army leaves the Black Hills region.

Under pressure from white citizens, President Ulysses S. Grant pulls the army out of the Black Hills (see entry for SUMMER 1874). The retreat shows that the government has no intention of protecting the area on behalf of the Lakota, despite the 1868 treaty promise that only officials authorized by the Indians would be "permitted to pass over, settle upon, or reside in the territory." Immediately

after the military leaves the Black Hills, the region is flooded by whites looking to take over the gold-rich lands.

The U.S. government attempts to concentrate the Apache on the San Carlos Reservation.

To open more land for whites, the United States announces plans to consolidate all Apache on the San Carlos Reservation, along the Gila River in present-day Arizona. San Carlos offers little to the Indians. The land is barren, and the area is a hotbed for malaria. Despite the terrible living conditions at San Carlos, most Apache agree to resettle there. The exceptions are about half of the Chiricahua, who escape to Mexico, and most of the Warm Springs Apache, who find refuge in the mountains.

United States v. Joseph gives individual Pueblo the right to sell land.

In the *United States v. Joseph,* the federal government attempts to prevent Pueblo individuals from selling lands without its consent. Because the Pueblo were given property rights by the Treaty of Guadalupe Hidalgo (see entry for FEBRUARY 2, 1848), the Supreme Court finds against the government, holding that the Pueblo should have the same rights as U.S. citizens to sell their land. Its ruling also cites that the Pueblo are unique among Indians because of their settled way of life, implying that they are superior to other Indian groups and hence deserve a greater amount of autonomy over their economic affairs. The Court will overturn this decision in *United States v. Sandoval* (see entry for 1913).

White hunters' slaughter of the northern Plains buffalo begins.

After having killed most of the buffalo of the southern Plains (see entry for 1875), professional hunters turn to the smaller herds to the north, which the Northern Pacific Railway has made accessible. During the early 1880s, more than 5,000 white hunters and skinners will come to the region. By 1883, they will have killed so many animals that the northern herds will have largely disappeared.

January 31

Plains Indians refuse to return to their reservations.

Despite a federal government ultimatum (see entry for DECEMBER 1875), several thousand Lakota Sioux and Northern Cheyenne, embittered by the invasion of the Black Hills (see entry for SUMMER 1874), refuse to report to their reservation agencies. In response, General Philip Sheridan sends out three columns of soldiers—led by General George Crook, Colonel John Gibbon, and General Alfred H. Terry—to subdue the Indians, now branded as "hostiles," and force them to live within reservation boundaries.

March 17

U.S. troops are defeated at the Battle of Powder River.

General George Crook orders Colonel Joseph J. Reynolds and his men to launch a surprise attack on a Lakota Sioux and Cheyenne village in the Powder River Valley, in what is now Montana. Confronted by Reynolds's forces at daybreak, the Indians, still dressed in nightclothes, flee into the frozen countryside. Having taken their weapons with them, the warriors of the village quickly regroup and return to fight the soldiers, who are torching the Indians' tipis and possessions. The warriors inflict heavy casualties and force the troops to retreat. Although an embarrassing defeat for the United States, the Battle of Powder River does succeed in alerting the Lakota Sioux and Cheyenne to the army's commitment to battling Indians found outside reservation borders (see entry for JANUARY 31, 1876).

April 12

The Canadian Parliament passes the Indian Act.

Enacted nine years after the confederation of Canada (see entry for JULY 1, 1867), the Indian Act of 1876 announces the new government's intention to uphold the paternalistic policies toward Indians that were initiated under British rule. The act applies only to people of full Indian descent, thereby excluding the Métis (a people of Indian and French ancestry) and the Inuit.

The Indian Act recognizes the Indian reserves established by treaty and allows for the creation of band councils. The real governing power on reserves, however, is to be held by agents, employees of Canada's Department of Indian Affairs. The department's goal is to "civilize" Canada's Indians by assimilating them into non-Indian society.

The act also creates for Indians a distinct legal status that is to be defined exclusively by the government. For example, the government's new definition of "Indianness" holds that an Indian man can give up his Indian status in exchange for citizenship and that an Indian woman who marries a non-Indian man forfeits her Indian status under the law. (See also entries for 1920; 1927; JUNE 20, 1951; and 1989.)

June 8

Sitting Bull has a vision of fallen soldiers.

While performing the Sun Dance, a traditional ritual of supplication, Lakota leader and holy man Sitting Bull hears a voice instructing that he study a vision that appears to him as he stares at the sun. Sitting Bull sees a great number of soldiers riding toward an Indian village. The soldiers and their horses are upside down, as are a few of the Indians. The voice tells him that the soldiers will all die, but Sitting Bull and his men must not plunder their bodies.

The vision is greeted with great enthusiasm by Sitting Bull's followers. It is interpreted as a prophesy that a great army of soldiers will descend on them. Although some Lakota will die in battle (as symbolized by the upside-down Indians), all of the soldiers will be killed. (See also JUNE 25 TO 26, 1876.)

June 17

U.S. troops meet Lakota Sioux and Cheyenne warriors in the Battle of the Rosebud.

From the Crow and Shoshone scouts accompanying his soldiers, General George Crook learns that a large group of Lakota Sioux and Cheyenne "hostiles" are occupying the Rosebud River Valley in Montana and moves his 1,200 soldiers there to confront them. While camped along the Rosebud, the soldiers are instead set upon by approximately an equal number of warriors led by Crazy Horse.

The attack leads to one of the largest battles of the Indian wars. After six hours of intense fighting along the three-mile river valley, the Indian forces end the battle. Crook declares a victory, but in fact the conflict is more of a draw, with both sides suffering relatively few casualties. The battle, however, largely incapacitates Crook's soldiers for two months, thus reducing the number of U.S. troops available to fight hostile Indians.

June 25 to 26

Lakota Sioux and Cheyenne warriors triumph at the Battle of Little Bighorn.

On orders from General Alfred H. Terry, Lieutenant Colonel George Armstrong Custer, commanding the Seventh Cavalry, travels up the Rosebud River to attack Lakota Sioux and Northern Cheyenne hostiles camped along the Little Bighorn River in Montana Territory.

Grossly underestimating the Indians' fighting forces, Custer divides his men into three battalions—one led by him, one headed by Major Marcus Reno, and the third assigned to Captain Frederick Benteen. Custer sends Benteen to scout the bluffs to the south, as Reno approaches the camp from the north and Custer moves toward it from the south. Reno and his men are met by a large Indian force, which compels them to retreat to the bluffs. Custer, meanwhile, leads more than 200 troops forward; they are met by an army of several thousand Lakota and Cheyenne warriors. Custer and all of his men are killed in the ensuing battle.

Although the victory has great symbolic meaning to the Indians, it gives them little advantage in the overall war the U.S. Army is waging against Indians in the northern plains. In fact, the Battle of Little Bighorn allows the popular press to demonize the Indians fighting to protect their territory and encourages the army to pursue its war against them with increased ferocity.

"Indians kept swirling round and round, and the soldiers killed only a few. Many soldiers fell. At last all horses killed but five.... [F]ive horsemen and the bunch of men, maybe forty, started toward the river.... One man all alone ran far down toward the river, then round up over the hill. I thought he was going to escape, but a Sioux fired and hit him in the head. He was the last man."

—Northern Cheyenne warrior Two Moons, describing the Battle of Little Bighorn

July 17

Yellow Hand is scalped by William F. Cody.

While serving as an army scout, William F. Cody, also known by the stage name Buffalo Bill, scalps the body of Yellow Hand, a Cheyenne chief shot in a skirmish with soldiers seeking to avenge the deaths of the cavalrymen led by George Armstrong Custer at the Battle of Little Bighorn (see entry for JUNE 25 TO 26, 1876). Wearing a garish Mexican vaquero outfit made of black velvet and trimmed with silver buttons and lace, Cody defiles the corpse.

Dressed in this costume, he replays the event in a play titled *The Red Right Hand; or the First Scalp for Custer,* which depicts Cody himself killing

A drawing of the Battle of Little Bighorn by a Lakota Sioux artist. War leader Crazy Horse is shown in the foreground, facing the viewer. *(Yale Collection of Western Americana, Beinecke Rare Book and Manuscript Library)*

Yellow Hand (renamed Yellow Hair in the play and in the popular press) in hand-to-hand combat. He also displays Yellow Hand's scalp for the audience. The success of the play will inspire Cody to launch his famous Wild West Show (see entry for MAY 17, 1883).

August 23

Canadian Indian leaders sign the "Medicine Chest" Treaty.

Cree and Assiniboine leaders in what are now Alberta and Saskatchewan agree to Treaty Six, which will become known as the "Medicine Chest" Treaty. In addition to promising extra rations to relieve famine in Indian settlements, the agreement states that "a medicine chest will be kept at the house of each Indian Agent for the use and benefit of all Indians." In the late 1960s, the Canadian government will agree to provide Indians with free health care on the basis of this treaty.

September 9

American Horse dies in a parley with U.S. troops.

Lakota Sioux war leader American Horse and his band are set upon by U.S. troops under the command of Anson Mills while the Indians are traveling south for the winter. In the ensuing conflict, later named the Battle of Slim Buttes, American Horse and 19 others are trapped in a cave. The troops are driven off by hundreds of warriors led by Sitting Bull and Gall, but not before American Horse is fatally wounded by a gunshot to his stomach. The troops possibly set out to kill American Horse because they believe (perhaps erroneously) that he had fought in the Battle of Little Bighorn (see entry for JUNE 25 TO 26, 1876).

October

Sitting Bull's followers escape to Canada.

Wanting to escape warfare but unwilling to be confined to a reservation, Sitting Bull and his followers set off for Canada. Although free from the threat of massacre by the U.S. Army, they find it difficult to replicate their traditional ways because there are too few buffaloes in the area. On the brink of starvation, the Canadian exile of Sitting Bull's people will end four and a half years later with their reluctant return to the United States (see entry for JULY 19, 1881).

November 25

Soldiers destroy Dull Knife's camp.

Eleven hundred troops led by Colonel Ranald Mackenzie attack Cheyenne leader Dull Knife's camp of 183 lodges along the Powder River, in present-day Wyoming. During the surprise assault, 40 Cheyenne are killed. The others watch helplessly as Mackenzie's soldiers set their camp and possessions ablaze. With the Indians' defeat, more than 1,000 Cheyenne are left without food or shelter in the dead of winter. The night after the attack, 11 infants freeze to death when temperatures fall to 30 below zero. (See also entry for SEPTEMBER 9, 1877.)

1877

The United States takes control of the Black Hills.

Eager to gain possession of the Black Hills (see entry for SUMMER 1874), Congress enacts the Black Hills Act, which amends the 1868 Treaty of Fort Laramie. By the terms of the original treaty, any amendment must be approved by three-fourths of the Lakota Sioux male population (see entry for NOVEMBER 7, 1868). A commission is sent to the Great Sioux Reservation to obtain the necessary signatures, but the number collected falls far short of this requirement. Through the Black Hills Act, therefore, the United States essentially confiscates 7.7 million acres legally held by the Lakota. The act offers the Indians no compensation for this gold-rich land.

Congress passes the Desert Land Act.

To encourage whites to settle in western desert lands, the Desert Land Act allows settlers to buy up to 640 acres of land for $1.25 per acre if they agree to irrigate the land within three years. The law will accelerate white settlement in Indian lands in the Southwest.

January 1 to 8

Cheyenne and Lakota Sioux forces fight the Battle of Wolf Mountains.

The Battle of Wolf Mountains is the last major conflict in the U.S. Army's war with the Cheyenne and Lakota Sioux (see entry for JANUARY 31, 1876). A series of skirmishes ends with a five-hour battle on January 8, during which soldiers under the command of Nelson A. Miles drive Indians led by Crazy Horse out of their camp in the Wolf Mountains. Their supplies depleted, Miles's exhausted men do not pursue the Indians, who also are suffering from fatigue and lack of food.

May 3

U.S. officials and Nez Perce leaders meet in council.

In 1863, the United States negotiated with Nez Perce leaders a treaty that reduced the tribe's reservation. Several tribal chiefs, including Old Joseph, refused to recognize the treaty. Their followers became known as "non-treaty" Nez Perce.

To convince the non-treaty Nez Perce to relocate to the reduced reservation, the U.S. government sends a commission headed by General Oliver O. Howard to meet with their leaders, including Chief Joseph (Heinmot Tooyalaket)—the son of Old Joseph (The Kakas), who became the leader of the elder chief's band after his death in 1871. As talks with Howard grow heated, Chief Joseph, hoping to avoid warfare, hesitantly agrees to move the non-treaty Nez Perce to the tribe's reservation by June 14. (See also entry for JUNE 15, 1877.)

May 6

Crazy Horse surrenders to the U.S. Army.

The vigorous military campaign against the Lakota Sioux of the previous winter compels band after band to give up the battlefield and return to the reservation. The last band to capitulate is Crazy Horse's. His followers, numbering more than 1,000, finally surrender to soldiers at Camp Robinson in Nebraska, an event that marks the end of the Sioux War. (See also entry for SEPTEMBER 5, 1877.)

May 7

Lame Deer is killed in the Battle of Muddy Creek.

Along the Muddy Creek in Montana, troops led by General Nelson A. Miles discover the village of Lame Deer, the leader of the Miniconjou band of the Lakota Sioux and a veteran of Red Cloud's War (see entry for JULY 1866) and the Battle of Little Bighorn (see entry for JUNE 24 TO 25, 1876). Without giving Lame Deer a chance to negotiate, Miles and his men rush the camp. As they approach, Lame Deer sets his rifle down to show his willingness to surrender, but the troops ignore the gesture and shoot at the unarmed warrior. Lame Deer grabs his rifle and begins returning fire, but along with about 10 other Lakota, he is killed in the ensuing battle. Their village set ablaze by the soldiers, the survivors will surrender to Miles several months later.

June 15

The Nez Perce War breaks out.

The day after Nez Perce leader Chief Joseph and his band are due to relocate to the tribe's reservation (see entry for MAY 3, 1877), a group of Nez Perce warriors kill four white settlers in Idaho. Troops are immediately sent out to counterattack. Although Chief Joseph tries to resolve the conflict peacefully, the soldiers open fire on the renegade band. In the ensuring battle, the Nez Perce kill nearly one-third of the troops and send the remainder fleeing.

When many more soldiers are dispatched to subdue the Indians, Chief Joseph and about 400 Nez Perce men, women, and children flee eastward. With hundreds of troops in pursuit, Chief Joseph's band begins an extraordinary four-month, 1,400-mile retreat over the Rocky Mountains and northward toward Canada, where they hope to find sanctuary in the camp of the Lakota leader Sitting Bull (see entry for OCTOBER 5, 1877).

September 2

Apache leader Victorio leads a mass escape from San Carlos.

Unable to endure the horrendous living conditions at the San Carlos Reservation (see entry for 1876), Mimbreno Apache leader Victorio escapes with more than 300 followers. For most, freedom is short-lived. Within a month, all but about 80 warriors, including Victorio, surrender at Fort Wingate in what is now New Mexico. Victorio and his men hide in the mountains as they try to negotiate for their return to their old reservation at Ojo Caliente.

September 5

Crazy Horse is killed.

Crazy Horse, after surrendering to the army (see entry for MAY 6, 1877), was compelled to live at Fort Robinson in Nebraska. With growing unrest at the fort, the commanding general orders the arrest of the great Lakota war leader, who resists being taken into custody. In the resulting scuffle, a guard stabs Crazy Horse with a bayonet. He dies of the wound later that day, at the age of 36.

September 9

Hundreds of Northern Cheyenne flee Indian Territory.

After surrendering to U.S. soldiers in the spring, Northern Cheyenne led by Dull Knife and Little Wolf (see entry for NOVEMBER 25, 1876) were sent to live on an Indian Territory reservation occupied by the Southern Cheyenne and Arapaho. By the fall they are starving from inadequate rations and weakened by a devastating malaria epidemic. In desperation, about 300 flee the reservation and set out for their old homeland in what is now Wyoming and Montana. Chased by more than 10,000 soldiers, the Northern Cheyenne led by Dull Knife are overpowered during a blizzard six weeks later. The army sends the captured Cheyenne to Fort Robinson in Nebraska, where they are held as prisoners. (See also entry for JANUARY 9, 1879.)

October 5

The Nez Perce War ends with Chief Joseph's surrender.

Ending one of the greatest campaigns during the Indian Wars in the West (see entry for JUNE 15, 1877), Chief Joseph of the Nez Perce surrenders to the U.S. Army. Only about 40 miles from the Canadian border, he and his followers were surprised and surrounded by an army led by Colonel Nelson A. Miles. During the five-day siege that followed, many Nez Perce warriors were killed, while the group's women and children starved in the freezing cold.

"I am tired of fighting. Our chiefs are killed.... My people, some of them, have run away to the hills and have no blankets, no food; no one knows where they are—perhaps freezing to death. I want to have time to look for my children and see how many I can find. Maybe I shall find them among the dead. Hear me, my chiefs. I am tired; my heart is sick and sad. From where the sun now stands I will fight no more forever."

—Nez Perce leader Chief Joseph as he surrenders to the U.S. Army

As Chief Joseph surrenders to Colonel Miles and General Oliver O. Howard, he makes a moving speech in which he mourns the dead and chronicles the enormous hardships suffered by his followers during the Nez Perce War. According to Chief Joseph's later claims, Miles promises that his followers will be able to return to their homeland. Instead, they are declared prisoners of war and will be sent first to Fort Leavenworth, Kansas, then to a reservation in Indian Territory, where many will die from disease. (See also entry for JANUARY 14, 1879.)

October 17

Sitting Bull meets with the Terry Commission.

As the presence of Sitting Bull and his followers north of the U.S. border (see entry for OCTOBER 1876) puts increasing strains on the United States's relationship with Canada, a commission headed by General Alfred Terry seeks an audience with the Lakota Sioux leader. With great reluctance, Sitting Bull agrees to meet with Terry, whom the Indians regard with contempt because of his past campaigns against them.

At the conference, Terry delivers a speech in which he tries to persuade Sitting Bull's people to give up their weapons and return to their reservation in the United States. After a long silence, Sitting Bull responds with an angry recitation of all the wrongs his people have suffered at the hands of Americans. He concludes with, "You come here to tell us lies, but we don't want to hear them." He then tells Terry to "go back home where you came from." (See also entry for JULY 19, 1881.)

1878

The Bureau of Indian Affairs establishes Indian police forces on reservations.

At the request of the secretary of the interior, Congress authorizes the Bureau of Indian Affairs to hire Indian men to police reservations. The Indian police forces are meant to replace U.S. troops in settling small disputes and subduing angry and starving Indians. Indian policemen will also serve as assistants to non-Indian agents by alerting them to reservation gossip and rumors and performing routine tasks, such as rounding up truant Indian students and forcing them to attend reservation schools.

Although intended to help keep the peace, Indian police forces often increase friction within reservation communities. Many of their fellow tribespeople resent following the orders of Indian policemen, whom they regard as traitors to their people. Indian police forces also undermine the authority of traditional leaders, who in the past had taken responsibility for settling intratribal disagreements.

The Hubbell Trading Post opens on the Navajo Reservation.

A former Spanish interpreter for the U.S. military, John Lorenzo Hubbell purchases a trading post in the Ganado area of the Navajo Indian Reservation. From the post, Hubbell offers the Navajo food and non-Indian manufactured merchandise for sale or for trade.

The non-Indian trader with the closest relationship and greatest influence on his Navajo (Dineh) customers, Hubbell encourages Navajo women to weave larger blankets for sale to whites for use as rugs, thus helping to create a new industry among the Navajo. Hubbell also redirects the traditional Navajo craft by encouraging weavers to use the patterns and colors most popular with his white clientele.

Hubbell exerts an even greater influence on Navajo craftwork by bringing silversmiths from Mexico to Ganado to instruct Navajo men. Although some Navajo are already familiar with silversmithing, it becomes a Navajo art only after Hubbell demonstrates to Navajo men that it can be a money-making enterprise. In addition to selling Navajo silverwork and rugs from his network of trading posts and stores, Hubbell offers the items in a mail-order catalog, thereby creating a demand for these wares among whites throughout the United States.

The first salmon cannery opens in southern Alaska.

With the opening of the first salmon cannery, the non-Indian-operated salmon industry begins to compete with Native fishers for the salmon catch in the waters of Alaska. As the industry grows it will take control of all major salmon streams, impoverishing the Alaska Natives who depended on fishing for their livelihood, and threatening their traditional culture.

Kiowa war leader Satanta dies from a fall.

Satanta, the Kiowa chief who most strongly resisted confinement on a reservation (see entry for MAY 1871), is imprisoned in Huntsville, Texas, for violating parole. When he falls headfirst from a second-story prison window, his death is ruled a suicide. The prison authorities refuse to allow an investigation of the incident by the Kiowa, who suspect Satanta was murdered.

April

The Hampton Institute admits Indian students.

Founded in 1868, the Hampton Institute in Hampton, Virginia, was established as a school for freed African-American slaves, who after graduation were encouraged to share their knowledge with others of their race. Wanting to extend this same educational philosophy to Native Americans, Hampton's administrators allow 17 Indian men to attend the institute.

The Indians were among the prisoners of war sent to Fort Marion, Florida, after their defeat in the Red River War (see entry for 1875). At the end of three years in jail under the watch of Richard Henry Pratt, a former army officer and Indian reformer who tried to introduce his charges to the ways of whites, the prisoners are offered the opportunity to stay in the East and receive non-Indian educations. Those who agreed are sent to Hampton, because it is the only school Pratt could convince to take Indian students. Quickly deemed a success by Pratt, the Hampton experiment in Indian education will inspire the establishment of boarding schools as a tool for assimilating Indians into non-Indian society. (See also entry for AUTUMN 1879.)

May to September

The Bannock War is fought.

To supplement their government rations, the Bannock Indians of present-day Idaho have relied on gathering camas roots that grow wild in their homeland. Although their right to gather these roots is guaranteed by treaty, white ranchers allow their hogs to trample and destroy the areas where the wild camas grow. Angered by this continuing threat to their food supply, the Bannock join with their Northern Paiute (Numu) relatives to rise up against non-Indians in their territory. Troops led by General Oliver O. Howard, a veteran of the Nez Perce War (see entry for JUNE 15, 1877, and for OCTOBER 5, 1877), are sent out to suppress the rebellion.

Although not all of the Bannock participated in the uprising, the United States decides to punish the entire tribe by disbanding their Malheur reservation. The Bannock are sent to live at the Yakima Indian Reservation in western Washington. The Yakama, however, are not eager to share their land with the Bannock. After five years of misery and conflict, the Bannock will be permitted to relocate to other reservations in present-day Oregon, Nevada, California, and Idaho.

1879

January 9

The U.S. Army slaughters the Northern Cheyenne led by Dull Knife.

About 150 Northern Cheyenne under the leadership of Dull Knife remain imprisoned at Fort Robinson in Nebraska after trying to escape their Indian Territory reservation (see entry for SEPTEMBER 9, 1877). The Cheyenne captives frustrate the officials at the fort by insisting that they would rather die than go back to the reservation. In order to force the defiant Indians into

submission, the troops chain the Cheyenne's barracks shut and, on January 3, stop giving them provisions. After six days with no food or water, the desperate prisoners burst from the barracks, jumping out of the building's high windows and racing for cover in the surrounding forests. About half escape; the others are gunned down by soldiers as they flee the fort.

Less than three weeks later, the survivors are discovered by U.S. troops at Antelope Creek. The Northern Cheyenne are defeated in the battle that follows. In the end, 78 of Dull Knife's followers are taken alive, 64 are dead, and only seven manage to escape.

> "We bowed to the will of the Great Father [president] and went far into the south where he told us to go. There we found a Cheyenne cannot live. Sickness came among us that made mourning in every lodge. Then the treaty promises were broken and our rations were short.... [W]e thought it better to die fighting to regain our old homes than to perish of sickness."
>
> —Northern Cheyenne leader Dull Knife on his followers' 1877 escape from their reservation

January 14

Chief Joseph lectures Congress on the plight of the Nez Perce.

After their surrender in the Nez Perce War (see entry for OCTOBER 5, 1877), the followers of Nez Perce leader Chief Joseph were sent to a reservation in Indian Territory. The conditions there are miserable. Already ill and weak with hunger, many of the Nez Perce die on the reservation. Among them are five of Chief Joseph's children.

Chief Joseph obtains permission to travel to Washington, D.C., to ask for the government's help. Before Congress, he delivers an eloquent speech recording the suffering of his people and the many injustices the United States has committed against them. His plea to be allowed to return to his homeland in Oregon's Wallowa Valley, however, is greeted with little enthusiasm by western congressmen. Chief Joseph's speech, however, does impress the members of the Indian Rights Association (see entry for DECEMBER 1882) and other eastern philanthropists. Widely circulating Chief Joseph's speeches, they will make the return of the Nez Perce to the Northwest a cause of national interest. (See also entry for MAY 22, 1885.)

March 3

The Bureau of Ethnology is established.

By an act of Congress, the Bureau of Ethnology (later renamed the Bureau of American Ethnology) is formed to collect information about American Indian tribes and their cultures. John Wesley Powell, a major in the U.S. Army, is chosen as the bureau's first director. Over the next 85 years, the organization will compile a huge amount of research material, although much of it will be colored by racial bias. The essays published by the bureau in its annual reports and bulletin will have a great influence on generations of scholars of Indian history and anthropology.

April 18

Standing Bear v. Crook defines Indians as human beings.

In January 1879, Ponca leader Standing Bear and 66 of his followers left their reservation in Indian Territory to return to their ancestral lands in present-day Nebraska. The Ponca had been forcibly

removed to Indian Territory two years earlier after U.S. officials negotiated a treaty in which they mistakenly granted the Ponca homeland to the Sioux. The Ponca suffered horribly during their removal: more than one-fourth of them died en route, including Standing Bear's children. Against the orders of the U.S. Army, he was determined to travel home in order to bury his son in Ponca territory.

About halfway there, Standing Bear and the other Ponca were stopped by General George Crook, who placed them under armed guard as he prepared to return them to Indian Territory. Newspaper accounts protested the harsh treatment of the Ponca, and several attorneys called for their release. The lawyers presented Crook with a writ of habeas corpus, demanding that he present his prisoners and declare the reason for their imprisonment. A U.S. attorney countered that habeas corpus could not apply to the Ponca because, as Indians, they were not legally considered human beings.

The dispute is resolved in court with the ruling in *Standing Bear v. Crook* that Indians are in fact people under U.S. law. Standing Bear's own testimony plays a crucial role in this landmark case. "My hand is not the same color as yours," he explains to the court, "but if you pierce it, I shall feel the pain. The blood will be the same color." (See also entries for OCTOBER 31, 1879, and for NOVEMBER TO DECEMBER 1879.)

May to October

The Sheepeater War is fought.

When five Chinese and two American prospectors are murdered in present-day Idaho, the army believes the culprits are the Sheepeaters, a group of about 30 Bannock and Shoshone Indians in the area. Troops sent out to subdue the Sheepeaters are met by a small war party that initially forces them to retreat. As the public clamors for the Sheepeaters' capture, more soldiers are dispatched. For months the Sheepeaters successfully evade the troops, but they are forced to abandon their property and food stores. Exhausted and hungry, most surrender in early October. Although they claim they are inno-cent of the murders, they are sent to prison in Vancouver, Washington Territory, then relocated to Idaho's Fort Hall Reservation.

Summer

Ethnologist Frank Hamilton Cushing comes to live among the Zuni.

A largely self-trained ethnologist employed by the Smithsonian Institution, Frank Hamilton Cush-ing, at age 22, travels to the Southwest as part of the Bureau of Ethnology's (see entry for MARCH 3, 1879) first expedition to the region. He is charged with collecting Zuni artifacts and learning as much as possible about the Indians' culture, a daunting task considering their reluc-tance to discuss their ways with non-Indians. To gain their confidence, Cushing leaves the expedi-tion's camp and moves into the house of the Zuni's governor. Cushing's willingness to adopt Zuni dress and customs and to learn their lan-guage endears him to the governor, who adopts him into his family. When, after two months, the expedition leaves the Zuni pueblo, Cushing chooses to remain behind.

For the next four years, Cushing will live as a Zuni, while taking notes about Zuni life, ways, and beliefs, particularly their complex mythology. Cushing's years among the Zuni will provide data for his later writings, which will be among the first in-depth anthropological studies of southwestern Indians. They will also establish a new model for the ethnologist as equal parts observer and partici-pant in the culture under study.

Autumn

The Carlisle Indian boarding school is founded.

The first non-reservation school sponsored by the U.S. government, the Carlisle Industrial Indian Boarding School is established in Carlisle, Pennsyl-vania, by Richard Henry Pratt. While serving in the army, Pratt supervised Indians held in a prisoner-of-war camp in St. Augustine, Florida (see entry for 1875). His experience convinced him that boarding schools could be the most effective tools for peace-ably assimilating Indians into non-Indian society. Only by taking children and young adults out of the "corrupting" environment of their own Indian communities, he reasoned, could they learn to pros-per in the mainstream. Pratt summarized his philosophy in the slogan "Kill the Indian and save the man."

When students arrive at Carlisle, they are for-bidden to speak their own language, wear Indian clothing, or practice any customs that appear too "Indian" to their non-Indian instructors. In addi-tion to receiving a modest academic education that stresses learning the English language, they are given vocational training to help them find manual work when they graduate. The boys are taught me-chanical skills and farming, while the girls learn to sew, cook, and do housework.

September

American troops defeat the Ute in the Ute War.

To force the Ute at the White River Agency in Col-orado to give up gambling and take up farming, their agent Nathan Meeker plows up their race track and prime horse pastures. Frightened by the infuriated Ute, Meeker asks the U.S. government to send troops to the agency to protect him. It re-sponds by dispatching 175 soldiers under the command of Major Thomas T. Thornburgh to sub-due the Indians.

When the troops reach White River, Ute war-riors led by Chief Jack (Nicaagat) attack them and kill Thornburgh in the Battle of Milk Creek. The Ute continue the battle for seven days, until American reinforcements arrive, forcing the In-dian warriors to retreat. The Ute War ends when a treaty is negotiated with the U.S. government by Ouray, the leader of the Uncompahgre Band. The treaty forces the Ute to cede their lands at White River and relocate to the Uintah Reservation in what is now Utah.

Carlisle Indian school students, photographed before and after their arrival at the institution. The photograph with the students wearing Indian dress shows, left to right, Richard Yellow Robe, Henry Standing Bear, and Chauncey Yellow Robe. In the photograph with them wearing uniforms, Chauncey is to the left and Richard is to the right. *(Cumberland County Historical Society, Carlisle, PA)*

September 4

Victorio's men attack a cavalry camp.

Led by Victorio (see entry for SEPTEMBER 2, 1877), 60 Apache warriors set upon the camp of cavalrymen outside the Indians' former reservation at Ojo Caliente. They kill eight soldiers and steal the troops' horses. The incident sparks an all-out war between Victorio's followers and the U.S. Army.

Joined by other renegade Apache, Victorio's forces will soon grow to 150 warriors. For more than a year, these fighters will inflict a reign of terror on American and Mexican settlements in Texas, northern Mexico, and what is now New Mexico and Arizona, all the while pursued by soldiers in-

tent on capturing the runaway Apache. (See also entry for OCTOBER 15 TO 16, 1880.)

October 31

Big Snake is murdered at the Ponca Indian Agency.

In *Standing Bear v. Crook* (see entry for APRIL 18, 1879), a federal judge ruled that the army cannot forcibly relocate Standing Bear and his band to the Ponca's reservation. Believing this ruling also applies to him, Big Snake, Standing Bear's brother, moves to a Cheyenne reservation about 100 miles away from the Ponca's assigned land. Troops arrest Big Snake and return him to his reservation. The agent there orders his imprisonment, but Big Snake, claiming he has committed no crime, refuses to go to the jail. After he shows the troops sent to capture him that he is unarmed, they beat him with rifle butts and shoot him dead.

November to December

Standing Bear travels through the East on a lecture tour.

Inspired by newspaper accounts sympathetic to his tribe's plight (see entry for APRIL 18, 1879), Ponca leader Standing Bear tours several cities in the East, delivering speeches about his people's removal from their homeland. To large audiences of non-Indians, he tells his story through the two translators, Omaha Indians Susette and Francis La Flesche. (Susette will later gain renown as an Indian activist, while her brother Francis will become one of the first Native American ethnologists.) Despite a public outcry for justice following Standing Bear's incarceration and tour, the Ponca in Indian Territory are forced to stay on their reservation.

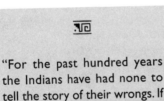

"For the past hundred years the Indians have had none to tell the story of their wrongs. If a white man did an injury to an Indian he had to suffer in silence, or being exasperated into revenge, the act of revenge has been spread abroad through the newspapers of the land as a causeless act, perpetrated on the whites just because the Indian delighted in being savage."

—Omaha activist Susette La Flesche during her 1879 lecture tour

1880

Indian University is established in the Cherokee Nation.

With a class of three, Indian University begins educating students in Indian Territory. Originally located in the town of Tahlequah in the Cherokee Nation, the school is founded by the American Baptist Home Mission Society. The university will quickly grow and move to a larger facility in Muskogee, where it will be renamed Bacone College.

October 15 to 16

Victorio's Apaches are defeated at the Battle of Tres Castillos.

Chased by American forces led by Colonel George Buell, the renegade Apache led by Victorio (see entry for SEPTEMBER 4, 1879) travel into Mexico's Chihuahua desert. There they are met by a 350-man militia of Mexicans and Tarahumara Indians. In the brutal two-day Battle of Tres Castillos, 78 Apache, including Victorio, are killed, and 62 more are captured. (See also entry for OCTOBER 1881.)

1881

Helen Hunt Jackson's *A Century of Dishonor* is published.

Inspired by the Standing Bear trial (see entry for APRIL 18, 1879), journalist Helen Hunt Jackson begins her career as an outspoken opponent of American Indian policy. Her book *A Century of Dishonor* chronicles the discrimination and injustices endured by Indians over the previous hundred years. Widely influential in intellectual circles, it represents one of the most vehement attacks any non-Indian has made upon the U.S. government for its mistreatment of Indian people. (See also entry for 1884.)

July 19

Sitting Bull and his followers surrender to the United States.

In the early months of the year, many members of Sitting Bull's camp in Canada (see entry for OCTOBER 1876), faced with starvation, crossed the border and make their way to the Lakota's reservations, where they can collect rations. A desperate Sitting Bull decided to follow suit and lead his diminishing band back to the United States.

Upon the arrival of Sitting Bull's followers at Fort Buford in Dakota Territory, they endure the humiliation of surrendering their weapons and horses to U.S. troops. The Indians expect to be confined to a reservation, but the army, still wary of Sitting Bull, instead sends the Indians to Fort Randall, where they will be imprisoned for two years.

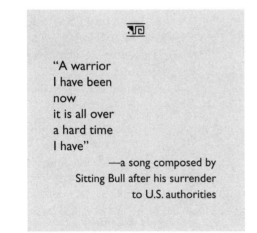

"A warrior
I have been
now
it is all over
a hard time
I have"

—a song composed by
Sitting Bull after his surrender
to U.S. authorities

August 5

Crow Dog kills Lakota Sioux leader.

During a heated dispute, a Lakota Sioux named Crow Dog shoots and kills his cousin Spotted Tail, an influential leader who had long sought peace by cooperating and negotiating with whites (see entry for JUNE 1866 and for APRIL TO AUGUST 1868). The tragic confrontation emerged from increasing tension between Spotted Tail and Crow Dog as Crow Dog began to challenge his friend's political authority.

A tribal court finds Crow Dog guilty and, in keeping with Sioux tradition, orders the killer to make restitution to Spotted Tail's family. The non-Indian press is outraged by the court's decision and demands that Crow Dog be imprisoned. The controversy will result in the landmark Supreme Court case *Ex Parte Crow Dog* (see entry for DECEMBER 17, 1883).

August 30

Apache prophet Nakaidoklini is murdered.

Among the White Mountain Apache, a prophet named Nakaidoklini preached that he could communicate with dead Apache and bring deceased leaders back to life. Fearing his growing following, Colonel Eugene A. Carr arrests Nakaidoklini at his village on Cibicue Creek and imprisons him at Fort Apache. Apache swarm around the fort, and amidst their protest fighting breaks out. Nakaidoklini is shot and killed by a soldier. Soon soldiers from throughout the Southwest rush to the Apache's San Carlos Reservation, responding to erroneous news reports that the Apache have massacred Carr and his troops.

October

Geronimo and his followers escape from San Carlos.

Alarmed by the increased military presence on the San Carlos Reservation (see entry for AUGUST 30, 1881), Apache leaders Geronimo, Juh, and Naiche and 74 followers flee to Mexico. There the runaways are reunited with the remnants of the Apache led by Victorio, who had escaped to Mexico five years earlier (see entry for SEPTEMBER 2, 1877).

1882

Traditionalists battle the Creek government in the Green Peach War.

Charged with misusing his office, tribal court judge Isparhechar is removed from his position by Samuel Checote, the principal chief of the Creek Nation.

An angry Isparhechar then joins the sizable faction of Creek traditionalists who demand that the tribal government be disbanded and replaced with one structured like a traditional Creek council. When the Creek police are sent to break up a meeting of Isparhechar's followers, the officers are shot. The conflict becomes known as the Green Peach War because it began in an orchard of unripened peaches.

Sent to track down the murderers, the Creek militia chase Isparhechar and several hundred of his followers to the Kiowa reservation. There U.S. troops capture the traditionalists, who are first sent to Fort Gibson but are later set free after Isparhechar and Checote make peace with one another.

Women's National Indian Association lobbies for an assimilation program.

Led by Amelia Stone Quinton, an influential advocate of temperance, the Women's National Indian Association demands in a petition that Congress initiate a program for assimilating Indians into non-Indian society. The association, composed largely of wealthy whites, endorses the division of tribally held land into individually owned allotments and the granting of citizenship to Indians.

The Omaha Allotment Act is passed.

With the encouragement of anthropologist Alice Fletcher, a faction of Omaha Indians lobby Congress to divide their reservation into individually owned allotments of land. Their efforts result in the passage of the Omaha Allotment Act. Although more assimilated than many tribes, the Omaha soon fall victim to their inexperience in owning private property. In time, two-thirds of the allotments will fall into the hands of non-Indians.

October 24 to 26

The U.S. Navy destroys the Tlingit village of Angoon.

The Tlingit of Angoon in southeast Alaska demand a payment of 200 blankets from the Northwest Trading Company. The goods are requested as compensation for the accidental deaths of two Tlingit men, including a shaman, who were killed while working for the trading firm. E. C. Merriman, the U.S. naval officer in charge of keeping peace in the region, meets with the Tlingit and tells them that they have no right to demand anything from whites. To punish them, he threatens to shell their village if they do not pay him a fee of 400 blankets.

When the Tlingit refuse, Merriman orders his men to demolish Angoon. Sailors fire a gatling gun into the village and set nearly all of its buildings on fire after looting the Tlingit's possessions. Six children die of smoke inhalation.

The destruction of Angoon is a disaster for Tlingit, who will spend more than 10 years rebuilding the village. Condemned by one congressman as "the greatest outrage ever committed in the United States upon any Indian tribe," the incident convinces the federal government to reorganize law enforcement in Alaska. (See also entries for 1973 and for OCTOBER 24 TO 26, 1982.)

December

Non-Indian philanthropists found the Indian Rights Association.

With offices in Philadelphia, the Indian Rights Association (IRA) is established to aid Native Americans. The organization is the brainchild of Herbert Welsh and Henry Panacoast, who attract many prominent and wealthy Easterners—the so-called Friends of the Indian—to their cause.

The IRA's mission is to protect Indians from the avarice of land-hungry whites until they can be fully assimilated into mainstream non-Indian culture. The tools the IRA advocates to assimilate Indians include non-Indian-style education, U.S. citizenship, Christianity, and the allotment of communal Indian lands into plots that individual Indians can own as private property.

The IRA quickly emerges as one of the most influential forces on U.S. Indian policy. The group maintains a high profile by organizing speeches, distributing pamphlets, and hiring a full-time lobbyist to present its views to those in power in Washington, D.C. The IRA's lobbying efforts will be instrumental in the passage of the General Allotment Act (see entry for FEBRUARY 8, 1887), which will result in the allotment of much of the tribally controlled land in the West. (See also entry for 1883.)

December 16

The Hopi Indian Reservation is established by executive order.

Responding to a series of Hopi delegations complaining of Navajo (Dineh) and Mormons moving onto their land, President Chester A. Arthur creates a reservation for the Hopi in a small area in the center of the tribe's ancestral homeland. Several Navajo families living within the new reservation's borders, however, refuse to surrender the region to the Hopi. The situation will lead to a Hopi-Navajo land dispute that will continue for more than 100 years.

1883

The first Lake Mohonk Conference is held.

Members of several religious and humanitarian groups devoted to reforming the government's dealings with Indians meet for the first of 35 annual conferences in the resort town of Lake Mohonk, New York. The conference participants, who call themselves "Friends of the Indian" (see entry for DECEMBER 1882), are mostly Protestant non-Indian reformers who believe the best way of protecting Native American rights and land is to encourage Indians to assimilate into mainstream American society.

During the late 19th and early 20th centuries, the Lake Mohonk conferences will have a great deal of influence on U.S. Indian policy and legislation. Their efforts will help lead to the passage of the General Allotment Act (see entry for FEBRUARY 8, 1887), which will aim to "civilize" Indian males by making them into private landowners.

"The Indian must be made to be intelligently selfish. . . . [He must be taken] out of . . . blankets and [put] into trousers —and trousers with a pocket in them, and a pocket that aches to be filled with dollars."

—Merrill Gates, the president of Amherst College, at the Lake Mohonk Conference of 1883

John Slocum founds the Indian Shaker Church.

Salish Indian John Slocum falls ill, prompting his father to ask an Indian healer for help. He does so against the wishes of Slocum's wife, Mary, who holds that Slocum had sworn off traditional medicine during another illness a year before. According to Slocum, the previous illness killed him but he rose up from the dead while his neighbors were searching for a coffin. During the experience, Slocum claims that he encountered God, who told Slocum that he would grant salvation to all Indians who swore off gambling, drinking, smoking, and consulting Indian healers. God also promised to give these Indians a far greater healing power than their medicine people possessed.

During Slocum's second illness, Mary begins to speak to God, weeping and shaking uncontrollably. As she prays over his body, Slocum recovers. He attributes his miraculous cure to Mary's shaking, which he sees as the promised medicine from God. Slocum spreads word of his revelation and cure, initiating the Indian Shaker movement, which will eventually spread through the Indian populations of Washington State, Oregon, northern California, and British Columbia. (See also entry for 1927.)

Mormon missionaries arrive among the Catawba.

Soon after their arrival on the Catawba's South Carolina reservation, representatives of the Mormon church find a large number of willing converts. The Catawba are attracted to Mormonism in part because, like themselves, the Mormons are discriminated against by their white neighbors. The missionaries also help establish schools for the Indians, who are barred from attending either white or black institutions in the area. Over the following decades, Mormonism will prove such a compelling force that it will help unify and revitalize the tribe.

Sarah Winnemucca's *Life among the Piutes* is published.

The first book published in English by an American Indian woman, *Life among the Piutes* combines a tribal history of the Northern Paiute with the autobiography of its author, Sarah Winnemucca. Winnemucca publishes the book to raise funds for an eastern lecture tour. Winnemucca tells her audiences, primarily wealthy whites, of the plight of her people, who were forced to leave their homeland following the Bannock War (see entry for MAY TO SEPTEMBER 1878). During the war, Winnemucca served as an interpreter for General Oliver O. Howard, who led U.S. troops against Bannock and Northern Paiute (Numu) rebels.

April 10

The Bureau of Indian Affairs (BIA) creates Courts of Indian Offenses.

Intended to punish Indians who violate a ban on holding traditional religious ceremonies such as the Sun Dance, the Bureau of Indian Affairs (BIA) establishes Courts of Indian Offenses on reservations. In the past, most reservation disputes were informally settled by non-Indian agents. The new courts allow the three highest-ranking members of a reservation's police force (see entry for 1878) to try residents for minor offenses. Recognizing the inher-

ent conflict in policemen serving as judges, Congress will soon provide funds for hiring three Indian judges for each tribal court.

Among the offenses the Indian courts are charged to try is the performance of what Secretary of the Interior H. M. Teller refers to as "old heathenish dances." Teller holds that in addition to being un-Christian, traditional ceremonies "stimulate the warlike passions" and are therefore a threat to the peace.

May 17

"Buffalo Bill's Wild West" premieres.

Masterminded by William "Buffalo Bill" Cody (see entry for JULY 17, 1876), "Buffalo Bill's Wild West and Congress of the Rough Riders" opens in Omaha, Nebraska. The show is one of about 50 traveling productions featuring sharpshooting, trick riding, and dramatic recreations of events in American history, particularly famous battles between the U.S. Army and Plains Indians.

"A Host of Western Celebrities; A Camp of Cheyenne, Arapahoe, Sioux and Pawnee Indians; A Group of Mexican Vaqueros; Round-up of Western Cow-Boys; Company of Prairie Scouts; A Herd of Wild Buffalos; A Corral of Indian Ponies; A Band of Mountain Elk; A Drove of Texas Steers; Pack-Train of Mexican Burros; Mountain Lions, Coyotes, Deer, Antelope, Mountain Sheep, etc."

—attractions on an 1886 program for "Buffalo Bill's Wild West"

Among the biggest draws of the show are the actual Indians and cowboys Cody hires as performers. The Indians enact scenes that reinforce white stereotypes of Indian people. The performers, however, benefit from the experience in several ways. At the very least, it offers them a source of income in an era when Plains Indians have few ways of making a living. Working in the show also gives Indians a chance to travel and, perhaps most importantly, a forum in which to display the superior horsemanship and marksmanship that has long been a source of intense pride for young Indian men of the Plains.

Cody, a former U.S. Army scout, is already a popular hero because of the embellished accounts of his exploits in the West written by "dime" novelist Ned Buntline. His show is an instant success, largely because of his skills at marketing his own image and because the myths of the "wild West" hold special appeal for his American and European audiences. (See also entry for JUNE TO OCTOBER 1885.)

June

U.S. troops penetrate an Apache mountain hideout.

Determined to end raids by the Apache followers of Geronimo (see entry for OCTOBER 1881), General George Crook enlists the assistance of Apache scouts. With their help, his men find and attack the Apache led by Chato in the Sierre Madre. The leaders of the runaway Apache, alarmed by Crook's ability to persuade fellow tribesmen to fight against

A 1907 publicity photograph of William "Buffalo Bill" Cody with his cast of Indian performers (*Wyoming State Museum*)

them, agree to meet with him in council. In the meeting, the general threatens to kill them all if they refuse to give themselves up. After much discussion among the leaders, Geronimo tells Crook that his people will surrender. (See also entry for MAY 1885.)

September

Sitting Bull speaks at the dedication of the Northern Pacific.

Perhaps the most famous Indian in the United States, Lakota chief Sitting Bull is invited to deliver a speech at a ceremony to dedicate the Northern Pacific Railroad in Bismarck, North Dakota. Speaking in his own language, Sitting Bull tells the crowd, "I hate all white people. You are thieves and liars. You have taken away our land and made us outcasts." His startled translator ignores Sitting Bull's actual words and reads from the laudatory prepared speech that Sitting Bull was supposed to have delivered. The speech receives a standing ovation from the audience.

December 17

The Supreme Court overturns the murder conviction of Crow Dog.

In 1881 a tribal court orders Crow Dog, a Lakota Sioux Indian convicted of killing of another Lakota, to make restitution to his victim's family (see entry for AUGUST 5, 1881). Seeking a harsher punishment, the territorial court of Dakota also indicted Crow Dog on murder charges. Crow Dog was again convicted and sentenced to death.

Claiming that the Dakota court has no jurisdiction over crimes committed by Indians on reservations, Crow Dog appeals the case to the Supreme Court. Determining that the Dakota court's action is a threat to Lakota sovereignty, the Supreme Court in *Ex Parte Crow Dog* overturns the conviction and death sentence. The ruling, which outrages the non-Indian legal community, will lead to the passage of the Major Crimes Act (see entry for MARCH 3, 1885).

1884

The Supreme Court denies Indians citizenship in *Elk v. Wilkins*.

John Elk, an assimilated Indian who does not live on Indian lands, is denied the right to vote in Nebraska. As a result, the Ponca Indian Committee initiates a lawsuit, arguing that because Elk has voluntarily chosen not to be a member of a tribe, he should be considered a U.S. citizen and be able to enjoy the rights of that status. The Supreme Court, however, rules in *Elk v. Wilkins* that the Fourteenth Amendment (see entry for JULY 8, 1868) does not apply to Indians, even those who renounce tribal membership.

The Organic Act recognizes land claims of Alaskan Natives.

In the Organic Act of 1884, Congress states that Natives of Alaska "shall not be disturbed in the possession of any lands" they use, occupy, or claim. The act adds, however, that future legislation will have to determine whether these peoples can be given legal title to their land.

Helen Hunt Jackson's *Ramona* is published.

Reformer and author of *A Century of Dishonor* (see entry for 1881), Helen Hunt Jackson writes the novel *Ramona* as a means of drawing attention to the injustices committed against California Indians. Loosely based on the life of Ramona Lubo, a Cahuilla basketmaker, *Ramona* is the sentimental story of a beautiful half-Mexican, half-Indian woman in love with an Indian man named Alessandro. As his tribe is dispossessed of its lands by settlers, Alessandro is driven insane and steals a white man's horse. Ramona watches as the man shoots down her beloved.

Largely because of its romantic, mythic view of California's past, *Ramona* is an enormous popular success and becomes a prototype for later stereotypical tales of lovelorn Indian "maidens." The novel will also provide the basis for four films and a play that is still performed annually in Hemet, California.

"[W]hen she reached the threshold, it was to hear a gunshot, to see Alessandro fall to the ground, to see, in the same second, a ruffianly man leap from his horse, and standing over Alessandro's body, fire his pistol again, once, twice, into the forehead, cheek. . . . As he rode away, he shook his fist at Ramona, who was kneeling on the ground, striving to lift Alessandro's head, and to staunch the blood flowing from the ghastly wounds. 'That'll teach you damned Indians to leave off stealing our horses!' he cried, and with another volley of ter-rible oaths was out of sight."

—from Helen Hunt Jackson's novel *Ramona*

The Canadian parliament passes the Indian Advancement Act.

The Indian Advancement Act sets forth provisions that will make the governments of assimilated Indian bands function like municipalities. The law gives band councils greater power to levy taxes, punish perpetrators of minor crimes, and control health care. The act also reduces the number of band councilors to six and calls for annual elections. Its most controversial provision allows representatives of the Canadian government to depose any council members deemed dishonest or immoral and prohibits bands from immediately reelecting leaders removed from their posts.

April 19

Canada outlaws the potlatch ceremony.

Under pressure from missionaries, the Canadian government makes it illegal for Indians living along the Pacific Coast to hold potlatches. In these traditional ceremonies, a wealthy family hosts a great feast and further demonstrates its generosity by distributing gifts to its guests. The increasingly elaborate gift giving, which plays a crucial role in the social and economic structure of these Indians' villages, is held suspect by missionaries and government officials, who feel the tradition is incompatible with Western concepts of personal property.

September 1

The United States Industrial Training School opens.

Located in Lawrence, Kansas, the United States Industrial Training School (renamed the Haskell Institute in 1894) admits its first class of 14 students. Like other Indian boarding schools operated by the Bureau of Indian Affairs, the school encourages assimilation by teaching students to abandon Indian ways and adopt non-Indian customs and beliefs in their place (see entry for AUTUMN 1879).

By the late 20th century, Haskell will become one of the largest Indian colleges. Renamed Haskell Indian Nations University in 1993, the institution will promote Indian sovereignty and self-determination among its approximately 100,000 students.

1885

William W. Warren's *History of the Ojibways* is published.

History of the Ojibways, Based upon Traditions and Oral Statements, by Minnesota state legislator William W. Warren, is published more than 30 years after his death. The son of a white trader and a French-Ojibway woman, Warren interviewed Ojibway elders to research the one-volume history.

> "When an Ojibway dies, his body is placed in a grave, generally in a sitting position, facing the west. . . . After camping out four nights, and traveling each day through a prairie country, the soul arrives in the land of spirits, where he finds his relatives accumulated since mankind was first created, all is rejoicing, singing and dancing, they live in a beautiful country interspersed with clear lakes and streams, forests and abounding in fruit and game[,] . . . all that the red man most covets in this life."
>
> —Ojibway author William W. Warren in *History of the Ojibways*

Washington Matthews begins recording Navajo (Dineh) ceremonies and songs.

Fearing that knowledge of traditional ceremonies, songs, and ceremonial dry paintings is in danger of being lost, Washington Matthews, the doctor at Fort Defiance, enlists the aid of Navajo (Dineh) leader Cree Dodge in recording these elements of tribal culture. The result of their efforts is a series of works, including *Navaho Legends* (1897) and *The Night Chant, a Navaho Ceremony* (1902).

March 3

Congress passes the Major Crimes Act.

Drafted as a result of the Supreme Court ruling in *Ex Parte Crow Dog* (see entry for DECEMBER 17, 1883), the Major Crimes Act establishes that Indians accused of committing major crimes on Indian reservations will be tried in U.S. courts, rather than in tribal courts. (The act defines "major crimes" as murder, manslaughter, arson, burglary, rape, larceny, and as- sault with the intent to kill.) It is the first piece of legislation to make Indians on tribally held lands subject to U.S. law. (See also entry for 1886.)

March 19

Louis Riel forms a Métis government in the Second Northwest Rebellion.

Following an unsuccessful Métis rebellion in Manitoba (see entry for NOVEMBER 2, 1869, and for AUGUST 24, 1870), rebel leader Louis Riel Jr. escaped Canadian authorities by moving to Montana, where he worked as a schoolteacher. As whites begin encroaching on the territory of the Saskatchewan Métis, a delegation led by Gabriel Dumont visits Riel in early 1884 and asks him to appeal to the Canadian government to recognize their land claims. While in exile, Riel has been elected to parliament three times but has been unable to take his seat for fear of arrest. When his appeal is ignored by the Canadian government, Riel organizes a second Métis uprising. He and his followers seize the church at Batoche, Northwest Territories (now in Saskatchewan), and establish an independent Métis government there. (See also entry for MAY 12 TO 15, 1885.)

May

Geronimo's band breaks out of the Apache reservation.

Forty-two men and 92 women led by Geronimo flee the San Carlos Reservation and head south to Mexico. Geronimo had surrendered less than two years earlier (see entry for JUNE 1883), but he found reservation life intolerable. Particularly bothersome to Geronimo are petty reservation rules that prohibit the consumption of tiswin, an alcoholic drink.

May 12 to 15

Canadian troops crush the Second Northwest Rebellion.

After the rebelling Métis at Batoche (see entry for MARCH 19, 1885) meet police in several skirmishes, the Canadian government sends federal troops to end the uprising. In a three-day battle, the rebels are defeated. While the Métis disperse, their leader, Louis Riel Jr., surrenders to Canadian authorities. For his role in the rebellion, Riel will be hanged for treason on November 16. After his death, he will become a martyr for both the Métis and the French Canadians in their efforts to force the Canadian government to recognize their sovereignty.

May 22

Chief Joseph's band of Nez Perce returns to the Northwest.

The 150 surviving followers of Chief Joseph board a train to take them from their reservation in Indian Territory to the Colville Indian Reservation in Washington State. Although they are not permitted to return to their homeland in the Wallowa Valley of Oregon, their return to the Northwest is considered a victory by the eastern non-Indian reformers who, impressed by Chief Joseph's passion and personal charisma, have taken up the Nez Perce cause (see JANUARY 14, 1879). Chief Joseph, however, is reportedly still despondent over his separation from the Wallowa Valley. At the Nez Perce leader's death in 1904, the doctor at Colville will maintain officially that Joseph died of a broken heart.

June to October

Sitting Bull appears in "Buffalo Bill's Wild West."

Vigorously courted by William Cody, the founder of "Buffalo Bill's Wild West" (see entry for MAY 17, 1883), Sitting Bull signs a contract to appear in the show's 1885 tour of the United States and Canada. As the Indian leader best known to the non-Indian public, Sitting Bull brings both jeers and cheers from the crowd as he parades on a beautiful gray circus horse through the arena in each show. In exchange for his performance, he receives $50 a week, a $125 bonus, and the exclusive right to sell his photograph and autograph to audiences.

Sitting Bull tells reporters that he enjoys show business but will decline Cody's invitation to stay with the show for a tour of England because he is needed on the Great Sioux Reservation. When Sitting Bull's contract ends, Cody, who has become a friend, gives him the gray horse.

1886

Mohawk Indians are first hired as ironworkers.

While constructing a bridge over the St. Lawrence River, the Dominion Bridge Company hires several Mohawk men from the nearby Kahnawake Reserve as day laborers. The men balance on and climb the high steel beams so adeptly and confidently that construction companies begin routinely hiring Mohawk as ironworkers on bridges and other steel structures. (See also entries for 1915 and for AUGUST 29, 1907.)

United States v. Kagama upholds the Major Crimes Act.

The legitimacy of the Major Crimes Act (see entry for MARCH 3, 1885), which gave federal courts jurisdiction over major crimes occurring on reservation land, is tested in *United States v. Kagama*. The case is brought against two Indians who in a federal court were convicted of killing another Indian on the Hoopa Valley Reservation in California. The criminals challenge the verdict, maintaining that despite the Major Crimes Act only a tribal court can try them for a crime committed on a reservation.

The Supreme Court dismisses their argument and decides that the conviction, and by extension the Major Crimes Act as well, are constitutional because Indians are legally wards of the U.S. government. The ruling reverses the Court's earlier controversial decision in *Ex Parte Crow Dog* (see entry for DECEMBER 17, 1883), which held that federal courts had no jurisdiction over criminal activity on Indian-held lands.

March to September

Geronimo surrenders to the U.S. Army.

Geronimo, exhausted by the military's efforts to subdue his renegade band, asks to meet with General George Crook—whom he had surrendered to nearly three years earlier (see entry for JUNE 1883)—at Canyon de los Embudos. Crook again threatens to kill all of Geronimo's people if they do not surrender. He insists that they will be sent to prison in the East but promises that after two years they will be allowed to return to the San Carlos Reservation, in present-day Arizona. On

March 25, after days of discussion, Geronimo accepts Crook's terms. In less than a week, however, he and Apache leader Nachez lead 20 men and 13 women back to their mountain hideaways in Mexico.

The Indians remain renegades for five months before Geronimo makes his final surrender to General Nelson A. Miles at Skeleton Canyon on September 4. Miles's terms are harsh: He insists that Geronimo's band be sent to deportation camps in Florida, along with all of the Chiricahua and Warm Spring Apache (including the army's Indian scouts) from the San Carlos Reservation. Geronimo's

Geronimo (front row, third from the right) and his followers, preparing to travel by rail to a Florida prison following their surrender to the U.S. Army *(National Archives, Neg. no. 111-SC-82320)*

surrender marks the end of the Apache's armed resistance to reservation life.

The Peabody Museum purchases the Great Serpent Mound.

Harvard University's Peabody Museum buys the farm of John Lovett in Adams County, Ohio. On the tract is the Great Serpent Mound—the largest effigy mound in North America (see entry for 1000 B.C. TO A.D. 700). The mound, which measures almost a mile long, was constructed by Indians of the Adena or Hopewell culture beginning about 3,000 years ago. The Peabody's purchase is made possible by a fund-raising campaign by museum employee F. W. Putnam, who wanted to ensure the mound would be preserved. The following year, the Peabody will open the area to the public as Serpent Mound Park.

Anthropologist Franz Boas begins his study of the Kwakiutl.

At 29, German-American anthropologist Franz Boas makes the first of many trips to British Columbia to observe and record the culture of the Kwakiutl people. Boas's research is aided by George Hunt, a man of mixed Tlingit and white ancestry who grew up among the Kwakiutl. Acting as a liaison between the Indians and the white anthropologist, Hunt helps Boas gain access to the winter ceremonials and other rituals that dominate Kwakiutl society.

Living among the Kwakiutl, Boas discovers the extreme complexity of their society. Able in the summer to catch and preserve enough fish to feed themselves year-round, the Kwakiutl are free throughout the winter to stage elaborate ceremonies, in which they dramatize their huge body of legends. Boas also learns of the complicated societal hierarchy by participating in potlatches, grand feasts during which wealthy Kwakiutl hosts confirm their rank in society by giving lavish gifts to their guests.

Largely through the publication of his research into Kwakiutl life, Boas will redefine anthropologists' approach toward the study of North American Indians. Rather than viewing Indians as "primitives" inferior to more "developed" peoples, Boas insists that the cultures of Indians he has observed are as sophisticated as so-called civilized societies. Boas's work will also emphasize the importance of collecting data about all aspects of a culture, from language to religion to art.

"Anyone who has lived with primitive tribes, who has shared their joys and sorrows, their privations and their luxuries, who sees in them not solely subjects of study to be examined like a cell under the microscope, but feeling and thinking human beings, will agree that there is no such thing as a 'primitive mind,' . . . but that each individual in 'primitive' society is a man, woman, a child of the same kind, of the same way of thinking, feeling and acting as man, woman or child in our own society."

—anthropologist Franz Boas on studying Indian cultures

Lakota George Bushotter is hired by the Bureau of American Ethnology.

A graduate of the Hampton Institute (see entry for APRIL 1878), George Bushotter, a Lakota Sioux, is recruited by anthropologist James Owen Dorsey to aid his research at the Bureau of American Ethnology (see entry for MARCH 3, 1879). During his 10 months there, Bushotter writes more than 1,000 pages about Lakota culture in the Lakota language and helps compile material on his language that will appear in the *Handbook of American Indians North of Mexico*. Bushotter will become known as the first Lakota ethnographer. Much of his work will later be translated by the Nakota Sioux linguist and novelist Ella Deloria (see entry for 1932).

February 8

The General Allotment Act is signed into law.

One of the most influential pieces of legislation in Native American history, the General Allotment Act (also known as the Dawes Act, after its sponsor Senator Henry L. Dawes) authorizes the president to survey Indian lands and compile tribal rolls in preparation for dividing reservations into 160-acres tracts called allotments. Unlike reservation land, which is owned communally by a tribe, allotments are to be held as private property. The act stipulates that when a reservation is allotted, the male head of each family will receive U.S. citizenship with his allotment. Because the government believes that most Indians are incompetent in business affairs, allotments are to be held in trust for 25 years, during which time they cannot be sold or leased by their Indian owners. Any land left over after all allotments are granted will be sold by the U.S. government.

The Allotment policy has broad support among non-Indians. Many reformers advocate Allotment as the best means of assimilating Indians: As landowners they will be better able to live like whites. Other "friends of the Indian" hold that Indians stand to lose all their lands to unscrupulous whites unless they own it as private property. The majority of whites, however, favor Allotment because the sale of the surplus lands will open huge areas to non-Indian settlement.

Few Indians support Allotment. Several large tribes—including the Five Civilized Tribes (the Cherokee, Chickasaw, Choctaw, Creek, and Seminole), the Osage, and the Seneca—are explicitly excluded from the General Allotment Act because their leaders have lobbied Congress to retain their tribally held lands and tribal government.

November 5

Crow warrior Sword Bearer is killed by U.S. troops.

A group of young Crow warriors, led by Sword Bearer, raid a camp of Blackfeet, who have stolen some of the Crow's horses. Recapturing the horses, the young men ride triumphantly through the town of Crow Agency, Montana. During the excitement, Sword Bearer fires his rifle into the agent's house and the town store. Fearing an uprising, the agent calls his superiors in Washington, D.C., to request military support. With the troops and local whites terrified of rebelling reservation Indians, the army orders Sword Bearer's arrest. A shoot-out follows, leaving eight Crow Indians, including Sword Bearer, dead.

1889

Susan La Flesche becomes the first female Native American physician.

Graduating first in her class, Omaha Indian Susan La Flesche is awarded a medical degree from the Women's College of Medicine in Philadelphia, Pennsylvania, thereby becoming the first Indian female to be fully trained in Western medicine. Her education has been funded by the Connecticut Indian Association, a group of pro-assimilation non-Indian reformers.

After graduation, La Flesche will return to the Omaha Reservation in Nebraska. There the Bureau of Indian Affairs will hire her as the reservation's physician, making her the only doctor available to the more than 1,000 reservation residents.

The Sioux Bill breaks up the Great Sioux Reservation.

Congress passes the Sioux Bill, which divides the Great Sioux Reservation established by the Treaty of Fort Laramie (see entry for NOVEMBER 7, 1868) into six smaller reservations: Standing Rock, Pine Ridge, Rosebud, Cheyenne River, Crow Creek, and

Lower Brulé. The law also opens nine million acres of former reservation land to settlement by whites and allows for remaining Sioux lands to be divided into 320-acre allotments to be owned by individual Indians.

January 1

Northern Paiute (Numu) prophet Wovoka founds a new Indian religion.

While cutting wood in tribal lands in western Nevada, a Northern Paiute (Numu) named Wovoka has a fever-induced vision. By his account, he dies and goes to heaven, where he encounters his dead ancestors. While in heaven, he is also given instruction from God on how Indians should live. They should avoid fighting, live in peace with whites, and perform the traditional Paiute Round Dance. Wovoka himself is given by God the power to control natural elements as well as the position of co-vice president of the United States. Wovoka's revelation will lead him to found the Ghost Dance movement, which will soon be embraced by the Indians throughout the Great Plains (see entry for SUMMER 1890).

"When the sun died, I went up to heaven and saw God and all the people who had died a long time ago. God told me to come back and tell my people they must be good and love one another, and not fight, or steal, or lie. He gave me this dance to give to my people."

—Northern Paiute (Numu) prophet Wovoka, on his religious revelation

April 22

The Unassigned Lands in Indian Territory are opened to non-Indians.

A 2-million-acre region in the center of Indian Territory that has not been assigned to an Indian group is opened to settlement by non-Indians. In the first of a series of rushes on former Indian Territory land, more than 50,000 non-Indians claim plots of land on this single day.

1890

February 8

Indian schools celebrate Indian Citizenship Day.

To commemorate the anniversary of the General Allotment Act (see entry for FEBRUARY 8, 1887), the commissioner of Indian affairs directs Indian schools to observe "Indian Citizenship Day." The celebration is intended to stir patriotism in Indian students by extolling the virtues of U.S. citizenship and private property, which will be granted to the residents of selected reservations through the Allotment act.

Indian Citizenship Day will become an annual school holiday, with speeches, pageants, and dramas featuring student performers. For example, in 1892, "Columbia's Roll Call," an extravaganza performed at Virginia's Hampton Institute (see entry for APRIL 1878), follows a mythic goddess "Columbia" as she meets Christopher Columbus, George Washington, and other legendary figures in American history. At the end of the parade of characters is a group of assimilated Indian tradesmen and farmers, on whom Columbia bestows the honor of citizenship.

May

Western Indian Territory becomes Oklahoma Territory.

The United States reorganizes the western portion of Indian Territory as the new territory of

Oklahoma. The federal government immediately begins the process of allotting the reservations in Oklahoma Territory so that any surplus lands can be sold to whites. With the formation of Oklahoma Territory, Indian Territory is reduced to the large reservations of the Five Civilized Tribes (Cherokee, Choctaw, Chickasaw, Creek, and Seminole) and several small reservations located in the extreme northeastern corner of the region.

Summer

The Ghost Dance is introduced to the Indians of the Plains.

Rumors of a messiah among the Northern Paiute (Numu) inspire a group of Lakota Sioux to seek out Wovoka, who claims to have traveled to heaven during a vision (see entry for JANUARY 1, 1889). Although Wovoka's divine revelation told him that Indians should cooperate with whites, the Lakota bring home to their people a version of the Wovoka's

"The whole world is coming.
A nation is coming, a nation is
    coming.
The Eagle has brought the
    message to the tribe.
The father says so, the father
    says so.
Over the whole earth they are
    coming.
The buffalo are coming, the
    buffalo are coming,
The Crow has brought the
    message to the tribe,
The father says so, the father
    says so."
            —a Lakota Sioux Ghost Dance
        song, recorded by anthropologist
                James Mooney in 1892

new religion that prophesies the death of all whites, the resurrection of their Indian ancestors, and the revival of traditional Indian ways of life. The converted begin to perform a version of the traditional Paiute Round Dance, which becomes known as the Ghost Dance.

The Ghost Dance movement quickly sweeps the Plains, finding followers in many tribes, including the Arapaho, Cheyenne, Shoshone, and Ute. Demoralized by reservation life, crop failures, and epidemic disease, eventually some 60,000 Indians will adopt the religion. The enthusiastic reception of the Ghost Dance frightens whites on the Plains, who fear its teachings will inspire Indians to band together and wage war against them. (See also entries for OCTOBER 1890 and for DECEMBER 29, 1890.)

October

The Pine Ridge agent requests U.S. troops to suppress the Ghost Dance.

The popularity of the Ghost Dance (see entry for SUMMER 1890), particularly its prediction of death for all whites, alarms Daniel F. Royer, the agent of the Lakota Sioux's Pine Ridge Reservation in South Dakota. When reservation Indians ignore his orders to stop dancing, he asks the U.S. government to send soldiers to restore order.

December 15

Sitting Bull is murdered by Indian police.

Amidst the panic caused by the Ghost Dance Religion (see entry for SUMMER 1890), government officials fear that the great Lakota leader Sitting Bull will lead the Ghost Dancers in a resistance movement against whites. On the recommendation of the commissioner of Indian affairs, the agent of the Standing Rock Reservation in North Dakota, James McLaughlin, orders Indian police to arrest Sitting Bull so he can be confined to a military prison. Some 100 U.S. troops from the Eighth Cavalry are dispatched to support the reservation police force.

Before daybreak, 39 Indian policemen storm Sitting Bull's cabin on the Grand River and place him under arrest. As he is being led away, an angry mob of Indians surrounds the police. In the panic that follows, a member of the crowd shoots the police commander in the leg. The police commander in turn shoots Sitting Bull in the side, while another Indian policeman fires a bullet into his head, killing the Lakota leader instantly. In the gunfight that follows, seven Lakota crowd members and six Indian policemen are killed before the U.S. soldiers can intervene.

December 29

U.S. soldiers massacre Lakota Indians at Wounded Knee.

As the Ghost Dance movement spreads through the Lakota Sioux (see entry for SUMMER 1890), some 3,000 Ghost Dancers camp together on the Pine Ridge Reservation. At the request of several leaders of the Oglala Lakota band, who fear that the United States will resort to a military campaign to break up the camp, most of the Ghost Dancers show their willingness to cooperate with authorities

A mass grave for the victims of the Wounded Knee Massacre of 1890 *(Courtesy of the Montana Historical Society, Helena)*

by voluntarily moving closer to the Pine Ridge Agency by late December.

Ghost Dancers led by Chief Big Foot are en route to the agency when they are confronted by the Seventh Cavalry near Wounded Knee Creek. Starving and freezing, the group—including about 100 men and 250 women and children—surrenders to the soldiers on December 28. The next morning, the troops exhausted after a night of celebratory drinking, attempt to disarm Big Foot's people. In the search for weapons, they treat the Indians, particularly the women, roughly and disrespectfully. As tensions rise, one warrior refuses to give up his gun. When the soldiers grab for it, the gun goes off. In the ensuing chaos, the troops begin firing into the crowd of Indians. The uninjured flee toward the surrounding woods, chased by soldiers. Bodies of women, children, and babies, riddled with bullets, will later be found as far as three miles away from the camp.

The hideous slaughter of Big Foot's band at Wounded Knee is one of the greatest tragedies in American Indian history. Though only one out of a series of Indian massacres committed by the U.S. Army, it will take on a larger symbolic importance. Often cited as the end of the Indian Wars, Wounded Knee will become an emblem of the centuries of injustices inflicted on Indian peoples and a rallying point for future Indian activists, particularly during the Red Power movement of the late 1960s and early 1970s (see entry for FEBRUARY 28, 1973).

7

1891 TO 1933
THE DISPOSSESSION YEARS

An exhausted Indian sits slumped forward from the waist atop his horse, the animal itself so weak that its legs are buckling beneath the weight of its burden. Cast in bronze, this allegorical figure achieved international renown as *The End of the Trail* (1915), a sculpture by James Earle Fraser. Its meaning was obvious: The Indian, once noble, had become a dying breed who would soon disappear forever.

Fraiser's warrior was only one of many popular images that predicted, and even celebrated, the demise of Indian peoples in the early 20th century. From the photographs of Edward Curtis to the novels of Zane Grey, Indians were said to be a "vanishing race." As Grey wrote in *The Vanishing American* (1925), "[The Indian's] deeds are done. His glory and dream are gone. His sun has set." For most Americans, an even more constant reminder of the Indian's eminent death was the Indian-head nickel, issued in 1913. Designed by Fraiser, it depicted an Indian man's profile on one side and a buffalo on the other—a none-too-subtle suggestion that the Indian, like the buffalo, was doomed to become a casualty of the United States's expansion westward.

As the prevalence of this imagery implies, the notion of the vanishing Indian was embraced by many non-Indians. It not only confirmed that the bloody and costly Indian Wars of the 19th century had in fact been won, but it promised that the victors need not worry over what to do about their defeated enemy. Centuries of bloodshed, disease, and forced assimilation had at last solved what policy makers had once called the Indian Problem.

The ultimate death of the Indian indeed seemed so certain that non-Indians could now afford to romanticize the peoples and cultures that they had long worked to destroy. Not surprisingly, the myth of the vanishing Indian blossomed simultaneously with the birth of the western film, the Boy Scouts' Indian merit badge, and a tourist industry that touted the remaining Indians in the West as an attraction for eastern vacationers.

There was, however, one obvious problem with the idea of the vanishing Indians: Indians were still very much alive. They had not become extinct; they had merely become easy to ignore. Owing largely to the federal Indian policies of the 19th century, by 1890 the Indian population of the United States had dropped to less than 250,000, an all-time low. Most lived in dire poverty, and many were landless. The immediate culprit of their misery was the policy of allotting tribally owned lands as individual plots to be held as private property. Lauded by some reformers as

225

the only means by which Indians could hold onto their remaining territory, the Allotment policy proved to have the opposite effect. Between 1887 and 1934, its implementation would lead Indians to lose some 90 million acres of land.

Although the poverty of most Indians rendered them invisible to the majority of Americans, some Indians gained prominence during the early years of the century. Those with the highest profiles were athletes, such as baseball player Louis Sockalexis, marathon runner Tom Longboat, and Olympic champion Jim Thorpe. A gold-medal winner in the 1912 decathlon and pentathlon, Thorpe would go on to play professional baseball and football in one of the most spectacular athletic careers in American history. Less well known today but significant in their time were Indian authors such as Charles A. Eastman, Mourning Dove, and John Joseph Mathews. Using non-Indian literary forms, these writers brought attention to the plight of Indians to generations of white readers.

Also influential were the many Indians who came together to resist government policies that were destroying Indian peoples and cultures. Traditionalists—such as the anti-Allotment Creek of the Crazy Snake movement—launched a number of resistance movements that openly rejected white customs and demanded a return to Indian ways. Others united to create such organizations as the Mission Indian Foundation and the All-Pueblo Council. While modeled after non-Indian political institutions, these and similar organizations provided powerful tools in the fight to protect Indian rights.

The most important Indian political organization of the era was the Society of American Indians (SAI). Founded in 1911, the group brought together prominent Indian advocates, including Carlos Montezuma, Gertrude Bonnin, Alfred C. Parker, and Laura Cornelius Kellogg. Many SAI members had been educated at boarding schools operated by the Bureau of Indian Affairs. Beginning in 1879 with the establishment of the Carlisle Indian Industrial Boarding School, these institutions sought to eliminate tribalism by instructing Indian children in the ways of white society. But for many students, their school experience redefined, rather than destroyed, their "Indianness." As the SAI bore witness, the schools produced a new generation of Indian leaders, whose knowledge of English, white customs, and mainstream institutions allowed them to deal effectively with non-Indian leaders and bureaucrats.

Although the agendas of individual members varied, the SAI took as its primary goals securing citizenship for all Indians and abolishing the Bureau of Indian Affairs, the government agency that had developed the policies largely responsible for the dispossession and poverty of American Indians. The group succeeded only in the former. In part as a reward for the military service of some 16,000 Indians during World War I, native-born Indians were made U.S. citizens in 1924. Citizenship, however, did little to improve the daily lot of Indian people. The SAI's more significant legacy was as a model for future political groups, such as the Indians of All Tribes and the American Indian Movement. Like the SAI, these were multitribal organizations whose members were willing to put aside tribal differences to work together to improve the lot of all Indians.

Spurred on by Indian activists and by an alarming series of Indian murders on the oil-rich Osage reservation, non-Indian progressives began to push for a reexamination of Indian policy. An early effort was the Committee of One Hundred, a group of Indians and non-Indians brought together by the Calvin Coolidge administration to discuss Indian affairs. The committee called for a wide variety of reforms—from improvements in Indian education to increased governmental tolerance for traditional Indian religion—but their recommendations were largely ignored. Far more significant to federal Indian policy was the Meriam Report, which was published in 1928. The document was the result of an extensive investigation of the living conditions of contemporary Indians. The findings were appalling: Indians were discovered to be the most impoverished American minority by every measure, including housing, health care, education, and diet.

By shining a light on Indian poverty, the Meriam Report revealed to all that Indians had never in fact vanished. They had merely been hidden from view. Its revelations would usher in a new era in which Indians and non-Indians alike would acknowledge the scope of problems facing modern Indians and the increasingly urgent need for a remedy.

1891

Sophia Alice Callahan's *A Child of the Forest* is published.

A Child of the Forest, by Sophia Alice Callahan, is possibly the first published novel written by an American Indian woman. A schoolteacher in Muskogee Indian Territory, the 23-year-old Callahan is the daughter of a prominent Creek merchant and farmer who was long involved in Creek politics. Her novel tells the story of a young Creek woman who learns to live comfortably in both the Creek and white worlds while under the tutelage of a white southern woman. Drawing on contemporary news stories, the last portion of the book shifts the focus to Lakota Sioux territory and castigates the U.S. government for its actions in the events leading up to the Wounded Knee Massacre (see entry for DECEMBER 29, 1890).

Alaskan Natives begin herding reindeer.

Serving as a Presbyterian missionary in Alaska, non-Indian Sheldon Jackson introduces reindeer herding to Inuit in the region. With whale harvest decreasing, Jackson hopes that reindeer will provide Inuit hunters with a new source of skins and meat. Eventually funded by the U.S. government, the missionary's efforts bring nearly 1,300 Siberian reindeer to Alaska. At local missions, the Inuit are instructed in caring for the animals by Sami, na-

Bering Strait Inuit corralling a reindeer herd, drawn with ink on hide by Inuit artist George Ahgupuk *(The Anchorage Museum of History and Art, 70-156-2 detail 4.2)*

tives of northern Norway whom Jackson recruits for his enterprise. Despite Jackson's enthusiasm and the United States's support, the plan to turn Alaskan Inuit into reindeer herders will ultimately fail, largely because of the Inuit's lack of interest.

The Act for the Relief of the Mission Indians is passed.

Congress offers federal protection to California Indian lands by passing the Act for the Relief of the Mission Indians. Through this law, the United States will establish 32 small reservations scattered throughout southern California over the next 18 years.

January 1

Nearly 150 Wounded Knee victims are buried.

Burial crews are sent to Wounded Knee to round up the bodies and search for any survivors of the

"The Whites, by law of conquest, by justice of civilization, are masters of the American continent, and the best safety of the frontier settlers will be secured by the total annihilation of the few remaining Indians. . . . Why not annihilation? Their glory has fled, their spirit broken, their manhood effaced, better that they should die than live the miserable wretches that they are."

—novelist and journalist L. Frank Baum, in the *Aberdeen Saturday Pioneer* one week after the 1890 massacre at Wounded Knee

massacre there three days earlier (see entry for DECEMBER 29, 1890). The frozen corpses of 146 men, women, and children are interred in a mass grave. Many of the bodies have been stripped of their Ghost Dance shirts and other paraphernalia by soldiers seeking souvenirs of the slaughter. The crews find few survivors. Most of the wounded have already been found and taken in by relatives before their arrival. Although estimates differ, probably at least 300 of the some 350 Indians at Wounded Knee died either at site or later under the care of their loved ones.

January 15

Ghost Dance advocate Kicking Bear surrenders to the U.S. Army.

Schooled in the Ghost Dance by its founder Wovoka (see entry for JANUARY 1, 1889), Oglala Sioux Kicking Bear is a strong advocate of the new Ghost Dance Religion embraced by many Plains tribes. Expelled from the Standing Rock Reservation, Kicking Bear and his people continue to perform the Ghost Dance on the Pine Ridge Reservation even after the army's slaughter of more than 300 adherents at Wounded Knee (see entry for DECEMBER 29, 1890). When army troops surround their encampment, Kicking Bear negotiates a peaceful surrender of about 5,000 Lakota Sioux to General Nelson A. Miles to avoid further bloodshed. The event is the last formal surrender by Indians to the U.S. Army in the Plains Indian Wars.

February 28

Congress amends the General Allotment Act.

The General Allotment Act (see entry for FEBRUARY 8, 1887) granted each head of a family 160 acres of land on an allotted reservation. The amendment to the act calls for 80-acre allotments to be given to every adult on the tribal roll. More important, the amendment allows Indians to lease allotments to non-Indians.

April 13

Civil service requirements are extended to Bureau of Indian Affairs employees.

President Benjamin Harrison declares that Bureau of Indian Affairs hiring for all medical and educational jobs must adhere to civil service requirements. His action is a response to reformers who have long maintained that the spoils system has placed corrupt agents in control of reservations.

April

Plenty Horses is acquitted of murder charges.

In Sioux Falls, South Dakota, a 22-year-old Sioux named Plenty Horses is tried for the murder of an army officer who was policing the Pine Ridge Reservation several days after the massacre at Wounded Knee (see entry for DECEMBER 29, 1890). In his testimony, Plenty Horses explains that his education at the Carlisle Indian school (see entry for AUTUMN 1879) in Pennsylvania had so divorced him from his Sioux friends and relatives that he felt compelled to earn their respect as a warrior. "I shot the lieutenant so I might make a place for myself among my people," the accused told the court. "Now I am one of them. . . . They will be proud of me. I am satisfied." In a controversial decision, the jury acquits Plenty Horses on the grounds that at the time of the shooting he was acting as a combatant during a state of war—the same justification the U.S. Army is using to avoid prosecuting the soldiers involved in the Wounded Knee Massacre.

1892

The federal government revises rules for tribal courts.

The U.S. government approves guidelines for tribal courts (see entry for APRIL 10, 1883) in

prosecuting several crimes, including the performance of "the sun dance, scalp dance, or war dance, or any other similar feast." Indians found guilty of these offenses can be imprisoned or have their food rations withheld for up to 30 days. The guidelines also define polygamous marriages and the rituals practiced by medicine men and women as offenses.

"Any Indian who shall engage in the practices of so-called medicine men, or shall resort to any artifice or device to keep the Indians of the reservation from adopting and following civilized habits and pursuits, . . . or shall use any arts of a conjurer to prevent Indians from abandoning their barbarous rites and customs, . . . upon conviction . . . shall be imprisoned for not less than ten nor more than thirty days."

—from the U.S. government's 1892 rules for Courts of Indian Offenses

July 23

The U.S. government forbids the sale of liquor in Indian country.

Throughout the history of contact, unscrupulous non-Indians have tried to take economic and political advantage of Indians by plying them with alcohol. Reformers objecting to this exploitation pressure Congress to pass the Intoxication in Indian Country Act. This law prohibits the sale or transportation of alcohol in Indian territory.

1893

The U.S. government forces an allotment agreement on the Quechan.

In negotiations with U.S. government representatives, the Quechan Indians of southern Arizona are compelled to cede much of the most fertile land along the Colorado River to the United States. Some of the signatures on the cession agreement are coerced; others are forged. According to the document's terms, the Quechan consent to take allotments and allow the government to sell "surplus" lands to whites. In exchange, the U.S. government agrees to irrigate the Indians' lands, but the promised irrigation system will never be built.

The Navajo (Dineh) agent compels Indian children to attend school.

Under the supervision of the Presbyterian Church, the Fort Defiance Boarding School is established for Navajo (Dineh) students. When few Navajo families allow their children to attend, Indian agent Dana Shipley tries to round up students and force them to go to school. Furious at Shipley, a headman named Black Horse and his followers confront the agent at the Round Rock Trading Post. They drag him from the building and beat him nearly to death before Navajo policemen are able to stop the assault.

March 3

Congress appoints the Dawes Commission.

Pressured by the flood of non-Indians into Oklahoma Territory (see entry for MAY 1890), the U.S. government seeks to open the neighboring Indian Territory to white settlement by allotting the reservations of the Five Civilized Tribes. Toward this end, Congress forms the Dawes Commission, headed by Henry Dawes, a former senator and the sponsor of the General Allotment Act (see entry for FEBRUARY 8, 1887). The commission is charged with evaluating the situation in Indian Territory and negotiating allotment agreements with Indian leaders. The Dawes Commission will be authorized to survey tribal lands in 1895 and to prepare rolls of tribal members in 1896.

"We ask every lover of justice, is it right that a great and powerful government, year by year, continue to demand cessions of land from weaker and dependent people. . . . We have lived with our people all our lives and believe that we know more about them than any Commission, however good and intelligent, could know from a few visits. . . . [The commissioners] care nothing for the fate of the Indian, so that their own greed can be gratified."

—Choctaw and Chickasaw leaders protesting the work of the Dawes Commission in an 1895 letter to the president and the Senate

July

Historian Frederick Jackson Turner presents his thesis of the "frontier."

As part of the World's Congress of Historians and Historical Students at the Columbian Exposition in Chicago, Frederick Jackson Turner, a historian at the University of Wisconsin, delivers a speech about the American frontier. He receives little response until the lecture is published later in the year as "The Significance of the Frontier in American History."

The essay cites American democracy as a direct outgrowth of the "existence of an area of free land, its continuous recession, and the advancement of American settlement westward." In Turner's eyes, the frontier is "the meeting point between savagery and civilization," with Indians on one side and whites on the other. Whites' movement westward, therefore, is celebrated as inevitable social progress, with superior, civilizing whites overtaking the inferior Indian savages that stand in their way. This thesis will be the dominant historical interpretation of Indian-white relations for the next 50 years.

September 16

The Cherokee Outlet is opened to white settlement.

In one of the most spectacular land rushes in American history, 100,000 American homesteaders frantically stake claims on the 6.5 million acres of land known as the Cherokee Outlet. Purchased by the United States from the Cherokee Nation for approximately $8.5 million, the Outlet is composed of lands forming what is now the panhandle of Oklahoma.

1894

Archaeological research proves the Moundbuilders were eastern Indians.

Working for the Smithsonian Institution, Cyrus Thomas publishes *Report on the Mound Explorations of the Bureau of Ethnology,* which outlines the results of his extensive research into the ancient burial mounds in eastern North America (see entries for CA. 1000 B.C. TO A.D. 200; CA. 200 B.C. TO A.D. 400; and CA. 700 TO 1550). Thomas provides conclusive evidence that the mounds were constructed by the Indians of the region, thus laying to rest a wide variety of far-fetched theories regarding the Moundbuilders' identity. Since the late 18th century, non-Indians were largely unable to believe that the "uncivilized" Indians native to North America could have acquired the technological knowledge to build the mounds (see entry for 1848). Displaying their racist notions of Indian inferiority, scholars speculated that the mounds were the creation of various foreign peoples, including Phoenicians, Egyptians, Aztec, Danes, and Hindus.

The Census Bureau reports the Indian population at an all-time low.

The Bureau of the Census releases *Report on Indians Taxed and Not Taxed in the United States (Except Alaska) at the Eleventh Census: 1890.* The publication holds that the Indian population has dropped to less than one-quarter million, down almost 40 percent from census figures for 1850. Although the figures may be inaccurately low, the 1890 census seems to confirm the view of many non-Indians that Indians are a "vanishing race" that will disappear in a matter of generations.

Thomas Edison produces the first film about Native Americans.

The Sioux Ghost Dance, the first motion picture to deal primarily with a Native American subject, is produced by Thomas Edison's film company. The company soon follows up its success with two more films about Indians—*Eagle Dance* (1898) and *Serving Rations to the Indians* (1898). Capitalizing on whites' fascination with Plains Indians, these short movies are privately viewed on Kinescope machines and run less than a minute. The films offer many Americans, particularly in the East, their first glimpse of Indian peoples.

1895

Quanah Parker is removed as a Court of Indian Offenses judge.

The well-respected Comanche leader Quanah Parker is stripped of his judgeship on his reservation's Court of Indian Offenses (see entry for APRIL 18, 1883). Over the objection of the reservation agent, Parker is removed on the order of Commissioner of Indian Affairs T. J. Morgan. A devout Christian, Morgan is opposed to Parker serving as a judge because, following tribal tradition, the affluent Comanche has several wives.

1896

May 18

Talton v. Mayes exempts tribal governments from upholding the Bill of Rights.

In the case of *Talton v. Mayes,* a Cherokee man convicted of murder in tribal court appeals to the Supreme Court on the grounds that the Cherokee grand jury that brought him to trial consisted of only five people, in violation of the Fifth Amendment. The Court finds that this is an inadequate basis for appeal because the Bill of Rights does not apply to tribal governments, which predated the Constitution. The principle established by the case—that tribal governments are not required to extend the rights guaranteed by the Constitution—will be observed until the passage of the Indian Civil Rights Act (see entry for APRIL 18, 1968).

August

The Klondike Gold Rush begins.

When gold is discovered in the Klondike region of Canada, thousands of white prospectors begin traveling north, flooding into the lands of Alaskan Natives. Although most prospectors will have little success, the luckiest involved in the Klondike Gold Rush will mine more than $100 million over the next decade. The Alaskan Natives will receive none of this money because the U.S. government will not give them mining grants for gold uncovered in their ancestral territories. They will, however, suffer from the presence of the miners, who indiscriminately overrun their lands and routinely commit acts of violence against them.

1897

Oil is discovered on the Osage reservation.

In 1895 the secretary of the interior granted a drilling company a 10-year oil lease on the eastern half of the Osage reservation in northern Indian Territory. Two years later, a test well finds oil under the tribe's land. The discovery will prompt the Osage to insist on retaining mineral rights when their reservation is allotted (see entry for 1906). (See also entry for 1921.)

The Indiana Miami lose their Indian status.

In 1846 the Miami tribe was divided, when approximately one-third of the tribe's members were forced to leave Indiana and move west, first to Kansas and later to Indian Territory. Acting on the advice of officials in the Bureau of Indian Affairs, the U.S. attorney general orders that the government no longer recognize the Indiana Miami and thereafter provide the benefits of tribal status only to the Western Miami in Indian Territory. As a result of the order, the newly unrecognized Miami will soon be driven from their Indiana homeland.

April 22

Louis Sockalexis begins his professional baseball career.

A Penobscot from Old Town, Maine, Louis Sockalexis, joins the Cleveland Spiders professional baseball team, becoming the first Indian player in the major leagues. Enduring racial taunts from fans, Sockalexis will play in the majors and minors until 1903, when his chronic problems with alcohol will end his career. (See also entry for 1914.)

April 23

The Choctaw and Chickasaw sign the Atoka Agreement.

Leaders of the Choctaw and Chickasaw end their resistance to the allotment of their lands in Indian Territory by signing the Atoka Agreement. Withstanding years of pressure to agree to Allotment, however, has allowed them to strike a far better deal with the United States than that offered most other Indian allottees. With Americans clamoring for the opening of Indian Territory to white settlement, the Choctaw and Chickasaw are able to negotiate for allotments of 320 acres—twice the size of those given to Indians outside of Indian Territory by the provisions of the General Allotment Act (see entry for February 8, 1887).

1898

Indians perform at the Trans-Mississippi Exposition.

In Omaha, Nebraska, the Trans-Mississippi Exposition features an exhibit of about 500 Indians from 23 tribes. Dressed in Indian garb, they perform traditional activities—such as dancing, weaving, and storytelling—for crowds of non-Indians. Anthropologist James Mooney of the Bureau of Ethnology praises the display as the "last opportunity" to see "the red man in his primitive glory." Richard Henry Pratt, the founder of the Carlisle Indian boarding school (see entry for AUTUMN 1879) and avid assimilationist, offers another view, condemning the spectacle as "a Wild West show of the most degenerate sort."

"Under the old Cherokee regime I spent the early days of my life on the farm up here of 300 acres, and arranged to be comfortable in my old age; but the allotment scheme came along.... I have 60 acres of land left me; the balance is all gone. ...And I am here to-day, a poor man upon the verge of starvation—my muscular energy gone, hope gone. I have nothing to charge my calamity to but the unwise legislation of Congress in reference to my Cherokee people."

—Cherokee allottee D. W. C. Duncan, testifying before the Senate in November 1906

June 28

The Curtis Act extends Allotment to the Five Civilized Tribes.

Sponsored by Charles Curtis, the Kaw Indian congressman from Kansas, the Curtis Act authorizes the Dawes Commission (see entry for 1893) to allot the lands of the Five Civilized Tribes in Indian Territory and to dissolve their governments without the tribes' permission. The act paves the way for Indian Territory's incorporation into the state of Oklahoma (see entry for NOVEMBER 16, 1907).

1899

Simon Pokagon's *O-Gi-Maw-Kwe Mit-I-Gwa-Ki* is published.

In the year of his death, Potawatomi scholar Simon Pokagon's autobiographical romance *O-Gi-Maw-Kwe Mit-I-Gwa-Ki* (Queen of the Forest) is postumously published. One of the few novels written by an American Indian during the 19th century, the book was originally written in the Potawatomi language and later translated into English.

1900

Autumn

Creek traditionalists join the Crazy Snake movement.

Creek town chief Chitto Harjo begins a campaign against the Allotment of the Creek Nation by gathering followers among the tribe's traditionalists. Chitto Harjo's name is translated as "recklessly brave snake" by Creek and as "crazy snake" by whites. The group becomes known as the Crazy Snakes.

The Crazy Snakes establish their own government, with its capital in the town of Hickory Ground. The new government drafts laws that forbid Allotment, discourages white settlement among the Creek, and creates a police force called the "lighthorse" to enforce them. Recruitment efforts draw many more Creek as well as disaffected Choctaw, Cherokee, and Seminole to Hickory Ground. (See also entry for JUNE 27, 1901.)

1901

The Sequoyah League is founded.
Non-Indian journalists George Bird Grinnell and Charles Lummi establish the Sequoyah League, a philanthropic organization based in New York and Los Angeles and named after the inventor of the Cherokee syllabary (see entry for 1821). Grinnell and Lummi advocate the preservation of traditional Indians ways but tend to view Indian peoples condescendingly. They oppose Indian schools and the allotment of Indian lands, not because they threaten Indians' autonomy but because Indians are too "backward" to benefit from these "civilizing" forces.

January 27

U.S. marshals arrest Crazy Snake followers.
Alarmed by the Crazy Snakes (see entry for AUTUMN 1900) and their threat to his leadership, Pleasant Porter, principal chief of the Creek, asks federal officials to send in troops to break up the radical movement. They respond by sending in U.S. marshals, who raid the Crazy Snake capital at Hickory Ground and arrest the rebel government's leader, Chitto Harjo, and 100 of his followers. In federal court in Muskogee, Indian Territory, the Creek agree to plead guilty on several counts in exchange for suspended fines and prison sentences. Although the judge warns them to stop their campaign against Allotment, most of those arrested continue their efforts after they return to Hickory Ground. (See also entry for FEBRUARY 1902.)

September

Geronimo attends the presidential inauguration.
The great Apache war leader Geronimo, who has been confined as a prisoner of war for 15 years (see entry for MARCH TO SEPTEMBER 1886), is temporarily freed and sent to Washington, D.C., to ride in the parade celebrating Theodore Roosevelt's inauguration. Geronimo takes the opportunity to ask the new president to release him and his fellow Apache prisoners from jail and to allow them to move back to their southwestern homeland. Roosevelt refuses, explaining that the people of Arizona Territory will not let them return.

1902

Eva Emery Dye's *The Conquest* is published.
In her novel *The Conquest: The True Story of the Lewis and Clark,* suffragette Eva Emery Dye recasts the legend of Sacagawea (Sacajawea), the Shoshone woman who accompanied the Lewis and Clark Expedition (see entry for APRIL 1804), to represent her as an emblem of a modern independent woman. Although Dye bases much of her book on the original journals of Meriwether Lewis and William Clark, she inaccurately elevates Sacagawea's role from a valued interpreter to a guide whose skills were responsible for the expedition's success.

The Reclamation Act calls for the irrigation of western lands.
Sponsored by Francis G. Newlands of Nevada, the Reclamation Act establishes the Reclamation Service, an agency authorized to build irrigation projects in 16 western states. The areas designated for development include large areas of Indian-held lands. As these lands become irrigated and thus more attractive to non-Indians, Indian control over them will be increasingly threatened.

Charles A. Eastman's *My Indian Boyhood* is published.
A graduate of Dartmouth and Boston College, physician and reformer Charles A. Eastman tells the

story of his traditional Dakota Sioux upbringing in *My Indian Boyhood.* The memoir is the first in a series of stories and books Eastman will write for a non-Indian readership with the aim of promoting respect for Indian cultures.

> 🔲
>
> "Almost every evening a myth, or a true story of some deed done in the past, was narrated by one of the parents or grandparents, while the boy listened with parted lips and glistening eyes. On the following evening he was usually required to repeat it. If he was not an apt scholar, he struggled long with his task; but, as a rule, the Indian boy was a good listener and had a good memory, so that the stories were tolerably well mastered. The household became his audience, by which he was alternately criticized and applauded."
>
> —Dakota Sioux author
> Charles A. Eastman in
> *My Indian Boyhood* (1902)

Creek satirist Alexander Posey begins writing the Fus Fixico Letters.

A noted poet and editor of the *Indian Journal,* Alexander Posey begins work on a collection of letters, supposedly written by a fictional character named Fus Fixico, about life in the Creek Nation. Using caricatures of actual leaders and other prominent Creeks, the Fus Fixico letters satirize Creek politics and humorously explore controversial issues such as Allotment and the pending incorporation of Indian Territory into the state of Oklahoma.

January 13

Indian men are ordered to cut their hair.

To accelerate assimilation, the commissioner of Indian affairs orders Indian agents to prohibit Indian males from wearing their hair long. Traditionally, long hair was a source of pride among young Indian men. If any Indians refuse to comply, the commissioner recommends withholding annuities due to them by treaty.

February

Crazy Snake leader Chitto Harjo is imprisoned.

Because of their refusal to disband the Crazy Snake movement (see entry for JANUARY 27, 1901), Creek radical leader Chitto Harjo and nine other Crazy Snakes are arrested and sent to the federal penitentiary in Leavenworth, Kansas. Harjo will remain imprisoned for nine months, during which time his followers begin to abandon their militant stance and seek political positions on the Creek tribal council.

May 27

The "Dead Indian Act" allows for the sale of inherited allotments.

The General Allotment Act (see entry for FEBRUARY 8, 1887) forbade Indians from selling allotments for 25 years. An amendment to this law, the so-called Dead Indian Act, allows the commissioner of Indian affairs to waive this restriction for Indians who have inherited land from original allottees. The act is passed in response to pressure from whites who want to buy Indian lands and from Indians, particularly those of mixed heritage, who want to be able to sell their own property.

1903

The U.S. government publishes Hopi kachina paintings.

Several hundred paintings and drawings of kachinas—the spirit beings of the Hopi and other Pueblo

Indians—are collected and reproduced in the *21st Annual Report of the Bureau of American Ethnology.* The images were commissioned from four Hopi men in the 1890s by anthropologist Jesse Walter Fewkes.

Intended only for ethnographic research, the works show carefully detailed figures against a blank background. They will have a great influence on the "Traditional Indian Style," a style of painting that will be adopted by Indian artists in the 1930s and become popular with non-Indian art collectors throughout the 20th century (see entry for SEPTEMBER 1932).

Lone Wolf v. Hitchcock establishes that Congress can abrogate Indian treaties.

Following the allotment of their reservation, the Kiowa Indians challenge the U.S. government's right to sell tribal lands left over after all allotments were assigned. In the lawsuit *Lone Wolf v. Hitchcock,* they cite the provisions of the Treaty of Medicine Lodge Creek (see entry for OCTOBER 21 TO 28, 1867), which stipulated that the reservation the Kiowa share with the Comanche could not be reduced without the approval of three-fourths of the reservation's male population. Because this vote was never taken, the Kiowa's reason that the sale of surplus reservation land is in direct violation of the treaty.

The Supreme Court, however, disagrees. It rules that Congress has "the power to abrogate the provisions of an Indian treaty." This ruling thereby gives Congress unlimited authority to ignore treaty agreements if it deems that by doing so it is acting "in the interest of the country and the Indians themselves."

May 12

The Cupeño are removed to the reservation at Pala.

After a protracted legal battle, the California Supreme Court finds that the small Cupeño tribe has no claim to its ancestral territory in present-day San Diego County. Over Cupeño opposition and public protest, the court orders the approximately 100 surviving tribe members to leave their village of Cupa and relocate to the Pala Reservation in Luiseño territory, 40 miles to the northwest. As most of the Cupeño pack their belongings in preparation for leaving their homeland forever, some elders refuse to make the move. One vows to stay "even if the Coyotes eat me."

1904

An Indian lawyer argues before the Supreme Court.

Working on behalf of his people, Omaha Indian Thomas L. Sloan becomes the first Indian lawyer to present a case to the Supreme Court of the United States. A graduate of Yale Law School, Sloan will later help found the Society of American Indians (see entry for OCTOBER 12, 1911) and offer advice on Indian affairs to the Harding administration as a member of the Committee of One Hundred (see entry for 1923).

March 11

Congress passes the Pipelines Act.

After oil is discovered in Oklahoma Territory, tribal leaders of neighboring Indian Territory resist the construction of pipelines to carry the oil through their lands. With the Pipelines Act, Congress subverts their authority by granting oil companies the right to build pipelines on reservation land without their residents' permission.

April to November

The St. Louis World's Fair features an Indian exhibit.

A celebration of the hundredth anniversary of the Louisiana Purchase (see entry for APRIL 3, 1803), the World's Fair in St. Louis touts displays of "strange animals and stranger peoples." Among the "stranger peoples" are representatives of more than 60 tribes. The massive Indian exhibit features replicas of Indian villages and buildings, where artisans offer baskets, beadwork, and other crafts for sale to non-Indian tourists. The star attraction is the

Apache war leader Geronimo, who sells his autograph for 10 cents. During the seven months the fair is in operation, more than three million people will visit the Indian exhibit.

1905

Indians of Indian Territory propose the state of Sequoyah.

Leaders in Indian Territory meet in a convention, draft a constitution, and present it to Congress with the request that the region enter the Union as a state named after Sequoyah, the creator of the Cherokee syllabary (see entry for 1821). The Indians fear plans for combining Indian Territory and Oklahoma Territory to form the state of Oklahoma, which will leave them outnumbered by non-Indian Oklahomans. Congress rejects the proposed Indian state, thereby paving the way for Indian Territory's incorporation into Oklahoma two years later (see entry for NOVEMBER 16, 1907).

The Pyramid Lake Paiute's water rights are violated by dam construction.

The Derby Dam, built on the Truckee River in Nevada, diverts so much water that Pyramid Lake, fed by the Truckee, is reduced to half its size. Even though the Paiute Indians living on the lake's banks have rights to the water, they are not consulted about the dam's construction. (See also entry for MARCH 28, 1970.)

United States v. Winans upholds Yakama fishing rights.

In Washington State, Indians have long objected to non-Indian landowners fencing in fishing sites that the Indians have used for centuries. The Yakama (formerly Yakima) take their complaints to the Supreme Court in the case *United States v. Winans*. The tribe argues that denying access to their ancient fishing areas along the Columbia River is a violation of the Yakama Treaty of 1855. In the treaty, the tribe ceded a portion of their land but retained the right to fish in "all usual and accustomed places."

The Supreme Court rules in the Yakama's favor, maintaining that the fishing rights guaranteed in the treaty are superior to the rights of the non-Indian owners of the fishing sites. The decision will become an important precedent cited in many fishing- and hunting-rights cases brought to court by Indian groups later in the century.

1906

Edward Curtis receives funding for his Indian photography.

At the suggestion by President Theodore Roosevelt, financier J. P. Morgan becomes the patron of Edward Curtis, a photographer best known for his portraits of American Indians. Beginning in the

Edward Curtis promoted the romantic myth of Indians "being one with nature" in carefully posed photographs such as this one, showing a Mandan Indian standing on a bluff above the Missouri River. *(Library of Congress, Neg. no. USZ62-46989)*

1890s, Curtis photographed the Indians living near his native Seattle. On the basis of this work, he was hired by the wealthy businessman E. H. Harriman to document an expedition to Alaska, and he was invited by artist George Bird Grinnell to photograph the Sun Dance of the Blackfeet.

Spending nearly a million dollars of Morgan's fortune, Curtis will devote the next 24 years to traveling through the West, persuading Indians from a large number of tribes and groups to sit for him. Trained as a society portraitist, he will photograph his subjects in soft focus, often dressing them in traditional clothing and posing them with cultural artifacts he has borrowed from museums.

"Instead of the painted features, the feathers, the arrows and the bow, we find [the Indian] in [the] blue jeans and cowboy hat of semi-civilization. . . . And so Edward S. Curtis, of Seattle, found him. . . . He unearthed the fantastic costumes of a bygone time. He won confidences, dispelling distrust. He took the present lowness of today and enshrined it in the romance of the past. . . . [H]e change the degenerated Indian of today into the fancy-free king of a yesterday that has long since been forgotten in the calendar of time."

—from an article on the photography of Edward S. Curtis in the November 15, 1903, issue of the *Seattle Times*

A selection of the nearly 40,000 photographs taken by Curtis will be published in the 20-volume *North American Indians.* Presented as documents of a "vanishing race" and its culture, Curtis's works create a romanticized view of Indians with great appeal to non-Indians. Rather than making whites confront the disastrous legacy of the dispossession and forced assimilation of Indian people, his photographs show defeated but noble savages who are conveniently disappearing to make way for "civilization."

Congress passes the Osage Allotment Act.

With the passage of the Osage Allotment Act, the Osage become the last tribe in Indian Territory to agree to the allotment of their reservation. The tribe negotiates for 500-acre allotments, far larger than the 160-acre allotments granted most other Indian Territory allottees. They are also allowed to retain communally held mineral rights to their land, where oil has been discovered (see entry for 1897).

Geronimo's Story of His Life is published.

In an "as-told-to" autobiography, the great Apache leader gives his own account of the Apache's military resistance to non-Indian encroachment on their homeland. The book is edited by S. M. Barrett, who was allowed to meet with Geronimo, still a prisoner of war, only by special permission from President Theodore Roosevelt (see entry for SEPTEMBER 1901). Barrett is aided in the project by Asa Daklugie, a close friend of Geronimo's, who translates his words. Geronimo refuses to answer any questions from Barrett, insisting instead that the white man merely "write what I have spoken."

Angel DeCora heads the art program at Carlisle.

Painter and illustrator Angel DeCora joins the faculty of the Carlisle Indian school (see entry for AUTUMN 1879) as the head of the institution's Department of Native American Art. A graduate of the Hampton Institute (see entry for APRIL 1878) and Smith College, DeCora was trained in non-Indian art and art history at Philadelphia's Drexel Institute, where she studied with illustrator Howard Pyle. At Carlisle, DeCora instructs her students in non-Indian art techniques but encourages them to research and experiment with designs and patterns used by potters, basketmakers, and other traditional Indian artisans. Through her teaching and her own art, DeCora will pioneer the integration of Indian and non-Indian art traditions and promote the academic study of Native American art.

May 8

The Burke Act amends the U.S. Allotment policy.

In response to perceived weaknesses of the General Allotment Act (see entry for FEBRUARY 8, 1887), Congress passes the Burke Act. The legislation gives control of Indian allotments held in trust to the federal government rather than to state governments. It also allows the president to extend the period in which allotments are held in trust (originally 25 years) if their Indian owners are deemed incompetent to handle their own affairs. Conversely, it gives the secretary of the interior the power to reduce the trust period for Indians who are considered able to take on the full responsibility of land ownership. Lastly, the Burke Act withholds citizenship from Indian landowners until the end of the trust period, rather than granting this right with each allotment.

The law is intended to protect incompetent (by which the government usually means unassimilated) Indians from being swindled by white land speculators, while giving competent (that is, assimilated) Indians the opportunity to lease or sell their land if they choose. In fact, the reduction of the trust period will, in most cases, leave Indians landless, often after being defrauded by unscrupulous white businessmen.

May 17

The Alaska Allotment Act is passed.

The Alaska Allotment Act extends the provisions of the General Allotment Act (see entry for FEBRUARY 8, 1887) to Indian lands in Alaska. The government will not put the act into effect, however, because there is little pressure from non-Indians to do so. The Indian-held territory in Alaska is so barren that few non-Indians have an interest in buying the surplus land that would be left over after allotment.

June 8

Congress passes the Antiquities Act.

Designed in part to prevent the wholesale looting of Indian archaeological sites, the Act for the Preservation of American Antiquities outlaws the appropriation or destruction of ancient ruins and artifacts found on federally owned lands. The law also authorizes the issuing of permits to conduct excavations on these sites by qualified archaeological researchers.

September 6

Hopi progressives drive traditionalists out of Oraibi.

A church and non-Indian-run school established by whites near the Hopi village of Oraibi (see entry for CA. 1150) splits the village population into two

> "Thereupon, the Friendlies set about clearing the village of Shungopovis. They began at the very spot where they stood; but every Friendly who laid hold of a Shungopovi to put him out of doors was attacked from behind by an Oraibi Hostile, so that the three went wrestling and struggling out of the door together. There was great commotion as the Friendlies carried out the Hostiles, pushing and pulling, the Hostiles resisting, struggling, kicking, and pull the hair of their adversaries."
>
> —Hopi Helen Sekaquaptewa on the 1906 battle between Hopi traditionalists and progressives at the village of Oraibi

factions: traditionalists (called "hostiles" by whites), who oppose the presence of whites in Hopi territory; and progressives (called "friendlies" by whites), who welcome the whites settling in their lands. The tension between the two groups comes to a head when the progressives expel the traditionalists from Oraibi by force and confiscate their property. Fearing retaliation from the traditionalists, U.S. officials intervene and arrest 75 "hostiles" when their leaders refuse to promise not to fight back. The violence at Oraibi will be remembered by future generations as one of the greatest tragedies of Hopi history.

November 23

Chitto Harjo testifies before Congress.

In a special Senate hearing held in Tulsa, Oklahoma, radical Creek leader Chitto Harjo (see entry for FEBRUARY 1902) delivers a speech that summarizes the history of the Creek's relations with the U.S. government. Harjo condemns the Allotment policy as a violation of the tribe's 1832 removal treaty, which guaranteed the Creek's right to self-government. A well-regarded orator among the Creek, Harjo impresses his listeners, one of whom later praises him as "the most wonderful speaker I ever heard." The Senate, however, ignores his demands for the end of Allotment.

1907

The Brooklyn Museum acquires important Maidu ceremonial paraphernalia.

Following the death of traditional Maidu leader Holi Lafonso, his ceremonial paraphernalia is sold to Stewart Culin of the Brooklyn Museum. The loss of these objects is a great blow to the Maidu's rich ceremonial life at Chico, a tribal center for traditional dances.

Anderson v. Matthews gives nonreservation Indians the right to vote.

Funded by the Indian Board of Cooperation, Ethan Anderson, a Pomo Indian, initiates a lawsuit charging that as a nonreservation Indian he has the right to register to vote in Mendocino County, California. *Anderson v. Matthews* is argued before the Supreme Court of California, which finds that Anderson is legally a citizen and therefore entitled to vote in the state.

January 23

Charles Curtis becomes the first Indian senator.

A Kaw Indian from Oklahoma, Charles Curtis begins his tenure as the first Native American in the U.S. Senate. Curtis, who previously has served eight terms as a Republican in the U.S. House of Representatives, will resign from the Senate after he wins his bid for the vice presidency on Herbert Hoover's ticket (see entry for NOVEMBER 1928).

April 19

Onondaga athlete Tom Longboat wins the Boston Marathon.

Dubbed the "Onondaga Wonder" by the press, long-distance running champion Tom Longboat from the Grand River Reserve in Ontario places first in Boston Marathon. He finishes the race in two hours and 24 minutes, besting the previous record time by a full five minutes.

August 29

Thirty-five Mohawk ironworkers are killed on the Quebec Bridge.

In the worst bridge-construction accident in history, 96 ironworkers die when the Quebec bridge they are building collapses. Thirty-five of the dead are Mohawk Indians from the Kahnawake Reserve. Famed for their ability to balance on steel beams and negotiate enormous heights with confidence, many Canadian Mohawk for decades have relied on ironwork for their livelihood (see entry for 1886).

November 16

Indian and Oklahoma territories become the state of Oklahoma.

Formed from Indian Territory and Oklahoma Territory, Oklahoma enters the Union as the 46th state. The new state takes its name from a Choctaw phrase meaning "home of the red people." With Oklahoma statehood, Indian Territory and the Indian nations within it cease to exist.

1908

Winters v. United States addresses Indian water rights on reservations.

At the request of the Bureau of Indian Affairs, the Department of Justice files suit in *Winters v. United States* to protect the water rights of the Indians of the Fort Belknap Reservation in Montana. The 600,000-acre reservation was established in 1888 by a treaty that called for the cession of the rest of the Indians' homelands to the United States. The treaty also provided the Fort Belknap Indians with money and supplies to help them learn to farm their reduced territory. By the time of the *Winters* suit, the Indians' ability to farm the reservation is threatened by a lack of water to irrigate their fields. The reservation is bound by the Milk River, but non-Indians who have settled on the river's opposite side are drawing much of the available water.

In *Winters,* the Department of Justice claims that the residents of Fort Belknap have a greater right to the water than the non-Indian settlers. Although the Indians' treaty with the government did not say so explicitly, the department argues that it implicitly gave them the right to enough water to farm their reservation. The Department of Justice wins the case, which in the future will become the basis for many water-rights claims of reservation populations.

Quick Bear v. Leupp supports federal funding for religious Indian schools.

A Protestant Lakota Sioux living on the Rosebud Reservation in South Dakota, Reuben Quick Bear opposes the federal government's requirement that reservation students attend a school operated by the Catholic Church. In a case that is eventually argued before the Supreme Court, Quick Bear argues that the government's funding of the school is a violation of the separation of church and state. The Court disagrees, maintaining that denying funds to the school would violate the rights of Roman Catholics to practice their religion. The decision is a blow to Indian religious freedom and educational choice.

The job of Indian agent is abolished.

To increase the pace of assimilation, Commissioner Francis E. Leupp eliminates the position of Indian agents in the Bureau of Indian Affairs (BIA). The administrative duties of agents on reservations are to be taken over by teachers and farmers employed by the BIA and referred to as "superintendents." Leupp maintains that these employees will be better equipped than agents to help Indians adjust to making their living from privately owned allotments.

The "Crime of 1908" allows whites to profit from Indian allotments.

In order to rescind restrictions placed on allotted Indian land, Congress passes legislation that allows for the sale of allotments owned by Indians of mixed ancestry and by Indians married to non-Indians. The law also permits county courts to appoint whites to act as guardians for other Indian allottees. Many of these guardians will charge Indians exorbitantly high fees for managing their lands. In fact, the law will result in so many fraudulent management schemes and dubious land deals that historians will later dub it the "Crime of 1908."

1909

The University of Wisconsin at Lacrosse adopts the name "Indians" for its sports teams.

By dubbing its teams "Indians," the University of Wisconsin at Lacrosse becomes the first of many sports organizations to use the warfare between Indians and non-Indians of previous centuries as a metaphor for the "battle" on the playing field. Further stereotyping Native Americans as aggressive savages, many other schools and sports organizations will follow the university's lead by adopting team names such as "Chiefs," "Braves," and "Redskins."

The "Last Great Indian Council" is called by the Bureau of Indian Affairs.

With the assistance of non-Indian businessmen Joseph K. Dixon and Rodman Wanamaker, the Bureau of Indian Affairs stages "one last great council" of selected Indian leaders, at the site of the Battle of Little Bighorn (see entry for JUNE 24 TO 25, 1876). Four years later, Dixon will publish a romantic account of the meeting titled *The Vanishing Race: The Last Great Indian Council.*

"To the man of mystery—the earth his mother—the sun his father—a child of the mountains and the Plains—a faithful worshipper in the great world cathedral—now a tragic soul haunting the shores of the western ocean—my brother the Indian."

—the dedication of Joseph K. Dixon's *The Vanishing Race: The Last Great Indian Council* (1913)

March 27

Chitto Harjo is shot by U.S. deputy marshals.

Several African Americans forced out of a nearby town by whites move to Hickory Ground, the capital of the Crazy Snake movement (see entry for AUTUMN 1900). When they are accused of stealing from local white families, the police arrive in the town to arrest them. Fifteen men are killed in the deadly shoot-out that follows.

Although uninvolved in the incident, Crazy Snake leader Chitto Harjo is blamed for the violence. Four U.S. deputy marshals come to Harjo's home to arrest him, again prompting an exchange of gunfire, during which Harjo is wounded. As a large posse gathers to capture Harjo, he escapes from Hickory Ground. Various accounts later emerge about Harjo's fate. Some claim he made his way to Mexico; others say he was hanged the next year in Oklahoma; still others maintain he died near his home from his gunshot wound.

April 9

Inuit explorers help Robert E. Peary reach the North Pole.

After trying six times, explorer Robert E. Peary becomes the first white man to reach the North Pole. Among the men in his exploration party are four Inuit—Coqueeh, Ootah, Eginwah, and Seegloo—and an African American, Matthew Henson.

Summer

The Four Mothers Society is founded.

Creek Indian Eufaula Harjo and Cherokee leader Redbird Smith form the Four Mothers Society, an organization dedicated to improving the political situation of Oklahoma Indian traditionalists. One of the first intertribal organizations, it draws its membership from the Creek, Cherokee, Choctaw, and Creek tribes, although the majority are the former followers of Chitto Harjo, the Creek leader of the Crazy Snake movement (see entry for MARCH 27, 1908). At its height the organization will have as many as 24,000 members. Among the society's goals are preserving communal ownership of tribal lands and pressuring Congress to remove restrictions on the sale of allotments.

September 26

Paiute Indian Willie Boy becomes a fugitive.

In Banning, California, a young Paiute man known as Willie Boy shoots a Chemehuevi Indian, William Mike, and runs away with his 14-year-old daughter Carlota. The murder launches a widely reported manhunt that makes Willie Boy into a folk hero. Chased by a posse that includes Indian trackers, Willie Boy kills Carlota and then, in the middle of a skirmish with his pursuers, shoots himself. In 1969 the legends surrounding Willie Boy will become the basis of the counterculture film *Tell Them Willie Boy Is Here,* starring non-Indian actor Robert Blake in the title role.

1910

June

The Omnibus Act creates "competency commissions."

To help open allotted Indian lands to non-Indians, Congress passed the Burke Act (see entry for MAY 8, 1906). Originally allotments were to be held in trust by the government for 25 years, during which time the land could not be sold. The Burke Act allowed the secretary of the interior to eliminate the trust period on lands whose owners were deemed "competent" to conduct their own affairs.

The Burke Act, however, required that Indians apply for competency, and very few did. As a response, Congress enacts the Omnibus Act, which allows the government to end the trust period on allotments owned by "competent" Indians, whether they want it removed or not. Under the law, "competency commissions" are sent to reservations to search out "competent" Indian landowners. Within two years, these commissions will take more than 200,000 acres of allotted land out of trust, sometimes without the knowledge of the Indians who own it.

1911

The Boy Scouts of America promotes instruction in Indian lore.

Founded in 1910 by Washington lawyer James E. West, the Boy Scouts of America merges with two other youth organizations—the Sons of Daniel Boone and the Woodcraft League of America—both of which focus on teaching non-Indian boys a romanticized view of Indian legends and lore. Based on these programs, the Boy Scouts institutes a highly popular Indian Lore merit badge, which constitutes one of the first organized attempts to instruct non-Indians in Native American history and culture.

Choate v. Trapp protects Oklahoma Indian allotments from taxation.

The Choctaw and Cherokee of Oklahoma take the state to court when it attempts to collect taxes on their allotments. In the case of *Choate v. Trapp,* the Supreme Court finds that the allottees are still wards of the U.S. government and therefore exempt from state taxes. Oklahoma's effort is one of many challenges the state's assimilationists have made to the terms of Allotment set forth under the General Allotment Act (see entry for FEBRUARY 8, 1887).

Soldiers force Hopi students to attend school.

U.S. troops are called in to capture Hopi children from the village of Hotevilla and take them to the Shonogopavi Day School. The experience further embitters traditionalist Hopi, who founded Hotevilla five years earlier when they were dispelled from the village of Oraibi by tribe members more accommodating to the growing white presence in their lands (see entry for SEPTEMBER 6, 1906).

August

Yahi Indian Ishi comes out of hiding.

An Indian man about 50 years old tentatively emerges from the foothills near Oroville, in northern California. He is the last surviving member of the Yahi tribe, most of whom had been killed either by Americans or by the diseases Europeans brought to North America. Unable to communicate with the non-Indians who find him, the man is placed in protective custody in the Oroville jail.

News of Ishi's discovery is widely reported. When anthropologist Alfred Kroeber hears the story, he arranges for the man to be transported to the University of California's museum in San Francisco. There he is named "Ishi," the Yahi word for man, and shares his knowledge of the Yahi language and culture with researchers. Ishi

continues to live at the museum until his death from tuberculosis in 1914.

October 12

The Society of American Indians (SAI) holds its first conference.

At a conference in Columbus, Ohio, held on Columbus Day for symbolic reasons, 50 Native American delegates found the Society of American Indians. The Society of American Indians (SAI) grows out of a meeting of prominent Indian men and women held

A Society of American Indians banquet held during the association's fourth annual meeting in 1914 (National Archives, Neg. no. RG75-M-3)

the previous spring and hosted by a non-Indian sociologist at Ohio State University. Among the participants were Dakota Sioux physician and writer Charles A. Eastman (see entry for 1902), Yavapai journalist Carlos Montezuma (see entry for APRIL 1916), and Oneida activist Laura Cornelius Kellogg.

These luminaries, like the majority of the SAI membership, are alumni of Indian and non-Indian schools and colleges. Not surprisingly, one of the major focuses of the new organization is Indian education. The members also hope to teach non-Indians to respect Native Americans and their ways. Although many SAI members are models of Assimilation, some in the organization outspokenly question the government's Assimilation policies, especially those that most directly threaten Indian values and culture.

> "To survive at all [the Indian] must become as other men, a contributing, self-sustaining member of society. This does not mean, necessarily, the loss of individuality, but the asserting of it. The true aim of educational effort should not be to make the Indian a white man, but simply a man normal to his environment. Every Indian who has succeeded is such a person. Hundreds of Indians have attained honorable positions and are ... in reality are the only Indians who can appreciate the true dignity and value of their race, and they alone are able to speak for it."
>
> —Society of the American Indian member Arthur C. Parker at the association's first conference

1912

The Alaska Native Brotherhood (ANB) is founded.

The most influential intertribal organization in Alaska before statehood, the Alaska Native Brotherhood is established to improve tribes' social conditions and increase their political power. Although the group presents itself as representing all Alaskan natives, the majority of members are from the Tlingit and Haida tribes. Initially, the Alaska Native Brotherhood (ANB) is most concerned with obtaining citizenship for Alaska Natives, but it will increasingly focus its attention on protecting fishing rights and promoting land claims.

Summer

Jim Thorpe wins two Olympic gold medals.

At the Fifth Olympiad in Stockholm, Sweden, 24-year-old Sac and Fox Indian Jim Thorpe thrills the audience by his amazing performance in two of the most grueling Olympic events—the decathlon and the pentathlon. Already a national sports star for his achievements on the football team of the Carlisle Indian school (see entry for AUTUMN 1879), Thorpe becomes world famous by winning the gold medal in both events. The Olympic crowd cheers wildly as Thorpe is given his awards by Swedish monarch Gustav V, who says to him, "Sir, you are the greatest athlete in the world." With a characteristic lack of pretension, Thorpe replies, "Thanks, King." (See also entry for JANUARY 1913.)

Summer

Louis Tawanima is awarded an Olympic silver medal.

Louis Tawanima, a Hopi Indian from the village of Shungopovi, comes in second in the Stockholm Olympics' 10,000-meter run. Four years earlier, Tawanima had competed in the Olympic Games in London, where he finished ninth in the marathon. In 1957 he will become the first athlete voted into the Arizona Hall of Fame.

1913

Jesse Cornplanter illustrates *The Code of Handsome Lake.*

A Seneca artist known for his drawings of Iroquois history and mythology, Jesse Cornplanter creates a series of illustrations for *The Code of Handsome Lake, A Seneca Prophet.* Compiled by Cornplanter's father and the ethnologist Alfred C. Parker, the book is a treatise about the code of conduct espoused by Handsome Lake, who founded the Longhouse Religion in the early 19th century (see entry for 1799). Cornplanter began his artistic career at age nine, when he was commissioned by New York State to draw sketches of traditional Iroquois life. Other examples of his work were published in *Iroquois Games and Dances* (1913) and *Iroquois Uses of Maize and Other Food Plants* (1910). (See also entry for APRIL TO OCTOBER 1939.)

United States v. Sandoval affirms federal supervision of Indian tribes.

In *United States v. Sandoval,* a white man named Sandoval is accused of selling alcohol to Pueblo Indians in New Mexico in violation of a federal law forbidding liquor sales in "Indian country" (see entry for JULY 23, 1892). Sandoval argues the Pueblo are too assimilated to be considered residents of a "dependent Indian community" and that therefore this law cannot be applied to their lands. The Supreme Court disagrees and finds that, as "a simple, uninformed and inferior people," the Pueblo still require the protection of the federal government. Notwithstanding its condescending language, the decision is a victory for Indians in that it confirms that their lands are subject only to federal law and are not under state jurisdiction.

The U.S. Mint issues the Indian-head nickel.

Issued supposedly to honor Indians, the Indian-head nickel features the head of a Plains Indian man in profile on one side and a buffalo on the reverse—with the clear implication that Indians, like buffalo, are a dying breed. The Indian profile, designed by famed sculptor James Earle Fraser (see entry for 1915), is a composite of the features of 13 Indian leaders.

The Chiricahua Apache return to the Southwest.

After the surrender of Geronimo's Chiricahua Apache followers (see entry for MARCH TO SEPTEMBER 1886), the U.S. Army treated them as prisoners of war. They were sent to live first at Fort Marion in Florida, then at the Mount Vernon Barracks in Alabama, and finally at Fort Sill in Oklahoma.

After being imprisoned for 17 years, they are at last given the chance to return to the Southwest by the U.S. government. While one-third opt to remain at Fort Sill, the majority of the prisoners agree to move to the Mescalero Apache's reservation in south-central New Mexico. Although initially the Chiricahua settle in their own area, over time they will become a powerful force in reservation politics.

January

Jim Thorpe is stripped of his Olympic medals.

The Amateur Athletic Union (AAU) decides that Jim Thorpe, a Sac and Fox Indian, was a professional athlete when he participated in the 1912 Olympics (see entry for SUMMER 1912). As a result, he is asked to return the gold medals he won after his

> "I did not play for the money ... but because I liked to play ball. I was not wise in the ways of the world and did not realize this was wrong, and that it would make me a professional in track sports. . . . I have always liked sports and only played or run races for the fun of the things and never to earn money."
>
> —Jim Thorpe in a letter to the Amateur Athletic Union, asking the organization not to revoke his amateur status

amazing performances in the decathlon and the pentathlon.

The AAU makes the decision six days after the *Worcester Telegram* in Worcester, Massachusetts, reports that Thorpe played professional baseball during the summer of 1910. The committee disregards a letter from Thorpe in which he pleas for leniency, explaining that he played not for the money but for the love of the game. The claim is particularly persuasive after it is reported that he received only $25 to $30 a week. Nationally and internationally, the public largely sides with Thorpe. The AAU is condemned as an elitist institution, and many contend that its decision to punish Thorpe smacks of racism. (See also entry for JANUARY 18, 1983.)

February 22

Work begins on Indian monument in New York City.

In a ceremony held on George Washington's birthday and attended by 32 Indian leaders, President William Howard Taft breaks ground at the future site of a bronze statue of a young Indian extending his hand in a gesture of peace. The monument, projected to be 15 feet taller than the Statue of Liberty, is the brainchild of department store owner Rodman Wanamaker (see entry for 1909). In a speech, Taft predicts that the statue will tell the "story of the march of empire and the progress of Christian civilization to the uttermost limits." Construction on Wanamaker's tribute to a "departed race" will be delayed because of a shortage of bronze during World War I, then abandoned due to a lack of funding and public interest.

1914

Louis Sockalexis is honored by Cleveland baseball fans.

When fans are asked to rename the Cleveland Spiders, they vote for "Indians." The new name is meant to honor Louis Sockalexis, who had become the first Indian to play major league baseball when he joined the Cleveland team (see entry for APRIL 22, 1897). Sockalexis died in obscurity on December 24, 1913.

The United States takes over the Northern Cheyenne's cattle.

Charging that the Northern Cheyenne's ranching operations are grossly mismanaged, the U.S. government takes control over the tribe's substantial herds, which grew from one to 12,000 head between 1903 and 1912. The action is encouraged by the Northern Cheyenne's non-Indian competitors, who are angry at being undersold in cattle markets by the tribe's ranchers. Under the government's watch, management errors—such as leaving cattle outside to freeze to death in the winter—will drastically reduce the herds. Within a decade, the number of cattle owned by tribe members will plummet to about 3,000. (See also entry for 1919.)

Actor Chauncey Yellow Robe attacks depictions of Indians on film.

Before a meeting of the Society of American Indians (SAI) (see entry for OCTOBER 12, 1911), the leading organization of Native American activists, Lakota Sioux actor Chauncey Yellow Robe speaks out against *The Indian Wars Refought* (1914), a motion picture produced by the film company of William "Buffalo Bill" Cody. Cody entered the film business after the public lost interest in his famous Wild West show, for which he hired Indian and non-Indian actors to re-create Plains Wars battles for a largely white audience (see entry for MAY 18, 1883).

As Yellow Robe tells the members of the SAI, he is appalled that *The Indian Wars Refought* presents the Wounded Knee Massacre—during which some 300 Lakota women, men, and children were slaughtered by the U.S. Army (see entry for DECEMBER 29, 1890)—as though it were a battle pitting noble American soldiers against bloodthirsty Lakota warriors. Yellow Robe also notes with dismay that the film, whose "technical advisor" is the notorious Indian fighter

General Nelson A. Miles, is being promoted for use in schools.

1915

Mohawk steelworkers begin working in New York City.

Hired to work on the Hell's Gate Bridge, John Diabo becomes New York City's first Mohawk steelworker (see entry for 1886). Nicknamed "Indian Joe," Diabo initially works with a team of Irish steelworkers but soon gathers his own crew of Mohawk workers from the Kahnawake Reserve. After several months, Diabo falls from a high beam and drowns in the river below. The rest of the crew returns to Kahnawake for good when they take his body back to the reserve. However, many other Mohawk, settling in Brooklyn, will become New York City steelworkers in the decades to come.

James Earle Fraser's *The End of the Trail* symbolizes the demise of the Indian.

At the Panama-Pacific International Exposition in San Francisco, *The End of the Trail,* a sculpture by James Earle Fraser (see entry for 1913), creates a sensation and wins a gold medal in the art competition. The sculpture depicts a Plains Indian warrior, slumped in exhaustion, mounted on a weary old pony. The work's popularity among non-Indians derives largely from its suggestion that the forces of "civilization" have finally subdued rebel Indian nations. Fraser himself explains, "It was [the] idea of a weaker race being steadily pushed to the wall by a stronger that I wanted to convey."

Autumn

Henry Roe Cloud founds an Indian prep school.

The only Indian-run high school in the United States, the Roe Indian Institute (later renamed the American Indian Institute) is established in Wichita, Kansas, to offer young Indian men a college-preparatory education. Funded through private sources, the school is the brainchild of Henry Roe Cloud, a Winnebago educator and Yale University graduate. Cloud will serve as the institute's president for 16 years.

1916

The Museum of the American Indian is built in New York City.

Beginning in 1897, New York businessman George Gustav Heye amassed a huge collection of Indian artifacts. To display his collection, he finances the construction of the Museum of the American Indian. He hires professional anthropological scholars to care for and document the objects in the museum. The museum is so small that it can display only about 5 percent of Heye's vast holdings.

United States v. Nice supports government restrictions on Indian citizens.

In the case of *United States v. Nice,* a white man is charged with selling alcohol to an Indian man, a violation of a federal law prohibiting the sale of liquor in Indian country (see entry for JULY 23, 1892). He argues that the sale was lawful because the Indian was given an allotment and, with it, U.S. citizenship.

In its decision in the case, the Supreme Court states that "citizenship is not incompatible with . . . continued guardianship." The decision, therefore, limits the meaning of citizenship for tribe members. In the words of the court, citizenship could "be conferred without completely emancipating the Indians" from government regulations made for their "protection."

April

Carlos Montezuma begins publishing *Wassaja.*

One of the leading Indian intellectuals of his day, Yavapai Indian Carlos Montezuma writes and publishes a newsletter, *Wassaja,* to voice his opinions on how Indian policy should be reformed. The publication's title is the name by which he was known as a boy before he was kidnapped by Akimel O'od-ham (Pima) Indians, who then sold him to a white guardian for $30.

Many of Montezuma's articles in *Wassaja* focus on the failings of the Bureau of Indian Affairs. In his opinion, the agency's policies had been so detrimental to the welfare of Indians that it should be disbanded. He also reports on the activities of the Society of American Indians, a pan-Indian political organization of educated Native Americans he helped to found (see entry for OCTOBER 12, 1911). Montezuma will continue to write the influential newsletter until 1922, the year before his death.

"The Indian Bureau system is wrong. The only way to adjust the wrong is to abolish it, and the only reform is to let my people go. After freeing the Indian from the shackles of government supervision, what is the Indian going to do: Leave that with the Indian, and it is none of your business."

—journalist Carlos Montezuma, speaking at the 1915 Society of American Indians Conference

Edited by Wassaja (Dr. Montezuma's Indian name, meaning "Signaling") an Apache Indian.

Vol. 3, No. 2   **ISSUED MONTHLY**   **May, 1918**

An illustration from Carlos Montezuma's newsletter *Wassaja*. Displaying Montezuma's contempt for the Bureau of Indian Affairs (BIA), the cartoon shows him leading a group of Indians in hammering down the door of the Indian Office (a popular name for the BIA) with a battering ram labeled "Freedom's Signal for the Indian." *(Photo Courtesy of the Newberry Library)*

May 13

Native Americans celebrate Indian Day.

The Society of American Indians, the leading Indian civil rights group in the United States (see entry for OCTOBER 12, 1911), declares May 13 to be "Indian Day." In addition to celebrating the achievements of Native Americans, the holiday is meant to bring awareness of the poverty and social problems plaguing Indian groups.

June

The Allied Tribes of British Columbia is formed.

At a conference in Vancouver organized by Squamish Andrew Paull and Haida Peter Kelly, the Allied Tribes of British Columbia is founded by representatives from Indian groups across the province. One of Canada's first multitribal Indian activist groups, the Allied Tribes dedicates itself to pursuing Indian land claims in British Columbia. When in 1927 a parliamentary committee denies the Indians' claims, the organization will fall into disarray.

1917

Indians serve in the military during World War I.

Although about half of male Indians are non-citizens and therefore not subject to the draft, approximately 16,000 Indians answer the call to join the military as the United States enters World War I. Their participation is at a rate nearly double that of the general population. Several Indian soldiers—including Sergeant Alfred Bailey, Corporal Nicholas E. Brown, and Private Joseph Oklahombi—will be hailed as war heroes. All Indians will later be made U.S. citizens in part as a reward for the Indian troops' distinguished service (see entries for NOVEMBER 16, 1919, and 1924).

Oklahoma Indians protest World War I in the Green Corn Rebellion.

Creek Indians and members of several other tribes in eastern Oklahoma join with impoverished whites and blacks in protesting the U.S. entrance into World War I, in a movement known as the Green Corn Rebellion. In addition to expressing their anger at their historical treatment by the U.S. government, the Indians involved oppose poor Americans' being called to fight a war that they believed would primarily benefit the rich. During a rally attended by 200 Creek, protest leader Ellen Perryman declares, "The Indians are not going to the slaughter fields of France." For telling Indians not to register for the draft, she will later be charged with violating the Espionage Act of 1917.

April

The Bureau of Indian Affairs removes restrictions on Indian land sales.

Commissioner of Indian Affairs Cato Sells announces a new policy of issuing patents-in-fee to any Indian landowner who is less than one-half Indian ancestry or judged competent to manage his or her own affairs. Once issued, the patents remove all restrictions that prohibit Indians from selling or leasing their lands. Sells's measure is inspired by a wartime shortage of farmland and the accompanying rise in agricultural prices. As predicted, large amounts of privately owned Indian land pass into the hands of whites soon after the policy is implemented.

1918

The Martinezes develop a black-on-black pottery style.

Maria and Julian Martinez, a couple from San Ildefonso Pueblo, create an innovative new style of pottery decoration. After Maria molds a pot, Julian paints designs, using slip—a mixture of white clay and water. They find that if while firing the clay they increase the amount of smoke by adding dung to the fire, the surface turns black. After polishing, the unpainted area takes on a shiny finish, while the painted designs remain matte. This black-on-black design scheme will become the trademark of the Martinezes' work and help to make Maria the most famous Indian potter in the world.

September to November

Choctaw Code Talkers participate in Meuse-Argonne campaign.

Fourteen Choctaw soldiers in the U.S. Army's 36th Division are chosen to send messages during the Meuse-Argonne campaign in France. Similar to the better-known Navajo Code Talkers of World War II (see entry for APRIL 1942), these men translate military communications into their native language so that they cannot be read if intercepted by the Germans. For their help in winning several key battles, the French government will later make the Choctaw Code Talkers Chevaliers de l'Ordre National du Mérite (see entry for NOVEMBER 3, 1989).

October 10

The Native American Church is incorporated.

Early in 1918, the U.S. House of Representatives defeats a bill that would outlaw all uses of peyote. Temporarily relieved but fearing the passage of such legislation in the future, adherents of peyotism try to legitimize their religious practices in the eye of non-Indians by incorporating themselves as the Native American Church of Oklahoma. (It will be renamed the Native American Church of North America in 1955.) The new religion, which developed in the late 19th century, is a blend of Indian beliefs and Christianity and focuses on the sacramental use of peyote. When ingested in a ceremonial setting, the button of the peyote cactus produces hallucinations that allow the church's followers to receive revelations from the Creator.

"[T]his corporation is formed . . . to foster and promote the religious belief of the several tribes of Indians in the State of Oklahoma, in the Christian religion with morality, sobriety, industry, kindly charity, and right living and to cultivate a spirit of self-respect and brotherly union among the members of the Native Race of Indians."

—from the corporate charter of Native American Church of Oklahoma

December

The League of Indians is founded.

The first conference of the League of Indians, the first pan-Indian political organization formed in Canada, is held on the Six Nations Reserve in Ontario. Modeling the organization on the Iroquois Confederacy (see entry for CA. 1400), Mohawk Indian Fred Loft forms the league to persuade the Canadian government to improve the educational opportunities available to Indians, but it soon expands its scope to address a wide variety of concerns and complaints of both bands and individual Indians. Highly respected among the Mohawk, Loft is a World War I veteran whose support for Britain during the war inspired many Indians to enlist.

Loft's efforts to organize Canadian Indians immediately brands him as a subversive in the eyes of the Department of Indian Affairs. The department's minister will attempt to silence Loft by trying to revoke his Indian status and bringing him up on criminal charges for raising money to fund the recognition of Indian land claims.

1919

The Bureau of Indian Affairs confiscates the Northern Cheyenne's horse herds.

The Bureau of Indian Affairs announces that the number of horses owned by the Northern Cheyenne must be reduced to free grazing land for their cattle. Ignoring the tribe's objections, officials arrange for many of their horses to be shot and the meat of the slaughtered animals to be served to the Indians as rations. Other horses are confiscated and sold, with none of the proceeds passed on to the horses' owners. (See also entry for 1914.)

November

The Mission Indian Federation is founded.

During a conference led by non-Indian Jonathan Tibbet at his home in Riverside, California, a group of southern California Indians forms the Mission Indian Federation (MIF). The MIF grows out of the Indians' anger with their past dealings with the federal government, specifically with the Bureau of Indian Affairs. The members are particularly incensed that California Indians have not been compensated for lands taken from them by treaty in exchange for reservations that the government never established. The organization is also committed to obtaining full citizenship for Indians and campaigning for the disbanding of the BIA. (See also entry for 1921.)

November 16

Congress grants citizenship to Indian veterans.

The U.S. government rewards Indians for service in the military during World War I (see entry for 1917) with the passage of the Indian Veteran's Citizenship Bill. The legislation, which gives citizenship to any honorably discharged Indian veteran who applies for it, paves the way for the Indian Citizenship Act, which will make citizens of all Indians born in the United States (see entry for JUNE 2, 1924).

1920

Navajo (Dineh) weaver Hosteen Klah creates the first dry painting rug.

An important religious leader among the Navajo (Dineh), Hosteen Klah weaves a rug called "The Whirling Log." Its design is based on a dry painting (often called sand painting)—an image formed from crushed minerals and made by Navajo holy men during healing ceremonies. Many Navajo object to Klah's creation of a permanent representation of a dry painting, which traditionally is destroyed after ceremonial use. Over their objections, Klah displays the rug at the Gallup Ceremonial. After it wins a blue ribbon at the art show, Klah sells it to a white tourist. Recognizing a large market for dry painting rugs, he will weave 24 more for sale to non-Indians and train two of his nieces in the new art form.

The Canadian government allows compulsory enfranchisement of Indians.

To promote assimilation, the Canadian government allows Indians to give up their Indian status in exchange for full citizenship and the right to vote. Because very few Indians apply for citizenship, parliament passes an amendment to the Indian Act (see entry for APRIL 12, 1876) giving the superintendent general the power to enfranchise Indians over the age of 21 and strip them of their Indian status without their consent. In the wake of Indian outrage over this threat to their autonomy, the government will repeal the amendment in 1922, only to reinstate it in 1933, with an added provision that enfranchisement cannot be forced on an Indian if the action violates a treaty promise.

1921

A rash of murders strikes the Osage reservation.

With the oil royalties on Osage lands in Oklahoma reaching approximately $20 million a year (see entry for 1897), wealthy tribe members increasingly become victims of non-Indian con men looking to swindle them out of their money in any way possible. In the three-year period beginning in 1921, many Osage are killed under mysterious circumstances, often with non-Indians named as their legal beneficiaries. While 24 murder cases are left unsolved, many other deaths are questionably ruled as suicides. This reign of terror among the Osage will lead Congress to pass the Osage Guardianship Act (see entry for 1925).

Mission Indian Federation members are arrested for conspiracy.

Angered by the hostility of Mission Indian Federation—a powerful California Indian advocacy group—toward the Bureau of Indian Affairs (see entry for NOVEMBER 1919), the Department of Justice orders the arrest of 57 federation members. They are charged with conspiracy against the U.S. government. Released without bail, the accused prepare for a long legal battle, but the charges will be dropped three years later after all Indians are granted citizenship (see entry for JUNE 2, 1924).

Non-Indian hobbyists perform the Snake Dance as the Smokis.

Established by the Prescott, Arizona, chamber of commerce to promote tourism, the Smokis are non-Indians who gather annually to dress up in Indian costumes and perform a version of the Hopi Snake Dance down the town's main street. Over the next 70 years the Smokis will develop into a secret society, with members taking Indian names and identifying themselves with small tattoos, called "snakebites," on their hands. The hobbyist group will continue to stage its annual Snake Dances until the early 1990s, when objections from the Hopi finally compel the Smokis to abandon the ceremony.

November 2

The Snyder Act provides funds services for Indians.

Responding to the dire health conditions in many Native American communities, Congress passes the Snyder Act. The act gives Congress the authority to authorize funds for health, social, and educational programs for Indian groups, even those for whom the United States is not required by treaty to provide such services.

November 11

Plenty Coups speaks at the Tomb of the Unknown Soldier dedication.

Joining President Warren G. Harding and many foreign dignitaries, Crow leader Plenty Coups marches in a procession to Arlington National Cemetery for the dedication of the Tomb of the Unknown Soldier. Before the soldier's body is placed in the tomb, Plenty Coups, in a scripted performance, emerges from the crowd to place his eagle-feathered headdress and coup stick on the coffin. Ignoring officials requests that he remain silent during the ceremony, the Indian leader then turns to the crowd and, speaking in Crow, pays tribute to the Indian warriors of the past and offers a brief prayer for peace.

"I am glad to represent all the Indians of the United States in placing on the grave of this noble warrior this coup stick and war bonnet, every eagle feather of which represents a deed of valor by my race....I hope that the Great Spirit will grant that these noble warriors have not given up their lives in vain and that there will be peace to all men hereafter."

—Crow chief Plenty Coups at the dedication ceremony for Tomb of the Unknown Soldier

December

Eighty Kwakiutl are arrested for holding a potlatch ceremony.

In a village near Alert Bay, off Vancouver Island, nearly 300 Kwakiutl Indians gather to hold a pot-latch—a ceremony that is outlawed by the Canadian government (see entry for APRIL 19, 1884). To assert his authority, the local agent arrests 80 of the most prominent participants. In the sub-sequent trial—conducted in English, a language most of the defendants do not understand—30 are sentenced to prison terms of up to a year. All are forced to promise never to attend another potlatch and to surrender goods that were to be distributed to guests at the potlatch feast.

The arrests effectively end illegal potlatching, but they also earn Canadian officials the enmity of the Kwakiutl people for decades to come. The Kwakiutl are also outraged by the confiscation of many treasured masks, costumes, and other pot-latch paraphernalia. Many of these objects will be placed on display at the Royal Ontario Museum, the National Museum in Ottawa, and the Museum of the American Indian in New York City (see entry for 1916).

1922

Emmet Starr's *History of the Cherokee Indians* is published.

After nearly 30 years of research and writing, Cherokee Emmet Starr completes a monumental history of his people. In addition to a comprehen-sive Cherokee genealogy and reproductions of primary documents, such as laws, treaties, and con-stitution, the book features descriptions of Cherokee life and important historical events both before and after the tribe's removal to Indian Terri-tory (see entry for MAY 1838). Starr's views of Cherokee history stand in stark contrast to those of white historians, who see the Cherokee Nation's dissolution in 1907 as the inevitable victory of "civ-ilization." Starr instead highlights the many political and social accomplishments of the Chero-kee and writes admiringly of traditional leaders.

Secretary of the Interior Albert B. Fall tries to take control of executive-order reservations.

Secretary of the Interior Albert B. Fall declares that all reservations formed by executive order, rather than by treaty, are public-domain lands. His state-ment is an attempt to take from tribes and give to the government all rights to these reservations. Fall is vigorously challenged by several Indian rights groups, including the Indian Rights Association (see entry for DECEMBER 1882) and the American Indian Defense Association (see entry for MAY 1923). The policy will be abandoned, partly be-cause of these groups' efforts and partly because of Fall's resignation under a cloud during the Harding administration's Teapot Dome scandal. In 1929, the former secretary will be convicted of accepting a bribe in exchange for leasing oil reserves at Teapot Dome, Wyoming, and Elk Hills, California.

Canadian Inuit are filmed in *Nanook of the North*.

Considered by cinema historians as the first great film documentary, *Nanook of the North* presents footage of Inuit living along Canada's Hudson's Bay. The director, Robert J. Flaherty, stages many of the vignettes, encouraging his subjects to act out tradi-tional activities performed before whites came to their lands. Much of the film focuses on one man, Nanook, and his struggles to hunt for food in the nearly barren Arctic environment. Two years after the filming, Nanook will die of starvation.

Spring

Cherokee Ruth Muskrat attends a Christian conference in China.

Cherokee activist Ruth Muskrat travels to Beijing, China, as the first Indian representative to the annual World's Student Christian Federation conference. A student at Mount Holyoke College, Muskrat, at 25, is the conference's youngest participant. She will later become instrumental in the creation of the National Congress of American Indians (see entry for NOVEMBER 1944), a national multitribal organization dedicated to defending Indian rights.

Summer

The first Gallup Inter-Tribal Indian Ceremonial is held.

In a large vacant lot on the edge of Gallup, New Mexico, Indians gather for the Gallup Inter-Tribal Indian Ceremonial. The event features ceremonial dances, a rodeo, and an open-air Indian arts and crafts market. The ceremonial will become one of the biggest annual Native American fairs in the United States.

October

The Eastern Association on Indian Affairs is founded.

A group of activists alarmed by growing threats to the Pueblo Indians' land base (see entry for NOVEMBER 5, 1922) founds the Eastern Association on Indian Affairs. Based in New York City, the organization joins other Indian rights group to help the Pueblo and to squelch Commissioner of Indian Affairs Charles Burke's efforts to prohibit southwestern and Plains Indians from performing traditional religious ceremonies. (See also entry for 1934.)

November 5

The All-Pueblo Council launches a campaign to defeat the Bursum Bill.

Organized by sociologist John C. Collier (see entries for MAY 1923 and for 1933), a meeting of 121 Pueblo Indians is held at Santo Domingo Pueblo. The issue at hand is the Bursum Bill, which aims to solve a land dispute between the Pueblo and non-Indians in the region. In 1848, a tract of Pueblo land was bought by Hispanic and white settlers, but in a later Supreme Court ruling (see entry for 1913) the Pueblo are still found to be wards of the federal government, which puts into question whether they can legally sell their own land. Despite the court's

decision, the non-Indians occupying the Pueblo's land refused to leave. The Bursum Bill, now before Congress, calls for the non-Indians to receive legal title to the land and for the Pueblo's water rights to be placed under the control of the state.

Alarmed by the proposed legislation, Collier organizes a movement to defeat it. He rallies support from such non-Indian groups as the General Federation of Women's Clubs, and he brings delegates from all pueblos to discuss the bill at the All-Pueblo Council. The delegates draft "An Appeal by the Pueblo Indians of New Mexico to the People of the United States," outlining how the Bursum Bill, if passed, would undermine traditional Pueblo life and traditions. Accompanied by Collier, representatives from the council travel to Washington, D.C., to testify before the Senate. Because of their impassioned pleas and public support for the Pueblo, the Bursum Bill will be defeated (see entry for JUNE 7, 1924).

1923

The Committee of One Hundred meets to discuss Indian affairs.

Organized by Secretary of the Interior Herbert Hoover, the Committee of One Hundred is created to propose reforms in Indian policy. The diverse group is composed of 100 Indian and non-Indian experts, scholars, and reformers. Among the Indians present are Cherokee activist and educator Ruth Muskrat Bronson (see entry for SPRING 1922); Dakota Sioux physician and author Charles A. Eastman (see entries for 1902 and for OCTOBER 12, 1911); and Seneca anthropologist Arthur C. Parker.

The committee calls for a wide variety of reforms, including improving Indian education, removing bans on Indian religious ceremonies, and protecting Indian ownership of mineral rights to their lands. Aside from their recommendation that the U.S. government resolve Pueblo land claims (see entry for NOVEMBER 5, 1922), the committee will have little effect on federal Indian policy. The meeting, however, will help set the stage for the progressive Indian policies of the New Deal era of the 1930s.

Cherokee delegate Ruth Muskrat presents President Calvin Coolidge with a book titled *The Red Man in the United States* during the 1923 meeting of the Committee of One Hundred. *(Library of Congress, Neg. no. USZ62-107775)*

The Lakota Sioux sue the United States for the illegal seizure of the Black Hills.

In a suit against the U.S. government filed in the Court of Claims, the Lakota Sioux call for the return of the Black Hills. Approximately 7.7 million acres in the Black Hills region were seized from the Sioux without compensation after the discovery of gold there (see entry for 1877). The land had been officially granted to the Indians as part of the formation of the Great Sioux Reservation by the 1868 Treaty of Fort Laramie.

The Iroquois seek recognition from the League of Nations.

As speaker for the council of the Iroquois confederacy, Cayuga leader Levi General travels to Geneva, Switzerland, to address the League of Nations. In his speech, General condemns the Canadian government's attempts to force citizenship on Indians (see entry for 1920). To reinforce Iroquois claims to sovereignty, he asks the league to formally recognize the confederacy, but the organization declines to do so.

February

The Bureau of Indian Affairs recommends restrictions on Indian ceremonies.

On the advice of a conference of missionaries, Commissioner of Indian Affairs Francis E. Leupp mandates that reservation superintendents should permit Indians to perform dances only once a month and that the dances should last no longer than one day. The "dance evil," as some reformers brand Indian ceremonies that feature dancing, is seen as one of the greatest obstacles to Assimilation. Leupp also indicates that dances should be attended only by Indians older than 50 and that the Bureau of Indian Affairs will use "careful propaganda" to gain public support for its suppression of Indian dancing.

May

The American Indian Defense Association is founded.

A small group of wealthy white liberals form the American Indian Defense Association to fight for a variety of Indian causes. The driving force behind the group is sociologist John C. Collier. Disillusioned with Western culture after the disaster of World War I, Collier was first fascinated by the tribal culture of the Pueblo Indians during a visit to Taos, New Mexico, in 1921. After helping the Pueblo defeat the Bursum Bill (see entry for NOVEMBER 5, 1922), which would have granted a large amount of Pueblo land to non-Indians, Collier decides to organize the AIDA to battle other governmental threats to Indian communities and cultures. Serving as the AIDA's executive secretary, Collier will spend the next 10 years lobbying Congress on issues such as Indian poverty, Native American religious freedom, and the diminishing power of tribal governments. (See also entry for 1933.)

July 7

The Navajo Business Council holds its first meeting.

In 1921 the Midwest Refining Company began negotiating with the Navajo (Dineh) to drill for oil on their reservation near Shiprock. The Navajo, however, had no formal government structure at the time, so it was unclear with whom the company should be negotiating. To remedy the situation, the Bureau of Indian Affairs (BIA) in 1922 appointed three prominent Navajo—Henry Chee Dodge, Charlie Mitchell, and Dugal Chee Bekiss— to handle Navajo business arrangements.

Seeking to make this arrangement more formal and permanent, the agency encourages the creation of a representative council. Following guidelines established by the BIA, the tribe elects 12 representatives and 12 alternates to serve as spokespeople for the Navajo as a whole. Henry Chee Dodge is chosen to be chair of the council. In its first annual meeting, the council concentrates on deciding the terms of oil leases. In years to come, it will broaden its focus to include a wide array of issues affecting the Navajo.

1924

Virginia passes the Racial Integrity Law.

With the Racial Integrity Law, the state of Virginia defines whites as people with no non-Caucasian ancestry. However, the law makes an exception for Caucasians with no more than one-sixteenth Indian blood. This provision is made to accommodate the socially prominent whites who proudly claim they are the descendants of Pocahontas (see entry for APRIL 5, 1614).

June 2

The Indian Citizenship Act makes all Indians citizens of the United States.

Drafted by the Indian Rights Association (see entry for 1882), the Indian Citizenship Act ex- tends U.S. citizenship to all Indians born in the United States. Before its passage, a series of congressional acts had already granted citizenship to more than two-thirds of the Indian population. In the aftermath of World War I, however, universal Indian citizenship became a focus of Indian rights organizations, who chastised the federal government for denying some Indians citizenship while allowing Indian soldiers to fight and die for the United States.

Despite the hopes of Indian activists, citizenship will leave Indians' relationship to the government largely unchanged. It will not alter their position as wards of the U.S. government, nor will it affect their tribal membership

"[I]t has [finally] pleased Congress to admit the descendants of the original American people to the same legal status as aliens who have gone through the necessary procedure after five years of continuous residence here.... If there are cynics among the Indians, they may receive the news of their new citizenship with wry smiles. The white race, having robbed them of a continent, and having sought to deprive them of freedom of actions, freedom of social custom and freedom of worship, now at last gives them the same legal basis as their conquerors."

—from an editorial in the *New York Times* on the granting of U.S. citizenship to Indians

June 7

The Pueblo Lands Act settles land disputes between Pueblo and non-Indians.

The Bursum Bill sought to give non-Indians title to lands they claimed in Pueblo territory, but the legislation was defeated owing to aggressive lobbying by Indian activists (see entry for NOVEMBER 5, 1922). To finally settle these disputes, Congress passes the Pueblo Lands Act. The law establishes the Pueblo Lands Board to examine the validity of the non-Indians' claims.

The board will grant title to a small number of non-Indian claimants and provide modest monetary compensation for the rest. The process of granting land titles and evicting non-Indians offered compensation only will continue until 1938.

Autumn

The final Big House Ceremony is held.

Near Copan, Oklahoma, the Lenni Lenape (Delaware) hold the last ceremony of the Big House Church. The most sacred religious rite of the Lenni Lenape, the Big House ceremony traditionally was held over 12 nights to celebrate the harvest and ensure good fortune during the year to come. The Lenni Lenape are forced to abandoned the Big House Church because their elder religious leaders are too old to perform it, while their children, now students in non-Indian schools, are prohibited from participating by their teachers.

1925

Zane Grey's *The Vanishing American* is published.

In his novel *The Vanishing American,* popular western writer Zane Grey tells a melodramatic love story about Nophaie, a Navajo (Dineh) man, and Marian, a white woman. Following the conventions of fictional interracial romance, the love affair ends with the death of Nophaie, symbolic of the demise of all Indian peoples. The title is perhaps drawn from a famous photograph taken by Edward Curtis (see entry for 1906) of a group of Navajo riding away into the desert. Read by a huge audience when serialized in *Ladies' Home Journal, The Vanishing American* will be made into a classic film western the following year.

> "[The Indian's] deeds are done. His glory and dream are gone. His sun has set. Those ... who survive the disease and drink and poverty ... must inevitably be absorbed by the race that has destroyed him. Red blood into the white! It means the white race will gain and the Indian vanish."
>
> —from Zane Grey's *The Vanishing American*

Congress tries to protect wealthy Osage with the Osage Guardianship Act.

Through the Osage Guardianship Act, the Osage County court and the Osage Agency are given joint responsibility for supervising guardians assigned to oversee Osage Indians' accounts and expenditures. Heralded in the press as "the richest people in the world," Osage born before 1907 are receiving approximately $13,000 a year each from the royalties given the tribe by oil companies drilling on its mineral-rich lands (see entry for 1897). Some tribe members have adopted a lavish lifestyle since they began receiving royalty income. Of more concern to Congress, however, is the large number of Osage who have been murdered by non-Indian swindlers after being tricked into naming these con men as their beneficiaries (see entry for 1921).

1926

The American Indian begins publication.

Indian progressives begin publishing *The American Indian,* a journal that focuses initially on the Indians of Oklahoma but soon expanded its scope to tribes across the United States. For the next five years, it will offer articles about socially prominent Indian families, accounts of games played by Indian school football teams, and biographies of successful Indians of the past and present.

Paleo-Indian studies begins with the excavation of the Folsom site.

Jesse Figgins, the director of the Colorado Museum of Natural History, organizes an archaeological dig near the small town of Folsom, New Mexico. A year before, a collection of old bones and stone points came into his possession. They had been discovered 17 years earlier by a black cowboy named George McJunkin on a Folsom ranch. Figgins identified the bones as those of an extinct species of bison that lived in the area at the end of the Ice Ages.

The excavation team uncovers more bones and several fluted projectile points (see entry for CA. 8500 TO 8000 B.C.), which provide evidence of humans in the area during the Stone Age. The find inaugurates the formal study of Paleo-Indians in North America.

The Fred Harvey Company offers tours of southwestern Indian lands.

The Fred Harvey Company, which operates luxury hotels throughout the West, makes the Southwest a major vacation destination, offering guided tours through the reservations of the Navajo (Dineh), Hopi, and Zuni. White vacationers, largely from the East and Midwest, travel west by railroad. Harvey Company cars meet them at the station, drive them through Indian Country by day, and return them to the comfort of a Harvey hotel at night.

Tourists quickly come to admire many of the objects the southwestern Indians make by hand, such as pots, kachina dolls, rattles, and other items used in religious ceremonies. Finding the visitors eager customers, southwestern Indians develop versions of these goods specifically for sale to whites.

The Indian Defense League of America is founded.

Organized by Tuscarora Clinton Rickard and Mohawk David Hill, the Indian Defense League of America brings together American and Canadian Iroquois in the battle to force the United States to honor Jay's Treaty, which gave the Iroquois the right to travel freely across the American-Canadian border (see entry for NOVEMBER 19, 1794). After a delegation from the organization convinces the U.S. government to respect the Iroquois' treaty rights in 1928, the league will organize the Border Crossing Celebration, an event held annually at Niagara Falls, New York.

The National Council of American Indians is established.

With the financial support of the General Federation of Women's Clubs, writer and activist Gertrude

"A number of glaring cases all show that in the activities of the informal organization of grafters, sex or age make no different; the young child, the adult, the incompetent (mentally or physically) are all robbed in the same thorough, nonchalant manner. The 'system' has but one object—GET THE MONEY AND GET IT QUICK!"
—Gertrude Bonnin in *Oklahoma's Poor Rich Indians* (1924), on non-Indian con men's theft of Indian land

Bonnin (Zitkala-Sa) founds the National Council of American Indians. Bonnin, who had been active in the Society of American Indians in its early years (see entry for OCTOBER 12, 1911), declares that the council's goals are to "create increased interest in behalf of the Indians, and secure for them added recognition of their personal and property rights."

Bonnin encourages Indians to participate in politics, particularly by exercising their newly won right to vote, and to look to education as a tool for freeing themselves from the paternalistic policies of the Bureau of Indian Affairs. Although the National Council's ideas will be greeted with little enthusiasm by tribes, Bonnin, under its auspices, will exercise a substantial influence over the drafting of the groundbreaking Indian Reorganization Act (see entry for JUNE 18, 1934).

Sam Blowsnake's *Crashing Thunder* is published.

With the encouragement and help of non-Indian anthropologist Paul Radin, Winnebago Indian Sam Blowsnake (also known as Crashing Thunder and Big Winnebago) tells his life history in *Crashing Thunder*. The book focuses on Blowsnake's search for religious truth, which he finally finds in peyotism (see entry for OCTOBER 10, 1918). A classic of ethnographic autobiography, the book will serve as a model for many future collaborations between Indians and anthropologists, including *Mountain Wolf Woman* (1961), the autobiography of Blowsnake's sister, edited by anthropologist Nancy Lurie.

1927

The Indian Act is amended to stymie Native political activity.

To suppress dissent among Native peoples, the Canadian government amends the Indian Act (see entry for APRIL 12, 1876) to outlaw the unauthorized solicitation of funds for Native political organizations. The measure effectively destroys Natives' efforts to band together to force the government to address their concerns, particularly their claims that land throughout Canada was seized from them illegally.

The Indian Shaker Church divides over a doctrine dispute.

The Indian Shaker Church (see entry for 1883) is mired in controversy when two groups of adherents

emerge in the church—those who want to use the Bible in their services and those who do not. The dispute comes to a head when a former bishop of the anti-Bible faction refuses to step down after a pro-Bible believer is elected to the position.

The conflict is resolved by the superior court of Snohomish County, Washington, which formally divides the church. The anti-Bible faction continues to be called the Indian Shaker Church; the pro-Bible faction is thereafter known as the Indian Full Gospel Church.

Mourning Dove's *Cogewea: The Half-Blood* is published.

Writing under the pen name Mourning Dove, Colville-Okanagan writer Christine Quintasket

"Cogewea seated on the veranda was endeavoring to interest herself in a book.... The scene opened [with] a half-blood 'brave' is in love with a white girl.... He deems himself beneath her.... But to cap the absurdity of the story, he weds the white 'princess' and slaves for her the rest of his life.

Cogewea leaned back in her chair with a sigh. 'Bosh,' she mused half aloud. 'Show me the Red "buck" who would *slave* for the most exclusive white "princess" that lives. Such hash may go with the white, but the Indian, both full bloods and the despised *breeds*, know differently.'"

—from Mourning Dove's *Cogewea: The Half-Blood*

achieves popular and critical success with the publication of *Cogewea: The Half-Blood,* one of the first novels published by an American Indian woman. Written over a 10-year period while Quintasket was working as a migrant laborer, the book tells a melodramatic story of Cogewea, a young mixed-blood woman trying to find her place in Indian and white society. Before her death in 1936, the author will publish one more book, *Coyote Stories* (1933), a collection of traditional Indian tales, many featuring the trickster character Coyote.

Patterson v. Seneca Nation upholds the right of tribes to set their own rules of membership.

Among the Seneca, ancestry is traced matrilineally, or through the mother's line. According to this tradition, the Seneca Nation does not extend tribal membership to children with Seneca fathers and white mothers. A Seneca man challenges the Seneca Nation's membership criteria in *Patterson v. Seneca Nation.* The Supreme Court finds for the tribe, citing that because of its tribal sovereignty the "Seneca Nation retains for itself the power of determining who are Senecas."

March 3

The Indian Oil Leasing Act is passed.

With the Indian Oil Leasing Act, Congress gives the secretary of the interior the ability to negotiate oil leases on behalf of Indian tribes. The legislation is supported by Indian groups, who want to ensure that tribes, and not the U.S. government, will receive oil royalties on their lands. Their right to this income was threatened after Secretary of the Interior Albert B. Fall tried to designate as public domain land all reservations formed by executive order (see entry for 1922). Although supported by Indian advocates, the act will work against the interests of many Indian tribes, as U.S. officials readily grant long-term leases that net these groups relatively little royalty income.

1928

The Kiowa Six develop a new Indian painting style.

At the urging of Susie Peters, the field matron at the Kiowa Agency, six young Kiowa enroll in art classes at the University of Oklahoma. The students are encouraged by art department head Oscar Jacobson to use European materials and techniques to paint images that reflect Native American values and beliefs. The result is a painting style that emphasizes brilliantly colored, monumental figures—most often warriors and dancers in ceremonial performances.

Soon after their arrival at the university, Jacobson will promote his students' work in an exhibition in Prague, Czechoslovakia, and a limited-edition French watercolor folio *Kiowa Indian Art* (1929). As their work becomes known nationally and internationally, the painters—Spencer Asah, James Auchiah, Jack Hokeah, Stephen Mopope, Lois Smoky, and Monroe Tsatoke—are dubbed the Kiowa Six. (See also entry for 1931.)

White-fox fur trade brings brief prosperity to the Inuit.

Beginning in the mid-1920s, Hudson's Bay Company and other trading firms establish posts in northern Canada to trade with Inuit for white fox pelts. The price of white fox rises rapidly, reaching its peak in about 1928. Abandoning their old ways to adopt new hunting technology introduced to them by non-Native traders, Inuit hunters initially profit greatly from the white fox trade. But in the mid-1930s, the price of furs will drop sharply. The sudden loss of income will devastate the Inuit, bringing many families to the brink of starvation.

February

The Meriam Commission issues its report on the status of American Indian life.

As a response to reformers' growing criticisms of federal Indian policies, the secretary of the interior commissions a team of social scientists, led by Lewis M. Meriam, to survey the living conditions of Indians in the United States. After eight months of fieldwork, the Meriam Commission assemble an 872-page report. Officially titled *The Problem of Indian Administration,* the document becomes known popularly as the Meriam Report.

The Meriam Report is a scathing indictment of federal Indian policy. It finds that the living conditions of Native Americans are the worst of any American ethnic group and far worse than those of the average non-Indian American. Indian diet, housing, and education are deemed substandard, but even more alarming is the state of health care among Indian populations. The report maintains that diseases such as measles and tuberculosis are epidemic on reservations and that the overall infant mortality approaches an appalling 19 percent.

"The work with and for the Indians must give consideration to the desires of the individual Indians. He who wishes to merge into the social and economic life of the prevailing civilization of this country should be given all practicable aid and advice in making the necessary adjustments. He who wants to remain an Indian and live according to his old culture should be aided in doing so....Whichever way the individual Indian may elect to face, work in his behalf must be designed not to do for him but to help him to do for himself."
—the Meriam Report's general recommendations for reforming Indian policy

The Meriam Commission places the blame for Indian poverty squarely on U.S. government policies toward Indians. It is particularly critical of Allotment, which in the 50 years since the passage of the General Allotment Act (see entry for FEBRUARY 8, 1887) has dispossessed Indians of more than 90 million acres of land. The report recommends that the United States reevaluate its federal Indian policies and that it overhaul the Bureau of Indian Affairs. The findings of the Meriam Commission will pave the way for radical reforms in the government's treatment of Indians in the 1930s (see entry for JUNE 18, 1934).

November

Kaw Indian Charles Curtis is elected vice president.

With the election of 1928, vice-presidential nominee Charles Curtis, on the Herbert Hoover ticket, becomes the only person of Indian ancestry ever chosen to occupy the second-highest position in the U.S. government.

Curtis is one-eighth Kaw Indian on his mother's side. He also has distant relatives among the Osage, owing to his great-great-grandfather's marriage to an Osage woman. Curtis spent some of his youth on Kaw lands in Kansas, but he was eliminated from the tribal roll in 1878 at age 18, because he had not permanently settled on the Kaw reservation in Indian Territory. He was reinstated as a tribal member in 1902, just in time to receive plots of land for himself and his children when the reservation was allotted.

Curtis, trained as a lawyer, spent 37 years in the U.S. Congress (1892–1907 in the House of Representatives, 1907–29 in the Senate). As a Republican congressman, he became an important figure in the formation of federal Indian policy. A stalwart supporter of Indian Assimilation into non-Indian society, he most notably sponsored the Curtis Act, which led the way for the dissolution of the governments of the Five Civilized Tribes and for the allotment of their lands in Indian Territory (see entry for JUNE 28, 1898). Throughout his one term in the vice presidency, he will continue to advocate Assimilationist policies.

1930

Oliver La Farge's *Laughing Boy* wins the Pulitzer Prize.

Awarded the 1930 Pulitzer Prize for fiction, *Laughing Boy,* a novel by non-Indian author Oliver La Farge, tells a sentimental story of the ill-fated romance between a young Navajo (Dineh) man and woman. A longtime advocate for Indian rights, La Farge will later become the president of the Eastern Association on Indian Affairs (see entry for OCTOBER 1922) and the subject of a biography by Chippewa author D'Arcy McNickle (see entry for 1936). (See also entry for 1931.)

The U.S. government establishes a college loan fund for Indians.

To help Indian students pursue postsecondary education, Congress authorizes an annual fund of $15,000 for educational loans for Indians admitted to college. One of the first students to receive a loan is Benjamin Reifel, who will later serve as a congressman from South Dakota.

1931

Lynn Riggs's *Green Grow the Lilacs* premieres.

At the Theater Guild in New York City, *Green Grow the Lilacs,* a play by poet and dramatist Lynn Riggs, begins an acclaimed run. Riggs's most successful work, the play is a nostalgic comedy about non-Indian farmers and ranchers in the early 20th century on the eve of Oklahoma statehood. Although the formation of Oklahoma led to the dissolution of the Cherokee Nation, where Riggs was born and raised, *Lilacs*—on which Rodgers and Hammerstein's musical *Oklahoma!* (1943) will

later be based—is largely sympathetic to the whites who settled in the Cherokee's western homeland. Riggs will later depict the history of the Cherokee in Indian Territory in the drama *Cherokee Nights* (1936).

The Exposition of Indian Tribal Arts opens in New York City.

Organized by Oliver La Farge (see entry for 1930), John Sloan, and Amelia White, the Exposition of Indian Tribal Arts is held at the galleries in New York City's Grand Central Station. The exhibit features works of 50 Indian artists from private and museum collections. Later traveling widely throughout the United States, the show will introduce many American museum-goers to the works of southwestern Indian painters, including Awa Tsireh, Fred Kabotie (see entry for 1932), and the Kiowa Six (see entry for 1928).

1932

John Joseph Mathews's *Wah'Kon-Tah* is published.

After spending many years studying and touring in Europe and Africa, Osage scholar John Joseph Mathews returns to his tribe's Oklahoma reservation to write *Wah'Kon-Tah: The Osage and the White Man's Road.* This tribal history is based on the journals of Major Laban J. Miles, who served as the Osage's agent for more than 30 years. With *Wah'Kon-Tah's* publication, Mathews begins a long literary career, during which he will document Osage history and culture in both fiction and nonfiction.

Fred Kabotie paints the Watchtower murals.

Hired by architect Mary Colter, Hopi painter Fred Kabotie begins work on a series of frescos on the walls of the Watchtower, a reconstruction of an Anasazi tower at the east entrance of the Grand Canyon. Kabotie's paintings, which depict Hopi legends, are based on murals found in kivas, the tribe's religious structures. The job is the first of several important commissions Kabotie will receive in the 1930s, including a mural series for Harvard's Peabody Museum and a collection of paintings recording Hopi life for the Museum of the American Indian (see entry for 1916) in New York City.

Black Elk's *Black Elk Speaks* is published.

A Lakota Sioux medicine man, Black Elk witnessed in his youth the destruction of Indian cultures by the Plains Wars and their aftermath. Although he was baptized as a Catholic, as an adult he was also involved in an underground movement to preserve Lakota religious traditions in the face of laws prohibiting Indian religious ceremonies, and of the U.S. policy of assimilating Indians into non-Indian society. Afraid that traditional religious knowledge would be lost to future generations of Lakota, Black Elk agreed to discuss Lakota religion, culture, and history with white poet John C. Neihardt, who began transcribing and reshaping Black Elk's story into a manuscript in the summer of 1930.

"You have noticed that everything an Indian does is in a circle, and that is because the Power of the World always works in circles, and everything tries to be round. In the old days when we were a strong and happy people, all our power came to us from the sacred hoop of the nation, and so long as the hoop was unbroken, the people flourished. The flowering tree was the living center of the hoop, and the circle or the four quarters nourished it."

—Lakota medicine man Black Elk
in his autobiography
Black Elk Speaks

The most literary of the 20th-century "as-told-to" autobiographies of Indians transcribed by non-Indian authors, *Black Elk Speaks* immediately finds a substantial readership among whites sympathetic to Indian issues. An underground classic for decades, the book will achieve renewed popularity during the years of the Red Power Movement in the late 1960s and early 1970s.

Ella Deloria's *Dakota Texts* is published.

Working with anthropologists Franz Boas (see entry for 1887) and Ruth Benedict, Dakota Sioux researcher Ella Deloria writes *Dakota Texts*, a compilation of Dakota legends and stories she collected during interviews with elders and translated into English. The collection will become a classic of anthropological literature. Deloria will also collaborate with Boas on *Dakota Grammar* (1941), an analysis of the structure of the Dakota Sioux language. (See also entry for 1887.)

April to July

Joseph White Bull makes a pictographic record of Lakota Sioux warfare.

While working on a biography of the great Oglala Lakota leader Sitting Bull, non-Indian author Stanley Vestal interviews Joseph White Bull, a Lakota Sioux who fought in many of the major battles of the Indian Wars. Interested in the old warrior's own story, Vestal offers White Bull $70 to create a series of drawings depicting his experiences in battle. Eight of the 40 drawings produced by White Bull will appear in Vestal's book *Warpath: The True Story of the Fighting Sioux Told in a Biography of Chief White Bull* (1934). Discovered in the University of Oklahoma Library archives in the 1990s, the entire series will be exhibited in 1994 with other drawings commissioned by Vestal from Sitting Bull's nephew Moses Old Bull.

September

The Studio is founded at the Santa Fe Indian School.

Conceived by non-Indian art teacher Dorothy Dunn, the Studio at the Santa Fe Indian School is established to "recover, maintain, and develop" Indian art. Under Dunn's tutelage, Santa Fe students, many in grade school, are taught to paint scenes of Indian life.

Students are encouraged to produce work in the "Studio style," in which flat, colorful figures are set against an empty or nearly empty background. This mode of representation will become known as "Traditional Indian Style," although it draws little from actual traditional Indian art. Studio-style paintings will become enormously popular with non-Indian collectors. The Studio will also become well known for instructing many of the most prominent Native American artists of the late 20th century, including Allen Houser, Oscar Howe, and Pablita Velarde. (See also entry for 1903.)

September

The first Southwest Indian Fair is held.

In conjunction with the Caddo County Fair, members of the Comanche, Kiowa-Apache, Caddo, Wichita, and Lenni Lenape (Delaware) tribes organize the Southwest Indian Fair in Anadarko, Oklahoma. Like most county fairs of the time, the event is a showcase for the participants' talents in domestic arts (such as canning and cooking), farming, and raising livestock. The fair, however, also features extensive displays of traditional Indian arts and crafts.

Renamed the American Indian Exposition in 1935, the fair will become an annual event attracting thousands of Indians and non-Indians each year. By the late 20th century, it will be owned and operated by 15 Plains tribes and will focus on exhibitions of Indian art, song, and dance.

1933

John C. Collier becomes the commissioner of Indian affairs.

Sociologist and executive secretary of the American Indian Defense Association (see entry for MAY 1923), John C. Collier is chosen by Secretary of the Interior Harold Ickes to head the Bureau of Indian Affairs (BIA). The appointment signals a new era for the BIA. A political progressive, Collier opposes the Assimilationist policies of the past, particularly the policy of Allotment. He instead supports government efforts to revitalize Indian cultures, settle Indian land claims, help revive tribal governments, protect religious freedom for Native Americans, and fund economic development in Indian communities. Collier's vision of federal Indian policy will be set into law with the passage of the Indian Reorganization Act (see entry for JUNE 18, 1934).

"If we can relieve the Indian of the unrealistic and fatal allotment system, if we can provide him with land and the means to work the land; if, through group organization and tribal incorporation, we can give him a real share in the management of his own affairs, he can develop normally in his own natural environment."

—Commissioner of Indian Affairs John C. Collier in his annual report for 1933

The U.S. government inaugurates a livestock reduction program on the Navajo (Dineh) reservation.

The United States becomes concerned about the erosion of the Navajo Indian Reservation when the amount of silt from the eroded lands in the Colorado River threatens the completion of Boulder Dam. The erosion is due to overgrazing by the Navajo's (Dineh) vast herds of sheep,

Commissioner of Indian Affairs John C. Collier with two Hopi men in the village of Oraibi *(National Archives, Neg. no. RG75-PU-WA-56)*

horses, and cattle. The U.S. government maintains the solution to the problem is for the Navajo to reduce their herds, particularly their number of sheep. The Navajo, however, maintain that the United States should give them more grazing land.

Although hesitantly, the Navajo Tribal Council agrees to cooperate with the government's livestock-reduction program. It asks each Navajo family to cut its herds by 10 percent. Commissioner of Indian Affairs John C. Collier allocates funds from the Federal Emergency Relief Administration to pay the Navajo a small sum for each animal they agreed to relinquish.

Despite the Navajo's cooperation, government officials often treat them harshly during the decade the program is in operation. Some agents take animals by force or shoot them when their owners refuse to surrender them voluntarily. For years to come, the program will leave the Navajo angry and bitter toward the U.S. government, with Collier as the principal target of their wrath.

The National League for Justice to American Indians is formed.

The Los Angeles–based National League for Justice to American Indians is created to campaign for the disbanding of the Bureau of Indian Affairs (BIA). Founder Marion Campbell maintains that BIA policies have kept Indians from assimilating into the general population and holds that Indians would be better served if states took over the administration of Indian affairs.

April

Franklin Roosevelt authorizes the Indian Emergency Conservation Work program.

Established as a part of the Civilian Conservation Corps (CCC), the Indian Emergency Conservation Work federal relief program hires Indian laborers to work on conservation projects on Indian lands. Projects of the IECW include protecting timber resources, improving rangelands, and controlling erosion on farmlands. (See also entry for 1937.)

8

1934 TO 1968
ON THE ROAD TO SELF-DETERMINATION

In the first decades of the 20th century, Indians found themselves drawn deeper and deeper into the mire of poverty. Even before the United States plunged into the Great Depression, only 4 percent of the Indian population earned annual incomes of more than $200. In an effort to address the needs of poor Indians, President Franklin Delano Roosevelt appointed John C. Collier as the head of the Bureau of Indian Affairs (BIA) in 1933. Collier struck many as a radical choice: a founding member of the American Indian Defense Association, a Washington-based lobbying group, Collier had long been one of the bureau's most virulent critics.

Collier's appointment indeed proved to be a watershed in contemporary Indian history. His work at the BIA helped to bring attention at last to the problems of Indian groups, which policy makers had long been happy to ignore. He also forced Washington to forge a new relationship with Indian peoples, in which they were given a greater say than ever before in policies that affected their lives.

Collier's new approach to federal Indian policy was presented in a 48-page bill that became the Indian Reorganization Act of 1934. Also known as the Indian New Deal, the IRA abolished Allotment, the policy that since the 1880s had robbed Indians of much of their remaining landholdings. It also offered loans for Indian students, established funds for tribal economic development, and provided for the purchase of new lands for the exclusive use of Indians. To help implement these and other social and economic programs, the IRA created guidelines by which groups could establish new tribal governments with elected leaders and written constitutions. Although many Indian groups resisted Collier's efforts to reorganize their governments following a non-Indian model, 92 tribes eventually adopted constitutions according to the IRA's provisions. Throughout the rest of the century, these new tribal governments would often be on the forefront of the continuing battle for Indian sovereignty.

As significant as the passage of the IRA was, the American involvement in World War II perhaps had an even greater impact on individual Indians. Soon after the attack on Pearl Harbor in December 1941, Indian men and women signed up for military service in unprecedented numbers, while thousands more from Indian communities joined the war effort on the home front. The experiences of these Indians, particularly those of servicemen sent overseas, profoundly affected their relationship to non-Indian society. Indian soldiers who had previously spent little time outside of reservations were suddenly in foreign nations, fighting side by side with non-Indian soldiers against a common enemy.

Such experiences left many Indian servicemen more confident and far less willing to accept unchallenged white prejudices against them and their people. For others, the war and its aftermath were more disorienting than empowering—a situation tragically illustrated by the death from alcoholism of Pima war hero Ira Hayes in 1955. The difficulty of many veterans in readjusting to reservation life after the war later provided the subject of N. Scott Momaday's *House Made of Dawn* (1968) and Leslie Marmon Silko's *Ceremony* (1977), two of the best Native American novels of the postwar era.

In addition to changing Indians' view of mainstream America, Indians' military experiences also changed how policy makers saw them. In the years immediately after the war, non-Indians in government came to question the special legal status of Indians and the logistics of the reservation system. In a complete reversal of Collier's progressive legislation, the new architects of federal Indian policy increasingly sought to get out of the "Indian business." This goal was often presented as a means of eliminating government interference in Indians' lives, although advocates often had far less benevolent motives. Faced with funding massively expensive federal programs for veterans, many Washington officials were eager to save the millions spent annually to administer reservations and to provide benefits and services guaranteed to Indians by treaty.

These aims resulted in the two dominant policies of the 1950s and early 1960s: Termination and Relocation. Most completely articulated in the House Concurrent Resolution 108 of 1953, Termination meant dissolving the reservations of specific tribes and thereby ending their special tribal status. In theory, Termination was to be applied only to relatively affluent tribes that could withstand the loss of tribal lands and the income they produced. In fact, few tribes had the resources to cope with Termination's economic costs. One of the most notorious instances was that of the Menominee of Wisconsin, who were an early target for Termination because they had more than $10 million of tribal funds in the U.S. Treasury. However, over the course of eight years, these funds were nearly depleted by the U.S. government in the process of implementing the policy. By the time the Menominee's Termination was official in 1961, they were desperately poor.

The Relocation policy was developed to help returning Indian veterans, who found few opportunities for employment on reservations or in other Indian communities. It sought to encourage these men to move to cities, where employees of the Bureau of Indian Affairs would help them find jobs and affordable housing. Some Indians were already eager to relocate, while others were persuaded by the promises of the government—promises that frequently proved empty. Many relocatees, unable to obtain either work or adequate homes, merely exchanged rural poverty for urban poverty.

For a large number of Indians, the effects of Termination and Relocation were devastating. Yet from these disastrous policies emerged a renewed fervor in and focus for Indian political activism. Largely to protest Termination, the National Congress of American Indians helped to organize the week-long American Indian Chicago Conference in 1961. Attended by more than 500 tribal representatives, the event sparked an increased commitment among Indian leaders from different tribes to band together to fight against the mistreatment of all Indians.

By the late 1960s, young Indians in urban areas also began to embrace a pan-Indian approach to protesting the government's policies. Many were the children of the original relocatees; born in the city, they often had almost no direct experience with traditional Indian societies. Gathering in Indian centers established to help new relocatees, this new generation of activists were drawn together by their shared anger at non-Indian authorities. From their ranks would emerge the American Indian Movement, the Indians of All Tribes, and other multitribal groups whose confrontational tactics and media savvy would draw international support for American Indian rights during the 1970s.

1934

The American Association on Indian Affairs is founded.

At the request of Commissioner of Indian Affairs John C. Collier, Oliver La Farge, the board president of the Eastern Association on Indian Affairs (see entry for OCTOBER 1922), merges his organization with another Indian rights advocacy group, the American Indian Defense Association (see entry for MAY 1923), to form the American Association on Indian Affairs (later renamed the Association on American Indian Affairs.) La Farge will serve as the association's president until his death in 1963.

April 16

The Johnson-O'Malley Act reforms Indian education.

The first piece of legislation to emerge from the reformist campaign of Commissioner John C. Collier (see entry for 1933), the Johnson-O'Malley Act allows the federal government to enter into contracts with states to offer various benefits to Indian groups, specifically education, health care, agricultural assistance, and social services. The act will have its greatest impact on Indian education. With the redirection of educational funds, Indian students will increasingly leave Indian schools run by the Bureau of Indian Affairs to attend public educational institutions.

June 18

The Indian Reorganization Act reforms federal Indian policy.

Perhaps the most important legislation affecting Indians in the 20th century, the Indian Reorganization Act sets forth a comprehensive plan to reform federal Indian policy and reorganize the Bureau of Indian Affairs (BIA). The IRA is the brainchild of John C. Collier, a longtime Indian rights activist and the new commissioner of Indian affairs. Because the act reflects the progressive agenda of the Roosevelt administration, it is popularly known as the Indian New Deal. (It is also called the Wheeler-Howard Act,

after its sponsors, Senator Burton K. Wheeler and Congressman Edgar Howard.)

The IRA's most significant provision calls for the end of the Allotment policy, which in the past 50 years has dispossessed Indians of some 90 million acres of land. The act also requires the U.S. government to return to tribes all unsold surplus lands on allotted reservations, establishes a fund to purchase additional land for Indian groups, and creates a program to conserve and rehabilitate tribal lands.

In addition, the IRA offers guidelines by which tribes can write constitutions and reorganize their governments. To promote economic and community development, tribes are also permitted to incorporate and to request loans from a fund set up for this purpose. Individual Indians may take out loans from the Bureau of Indian Affairs to finance their educations, and they are to be given preference in hiring for BIA jobs.

Before passing the IRA, Congress adds a provision that tribes must vote on whether to accept or reject the act's provisions. Eventually, more than two-thirds of Indian nations will accept the IRA. (A notable exception will be the largest U.S. tribal group, the Navajo [Dineh], who resent Collier's efforts to prevent erosion of reservation lands by reducing their sheep herds [see entries for 1933 and for 1935]). Thirty-six percent of tribes will write new constitutions based on IRA guidelines, while 28 percent will incorporate for business purposes.

August

The American Indian Federation is formed.

Formed in Gallup, New Mexico, by several wealthy Indian conservatives who advocate Assimilation, the American Indian Federation is founded to speak out against the views of the new commissioner of Indian affairs John C. Collier (see entry for 1933), a political liberal who wants to revive Indian tribalism. The AIF's ultimate goal, however, is to bring about the dismantling of the Bureau of Indian Affairs (BIA). Although it receives support from several right-wing organizations (including the Daughters of the American Revolution), the AIF will fall into disarray in the mid-1940s after the group's repeated efforts to destroy the BIA fail.

1935

The Navajo (Dineh) reject the Indian Reorganization Act.

The largest tribe in the United States, the Navajo (Dineh) vote against adopting a constitution and creating a tribal government under the guidelines set out in the Indian Reorganization Act (IRA) (see entry for JUNE 18, 1934). Although the act is seen by many Indians as a tool toward greater tribal independence, the IRA is rejected by the Navajo largely because it was masterminded by Commissioner of Indian Affairs John C. Collier. The tribe blames Collier for formulating the much-resented livestock-reduction policy, through which Bureau of Indian Affairs employees have confiscated or killed many of the Navajo's sheep and horses (see entry for 1933).

January 24

The Santa Clara Pueblo adopt a written constitution.

Traditionally, the Santa Clara Pueblo were led by the headmen of the summer kiva group in spring and summer and by those of the winter kiva group in fall and winter. By the 1930s, relations between the two groups have deteriorated as the Summers became more conservative and the Winters become more progressive. To re-create their ailing government, the Santa Clara embrace the guidelines for forming tribal councils as set out in the Indian Reorganization Act (see entry for JUNE 18, 1934). They are the first tribe to draft a constitution as called for in the new legislation.

August 15

Cherokee humorist Will Rogers dies in a plane crash.

The American public is stunned and saddened by the news that Will Rogers has been killed in a plane crash in Alaska. A star of vaudeville, theater, and film, Rogers at the time is the most famous Native American in the United States as well as one of the country's most beloved performers. His funeral in Los Angeles will be attended by an astounding 50,000 mourners. A smaller service will be held in Claremont, Oklahoma, the small town in the former Cherokee Nation where Rogers was born and raised.

> "They sent the Indians to Oklahoma. They had a treaty that said, 'You shall have this land as long as grass grows and water flows.' It was not only a good rhyme but looked like a good treaty, and it was till they struck oil. Then the government took it away from us again. They said the treaty only refers to 'water and grass; it don't say anything about oil.'"
>
> —Cherokee humorist Will Rogers in a 1928 syndicated column

August 27

Congress establishes the Indian Arts and Crafts Board.

"To promote the development of Indian arts and crafts," Congress creates the Indian Arts and Crafts Board as a new agency under the Department of the Interior. Another goal of the board is to prevent non-Indian artisans from marketing their works as Indian-made.

The board's first general manager, Rene d'Harnoncourt, begins surveying Indian country to determine which Indian arts are still being produced. Working for the board over the next 26 years, he will encourage Indian artists to produce items of the highest possible quality and will organize several exhibitions that encourage non-Indians to see the Indians' work as art rather than just objects of ethnographic interest (see entry for MARCH 1941).

1936

Autobiography of a Papago Woman is published.

In the early 1930s, anthropologist Ruth Underhill, a student of Franz Boas (see entry for 1887), began interviewing Maria Chona, an elder of the Papago (now the Tohono O'odham), while gathering information for an anthropological study of her tribe. Speaking through an interpreter, Chona told Underhill the fascinating story of her life, which Underhill recognized as a book in itself.

From their conversations, Underhill crafts *Autobiography of a Papago Woman* (later reissued as *Papago Woman*). The book describes the life of a strong woman who manages to satisfy her ambition to become a medicine women while observing the often constricting roles assigned to women among the Papago. Owing to Chona's compelling story and Underhill's mastery as a writer and an editor, *Papago Woman* will become a landmark in both anthropological and Native American literature.

> "You see, we *have* power. Men have to dream to get power from the spirits and they think of everything they can—song and speeches and marching around, hoping that the spirits will notice them and give them some power. But we *have* power. . . . Can any warrior make a child, no matter how brave and wonderful he is?"
>
> —medicine woman Maria Chona
> in *Autobiography of a Papago Woman*

The Indian Actors Association is founded.

Affiliated with the Screen Actors Guild, the leading union for film actors, the Indian Actors Association is established in Hollywood. The organization protects the interests of Indian actors by lobbying for better pay and benefits and by encouraging casting agents to hire Indians to play Indian roles. Among the association's founding members are star athlete Jim Thorpe (see entry for SUMMER 1912) and writer and performer Luther Standing Bear.

D'Arcy McNickle's *The Surrounded* is published.

The Surrounded, the story of the struggles of an Indian of mixed ancestry living on the Flathead Indian Reservation, is published as the first novel of Chippewa-Cree writer D'Arcy McNickle. Later trained in anthropology, McNickle will help implement the Indian Reorganization Act (see entry for JUNE 18, 1934) while working for the Bureau of Indian Affairs. Decades later, he will also be instrumental in organizing the seminal conference of the National Congress of American Indians (see entry for JUNE 13 TO 20, 1961).

May 1

The Alaska Native Reorganization Act extends the Indian Reorganization Act (IRA) to Alaskan Natives.

By order of Congress, the Natives of Alaska were excluded from the Indian Reorganization Act (IRA) (see entry for JUNE 18, 1934), largely because unlike other Native groups they receive government services from the Bureau of Education in the Alaska territorial government instead of from the Bureau of Indian Affairs. By extending the IRA's provisions to Alaskan groups, the Alaska Native Reorganization Act creates new federally funded programs for self-government and economic development, thereby redefining the relationship between Alaska's Native population and the U.S. government.

June 26

Congress passed the Oklahoma Indian Welfare Act.

Because the governments of the large Indian tribes of Oklahoma were dissolved when it became a state, Congress specifically excluded them from the landmark Indian Reorganization Act (IRA) (JUNE 18, 1934). With the passage of the Oklahoma Indian Welfare Act, this decision is reversed. The act gives Oklahoma Indians the same benefits that the IRA awarded to the rest of the Native American population.

1937

The Indian Civilian Conservation Corps is established.

The Indian Emergency Conservation Work program (see entry for APRIL 1933) is renamed the Indian Civilian Conservation Corps (ICCC). The new program offers increased on-the-job training and vocational education for Indian laborers hired by the corps. Before the program is disbanded in 1942, the ICCC will employ 85,000 Native Americans and train thousands for wartime jobs.

1938

The federal government creates a new Navajo (Dineh) council.

Although the Navajo (Dineh) voted against accepting the Indian Reorganization Act, which set guidelines for drafting tribal constitutions (see entry for 1935), they choose to hold a constitutional convention on their own terms. The resulting constitution, which declares the tribe's independence from the Bureau of Indian Affairs, is rejected by the U.S. government, which instead establishes a set of bylaws—nicknamed the "Rules of 1938"—that creates a new tribal council consisting of 74 elected representatives.

The Museum of the American Indian returns a Hidatsa medicine bundle.

The Museum of the American Indian (see entry for 1916) in New York City becomes the first institution to repatriate a sacred Indian object when it returns a medicine bundle to the Midipadi clan of the Hidatsa. Four years earlier, following the death of Wolf Chief, the clan asked to have the medicine bundle back. Under pressure from missionaries and government officials to abandon his traditional religion, Wolf Chief in 1907 had sold the bundle to anthropologist Gilbert L. Wilson, who in turn gave it to the museum.

May 2

The first tribal museum opens.

During a ceremony overseen by Osage chief Fred Lookout, the Osage Tribal Museum in Pawhuska, Oklahoma, is opened to the public. The museum, which chronicles the history of the Osage and serves as a cultural center, is the first to be owned and operated by an American Indian tribe.

May 11

Congress allows for the leasing of reservation land to mining companies.

At the urging of Commissioner of Indian Affairs John C. Collier, Congress passes the Indian Lands Mining Act, which permits reservation lands to be leased to commercial mining companies. Collier holds that the leases will provide much-needed jobs and royalty income for reservation residents. However, many of the long-term mining leases approved by the secretary of the interior will destroy Indian resources while offering only extremely low royalties fixed at levels set during the Great Depression.

1939

The Tekakwitha Conference is founded.

Headquartered in Great Falls, Minnesota, the Tekakwitha Conference is established by several non-Indian missionaries to increase awareness of the special concerns of the Native American Catholics among Roman Catholic Church authorities. The organization is named after a 17th-century Mohawk nun Kateri Tekakwitha (see entry for APRIL 17, 1680). (See also entry for 1977.)

April to October

The work of Seneca artists is featured at the World's Fair.

With the support of the Indian Arts Project, organized under the Federal Works Progress Administration, the Seneca of the Tonawanda and Cattarugus Reservations experienced an artistic renaissance during the mid-1930s. Seneca artists involved in the WPA program revived traditional arts, including woodcarving, basketry, and quillwork, while others explored the non-Indian media of painting and drawing. The work of artists such as Jesse Cornplanter (see entry for 1913), Ernest Smith, and Sarah Hill are brought to the attention of an international audience when they are displayed in the New York State Pavilion at the World's Fair in New York City.

April 5

In Re Eskimo clarifies the legal status of Canadian Inuit.

The Canadian Supreme Court decides in *In Re Eskimo* that the word *Indian* in the British North America Act (see entry for JULY 1, 1867) should be understood to include the Inuit of Canada. The ruling therefore establishes that the Canadian government has the same relationship with the Inuit as it does with Indians.

May 19

Kateri Tekakwitha is declared venerable.

Pope Pius XII declares Kateri Tekakwitha, a Mohawk nun renowned for centuries for her devoutness, to be venerable. She is the first Native American to be so honored by the Catholic Church. Since Tekakwitha's death (see entry for APRIL 17, 1680), many miracles have been attributed to her intervention. (See also entries for 1939 and for JUNE 22, 1980.)

1940

The Eagle Protection Act is passed.

With the Eagle Protection Act, Congress authorizes the Department of the Interior's Fish and Wildlife Service to restrict the killing of bald eagles or the taking of their parts. The law threatens many Indian groups' ability to practice their native religion because eagle feathers are needed to make sacred religious paraphernalia. (See also entry for 1986.)

February

Southwestern Indian artisans reject the swastika motif.

To protest the Nazi Party in Germany, Indian artisans from the Navajo (Dineh), Hopi, Papago (now the Tohono O'odham), and Apache peoples sign an agreement to stop using swastika designs in their work. Before the swastika was adopted as a Nazi symbol, it was a common design motif in southwestern silverwork, basketry, and textiles.

October

American Indians register for the draft.

For the first time in American history, all young Indian men are called upon to register for the draft as the United States prepares to enter World War II. (Because Indians did not receive U.S. citizenship until 1924, most were not subject to the draft during World War I.) Before the end of World War II, approximately 25,000 Indians will serve in the U.S. military, while about 45,000 will contribute their labor to wartime industries. Three Indian soldiers—Jack C. Montgomery (Cherokee), Ernest Childers (Creek), and Van Barfoot (Choctaw)—will be awarded the Medal of Honor.

"When I went to Germany I never thought about war honors, or the four 'coups' which an old-time Crow warrior had to earn in battle. Those days were gone. But afterwards, when I came back and went though this telling of the war deeds ceremony, why, I told my war deeds, and lo and behold I completed the four requirements to become a chief."
—Crow veteran Joseph Medicine Crow on his experiences as a soldier in World War II

December 27

Iroquois protest the draft.

Outside the main post office in Buffalo, New York, protesters led by Tuscarora leader Clinton Rickard speak out against the drafting of the Iroquois men to serve in World War II. The group maintains that Iroquois should not be subject to the draft because they are citizens of their own sovereign nation, not of the United States. Rickard does not object to Iroquois serving in the military, but he counsels those of drafting age to register as "alien non-residents" rather than as citizens. (See also entry for 1941.)

1941

Ex Parte Green affirms the United States's right to draft Indians.

Onondaga Warren Green brings a suit against the United States, claiming that the Selective Service Act cannot be applied to Indians because they are citizens of sovereign Indian nations. After the U.S. Court of Appeals finds against Green, the negative

publicity surrounding the suit will move several prominent Iroquois to make an exaggerated show of patriotism (see entry for JUNE 11, 1942). (See also entry for DECEMBER 17, 1940.)

Hopi men resist the draft.

Five Hopi men from the village of Hotevilla are prosecuted in federal court for refusing to register for the draft. In their defense, they explain, "We have a stone tablet [that] . . . says there will come a time when there will be great trouble involving many nations. The Hopi are to show their bows and arrows to no one at that time." They are sentenced to a year and a day in jail.

March

An Indian art exhibit opens at the Museum of Modern Art.

New York City's Museum of Modern Art, in co-operation with the Indian Arts and Crafts Board (see entry for AUGUST 27, 1935), organizes an exhibition entitled "Indian Art in the United States." The influential exhibit presents Indian-made objects not only as sources of anthropological data but also as works of art. Enthusiastically received by the public, the show also attempts to counter the myth that indigenous art was uniformly corrupted after Indians came in contact with non-Indians. In the exhibit catalog, the curators maintain that "invention or adoption of new forms does not necessarily mean repudiation of tradition but is often a source of its enrichment."

April

The Inter-American Institute is created.

To promote the study and preservation of indigenous cultures, representatives from countries throughout North and South America gather in Patzcuaro, Mexico, for the first Inter-American Conference on Indian Life. Sponsored by the Pan American Union, the conference leads to the formation of the Inter-American Institute in Mexico

City. The institute's goal is to negotiate formal agreements with the nations of the Pan American Union, in which each nation promises to establish a National Indian Institute to aid its native population.

Represented by Commissioner of Indian Affairs John C. Collier, the United States is initially enthusiastic about establishing the U.S. Indian Institute, as a means of improving relations with Latin America. After the end of World War II, however, Congress will sharply cut funding to the organization.

June

The Sun Dance is revived among the Crow.

Seeking a way to preserve Indian traditions in the modern era, a Crow man named William Big Day travels to the Wind River Reservation in Wyoming to participate in the Shoshone's annual Sun Dance. After receiving instruction from a Shoshone religious leader in how to stage the ceremony, Big Day performs a Shoshone version of the Sun Dance on the Crow's Montana reservation, an event that will lead to the revival of the dance among his own people.

1942

Felix S. Cohen's *Handbook of Federal Indian Law* is published.

Written by Felix S. Cohen, a lawyer with the Department of the Interior, *The Handbook of Federal Indian Law* provides a long-needed comprehensive resource on the history of Indian law. Included in this monumental work are the texts of treaties, laws, executive orders, court cases, court rulings, and other documents from the first encounters between Indians and non-Indians to the present. In the decades to come, the *Handbook* will provide many activists—both Indian and non-Indian—with historical and legal information needed to challenge federal Indian policies and their administration.

"One who attempts to survey the legal problems raised by Indian treaties must at the outset dispose of the objection that such treaties are somehow of inferior validity or are of purely antiquarian interest. . . . Such an assumption is unfounded. . . . That treaties with Indian tribes are of the same dignity as treaties with foreign nations is a view which has been repeatedly confirmed by the federal courts and never successfully challenged."

—from Felix S. Cohen's
Handbook of Federal Indian Law

Tulee v. Washington limits state regulation of Indian fishing.

In *Tulee v. Washington,* the state of Washington sues Tulee, a Yakama man, for fishing outside of the Yakima (later Yakama) Reservation without a fishing license. Tulee argues in his defense that as an Indian, he is not subject to state law. He is convicted in state court, but the Supreme Court overturns the verdict. The case will be cited as a precedent in later suits involving Indian fishing and hunting rights.

The Lakota Sioux at Standing Rock revive the Sun Dance.

For the first time in 50 years, the Lakota Sioux of the Standing Rock Indian Reservation in North Dakota hold a Sun Dance. This ceremony was traditionally performed to enhance the spiritual health and strength of the dancers and their families. At Standing Rock, participants pray for an Allied victory in World War II and for the safe return of the more than 2,000 Lakota Sioux serving in the armed forces.

January

The Seneca demand payment from non-Indians leasing their lands.

On behalf of the Seneca, the United States in *United States v. Forness* brings suit against non-Indian lessees of Seneca land in Salamanca, New York, on the Allegany Reservation. Many of the lease-holders are long delinquent in payments, but more galling to the Seneca are the financial provisions of the long-term leases, which were negotiated by the U.S. government in 1892. A white garage operator, for instance, has not made payments to the Seneca for 11 years, but his back rent amounts to only $44. The U.S. Court of Appeals in New York State finds in favor of the Seneca and allows them to cancel the unfair leases. (See also entry for AUTUMN 1991.)

March

Construction on the Alaska Highway begins.

The U.S. Army Corps of Engineers begins work on a 1,500-mile highway stretching from Dawson Creek, British Columbia, to Fairbanks, Alaska. Although the project offers employment to some Alaskan Natives, it has tragic consequences for many more, as epidemics of non-Indian diseases previously unknown in Alaska spread through Native communities. When opened to unrestricted traffic in 1947, the highway will also disrupt Native societies by making their homelands easily accessible by whites.

April

The Marine Corps recruits Code Talkers on the Navajo (Dineh) reservation.

At the suggestion of Navajo (Dineh) engineer Philip Johnston, the marines decide to use the Navajo language as the basis for a code for transmitting sensitive information in the Pacific theater. Other Indian languages—including Choctaw, Comanche, and Creek—had earlier been used as codes (see entry for SEPTEMBER TO NOVEMBER 1918), but all had been broken. The Navajo language,

however, is so complex that, Johnston maintains, a Navajo code would be unbreakable.

To investigate the idea, Marine Corps ecruiters travel to the Navajo reservation and sign up 29 young Navajo men to develop and use the code. The experiment proves so effective that the marines soon expand the program, eventually training more than 400 Navajo for the elite group.

May 8

A Japanese internment camp is constructed on the Colorado River Reservation.

In February, President Franklin Roosevelt orders the wartime internment of Japanese Americans. One of the 10 internment camps built is located on the Colorado River Reservation of the Mojave and Chemehuevi. In exchange for not opposing the presence of the camp, the U.S. government finances land improvements and an irrigation system on the reservation.

June

The Aleutian Islands are attacked by the Japanese.

Japanese soldiers invade the Aleutian Islands and attack the village of Annu. When Annu's residents are captured and taken to Japan, the U.S. Navy decides to evacuate the Aleut's villages on the Pribilof Islands. The refugees are sent to live in abandoned canneries, without heat, in southeastern Alaska for the remainder of the war. With little food or medical care, many of the Aleut, especially elders, fall victim to disease. Living conditions are so wretched that a group of Aleut women petitions the U.S. government in October to move them elsewhere, but their pleas are ignored. (See also entry for MAY 1944.)

June 11

The Iroquois declare war against the Axis powers.

On the steps of the U.S. Capitol in Washington, D.C., a delegation of six Iroquois leaders declares war on Germany, Italy, and Japan. The declaration, made without the full consent of the Iroquois council, is an effort to stave off criticism resulting from Iroquois resistance to the draft (see entries for DECEMBER 27, 1940, and for 1941). Some Iroquois refuse to register because they do not regard themselves as U.S. citizens. Many non-Indians, however, interpret their opposition to the draft as a lack of patriotism, rather than as a statement of Indian sovereignty.

The Department of the Interior sees the Iroquois declaration of war as a public relations opportunity. To help generate popular support for the war, government officials orchestrate the delegation's visit to Washington as a media event and book the leaders on the CBS radio program *We, the People at War,* on which they read the declaration to a large non-Indian audience.

> "The New York Indians, in making a separate declaration of war against the Axis powers do not question the sovereignty of the United States Government but they are simply giving full expression, in their democratic traditions, to a supreme cause which has upset the internal affairs of the various members of the historic Confederacy. Like millions of families throughout the United States, the New York Indians have sent their sons into the armed forces and their daughters into war jobs off the reservation."
>
> —from a press release issued by Commissioner of Indian Affair John Collier on the Iroquois declaration of war

1943

The Indian Scouting Service is disbanded.

The Indian Scouting Service, formed to assist the U.S. Army's campaigns against western Indians (see entry for 1866), is eliminated as a branch of the American military. In the late 19th century, 16 scouts were given the Congressional Medal of Honor for their participation in the Indian Wars. During the service's 77-year history, Indian scouts also served in several of the United States's foreign wars, including the Spanish-American War and World War I.

Lakota Sioux reservation land is seized for a wartime gunnery range.

Officials from the U.S. government order Lakota Sioux living on a 3-million-acre area of South Dakota's Pine Ridge Reservation to move in order to make way for an aerial gunnery range. According to one evacuee, the reservation's superintendent threatens that the Indians will be shot if they do not leave their homes within a 30-day period. The government offers the displaced Lakota only 75¢ for each acre of land taken from them.

1944

May

The Pribilof Island Aleut return home.

After the Japanese evacuate the Aleutian Islands, the Aleut of the Pribilof Islands are sent home by the federal government. Nearly two years earlier, they were removed from the region by the U.S. Navy and relocated and held against their will in an unsanitary camp (see entry for JUNE 1942). Upon reaching the Pribilofs, the Aleut find that in their absence many of their houses have been looted and destroyed by U.S. military personnel. The damage is so great that several ancient villages are abandoned forever.

November

The National Congress of American Indians is founded.

Eighty Indians representing 50 tribes convene in Denver, Colorado, for the first meeting of the National Congress of American Indians (NCAI). The idea for the congress had originated at a 1942 meeting of Indian employees of the Bureau of Indian Affairs, who realized the need for a national organization through which Indians from all tribes could voice their concerns. Particularly instrumental in its formation was D'Arcy McNickle (see entry for 1936), a Flathead anthropologist who was then serving as special assistant to Commissioner of Indian Affairs John C. Collier.

Like the Society of American Indians (SAI)—an earlier pan-Indian organization (see entry for OCTOBER 12, 1911)—the members of the NCAI are largely well-educated professionals. Unlike the SAI, however, the new group is concerned with tribal as well as civil rights. In addition to working "to secure and to preserve Indian rights under Indian treaties," the Denver conference delegates name the preservation of "Indian cultural values" as one of their primary goals. The representatives also call for the creation of a U.S. government commission to settle Indian land claims. (See also entry for JUNE 13 TO 20, 1961.)

1945

John C. Collier resigns as the commissioner of Indian affairs.

Recognizing a change in the federal government's goals for Indian policy, Commissioner John C. Collier steps down from his position as head of the Bureau of Indian Affairs (BIA). Collier had held the post for 12 years, what was then the longest tenure of any commissioner (see entry for 1933). In keeping with Roosevelt's progressive policies, Collier's Indian Reorganization Act (see entry for JUNE 18, 1934) ended the Allotment policy, which had stripped many tribes of their land, and encouraged the preservation of tribal cultures.

As Collier's years as commissioner were coming to an end, many in government had already begun to gravitate toward a more conservative federal Indian policy. Encouraged by western business leaders seeking control over Indian lands and resources, the post-Collier BIA will focus on assimilating individual Indians into mainstream society while attempting to terminate the government's financial responsibilities to tribes.

February 24

Ira Hayes raises the American flag on the island of Iwo Jima.

During the Battle of Iwo Jima, Marine Private First Class Ira Hayes, a Pima (Akimel O'odham) Indian, is one of the first American soldiers to reach the summit of Mount Suribachi, an extinct volcano at Iwo Jima's southern tip. To mark the American victory in this pivotal battle, Hayes and five other marines raise a U.S. flag. The moment (actually a second flag-raising soon after) is captured in a photograph by the Associated Press's Joe Rosenthal. The photograph will become one of the most famous

World War II hero Ira Hayes identifies himself in the famous Associated Press photograph of U.S. soldiers raising the American flag on the Japanese-held island of Iwo Jima. *(Princeton University Library)*

and widely reproduced images of World War II. (See also entry for JANUARY 23, 1955.)

1946

The United States forms the Bureau of Land Management (BLM).

The General Land Office and the Grazing Service are merged to form the Bureau of Land Management (BLM). As the agency charged with overseeing the use of federal lands and its natural resources, the BLM is given responsibility for dealing with Indians on issues relating to reservation land, water rights, and mineral rights.

The Fort Berthold Indian Defense Association is founded.

In response to the Garrison Dam Act, members of the Mandan, Arikara, and Hidatsa establish the Fort

"We did not want Garrison Dam built. We pleaded with you to find another place to build a dam. It was not that we wished to hamper progress. In fact, we voluntarily offered some of our other lands which were not so vital to our life as a place to be used to construct the dam. Our prayers and pleas were fruitless. The Government told us 'Either you agree to some terms, or we'll take the land without your consent.'"

—Fort Berthold Reservation chairman Carl Whitman Jr. testifying before Congress in 1949 on Indian opposition to the Garrison Dam

Berthold Indian Defense Association. The organization launches a campaign to stop the federal government from constructing a dam across the Upper Missouri River, which threatens to flood 275,000 acres of land on the tribes' Fort Berthold Reservation in North Dakota. Despite their efforts, the government will proceed with the Garrison Dam, which will profoundly disrupt reservation life.

August 13

Congress establishes the Indian Claims Commission.

The Indian Claims Commission (ICC), formed by an act of Congress, is charged with reviewing and resolving all outstanding land claims of Indians living within the continental United States. The commission is meant to free the U.S. Court of Claims from hearing Indian land claims. Since 1881 the court has been inundated with more than 200 cases, only 35 of which it has been able to settle. In addition to settling land disputes, the ICC is created to address a need felt by many non-Indians, both inside and outside of the government, to right the moral wrongs committed by the United States in its unjust treatment of Native Americans in the past. (See also entry for SEPTEMBER 30, 1978.)

1947

The Mormons establish the Indian Student Placement Program.

The Church of Jesus Christ of Latter-Day Saints initiates the Indian Student Placement Program, with the goal of placing Native American children in Mormon foster homes, where they can be trained in the Mormon faith throughout the school year. During the next 30 years, more than 20,000 Indian students will participate in the program. Their Indian parents agree to the placements by signing a consent form in English, a language many cannot read. They are discouraged from visiting their children, who are as young as eight when they are taken from their homes.

1948

Uranium is first mined on the Navajo (Dineh) reservation.

The Kerr-McGee Company begins mining the vast uranium resources on the Navajo (Dineh) reservation. The firm takes advantage of the reservation's lack of health regulations and the large available labor force. Many returning Navajo veterans sign on to work in the mines, where they will routinely handle radioactive ore and suffer exposure to more than 100 times the legal limit of radon gas. A large number will subsequently die of cancer.

The Bureau of Indian Affairs initiates an education grant program.

Beginning in 1930, Congress established a loan fund for Indians students pursuing college degrees. By 1944, however, so many Indian graduates were unable to repay their loans that Congress stopped authorizing money for the fund.

Taking a new approach, the Bureau of Indian Affairs creates the Higher Education Grant Program to offer nonrepayable grants for tuition and other student costs. Although initially modest in scope, by the 1990s the program will grow to become the primary source for federal funding for Indian college students.

Arizona enfranchises its Indian population.

In *Harrison v. Laveen,* the state supreme court of Arizona upholds the right of Indian residents to vote in local and state elections. The decision reverses a 20-year-old ruling in which the court found that Indians should not be allowed to vote because they are under the guardianship of the federal government. The court equated this status with that of "people with disabilities."

The Bureau of Indian Affairs (BIA) encourages Navajo (Dineh) to move to cities.

Concerned that the Navajo (Dineh) reservation economy cannot support its growing population, the Bureau of Indian Affairs (BIA) develops a program to encourage Navajo to move to urban areas.

Participants are sent to relocation offices in Los Angeles, Denver, and Salt Lake City, where BIA employees try to place them in temporary or permanent jobs. The program's success will later inspire the BIA to extend the Relocation policy to reservation populations across the United States (see entry for 1952).

1948

May 6

The *Straight Arrow* radio series is first broadcast.

Sponsored by the National Biscuit Company (Nabisco), *Straight Arrow*, an action radio series, is aired on the Don Lee Network. *Straight Arrow* recounts the adventures of a Comanche warrior who disguises himself as a white cattle rancher named Steve Adams. Before its cancellation in 1951, the popular series will spawn a comic book and syndicated newspaper strip. It will also inspire Nabisco to include "Injun-Uity Cards" in boxes of its Shredded Wheat cereal. These cheaply printed collectable cards will feature information for children on Indian customs and lore.

May 27

Korczak Ziolkowski begins work on his monument to Crazy Horse.

Non-Indian sculptor Korczak Ziolkowski starts to carve a figure of the legendary Lakota Sioux warrior Crazy Horse (see entry for MAY 6, 1877) into Thunderhead Mountain in the Black Hills, a complex of mountains sacred to the Lakota Sioux. Because Crazy Horse was never photographed, the sculptor works from his imagination to design the figure, which sits astride a stallion with his arm outstretched and finger pointing to his burial site. The flamboyant Ziolkowski plans for the sculpture to be the largest ever created on earth. If stacked, the four heads of the nearby Mount Rushmore would measure only as high as Crazy Horse's massive face.

Following Ziolkowski's death in 1982, his widow and children will take over the project, which is projected to continue well into the 21st century. The work is funded largely by admission fees paid by the thousands of tourists who visit the site every year.

"The purpose of Crazy Horse is noble. There are many people who do not see its nobility at present, and even in your time—and maybe in your children's time—the vision of Crazy Horse might be clouded to some people; but if you wish to dedicate your life as to carry out my dreams ... they will then also be your dreams some day."
—Crazy Horse memorial sculptor Korczak Ziolkowski in a 1952 letter to his children

August

The Oahe Dam floods two Lakota Sioux reservations.

As part of the federal government's damming of the Missouri River, the U.S. Army Corps of Engineers builds the Oahe Dam near Pierre, South Dakota. The project floods more than 160,000 acres on the Lakota Sioux's Standing Rock and Cheyenne River Reservations. The flooded area includes the Lakota's best rangeland and farms and most of their timberlands.

1949

The Gilcrease Museum opens.

Owner of the Gilcrease Oil Company, Creek businessman Thomas Gilcrease establishes the Gilcrease Museum in Tulsa, Oklahoma. According to its corporate charter, the museum is "devoted to the preservation for public use and enjoyment the artistic, cultural, and historical records of the American Indian." The institution will eventually house one of the largest collections of Native American art and artifacts in the world.

The Bureau of Indian Affairs creates 11 area offices.

To streamline its organization, the Bureau of Indian Affairs establishes 11 area offices throughout the country. Each area office is given responsibility for operating programs and performing routine administrative tasks, freeing the central office in Washington, D.C., to focus on larger policy issues.

The Hoover Commission advocates Termination and Relocation.

Charged with improving efficiency in the U.S. government, the Hoover Commission, headed by former president Herbert Hoover, recommends the "discontinuance of all specialized Indian activity on the part of the federal government." As a necessary step toward fully assimilating Indians, the commission suggests that programs administered by the Bureau of Indian Affairs be transferred to other federal agencies or made the responsibility of state governments. It also promotes the Termination of tribal status and Relocation of reservation Indians to urban areas—the two goals that, to the detriment of Indian people, will come to dominate federal Indian policy in the 1950s (see entries for 1952 and for AUGUST 1, 1953).

1950

Jim Thorpe is named the greatest athlete of the half-century.

In an Associated Press poll, 381 sportwriters and sportscasters are asked to name the best all-around athlete of the past 50 years. Olympic champion (see entry for SUMMER 1912), football phenomenon, and member of the Sac and Fox tribe Jim Thorpe is far and away the winner. He is the first choice of 252 respondents, while baseball great Babe Ruth, the athlete in the second place, receives only 86 first-place votes.

April 19

Congress passes the Navajo-Hopi Rehabilitation Act.

Following the end of wartime jobs, the residents of the Navajo (Dineh) and the Hopi reservations, particularly returning veterans, have had difficulty finding work. The problem was compounded by a severe drought in 1946 and 1947, which drew the reservations into economic chaos. After lengthy study into how the reservation economies could be rehabilitated, Congress passes the Navajo-Hopi Rehabilitation Act. The legislation allocates $88 million over the next 10 years to improve the reservations' infrastructure, including roads, schools, and irrigation operations. In the years to follow, the improvements, particularly those to roads and highways, will greatly increase Navajo and Hopi interaction with non-Indian society.

August 1

Broken Arrow counters the Hollywood stereotype of the "Indian savage."

Popular with audiences and critics, *Broken Arrow* is recognized as a new type of Hollywood western.

A scene from *Broken Arrow* (1950), an acclaimed film dramatizing the friendship between Apache leader Cochise (Jeff Chandler) and his non-Indian friend Thomas Jeffords (James Stewart) *(Courtesy of the Museum of Modern Art Film Stills Archive)*

Rather than dismissing Indians as savage, uncivilized killers, it offers a complex Indian character in Cochise, the legendary Apache warrior, played by non-Indian actor Jeff Chandler. The film focuses on Cochise's friendship with the white adventurer Thomas Jeffords (see entry for OCTOBER 1 TO 11, 1872), who is depicted by James Stewart. In addition to expressing a degree of sympathy for Cochise's desire to save his people's land from being overrun by non-Indians, it includes a controversial scene in which Jeffords marries an Indian women. *Broken Arrow* is the most successful of several movies of the post–World War II era that attempt (though often awkwardly) to present a more balanced view of Indian-white relations than the blatantly racist westerns of the past.

November 5

A Winnebago soldier saves his company in Korea.

Mitchell Red Cloud Jr., a Winnebago soldier serving in Korea, sights a Communist force preparing to attack his company while he is standing guard. He sounds an alarm and, with an automatic rifle, single-handedly holds off the attacking enemy long enough for his fellow soldiers to prepare to defend themselves. During the ensuing battle, Red Cloud is killed. Later, he and Charles George, a Cherokee who died throwing himself on a grenade to protect his comrades, will become the two Indian soldiers serving during the Korean War to be awarded the Medal of Honor.

1951

The Menominee receive an $8.5 million settlement from the United States.

Since the late 19th century, the lumber industry has provided most of the Menominee, a Wisconsin tribe, with their livelihoods. Alleging that the U.S. government has mismanaged their forest lands, the tribe sued the United States in 1934. Seventeen years later, the Menominee are awarded $8.5 million in compensation, a settlement that will soon encourage the U.S.

government to target the tribe as an early candidate for Termination (see entry for AUGUST 1, 1953).

Annie Dodge Wauneka is elected to the Navajo Tribal Council.

The daughter of former Navajo (Dineh) chairman, Henry Chee Dodge (see entry for JULY 7, 1923), Annie Dodge Wauneka becomes the first woman to serve on the tribal council of the Navajo, whose political leaders traditionally have been men. With a special interest in improving health care on the Navajo reservation, Wauneka will serve three terms in office, becoming one of the most influential council members. (See also entry for DECEMBER 2, 1963.)

"Ever since the development of political machinery and bureaucratic organizations among Indians, there has been a sudden perspective of women—and the roles of women—as second-class citizens. The basic reason for discrimination against Indian women stems from the Federal government's intervention in Indian affairs.

To offset the second-class role, Indian women must become more active in politics and become aware of the education opportunities open to Native American Women."

—Annie Dodge Wauneka in a speech at the 1975 Southwest Indian Women's Conference

Western Shoshone land becomes a nuclear testing site.

President Harry S. Truman names a 1,350-square mile area in Nevada as the official site for the

United State's testing of nuclear bombs. The land belongs to the Western Shoshone, who are not consulted about the president's appropriation of their land.

Canyon Records is founded.

In Phoenix, Arizona, Ray and Mary Boley establish Canyon Records, the first recording company to market Native American music to a Native American audience. Their first album is *Natay, Navajo Singer,* which includes eight songs by Ed Lee Natay. Canyon will eventually feature a catalog of more than 400 contemporary and traditional recordings, including those of the popular Navajo-Ute flutist R. Carlos Nakai.

June 20

Canada's Indian Act is revised.

The valor of Native soldiers in the Canadian military in World War II prompts Natives and government officials alike to reexamine Indian policy. One result is the first major revision of the Indian Act, which consolidated Canada's policies regarding Natives (see entry for APRIL 12, 1876). The 1951 revision ends the prohibition of Indian ceremonies, such as the Sun Dance and the potlatch, and allows the consumption of alcohol by Natives outside of reserve borders. It also extends voting rights to more Natives and rescinds a provision that forbids Native political organizations from raising funds without the permission of the Department of Indian Affairs (see ENTRY FOR 1927).

1952

The Relocation program is expanded.

With an allocation of $500,000 from Congress, Commissioner of Indian Affairs Dillon Myers establishes a branch of the Bureau of Indian Affairs (BIA) dedicated to "relocation services," allowing Myers to expand nationwide the Relocation program first established for the Navajo (Dineh) (see entry for 1948). The Relocation program encour-

ages reservation Indians to move to cities, where employees of the BIA assist them in finding jobs and housing. The BIA maintains that Relocation will greatly improve the quality of life of Indians, particularly those living on the poorest reservations. The federal government, however, also sees Relocation as a means of reducing the high cost of operating the reservation system.

Between 1952 and 1957, annual Relocation funding will grow to $3.5 million, and more than 17,000 Indians will receive assistance from the BIA's Relocation services. Although some will find the good jobs and comfortable homes promised them by the BIA, many others will merely exchange rural poverty for urban poverty.

Summer

Creek pitcher Allie P. Reynolds plays his best season.

A Creek Indian star pitcher for the New York Yankees, Allie P. Reynolds leads the American League in strikeouts and in earned-run average. After attending Oklahoma State University on a track scholarship, Reynolds began playing professional baseball in 1942 for the Cleveland Indians. In 1972, he will be honored as one of the first inductees into the American Indian Athletic Hall of Fame (see entry for NOVEMBER 25, 1972).

1953

Chief Bender is elected to the Baseball Hall of Fame.

The year before his death, Charles Alfred "Chief" Bender is admitted into the Baseball Hall of Fame—the first Indian to be so honored. From 1903 to 1917, Bender was a pitcher for major league teams,

Opposite page: A poster produced by the Bureau of Indian Affairs to encourage Indians to move to Denver, Colorado, as part of its relocation program *(National Archives, Neg. no. RG75N-Reloc-G)*

COME TO DENVER

THE CHANCE OF YOUR LIFETIME!

Good Jobs

Retail Trade

Manufacturing

Government–Federal, State, Local
Wholesale Trade

Construction of Buildings, Etc.

Happy Homes

Beautiful Houses

Many Churches

Exciting Community Life.

Over Half of Homes Owned by Residents

Convenient Stores–Shopping Centers

Training

Vocational Training
Auto Mech., Beauty Shop, Drafting,
Nursing, Office Work, Watchmaking
Adult Education
Evening High School, Arts and Crafts
Job Improvement, Home-making

Beautiful Colorado

"Tallest" State, 48 Mt. Peaks Over 14,000 Ft.

350 Days Sunshine, Mild Winters

Zoos, Museums, Mountain Parks, Drives

Picnic Areas, Lakes, Amusement Parks

Big Game Hunting, Trout Fishing, Camping

spending most of his active years with the Philadelphia Athletics. Although racism was rampant in the early ball clubs, Bender took this tension in stride. He was known for responding to racist taunts from fans by shouting "Foreigners! Foreigners!" at hecklers in the bleachers. After leaving the major leagues, Bender had a successful second career managing and coaching in the minors.

The Indian Claims Commission makes its first lands claim settlement.

The Otoe-Missouria of Oklahoma becomes the first Indian tribe granted title to their lands by right of occupancy by the Indian Claims Commission (ICC) (see entry for AUGUST 12, 1946). The ICC awards the Otoe-Missouria $1.5 million dollars, which the tribe elects to distribute per capita to tribal members.

The prohibitions on the sale of alcohol to Indians are removed.

As part of the federal government's efforts during the 1950s to end its supervision over Indian tribes, Congress repeals all laws prohibiting Indians from purchasing alcohol. Some reservations, however, will institute their own bans on liquor sales and consumption to keep alcohol out of their communities.

August 1

House Concurrent Resolution 108 formally implements the Termination policy.

As a response against the pluralistic Indian policies of the New Deal era, many conservative legislators have long advocated that the federal government get out of the "Indian business." Their ideas for reform, collectively known as the Termination policy, are codified in House Concurrent Resolution 108.

The resolution calls for Congress to draft 60 Termination bills over the next nine years. The goal of these bills is to terminate the tribal status of Indian groups that Congress deems capable and affluent enough to survive without the special protection given wards of the U.S. government. As a prelude to Termination, a roll of tribal members is to be taken. Tribal assets will then be liquidated,

and the proceeds will be distributed to individual tribal members.

Although presented as a means to "emancipate" Indians from the control of the federal government, the Termination policy is largely intended to save funds due to Indian groups, often guaranteed by treaty. Termination is also supported by private companies that want access to natural resources on Indian-held lands, and by state and local governments that will be able to tax Indians living within their borders after the tribes have been terminated. (See also entry for APRIL 28, 1988.)

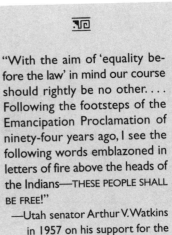

"With the aim of 'equality before the law' in mind our course should rightly be no other. . . . Following the footsteps of the Emancipation Proclamation of ninety-four years ago, I see the following words emblazoned in letters of fire above the heads of the Indians—THESE PEOPLE SHALL BE FREE!"

—Utah senator Arthur V. Watkins in 1957 on his support for the Termination policy

August 15

Congress passes Public Law 280.

In keeping with the goals of the Termination policy, Public Law 280 places most of the reservations in California, Minnesota, Nebraska, Oregon, and Wisconsin under the jurisdiction of these states' civil and criminal legal systems. Previously, the Federal Bureau of Investigation was in charge of investigating major crimes, while the Bureau of Indian Affairs and tribal police forces were responsible for dealing with all lesser offenses. The law also allows for other states to extend their jurisdictions over Indians living within their borders, without the Indians' consent.

Indian rights groups strongly object to the legislation, which they see as a major threat to tribes' right to self-government. Despite their opposition, the provisions of Public Law 280 will remain in place until the passage of the Indian Civil Rights Act (see entry for APRIL 18, 1968).

1954

The Cahuilla elect an all-woman tribal council.

Although traditionally Cahuilla women were not involved in the leadership of the tribe, a dwindling male population forces the Cahuilla of Palm Springs, California, either to elect female leaders or allow the Bureau of Indian Affairs (BIA) to handle their business affairs. The Cahuilla choose the former path, electing five women to a five-member tribal council. Its head, Vyola Olinger, will prove to be adept at negotiating with BIA representatives.

May

A Pennsylvania town names itself after Jim Thorpe.

A year after the death of Sac and Fox sports hero Jim Thorpe (see entry for SUMMER 1912), the town of Mauch Chunk, Pennsylvania, votes to change its name to Jim Thorpe. The idea is proposed by Thorpe's widow, Patricia, who arranges for his body to be buried in Mauch Chunk, against the wishes of his children. The Jim Thorpe grave site is the focus of the town's attempt to bring tourists and new industries to the economically depressed area.

October 11

Maria Tallchief appears on the cover of *Newsweek*.

In a cover story, *Newsweek* magazine profiles Osage ballerina Maria Tallchief. The story focuses on her new salary of $2,000 a week, which the Ballet Russe used to lure her away from the New York City Ballet. Hailed as the only living dancer who can rival in technical mastery the greatest European and Rus-

sian ballerinas, Tallchief, the article notes, is now the highest-paid ballerina in the world. (See also entry for DECEMBER 1996.)

1955

January 23

War hero Ira Hayes is found dead on the Pima reservation.

The body of 33-year-old Ira Hayes, the most celebrated Indian soldier during World War II (see entry for FEBRUARY 24, 1945), is found on the Gila River Reservation in Arizona. Following a night of drinking, he apparently passed out about a mile away from his parents' house and died of exposure.

The tragedy of Hayes's death becomes a public symbol of the difficulties many Indian soldiers have faced after returning to the United States after the war. In the military they had been treated with respect, but at home they found that, despite their service and sacrifice, they were largely regarded with contempt, as members of one of America's most hated minorities.

July 1

The U.S. Public Health Service takes over Indian health care.

The federal government transfers responsibility for Indian health care from the Bureau of Indian Affairs to the U.S. Public Health Service. Administered under the newly created Division of Indian Health, funds spent on Indian health care will dramatically increase over the next several decades. Nevertheless, the health of most Indians will remain below the national average.

1956

A Lakota tax on non-Indian ranchers is upheld in federal court.

The Lakota Sioux outrage white ranchers when they levy a tax on all non-Indians leasing land on South

Dakota's Pine Ridge Reservation. The ranchers fight the tax in federal court, where their lawyer angrily claims the Lakota are behaving like a "foreign nation." Judge George T. Mickelson agrees, maintaining they have every right to do so. Finding for the Lakota, he states that Indian tribes are "sovereign powers and as sovereign powers can levy taxes."

March 10

The Dalles Dam destroys Celilo Falls.

Construction on the Dalles Dam on the Columbia River floods the ancient spiritual and trading center at Celilo Falls. For thousands of years, this area has been sacred to many northwestern Indian groups, including the Umatilla, Nez Perce, Yakama, and Warm Springs Indians. Destroyed as well are important fishing sites guaranteed to these groups by treaty.

"The Pacific Northwest is renowned for its natural beauty and livability, but the riches of our homeland are being spent without conscience or regard for its long history of its people....The unconscionable drowning of Wyam—Celilo Falls—marks a crucial point in our collective history. It destroyed a major cultural site and rent a multimillennial relationship of a people to a place....It was like a mother, nourishing us, and is remembered as a place of great peace."

—Warm Springs–Wasco–Navajo poet Elizabeth Woody on the cultural meaning of the flooding of Celilo Falls

June 7

Congress passes the Lumbee Recognition Act.

After years of requests for acknowledgment from the federal government, the Lumbee Indians of North Carolina are formally recognized by an act of Congress. The act, however, specifically bars the Lumbee from receiving federal funds and services offered to other tribes. The legislation will prompt a series of legal battles, through which the Lumbee and other North Carolina groups will seek the full benefits of recognition.

1957

The U.S. government rejects a petition to create a reservation at Hill 57.

Senator James E. Murray of Montana launches an unsuccessful campaign to persuade the federal government to declare "Hill 57" in Great Falls a reservation. This Indian community, named after a nearby billboard that advertises 57 varieties of pickles, was settled in the 1940s by landless Cree, Ojibway, and Métis, who came to Great Falls looking for wage work. Poor and homeless, many squatted in Hill 57 in squalid conditions that came to symbolize the poverty of the many Indians driven to cities by the Relocation and Termination policies. The United States rejects Murray's petition, maintaining that the squatters should return to their reservations or relocate to other urban areas.

The Indian Vocational Training Act is passed.

Through the Indian Vocational Training Act, Congress authorizes the creation of job training centers near reservations and in some cities. The centers are to provide free vocational education to Indians to help prepare them for jobs in urban areas. Many unemployed Indians, even those resisting relocation to cities, welcome the opportunity to train for trades.

State of Washington v. Satiacum encourages northwestern Indian fishing.

The Washington State Supreme Court hears *State of Washington v. Satiacum*, a case involving the arrest of Robert Satiacum, a Puyallup and Yakama Indian who is accused of fishing steelhead trout with gill nets out of season. The court dismisses the charges, which will encourage many northwestern Indians to start taking more advantage to the fishing rights granted to their ancestors by treaties with the United States.

1958

The Seneca object to the construction of the Kinzua Dam.

The Seneca begin a campaign to stop work by the U.S. Army Corps of Engineers on the Kinzua Dam.

> "I would like to point out that the 1794 Treaty was signed by the *Seneca Nation,* . . . [which] remains today exactly what it was 165 years ago—in the words of the court . . . a 'quasi-sovereign independent nation.' . . . I know it will sound simple and perhaps silly but the truth of the matter is that my people really believe that George Washington read the 1794 Treaty before he signed it, and that he meant exactly what he wrote."
>
> —Seneca Nation president George D. Heron, speaking out against the Kinzua Dam project before the House Subcommittee on Indian Affairs in 1960

First proposed in 1908, the dam is intended to control flooding along the Ohio and Allegheny Rivers, but its reservoir would flood two Seneca reservations, one in Pennsylvania and one in New York, forcing the relocation of some 130 tribe members. The dam would also destroy the Cold Spring Longhouse, the Seneca's spiritual center, and flood the cemetery where 18th-century Seneca leader Cornplanter is buried.

In the media and the courts, the Seneca claim that building the dam is a direct violation of the 1794 Treaty of Canandaigua, which gave the Iroquois possession of the lands that would be damaged by the redirected waters. The tribe also hires engineers to find an alternate site where the dam could more effectively control flooding without threatening the Seneca's reservations. Ignoring their efforts, the U.S. government will move ahead with the dam's construction (see entry for OCTOBER 1964).

Mungo Martin creates a totem pole for the British Columbia centennial.

Kwakiutl artist Mungo Martin is honored by Queen Elizabeth of England with a commission to create 100-foot totem pole for Windsor Great Park as part of British Columbia's centennial celebration. Despite the Canadian government's ban on the potlatch ceremony (see entry for APRIL 19, 1884), Martin has devoted his life to making ceremonial carvings that, in large measure, have been responsible for keeping the Kwakiutl's artistic traditions alive.

The Tuscarora fight to prevent the New York State Power Authority from seizing their land.

To the ire of the Tuscarora, the New York State Power Authority announces a plan to locate a reservoir on a large portion of their land near Niagara Falls. The Tuscarora Tribal Council rejects an offer of monetary compensation, maintaining that the land is more important to them than money. The council decides to take its case to court (see entry for MARCH 7, 1960).

Tuscarora activists William Rickard, John Hewitt, and Wallace "Mad Bear" Anderson erect a sign protesting the New York State Power Authority's plan to build a reservoir on tribal lands. *(Buffalo and Erie County Historical Society)*

Kiowa veterans revive the Black Legs warrior society.

A group of Kiowa veterans of World War II and the Korean War meet in Carnegie, Oklahoma, to re-form the Black Legs warrior society. Traditionally, membership in warrior societies had given Kiowa men special prestige in their society. The revived society is open only to men who have been in the armed services. Their female relatives, however, participate in the biannual ceremonies by performing the Scalp Dance, a ritual that welcomes warriors back into the community after they return from battle.

Thirty-six California Indian groups agree to Termination.

With the passage of the Rancheria Act, the Indians living on 41 small California reservations known as rancherias are targeted for Termination (see entry for AUGUST 1, 1953). The act provides that rancheria residents must vote on whether or not to be terminated. To persuade the Indians to accept Termination, federal officials visit the rancherias and promote the policy, often with exaggerated claims of its benefits. Largely because of their efforts, 36 groups vote in favor of Termination. In the years to come, their loss of Indian status will irrevocably damage their social and cultural unity. In addition, it will cause more than 5,000 acres of Indian lands to pass into non-Indian hands.

The Bureau of Indian Affairs promotes Indian adoptions.

In cooperation with the Child Welfare League of America, the Bureau of Indian Affairs launches a campaign to encourage white families to adopt Indian children. During the next 10 years, the agency will place in non-Indian homes approximately 400 children, sometimes without their relatives' consent or full understanding of legal adoption.

The Navajo (Dineh) and Hopi are given permission to sue one another.

For the first time in American history, two Indian groups—the Navajo (Dineh) and the Hopi—ask Congress for permission to sue one another in federal court. The dispute between the tribes revolves around an area of land on the Hopi Indian Reservation that is occupied by Navajo families (see entry for DECEMBER 16, 1882). Congress approves their request and assigns the case, *Healing v. Jones* (see entry for 1962), to a three-judge district court.

January 18

The Lumbee Indians break up a Ku Klux Klan rally.

To intimidate the Lumbee of Robeson County in North Carolina, the Ku Klux Klan schedule a nighttime rally in a field on Lumbee lands. The rally is likely a response to rumors of a romantic relationship between an Indian woman and a white man, which the KKK perceives as a threat to the informal segregation of Robeson County's Indian, white, and African-American populations.

As some 75 Klansmen gather, they are approached by more than 300 Lumbee, some armed with rifles. One Lumbee shoots out a lightbulb strung over the field, prompting others to fire their guns in the air. Outnumbered and terrified, the Klansmen frantically flee the scene, as Indians try to shoot out the tires of their cars. No one is injured in the melee, although two members of the Klan are later prosecuted for inciting a riot. Their action is reported throughout the nation, and the Lumbee are hailed in Indian Country for their successful resistance against racist oppressors.

1959

Williams v. Lee prohibits state courts from hearing civil cases originating on reservations.

A white general-store owner sold goods on credit to a Navajo (Dineh) man. When the Navajo did not pay the bill, the store owner successfully sued him in Arizona state court. The Navajo man appeals the decision in *Williams v. Lee* to the U.S. Supreme Court, before which he argues that an Arizona court could not settle the case, because the general store is located on the Navajo Indian Reservation. The Supreme Court agrees and reverses the state court's ruling, explaining that a state has no power to regulate transactions occurring on reservation land.

Kahnawake Mohawk address the United Nations.

A delegation of Kahnawake Mohawk appears before the United Nations to claim that their human rights have been violated by the Canadian government. At issue is the government's confiscation of 1,260 acres of Kahnawake land along the St. Lawrence River. The land was taken in preparation for the construction of the St. Lawrence Seaway, which will connect the Atlantic Ocean to the Great Lakes. Although the government offered the Indians monetary compensation, the Mohawk refused, maintaining that the money offered was far lower than the amounts given to non-Indian landowners for land along the river. The UN delegates express sympathy for the Mohawk but ignore their request that the United Nations pressure Canada to end its encroachment on the reserve.

January 3

Alaska becomes a state.

With the passage of the Alaska Statehood Act, Alaska becomes the 49th state of the Union. The act allows the new state to appropriate 108 million of the 375 million acres within Alaska's borders for the state's own use. The state subsequently identifies as its property many hunting and fishing areas frequented by Alaska's Natives.

March 5

Traditional Iroquois rebel against the tribal council at Ohsweken.

On the Six Nations Reserve in Ontario, Canada, a group of Iroquois traditionalists, declaring themselves the true governing body of the reserve, seize the council house at Ohsweken, the meeting place of the reserve council set in place by the Canadian government in 1924. The revolt ends when 50 Royal Canadian Mounted Police raid the council house and restore the officially sanctioned council to power.

Spring

The Cape Dorset Inuit establish the West Baffin Eskimo Co-operative.

In the mid-1950s, non-Indian adventurer and writer James Houston traveled to the village of Cape Dorset on Canada's Baffin Island, where he taught the Inuit the art of printmaking. Using simple designs that traditionally decorated their sealskin robes, the Cape Dorset Inuit quickly took to making high-quality prints that they could sell to whites. To capitalize fully on non-Indian demands for their works, Houston encourages the Inuit printmakers to create the West Baffin Eskimo Co-operative. Artists can buy shares in the co-operative, which operates a studio where they can work and a store where they can sell their prints. (See also entry for 1967.)

1960

A Norse village is discovered in Newfoundland.

Norwegian author Helge Ingstad discovers the ruins of an ancient settlement near the village of L'Anse aux Meadows, in northern Newfoundland. The remains include multiroom houses built using 3,000-year-old Norse technology. The date is consistent with Norse sagas of the 12th and 13th centuries that tell of the travels of Norse seamen from Greenland and Iceland to a location they called Vinland (see entry for CA. 1000). Many scholars have identified Vinland as Newfoundland, but the discovery of L'Anse aux Meadows is the first evidence of pre-Columbian Norse settlement in North America that is widely accepted by archaeologists.

Half a million Americans identify themselves as Indians in the U.S. Census.

For the first time in American history, the U.S. Census Bureau allows Americans to report their own racial origins as "Indian." Approximately, 513,500 people identify themselves as Indian, and an additional 28,000 Alaskans call themselves Aleut or Eskimo. Over the next few decades, the new system of self-identification will help account for a rapid rise in the official Indian population (reported as 1.9 million in the 1990 census).

March 7

The Tuscarora lose their lawsuit against the New York State Power Authority.

The Tuscarora tribe's legal case against the New York State Power Authority (see entry for 1958), which is attempting to seize a large portion of their land to build a reservoir, goes before the Supreme Court. In a split decision, the Court rules against the Tuscarora. The ruling is an enormous blow to the tribe, which staged many highly publicized protests while the case was in the courts. Although their fight ends in defeat, their protests will inspire other Indian groups to use the media to bring attention to their own causes.

1961

May 1

The Menominee tribe is terminated.

The Menominee of Wisconsin lose their Indian status when they are terminated by the U.S. government (see entry for AUGUST 1, 1953). In the years since 1954, when the Menominee were first targeted for Termination, the some $10 million the tribe held in the U.S. Treasury is largely depleted by the costs of implementing the policy. As their once-prosperous reservation is dissolved, Wisconsin officials declare that the new Menominee County formed from tribal lands is "an instant pocket of poverty."

June 13 to 20

The American Indian Chicago Conference ushers in a new era of Indian activism.

In a week-long conference, 500 representatives from 90 Indian communities come together at the University of Chicago to develop a plan for making their voices heard in the formulation of Indian policy. The largest multitribal gathering in decades, the success of the Chicago conference will encourage

Indian groups to work together to solve their common problems.

The conference was first conceived by Sol Tax, chairman of the Department of Anthropology at the University of Chicago, and his assistant Nancy Lurie. With the heavy involvement of the National Congress of American Indians (see entry for NOVEMBER 1944), Tax coordinated many preliminary meetings to define a program for Indian affairs that would serve the needs and address the concerns of both reservation and urban Indians.

"When Indians speak of the continent they yielded, they are not referring only to the loss of some millions of acres in real estate. They have in mind that the land supported a universe of things they valued, and loved. With that continent gone, except for the parcels they will retain, the basis of life is precariously held, but they mean to hold the scraps and parcels as earnestly as any small nation of ethnic groups was ever determined to hold to identity and survival."

—from the Declaration of Indian Purpose, issued at the American Indian Chicago Conference

These ideas are incorporated into the Declaration of Indian Purpose, which the delegates to the meeting approve. The declaration calls for an end to the Termination policy (see entry for AUGUST 1, 1953), which it condemns as "the greatest threat to Indian survival since the military campaigns of the 1800s." It also demands improved education and health services, greater economic development of

Indian communities, increased tribal control of natural resources, and the disbanding of 10 regional Bureau of Indian Affairs offices.

July

The first World Eskimo-Indian Olympics are held.

In what will become an annual event, Inuit, Aleut, and Indian athletes gather in Fairbanks, Alaska, to participate in the World Eskimo-Indian Olympics. The four-day competition includes games, such as the arm pull and blanket toss, that were traditionally played by Alaskan Natives to build their strength and stamina. The event also features traditional dance contests and displays of Native arts and artifacts.

July 10

The Keeler Commission issues a report on Indian policy.

In February, Secretary of the Interior Stewart Udall appointed a five-person special task force to investigate how to implement an Indian policy of self-determination. Chaired by William Wayne Keeler, the principal chief of the Cherokee, the commission five months later issues a 77-page report recommending that the Bureau of Indian Affairs abandon the Termination policy (see entry for AUGUST 1, 1953) and instead work to promote economic development in Indian communities. Specifically, it encourages the government to find ways of attracting businesses to reservations, offer increased job training and placement to Native Americans, and quickly settle outstanding Indian land claims.

August

The National Indian Youth Council is founded.

Ten young Indian activists—most of whom are college students—meet in Gallup, New Mexico, to form a new pan-Indian organization, the National Indian Youth Council. The council is founded in part as a response to the conference endorsed by the National Congress of American Indians held two months earlier in Chicago (see entry for JUNE 13 TO 20, 1961). The youths had appeared at the meeting uninvited, but the delegates allowed them to voice their views, some of which were reflected in the Declaration of Indian Purpose produced at the conference.

Nevertheless, the young activists found the delegates' approach to Indian policy reform overly conservative, prompting them, with the encouragement of many tribal elders, to create an organization through which they could express their more radical opinions. In the years to come, NIYC will be instrumental in organizing protests, including the "fish-ins" held in Washington State to demand the recognition of Indian fishing rights (see entry for MARCH 1964).

"[The] weapons employed by the dominant society have become subtler and more dangerous than guns—these, in the form of educational, religious, and social reform, have attacked the very centers of Indian life by attempting to replace native institutions with those of the white man.... Our viewpoint, based in a tribal perspective, realizes literally, that the Indian problem is the white man, and, further, realizes that poverty, educational drop-out, unemployment, etc., reflect only symptoms of a social-contact situation that is directed at unilateral cultural extinction."

—the National Indian Youth Council in its Statement of Policy at the 1961 Gallup conference

December

The National Indian Council is formed.

The first major pan-Native organization in Canada since the demise of the League of Indians (see entry for DECEMBER 1918), the National Indian Council is founded as a national lobbying group representing status Indians (i.e., people registered as Indian under the Canadian Indian Act [see entry for APRIL 12, 1876]), nonstatus Indians, and the Métis. The organization identifies its purpose as the promotion of "unity among all Indian people."

1962

Edward Spicer's *Cycles of Conquest* is published.

In *Cycles of Conquest: The Impact of Spain, Mexico, and the United States on the Indians of the Southwest, 1533–1960,* cultural anthropologist Edward Spicer documents the ineffectiveness of foreigners' efforts to assimilate southwestern Indian peoples throughout recorded history. His emphasis on the persistence of Indian traditional cultures counters theories that present Indians represent a "vanishing race."

The Indian Claims Commission offers compensation for Shoshone land.

After a 15-year court battle, the Indian Claims Commission (see entry for AUGUST 12, 1946) rules that certain lands of the Western Shoshones were taken from them by gradual encroachment by whites. The United States holds that the Western Shoshone are entitled to monetary compensation but not to the lost land itself. The decision will cause a division in the tribe, as some tribe members decide to accept compensation whereas others, led by sisters Mary and Carrie Dann, continue to fight to regain their land. (See also entries for 1973 and FEBRUARY 20, 1985.)

Healing v. Jones addresses Hopi and Navajo (Dineh) land claims.

A federal court ruling in *Healing v. Jones* attempts to settle a land dispute between the Hopi and Navajo (Dineh) that dates back to the late 19th century, when an executive order established the Hopi Indian Reservation (see entry for DECEMBER 16, 1882). Within its borders lived a large number of Navajo who refused to move. As the Najavo's population expanded, more and more land on the Hopi reservation was occupied by Navajo.

Healing v. Jones determines that most of the disputed land belongs to both the Hopi and the Navajo. Aside from a half-million-acre grazing area to be exclusively owned by the Hopi, the land in question, measuring approximately two million acres, is to be used jointly by both groups. Far from settling the dispute, this compromise decision angers the Hopi and Navajo alike.

The Atomic Energy Commission (AEC) begins dumping nuclear waste on Inuit land.

In the late 1950s, the Atomic Energy Commission (AEC) proposed to demonstrate peacetime uses of atomic energy by using atomic weapons to blast a new harbor near the Inuit village of Point Hope in Alaska. The Point Hope Inuit strongly objected to the project (named Operation Chariot) and wrote letters of protest to President John F. Kennedy.

In light of the opposition, the AEC abandons Operation Chariot and instead embarks on an experiment to determine the toxicity of radioactive material on Arctic plants and animals. Without informing the Inuit, the agency dumps near Point Hope 15,000 pounds of radioactive waste from the U.S. nuclear testing site in Nevada. The waste is not placed in protective containers but is inserted into holes in the ground and covered with gravel. The AEC's actions will not come to light until the 1980s, when scholars will link the secret waste dump to the extremely high incidence of cancer suffered by the Inuit at Point Hope.

Montoya v. Bolack confirms the enfranchisement of New Mexico Indians.

After narrowly losing a race for lieutenant governor of New Mexico, Joe Montoya insists that the votes of Navajo reservation residents should be discounted because they do not pay state taxes or live on state property. In the resulting court case, *Montoya v. Bolack,* a New Mexico court finds against Montoya and upholds the right of the Navajo to vote in state elections. The decision draws on an earlier Arizona court ruling, in *Harrison v. Laveen* (see entry for 1948), that similarly maintained that that state could not deny the vote to Indian residents.

July 1

The Catawba's tribal status is terminated.

The United States ceases to recognize the Catawba of North Carolina as a tribe after the members of the Catawba Tribal Council vote nearly two to one to accept Termination (see entry for AUGUST 1, 1953). Some who favor Termination resent their previous status as wards of the federal government; others want deeds to their land allotments so they can obtain loans to improve their property. Despite predictions that the Catawba will lose their tribal identity after Termination, tribe members will remain united through sharing the 630-acre state reservation and through their strong connection to the Mormon church (see entry for 1883). (See also entry for NOVEMBER 29, 1993.)

August 15

Indian activists meet with President John F. Kennedy.

Thirty-two of the delegates from the previous summer's American Indian Chicago Conference (see entry for JUNE 13 TO 20, 1961) travel to Washington, D.C., to meet with President John F. Kennedy, Vice President Lyndon B. Johnson, and congressional leaders to recommend changes in Indian policy. The delegates present Kennedy with the "Declaration of Indian Purpose," a document drafted at the Chicago conference that condemns the present policy of terminating the government's financial responsibilities to tribes.

October 1

The Institute of American Indian Arts is established.

The first government-sponsored Indian art school, the Institute of American Indian Arts opens at the Santa Fe Indian School. Created by the Indian Arts and Crafts Board (see entry for AUGUST 17, 1935) and the Bureau of Indian Affairs, the IAIA is dedicated to teaching Indian students to appreciate the artistic traditions of Native Americans and to create innovative new work drawing upon them. Its director is Cherokee artist Lloyd Kiva New. The curriculum includes textiles, ceramics, sculpture, painting, metals, creative writing, music, and performance.

1963

Indian water rights are addressed in *Arizona v. California.*

The Supreme Court finds in *Arizona v. California* that five tribes living along the lower Colorado River are entitled to a substantial quantity of the river's water for irrigation. The court determines the Indians' share of the water by multiplying their reservations' acreage by the amount of water needed to make one acre farmable. This method will be used to define tribal shares of water sources in several future water-rights cases.

December

The American Indian Arts Center is established.

The American Indian Arts Center opens in New York City, to promote the aesthetic quality and excellent craftsmanship of Indian arts and crafts to non-Indian collectors. Within a few months, the center will display work of artists from more than 50 tribes.

December 2

Annie Dodge Wauneka receives the Medal of Freedom.

In a ceremony at the White House, President Lyndon B. Johnson presents Navajo (Dineh) political leader and health care advocate Annie Dodge Wauneka (see entry for 1951) with the Presidential Medal of Freedom, the highest honor the U.S. government can bestow on a civilian. The first American Indian to be so honored, Wauneka will be nicknamed "Badge Woman" by the Navajo as she takes to wearing the medal on her blouse.

1964

The American Indian Historical Society is founded.

Formed in San Francisco, the Indian-run American Indian Historical Society dedicates itself to producing materials about Indian issues and history from the Native American perspective. In the next two decades, it will publish several periodicals, including a journal (*The Indian Historian,* 1964–80), a newspaper (*Wassaja,* 1972–84), and a children's magazine (*The Weewish Tree,* 1974–83). Beginning in 1970, the society will also operate the Indian Historian Press, whose published titles will include *Tsali* and *Textbooks and the American Indian.*

Pueblo potter Helen Cordero first displays storytelling dolls.

At the New Mexico State Fair, Helen Cordero, a potter from Cochiti Pueblo, exhibits her "storytelling dolls," which she has developed from earlier and largely extinct Pueblo effigy figures. The clay figurines show a storyteller, with eyes closed and mouth wide open, on whom several smaller figures of children are crawling. The figurine style creates a sensation and garners the

fair's first, second, and third prizes. In addition to making an active career for Cordero, storytelling dolls prove so popular that their creation will become an industry for future generations of the Pueblo artists.

> "I don't know why people go for my work the way they do. Maybe it's because to me [my sculptures] aren't just pretty things that I make for money. All my potteries come out of my heart. They're my little people. I talk to them and they're singing. If you're listening, you can hear them."
>
> —Cochiti Pueblo sculptor Helen Cordero on the appeal of her storytelling dolls

Economic Opportunity Act funds tribal social programs.

As a part of the Johnson administration's "War on Poverty," Congress passes the Economic Opportunity Act, which establishes funds for Community Action Agencies (CAA) to fight poverty on a local level. Under the act, tribal governments can declare themselves as CAAs and receive federal money to finance education, employment, health, and community development programs.

The Department of the Interior exhibits Indian paintings.

The First Annual Invitational Exhibition of American Indian Painting is hung in the art gallery of the Department of the Interior building in Washington, D.C. The show features 132 works, the majority by contemporary artists, including some graduates of the new government-sponsored Institute of American Indian Arts (see entry for

OCTOBER 1, 1962). The exhibition catalog singles out these painters' works as exemplifying "the new spirit of experimentation and invention which has resulted in a wide latitude of styles and media now at the command of Native American artists."

Cree singer Buffy Sainte-Marie releases her first album.

Already well known on the folk circuit, Cree Indian Buffy Sainte-Marie reaches a mass audience with her first album *It's My Way.* Named the "Best New Artist of the Year" by *Billboard* magazine, Sainte-Marie uses many of her songs—including "Native American Child," "Now That the Buffalo's Gone," and "My Country 'Tis of Thy People You're Dying"—to protest the United States's mistreatment of Native Americans. As an activist, she also uses her notoriety to bring attention to a variety of Indian causes and to speak out against the Vietnam War. Her song "Universal Soldier" will become the unofficial anthem of the Vietnam War protest movement. (See also entry for 1996.)

Lakota Sioux protesters occupy Alcatraz Island.

Six Lakota Sioux men take over the closed federal prison on Alcatraz Island in San Francisco Bay to protest the seizure of Indian lands. The protesters claim the area, citing the Treaty of Fort Laramie (see entry for NOVEMBER 7, 1868) between the Lakota and the United States. The treaty included a provision stating that ownership of federal lands abandoned by the government is to revert back to the Indians. Although treated as a joke by the media, the protest sets the stage for the later occupation of Alcatraz by the Indians of All Tribes (see entry for NOVEMBER 20, 1969).

March

The National Indian Youth Council organizes the first "fish-in."

To protest illegal fishing restrictions placed on many small tribes in western Washington State, the National Indian Youth Council (see entry for AUGUST 1961) recruits volunteers for a "fish-in." In violation of state regulation, the participants fish in the waters of Quillayute River. As the state police arrives to arrest the protesters, local Indians step in to take their place. When hundreds of Indian join in the protest, the police are forced to stop making arrests. The success of this new type of protest will spark a rash of "fish-ins" held by Indians whose fishing rights are being violated.

March 27

Aleut villages are destroyed by an earthquake.

A massive earthquake in Alaska levels several Aleut villages, including Old Harbor and Kaguyak on Kodiak Island and Afognak on Afognak Island. The disaster also kills 23 people at the village of Chenega in Prince William Sound. It will take the survivors 20 years to rebuild their settlement (now called Chenega Bay).

August

The California Supreme Court protects the ceremonial use of peyote.

In 1962, three Navajo (Dineh) men were arrested in California for distributing peyote, a hallucinogen used in the rituals of the Native American Church (see entry for OCTOBER 10, 1918). Two years later, the California Supreme Court finds that preventing the men from using peyote is a violation of their First Amendment rights to freedom of religion. The ruling will discourage federal officials from prosecuting Indians for using peyote in religious rituals.

October

The United States starts construction of the Kinzua Dam over Seneca objections.

For several years, the Seneca have staged a campaign in the media and the courts to stop the construction of the Kinzua Dam on the

Allegheny River (see entry for 1958). Over their objections, the U.S. Army Corps of Engineers begins work on the dam, which leads to the flooding of more than 10,000 acres of land on the tribe's lands in Pennsylvania and New York State. Although the United States pays the Seneca $15 million in compensation, the destruction of the land is a disaster for the tribe. Some 130 families have to leave their homes—a forced relocation that many elders describe as a "trail of tears." The dam also destroys the Cold Spring Longhouse, the Seneca's spiritual center, and floods the grave site of the 18th-century Seneca leader Cornplanter (see entry for 1790) (the grave itself is moved to a new cemetery).

October 14

Lakota Sioux Billy Mills wins an Olympic Gold Medal.

Billy Mills, a Lakota Sioux from South Dakota's Pine Ridge Reservation, was a track star at the Haskell Institute and the University of Kansas. While serving as an officer in the marines, he is selected to represent the United States in the 10,000-meter run in the 1964 Summer Olympics in Tokyo. In an upset victory, Mills beats the favored runners in the race. In addition to winning the gold medal, he sets an Olympic record in the event.

1965

The Supreme Court challenges states' rights to collect taxes on reservations.

In *Warren Trading Post Co. v. Arizona Tax Commission,* the non-Indian owner of a reservation trading post challenges Arizona's attempts to collect taxes on purchases made by his Indian customers. The Supreme Court finds that the state's actions violate Congress's right to regulate Indian commerce on reservations. It rules that reservation trading posts can collect sales tax only from non-Indians.

September

Taos leaders reject $10 million settlement offer for Blue Lake.

In 1906 the federal government confiscated 48,000 acres surrounding Blue Lake in northwestern New Mexico and made it part of the Kit Carson National Forest. The Taos Indians, to whom the Blue Lake area is sacred, have spent decades trying to recover the land. After hearing their case, the Indian Claims Commission (see entry for AUGUST 12, 1946) offers the Taos 3,000 acres and $10 million in compensation. Taos leaders, however, refuse to take the settlement and vow to continue to fight for the return of the lake and all 48,000 acres.

> "We don't have gold temples in this lake, but we have a sign of a living God to whom we pray—the living trees, the evergreen and spruce and the beautiful flowers and the beautiful rocks and the lake itself.... We are taking that water to give us strength so we can gain in knowledge and wisdom.... That is the reason this Blue Lake is so important to us."
>
> —Taos spokesperson at a 1961 Association on American Indian Affairs meeting

1966

The Indian Actors' Workshop is founded.

A longtime critic of stereotyped Indian characters in film, Jay Silverheels (see entry for JULY 12, 1979), the Mohawk actor best known for portraying Tonto on the *Lone Ranger* television series, establishes the

Indian Actors' Workshop at the Los Angeles Indian Center. The workshop calls for more accurate portrayals of Indians in television and film, and it advocates the casting of Indians in Indian roles.

April 27

Oneida Indian Robert Bennett becomes commissioner of Indian affairs.

Stating that "the time has come to put the first Americans first on our agenda," President Lyndon B. Johnson swears in Robert Bennett, the first Indian chosen to head the Bureau of Indian Affairs (BIA) in nearly a century. (Ely S. Parker, a Seneca, had earlier served as commissioner of Indian affairs; see entries for 1869 and 1871.) To increase Indian representation in the BIA, Indians will be selected to hold the agency's top position throughout the rest of the 20th century.

Spring

The Rough Rock Demonstration School is established.

Headed by educator Ned Hatathi, the non-profit organization Demonstration in Navajo Education (DINE) founds the Rough Rock Demonstration

"I am glad our children are learning to read and write English, but I'm also very glad they're learning about the Navajo culture and the Navajo way. We want our children to be proud they are Navajo and this is what our school is doing."

—Navajo school board member Ada Singer on the Rough Rock Demonstration School

School, the first American Indian school completely controlled by Indians. The institution is funded through a contract with the Bureau of Indian Affairs (BIA) and the Office of Educational Opportunity. With a curriculum shaped by Navajo (Dineh) traditions and classes taught in Navajo and English, Rough Rock encourages the Navajo community to participate in making decisions affecting the school. A great success, the school will inspire Indian tribes across the country to negotiate with the BIA to found their own contract schools.

October

The Alaska Federation of Natives is formed.

After joining the Union, Alaska was authorized by the U.S. government to select 108 million acres of territory for its own use (see entry for JANUARY 3, 1958). Native Alaskans, however, still claimed all the land appropriated by the state. To bring attention to these land claims and halt further appropriations, the Natives of Alaska join together to establish the Alaska Federation of Natives. Its lobbying efforts will lead to the passage of the Alaska Native Claims Settlement Act (see entry for DECEMBER 18, 1971).

October

The Canadian government issues the Hawthorne Report.

In 1963, the Canadian government appointed anthropologist Harry B. Hawthorne to investigate the social, economic, and educational conditions of the country's Indian population. His findings are published as *The Survey of the Contemporary Indians of Canada,* popularly known as the Hawthorne Report.

The Hawthorne Report states that Canadian Indians are in general much worse off than non-Indian citizens. In opposition to Canada's long-held policy of Assimilation, the document also maintains that the economic condition of Indians is not likely to be improved by forcing them to "acquire those values of the major society [they do] not hold or wish to acquire." Instead, its authors state that Indian communities need more control over government trust funds and revenues from land leases and mineral rights. Well received by most Canadian Indian leaders, the Hawthorne Report also introduces the concept of a "citizens plus" status for Indians, explaining that "in addition to the normal rights and duties of citizenship, Indians possess certain additional rights as charter members of the Canadian community."

1967

The Omnibus Bill is defeated in the wake of Indian opposition.

The Indian Resources Development Act, popularly known as the Omnibus Bill, fails to pass Congress after pan-Indian groups speak out against it. The proposed law would have given the federal government more control over transactions involving Indian land and resources. In addition to their opposition to the bill's provisions, Indian activists were also infuriated by their treatment by the federal government while the bill was being drafted. Commissioner of Indian Affairs Robert Bennett (see entry for APRIL 27, 1966) and several other officials were sent to Indian communities throughout the nation, supposedly to discuss with Indian leaders what they would like to see in the legislation. The Indians soon discovered, to their ire, that the bill had already been written and that the officials' "consultations" with them were merely a ruse to help win Indian support for the bill.

The American Indian Law Center is established.

Located at the University of New Mexico Law School, the American Indian Law Center is created to sponsor courses in Native American law and provide tribal governments with legal assistance. In the years to come, one of the center's most successful programs will be the Pre-Law Summer Institute, which encourages and helps prepare Indian students to attend law school.

Inuit artist Kenojuak is awarded the Order of Canada.

In the late 1950s, the Inuit of the Canadian settlement of Cape Dorset began making prints for sale to non-Indians (see entry for SPRING 1959). Among the most accomplished of the Cape Dorset printmakers is Kenojuak, who, in recognition of her contributions to art, becomes the first Native to receive the Order of Canada, the highest honor given to civilians by the Canadian government. The government will later honor Kenojuak by reproducing two of her most famous works—*The Enchanted Owl* (1960) and *Return of the Sun* (1961)—on postage stamps.

"I may start off at one end of a form not even knowing what the entirety of the form is going to be; just drawing as I am thinking, thinking as I am drawing.... And rather what I do is I try to make things which satisfy my eye, which satisfy my sense of form and colour. It's more an interplay of form and colour which I enjoy performing and I do it until it satisfies my eye and then I am on to something else."

—Inuit printmaker Kenojuak in 1980 on her working methods

The Seminole elect the first female tribal chief.

After serving several years on the Seminole Tribal Council, Betty Mae Jumper is elected tribal chief of the Seminole. She is the first woman to hold such a high position in any modern tribal government. As chief, Jumper will focus her energy on improving the Seminole's economy, health care, educational opportunities, and housing. She is also one of the founders of the United South and Eastern Tribes, an organization that brings together more than 20 Indian groups to solve shared economic and social problems.

April to October

Canadian Natives air their grievances at Expo '67.

With funding from the federal government, the National Indian Council (see entry for DECEMBER 1961) organizes the Canadian Indian Pavilion at Expo '67, the world's fair held in Montreal to celebrate the centennial of Canadian Confederation. Natives at the fair use the pavilion as a forum in which they recount the history of abuses they have suffered at the hands of the government. The event helps bring international attention to Native Canadians' continuing struggle for basic rights.

October 9

The Navajo Tribal Council lifts ban on ceremonial peyote use.

In a victory for religious freedom, the Navajo Tribal Council exempts members of the Native American Church (see entry for OCTOBER 10, 1918) from prosecution for eating the buttons of the peyote cactus during religious ceremonies. Led by traditionalists who feared the spread of peyotism on the Navajo (Dineh) reservation, the council had outlawed the possession, sale, or use of peyote within the reservation borders in 1940. Those convicted of peyote use could be sentenced to nine months of labor, a fine of $100,000, or both.

November

Louis Ballad's *Four Moons* ballet is produced.

As part of a year-long 60th-anniversary celebration of Oklahoma statehood, *The Four Moons,* a ballet by Quapaw-Cherokee composer Louis Ballard, is performed in Oklahoma City. The star performers are four noted Oklahoma ballerinas of American Indian

descent—Rosella Hightower, Marjorie Tallchief, Yvonne Chouteau, and Moscelyne Larkin.

1968

Tom Little Bear initiates a revitalization movement among the Esselen.

At eight years old, Tom Little Bear, a member of the small Esselen tribe of California, begins having visions, which tell him that he has been chosen to resurrect the group's traditional life. With the help of Esselen elders, Little Bear begins a campaign to revitalize his tribe's old ways.

Akwesasne Notes begins publication.

The Mohawk on the Akwesasne Reservation in New York begin publishing a newspaper, *Akwesasne Notes.* Reprinting stories dealing with a wide variety of Native American issues and protests, the paper will become an important source of information for Indians involved in the Red Power Movement during the late 1960s and early 1970s. (See also entry for JANUARY 9, 1988.)

February

The National Indian Council splits into two organizations.

Unable to find common ground, the three Native groups represented by the National Indian Council (see entry for DECEMBER 1961) agree to disband it and create two new lobbying organizations in its place: the National Indian Brotherhood for status Indians and the Native Council of Canada for non-status Indians and the Métis. (See also entry for 1982.)

March 6

President Lyndon B. Johnson announces new Indian policy goals.

In a special message to Congress on "the problem of the American Indian," President Johnson sets out three goals for his administration's federal Indian policy. First, he cites the need to bring Indians' standard of living up to the same level as that of other Americans. Second, the president comes out against the Relocation policy (see entry for 1952), insisting that Indians be given "freedom of choice" to live in urban areas or in traditional Indian communities. Third, Johnson wants Indians to experience "full participation in modern America," noting a lack of economic opportunities and "social justice" as the main obstacles.

"• In 1970, when men have landed on the moon, many American Indians still do not have adequate roads to the nearest market.

• In 1970, when almost every American baby can look forward to a life expectancy of 70 years, the Indian infant mortality rate is three times higher than the national average after the first month of life.

• In 1970, when personal income in America is at an unprecedented level, unemployment among American Indians runs as high as 60%."

—from a statement presented to Vice President Spiro Agnew by the National Council on Indian Opportunity in 1970

March 6

The National Council on Indian Opportunity is formed.

To promote its Self-determination policy, the Johnson administration establishes the National Council on Indian Opportunity. Composed of representatives of several cabinet departments and headed by Vice President Hubert Humphrey, the council is charged with recommending reforms to increase American Indians' involvement in federal programs meant to benefit them.

April 18

American Indian Civil Rights Act applies constitutional protections to tribal governments.

After six years of hearings, Congress passes the American Indian Civil Rights Act, as Title II of the Civil Rights Act. The legislation extends most of the protections granted to American citizens by the Bill of Rights to people—Indian and non-Indian—under the jurisdiction of tribal governments. For example, the act orders that tribal governments cannot deny the freedoms of speech, religion, press, and assembly. Among the rights it does not enforce are the constitutional guarantee of a republican form of government, which could interfere with traditional Indian forms of government, and the right to free legal counsel, which is considered too great an expense for tribal courts.

One of the greatest and most immediate consequences of the Indian Civil Rights Act will be a flurry of lawsuits against Indian tribes by individuals who maintain the tribes are violating their civil rights. Suits will challenge tribes on such issues as election and voting procedures, job discrimination, and tribal enrollment.

July

The American Indian Movement (AIM) is founded in Minneapolis, Minnesota.

In response to police brutality, a group of young Minneapolis Indians—led by Dennis Banks and Clyde Bellecourt—form the American Indian Movement (AIM). The organization, modeled on the Black Panthers, begins to monitor the city's non-Indian police force, which AIM contends systematically harasses Minneapolis Indians. Within a year, AIM's efforts will reduce Indian arrests in Minneapolis by 50 percent. AIM's early victories will attract members from urban Indian populations from across the country, quickly making it the most influential national Indian activist organization.

November 18

Mohawk protesters blockade the Cornwall-Massena International Bridge.

In order to build the Cornwall-Massena International Bridge over the St. Lawrence River, Canada appropriated Akwesasne Mohawk land, where the country intended to build a customs station and tollbooths. The Canadian Akwesasne Mohawk challenged the action, invoking Jay's Treaty (see entry for NOVEMBER 19, 1794), which gave the Mohawk the right to travel back and forth between the United States and Canada at will. Canada ignored their demands and required them to pay tolls while crossing the bridge.

After years of objecting to the toll, the Mohawk bring attention to their cause by staging a dramatic protest, during which they blockade the bridge. None of the participants are prosecuted, and the following February the Akwesasne Mohawk of Canada are issued passes so that they can cross the bridge at no cost.

9

1969 TO 1979
PROTEST AND REVITALIZATION

In the early morning hours of November 20, 1969, 78 young Indians arrived on Alcatraz, in San Francisco Bay, and declared that the island was now Indian land. Only five years earlier, six Lakota men had taken over the abandoned federal prison on the island, similarly claiming it for their people. That protest was treated as a joke by the government, the public, and the media. By the late 1960s, however, Indian activists were not so easily dismissed. Drawing from the example of the African-American civil rights movement, they had become far more confident and determined. Reflecting the new sophistication in Indian activism, the second occupation drew a far different response than the first. For 19 months, the second group of Alcatraz protesters were able to air their many grievances to the world, as reporters, attracted by their photogenic and articulate spokespeople, flocked to cover the standoff.

The success of Alcatraz inspired Indians across the United States to organize protests to demand better treatment from the government and non-Indian society. In 1970 alone, Indians staged scores of takeovers, including the seizure of the Bureau of Indian Affairs headquarters in Washington, D.C., the establishment of a protest camp at the Badlands National Monument, and the symbolic occupations of Mount Rushmore and Plymouth Rock. But the most dramatic protest in the aftermath of Alcatraz occurred in 1973 at Wounded Knee, South Dakota, the site of an 1890 massacre of more than 300 Lakota at the hands of U.S. soldiers. Supported by Lakota elders, young urban activists of the American Indian Movement took over Wounded Knee, to speak out against the tribal government of South Dakota's Pine Ridge Reservation, which the protesters accused of systematically harassing the reservation's traditionalist faction. News reports of the event showed hundreds of heavily armed FBI agents swarming on Wounded Knee during the two-month protest—an image that only helped to reinforce the protesters' claims of abuses perpetrated by the FBI-supported Pine Ridge government.

By the mid-1970s, the frequency of Indian protests had declined, but their influence was increasingly felt in federal Indian policy. In part due to the public's sympathy for the demands of Indian protesters, President Richard Nixon expressed his commitment to Indian Self-determination.

Originally set forth in a special message to Congress in 1970, the new policy was intended as a complete reversal of Termination, through which the government had attempted to dismantle the reservation system in the 1950s and 1960s. Rather than trying to get out of the "Indian business," the Bureau of Indian Affairs was now charged with administering more programs to improve Indian health care, housing, and education and to stimulate economic development in reservation communities. Integral to Self-determination was the idea that Indians should be more active participants in deciding what programs they needed and how they should be operated. As Nixon told Congress, "It is long past time that the Indian policies of the Federal government began to recognize and build upon the capacities and insights of the Indian people."

The Self-determination policy had perhaps its most immediate effect on Indian education. In 1969, a report on Senate hearings titled *Indian Education: A National Tragedy–A National Challenge* revealed to the nation what had long been clear to Indian parents—that the Indian education system did not serve their children well. The report's conclusions were put into action three years later with the passage of the Indian Education Act. In addition to provide extra funding for Indian schools, it helped reverse a 100-year legacy of paternalism by calling for Indians themselves to determine what and how their children should be taught. Another crucial improvement in education opportunities open to Indians began with the opening of the Navajo Community College (now Diné College) in 1968. With the subsequent development of the tribal community college system, Indian students for the first time were given the chance to obtain advanced degrees while still living in a Native American community.

In the 1970s, Indians also seized on the court system as another important vehicle for change. Through landmark decisions such as *United States v. State of Washington* (1974), courts confirmed Indian hunting, fishing, and mineral rights. Many Indian tribes also pursued lawsuits to resolve long-standing land claims disputes. For instance, in *Passamaquoddy v. Morton* (1975), the Passamaquoddy and the Penobscot successfully sued the U.S. government for allowing their aboriginal lands to be overrun by whites, and in *United States v. Sioux Nation* (1980), the Lakota were awarded a judgment of more than $100 million in compensation for the United States's illegal seizure of the Black Hills. Monetary awards won in court, however, were far from satisfying to many tribes seeking redress to past wrongs. The Lakota, for instance, refused the court's award, deciding instead to continue their battle for the return of their sacred lands.

1969

Vine Deloria Jr.'s *Custer Died for Your Sins* is published.

A Dakota lawyer, activist, and former executive director of the National Congress of American Indians (see entry for NOVEMBER 1944), Vine Deloria Jr. writes with equal parts of wit and venom a scathing account of the injustices committed against Indians throughout U.S. history, in his first book, *Custer Died for Your Sins*. The book finds a mass audience in non-Indian readers looking to understand the roots and goals of the growing Red Power Movement. Deloria's follow-up to *Custer—We Talk, You Listen* (1970)—will also be a best-seller.

Floyd Westerman records *Custer Died for Your Sins*.

Dakota activist Floyd Westerman emerges as celebrated folksinger-songwriter with his first album, *Custer Died for Your Sins*. Like the book by Vine Deloria Jr. of the same name, Westerman's album explores the lives of contemporary Indians and attacks non-Indian efforts to dictate Indian conduct. His songs include "Here Come the Anthros," "B.I.A.," and "They Don't Listen." On the album cover, Deloria calls Westerman's work "the badly needed war songs that thousands have waited to hear."

The Navajo Tribal Council is tried in federal court.

In *Dodge v. Nakai*, a non-Indian lawyer brings suit against Raymond Nakai, the chairman of the Navajo (Dineh) tribal council, to settle a dispute with the tribal government. The Navajo's lawyers assume the case has no basis because the Navajo government is not subject to federal law. The federal court, however, holds that the case can be tried because the Indian Civil Rights Act (see entry for APRIL 18, 1968) has given the court jurisdiction over the matter. The court's interpretation of the act is derided as a threat to Indian sovereignty.

The United Southeastern Tribes is founded.

Leaders of the Eastern Cherokee of North Carolina, the Choctaw of Mississippi, and the Seminole and Miccosukee of Florida band together to form the United Southeastern Tribes. The organization is concerned about plans of the federal government to transfer responsibility for some Indian programs to the states. Because historically southeastern tribes have received little or no recognition from state governments, the United Southeastern Tribes lobbies for the federal government to retain authority over programs organized for their benefit.

January 21

The Navajo Community College begins holding classes.

Founded and chartered by the Navajo Nation in 1968, the Navajo Community College (now Diné College) opens its doors to Navajo (Dineh) students. The institution is the first Indian-controlled and reservation-based postsecondary school in the United States. Its curriculum includes courses in Navajo history, culture, and language.

May 5

N. Scott Momaday's *House Made of Dawn* wins the Pulitzer Prize.

An enormous critical success, *House Made of Dawn* (1968) by Kiowa author N. Scott Momaday is awarded the Pulitzer Prize for literature, becoming the first book by a Native American to be so honored. The novel deals with the spiritual crisis of Abel, a part-Indian, part-white World War II veteran as he struggles to readjust to reservation life following the war. Through its nonlineal structure, the book employs traditional Native American styles of storytelling. The success of *Dawn* will initiate a Native American literary renaissance by inspiring many young Indians to use the non-Indian form of the novel to tell stories of contemporary Indian life.

June 25

The Canadian government issues the White Paper on Indian Affairs.

Canadian minister of Indian affairs Jean Chrétien releases a report titled "Statement of the Government of Canada on Indian Policy, 1969," which will later be known simply as the White Paper. The report announces the government's intention to pursue a policy similar to Termination, the largely discredited Indian policy that was dominant in the United States during the 1950s (see entry for AUGUST 1, 1953). According to the White Paper, Canada plans to eliminate the special status of all Native groups within its borders. Reserves are to be broken into individually owned plots, the Indian Act (see entry for APRIL 12, 1876) is to be repealed, and the Ministry of Indian Affairs is to be disbanded.

The Natives of Canada respond to the White Paper with shock, then anger. Their determination to keep the government from disregarding their unique status and rights ushers in a new era of Native activism.

> "We view this as a policy designed to divest us of our aboriginal, residual, and statutory rights. If we accept this policy, and in the process lose our rights and our lands, we become willing partners in cultural genocide. This we cannot do."
>
> —the National Indian Brotherhood, in response to the White Paper

August 26

The Quinault close beaches to non-Indians.

Living on the Pacific coast of Washington State, the small Quinault tribe refuses to allow non-Indians to visit their reservation beaches. The Quinault maintain that non-Indian vacationers have stolen fishing equipment from them and littered the area. Later in the year, the tribe will again exercise their sovereignty by blocking construction on a state road through the reservation after Washington refuses to grant them the right to control access to the road.

September 6

The Fairchild Semiconductor Factory opens on the Navajo (Dineh) reservation.

The largest factory in New Mexico, the Fairchild Semiconductor Factory is dedicated in a ceremony attended by the commissioner of Indian affairs, Louis R. Bruce. Located on the Navajo (Dineh) reservation, the plant will eventually employ more than 1,200 Indians, the highest number of Indian employees of any factory in the United States. (See also entry for FEBRUARY 24, 1975.)

October

The National Indian Youth Council founds AMERIND.

After several Indians applying for jobs with the federal government complain of employment discrimination based on race, AMERIND is formed as an offshoot of the National Indian Youth Council (see entry for AUGUST 1961). The organization is charged with fighting discrimination against Native Americans in hiring within government agencies, particularly the Bureau of Indian Affairs and the U.S. Public Health Service.

October 12

Dartmouth College abandons its Indian mascot.

Bowing to student pressure, Dartmouth College agrees to stop using an Indian mascot for its sports teams. Originally founded to educate Indian youths (see entry for 1769), the prestigious school recently committed itself to recruiting more Indian students, with the ultimate goal of raising Indian enrollment to 3 percent of the student body.

November

The National Indian Education Association is founded.

In Minneapolis, Minnesota, during the first national conference of Indian education, the National Indian Education Association is established to improve the quality of schooling available to Indian students. At the request of Senators Edward Kennedy and Walter Mondale, representatives in the association will be actively involved in the drafting of the landmark Indian Education Act (see entry for SPRING 1972).

November 3

The Senate issues the Kennedy Report on Indian education.

Information gleaned during hearings of the Special Senate Subcommittee on Indian Education is summarized in *Indian Education: A National Tragedy—A National Challenge.* The document becomes informally known as the Kennedy Report after the chairs of the subcommittee, Senators Robert F. Kennedy and Edward Kennedy. The Kennedy Report concludes that Indian students are poorly served by Indian schools and recommends several changes, including teaching Native American history and heritage as part of the curriculum and allowing Indian parents more involvement in their children's schooling. (See also entry for SPRING 1972.)

November 10

The American Indian Task Force meets with Vice President Spiro Agnew.

The American Indian Task Force—an organization composed of 42 prominent Indian leaders, including Dennis Banks, D'Arcy McNickle, and Peter McDonald—travels to Washington, D.C., to discuss Indian affairs with Vice President Spiro Agnew and other Nixon administration officials. The group's primary goal is to promote more Indian involvement in the formation of federal Indian policy.

The task force is an outgrowth of *Our Brother's Keeper: The Indian in White America,* a published study produced by Indian and non-Indian researchers and writers funded by the Citizens' Advocate Center. *Keeper* condemned the federal government, particularly the Bureau of Indian Affairs, for failure to live up to its responsibilities to Indian peoples.

"1. It is isolated from modern facilities, and without adequate means of transportation.

2. It has no fresh running water.

3. It has inadequate sanitation facilities.

4. There are no oil or mineral rights.

5. There is no industry, and so unemployment is very great.

6. There are no health care facilities.

7. The soil is rocky and unproductive; and the land does not support game.

8. There are no educational facilities.

9. The population has always exceeded the land base.

10. The population has always been held as prisoners and kept dependent upon others."

—from a proclamation issued by the Indians of All Tribes occupying Alcatraz Island, listing Alcatraz's similarities to an Indian reservation

A protester outside a tipi erected on Alcatraz during the Indians of All Tribes's 19-month occupation of the island (*CORBIS/Bettmann*)

November 20

The Indians of All Tribes takes over Alcatraz Island.

Led by Adam Fortunate Eagle and Richard Oakes, 78 Native American activists arrive on the island of Alcatraz in San Francisco Bay to draw attention to a variety of Indian issues, including the relocation of Indians to urban areas and the substandard living conditions on reservations. Their demands are outlined in the "Proclamation of Indians of All Tribes," in which, in an allusion to the supposed purchase price paid to Indians for Manhattan (see entry for MAY 6, 1626), they offer the government $24 worth of glass beads and red cloth for the island. The document also calls for converting the abandoned Alcatraz prison into an Indian educational and cultural center. The Alcatraz occupation, which will last for 19 months, will attract worldwide media attention and public sympathy for the plight of urban and reservation Indians. (See also entry for JUNE 11, 1971.)

1970

The University of Oklahoma abandons the Little Red mascot.

Led by the Norman, Oklahoma, chapter of the National Indian Youth Council (see entry for AUGUST 1961), Indian students speak out against the University of Oklahoma's mascot, Little Red. During sports games, the student portraying Little Red dances and whoops wearing a breechcloth bearing the school's name. Although Little Red was traditionally depicted by a young white man, the university begins choosing Indian students to play the mascot, as a misguided attempt to address the protesters' concerns. The plan backfires when Navajo Ron Benally refuses to perform as Little Red at the school's Thanksgiving Day football game, in consideration of the concerns of his fellow Indian students. After protesters stage a sit-in at the university president's office, the school finally agrees to abolish the Little Red tradition.

Harvard's school of education recruits Indian students.

With funds provided in part by a grant from the federal government, Harvard University establishes the American Indian Program (later renamed the Harvard Native American Program) in its Graduate School of Education. The program is intended to recruit Indian and Inuit students to the school and train them to be leaders in the field of education. Since the program's inception, Harvard has conferred on Indians more than 180 advanced degrees in education.

LaDonna Harris founds Americans for Indian Opportunity.

Americans for Indian Opportunity is formed by LaDonna Harris, a Comanche public servant and activist. An outgrowth of her previous organization, Oklahomans for Indian Opportunity, AIO is a non-profit group dedicated to improving the economic, political, and cultural self-sufficiency of Indian tribes throughout the United States.

Determination of the Rights and Unity for Menominee Shareholders (DRUMS) is founded to fight land sales.

To prevent Menominee leaders from selling land to pay property taxes, a group of activists headed by Ada Deer form Determination of the Rights and Unity for Menominee Shareholders (DRUMS). DRUMS will later take on the larger goal of fighting to restore the Menominee's tribal status, which was terminated by the United States (see entry for MAY 1, 1961).

"The immediate effect of termination on our tribe was the loss of most of our hundred-year-old treaty rights, protections, and services. No amount of explanation or imagination prior to termination could have prepared us for the shock of what these losses meant.... We hope you can appreciate the magnitude of these treaty losses to us. Visualize a situation similar to ours happening to one of your home states. Imagine the outrage of the people in one of your own communities if Congress should attempt to terminate their basic property, inheritance, and civil rights."

—DRUMS representatives protesting the Menominee's termination before the Senate Committee on Interior and Insular Affairs in 1971

The Makah village of Ozette is uncovered.

A severe storm in northern Washington State uncovers a portion of the ancient Makah Indian village of Ozette, which had been destroyed in a mudslide before the Makah came into contact with whites. Well preserved in the mud are thousands of artifacts. With the help of Washington State University, the Makah will eventually unearth more than 55,000 objects, forming the largest collection of artifacts ever assembled from a precontact site. (See also entry for 1979.)

The Native American Rights Fund is founded.

With a grant from the Ford Foundation, the Native American Rights Fund is created to provide legal aid to Indians and Indian groups that otherwise could not afford representation. The organization is an outgrowth of the California Indian Legal Service, which was established in the 1960s as part of the Johnson administration's War on Poverty.

Cree leader William I. C. Wuttunee defends the White Paper.

Because of his support for the White Paper (see entry for JUNE 25, 1969), the Canadian government appoints Cree lawyer William I. C. Wuttunee as the commissioner of Indian land claims. Wuttunee's encouragement of Native participation in white society earns him the enmity of many Natives, including those of his own band, who ban him from their reserve. Wuttunee will soon resign his post and write *Ruffled Feathers*, in which he tells Natives to work to improve their own lives and stop "cry[ing] about broken promises and broken treaties."

The "crying Indian" television spot is first aired.

Keep America Beautiful sponsors a public-service television announcement against littering, a spot that features veteran western actor Iron Eyes Cody. Wearing a feather in his hair and dressed in buckskin, Cody stands by the side of a highway as trash tossed from a passing car falls at the actor's feet. In an extreme close-up on his face, a single tear slowly drips down.

Produced by the Ad Council, the spot becomes one of the most effective and famous public service announcements ever telecast. The advertisement, however, is criticized by some Indians, who see it as propagating the romantic stereotype of Indians as "children of nature." Others later accuse Cody of fabricating his Indian ancestry, a charge he denies until his death in 1999.

The National American Indian Court Judges Association is established.

To improve the quality of legal services offered by reservation court systems, the National American Indian Court Judges Association is created. Over the next several decades, the organization will offer training sessions in federal, state, and constitutional law to hundreds of tribal court judges.

March to April

Protesters seize Bureau of Indian Affairs (BIA) offices.

On March 14, a group of Indian activists take over the Bureau of Indian Affairs (BIA) office in Denver, Colorado, to protest the BIA's hiring practices. The specific cause of their anger is the case of an Indian woman in Littleton, Colorado, who was turned down for a job teaching Indian children despite her solid credentials.

The Denver protest sparks a wave of demonstrations and sit-ins at BIA offices throughout the United States. Protests are held in Albuquerque, Cleveland, Chicago, Dallas, Los Angeles, Minneapolis, and Santa Fe.

March 8

A California march protests the shooting death of an Indian student.

A group of Indians marches on the California state capitol in Sacramento to draw attention to the death of Michael Ferris, a Hupa Indian student at the University of California at Los Angeles. Ferris was shot to death by a non-Indian at a bar in nearby Will Creek in December 1969. The Sacramento protest is led by Lehman Brightman, later the director of the Native American Studies program at the University of California at Berkeley.

March 8 and 15

United Indians of All Tribes occupy Fort Lawton.

Inspired by the occupation of Alcatraz (see entry for NOVEMBER 20, 1969), Indian activists calling themselves the United Indians of All Tribes take over Fort Lawton, a federal land area about 50 miles south of Seattle, Washington. Seattle Indians had asked for title to Fort Lawton, which was due to be declared surplus land, but their requests were ignored. Military police arrest 77 Indians and use clubs to disperse the protesters, who include non-Indian actress and activist Jane Fonda.

A week later, activists reoccupy the fort and are again routed by the U.S. Army. The protest makes the international news, and stories about the Fort Lawson and Alcatraz occupations are featured on the covers of *Time* and *Newsweek* magazines.

March 16

Indian protesters attempt to take over Ellis Island.

Activists from 14 tribes led by Bruce Oakes and David Leach plan to establish a camp on New York City's Ellis Island, an action modeled after the Alcatraz occupation (see entry for NOVEMBER 20, 1969). The attempt fails, however, when winter temperatures freeze the fuel lines of the boats meant to carry them to the island. While the group is stranded on the New Jersey shore, news of the planned occupation is leaked to the press, alerting the police to a possible takeover and thus spoiling the protesters' plans to try again the following day.

March 23 to 26

The first Convocation of American Indian Scholars is held.

Indian academics, students, and tribal leaders gather at Princeton University for the Convocation of American Indian Scholars. Sponsored by the American Indian Historical Society (see entry for 1964), the participants discuss the issues facing contemporary Indians and explore means of preserving Indian cultures and traditions in the future.

March 28

The Indians of All Tribes show support for the Pyramid Lake Paiute.

Forty of the protesters occupying Alcatraz Island (see entry for NOVEMBER 20, 1969) form a caravan and travel to Nevada to bring attention to the plight of the Paiute of Pyramid Lake. For 65 years, water has been diverted from the Truckee River, which feeds into the lake, so that it can be used to irrigate nearby farms owned by non-Indians (see entry for 1905). Although Pyramid Lake threatens to dry up completely, the Department of the Interior continues to ignore the Paiute requests for help.

April 27

Indian activists protest *A Man Called Horse.*

In Minneapolis, Minnesota, members of the American Indian Movement (see entry for JULY 1968) picket the premiere of *A Man Called Horse,* a film directed by Elliot Silverstein and starring British actor Richard Harris. Harris plays an English gentleman captured by the Lakota Sioux during the Plains Wars. When the Englishman valiantly withstands the Lakota's torture, he is adopted into the tribe and leads them into battle against their Shoshone enemies. The protesters particularly object to the presentation of Harris's character as the Lakota's superior, and to a gory and inaccurate depiction of the Sun Dance, a traditional religious ritual.

May

Mercury poisoning leads to a fishing ban on an Ojibway reserve.

The Grassy Narrows Ojibway of Ontario are forced to close their commercial fishing operations after rivers on their reserve are found to be contaminated with methyl mercury. The methyl mercury had been dumped by the Reed Paper Company, an English mill located 100 miles upriver.

When the Canadian government is slow to react to concerns about related health problems among the Ojibway, the Indians themselves hire experts from Minamata, Japan, where rivers have been similarly poisoned. They confirm that some Ojibway are suffering from "Minamata disease," a nervous disorder caused by exposure to mercury.

May 1 to 3

Pomo occupy burial grounds and an army base.

On May 1, Pomo protesters take over their ancient burial grounds on Rattlesnake Island near Clear Lake, California. The island is owned by the Boise-Cascade Lumber Company, which intends to develop the area as a vacation resort.

The next day, Pomo activists seize a surplus army radio station near Middletown, California. Their demands that the buildings be made into a Pomo education and cultural facility will lead to the establishment of the Ya-Ka-Ama (meaning "our land") Center.

June 4

Canadian Natives issue the Red Paper.

As a response to the Canadian government's White Paper (see entry for JUNE 25, 1969), which advocated the termination of Native groups, Native leaders endorse the opinions offered in *Citizens Plus,* a report drafted by Cree Indian Harold Cardinal and issued by the Indian Association of Alberta. Also known as the Red Paper, *Citizens Plus* maintains that Natives should retain their special status as defined by past treaties. It also insists that the Ministry of Indian Affairs be reorganized and that the Canadian government recognize Native land claims.

June 6

The Pit River Indians occupy Lassen National Forest.

The Pit River Indians take over the Pacific Gas and Electric Company campgrounds in Lassen National Forest, in northern California. The tribe claims that the forest was illegally seized from them in 1853. Joining them in the protest are members of the American Indian Movement (see entry for JULY 1968), including Richard Oakes and Grace Thorpe (the daughter of sports star Jim Thorpe). On the second day of the occupation,

U.S. marshals in full riot gear oust the protesters and place more than one hundred of them under arrest for trespassing. (See also entry for OCTOBER 1970.)

> "We believe that money cannot buy the Mother Earth. She has sheltered and clothed, nourished and protected us. We have endured. We are Indians.
>
> We are the rightful and legal owners of the land. Therefore, we reclaim all the resourceful land that has traditionally been ours, with the exception of that 'owned' by private individuals.
>
> On this land we will set up our own economic and social structure, retaining all the values that are commensurate with Indian life."
>
> —from a proclamation issued by the Pit River Indians during the Pacific Gas and Electric Company occupation

July 8

President Richard M. Nixon declares his support of Self-determination.

In a special message to Congress, President Richard M. Nixon announces his intention to support a federal Indian policy of Self-determination, which would give Indian groups more control over their political and economic affairs. He states that the government should "break decisively with the past and create the conditions of a new era in which the Indian future is determined by Indian acts and Indian decisions."

Autumn

Activists stage a protest at Mount Rushmore.

In a symbolic protest, Indian activists calling themselves the Black Hills National Monument Movement seize portions of Mount Rushmore in South Dakota. The famous monument has long been resented by Indians, because it was carved from a mountain in the Black Hills, an area sacred to the Lakota Sioux and other peoples of the Plains. The protest will continue through the following spring.

October

Lakota Sioux establish a protest camp at the Badlands National Monument.

Lakota Sioux protesters at South Dakota's Badlands National Monument demand the return of Sheep Mountain, an area that is sacred to the Indians. The U.S. government took Sheep Mountain from the Lakota without compensation during World War II for use as a gunnery range (see entry for 1943). (Badlands National Monument became a national park in 1978.)

October

The Pit River Indians meet federal troops at Four Corners.

During the trial of the Pit River activists arrested in Lassen National Forest (see entry for JUNE 6, 1971), Indian supporters establish a camp at Four Corners, near Burney, California. When they begin cutting up felled trees to build cabins at the site, a team of federal troops, U.S. marshals, and Forestry Service officials storm the camp. The activists try to defend themselves with sticks as the troops spray them with mace and bludgeon them with clubs and rifle butts. Thirty-eight Indians are arrested, but the charges will later be dropped against all but five. Those who stand trial for assault will be found not guilty in 1972.

November 3

Indian protesters occupy University of California land.

A group of Indian activists take over a 650-acre plot of land near Davis, California, after the University of California announces plans to establish a primate research center on the site. The board of trustees of the Deganawida-Quetzalcoatl University, planned to be the first Indian-run college for Native Americans of all tribes, had applied to the Department of Health, Education, and Welfare to use the site—formerly an army communications center—but the request had been denied. Largely because of the protest, the federal government will be persuaded to award the university title to the land the following January. (See also entry for JULY 7, 1971.)

November 26

American Indian Movement (AIM) activists stage a protest at Plymouth Rock.

Declaring Thanksgiving "a national day of mourning," members of the American Indian Movement (AIM) led by Russell Means and Dennis Banks stage a protest in Plymouth, Massachusetts. The activists paint the historic Plymouth Rock red and take over *Mayflower II,* a replica of the ship that transported the Pilgrims to North America. Using the ship as a podium, Means speaks out against the United States's treatment of Indians. The event is the first AIM protest intended to focus the attention of the public nationwide on contemporary Indian issues and grievances.

December 15

The U.S. government returns the Blue Lake area to the Taos Pueblo.

In the culmination of a 64-year legal battle, the people of Taos Pueblo regain control over Blue Lake and the surrounding area in New Mexico. The land was seized by the United States in 1906, when it was incorporated into the Carson National Forest. The Indian Claims Commission offered monetary compensation for Blue Lake, a sacred site to the people of Taos, but they refused the money and continued to fight for the land's return (see entry for SEPTEMBER 1965). A landmark in the history of Indian land claims, Congress's decision to give the 48,000-acre Blue Lake area back to the Taos marks the first time the United States has ever returned land to an Indian group.

> "I can only say that in signing the bill I trust that this will mark one of those periods in American history where, after a very, very long time, and at times a very sad history of injustice, that we started on a new road—a new road which leads us to justice in the treatment of those who were the first Americans, of our working together for the better nation that we want this great and good country of ours to become."
>
> —President Richard M. Nixon, upon signing the bill mandating the return of Blue Lake to the Taos Indians

1971

Dee Brown's *Bury My Heart at Wounded Knee* is published.

Subtitled "An Indian History of the American West," *Bury My Heart at Wounded Knee,* by Dee Brown, documents the systematic destruction of Indian nations and cultures in the latter half of the 19th century. The book becomes an immediate best-seller and will sell more than one million copies in hardcover and four million in paperback.

Bury My Heart also makes non-Indian readers familiar with the tragedy of the Wounded Knee Massacre, during which the U.S. Army murdered nearly 300 unarmed Lakota Sioux men, women, and children (see entry for DECEMBER 29, 1890). Long a symbol for Indian people, Wounded Knee now takes on similar meaning for non-Indian Americans, thus inspiring the American Indian Movement to chose the site two years later for its most dramatic protest (see entry for FEBRUARY 28, 1973).

February

The American Indian Movement protests the murder of Oglala Lakota Raymond Yellow Thunder.

In a 200-car caravan, a group of activists organized by the American Indian Movement (AIM) descends on the small town of Gordon, Nebraska. The group means to pressure the local police to press charges against two white men who beat Raymond Yellow Thunder, an Oglala Sioux man from the Pine Ridge Reservation in South Dakota, and paraded his battered body through an American Legion dance hall. Yellow Thunder later died of his injuries.

Confronted by the protesters, the police finally arrest the accused, who will become the first whites in Nebraska sentenced to a jail term for the murder of an Indian. This victory for AIM will give the organization new legitimacy in the eyes of many reservation residents in the region.

February 19 to 20

The National Tribal Chairmen's Association is formed.

At a meeting in Billings, Montana, tribal leaders from 50 reservations establish the National Tribal Chairman's Association. Formed with the support of the Bureau of Indian Affairs, the organization is intended to help give tribal chairmen more of a voice in federal Indian policy, which reservation leaders fear is influenced too greatly by the demands of urban Indian activists.

February 22

Chief Dan George is nominated for an Academy Award.

When the 1970 Oscar nominations are announced, 71-year old Salish actor Chief Dan George becomes the first Native American to compete for the award. George is nominated for a Best Supporting Actor Oscar for his portrayal of Old Lodge Skins, a wise and witty Cheyenne elder in the comic western epic *Little Big Man.* George will not win the Oscar, but he will be honored as Best Supporting Actor by the prestigious New York Film Critics Circle.

March 17

The Canadian government withdraws the White Paper.

Under intense pressure from pan-Native organizations, the administration of Prime Minister Pierre Trudeau officially disavows the White Paper (see entry for JUNE 25, 1969), which recommended the Termination of Canadian Natives. With the withdrawal of this new policy, the Indian Act (see entries for APRIL 12, 1876, and for JUNE 20, 1951) resumes effect.

April 30

The James Bay Hydroelectric Project threatens the lands of the Cree and Inuit.

Quebec announces plans to build the James Bay Hydroelectric Project, which calls for rivers in the James Bay region to be dammed or diverted. As a result, the lands of Cree Indians and Inuit in the area will be flooded. When the Cree and Inuit object to the plan, the provincial government ignores them and maintains that they have no claims to the territory that they have occupied for centuries. To make their grievances heard, the Natives will turn to the courts to uphold their rights to their ancestral lands (see entry for NOVEMBER 1972).

May 15

Hopi traditionalists file suit to stop strip-mining.

In 1966 the Hopi Tribal Council signed a contract with the Peabody Coal Company permitting it to strip-mine for coal in the Joint Use Area, an area shared by the Hopi and the Navajo (Dineh) (see entry for 1962). Four years later mining began on Black Mesa, prompting traditionalists to band together to object to the desecration of this sacred area. With the support of non-Indian conservationists and the Native American Rights Fund (see entry for 1970), 64 traditional Hopi file a lawsuit, *Lomayaktewa v. Morton,* to stop the mining on the grounds that it violates their religious freedom.

> "The white man's desire for material possessions and power has blinded him to the pain he has caused Mother Earth by his quest for what he calls natural resources. . . . Today the sacred lands where the Hopi live are being desecrated by men who seek coal and water from our soil that they may create more power for the white man's cities. This must not be allowed to continue for if it does, Mother Nature will react in such a way that almost all men will suffer the end of life as they now know it."
>
> —Hopi religious leaders in a letter to President Richard M. Nixon protesting the strip-mining of Black Mesa

May 16

American Indian Movement members take over an abandoned naval station.

American Indian Movement protesters seize an abandoned naval station near Minneapolis, Minnesota. Claiming their right to the area by the Treaty of Fort Laramie (see entry for NOVEMBER 7, 1868), they announce that they want to make the station into an Indian school and cultural center. The protesters are forcibly removed on May 21, when U.S. marshals storm the site.

June 11

The Indian occupation of Alcatraz ends.

Twenty armed federal marshals arrive on Alcatraz, forcing the less than 30 Indian protesters remaining on the island to leave. The event ends the Indian occupation of Alcatraz, which had begun 19 months earlier (see entry for NOVEMBER 20, 1969). The number of protesters fluctuated throughout that period, but at its height more than 400 people occupied the island, while many others on the mainland gathered supplies for the protesters and focused media attention on the event.

In the end, no Indian policies will be changed as a direct result of the protest. The occupation will, however, heighten international awareness of a wide variety of Indian issues. It will also prove to young Indian activists the power of collective protest and therefore lead to similar multitribal actions, including the Trail of Broken Treaties (see entry for NOVEMBER 2 TO 8, 1972) and the Wounded Knee occupation (see entry for FEBRUARY 28, 1973).

June 14

The Indians of All Tribes take over a San Francisco Bay missile base.

Activists ousted from Alcatraz Island (see entry for JUNE 11, 1971) move their protest to an abandoned Nike missile base in the Berkeley Hills on San Francisco Bay. The protesters intend to occupy the base indefinitely, but truckloads of military police de-

scend on their camp, forcing them to leave the base three days after the takeover begins.

July 7

Deganawida-Quetzalcoatl University begins holding classes.

Established at a former army communications station near Davis, California (see entry for NOVEMBER 3, 1970), Deganawida-Quetzalcoatl University (also known as D-Q University) opens its doors to Indian students. Unique among Indian-operated universities, Deganawida-Quetzalcoatl University is not located on a reservation or affiliated with a single tribe. Instead it is founded to serve indigenous peoples throughout North and Central America. Its diverse student body and educational vision is reflected in its name: Deganawida was the great Peacemaker of Iroquois oral tradition (see entry for CA. 1400), while Quetzalcoatl was a god of several Mesoamerican peoples, including the Toltec, Maya, and Aztec (see entry for CA. 900 TO 1200).

August

The Iroquois protest interstate construction.

Protesters from the Onondaga, Oneida, Mohawk, and Tuscarora tribes lie down on Interstate 81 to prevent New York State from building an additional lane on lands owned by the Onondaga. Following meetings between Onondaga leaders and Governor Nelson Rockefeller, the conflict ends when the state abandons its plans to widen the highway and agrees to consult with the Onondaga Council about any future construction.

December 18

The Alaska Native Claims Settlement Act is signed into law.

Under pressure from the Alaska Federation of Natives (see entry for OCTOBER 1966) and several large energy corporations, Congress passes the

Alaska Native Claims Settlement Act (ANCSA). The goal of the legislation is to settle long outstanding land claims disputes between the Alaskan Natives and the state of Alaska. After becoming a state, Alaska was authorized by the federal government to take control of more than a quarter of the state's land base for its own use (see entry for JANUARY 3, 1958). The Natives of this land, however, have never formally relinquished their claims to this territory.

The ANCSA gives Native groups title to 44 million of Alaska's 375 million acres. In compensation for the remaining land, the Natives are awarded $462.5 million and mineral royalties worth $500 million. In a radical departure from earlier policies, the Native lands in Alaska are not established as reservations held in trust by the U.S. government. Instead, in an effort to assimilate Alaskan Natives into the larger economy, Native groups are granted fee simple patents to their 44 million acres. These lands are to be managed by for-profit corporations, the shares of which are owned exclusively by Native peoples. The ANCSA calls for the creation of 12 regional corporations and about 200 village corporations. (See also entry for FEBRUARY 3, 1987.)

1972

The first Indian radio station begins broadcasting.

KTDB-FM becomes the first radio station owned and operated by Indians. Based in Ramah, New Mexico, the station defines its mission as providing local, state, and national news and educational programming in the Navajo (Dineh) language. Its call letters stand for the Navajo words "Te'ochini Dinee Bi-Radio," meaning "Radio Voice of the People."

Indian groups speak out against Indian mascots.

Indian organizations, such as the American Indian Movement (AIM), launch a campaign against sports teams that make use of offensive Indian mascots. AIM leader Russell Means threatens to sue the Atlanta Braves (whose Chief-Noc-a-Homa emerges from a tipi and whoops every time the team scores a run) and the Cleveland Indians (whose mascot, Chief Wahoo, performs similar on-field antics). AIM, the National Congress of American Indians (see entry for NOVEMBER 1944), and Americans for Indian Opportunity (see entry for 1970) also send representatives to meet with the owner of the Washington Redskins to persuade him to change the team's name. Aside from drawing attention to the issue of Indian mascots, their efforts are largely unsuccessful. (See also entry for APRIL 2, 1999.)

The Heart of the Earth Survival School is founded.

Responding to the alarming dropout rate of Indian high school students, members of the American Indian Movement found the Heart of the Earth Survival School. The school teaches Indian students about their culture and history from an Indian perspective. The institution will serve as a model for other "survival schools" established by Indian activists throughout the United States.

The Smithsonian Institution establishes the Native American Cultural Resources Training Program.

In response to Indian demands for access to tribal artifacts and records, the Smithsonian's Department of Anthropology creates the Native American Cultural Resources Training Program. The program allows Indians to come to Washington, D.C., for up to six months to research their tribes using the resources of the Smithsonian, National Archives, and Library of Congress. During the next 10 years, about 90 Indians from 55 tribes will participate in the program, including a Tunica-Biloxi intern who will find documents to help support the tribe's application for federal recognition.

The paintings of Indian artists T. C. Cannon and Fritz Scholder are showcased in a Smithsonian exhibition.

The Smithsonian's National Collection of Fine Art in Washington, D.C., presents *Two American Painters,* an exhibition of the works of T. C. Cannon, a Caddo-Kiowa Indian, and Fritz Scholder, a member of the Luiseño tribe. Their clever and ironic representations of Indians of the past and present are well received by the international art world. In part because of the success of the show, Cannon and Scholder will emerge as the leading figures in a revival of interest in contemporary Native American art.

The American Indian Higher Education Consortium holds its first meeting.

Representatives from seven tribally run colleges and three postsecondary schools operated by the Bureau of Indian Affairs meet to share information and discuss ways to improve educational options for Indian college students. The group, named the American Indian Higher Education Consortium, will help move tribal colleges into the forefront of the movement to preserve Indian cultures and values. Concerned with increasing funding for tribal colleges, the consortium will also be instrumental in the passage of the Tribally Controlled Community College Act (see entry for OCTOBER 17, 1978).

The Grand Council of the Crees is formed.

The eight Cree communities of Canada, which have always been politically autonomous, come together to found the Grand Council of the Crees. The council is created in response to the threat posed to Cree lands along James Bay by the construction of the James Bay Project, a hydroelectric plant (see entry for APRIL 30, 1971). The organization will launch a series of legal battles in an attempt to halt the project.

Spring

The Indian Education Act is passed.

The Senate Special Subcommittee on Indian Education called for major reforms in its study *Indian Education: A National Tragedy—A National Challenge* (see entry for 1969). As a response, Congress passes the Indian Education Act, which will become known informally as Title V. The act provides additional funds for public schools with a large number of In-

dian students and requires increased parental involvement in educational programs for Indian children. It also offers educational grants to tribes and other nonprofit organizations serving Indians, allocates money for adult job training programs, and calls for the formation of an Office of Indian Education within the U.S. government. As a direct result of this legislation, Indians throughout the country will see a substantial improvement in their educational opportunities. (See also entry for NOVEMBER 1, 1978.)

> "We have concluded that our national policies for educating American Indians are a failure of major proportions. They have not offered Indian children—either in years past or today—an educational opportunity anywhere near equal to that offered the great bulk of American children.... Our own general thus faces a challenge— ... [to] recognize our failures, renew our commitments, and reinvest our efforts with new energy."
>
> —from *Indian Education: A National Tragedy—A National Challenge* (1969)

May 20

Mount Adams is returned to the Yakama.

Acknowledging the wrongdoing of the United States, President Richard M. Nixon signs an executive order to return 21,000 acres of land in the Gifford Pinchot National Forest to the Yakama of central Washington State. The area includes Mount Adams, a site of great religious importance to the tribe. The land was part of a 121,000-acre parcel of Yakama territory illegally seized by the U.S. government in 1897.

September 21

Indians of All Tribes leader Richard Oakes is murdered.

During an altercation with an employee of a YMCA camp, Mohawk Indian activist Richard Oakes is shot and killed. While a student from San Francisco, Oakes emerged as the leading spokesperson for the Indians of All Tribes during its occupation of Alcatraz Island (see entries for NOVEMBER 20, 1969, and for JUNE 11, 1971). The shock of his sudden death helps unify participants of the growing Red Power Movement.

November

Quebec rejects Cree and Inuit land claims.

The Grand Council of the Crees (see entry for 1972) and the Northern Quebec Inuit Association apply for an injunction to halt the construction of the James Bay hydroelectric project (see entry for APRIL 30, 1971). The injunction is granted, but it is withheld a week later by the Quebec Court of Appeals, which maintains that Native rights in Quebec were extinguished by the Hudson's Bay Company charter (see entry for 1670). The decision prompts a storm of protest and moves Quebec Natives to come together to demand recognition of their claim to lands in the province. (See also entry for NOVEMBER 11, 1975.)

November 2 to 8

The Trail of Broken Treaties protesters occupy the Bureau of Indian Affairs headquarters.

Starting from the Rosebud Reservation in South Dakota, a contingent of nearly 1,000 Indian activists, including many American Indian Movement members, travel to Washington, D.C., in a caravan they dub the Trail of Broken Treaties. The activists bring a 20-point platform on Indian rights, which they intend to present to President Richard M. Nixon during a massive demonstration. The majority of the platform deals with treaty rights, including a demand that the U.S. government reinstate the treaty-making process (see entry for MARCH 3, 1871). Other portions of the document call for the dissolution of the Bureau of Indian Affairs (BIA), the end of state interference in civil and legal matters on Indian territory, and a formal repeal of the Termination policy (see entry for AUGUST 1, 1953).

When the caravan reaches Washington, about 400 activists enter the government building that houses the BIA, while representatives of the group meet with bureau officials to discuss the demonstration. When guards try to expel the activists, they fight back and take over the building. No one is hurt during their six-day standoff with police, which ends peacefully when the Nixon administration agrees not to prosecute the activists and promises to give a written response to each point in their platform.

November 25

The American Indian Athletic Hall of Fame admits its first inductees.

Located at the Haskell Indian Nations University in Lawrence, Kansas, the American Indian Athletic Hall of Fame is established to celebrate the achievements of Indians in football, baseball, basketball, and track. At its first induction ceremony, 14 athletes—including Charles "Chief" Bender (see entry for 1953), Joseph Guyon, and Allie P. Reynolds (see entry for SUMMER 1942)—are admitted into the hall of fame.

1973

The Tlingit are compensated for the bombing of Angoon.

The Tlingit of southeastern Alaska accept a settlement of $90,000 from the Indian Claims Commission (see entry for AUGUST 12, 1946) in compensation for the destruction of Angoon. With little provocation, the U.S. Navy shelled and set fire to the Tlingit village nearly 100 years earlier (see entry for OCTOBER 24 TO 26, 1882).

The American Indian National Bank is founded.

With Crow educator and Bureau of Indian Affairs administrator Barney Old Coyote as its first president, the American Indian Nation Bank is established to help provide Indian businesspeople and tribes with needed capital. The bank issues one hundred thousand shares of stock, all of which are Indian owned. Old Coyote announces that the institution represents "the first real opportunity for Indians to put their money to work for themselves and for others in the Indian community."

The Dann family of the Western Shoshone is accused of trespassing on federal lands.

The Bureau of Land Management orders the Danns, a ranching family on the Western Shoshone Reservation, to remove their cattle from a grazing area in Nevada that the bureau regards as federally owned rangeland. The Danns refuse to round up their herds or to purchase grazing permits. They maintain that they never agreed to a Court of Claims settlement cited by the BLM (see entry for 1962), in which one band of the Western Shoshone took monetary compensation in exchange for some 24 million acres of land, including the Danns's grazing lands. The BLM ignore the Danns's claims and sends federal agents to impound their cattle. (See also entry for FEBRUARY 20, 1985.)

McClanahan v. Arizona State Tax Commission confirms Indians' state tax exemption.

A Navajo (Dineh) woman named McClanahan sued Arizona for a tax refund after it withheld taxes from her salary in 1967. All of her wages that year had been earned on the Navajo Indian Reservation, which she maintains made that income nontaxable. When Arizona courts refused to grant her the refund, McClanahan appeals to the Supreme Court. After a review of the Navajo's treaties, which include no provision allowing Arizona to collect taxes from tribe members, the Court finds in McClanahan's favor.

The old Narragansett reservation is listed on the National Register of Historic Places.

The remains of a Narragansett village on the tribe's old reservation in the Charlestown section of Boston is protected from destruction by its addi-tion to the National Register of Historic Places. This historic site includes the Narragansett Indian Church, built by Indian masons in 1859, and the ruins of many Narragansett houses constructed during the 18th and 19th centuries.

January 31

Calder v. Attorney General of British Columbia upholds Canadian Natives' land claims.

In the case of *Calder v. Attorney General of British Columbia,* Frank Calder, the president of the Nishga Tribal Council, claims before the Canadian Supreme Court that his people have never formally given up control of their lands in British Columbia. In a lower-court hearing, Calder stated, "What we don't like about the government is their saying this: 'We will give you this much land.' How can they give it when it is our own?"

Although the Canadian Supreme Court rules against Calder on a technicality, it does recognize that Canada's Natives had a legal claim to their lands before the arrival of Europeans in North America—a claim that can only be extinguished through legal means, such as treaties or land purchases.

February 6

American Indian Movement protesters are arrested following a riot in Custer, South Dakota.

About 200 members of American Indian Movement (AIM) travel to the town of Custer, South Dakota, to protest the local police's actions following the death of Wesley Bad Heart Bull, a young Indian man. Bad Heart Bull was brutally stabbed to death by a white man at a local bar, but his assailant was charged with involuntary manslaughter rather than with murder.

Seeking justice, the protesters confront the police on the steps of the Custer courthouse. The heavily armed officers, who decide to allow only AIM leaders to enter the building, forcibly hold back Sarah Bad Heart Bull, the victim's mother.

The police send tear gas into the crowd, and the protesters begin to riot. Although no one is killed, several AIM members are beaten, and a nearby city building is burned to the ground. In the aftermath, 27 protesters, including Sarah Bad Heart Bull, are arrested for rioting.

February 28

American Indian Movement (AIM) activists take over Wounded Knee.

Some 200 Oglala Lakota traditionalists and members of the American Indian Movement (AIM) seize control of a Catholic church, a trading post, and a museum near the site of the Wounded Knee Massacre, during which nearly 300 Lakota were slaughtered by the U.S. Army (see entry for DE-CEMBER 29, 1890). The action is intended to bring attention to the campaign of terror launched by tribal chairman Dick Wilson against traditional Indians and other political opponents on the Pine Ridge Reservation in South Dakota. With funds from a government grant, Wilson assembled a heavily armed force of policemen who refer to themselves as "goons" (an acronym for "Guardians of the Oglala Nation"). To protect themselves from the goons, the reservation's traditionalists and elders formed the Oglala Sioux Civil Rights Organization. The group asked the Justice Department for help and tried to impeach Wilson. When both efforts failed, the traditionalists turned to the young activists of AIM, who on the suggestion of several female elders decide to take over the symbolically charged site of Wounded Knee.

Two members of the American Indian Movement stand guard during the 1973 Wounded Knee takeover. (CORBIS/Bettmann)

The morning after the takeover, Wounded Knee is surrounded by more than 200 FBI agents and Bureau of Indian Affairs officials with machine guns and armored cars. The standoff between the Indian protesters and the U.S. government will continue for more than two months and become a news event of international importance. (See also entry for MAY 8, 1973.)

"I thought of the old warrior societies. . . . The Kit Foxes—the Tokalas—used to wear long sashes. In the midst of battle, a Tokala would sometimes dismount and pin the end of his sash to the earth. By this he signified his determination to stay and fight on his chosen spot until he was dead, or until a friend rode up and unpinned him, or until victory. . . . None of us had any illusions that we could take over Wounded Knee unopposed. Our message to the government was: 'Come and discuss our demands or kill us!'"

—Lakota Sioux activist Mary Brave Bird on the decision to occupy Wounded Knee

March 27

Marlon Brando refuses the Academy Award to protest Hollywood's portrayal of Indians.

At the 1972 Academy Awards ceremony, Marlon Brando is named best actor for his performance in *The Godfather*. When his name is announced, a young woman wearing a Plains Indian costume walks on stage in his behalf and pushes away the Oscar statuette offered to her by presenter Roger Moore. In her "acceptance" speech, she explains that she is Sacheen Littlefeather, an Apache representative of the National Native American Affirmative Image Committee. Acting for Brando, she refuses the Oscar because of "the treatment of American Indians today by the film industry and on television in movie reruns and also . . . the recent happenings at Wounded Knee" (see entry for FEBRUARY 28, 1973).

The protest is widely criticized as inappropriate to the awards ceremony. Representative of the entertainment industry's response is the remark of actor Charlton Heston, a political conservative: "It was childish. The American Indian needs better friends than that." Sacheen Littlefeather—actually a professional actress named Maria Cruz—is personally criticized when she exploits her fame by appearing as "Pocahontas-in-the-buff" in an issue of *Playboy* magazine.

May 8

The Wounded Knee occupation ends.

After more than two months, American Indian Movement (AIM) members and other protesters agree to leave the site of Wounded Knee (see entry for FEBRUARY 28, 1973). In the "peace pact" that ends the occupation, the U.S. government guarantees that the activists will be treated fairly. However, the FBI, embarrassed by the standoff with AIM, will push for the arrest of 562 people in connection with the protest. Only 15 will be convicted of a crime.

The Wounded Knee occupation succeeds in bringing worldwide attention to Indian disputes with the United States, but it fails in its original intention to end tribal chairman Dick Wilson's harassment of Indian traditionalists on the Pine Ridge Reservation. In the next three years, 69 people affiliated with the resistance effort will be killed. Although Wilson's police force will be implicated in many of the murders, every case will remain unsolved by the FBI.

August 27

The Canadian Supreme Court decides the Lavell case.

In *Attorney General Canada v. Lavell,* Jeannette Lavell, an Ojibway Indian, challenges the provision in Canada's Indian Act (see entry for APRIL 12, 1876) that revokes an Indian woman's Indian status when she marries a non-Indian. The Canadian Supreme Court finds against Lavell and holds that the Indian Act does not violate the guarantee of equality provided for in Canada's Bill of Rights.

November 19

The Supreme Court brands Washington fishing regulations as discriminatory.

In *Puyallup Tribe, Inc. v. Department of Game,* the Supreme Court rules that the state of Washington's regulations on Puyallup fishermen discriminate against Indians. The state bans net fishing, an Indian fishing technology, but not hook-and-line fishing, the method most often used by non-Indians. Although the ruling reaffirms Washington's right to impose nondiscriminatory regulations on Indian fisherman, the ruling is considered a victory in the Puyallup's long battle to exercise their fishing rights.

September 24

A Chippewa leader claims Italy "by right of discovery."

Adam Nordwall, a Chippewa leader who participated in the Alcatraz occupation (see entries for NOVEMBER 20, 1969, and for JUNE 11, 1971), steps out of a plane after landing at Rome's Fiumicino airport, declares that he has discovered Italy, and claims it for his people. The tongue-in-cheek gesture is meant to illustrate the absurdity of the claims of Christopher Columbus and other non-Indian explorers to Indian land by right of discovery. Nordwall explains to the press that the only difference between his claim and Columbus's is that the Italian explorer "came to conquer a country by force where a peaceful people were living, while I am on a mission of peace and goodwill."

December 22

The Menominee Restoration Act reinstates the Menominees' tribal status.

Twelve years after the termination of the Menominee's tribal status, the Menominee Restoration Act formally recognizes the Menominee as a tribe and reestablishes the Menominee Indian Reservation in Wisconsin. The restoration of the Menominee is largely due to the lobbying efforts of Ada Deer and other members of Determination of the Rights and Unity for Menominee Shareholders (see entry for 1970), a group of Menominee activists who lobbied Congress and spoke out in the press about the disastrous effects Termination has had on the Menominee both economically and culturally. Through the act, the U.S. government acknowledges that Termination was ill conceived and signals its formal abandonment of the policy.

December 28

The Comprehensive Employment and Training Act (CETA) program provides funds for Indian groups.

Congress passes the Comprehensive Employment and Training Act, which offers grants to increase employment for underprivileged Americans. Many Indian groups, which under the law are eligible to apply for CETA grants, acquire CETA funds to help create jobs and finance job training in Indian communities, both on reservations and in cities. CETA will soon become a leading source of money for Indian self-help programs.

1974

Women of All Red Nations (WARN) is founded.

Female activists in the American Indian Movement found the Women of All Red Nations (WARN), an organization dedicated to fighting for the rights of all Indian people. Based on the Rosebud Reservation in South Dakota, WARN will focus on many issues of particular relevance to women and children, such as the forced sterilization of Indian women and the adoption of Indian children by non-Indians. It will also encourage women to seek leadership positions within tribes.

The Canadian prime minister authorizes the Mackenzie Valley Pipeline Inquiry.

As the Canadian government plans to build an oil pipeline in the Mackenzie Valley, Natives in the area challenge that their claims to the valley have never been extinguished by treaty. To investigate their land claims, Prime Minister Pierre Trudeau initiates the Mackenzie Valley Pipeline Inquiry and appoints Justice Thomas Berger to head the investigation. (See also entry for APRIL 15, 1977.)

"I wonder how people in Toronto would react if the people of Old Crow went down to Toronto and said, 'Well, look, we are going to knock down all those skyscrapers and high rises[,] . . . blast a few holes to make lakes for muskrat trapping, and you people are just going to have to move out and stop driving cars and move into cabins.'"

—testimony during the Berger Inquiry Hearings on the Mackenzie Valley Pipeline

The Archaeological Recovery Act is passed.

An amendment to the Reservoir Salvage Act of 1960, the Archaeological Recovery Act sets aside funds to recover or salvage Indian burial grounds and other important archaeological sites endangered by dam construction and other federal projects. The act is the first major piece of legislation that calls for the protection of Indian sites of historical and cultural significance.

The Indian Claims Commission offers compensation for the Black Hills.

Twenty-four years after their case first came before the Indian Claims Commission, the Lakota Sioux receive a favorable decision on their complaint regarding the United States's illegal seizure of the Black Hills in South Dakota, an area sacred to the Lakota (see entry for 1877). The commission determines that the land and the gold mined from the area was worth $17.5 million at the time the Black Hills were appropriated. It also finds that the Lakota are entitled to 5 percent annual interest, since the U.S. actions violated their Fifth Amendment rights.

The victory for the Lakota will be short-lived. The next year, the U.S. Court of Claims will reverse the decision. It will rule that the Indian Claims Commission cannot determine the case, because it had already been heard and dismissed by the U.S. Court of Claims in 1942. Despite this setback, the Lakota will continue their legal battle throughout the 1970s.

February 7

AIM leader Russell Means loses the election for Pine Ridge tribal chairman.

In an election for tribal chairman of the Pine Ridge Reservation, incumbent Dick Wilson defeats Russell Means, a leader of the American Indian Movement (AIM) activists who took over Wounded Knee the previous year to protest Wilson's systematic harassment of Indian traditionalists (see entry for FEBRUARY 28, 1973). In a later investigation of the election, the U.S. Commission on Civil Rights will find that nearly one-third of the votes were "tainted," but the Justice Department will take no action against Wilson.

February 12

The Boldt Decision confirms Northwest Indian fishing rights.

A long series of protests and court battles regarding fishing rights culminates in *United States v. State of Washington*. In the case, many Indian groups challenge the right of the Washington State government to regulate and restrict Indian fishing. These regulations were instituted beginning in the early 20th century to placate non-Indian commercial fishing concerns and sports fishermen. In their argument, the Indians refer to the treaties by which they were forced to cede their lands (see entry for MAY 24 TO JUNE 11, 1855). These documents explicitly stated that the Indian groups retained the right to fish at their "usual and accustomed" fishing areas, whether these were on or off reservations, without interference by the state.

A landmark victory in the battle for Indian fishing rights, the ruling in the case (known as the Boldt Decision, after the presiding judge, George Boldt) states that the Indian groups that signed these treaties have a right to half the catch taken in the state of Washington. It also holds that for conservation purposes the state can limit the overall catch, but it cannot impose rules on Indian fishers regarding their fishing methods.

April 12

The Indian Financing Act provides loans for Indian-run businesses.

With the Indian Financing Act, Congress establishes a fund from which Indians can draw loans to finance business ventures. The law is a response to the difficulty many Indians have encountered borrowing money from banks that refuse to accept as collateral tribal lands held in trust by the government.

May

Mohawk activists occupy Ganienkeh.

Claiming the land belongs to them, a group of Mohawk from the Akwesasne and Kahnawake reservations occupy 612 acres owned by New York State at Eagle Bay, near Moss Lake in the Adirondacks. They rename the land "Ganienkeh," meaning "Land of Flintstone." The occupation begins a lengthy standoff between the activists and local authorities. (See also entry for MAY 13, 1977.)

June

The International Indian Treaty Council is founded.

The First International Indian Treaty Conference results in the formation of the International Indian

"Might does not make right. Sovereign people of varying cultures have the absolute right to live in harmony with Mother Earth so long as they do not infringe upon this same right of other people. The denial of this right to any sovereign people, such as the Native American Indian Nations, must be challenged by truth and action. World concern must focus on all colonial governments to the end that sovereign people everywhere shall live as they choose, in peace with dignity and freedom."

—from the International Indian Treaty Council's "Declaration of Continuing Independence"

Treaty Council. The conference, held on the Standing Rock Reservation in North Dakota, is organized by the American Indian Movement and attended by several thousand Indians from 97 Indian groups from North, Central, and South America. The participants outline IITC's philosophy in "The Declaration of Continuing Independence," which calls on governments throughout the world to recognize and respect the sovereignty of indigenous peoples. (See also entry for JULY 1977.)

June 17

Morton v. Mancari et al. upholds preference to Indian applicants for Bureau of Indian Affairs jobs.

In *Morton v. Mancari et al.,* the legality of the Bureau of Indian Affairs' time-honored policy of giving Indian job applicants preferential treatment is challenged as unconstitutional. A Supreme Court ruling, however, states that this preference does not violate the U.S. Constitution's prohibition on racial discrimination but rather emerges naturally from the federal government's responsibility to allow and encourage Indians to govern themselves. The decision thus implies that because of the unique historical relationship between Indian nations and the United States, Congress may grant preferences to Indians in other areas as well.

Long criticized for its lack of Indian representation, the staff of the BIA will radically change its racial make-up in the wake of *Morton v. Mancari.* By the beginning of the 1980s, more than 75 percent of BIA positions will be staffed by Indians.

July

Canada establishes the Office of Native Claims.

As a result of the Canadian Supreme Court's ruling in *Calder v. Attorney General* (see entry for JANUARY 31, 1973), the Canadian government creates the Office of Native Claims. Like the Indian Claims Commission (see entry for AUGUST 12, 1946) in the United States, the Office of Native Claims will hear Indian land claims cases and offer restitution to Native groups whose ancestral lands were taken from them illegally.

July 22 to August 28

The Ojibwa Warrior Society seizes an Ontario park.

A radical group modeled after the American Indian Movement, the Ojibwa Warrior Society begins a four-week occupation of Anishinabe Park in Kenora, Ontario. The park sits on 14 acres of land that the Canadian Department of Indian Affairs purchased to create a camping area for Indian use. Without the Indians' permission, the government sold the land to the town of Kenora, which developed it as a tourist area. The protest forces town authorities to enter into negotiations with the Ojibway, but it elicits little support from most Canadian Indians, who are uneasy with the Ojibwa Warrior Society's confrontational tactics.

December 22

Congress passes the Hopi-Navajo Land Settlement Act.

A two-million-acre area of the Hopi Indian Reservation is occupied by both the Hopi and the Navajo (Dineh) (see entry for 1962). The two groups, however, have great difficulty jointly managing the land, which leads Congress to pass the Hopi-Navajo Land Settlement Act. The act grants roughly half of the area to the Navajo, with the transfer to take place in 1977. The partitioning of the Joint Use Area calls for the eventual relocation of several hundred Hopi and nearly 5,000 Navajo.

1975

The Council of Energy Resource Tribes (CERT) is created.

To help tribes assert more control over the development of mineral resources on their lands, 26 tribal governments form the Council of Energy Resource Tribes (CERT) in Denver, Colorado. CERT research determines that one-third of all coal and uranium in the United States is found on Indian land. It also reviews the Bureau of Indian Affairs's

(BIA) past efforts to develop these resources and determines that many decisions made by the BIA were based on inaccurate or incomplete information. CERT takes on the goal of providing tribes with the knowledge needed to negotiate leases with energy and power companies for the groups' maximum benefit.

Dennis Banks is convicted of rioting and assault.

A South Dakota court finds American Indian Movement leader Dennis Banks guilty of rioting and assault with a deadly weapon. The charges stem from his participation in a demonstration held in the town of Custer (see entry for FEBRUARY 6, 1973). Banks flees the state before sentencing and becomes a fugitive in Oregon. (See also entries for APRIL 19, 1978, and for SEPTEMBER 13, 1984.)

Passamaquoddy v. Morton holds the United States responsible for lost tribal lands.

In *Passamaquoddy v. Morton,* the Passamaquoddy and Penobscot of Maine bring suit against the secretary of the interior, Robert Morton. They maintain that, even though they are not formally recognized as tribes by the U.S. government, the United States was negligent in allowing their tribal lands to be overrun by whites. The basis of their claim is the Trade and Intercourse Act (see entry for 1790), which forbade the sale of Indian land without the permission of the U.S. government. The Passamaquoddy and Penobscot had lost most of their ancestral lands through a treaty with the Commonwealth of Massachusetts, which purchased the land without authorization from the federal government.

Confirming a lower-court decision, a U.S. Court of Appeals finds in the tribes' favor. In addition to suggesting that the tribes have a claim to much of the land in the state of Maine, the ruling also maintains that the federal government has a responsibility to protect Indian land claims, whether or not the Indians are recognized. (See also entry for OCTOBER 10, 1980.)

United States v. Mazurie addresses tribes' rights to regulate alcohol on reservations.

Tribal police on the Wyoming's Wind River Reservation arrested Robert Mazurie, a non-India, for operating a liquor store on reservation land. Because the tribal council had refused to give him a liquor license, Mazurie was convicted of selling liquor illegally. In *United States v. Mazurie,* Mazurie challenges his conviction by arguing that he had a state liquor license and that his store was located on land he had purchased from a reservation resident and therefore was no longer part of the reservation. The court rules against Mazurie and affirms the right of the Wind River tribal council to set regulations on alcohol within the reservation that apply to Indians and non-Indians alike.

The Northwest Indian Fisheries Commission is founded.

In response to the Boldt Decision (see entry for FEBRUARY 12, 1974), which granted Washington Indians one-half of the fishing catch of area waters, 28 tribes band together to found the Northwest Indian Fisheries Commission. The commission is charged with negotiating the size of the Indians' share of the catch and offering the technical expertise that member tribes need to manage their fishing resources.

The American Indian Film Institute is established.

To promote the work of Native American actors and filmmakers, the American Indian Film Institute is founded by Choctaw Michael Smith in Culver City, California. The institute organizes the first American Indian Film Festival in Seattle, Washington (later festivals are held in San Francisco, California). The presentation of the prestigious American Indian Motion Picture Awards will become an annual event.

January 1

Menominee Warrior Society takes over Wisconsin abbey.

Forty-five activists calling themselves the Menominee Warrior Society occupy an unused 225-acre abbey of the Alexian Brothers Novitiate in Gresham, Wisconsin. The protesters demand that they be permitted to turn the abbey into an Indian health center. They remain in a standoff with the Wisconsin National Guard until February 4. The Alexian Brothers then agree to deed the abbey complex to the Menominee, but in July they will rescind their offer.

January 2

The American Indian Policy Review Commission is established.

Congress authorizes the formation of the American Indian Policy Review Commission to review the

> "Sovereignty means the authority to govern; to exercise those powers necessary to maintain an orderly society[;] . . . the power to enact laws; the power to establish court systems; the power to require people to abide by established laws; the power to tax; the power to grant marriages and divorces; the power to provide for the adoption of children; the power to zone property; the power to regulate hunting and fishing. . . . When we talk about tribal sovereignty, thus, we are saying a very simple but deeply fundamental thing: Indian Tribes are governments."
>
> —from the 1977 report of the American Indian Policy Review Commission

historical and legal factors that have influenced the relationship between Indians and the federal government. The commission is established in part as a response to the protests of Indian activists, particularly the takeover of Wounded Knee (see entry for FEBRUARY 28, 1973). Charged with making recommendations for policy changes "by Indians for Indians," it consists of five Native Americans, three senators, and three congressmen. (See also entry for MAY 17, 1977.)

January 4

Indian Self-Determination and Education Assistance Act redirects funds for Indian education.

By the 1970s, Indian groups increasingly voiced concern that educational funds due to Indian students under the Johnson-O'Malley Act (see entry for APRIL 16, 1934) were being used for general purposes by state-run schools. To address these abuses, Congress passes the Indian Self-Determination and Education Assistance Act. The legislation allows Indian groups to take an unprecedented amount of control over educational programs and other services they receive from the U.S. government. Denouncing the paternalistic policies of the past, the act recognizes that these services will be "responsive to the needs and desires of [Indian] communities" only if Indians themselves are given more say in determining how they are administered.

February 25

Activists take over the Fairchild factory on the Navajo reservation.

American Indian Movement (AIM) members led by John Trudell take over the Fairchild Corporation's electronics plant at Shiprock, New Mexico, on the Navajo Indian Reservation (see entry for SEPTEMBER 6, 1969). The activists are protesting Fairchild's firing of 140 Navajo employees who were attempting to organize a union to demand better wages.

The protest ends peaceably on March 3. Ten days later, the Fairchild Corporation announces that it will close the Shiprock plant because it "couldn't be reasonably assured that future disruptions wouldn't occur." The factory closing will put out of work hundreds of reservation residents and cost AIM much of its support among the Navajo.

June 26

One Indian and two FBI agents die in a Pine Ridge Reservation shoot-out.

On South Dakota's Pine Ridge Reservation, agents of the FBI stake out the Jumping Bull camp, where several fugitives affiliated with the American Indian Movement are rumored to be staying. A firefight breaks out, during which two FBI agents and one Indian activist are killed. The incident is the culmination of months of tension and violence between AIM and the reservation police force. Supervised by tribal chairman Dick Wilson and possibly funded and trained by the FBI, the police were allegedly involved in more than 60 murders of and 350 assaults on reservation residents.

Immediately after the shootings, swarms of FBI agents, determined to find the killers, descend on Pine Ridge. The agents begin arresting hundreds of AIM members, often on dubious charges, thereby escalating the atmosphere of suspicion and hostility throughout the reservation. (See also entries for JULY 16, 1976, and for APRIL 18, 1977.)

July 19

Northwest Territories Natives issue the Dene Declaration.

Calling themselves the Dene Nation, the Indians and Métis of the Northwest Territories assert their sovereignty with the Dene Declaration. The document states, "We the Dene of the N.W.T. insist on the right to be regarded by ourselves and the world as a nation." Minister of Indian Affairs Judd Buchanan dismisses the declaration as "gobbledygook," prompting the Dene to demand his resignation.

November 11

Canada negotiates the James Bay and Northern Quebec Agreement.

In response to Cree, Inuit, and Innu opposition to the construction of the James Bay hydroelectric project (see entry for APRIL 30, 1971), the Canadian government negotiates the James Bay and Northern Quebec Agreement with these groups. The first Native claims settlement in modern Canada, it awards the Cree, Inuit, and Innu $232.5 million and allows them to retain ownership of 2,140 square miles of land surrounding their communities in Quebec. The Natives are also granted hunting and fishing rights in other areas.

1976

The Catawba Pottery Association is founded.

The Catawba form the Catawba Pottery Association to sponsor classes for tribal members in making traditional Catawba pottery, known for its distinctive orange, brown, and black coloring. By giving master potters a chance to instruct a new generation in this 4,000-year-old art, the association will help the Catawba become the only eastern tribe to retain the pottery traditions of ancient ancestors.

January 31

Byron DeSersa is killed by Pine Ridge police.

In a January 17 vote, incumbent Dick Wilson lost his bid for reelection as tribal council president of the Lakota's Pine Ridge Reservation (see entry for FEBRUARY 28, 1973). With his term not officially to end until April, he sends 15 tribal policemen into the new president Al Trimble's hometown of Wanblee. After a four-mile, high-speed chase, the police open fire on a car driven by Byron DeSersa—the son of the editor of a reservation newspaper highly critical of Wilson and the great-grandson of the famous Lakota medicine man Black Elk (see entry for 1932). The car's five passengers manage to flee, but DeSersa, shot in the leg, is left to bleed to death while the policemen look on. Two of the policemen will later serve two years in jail for the murder. Two others accused of the crime will be acquitted after claiming they acted in self-defense, even though no one in DeSersa's car was armed.

February 24

The corpse of American Indian Movement activist Anna Mae Aquash is found.

The badly decomposed body of a young woman is discovered on a ranch near South Dakota's Pine Ridge Reservation. A doctor for the Bureau of Indian Affairs (BIA) concludes that the woman died of exposure, possibly after passing out during a night of heavy drinking. For reasons unclear, the corpse's hands are cut off and shipped to FBI headquarters in Washington, D.C., before the body is buried in an unmarked grave.

In Washington, the fingerprints on the hands allow the BIA to identify the woman as AIM activist Anna Mae Aquash. At the demand of her family, a second autopsy is performed. It reveals that Aquash was shot point-blank at the base of her skull. Many accuse the FBI of murdering Aquash; others suggest that she was killed by AIM members who believed that she was spying on AIM for the FBI.

April 16

United National Indian Tribal Youth is incorporated.

Growing out of programs for Indian youth directed by Cherokee J. R. Cook, United National Indian Tribal Youth (UNITY) is incorporated in Oklahoma as a first step toward becoming a national organization. UNITY's goal is to raise the self-esteem of young Indians by involving them in community service projects and celebrations of Native American heritage.

May 29

The Major Crimes Act is amended.

The Major Crimes Act (see entry for MARCH 3, 1885) established that an Indian who commits a major crime on a reservation will be tried in federal court, rather than tribal court. Congress amends the act to add five new offenses (kidnapping, statutory rape, incest, assault with intent to commit rape, and assault with a deadly weapon) to the list of major crimes cited in the original legislation.

July 16

Bob Robideau and Dino Butler are acquitted of charges in the Pine Ridge shooting.

In Cedar Rapids, Iowa, American Indian Movement members Bob Robideau and Darrelle "Dino" Butler stand trial in the shooting deaths of two FBI agents on the Pine Ridge Reservation (see entry for JUNE 26, 1975). The defendants both admit to shooting at the agents, but their lawyers argue that they did so in self-defense. The defense theory holds that, based on the FBI's thuggish conduct on the reservation, Robideau and Butler were reasonable in fearing for their lives when confronted with armed agents. An all-white jury agrees and acquits the men both of murder and of aiding and abetting murder.

September 16

The Indian Health Care Improvement Act is passed.

Recognizing that the "health status of the Indians is far below that of the general population of the United States," Congress passes the Indian Health Care Improvement Act. The legislation substantially increases federal funding for health facilities, including clinics and hospitals, in Indian communities. In keeping with the policy of Self-determination, the act encourages Indians to participate in their health care programs. One of the most significant provisions establishes special scholarships for Indians for education and training in health care professions.

November

The first Indian National Finals Rodeo is held.

Rodeo fans gather in Albuquerque, New Mexico, to see the first Indian National Finals Rodeo. The rodeo will become an annual event, bringing together the best of the 2,000 contestants who compete in the some 150 regional all-Indian rodeos held throughout North America.

1977

The American Science and Engineering Society is founded.

Andy Anderson, a Mohawk engineer, calls the first meeting of the American Indian Science and Engineering Society in Wind Rock, Arizona. The organization is created in response to the high dropout rate among Native American students and their extreme underrepresentation in the science and engineering fields. To encourage Indian students to study science and engineering and use this knowledge to protect Native American lands and natural resources, ASES will develop a variety of educational programs and establish a substantial scholarship fund. Beginning in 1986, the society will also publish *Winds of Change*, a national magazine focusing on career and educational issues relating to Indians across the United States.

The Columbia River Inter-Tribal Fish Commission is founded.

To protect Indian fishing resources in the Northwest, the Columbia River Inter-Tribal Fish Commission is formed by the Nez Perce, the Yakama, and the tribes of Oregon's Umatilla Reservation and Warm Springs Reservation. The organization will become a leading force in lobbying for Indian fishing rights.

Leslie Marmon Silko's *Ceremony* is published.

Upon the publication of her first novel, *Ceremony*, Laguna Pueblo poet Leslie Marmon Silko is named "the most accomplished Indian writer of her generation" by the *New York Times Book Review*. Like N. Scott Momaday's acclaimed *House Made of Dawn* (see entry for MAY 5, 1969), *Ceremony* tells of a World War II Indian veteran's struggle to readjust to reservation life. With the help of a medicine man, the protagonist, Tayo, finally finds salvation by performing his tribe's ancient ceremonies. Silko's innovative narrative style interweaves Tayo's story with retellings of traditional Pueblo legends.

The Tekakwitha Conference opens membership to Native American Catholics.

The Tekakwitha Conference, founded by non-Indian missionaries (see entry for 1939), is devoted to promoting the interests of Indian Catholics to the authorities of the church. After 38 years of operation, the organization invites Indian Catholics to join its ranks. Its Indian membership will grow quickly: By the early 1980s, more than 3,000 members, the majority Indians, will participate in the Tekakwitha Conference's annual conventions.

April 15

The Berger Report recommends the postponement of the Mackenzie Valley Pipeline.

Prime Minister Pierre Trudeau appointed Justice Thomas Berger to head an inquiry board to investigate Native land claims to the Mackenzie Valley, where the Canadian government intends to build a pipeline (see entry for 1974.). After three years of interviewing Natives of the region, the Berger inquiry issues the results of its study as *Northern Frontier, Northern Homeland*. Informally known as the Berger Report, the published document receives a great deal of media attention and becomes a Canadian best-seller. It recommends that the pipeline's construction be put on hold for 10 years in order to explore Native objections more fully.

April 18

Leonard Peltier is found guilty of murdering two FBI agents.

Extradited from Canada, Leonard Peltier, an American Indian Movement activist, is put on trial for the murder of two FBI agents on Pine Ridge Reservation (see entry for JUNE 26, 1975).

Unlike Bob Robideau and Darrelle "Dino" Butler, who were tried and acquitted of the same crime (see entry for JULY 16, 1976), Peltier is not permitted by the court to argue that he acted in self-defense. The jury finds Peltier guilty of both murders, and he is sentenced to two consecutive life terms.

The verdict will be called into question as charges of misconduct are launched against the prosecution. In the years to come, the Peltier case will become an international cause célèbre, with his many supporters worldwide claiming that he is being held as a political prisoner by the U.S. government. (See also entry for JULY 20, 1979, DECEMBER 15, 2000, and for JANUARY 20, 2001.)

> "I stand before you as a proud man; I feel no guilt! I have done nothing to feel guilty about!.... No, I'm not the guilty one here; I'm not the one who should be called a criminal—white racist America is the criminal for the destruction of our lands and my people; to hide your guilt from the decent human beings in America and around the world, you will sentence me to two consecutive life terms without any hesitation."
>
> —Leonard Peltier on his sentence for the murder of two FBI agents

American Indian Movement activist Leonard Peltier, escorted by police after being deported from Canada in 1976. The next year Peltier was convicted of murdering two FBI agents on the Pine Ridge Reservation. *(CORBIS/Bettmann)*

May 13

The Mohawk end the Adirondack occupation.

For three years, a group of Mohawk have occupied a 600-acre area of the Adirondack Mountains, which they call Ganienkeh (see entry for MAY 1974). In negotiations with the state of New York, the Mohawk finally agree to vacate Ganienkeh in exchange for 5,000 acres of land in Macomb State Park and 700 acres near Altoona, New York.

May 17

The American Indian Policy Review Commission issues a report on federal Indian policy.

Two and a half years after its formation, the American Indian Policy Review Commission (see entry for JANUARY 2, 1975) issues a 923-page report that maintains the government should abandon the assimilationist goals it has long-promoted. It holds that the United States should instead recognize Indian tribes as sovereign political institutions with an inherent right to choose their own form of government. Some specific recommendations in the report will lead to the passage of several important pieces of legislation, including the Indian Child Welfare Act (see entry for NOVEMBER 8, 1978) and the American Indian Religious Freedom Act (see entry for AUGUST 11, 1978). Many more of the report's 200 recommendations, however, will not be acted on by Congress.

June

Inuit Circumpolar Conference (ICC) is founded to protect Inuit rights.

An international contingent of Inuit meet at the first Inuit Circumpolar Conference. The meeting marks the first time Inuit from Alaska, Canada, and Greenland have come together to form a political organization. Among the ICC's goals are to protect the rights of all Inuit, increase Inuit input in political decisions concerning them, and promote self-sufficiency within their communities.

July

The United Nations hosts a conference of indigenous peoples.

Founded by members of the American Indian Movement, the International Indian Treaty Council (IITC) (see entry for JUNE 1974) organizes the 1977 International Non-Governmental Organizations' Conference on Indigenous Peoples of the Americas. The conference is held at the offices of the United Nations in Geneva, Switzerland, and is attended by approximately 100 representatives of indigenous groups from throughout the Western Hemisphere.

Among the participants' recommendations to the UN is the creation of the Working Group on Indigenous Populations. The organization will be created in 1981 to draft a declaration of rights of indigenous peoples throughout the world.

During the conference, the IITC is named a nongovernmental organization (NGO), the first group to be given this designation by the UN. NGO status makes the IITC an official consultant of the Economic and Social Council of the United Nations.

August 15

The Native American Public Broadcasting Consortium is founded.

Located in Lincoln, Nebraska, the Native American Public Broadcasting Consortium is established to fund and produce public television programs about American Indians. The organization also offers to review PBS-produced shows with Native American content for accuracy and begins building a library of Indian-related films and videos.

September

The Alaskan Eskimo Whaling Commission is founded.

In response to a ban placed on subsistence hunting of bowhead whales by the International Whaling Commission, (INC) eight Iñupiat communities in northern Alaska form the Alaskan Eskimo Whaling Commission. The commission is charged with educating the IWC about the bowhead population and their whaling traditions. To convince the IWC that the number of bowheads is far larger than their estimates, the Iñupiat group initiates an ambitious census of the whale population. Their evidence will eventually convince the IWC to replace the ban on whaling with a quota on the number of bowhead that can be hunted.

October 13

The Bureau of Indian Affairs head becomes an assistant secretary.

Since 1832, the head of the Bureau of Indian Affairs has been referred to as a "commissioner." With the appointment of Forrest J. Gerard, President Jimmy Carter symbolically elevates this position by renaming it "assistant secretary," the same title given to the administrators of other agencies in the Department of the Interior.

1978

February to July

Indian activists stage the "Longest Walk" protest.

Reminiscent of the Trail of Broken Treaties (see entry for NOVEMBER 2 TO 8, 1972), a group of Indian activists, led by the American Indian Movement leader Dennis Banks, marches on the "Longest Walk"—a 3,000-mile trek from San Francisco to Washington, D.C.—to draw attention to Indian issues. The protest is in part inspired by the government's removal of Navajo (Dineh) traditionalists from their lands on the Hopi Reservation (see entry for DECEMBER 22, 1974). After the group reaches Washington, the several hundred protesters representing some 90 Indian groups hold a rally near the Washington Monument on July 25. The "Longest Walk" will be AIM's last national protest effort.

"We ask each and every one of you to pray with us for the next four days. We want to meet your community, we want to talk to your people, and we want to change the image that has been portrayed by John Wayne, the media, and the history books. We want to portray the truth. We the Indian people, the Red Man of the Western Hemisphere, are the truth of the Western Hemisphere!"

—activist Clyde Bellecourt, in a speech given in Washington, D.C., during the "Longest Walk" protest

March 6

Oliphant v. Suquamish Indian Tribe determines that tribal courts cannot try non-Indians.

David Oliphant, a non-Indian, assaults a Suquamish police officer and is subsequently arrested by tribal police. The case against him goes before the Supreme Court, which finds that the Suquamish tribal court cannot try Oliphant because he is a non-Indian. The decision challenges the long-assumed right of Indian nations to prosecute all people who commit criminal acts within their borders. The ruling is controversial, not only because it substantially weakens Indian control over reservations, but also because it challenges the very concept of Indian sovereignty.

March 22

United States v. Wheeler establishes that a tribal and federal court can try the same crime.

A man named Wheeler pleads guilty to disorderly conduct and contributing to the delinquency of a minor in Navajo (Dineh) tribal court. After his conviction, he is charged with rape for the same incident by a federal court. In a subsequent lawsuit, *United States v. Wheeler,* Wheeler's lawyers allege that he is being tried twice for the same crime, a violation of the U.S. Constitution prohibition of double jeopardy. When the case is presented before the Supreme Court, the judges rule that because the United States and Indian tribes are separate sovereignties, they may both prosecute an accused criminal for the same crime.

April 17

Navajo (Dineh) protesters occupy oilfields in Aneth, Utah.

A group of Navajo (Dineh) protest the behavior of oil workers hired by four oil companies—Conoco, Phillips, Superior Oil, and Texaco. They claim they have used alcohol on the Navajo reservation and have harassed Navajo women. The protesters also demand that Indians be given preference in hiring.

April 19

The California governor blocks Dennis Banks's extradition.

To escape imprisonment in South Dakota for rioting and assault, American Indian Movement leader Dennis Banks fled first to Oregon and then to California (see entry for 1975). When South Dakota governor Richard F. Kneip requests his extradition, Jerry Brown, the governor of California, refuses, citing the undue hostility toward AIM members in Kneip's state. The California Supreme Court upholds Brown's decision.

May 15

Santa Clara v. Martinez confirms the right of tribes to set criteria for tribal membership.

In *Santa Clara v. Martinez,* the Santa Clara Pueblo are sued by Julia Martinez, a tribal member who wants to will her house to her daughters. The Santa Clara tribal council declares that the children cannot inherit property within the pueblo because their father is a Navajo. Martinez and her supporters counter that the council's definition for tribal membership disregards Pueblo tradition: The policy reflects the European practice of tracing ancestry through the father's line, not the Pueblo custom of tracing it through the mother's.

In the suit, Martinez maintains that the Indian Civil Rights Act (see entry for APRIL 18, 1968) guarantees her daughters equal protection under federal law. In a seven-to-one decision, the Supreme Court, however, concludes that, as sovereign governments, Indian tribes have the right to determine for themselves their own criteria for tribal membership.

Effectively the *Martinez* decision prohibits federal courts from hearing future claims against tribal governments. Critics hold that the Supreme Court is eliminating the best legal means Indian people have of protecting themselves from corrupt tribal governments.

May 20

The Chumash protest natural gas extraction on a burial site.

Twenty-five members of the small Chumash tribe take over Little Cohu Bay near Point Conception, California, to protest a utility company's plan to extract natural gas in the area. The Chumash demand protection of the site, which is the location of ancient burial grounds of the tribe. The utility company agrees to allow six Chumash to oversee the excavation of the site and to provide the tribe access to the area for religious purposes.

May 24

Indian activists are acquitted of a cab driver's murder.

After a long, sensational trial, Paul "Skyhorse" Durant and Richard "Mohawk" Billings are acquitted of the 1974 stabbing death of a Los Angeles cab driver on Camp 13, a campsite affiliated with the American Indian Movement (AIM). AIM members allege that the FBI attempted to frame the two men in order to discredit the Indian rights group.

August 11

The American Indian Religious Freedom Act reinforces Indians' right to practice traditional religions.

A joint resolution of both houses of Congress, the American Indian Religious Freedom Act establishes the protection and preservation of Indian religions as an important goal of federal Indian policy. The resolution is seen as a reversal of past policies that discouraged and sometimes outlawed the practice of Native American religions. The resolution explicitly states that Indians have the inherent right to access sites of religious importance, to the use and possession of sacred objects, and to worship through traditional ceremonies and rites. It does not, however, offer any procedures for enforcing these provisions (see entry for APRIL 19, 1988). (See also entry for 1994.)

September 30

The Indian Claims Commission (ICC) ceases operation.

The Indian Claims Commission (ICC) is disbanded after 32 years of operation (see entry for AUGUST 13, 1946). Charged with resolving all Indian land claims, it heard about 300 cases and awarded Indian groups approximately $800 million in compensation for lost lands. The 66 claims still pending are referred to the U.S. Court of Claims for resolution.

The ICC is judged on some levels a failure, on others a success. The federal government had intended the commission to clear up not only land claims but also satisfy its moral obligations to compensate Indians for the injustices committed against them by the United States. Instead of settling past wrongs, the ICC merely brought more to light, as Indian groups researched tribal histories in preparation for bringing their cases before the commission. Many Indians were disappointed by the ICC, sometimes because it offered inadequate compensation, other times because groups wanted land and justice, not just money. Settlements from the ICC, however, did funnel much-needed funds into tribal governments and communities. Dealing with the commission also taught many Indian leaders about the legal system, allowing them to use other courts more effectively to fight for their rights.

October 1

The Department of the Interior reexamines tribal status criteria.

After more than 400 hearings to gather information, the Department of the Interior puts into effect seven criteria an Indian group must meet to be considered a tribe by the federal government. If acknowledged as a tribe, an Indian group is eligible for certain federal funds and benefits.

The new rules for acknowledgment require that a tribe be "identified from historical times until the present on a substantially continuous basis, as 'American Indian,' or 'Aboriginal.'" A group must also document that it is socially distinct from other tribes and that it has been politically autonomous throughout the course of history.

October 17

The Tribally Controlled Community College Act is passed.

Responding to the lobbying of the American Indian Higher Education Consortium (see entry for 1972), Congress votes to increase federal funds to Indian schools by passing the Tribally Controlled Community College Act. The act helps finance the operation of colleges run by tribal governments as well as elementary and secondary public schools with large numbers of Indian students.

November 1

Congress amends the Indian Education Act.

Concerned that the Indian Education Act (see entry for SPRING 1972) is not being properly implemented, Congress appoints the Advisory Study Group on Indian Education. This group will find that Indian education could be improved by increasing funding and parental involvement, creating educational standards, and raising the number of qualified teachers for Indian students. Congress will respond to its recommendations by passing several amendments to the original act designed to increase Indian participation in education. For example, the amendments tie the funds available to an Indian school to the amount of influence Indians have in decisions affecting the institution.

November 8

Indian Child Welfare Act encourages the adoption of Indian children by Indian adults.

In the best interest of the child, the Indian Child Welfare Act states that Indian children should be adopted by Indian adults whenever possible—a policy that reverses a long-held conviction of non-Indian social service agencies that adopted Indian children are better placed with white families. The act gives preference first to a child's extended family, next to families with the same tribal affiliation as the child, and finally to families of other tribes. It also moves custody hearings regarding Indian children from state to tribal courts and gives tribal governments the authority to settle custody disputes.

1979

The Ohoyo Resource Center is founded.

Choctaw activist Owanah Anderson establishes the Ohoyo Resource Center to improve educational and employment opportunities for Native American women. Founded with the support of the Department of Education, the center sponsors conferences and leadership training. Before closing in 1983, it will also produce the *Ohoyo One Thousand,* a directory of more than 1,000 Indian women working in professional fields, such as business, communications, education, and law.

The Federal Acknowledgment Project is founded.

The Department of the Interior creates the Federal Acknowledgment Project to investigate and rule on applications for tribal status. This new agency (later renamed the Branch of Acknowledgment and Research) is to base its decisions on documentation submitted by groups in support of their contentions that they meet the specific criteria for tribal status established by the department (see entry for OCTOBER 1, 1978). The Federal Acknowledgment Project is also required to publish the "Federal Register," an annual listing of tribes recognized as eligible for federal funds and services by the secretary of the interior.

The Supreme Court affirms Indians' right to use modern fishing methods.

Pressured by non-Indian sports fishermen, the legislatures of Washington, Oregon, and Califor-

nia outlaw large gillnets, which commercial Indian fishermen use to catch large numbers of steelhead trout. The Indian fishermen sue in state court, claiming that these laws violate their tribes' fishing rights as confirmed by treaty (see entry for MAY 24 TO JUNE 11, 1855).

In *Washington v. Washington State Commercial Passenger Fishing Vessel Association,* the Washington state court rules against them on the rationale that gillnets, a 20th-century fishing technology, did not exist when the treaties were made. The Supreme Court, however, reverses this decision. It maintains that the Indians' fishing methods do not affect their right to fish in their traditional areas.

The Makah open a cultural center.

Developed with tribal funds, the Makah Cultural and Research Center opens in the village of Neah Bay in Washington State. The facility houses an exhibit gallery and a laboratory, which preserves more than 80,000 artifacts, including 55,000 collected at the Ozette site (see entry for 1970). The center also manages a highly successful program through which Makah elders instruct preschoolers and kindergartners in the tribe's language.

February 12

The family of American Indian Movement activist John Trudell dies in a fire.

At a demonstration outside the FBI headquarters in Washington, D.C., John Trudell, the national chairman of the American Indian Movement, denounces the federal agency and burns an American flag. Twelve hours later, the house of Trudell's father-in-law on the Duck Valley Reservation in Nevada is engulfed in flames. Killed in the fire are Trudell's wife, three children, and mother-in-law. The FBI investigates and determines the fire was an accident; Trudell accuses his political adversaries of setting the blaze.

> ᓚᓄ
>
> "We are statistics that everyone has heard about, the unemployed, uneducated, alcoholics, welfare recipients. . . . [The American Indian Movement's] functions have been to educate our own people and to try and educate the white Americans as to the fact that we exist today. . . . We are concerned about what is happening to our people now, because, you know, we don't like to be a statistic."
>
> —John Trudell in a 1975 statement on the AIM's purpose

May 29

Mohawk traditionalists take over the Akwesasne police station.

On the Akwesasne reservation, tribal police arrest Loran Thompson, a traditional Mohawk leader, on a minor charge. Outraged by the policemen's actions, other traditionalists demand they resign but the policemen refuse. The traditionalists then take over the tribal police station in protest, prompting the tribal government to request New York State to send troops in to help resolve the conflict. The standoff reflects a long feud between two factions on Akwesasne—one that recognizes only the authority of traditional leaders and one that accepts the leadership of the tribal council supported by the United States. The incident will be diffused when the tribal police force is disbanded in 1981, but the tension on the reservation will continue (see entry for April 24, 1990).

July

A Canadian Native delegation is denied an audience with Elizabeth II.

In an effort to secure recognition of the treaty rights of Natives in the Canadian constitution, a delegation of 300 Natives travels to London and asks to present its case to Queen Elizabeth. The delegation hopes that she, as a member of the monarchy that had been an original party to the treaties, will be persuaded to support their cause and use her influence to make Canadian officials listen to Native demands. The Tory government, however, will not allow the delegation to meet with the Queen.

July 12

Jay Silverheels is honored with a Hollywood "star."

Mohawk actor Jay Silverheels, costar of the *Lone Ranger* television series of the 1950s, becomes the first American Indian to receive a "star" on the Hollywood Walk of Fame. Throughout his career, Silverheels has chosen roles in television shows and films that depict Indians and whites cooperating with one another. He is widely credited with changing public perceptions of Indians by refusing to play the stereotypical savage Indian warrior. (See also entry for 1966.)

July 16

Radioactive material escapes from a Navajo (Dineh) reservation mine.

In one of the largest nuclear accidents in American history, more than 11,000 tons of uranium mining wastes escape from a mine on the Navajo Indian Reservation. Some 100 gallons of polluted water rush through a dam near Church Rock, New Mexico, and contaminate the Rio Puerco. Shortly after the accident, the river is measured as having 7,000 times the acceptable level of radioactivity for drinking water.

July 20

Leonard Peltier attempts a prison escape.

Amidst rumors that he is targeted for assassination, Leonard Peltier escapes with two other inmates from the federal prison in Lompoc, California. A member of the American Indian Movement, Peltier was convicted of murdering two FBI agents on the Pine Ridge Reservation (see entry for APRIL 18, 1977) but has long maintained his innocence. The police soon recapture Peltier and return him to Lompoc. The next year, for his escape attempt, seven years will be added to the two life sentences he is already serving.(See also entry for DECEMBER 15, 2000, and for JANUARY 20, 2001).

October 31

The Archaeological Resources Protection Act regulates excavations on federal lands.

Through the passage of the Archaeological Resources Protection Act, Congress exerts greater control over archaeological excavations on federal lands. It requires excavators to apply for permits before digging at sites and to keep thorough records of their findings. The act is the first federal law designed to prevent the archaeological looting that historically has robbed Indian groups of many of their ancestors' remains, sacred objects, and other artifacts.

Autumn

The first Native American Film and Video Festival is held.

To showcase films and videos by and about American Indians, the Native American Film and Video Festival is held in New York City. The festival will become a biennial event sponsored by the Film and Video Center of the National Museum of the American Indian (see entry for NOVEMBER 28, 1989). The center provides information about Indian productions and film professionals to the mainstream film and video industries.

10

1980 TO THE PRESENT
INTO THE FUTURE

With the election of President Ronald Reagan in 1980, Indians faced a new challenge. Once in office, Reagan almost immediately attempted to slash the funds available to Indian groups. Although some of the most dramatic cuts were blocked, by the mid-1980s, the federal budget for crucial programs to better Indian health and education had been greatly diminished.

The drop in government funds created an increased urgency to find new sources of tribal income. Tribal governments, often against the wishes of their people, considered housing nuclear waste on reservations and allowing mineral companies to strip-mine their lands. Equally controversial was the growing number of gambling parlors established by tribes. Especially after the passage of the 1988 Indian Gaming Regulatory Act, which legalized some forms of gambling on reservations, many Indians groups began to operate casinos, both to increase tribal revenues and to bring jobs to their communities. Although the establishments have met opposition by both Indians and non-Indians, they have helped to revitalize several tribes. Perhaps the most dramatic example is the small Mashantucket Pequot tribe of Connecticut, which uses its annual casino revenues of more than $1 billion to aid poorer Indian groups and to operate the impressive Mashantucket Pequot museum and research center.

Despite these new sources of revenue, according to the 1990 census Indians continued to be the most impoverished minority in the United States. The census, however, also revealed an encouraging trend: The American Indian population was growing, and growing quickly. In 1990, more than two million Americans identified themselves as Indians, up 40 percent from only a decade earlier.

The figure certainly revealed that Indians were far from being the "vanishing race" they were said to be at the century's beginning. But demographic scholars noted that the number probably also reflected a change in attitudes toward "Indianness." People who in the past may have hidden their Indian ancestry for fear of discrimination were now proud to announce their heritage. In some non-Indian circles, fabricating Indian roots had even become fashionable, and in some cases lucrative. Actual Indians naturally grew resentful of Indian impostors, particularly those who made and sold "Indian" art. Responding to Indians' complaints, Congress in 1990 passed a revision of the

Indian Arts and Crafts Act, criminalizing such misrepresentation.

In the last years of the 20th century, many non-Indians adopted a heartfelt (if disconcertingly superficial) respect for Indian peoples and societies. However misguided and inauthentic, popular movies such as *Dances with Wolves* (1990) and *Pocahontas* (1995), and New Age–influenced interpretations of Indian religious beliefs, at least revealed a desire to learn about, rather than suppress or destroy, Indian cultures.

Some recent legislation also reflected this shift. The United States offered new protections for sacred Indian sites with 1990's Native American Grave Protection and Repatriation Act (NAGPR). This landmark law also called for the return to tribes of all Indian remains and artifacts collected from burial grounds that were held in the collections of government agencies. Enforcement of NAGPR has led to the repatriation of thousands of bones and ceremonial objects, as well as sparking a number of new controversies. Five tribal groups in the Northwest, for instance, have used NAGPR to make claims to Kennewick Man, the 9,000-year-old skeleton found along the banks of the Columbia River. Their requests for repatriation of Kennewick Man's remains have pitted them against non-Indian scientists intent on conducting research on the ancient skeleton.

Another pivotal piece of legislation was the National Museum of the American Indian Act, also passed in 1989. This law called for the construction of a new museum on the Mall in Washington, D.C., to promote the appreciation of Indian art and culture. The museum, which is scheduled to open in 2002, and the Cultural Resources Center being built in Scotland, Maryland, will offer display space for the vast collection formerly held by the Museum of the American Indian in New York City. This new showcase has galvanized the already burgeoning market for both contempory and traditional Native American art, helping it to become a $1 billion industry.

Perhaps the most significant event to Indian peoples' of the last years of the twentieth century was Canada's return to Native control of nearly one-fifth of the country's land mass through the formation of the new territory of Nunavut in 1999. Governed by an Inuit-dominated parliament, Nunavut represents an impressive victory for Indian demands for a return to self-government. Yet, it is only one battle of many still being fought by Indians seeking more control over their lives, their lands, and their destinies. And, increasingly, these are battles that both Indians and non-Indians are fighting together. As activist Suzan Shown Harjo wrote on the occasion of the Columbus Quincentennial, "It is necessary and well past time for others to amplify our voices and find their own to tell their neighbors and institutions that 500 years of this history is more than enough and must come to an end."

1980

April 15

Cherokee's Tellico Dam suit is dismissed.

To stop the Tennessee Valley Authority's construction of the Tellico Dam on the Tennessee River, the Eastern Branch of the Cherokee file a lawsuit charging that the dam will flood sites sacred to them and therefore violate their freedom of religion. The U.S. Court of Appeals will dismiss the suit, ruling that the sites are not essential to the Cherokee's religious practices.

June 22

Mohawk nun Kateri Tekakwitha is beatified.

The Catholic Church beatifies Kateri Tekakwitha (see entry for APRIL 17, 1680), the second step toward canonization. Tekakwitha, an early Mohawk convert who was known for her intense piety, is an important symbol to Native American Catholics. Many are involved in the Kateri Tekakwitha Movement, which embraces an integration of Catholicism and Indian religious traditions. (See also entries for 1939 and 1977.)

June 30

The U.S. Supreme Court settles the Sioux's Black Hills case.

Beginning in 1923, the Lakota Sioux have repeatedly attempted to sue the United States for its illegal seizure of the sacred Black Hills (see entry for 1877). The Supreme Court finally gives its decision on the dispute, ruling in favor of the Lakota in the *United States v. Sioux Nation of Indians.* It upholds the Court of Claims's earlier decision to award the Indians $17.5 million plus interest for a total of $106 million (see entry for 1974)—the largest Indian lands–claim settlement to date. Although much of the Lakota population lives in poverty, all tribal groups will decide to reject the award and instead continue to fight for the return of the Black Hills.

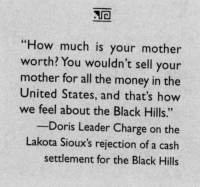

"How much is your mother worth? You wouldn't sell your mother for all the money in the United States, and that's how we feel about the Black Hills."
—Doris Leader Charge on the Lakota Sioux's rejection of a cash settlement for the Black Hills

July 8

The Hopi-Navajo Relocation Act is passed.

Through the Hopi-Navajo Relocation Act, Congress allocates funds to purchase new lands for Navajo families living on the Hopi reservation. An earlier law (see entry for DECEMBER 22, 1974) required the relocation of these families in order to resolve a Hopi-Navajo land dispute dating from the formation of the Hopi Indian Reservation nearly 100 years before (see entry for DECEMBER 16, 1882).

October 10

Maine awards the Penobscot and Passamaquoddy $81 million.

With the Maine Indian Claims Settlement Act, the Penobscot and Passamaquoddy tribes agree to give up their claim to 12.5 million acres of land in the state. The law is the culmination of a protracted legal battle, in which the tribes maintained that Maine had illegally confiscated two-thirds of the state's lands from these Indian groups, in violation of the Trade and Intercourse Act of 1790 (see entry for 1975).

In exchange for relinquishing their land claims, the Penobscot and Passamaquoddy receive a cash payment of $81 million. Part of the award is to be set aside for the purchase of 300,000 acres of land. The act also gives the tribes' reservations the powers

Leaders from the Passamaquoddy and Penobscot tribes (far right) look on as President Jimmy Carter signs the Maine Indian Claims Settlement Act, which granted the tribes $81 million in compensation for land they lost in the late 18th century. *(CORBIS/Bettmann)*

granted municipalities. In the words of the Native American Civil Rights Fund, the settlement was "far and away the greatest Indian victory of its kind in the history of the United States."

November

The Fourth Russell Tribunal brings attention to a Western Shoshone land dispute.

Supported by the Russell Peace Foundation and organized by a group of Dutch activists, the Fourth Russell Tribunal on Rights of the Indians of the Americas is held in Rotterdam, in the Netherlands. The tribunal, composed of international experts, listens to 14 cases of government abuse submitted by Indian groups from throughout the Western Hemisphere.

One case explores complaints of the Western Shoshone that the U.S. government is using lands granted to them by treaty to construct an MX missile system. In addition to the tribes' objections to having an enormous weapons system on their land, they charge that the construction project will sap their water supply. The tribunal brings publicity to the Western Shoshone's plight. Under public pressure, the United States will postpone the MX project.

December 2

The Alaska National Interest Lands Conservation Act is signed into law.

President Jimmy Carter signs the Alaska National Interest Lands Conservation Act, which sets aside one hundred million acres of land in Alaska for national parks and forest lands. The law also gives Native Alaskans the right to gather food in this area.

1981

The Okanagan Tribal Council establishes the En'owkin Centre.

Affiliated with the University of Victoria, the En'owkin Centre is founded in Penticton, British Columbia, by the Okanagan Tribal Council. In addition to offering classes in the Okanagan language and visual arts, this cultural center will later operate Theytus Books, a publishing company focusing on the works of Native writers. It will also establish the International School of Writing, the first Indian-run writing school, with Okanagan novelist Jeannette Armstrong as its director.

Reagan recommends enormous cuts in Indian spending.

In his first budget, President Ronald Reagan proposes cuts in federal funds to Indians amounting to $1 billion—approximately one-third of the total budget for programs benefiting Indian peoples. The Reagan administration also endorses transferring responsibilities for Indian education and resources to state governments. Although Indian leaders and the Senate Subcommittee on Indian Affairs will resist these measures, funding to Indian programs will be slashed by more than $100 million during Reagan's tenure in the White House.

April 4

Activists establish Camp Yellow Thunder in the Black Hills.

In a 20-car caravan, a contingent of Indian activists led by Russell and Bill Means enters the Victoria

Creek Canyon in the Black Hills. There they set up a tent settlement that they call Camp Yellow Thunder. The camp is named after Raymond Yellow Thunder, an Oglala Lakota murdered by a white man in Gordon, Nebraska (see entry for FEBRUARY 1971).

The activists declare that their right to occupy the area dates back to the Treaty of Fort Laramie (see entry for NOVEMBER 7, 1868), which guaranteed the Lakota Sioux "undisturbed use" of the Black Hills, lands sacred to the Lakota people. The protest is meant to draw attention to the Sioux's recent decision to reject a $106 million land claim settlement from the U.S. government for the Black Hills in favor of continuing their fight for the return of the land (see entry for JUNE 30, 1980).

Camp Yellow Thunder will remain in operation for four years. The peaceful protest will compel the federal government to reexamine the Lakota's claims to the Black Hills region.

May 29

Montana v. United States denies the Crow's right to prohibit non-Indian hunting and fishing.

In *Montana v. United States,* the Crow tribe of Montana seeks to stop non-Indians from hunting and fishing within its reservation borders, even on land non-Indians have purchased from the Crow. The Supreme Court, however, rules that the Crow have no tribal jurisdiction over these non-Indians. The court concedes that earlier cases have given tribes authority over non-Indians on their reservations in some matters but maintains that non-Indian hunting and fishing does not "so threaten the Tribe's political and economic security as to justify tribal regulations."

July 1

The *Lakota Times* begins publication.

The *Lakota Times* is founded by editor Tim Giago, an Oglala Sioux, to report the news of the Pine Ridge Reservation in South Dakota. As other reservations request coverage, the weekly newspaper will broaden its focus. In 1992 the *Lakota Times* will be renamed *Indian Country Today,* to reflect its status as one of the leading news sources about Indian affairs nationwide.

September 2

The United Nations condemns Canada's Indian status laws.

Sandra Lovelace, a Maliseet Indian, appears before the Human Rights Commission of the United Nations to protest Canada's laws for determining Indian status. When Lovelace married a non-Indian man, by law she lost her Indian status and was therefore barred from living on a reserve. If she had been a man married to a non-Indian woman, however, she would still have been regarded as an Indian by the Canadian government.

After hearing Lovelace's testimony, the committee agrees that Canada's actions constitute "an unjustifiable denial of her rights" under the United Nations' Covenant on Civil and Political Rights. Although the statement does nothing to change Lovelace's situation, it does bring attention to issue of gender discrimination in the Canadian definition of Indian status.

1982

The National Indian Brotherhood is reorganized as the Assembly of First Nations.

Long the most prominent pan-Indian lobbying group in Canada, the National Indian Brotherhood (see entry for FEBRUARY 1968) is restructured as an assembly of chiefs. With the shift from being an organization of "representatives from regions" to one of "First Nations Government Leaders," the group declares that it will now be known as the Assembly of First Nations.

The U.S. Postal Service issues a Crazy Horse stamp.

As part of its "Great Americans" series, the U.S. Postal Service issues a 13¢ stamp bearing the face of

Crazy Horse, the famous Lakota Sioux war leader who fought at the Battle of Little Bighorn (see entry for JUNE 24 TO 25, 1876). Because Crazy Horse refused to be photographed during his lifetime, the portrait is based on a design by Korczak Ziolkowksi, whose massive Crazy Horse sculpture is being carved into the Black Hills of South Dakota (see entry for MAY 27, 1948).

Congress passes legislation to protect tribal energy resources income.

Largely through the lobbying of the Council of Energy Resource Tribes (see entry for 1975), Congress passes the Federal Oil and Gas Royalty Management Act and the Indian Mining Development Act. The laws are intended to help tribes with energy-rich lands receive fair royalties for oil, natural gas, uranium, and coal. Many tribes were burdened by long-term leases (negotiated by the Bureau of Indian Affairs) that paid them far less than market price, especially after the rise of energy costs during the energy crisis of the 1970s. The act offers provisions for the renegotiation of these contracts, guidance in forging direct relationships between tribes and energy companies, and funds for educating tribal members in managing their natural resources.

A Cherokee prisoner wins the right to wear long hair.

A Cherokee inmate refuses to allow prison authorities to cut his hair, maintaining that wearing his hair long has religious significance for him. In the subsequent case *Gallahan v. Holyfield,* the Supreme Court finds in favor of the prisoner, largely because the prison has not adequately justified its policy of cutting inmates' hair for security reasons.

Peter John Powell's *Sweet Medicine* is published.

An Episcopal missionary dedicated to helping Indian preserve their traditional ways, Peter John Powell is given permission by Cheyenne leaders to research the history of the tribe. The result of his work is *Sweet Medicine,* which chronicles the life of this Cheyenne prophet and records the tribe's religious traditions.

Adopted by both the Northern and Southern Cheyenne, Powell is given the name Stone Forehead, after one of their most revered ancestors.

> "I shall not be with you long now.... Now I am growing old and have lived as long as I want to live. Before I die I have something to tell you. Now, my people, you must not forget what I am telling you today. You must not forget all that I have told you and taught you. When I am dead, you must come together often, and talk about these things. When you do this, always call my name."
>
> —the words of Cheyenne prophet Sweet Medicine, as recorded by Peter John Powell

April 17

Canada's Constitution Act affirms "existing aboriginal and treaty rights."

With the signing of the Constitution Act, a new Canadian constitution replaces the British North America Act (see entry for JULY 1, 1867) as the supreme law of Canada. In section 35 of the new constitution, the Natives of Canada are defined as the "Indian, Inuit and Métis people," thus recognizing both the Inuit and the Métis as culturally distinct aboriginal peoples.

The new constitution also states that "existing aboriginal and treaty rights" of Canada's Natives are "recognized and confirmed." The vague wording of this confirmation is highly criticized by Native leaders, who are also angry that they were excluded from the drafting of the revised constitution. To answer their concerns, the prime minister agrees to meet with aboriginal leaders to discuss and define Native rights, in a series of annual conferences.

October 24 to 26

The Tlingit commemorate the bombing of Angoon.

The Tlingit hold a series of ceremonies to commemorate the centennial of the U.S. Navy's destruction of the village of Angoon (see entry for OCTOBER 24 TO 26, 1882). During the commemoration, totem poles are erected in the center of Angoon to the memory of the six children who were killed in the unwarranted attack.

1983

Yakama activist David Sohappy Sr. is convicted of violating fishing regulations.

Working undercover, federal agents buy 317 fish caught out of season from David Sohappy Sr. Long active in the campaign for Indian fishing rights, Sohappy is best known for using the courts to challenge regulations on fishing in the Columbia River in the case *Sohappy v. Smith.* After he is convicted, Sohappy is sentenced to serve 18 months in prison.

The Office of Intergovernmental Affairs is charged with dealings with Indians.

President Ronald Reagan transfers responsibility for the White House's dealings with Indians from the Office of Liaison to the Office of Intergovernmental Affairs. Through the change, the Reagan administration implies a shift in attitude toward Indian tribes: Instead of considering them as minority groups, the White House will treat them as sovereign nations.

The Samish erect the "Maiden of Deception."

In 1979 the Samish, a small group of Coast Salish Indians in northwestern Washington State, filed a petition for federal recognition as a tribe. When, four years later, the government decides to deny them recognition, the Samish protest the decision

by commissioning a sculpture of the "maiden of deception," an important figure in Samish legends. To show their solidarity despite their "unrecognized" status, they erect the statue by holding a traditional potlatch feast, with neighboring tribes as their guests.

The *Fool's Crow v. Gullett* court decision threatens the sacred site of Bear Butte.

When the federal government made plans to build roads and parking lots in the Bear Butte area of South Dakota, several Plains tribes object in federal court. They hold that, by facilitating non-Indian tourism in the region, the government's projects will destroy a site the Indians regard as sacred. In *Fool's Crow v. Gullett,* the tribes claim that the government is violating their First Amendment rights to religious freedom, but the court finds for the government, allowing it to proceed with the proposed construction.

January 14

The Indian Tribal Governmental Tax Status Act is passed.

Through the Indian Tribal Governmental Tax Status Act, Congress confirms that tribes are not taxable entities. The act also gives tribes many of the tax benefits available to state and local governments. For instance, it allows tribes to finance commercial and governmental ventures by issuing tax-exempt bonds.

January 18

Jim Thorpe's Olympic records and medals are restored.

The International Olympic Committee (IOC) reinstates Jim Thorpe's amateur status 30 years after his death and gives his children duplicates of the two gold medals he won in the Olympics (see entry for SUMMER 1912). The IOC's reversal is largely due to the urging of the Jim Thorpe Foundation, led by Thorpe's daughters Grace and Charlotte, and the U.S. Olympic Committee. A Sac and Fox

Indian, Thorpe had been stripped of his medals when it was discovered that he had played semiprofessional baseball in the summer of 1910 (see entry for JANUARY 1913).

January 19

James Watts brands reservations as "socialist."

In a television interview, Secretary of the Interior James Watts states, "If you want an example of the failures of socialism, don't go to Russia. Come to America, and see the American Indian reservations." Watts goes on to say that reservation "socialism" has led to "alcoholism, unemployment, venereal disease, and drug addiction." Indian leaders across the United States denounce the secretary's equation of tribalism with socialism and his grossly negative characterization of reservation life.

January 25

The Voigt Decision affirms Ojibway fishing and hunting rights.

A U.S. Court of Appeals rules in *Lac Courte Oreilles Band of Lake Superior Chippewa Indians v. Voigt* (also known as the Voigt decision) that the Ojibway of Wisconsin have a right to fish, hunt, and gather wild foods in their former homeland, even though the area was ceded to the United States by treaty. The decision will inspire an Ojibway movement to defend their treaty rights, breeding increasing tension between Indians and non-Indians in Wisconsin.

February 27

KILI opens as a radio station serving the Lakota Sioux.

On the 10th anniversary of the takeover of Wounded Knee (see entry to FEBRUARY 28, 1973), public radio station KILI begins broadcasting in Porcupine, South Dakota. Managed by Dale Means, the brother of American Indian Movement leader Russell Means, the station features local programs, high school reports, and tribal news in both English and Lakota. Reaching more than 22,000 Lakota Sioux throughout the state, the enterprise is conceived as a relatively inexpensive way of disseminating information from an Indian perspective.

May 10

Micmac prisoner Donald Marshall is exonerated.

The Supreme Court of Nova Scotia acquits Donald Marshall, a Micmac who has served 11 years in prison for a murder he did not commit. The case brings attention to the inequities of the Canadian justice system, which is three times more likely to imprison a Native than a non-Native accused of a crime.

June 13

The Mescalero Apache retain control over reservation hunting and fishing.

The Mescalero Apache and the state of New Mexico dispute which party has the right to regulate non-Indian hunting and fishing on the tribe's reservation. The matter is settled by the Supreme Court in *New Mexico v. Mescalero Apache Tribe*. The court holds that because the tribe has invested heavily in developing the reservations' hunting and fishing resources, it may dictate how they are used by Indians and non-Indians alike.

July 15

The Supreme Court allows Indian water rights disputes to be heard in state courts.

In *Arizona et al. v. San Carlos Apache Tribe,* the Supreme Court backs away from the stance on Indian water rights it set in *Winters v. United States* (see entry for 1908). Its decision in the *Winters* case stated that Indians had a right to their reservations' water sources. In *Arizona,* however, the Court finds that tribes can be forced to settle disputes with non-Indians over water rights in state courts rather than in federal courts. The ruling threatens Indian water rights because state courts are far less sympathetic to the position of tribes.

September

The Alaska Native Review Commission is formed.

To investigate the impact of the Alaska Native Claims Settlement Act (see entry for DECEMBER 18, 1971), Inuit activists establish the Alaska Native Review Commission. The commission begins holding hearings at 62 villages throughout Alaska. The transcribed testimony of nearly 15,000 Natives will eventually be collected into 98 volumes (see entry for SEPTEMBER 1985).

October 1

The American Indian Registry for the Performing Arts is founded.

In Los Angeles, the American Indian Registry for the Performing Arts is established to help Indians find work as actors, directors, producers, and technical staff in film and television productions. The organization also works to promote the casting of Indians as Indian characters and to improve the accuracy of representations of Native Americans in movies and television.

1984

Ponca Indian David Pensoneau becomes the Oklahoma Chess Champion.

At 25, David Pensoneau, a member of the Ponca tribe, wins the Oklahoma Chess Championship Tournament. Pensoneau started entering tournaments when he was 14, with an eye toward becoming a U.S. Chess Federation National Master, a goal he will reach later in the year. As a master, Pensoneau will become a devoted chess teacher to young Indians.

The Native American Journalists Association (NAJA) is founded.

Indian journalists working in print, radio, and television establish the Native American Journalists Association (NAJA) in Minneapolis, Minnesota.

The association seeks to promote the exchange of ideas among Indian journalists and strengthen relations between the Indian press and non-Indian public. NAJA also encourages young Indians to pursue careers in journalism by offering financial assistance for college and information about jobs and internships, in its newsletter *Medium Rare*.

Louise Erdrich's *Love Medicine* is published.

Chippewa fiction writer and poet Louise Erdrich publishes her first novel, *Love Medicine,* to great acclaim. Through 14 self-contained stories, each narrated by a different character, the work tells the story of several Chippewa families living on the Turtle Mountain Reservation between 1934 and 1983. In addition to appearing on several best-seller lists, *Love Medicine* also receives the prestigious National Book Critics Circle Award and *Los Angeles Times* Book Prize.

"People in [American Indian] families make everything into a story.... People just sit and the stories start coming, one after another. I suppose that when you grow up constantly hearing the stories rise, break, and fall, it gets into you somehow."

—novelist and poet Louise Erdrich, on the inspiration for her work

The Great Lakes Indian Fish and Wildlife Commission is formed.

Founded by activist Thomas Maulsen, the Great Lakes Indian Fish and Wildlife Commission (GLIFWC) organizes the Ojibway of Wisconsin so that they can better exercise their treaty rights to fish and hunt in their former homeland. The GLIFWC, based on the Bad River Reservation, also offers Ojibway bands information and technological expertise to help them manage their resources.

April 7

Eastern and Western Cherokee meet in a joint council.

Leaders of the two branches of the Cherokee—those in Oklahoma and those in North Carolina and Tennessee—come together in Red Clay, Tennessee, to hold the first joint council since 1838. In that year, the majority of the Cherokee were forced to journey on the tragic Trail of Tears to Indian Territory (see entry for MAY 1838), while a minority, hiding in the hills from white authorities, remained in their southeastern homeland. Approximately 10,000 Cherokee gather in Red Clay to celebrate the reunion of the tribe.

June 6

The Senate establishes a permanent committee on Indian affairs.

By Senate vote, the Senate Select Committee on Indian Affairs becomes a permanent organization. Charged with studying Indian issues and developing new federal Indian policy, the committee was first established in 1820 but disbanded after World War II, only to be reestablished in 1977 as a response to the Indian activism of the late 1960s and early 1970s.

Summer

Indian athletes participate in the "Longest Run."

Ojibway activist Dennis Banks, while living as a fugitive on the Onondaga Reservation in New York State (see entry for SEPTEMBER 13, 1984), organizes the Jim Thorpe Longest Run. During this event, teams of Indian runners run a relay from the reservation to Los Angeles, California, the site of the summer Olympic Games. At the Olympics, the Indians hold a powwow to honor Jim Thorpe, the great Sac and Fox athlete who won gold medals for the decathlon and pentathlon at the Olympics in Stockholm, Sweden (see entry for SUMMER 1912).

September 13

Activist Dennis Banks surrenders to the South Dakota police.

Stating that he wants to "get on with his life," American Indian Movement (AIM) leader Dennis Banks turns himself in to state and local law enforcement officers in South Dakota. Banks was convicted on riot and assault charges stemming from his involvement in AIM protest outside the courthouse in the town of Custer (see entry for FEBRUARY 6, 1973). To avoid a jail term, he first went underground and later moved to California, where he was given amnesty by Governor Jerry Brown (see entry for APRIL 19, 1978). When Brown left office, the Onondaga Reservation in New York offered the activist sanctuary before he decided to surrender to authorities.

On October 3, Banks is sentenced to two concurrent terms of three years in prison. Released after serving 18 months, he will move to South Dakota's Pine Ridge Reservation, where he will work as a drug and alcohol counselor.

September 23

Lawsuit forces a newspaper to apologize for publishing photographs of a Pueblo dance.

Ignoring the Pueblo's ban on photographing their religious observances, a Santa Fe newspaper, the New Mexican, prints two photographs taken from a low-flying plane of a ceremonial dance performed at Santa Domingo Pueblo. The editors of the New Mexican apologize to the Santa Domingo community only after its leaders threaten to file a $3.5 million lawsuit against the newspaper.

November

Navajo (Dineh) weavers form the Ramah Navajo Weavers Association.

Founded by 17 women on the Ramah Navajo Reservation, the Ramah Navajo Weavers Association is a cooperative dedicated to combining modern business practices with the 19th-century craft of Navajo (Dineh) textile-making. Through the association, the women intend to market their rugs and other textiles to customers directly, thus cutting out the non-Indian dealers and traders who previously have reaped the largest portion of the profits from sales of their works.

1985

Northwest Indians agree to the Pacific Salmon Treaty.

The governments of the United States, Canada, and several Northwest Indian groups negotiate the Pacific Salmon Treaty. The agreement is a response to the dwindling numbers of salmon in the waters of the Pacific Northwest. The salmon population is threatened by increasing commercial and recreational fishing in the area. All parties in the treaty agree to create a commission to oversee efforts to conserve and manage their shared salmon resources.

Junípero Serra is declared venerable over Indian objections.

The Catholic Church venerates Junipero Serra, the Franciscan priest who pioneered the mission system in California (see entry for 1769). The veneration was opposed by many California Indians and such groups as the Tekakwitha Conference (see entry for 1939) and the American Indian Historical Society (see entry for 1964). They charge that Serra advocated seizing Indian land, placing Indians in virtual slavery, suppressing their traditional religions, and converting them to Catholicism by force. Ignoring these continuing objections, the church in 1988 will declare Serra beatified, the second of the three steps toward canonization.

The Canadian Native Arts Foundation is founded.

Mohawk John Kim Bell, the first Indian to become a professional symphony conductor, establishes the Canadian Native Arts Foundation when, following an appearance in a 1983 television documentary, he is inundated with requests from Indian parents ask-

ing how their children can obtain training in the arts. The foundation, which grants college scholarships to Indian students, is financed through fund-raising performances of Native talent.

The Indigenous Women's Network (IWN) is formed.

Organized by Oneida Ingrid Washinawakatak, a coalition of American Indian women comes together to create the Indigenous Women's Network (IWN). The nonprofit organization's goals are the revitalization of Indian languages, the protection of religious and cultural practices, environmental conservation, and the return of Indian land to Indian control. The IWN takes the stance that problems facing contemporary indigenous women around the world are best solved by reviving and applying traditional values and practices.

February 20

The Supreme Court reverses the Dann decision.

In *United States v. Dann*, the Western Shoshone Dann family, led by sisters Mary and Carrie, brought suit against the United States, because the government refused to allow the Danns to use their traditional grazing land near Beowawe, Nevada. The United States claimed it had gained possession of the land as a result of an Indian Claims Court settlement with the Western Shoshone (see entry for 1962). The Danns, however, maintained that they had never agreed to extinguish their land title. A federal court found in favor of the Danns, but the Supreme Court now reverses its decision. It holds that because the Western Shoshone as a group accepted the settlement, the Danns no longer own the lands they occupy.

March 4

The Supreme Court allows the Oneida to sue New York State.

In *County of Oneida v. Oneida Nation*, the Oneida Nation argues that the state of New York violated the Trade and Intercourse Act (see entry for 1790) by seizing 100,000 acres of Oneida territory in 1795 without federal approval. The Supreme Court agrees and further finds that there is no statute of limitations to prevent the Oneida from pursuing their land claims in court. The landmark decision will open the door for eastern Indian groups to sue for lands taken from them in the 18th and 19th centuries.

August to September

The Wind River Reservation suffers a rash of suicides.

Ranging in age from 18 to 25, nine young men— eight Arapaho and one Shoshone—kill themselves on the Wind River Reservation in central Wyoming. The deaths are attributed to poverty, alcoholism, and an overwhelming sense of hopelessness among the reservation's young. To end the suicides, elders call the 5,000 Wind River residents together to perform the Paint Ceremony, a powerful cleansing ritual that was last held in 1918 to stem a lethal flu epidemic.

September

Alaska Native Review Commission issues its report on Native land issues.

Formed to study the effects of the Alaska Native Claims Settlement Act, (ANCSA) the Alaska Native Review Commission (see entry for SEPTEMBER 1983) summarizes its findings in *Village Journey*. Based on the testimony of approximately 15,000 Natives, the report records their concerns about maintaining control over their lands, protecting their natural resources, and preserving their culture. In the commission's analysis of their comments, it finds fault with the ANCSA for forming corporations as the legal owners of the 44 million acres the act awarded to Natives (see entry for DECEMBER 18, 1971). It recommends that the land title be transferred to tribal governments, so that land and water use can be regulated in a way more in keeping with traditional beliefs and customs.

December 14

Wilma Mankiller becomes the first female principal chief of the Cherokee.

In 1983 activist and administrator Wilma Mankiller became the first woman elected deputy chief, the second-highest position in the Cherokee tribal government. Two years later, she makes history again when she becomes the first female principal chief. The post was held by Ross Swimmer, who resigns when he is appointed the assistant secretary of the Bureau of Indian Affairs.

Although initially greeted with skepticism by more conservative Cherokee, Mankiller will prove to be a highly popular chief. She will be reelected in 1987 and 1991, winning the latter election with 82 percent of the vote.

"With all of the progressive work we do in economic development, protection of tribal rights and in running a very complex organization, we must not forget who we are. We must pay attention to the protection and preservation of tribal culture. . . . In the past, promotion of tribal culture has been viewed as a function of the community and family, not of tribal government. But we've reached a point where we need to assume a leadership role. We need to explore what we as a government can do to promote and protect our culture."

—Wilma Mankiller at her 1987 inaugural as principal chief of the Cherokee

1986

The Hopi prohibit non-Indians from viewing the Snake Dance.

The Snake Dance is an ancient ceremony of the Hopi performed to bring prayers for rain to the underworld. At the end of the dance, members of the Snake clan dance with washed snakes in their mouths as members of the Antelope clan whip the snakes with eagle feathers to keep them from biting the dancers. This spectacle, widely recorded in anthropological literature, so intrigues non-Indian tourists that the dance becomes the most photographed Indian ceremony. The visitors, however, are not always respectful of religious ritual. Annoyed by their interruptions and inappropriate behavior, the Hopi decide to ban all non-Indian spectators from Snake Dance ceremonies.

The Pikuni Traditionalists Association is formed to protect Blackfeet religious rites.

Seven Blackfeet leaders organize the Pikuni Traditionalists Association in response to the U.S. Forestry Service's plans to allow oil and gas drilling near Badger–Two Medicine, a sacred site of enormous religious importance to the tribe. The Blackfeet ceded the area to the United States in 1896, but in the treaty they retained the right to use Badger–Two Medicine for ceremonies.

United States v. Dion upholds the Eagle Protection Act.

In *United States v. Dion,* Dwight Dion Sr., a Nakota Sioux, sues the U.S. government after he is convicted of violating the Eagle Protection Act (see entry for 1940). The law forbade the killing of endangered species of eagles but was amended in 1962 to allow Indians who needed eagle feathers for ritual use to obtain a special eagle hunting license from the secretary of the interior. Dion was found guilty of killing four bald eagles because he did not have such a license.

In his suit, Dion argues that his right to hunt bald eagles without a license is protected by the First Amendment, the Indian Civil Rights Act (see entry for APRIL 18, 1968), and the Yankton Sioux Treaty of 1858. In a controversial decision that angers many advocates of Indian religious freedom, the Supreme Court upholds his conviction and maintains that the Eagle Protection Act supersedes the provisions of the earlier treaty.

The U.S. Civil Rights Commission studies tribal courts.

The U.S. Civil Rights Commission launches an investigation into the implementation of the Indian Civil Rights Act (see entry for APRIL 18, 1968) in the tribal court system. In a report to Congress, the commission discusses complaints that tribal officials have interfered with or disregarded the decisions of tribal court judges. The report attributes these problems to the inadequate funds available to tribal courts.

Paula Gunn Allen's *Sacred Hoop* is published.

In *The Sacred Hoop: Recovering the Feminine in American Indian Traditions,* scholar and novelist Paula Gunn Allen examines the central role of women in tribal traditions and their long-ignored significance in Indians' cultural and literary history. The essay collection will have a great influence on the teaching of Native American cultures and literatures.

October

The Tunica-Biloxi are awarded the Tunica Treasure.

In the late 1960s, a non-Indian treasure hunter dug up an Indian graveyard in lands in Louisiana that were occupied by the Tunica between 1731 and 1764. He unearthed an enormous collection of artifacts made by the 18th-century Tunica or obtained through trade with the French and other Indian groups. Nicknamed the Tunica Treasure, the collection becomes the focus of a legal battle, as the Tunica-Biloxi demand that they are the rightful owners of their ancestors' goods. A U.S. Court of Appeals affirms a lower-court ruling that awarded the Tunica Treasure to the tribe.

November 19

The Native American Vietnam Veterans Memorial is dedicated.

A plaque placed near the grave site of World War II hero Ira Hayes (see entries for FEBRUARY 24, 1945, and for JANUARY 23, 1955) is dedicated as the first national memorial for Native American veterans. The two-by-three-foot bronze slab is engraved with the words, "Dedicated To Our Indian Warriors and Their Brothers Who Have Served Us So Well—The Vietnam Era Veterans—We Are Honored To Remember You—The Indigenous People of America." Designed and cast by Crow Indian Bob Kelly, the plaque was originally donated to the Bureau of Indian Affairs in 1979. Only after seven years of pressure from Indian veterans groups does the Arlington National Cemetery finally agree to establish the memorial.

1987

The American Indian Dance Theater is founded.

To provide a showcase for Indian dance, theater producer Barbara Schwei and Kiowa playwright and theater professor Hanay Geiogamah organize the American Indian Dance Theater. Representing many tribes, the company's dancers will introduce traditional dances as well as powwow "fancy" dancing to non-Indian audiences by touring throughout the United States and abroad. The troupe will also be the subject of two PBS television specials.

Wings of America is established.

The Full Moon Foundation of Santa Fe, New Mexico, founds Wings of America. The organization sends teams of athletes to reservations in the West and Midwest to conduct running camps for Indian children and teenagers. The goal of the camps is to resurrect Indian running traditions and teach young Indians about health and fitness. Wings of America also sponsors regional teams to attend national championship track meets.

Congress considers opening an Arctic refuge to oil companies.

The Reagan administration lends its support to legislation that would open up the coastal plain of the Arctic National Wildlife Refuge to oil drilling. Created in the 1950s, the 20-million acre refuge is one of the largest protected wilderness areas in the United States. It is also the home of the Gwich'in people, who have lived in northeastern Alaska for approximately 1,200 years. Like their ancestors, they survive on subsistence hunting of a great caribou herd. The area slated for oil development includes the grounds where the caribou give birth and raise most of their calves.

Fearing that oil drilling would destroy these grounds and thus decimate the caribou herd, the Gwich'in form the Gwich'in Steering Committee to publicize their concerns worldwide. Despite their efforts, the proposed legislation will be close to passing when the *Exxon Valdez* disaster (see entry for MARCH 24, 1989) temporary deflates congressional enthusiasm for further oil development in Alaska. (See also entry for 1995.)

January 5

The *National Native News* is first broadcast.

Produced by the Alaska Public Radio Network, the *National Native News* becomes the first daily radio program to focus on news concerning Native Americans. Originally broadcast primarily in Alaska, the news service will eventually be used by more than 150 public and tribal radio stations throughout the United States.

February 3

The Alaska Native Claims Settlement Act is amended.

The Alaska Native Claims Settlement Act (ANCSA) (see entry for DECEMBER 18, 1971) is amended to satisfy the demands of many Native groups. Originally, the ANCSA called for the establishment of corporations to manage property communally owned by Alaska Natives, who then held the shares in these corporations. The amendment permits shareholders to vote whether to offer new shares to Native children born after 1971, to give additional dividends to elderly shareholders, and to extend restrictions on the sale of shares.

February 25

California v. Cabazon Band allows for unregulated Indian gaming houses.

In *California v. Cabazon Band of Mission Indians,* the state of California takes the Cabazon band of Indians to court for operating bingo and poker games whose prizes exceed the $250-per-game limit allowed by California gaming regulations. Upholding a lower-court ruling, the Supreme Court finds that California cannot prohibit or regulate these forms of gambling on Indian reservations because it allows them on non-Indian lands. It could, however, prohibit a form of gambling on reservations if it were also prohibited elsewhere in the state.

The decision establishes that Indian groups throughout the United States can operate unregulated gaming enterprises as long as the types of gambling they offer customers are legal in their states. This clarification of gambling law leads many Indian tribes to consider opening casino and gambling parlors to bolster their tribal income.

April 30

The Canadian government proposes the Meech Lake Accord.

At Meech Lake, Quebec, Prime Minister Brian Mulroney and 10 provincial premiers meet to amend Canada's Constitution Act (see entry for APRIL 17, 1982). The meeting results in a proposal called the Meech Lake Accord, which recognizes French-speaking Quebec as a "distinct society." The accord infuriates Native leaders. They resent the willingness of Canadian officials to grant a group of citizens of European descent the special status that Canada's aboriginal peoples have long been denied. Despite their protests, the accord is sent on to the provincial legislatures for ratification (see entry for JUNE 23, 1990).

June

The first Red Earth Festival is held in Oklahoma City.

Thousands attend the three-day Red Earth Festival, a celebration of Indian cultures sponsored by the Oklahoma Department of Tourism. The festival—which includes dance performances, art shows, an Indian powwow, and a parade through the center of Oklahoma City—will become an annual event that attracts non-Indian tourists from around the world.

October 8

Seminole leader is acquitted of killing an endangered panther.

Seminole councilman James Billie is tried for violating the Endangered Species Act after shooting a panther of a rare Florida species. Billie is acquitted after he claims that the Seminole's 1847 treaty with the U.S. government gave him the right to hunt in their lands. The jury also questions whether Billie knew the animal was a panther before he fired his gun.

"We have frequently been unconscious and insensitive and not come to your aid when you have been victimized by unjust Federal policies and practices. In many other circumstances we reflected the rampant racism and prejudice of the dominant culture with which we too willingly identified. During this 200th Anniversary year of the United States Constitution we, as leaders of our churches in the Pacific Northwest, extend our apology. We ask for your forgiveness and blessing."

—from the "Thanksgiving Day Proclamation" to northwestern American Indians

November 21

Church leaders apologize to northwestern Indians.

In a meeting at an Indian burial site outside of Seattle, Washington, Christian leaders from 1,800 congregations and nine denominations apologize to representatives from 36 northwestern tribes for the church's historical attempts to destroy Indian religions. The clergy involved issue a document, known as the Thanksgiving Day Proclamation, in which they also vow to defend Indian religious traditions and to help Indians recover sacred objects and protect sacred sites.

1988

Studies show Canadian Inuit suffer high levels of PCB contamination.

Canadian researchers discover that the milk of Inuit mothers in the Hudson Bay region contains more than twice the amount of the toxic chemical PCB (polychlorinated biphenyl) considered safe by the Canadian government. The Inuit have been exposed to the carcinogen by eating fish contaminated by PCBs emitted into the atmosphere in warmer regions to the south. PCBs were also dumped into the Arctic by military installations.

January 9

The offices of *Akwesasne Notes* are bombed.

Amidst disputes among various Mohawk factions on the Akwesasne reservation in New York State, a firebomb destroys the Nation House, the building that houses the offices of *Akwesasne Notes* (see entry for 1968). The most widely read Indian-operated newspaper, *Akwesasne Notes* has reported on indigenous resistance movements throughout North and South America for 20 years. In its first issue after resuming publication, the paper condemns the rebel faction suspected of the bombing.

"With the gambling, the cigarette smuggling, the violence[,] ... it is understandable why those criminal elements amongst us are opposed to a free press disseminating information about the illegal and immoral activities around us.... They almost succeeded in putting us out of business[,] ... but we will survive."

—from an *Akwesasne Notes* editorial following the firebombing of the newspaper's office

February

The Lubicon protest Glenbow Museum exhibit.

The Indians of the Lubicon Lake band protest against *The Spirit Sings,* an exhibition at the Glenbow Museum in Calgary, Alberta, created to coincide with the Calgary Winter Olympics. One of the show's corporate sponsors is involved in commercial enterprises on lands claimed by the Lubicon. In the 1930s, the Canadian government promised the band's traditional homeland would be set aside for them as a reserve, but it allowed non-Indians to overrun the area after oil and mineral deposits were discovered there.

February 1

Two Tuscarora take over a newspaper office.

Two Tuscarora Indians, Eddie Hatcher and Timothy Jacobs, hold 17 people hostage for 10 hours in the office of the *Robesonian,* a newspaper serving

Lumberton, North Carolina, in the center of Lumbee Indian territory. The men claim to have uncovered a drug ring involving several prominent people in the town and demand that the paper investigate injustices committed by local police to Indians and African Americans in the area. Several hostages later express their sympathy for their captors and their cause. In another show of support, an editorial in the *Robesonian* refers to Hatcher and Jacobs as "our conscience."

March

Native leader J. J. Harper is killed by non-Indian policemen.

J. J. Harper, the executive director of the Island Lake Tribal Council in northeastern Manitoba, is shot to death by policeman Robert Cross, who is pursuing two Indian youths suspected of stealing a car. Although Cross maintains that his gun went off accidentally, the shooting prompts the provincial government to launch a sweeping inquiry into the treatment of Natives by the Manitoba justice system.

March 26

Lumbee superior court judge candidate Julian Pierce is murdered.

Lumbee attorney Julian Pierce is shot to death at point-blank range at his home in Wakulla, North Carolina. Within four days, the police investigation concludes that Pierce was murdered in a domestic dispute by the boyfriend of his fiancée's daughter, who then killed himself. The speedy findings breed anger and suspicion among the Lumbee, who strongly supported Pierce in his campaign for a superior court judgeship created the previous year by the North Carolina legislature to provide better representation for Lumbee County's Indian and African-American populations. Another candidate for the position is Joe Freeman Britt, the white district attorney, in charge of the prosecution of the Pierce case.

April 19

The Supreme Court rules against the preservation of sacred sites on federal land.

Representatives of the Yurok, Karok, and Tolowa Indians formed the Northwest Indian Cemetery Protective Association to protest the proposed construction of a road through national forest lands in northern California. The association maintained that traffic along the road will disrupt the religious practices their tribal members perform at sacred sites within the forest. In the American Indian Religious Freedom Act (AIRFA) (see entry for AUGUST 11, 1978) the federal government resolved to protect and preserve Indian religions, but the U.S. Forest Service decided to build the road anyway, to improve access to timber resources and recreational areas.

In a subsequent suit filed by the association—*Lyng v. Northwest Indian Cemeteries Assn.*—federal and appellate courts prohibited the road's construction, maintaining that the negative impact the road will have on the tribes' religious freedom outweighed the benefits it would provide the U.S. government. The Supreme Court, however, reverses the decisions of the lower courts and finds in favor of the Forest Service. The Court ignores the policies articulated in AIRFA—a law it says "has no teeth," in that it offers tribes no legal means of challenging federal actions that violate American Indian religious sites.

April 28

The Termination resolution is repealed.

With Public Law 100-297, Congress formally repeals House Concurrent Resolution 108 (see entry for AUGUST 1, 1953), which allowed the government to terminate Indian tribes. Through Termination, the dominant federal Indian policy of the 1950s, the U.S. government attempted to sever its financial responsibilities to more than 100 tribes without their consent. Most terminated tribes were plunged into poverty, causing the government largely to disavow the policy by the late 1960s.

May 30

President Ronald Reagan disparages Indians while visiting the USSR.

At a meeting with students at Moscow University, President Ronald Reagan is questioned about the suppression of dissent among American minority groups. In his response, Reagan suggests that the United States should not have "humored" Indians by letting them "live a primitive lifestyle." His comment leads to a storm of protest from Indian leaders and activists, who castigate the president for promoting negative Indian stereotypes. Ignoring their complaints, Reagan refuses to apologize for the statement. (See also entry for DECEMBER 12, 1988.)

October 17

The Indian Gaming Regulatory Act provides guidelines for Indian gambling.

In response to *California v. Cabazon Band of Mission Indians* (see entry for FEBRUARY 25, 1987), in which the Supreme Court held that Indian gaming could be regulated only by a congressional act, Congress passes the Indian Gaming Regulatory Act. The act acknowledges that Indian-run gambling operations are a "means of promoting tribal economic development, self-sufficiency, and strong tribal government"—all primary goals of contemporary Indian policy.

The Indian Gaming Regulatory Act divides games into three classes. In Class I are traditional games, which are to be regulated solely by tribes. Class II includes bingo and lotto games, which are to be governed by the National Indian Gaming Commission—a three-person board of which two members must be Indians. Composing Class III are all high-stakes, casino-style games. Tribes may operate Class III games only if the games are not prohibited by the state in which the Indian group lives. The group must also negotiate with the state a formal agreement that outlines rules for operating any Class III game.

October 29

Indians buried in the Congressional Cemetery are honored.

The "Celebration of Native American Life" draws several hundred people to Washington, D.C., to pay tribute to the Indians buried in the Congressional Cemetery. Wilma Mankiller, the principal chief of the Cherokee (see entry for DECEMBER 14, 1987), delivers the event's keynote speech.

November

The Mount Graham observatory is approved for construction on a sacred Apache site.

Congress agrees to allow the construction of the Mount Graham International Observatory in the Coronado National Forest in Arizona. The decision is criticized by many San Carlos Apache, who regard the mountain as a sacred site. In light of Indian opposition, the observatory's sponsors—which include the Vatican and the Arcetri Astrophysical Observatory in Italy—decide to abandon the name "The Columbus Project" for the astronomical research center.

December 12

Reagan meets with Indian leaders.

President Ronald Reagan invites 16 Indian leaders to Washington, D.C., hoping to ease the tension created by a speech he delivered earlier in the year, in which he belittled Indians' "primitive lifestyle" (see entry for MAY 30, 1988). The 20-minute meeting marks the first time in recent history that Indians have been in council with the president in the White House.

1989

Tribes object to tourists at the Medicine Wheel.

When the Forestry Service begins to promote the Medicine Wheel at the Big Horn National Forest as a tourist attraction, tribal elders on the Wind River

Reservation organize a multitribal campaign to protect the site. The circle of large boulders has been a sacred site for many Indian groups for hundreds, if not thousands of years. In addition to insisting on 12 days of exclusive use of the Medicine Wheel for seasonal ceremonies, the Indians demand protection for the natural habitat within a 2.5-mile radius of the site, and they oppose the construction of a visitor's center and a new road to the site.

Canada amends the Indian Act.

The Indian Act (see entry for APRIL 12, 1876) is amended by the Canadian parliament to address several contemporary concerns of Canada's Natives. The amended act acknowledges band councils as the only authorities having the right to assign to individuals specific tracts of land on reserves. It also restricts the government's right to appropriate reserve lands for such projects as roads and bridges, and it requires Indian children to attend school up to a certain age.

Michael Dorris's *The Broken Cord* increases public awareness of fetal alcohol syndrome.

An anthropologist of Modoc heritage and husband of novelist Louise Erdrich (see entry for 1984), Michael Dorris chronicles in *The Broken Cord* his experiences as an adoptive father of a boy with fetal alcohol syndrome (FAS). The syndrome, which is linked to maternal drinking during pregnancy, impairs a child's ability to think abstractly and make reasoned choices. The book, which will be made into a television movie, draws attention to the prevalence of FAS on Indian reservations and in other impoverished communities. (See also entry for APRIL 10, 1997.)

Nebraska agrees to return Indian skeletal remains.

With the Unmarked Human Burial Sites and Skeletal Remains Protection Act, Nebraska becomes the first state to pass legislation calling for the repatriation of human remains and burial goods to Indian tribes. The law guarantees that remains found in public sites will be returned within one year of a tribal request and that unmarked grave sites will be protected from looting and destruction.

March 2

A Navajo Code Talker statue is dedicated.

In Phoenix, Arizona, a ceremony is held to dedicate a monumental 14-foot statue of a Navajo Code Talker—one of the elite corps of Navajo (Dineh) marines who delivered messages in code during World War II (see entry for APRIL 1942). The statue, designed by Douglas Hyde and titled *Tribute to Navajo Code Talkers,* depicts a young Navajo holding a flute, traditionally an instrument used to signal the coming of peace.

March 24

The *Exxon Valdez* oil spill destroys lands of the Aleut.

In the early morning, the *Exxon Valdez,* an oil tanker nearly a fifth of a mile long, runs aground on Alaska's Blight Reef. During the next two weeks, 11 million gallons of oil will spill out of a massive hole in the supertanker and into Prince Island Sound near the Aleut village of Tatiklek. As the oil spreads onto the surrounding beaches, much of the area's sea life, on which the Aleut depend for sustenance, will be killed.

Spring

Wisconsin whites harass Chippewa fishermen.

The Chippewa of northern Wisconsin face growing resentment from area whites for exercising their treaty right to spearfish walleyed pike outside of their reservations. Many are harassed by whites throwing rocks, shooting guns in their direction, and shouting racist slogans, such as "Save a walleye. Spear a pregnant squaw." Some white protesters are members of Protect American Rights and Resources. The group's animosity toward the Chippewa is largely triggered by the fear that

Douglas Hyde's bronze 14-foot sculpture of a Navajo Code Talker, installed in Phoenix, Arizona, is one of the largest works of public art ever commissioned from an American Indian artist. *(CORBIS/Buddy Mays)*

increased Indian fishing will drive off sports fishermen and other tourists, on whose business many whites rely for their livelihoods.

April 3

The Supreme Court strengthens the role of tribes in Indian adoptions.

In 1985 two children were born to unmarried Mississippi Choctaw parents outside of the band's reservation. The couple decided to give the children up for adoption through the social service division of Mississippi state and signed an agreement allowing them to be placed with non-Indian parents. The Mississippi Choctaw objected to the couple's decision and took them to court to ensure that the children were adopted by Indians.

The case, *Mississippi Band of Choctaw Indians v. Holyfield et al.,* reaches the Supreme Court four years later. The Mississippi Choctaw maintain that the provisions of the Indian Child Welfare Act (see

entry for NOVEMBER 8, 1978) gives them the right to be involved in the adoption procedure. This law was enacted to give tribes more control over Indian adoptions and to hamper social service organizations that believe Indian adoptees are best placed by non-Indian adults. Ruling in favor of the Choctaw, the Supreme Court echoes the sentiment of the act, which maintained that Indian children could suffer substantial psychological damage if separated from their cultural roots.

May 10

The Cree file suit to stop the Great Whale Project.

As the second phase of the James Bay Hydroelectric Project (see entry for APRIL 30, 1971), the province of Quebec plans to build the Great Whale Project. The reservoirs created by the first phase contain mercury levels nine times higher than that judged safe for humans. To prevent further destruction of their homeland, the Cree of northern Quebec take the province to court to try to halt the new construction. (See also entry for 1994.)

Summer

Northwest Coast Indians stage the "Paddle to Seattle."

Representatives from 17 Indian groups in the Pacific Northwest travel in dugout canoes from their communities to Seattle, Washington, during the "Paddle to Seattle." Part of Washington State's centennial celebration, the event is intended to help revive canoe building among tribes who traditionally relied on these boats as their primary mode of transportation.

Summer

A lawsuit against author Peter Mattiessen is dismissed.

A federal court of appeals dismisses a lawsuit against Peter Mattiessen, author of *In the Spirit of Crazy*

"Those guilty of the crimes perpetrated against the Indians of Pine Ridge have gone unpunished. But that's not the moral of the story. The point to remember is, if the FBI lied about what it was doing then, at the height of its supposed self-reformation, it could certainly be doing the same thing now.

]The victory over censorship in the *Crazy Horse* case is real enough. But it's no time for complacency."

—Cherokee scholar Ward Churchill on the suppression of *In the Spirit of Crazy Horse*

Horse (1983), a scathing indictment of the FBI's dealings with the American Indian Movement on South Dakota's Pine Ridge Reservation in the 1970s. The suit, brought by FBI agent David Price, held that the book defames Price's character and demanded $20 million in punitive damages. It also blocked the publication of the book in a paperback format and in foreign editions. Following the 1988 dismissal of a similar suit brought by South Dakota governor William Janklow, the conclusion of the Price case allows the sale of Mattiessen's book for the first time since its original publication.

July 21

The Supreme Court restricts the zoning of reservation land.

In *Brendale v. Confederated Tribes and Bands of the Yakima Indian Nation,* Yakama Indian Philip Brendale and non-Indian Stanley Wilkinson take the Yakama Nation to court to force it to lift its zoning restrictions on their land on the Yakima (now Yakama) Reservation in central Washington State. Brendale and Wilkinson want to divide their land into small house plots, which adheres to the zoning laws of the county but violates those of the Yakama Nation. Because Wilkinson's land is in an area of the reservation with a largely non-Indian population, the Supreme Court finds in his favor. Because it limits tribal control over reservation land occupied by non-Indians, the decision is seen by many Native American leaders as a blow to Indian self-determination.

July 22

Two Navajo (Dineh) are killed at a political rally.

Two Navajo (Dineh) are killed and nine others are injured during a clash with police at the Navajo Nation capital of Window Rock, Arizona. The violence occurs at a rally of supporters of former tribal chairman Peter MacDonald. Five days earlier, Macdonald was placed on involuntary leave by the tribal council, which is investigating charges that he had taken bribes. (See also entry for OCTOBER 1990.)

August 21

Harvard's Peabody Museum returns the Omaha's Sacred Pole.

Pressured by Omaha tribal chairman Dorris Morris and historian Dennis Hastings, the Peabody Museum at Harvard University gives the Sacred Pole, an important Omaha artifact, back to the tribe. The Sacred Pole was placed in the museum collection by Omaha anthropologist Francis La Flesche in the late 19th century.

Autumn

Native-L offers information about Indians on the Internet.

After attending the Tribal Lands Conference, Gary Trujillo of Smith College develops Native-L, an Internet forum to discuss endangered land bases of indigenous peoples around the world. As the mailing list for Native-L grows, the range of information and inquiries broadens to all issues relating to indigenous peoples. With the explosion of the Internet in the mid-1990s, Native-L will emerge as the leading Internet "community" dealing with the concerns of Indians.

September 1

George P. Lee is excommunicated from the Mormon Church.

Navajo (Dineh) George P. Lee, a devout Mormon but an outspoken critic of the role assigned to American Indians in his church, is excommunicated for apostasy (abandonment of religious faith). As a member of the First Quorum of Seventy, Lee had been the highest-ranking American Indian in the Church of Jesus Christ of Latter-Day Saints. He became a Mormon when he was enrolled in the Indian Student Placement Program (see entry for 1947), which placed boarding school students in the homes of Mormon families to be educated about Mormonism.

October 13

The New York State Museum returns wampum belts to the Onondaga.

In a ceremony in Albany, the leaders of the Onondaga are given 12 wampum belts by representatives of the New York State Museum. In 1898 the Onondaga had placed five belts in the museum for safekeeping and later named the institution's director the official Keeper of the Wampum. Three belts were purchased by the museum with the Onondaga's consent, while the four others were donated by a collector in 1927.

November 3

The French government honors the Choctaw Code Talkers.

The first Indian soldiers to use their native language as a code for communicating top secret messages, the Choctaw Code Talkers were instrumental in the Meuse-Argonne campaign in France during World War I (see entry for SEPTEMBER TO NOVEMBER 1918). In appreciation, officials of the French government make Choctaw leader Hollis E. Roberts a Chevalier de l'Ordre National du Mérite (a Knight of the National Order of Merit), their country's highest honor.

November 17

The Senate reports mismanagement of Indian land and resources.

Following a two-year investigation, a report issued by the Senate Select Committee on Indian Affairs examines the Bureau of Indian Affairs's (BIA) mismanagement of Indian lands and funds. Among its many allegations of corruption within the agency, the document reveals that oil companies have routinely stolen oil from Indian tribes by underreporting the amount of oil they drilled on reservations. Aware of these practices, the BIA took no action to stop them. The committee concludes that Indians should be given more control over federal funds and programs.

November 28

Congress votes to fund a Native American museum in Washington, D.C.

With the National Museum of the American Indian Act, Congress authorizes funding for a national museum of Indian culture and history. This museum will be part of the Smithsonian Institution and will be built on the last remaining plot on the Mall in Washington, D.C. Intended as a "living memorial to Native Americans and their traditions," it will house a vast collection of Indian art and artifacts, including those of New York's Museum of the American Indian (see entry for 1916), which merged with the Smithsonian on May 8. An additional facility for the conservation and storage of items on display will be constructed at the Smithsonian's Museum Support Center in Maryland. The act also calls for the Smithsonian to return Native American human remains and funerary objects in its collections to the tribal groups to whom they belong. (See also entry for 1993.)

1990

The Working Group on Indigenous Populations refuses to celebrate the Columbus Quincentenary.

Through the lobbying efforts of the International Indian Treaty Council, the United Nations Working Group on Indigenous Populations (see entry for JULY 1977) announces that it will reject all plans for celebrating the upcoming quincentenary of Christopher Columbus's arrival in North America. The Working Group maintains that such a celebration would negate "our existence, our systems of government, our cultures, and our pre-Columbian and pre-colonial history."

The film *Dances with Wolves* premieres.

Dances with Wolves, a three-hour epic starring and directed by non-Indian actor Kevin Costner, opens to wide acclaim from the public and critics. The movie tells the story of a white army officer who goes to live among the Lakota Sioux during the Plains Indian Wars of the late 19th century. In addition to being one of the year's biggest box-office hits, the film will receive the 1990 Academy Award for Best Picture.

The film is praised among Indians for its sympathetic view of the plight of the 19th-century Lakota and for its casting of Indian actors, such as Rodney Grant, Tantoo Cardinal, and Graham Greene (who will be nominated for an Oscar for Best Supporting Actor). Some Indians, however, fault the movie for taking an overly romantic view of the Lakota Sioux and for perpetuating the myth of Indians as a "vanishing race," inevitably doomed to extinction. The film is also criticized for presenting Indian life through the eyes of a white man rather than from the perspective of the Indian characters. (See also entry for FEBRUARY 1993.)

> "*Dances with Wolves* is first and foremost a movie, and should be seen as one. . . . It wasn't made to manipulate your feelings, to reinvent the past, or to set the historical record straight. It's a romantic look at a terrible time in our history, when expansion in the name of progress brought us very little and, in fact, cost us deeply."
>
> —actor-director Kevin Costner on his film *Dances with Wolves*

The North American Indian Prose Award is established.

The University of Nebraska Press, in conjunction with the Native American studies programs of the University of California at Berkeley and the University of New Mexico, announces that it will sponsor the North American Indian Prose Award.

This literary prize is to be given annually to a non-fiction manuscript by an Indian author. Part of the award is publication of the manuscript by University of Nebraska Press. Future winners will include *Claiming Breath,* by essayist Diane Glancy, and *They Called It Prairie Light,* by historian K. Tsianina Lomawaima.

The Rosebud Reservation becomes a landfill site.

The Lakota tribal council of South Dakota's Rosebud Reservation approves a proposal by O&G Industries to construct a landfill on 5,700 acres of reservation land. Under the agreement, Rosebud residents will receive one dollar for every ton of trash dumped in the enormous landfill. Fearing environmental damage, the council of the Pine Ridge Lakota has rejected a similar landfill proposed for its nearby reservation.

The Department of Education creates the Indian Nations at Risk Task Force.

Concerned with modern threats to Indian traditions, the Department of Education appoints a task force to examine ways that schools can help to preserve and protect tribal cultures. The Indian Nations at Risk Task Force makes a number of recommendations, including training more Indian teachers, teaching Indian languages in public schools, and bringing schools, parents, tribes, and social service organizations together in an effort to improve Indian education.

Mary Crow Dog's *Lakota Woman* is published.

In *Lakota Woman,* activist Mary Crow Dog tells of her involvement in the American Indian Movement in the 1970s. Working with non-Indian author Richard Erdoes, Crow Dog first wrote the autobiography in 1979, but the manuscript was abandoned by its publisher, which deemed the material too controversial. Finally published 11 years later, the book is an immediate popular and critical success and is named the winner of the American Book Award from the Before Columbus Foundation. Following the success of *Lakota*

Woman, Crow Dog (then calling herself Mary Brave Bird) and Erdoes will collaborate on its sequel, *Ohitika Woman* (1993).

The Iroquois National Lacrosse Club becomes a national team.

Formed in 1983, the Iroquois National Lacrosse Club lobbies successfully to join the membership of the International Lacrosse Federation as a national team. The Iroquois team is therefore allowed to enter the world championships in Australia on an equal status with all other member teams, including that sent by the United States. A traditional Indian sport, lacrosse has been played by the Iroquois for hundreds of years.

The Turtle Mountain Ojibway begin operating Uniband Data Entry.

The Turtle Mountain Ojibway of North Dakota purchase Uniband, a data entry–services corporation. By soliciting government contracts as a minority-owned business, Uniband will grow quickly and provide increased employment opportunities for the tribe. The business will eventually have more than 800 employees throughout the country.

March

A site near the Akwesasne reservation is named America's worst toxic dump.

Following five years of environmental studies initiated by the Mohawk of New York State, the Environmental Protection Agency (EPA) releases a Superfund report that sets aside $138 million to clean up the General Motors waste dumps near the tribe's Akwesasne reservation. The massive cleanup plan identifies the dumps as the worst toxic site in the United States. As the EPA begins work, the dumps have already leaked PCBs, insecticides, and other toxins into the surrounding region, affecting the Akwesasne Mohawk's health and economy. The level of pollution is so great that fishing, a traditional Mohawk means of making a livelihood, in no longer viable in many area waters.

March 30

Shots are fired at an army helicopter over Ganienkeh.

While passing over the Mohawk community at Ganienkeh (see entry for MAY 13, 1977), an Army National Guard helicopter is struck by three bullets, one of which wounds an army doctor on board. When the state police attempt to investigate the shooting, the Ganienkeh Mohawk will refuse to cooperate, maintaining that their sovereignty prohibits state interference in their affairs. The Indians form a barricade to keep the police out and exchange gunfire with troops that attempt to enter Ganienkeh.

April 17

Oregon v. Smith supports laws against peyote use.

In the case *Employment Division, Department of Human Resources of Oregon v. Smith,* two Indian drug and alcohol counselors, Alfred Smith and Galen Black, sue Oregon's human resources department when they are denied unemployment compensation. The men were fired from their jobs after ingesting peyote as part of a religious ceremony held by the Native American Church (see entry for OCTOBER 10, 1918), which Oregon defined as "misconduct" that disqualified them for benefits by state law.

Maintaining that Oregon's laws against peyote use do not contradict the First Amendment's protection of religious freedom, the Supreme Court finds in favor of Oregon. The decision is criticized by many Native American leaders, who see it as inconsistent with the religious rights guaranteed by the American Indian Religious Freedom Act (see entry for AUGUST 11, 1978).

April 24

A militant Mohawk faction takes over the Akwesasne reservation.

On the Mohawk's Akwesasne reservation on the border of New York State and Canada, members of the heavily armed Mohawk Warrior Society over-run roadblocks set up by the Antis, a group of antigambling traditionalists, to prevent non-Indians from patronizing the reservation's gambling parlors. The Mohawk Warrior Society is a radical political force that favors tribal gambling operations and opposes the Iroquois leadership structure represented by the various tribal councils.

As the Mohawk Warrior Society takes control of the reservation, about 2,000 Antis flee from Akwesasne, fearing for their lives. The standoff continues for four days, during which two men are killed in a gun fight. The shooting stops only after hundreds of New York state troopers storm the area and restore order.

May 29

Duro v. Reina weakens the power of tribal courts.

In the case of *Duro v. Reina,* the Supreme Court finds that the tribal court of the Quinault's reservation in Washington State does not have jurisdiction over Indians who live on the reservation but are not enrolled in the tribe. The decision threatens the ability of tribal courts to maintain law and order, especially on reservations on which nonenrolled Indians make up a large percentage of the population.

June 23

The Meech Lake Accord is defeated.

The Meech Lake Accord, which proposes that the Canadian government consider Quebec a "distinct society" (see entry for APRIL 30, 1987), has earned the contempt of Native leaders who believe Native groups deserve the same recognition. The accord must be approved by all provincial legislatures by June 23, 1990, to be accepted as law.

As the deadline approaches, the only holdout is Manitoba, where by law the accord must be approved by all legislators. Cree Indian Elijah Harper, the province's only Native legislator, refuses to participate in a debate of the issue. When asked for his vote, he holds up a white feather and declines to answer. With Harper's abstention, the accord is not approved by the Manitoba legislature and thereby fails to pass. Its defeat is considered a victory in the fight for Native rights.

Summer

Mohawk activists and Canadian police face-off in Oka, Quebec.

The mayor of the town of Oka, Quebec, located 25 miles west of Montreal, approves a plan to expand a municipal golf course into a neighboring forest. The forest, however, lies in lands, including an Indian graveyard, that were traditionally claimed by the Mohawk. To prevent the local government from taking control of the area, Mohawk activists arm themselves and block the entrance into the forest.

On July 11, the Quebec police force storms the blockade. One officer is killed in the gunfire exchanged between the Mohawk and police. In a desperate attempt to end the conflict, the Canadian government sends 3,700 troops to Oka to surround the protesters. The tense standoff finally ends on September 26 without further bloodshed. The incident at Oka is reported internationally during the summer of 1990, thus bringing worldwide attention to the land claims of Canadian Natives.

"Everyone thinks that July 11, it just started. It didn't. . . . You think this came out of nowhere? What that one day we said we are going to put up barricades? This wasn't something new. It went back hundreds of years. It wasn't a new struggle, it was part of an old one, a continuous one. Look at the history, it's there."

—Mohawk protester Debra Etienne on the Oka occupation

July

The United States admits the Yakama have been exposed to radioactive waste.

A federal government spokesperson acknowledges that since the 1950s radioactive waste from a nuclear facility at Hanford, Washington, on the border of the Yakima (Yakama) Reservation has contaminated local ground water sources. Residents in the area have been exposed to about 2,000 times the amount of nuclear waste deemed safe—a greater exposure than that experienced by Soviets living near Chernobyl after the 1986 nuclear accident there.

August

The first North American Indigenous Games are held.

In Edmonton, Alberta, thousands of Native athletes gather to compete in the North American Indigenous Games. The competition, which will become a biannual event by the end of the decade, is intended to promote pride in Canadian Native youths by showcasing their athletic talents in eight sports, including baseball, soccer, and lacrosse—a game first played by Native peoples.

October

Peter MacDonald is convicted of bribery.

Navajo Tribal Chairman Peter MacDonald and his son are found guilty of taking bribes in the Navajo (Dineh) tribal court. In addition to being barred from holding political office for four years, MacDonald is sentenced to a six-year prison sentence and fined $11,000. His son is sent to prison for 18 months and fined $2,500. (See also entry for JULY 22, 1989.)

October 30

The Native American Languages Act encourages the use and study of Indian languages.

The warnings of Native American language scholars that many Indian languages are in danger of becoming extinct moves Congress to pass the Native American Languages Act. The law recognizes Indian languages as an important part of American culture and makes their preservation a goal of U.S. policy. More specifically, the act states that Indian languages should be taught and used in government-run Native American educational programs. This provision reverses the century-old policy of forbidding Indian students from speaking their own languages in institutions operated by the Bureau of Indian Affairs.

November 16

The Native American Graves Protection and Repatriation Act is passed.

Despite opposition from the Society of American Archaeology, Congress passes the Native American Graves Protection and Repatriation Act. The legislation is a response to Indians' demands for repatriation—the return to Indian tribes of Native American remains and artifacts collected by non-Indians from grave sites.

The act increases legal protection of Indian burial grounds by citing penalties for tampering with graves and selling objects collected from them. It also requires all federal agencies and institutions that receive funds from the U.S. government to inventory the Indian remains, funerary objects, sacred objects, and items of central ceremonial significance in their collections. These institutions are also responsible for contacting the appropriate Indian groups about the objects held. The groups may then submit applications requesting that any or all of these items be returned.

November 29

The Indian Arts and Crafts Act criminalizes nonauthentic Indian art.

With the rapid growth of the Indian art industry, many non-Indian craftspeople have tried to increase sales by marketing their work as Indian art. Responding to pressure from Indian leaders to stop this practice, Congress passes a revision of the Indian Arts and Crafts Act (see entry for AUGUST 27, 1935), establishing means to punish impostor Indian artists. The act allows the Indian Arts and Crafts Board to bring civil and criminal suits against artists not enrolled in a federally recognized Indian tribe who represent themselves as Indians to their customers. (Indian artists belonging to tribes not formally recognized by the federal government can obtain special certification.) It also prohibits galleries from selling nonenrolled artists' works as Indian art.

December 23 to 29

The Big Foot Memorial Riders commemorate the Wounded Knee Massacre.

In recognition of the hundred-year anniversary of the massacre at Wounded Knee (see entry for DECEMBER 29, 1890), 200 Lakota horsemen calling themselves the Big Foot Memorial Riders retrace the 150-mile route taken by Chief Big Foot's band from their Cheyenne River Reservation to the massacre site. Throughout the ride, participants say prayers to ensure the survival of the Lakota and their culture. Describing the event's purpose, one participant later explains, "The Lakota Nation's greatest tragedy was used to build the people's strength."

1991

Author Forrest Carter is revealed to be an Indian impostor.

The Education of Little Tree is exposed as the work of a non-Indian who had been a speechwriter for Alabama governor George Wallace and a member of the Ku Klux Klan. The author, Asa Earl Carter (a.k.a. Forrest Carter), who died in 1979, presented himself as a Cherokee and his book as the true story of how he learned the traditions of his tribe from his traditional grandparents.

First published in 1976 and reissued 1986, the book was embraced by teachers faced with developing multicultural curricula in the late 1980s. The book became an unlikely best-seller and in 1990 was awarded the American Booksellers Award, an honor annually bestowed on the favorite book of booksellers across the United States.

The Supreme Court grants states the right to tax Indian cigarette sales to non-Indians.

In the case of *Oklahoma Tax Commission v. Citizen Band Potawatomi Indian Tribe,* the state of Oklahoma maintains that the Potawatomi owe state tax on any sales of cigarettes to non-tribal members on their reservation. The Supreme Court agrees but also holds that because of the sovereign status of the Potawatomi, Oklahoma cannot sue the tribe for the amount owed. The decision, therefore, in practice is a victory for the Potawatomi: Although the Court upholds Oklahoma's right to this tax income, it gives the state no means to force the Indians to pay.

Tribal leaders are asked to use reservation land to store nuclear waste.

At the annual conference of the National Congress of American Indians (see entry for JUNE 13 TO 20, 1961), David Leroy, the head of the U.S. Office of Nuclear Waste, encourages Indian tribal leaders to allow the United States to store nuclear waste on their reservations. Leroy offers a $100,000 grant to any tribe that agrees to consider housing waste for 40 years. For tribes prepared to pursue waste storage, the United States promises another $200,000 for study of appropriate sites and $2.8 million once negotiations are finalized.

Over the objections of many tribal members and others concerned about the possible health risks, 20 tribes will apply for the $100,000 grants within six months. Several leaders, however, will be forced to return the money by pressure from their people.

February

The InterTribal Bison Cooperative is founded.

Hosted by the Native American Fish and Wildlife Society, representatives of 19 tribes come together in the Black Hills of South Dakota to find ways in which tribes can work with one another to increase the buffalo population. From this meeting emerges the InterTribal Bison Cooperative, a nonprofit organization that offers Indian tribes information and the funds needed to maintain buffalo herds and develops educational programs to teach the importance of the buffalo in Indian cultures.

April 4

The 1990 census shows a growing Indian population.

The U.S. Census Bureau releases its 1990 figures, which set the population of Indians and Alaskan Natives at almost two million. The number represents a 40 percent increase since 1980. Although the Indian population in the United States is clearly growing, much of the increase is attributed to the diminishing stigma on Indianness, which previously had prevented many people from identifying themselves as Indians.

June 6

Canada's Studio One promotes Native filmmaking.

Founded by the National Film Board of Canada, Studio One in Edmonton, Alberta, is founded as the first Native-operated studio for film production. The studio, dedicated to producing films that counter stereotypes about Canada's Natives, offers aspiring filmmakers instruction and access to production facilities.

Summer

Indians protest against the Atlanta Braves at the World Series.

During the World Series between the Atlanta Braves and Minnesota Twins, protests are held at the stadiums of both teams to denounce Atlanta's team name and the "tomahawk chop" performed by its fans. To show support for the Braves, fans make a chopping motion with their hands to the beat of a drum—a gesture that the protesters criticize as belittling to Indian peoples and cultures. Over their objections, many spectators still make a modified version of the "tomahawk chop"—among them former President Jimmy Carter and the wife of the Atlanta Braves's owner Ted Turner, Jane Fonda, who had been a celebrity advocate for Indian rights in the 1960s and 1970s.

"When we see these folks dressed as Indians and wearing war paint, the stereotypes of Indians come out. They wear headdresses, which are very spiritual in nature, very cere-monial. It would be like if we went to a game with a lot of Catholics and started giving communion in the stands or hearing confessions. It wouldn't show respect."

—Roger Head, head of the Minnesota Indian Affairs Council, on the 1991 World Series protest against the Atlanta Braves

Autumn

The Seneca agree to a renewal of the Salamanca lease.

Several months before its expiration, the lease on lands in the town of Salamanca, New York, on the Seneca's Allegany Reservation is renewed for 40 years. The original hundred-year lease was negoti-ated in 1892, when the United States, eager to take control of the growing railroad town, pressured the Seneca to sign an agreement that yielded them very little income; on some parcels of land, rents were as low as a dollar a year for the life of the lease. As leg-islated by Congress, the new lease grants the Seneca Nation $60 million in compensation for the previ-ous unfair agreement and allows for rent increases of $750,000 a year. It also names the Seneca as the owners of "improvements"—including homes and other buildings— on the leased land. The new lease infuriates many residents of Salamanca and in-creases tension between the Seneca and their non-Indian neighbors. (See also entry for JANUARY 1942.)

September

Aleut skeletal remains are reburied on Kodiak Island.

Under the terms of the National Museum of the American Indian Act (see entry for NOVEMBER 28, 1989), the Smithsonian returns 756 skeletal re-mains for reburial to the Aleut of Larsen Bay, on Kodiak Island in Alaska. In addition to 5,000 arti-facts, the remains were collected on Kodiak Island in the 1930s by anthropologist Ales Hrdlicka while employed by the Smithsonian Institution.

November 26

The U.S. government renames the Custer Battlefield National Monument.

Under pressure by Indian groups, Congress enacts Public Law 102-201, which changes the name of the Custer Battlefield National Monument in Mon-tana to the Little Bighorn Battlefield National Monument. The law also calls for the construction of a monument to memorialize the Lakota Sioux, Cheyenne, and Arapaho warriors who defeated the Seventh Cavalry, led by Lieutenant Colonel George Armstrong Custer, during the Battle of Little Bighorn (see entry for JUNE 24 TO 25, 1876). (See also entry for FEBRUARY 1997.)

December 16

Canada announces its plan to create the new territory of Nunavut.

Acting on a proposal first presented to the govern-ment in 1976, Canada declares that it will create the territory of Nunavut, which will be composed of 350,000 square kilometers of land in the eastern half of the Northwest Territories. Approximately 85 percent of the population of the new territory will be Inuit. The Canadian government also allocates $580 million to fund the territorial government and new Inuit businesses in the territory. In exchange for the creation of Nunavut, the Inuit of the eastern and central Arctic agree to relinquish their aboriginal claims to more than 1 million square miles of territory.

1992

Ben Nighthorse Campbell joins the Senate.

After serving in the Colorado legislature and the U.S. House of Representatives, Ben Nighthorse Campbell, a Northern Cheyenne from Colorado, is elected to the U.S. Senate. Campbell was a judo champion, jewelry maker, rancher, and tribal councilman before he entered U.S. politics in 1983.

"I am convinced that America, which has failed so miserably in fighting social evils from drugs to crime, from prostitution to hunger, is *ready* to learn values of traditional Native American ways.... We need to help lead this nation. We need not abandon our traditional values— that's what makes our people so unique in this nation—we need to affect public policy to recognize those values."

—Northern Cheyenne politician Ben Nighthorse Campbell in a 1991 speech to graduates of Haskell Indian Nations University

Elected to the Senate in 1992, Northern Cheyenne politician Ben Nighthorse Campbell dons a beaded headdress at a 1984 parade. *(CORBIS/Dave Bartruff)*

A sculpture by Bill Reid is displayed in the Canadian embassy.

After five years of work, Bill Reid's massive bronze sculpture of a canoe full of figures from Haida mythology is installed in the Canadian embassy in Washington, D.C. A member of the Haida Tribe, Reid is a central figure in the revival of traditional woodcarving arts among the Indians of the Pacific Northwest.

A Superfund cleanup begins on Coeur d'Alene lands.

The U.S. government begins a Superfund cleanup of a three-by-seven-mile area in Kellogg, Idaho, on the Coeur d'Alene reservation. The area is contaminated with lead dumped by silver-mining companies, which began operating in the area in the 1880s. Their activities were largely unregulated until the passage of the Clean Water Act in 1972.

The second-largest project in Superfund history, the 10-year cleanup will cost $150 million. The Coeur d'Alene, however, are disappointed by the scope of the project and advocate a much larger cleanup of their reservation. (See also entries for 1996 and FEBRUARY 1998.)

January 26

Innu adolescents attempt mass suicide.

Six youths, age 12 to 14, from the small Innu village of Davis Inlet in Labrador, Canada, are discovered in an abandoned shack, where they attempted to commit suicide by sniffing gasoline. The event focuses media attention on the epidemic proportions of suicide and substance abuse among the grossly impoverished Davis Inlet Innu. The social problems of the Innu are widely credited to the government's relocation of the band in 1967. The Innu were lured to their new home with promises of work and adequate housing, but few ever found jobs or houses with indoor plumbing or running water.

February 12

The Pequot open the Foxwoods resort and casino complex.

Inspired by the success of the bingo parlor they opened in 1986, the small Pequot tribe builds Foxwoods—a huge complex that includes a hotel, shopping center, and two casinos—on their reservation in Connecticut. Employing more than 9,000 people, Foxwoods will soon boost tribal revenues by 1 billion dollars a year and become one of the largest employers in the state. The money will be used to provide income and services to the Pequot and to invest in businesses, including gambling operations, run by other tribes. (See also entries for MARCH 1997 and for AUGUST 11, 1998.)

April

A children's book featuring the "Chief Seattle speech" comes under attack.

A front-page article in the *New York Times* questions the authenticity of the text of the best-selling children's book, *Brother Eagle, Sister Sky: A Message from Chief Seattle.* The book features a version of a speech credited to Chief Seattle of the Suquamish tribe. The speech, supposedly delivered during the negotiation of the Treaty of Point Elliot (see entry for DECEMBER 1854), extols the virtues of living in harmony with nature and has long been embraced by the environmental movement.

Although eyewitness accounts confirm that Seattle spoke with great eloquence at the treaty negotiations, the words attributed to him did not appear in print until 30 years later, prompting speculation that they were actually written by their non-Indian "translator," Henry Smith. Well into the 20th century, Smith's version of the Seattle speech will be adapted freely, often by environmentalists seeking support for their cause.

July 7 to 10

Native American writers participate in the Returning the Gift festival.

Chaired by Abenaki writer Joseph Bruchac, the Returning the Gift festival brings together 400 Indian fiction writers, poets, and playwrights for a four-day conference at the University of Oklahoma. The festival's goal is to create a setting where Native American writers—both published and unpublished—can meet one another and share ideas.

During the conference, two organizations are formed: the Native Writers' Circle and the Wordcraft Circle. The Native Writers' Circle, a professional association, gives its first annual lifetime achievement award to Pulitzer Prize–winning Kiowa novelist N. Scott Momaday (see entry for MAY 5, 1969). The organization also establishes the First Book Awards, which are to be given annually in the fields of poetry, prose, creative nonfiction, and drama to writers who have not yet published a full-length book. The Wordcraft Circle is founded to place young writers in contact with more established authors and to help them get their work in print.

September 17

A Pentagon exhibit honors the Navajo Code Talkers.

At the Pentagon in Washington, D.C., 35 Navajo (Dineh) veterans are honored for their service as Code Talkers during World War II. The Code Talkers transmitted top secret messages using an unbreakable code based on the Navajo language (see entry for APRIL 1942). The Pentagon recognizes their contribution to the war effort with an exhibit featuring photographs of the Code Talkers, a display of their equipment, and an explanation of how the code was used.

October 12

Indians oppose the celebration of the Columbus Quincentenary.

The celebration of the five hundredth anniversary of the arrival of Columbus in the Americas (see entry for OCTOBER 12, 1492) provokes opposition by many Indians and Indian groups. A survey of indigenous peoples in North, South, and Central America conducted by the Cornell University American Indian Program finds that about three-quarters of those responding view the quincentenary as a tribute to "500 years of Native People's resistance to colonization, or an anniversary of a holocaust." The Assembly of First Nations (see entry for 1982) of Canada denounces the quincentenary, maintaining that "for the First Nations to celebrate the near destruction of our culture and identity would be insane." In *Newsweek* magazine, Cheyenne-Muskogee activist Suzan Shown Harjo contributes an editorial titled, "I Won't Be Celebrating Columbus Day," in which she calls on Indians and non-Indians alike "to turn our attention to making the next 500 years different from the past ones: to enter into a time of grace and healing."

October 26

The Charlottestown Accord is defeated.

The Charlottestown Accord, which acknowledges the right of Canadian Natives to self-government, is brought before the electorate for a vote. The provisions dealing with Natives are widely supported by Native leaders. According to opinion polls, the majority of non-Indian voters approve of them as well. The accord as a whole, however, focuses on allowing the province of Quebec greater autonomy. Due to these provisions, which are not as strongly supported by the populace, the accord is defeated.

November

Hopi and Navajo (Dineh) announce an agreement over disputed lands.

After more than a century of discord, the Hopi agree to allow about 450 Navajo (Dineh) families living on their reservation to stay in their homes (see entry for 1962). By the proposed agreement, mediated in federal court, these Navajo will be permitted to lease the land from the Hopi for 75 years. In exchange, the Hopi will receive approximately 400,000 acres of land in the San Francisco Peaks area. Also by its terms, the U.S. government promises to settle several outstanding lawsuits with the Hopis for $15 million.

The agreement is opposed by many white landowners in Arizona. They fear that the new Hopi land acquisitions will reduce their property values and limit their access to hunting and fishing sites on nearby public lands.

1993

Douglas Cardinal is hired to design the Smithsonian's Indian museum.

The Smithsonian Institution selects Canadian Douglas Cardinal, an Indian of Blackfoot and Metís ancestry, to be the lead architect of the National Museum of the American Indian (see entry for NOVE BER 28, 1989), slated to open on the Mall in Washington, D.C., in 2002. Cardinal is best known for his design of the Canadian Museum of Civilization in Quebec and of the Institute of American Indian Arts in Santa Fe. Cardinal's architectural firm has worked with many Native groups using a consensual design process, through which Cardinal asks for input from elders and other representatives of Native communities.

February

Actor Kevin Costner unveils plans for a Black Hills resort.

Announcing what is projected to be the largest private building project in South Dakota history, non-Indian actor Kevin Costner and his brother Dan plan to open Dunbar, a $95 million resort, in the town of Deadwood. Located in the Black Hills, an area sacred to the Lakota Sioux, the resort complex is to feature 430,000-square-foot hotel and recreation facilities, including golf courses, billiard halls, squash and tennis courses, and movie theaters.

The resort is named after Costner's character in *Dances with Wolves,* a film he directed and starred in (see entry for 1990). Winner of the Academy Award for Best Picture, the enormously successful movie addressed the Lakota's battles for their land in the late 19th century. Although the tribe largely endorsed Costner's film, most Lakota are outraged by his plans to develop their sacred lands into a tourist attraction for non-Indians. Echoing the sentiment of many tribal members, Madonna Thunder Hawk of the Black Hills Protection Committee later says, "Kevin Costner only likes his romantic idea of the Indians. He's not interested in real Indians and our modern problems."

February 6

The first First Americans in the Arts (FAITA) Awards are held.

Created by Creek-Seminole actor Bob Hicks, the First Americans in the Arts (FAITA) awards are held in Los Angeles, California. In what will become an annual event, FAITA awards are given to Indian performers who have excelled in film, music, and television, and scholarships are presented to outstanding Indian students interested in careers in the arts. Among the evening's winners are Dakota Sioux actor-singer John Trudell, Oneida actor Graham Greene (see entry for 1990), and Kiowa playwright Hanay Geiogamah.

May to July

The hantavirus epidemic breaks out on the Navajo reservation.

A 19-year-old Navajo (Dineh) man is rushed to Indian Medical Center in Gallup, New Mexico, with severe flu symptoms. Soon the patient, unable to breathe, dies. Learning of several similar cases, area doctors consult with the Center of Disease Control (CDC). Within a few days, the CDC identifies the mysterious illness as hantavirus, a virus that has never before caused disease in humans in the Americas.

The disease claims the lives of 16 Navajo before the virus's carrier is discovered to be the wild deer mouse, whose population has exploded after heavy rains produced an especially large crop of the pinon nuts on which the animals feed. The government immediately launches a public information campaign in English, Spanish, and Navajo in the Four Corners area to inform residents how to avoid contamination.

May 23

Indian canoeists set off on the Enatai on Alki.

To help revive their cultural traditions surrounding canoe travel, 15 representatives of seven Pacific Northwest tribes begin a month-long journey from the Puget Sound to Bella Bella, British Columbia. The participants call the grueling 1,000-mile trip the Enatai on *Alki,* which means "a crossing into the future" in Chinook. When the canoeists arrive in Bella Bella, they join in a potlatch ceremony attended by thousands as part of a Washington State Day celebration.

August 7

Ada Deer is sworn in as the head of the Bureau of Indian Affairs.

Following his election to the presidency, Bill Clinton names Menominee scholar and activist Ada

Deer the assistant secretary of the Bureau of Indian Affairs (BIA). During the congressional hearing on her appointment, the Senate gives her a standing ovation, a gesture that displays the popularity she earned while lobbying in Washington on behalf of her tribe (see entry for 1970). As her nomination is confirmed, Ada Deer becomes the first Native American woman ever to head the BIA.

> ᛤᛁᛈ
>
> "My vision for the Bureau of Indian Affairs is to create a progressive federal/tribal partnership. First and foremost, the heart of Indian policy must be strong, effective tribal sovereignty. There is no reason for me or for any of you to be reluctant to support the permanency of tribal sovereignty any more than we would be reluctant to support the permanency of federal or state sovereignty. ...The role of the federal government should be to support and to implement tribally-inspired solutions to tribally-defined problems. The days of federal paternalism are over."
>
> —Ada Deer, speaking before Congress following her nomination for the assistant secretary of Indian affairs

October 28

The House recognizes the Lumbee tribe.
The Lumbee Indians of North Carolina are formally recognized by the House of Representatives. With recognition, the Lumbee are permitted to adopt a constitution, but they are still not eligible for federal funding (see entry for JULY 7, 1956). Recognized by the state of North Carolina in 1885, the tribe has been seeking full federal recognition since 1890.

November 29

The Catawba's federal recognition is restored.
After 13 years of negotiation between the United States and the Native American Rights Fund, Catawba chief Gilbert Blue signs an agreement that settles the claim to lands in South Carolina taken from the Catawba by the Treaty of Nation Ford of 1840. As part of the settlement, the United States restores federal recognition to the Catawba tribe (see entry for JULY 1, 1962), making it eligible for government services reserved for Indians. Congress also awards the Catawba $50 million to purchase land, fund economic and social programs, and make payments to tribal members.

December

The Turner Network Television network launches a series of programs about Indians.
Initiated by Ted Turner, owner of Turner Network Television, the cable network begins a year of programming about Native Americans, starting with the airing of *Geronimo*, a television movie biography of the 19th-century Apache leader. The project will include six movies about historical Indian figures and a six-hour documentary on Indian history titled *The Native Americans*. Turner's Cable News Network (CNN) will also produce *The Invisible People*, a 20-part series of reports about contemporary Indian issues.

1994

Cree protests halt the James Bay Project.
With the support of environmental groups, Cree convince Hydro-Quebec to postpone the second

phase of the James Bay Project (see entry for MAY 10, 1989), the construction of a hydroelectric plant that threatens the Cree's lands along James Bay. They cite the environmental chaos the first phrase of the project, completed in 1985, wreaked in Cree territory: Ancient burial grounds and fishing sites were flooded, drinking water became polluted, and the migration routes of caribou hunted by the Cree were disturbed. Perhaps most detrimental to the Cree, fish in area rivers were poisoned with mercury. A 1990 study found that some Cree elders, dependent on fish as their major source of food, had as much as 20 times the safe level of mercury in their bodies.

The Native American Religious Freedom Act is amended to protect religious peyote use.

To address contradictions between state laws and federal policy, an amendment to the Native American Religious Freedom Act (see entry for AUGUST 11, 1978) allows Indians to use peyote in a ceremonial context without fear of arrest and prosecution under state drug laws.

January

South Dakota bank pays damages for discriminating against Indians.

The Blackpipe State Bank of Martin, South Dakota, settles with the Justice Department for discriminating against Indian customers. The bank was accused of applying higher finance charges and interest rates to Indian borrowers than to whites. As part of the settlement, Blackpipe is required to establish a $125,000 fund to compensate loan applicants whom it had rejected because of their race.

February 15

The Mescalero Apache agree to a nuclear waste dump on their reservation.

Mescalero Apache leaders sign an agreement with Northern States Power that will allow the Minnesota company to store nuclear waste on the tribe's New Mexico reservation. Citing health risks, the governor of New Mexico, Bruce King, joins with the Indigenous Environmental Network in objecting to the waste site. The Apache tribal council, however, says its decision was made after careful study and emphasizes that the waste storage facility will provide jobs for reservation residents for the next 40 years. (See also entry for MARCH 9, 1995.)

February 11 to July 15

Indian protesters stage the Walk for Justice.

American Indian Movement activists Dennis Banks and Mary Jane Wilson-Medrano organize the Walk for Justice, a protest march from Alcatraz Island in San Francisco Bay, California, to Washington, D.C. The protesters hope to bring public attention to an array of contemporary Indian issues, foremost of which is the fight for clemency for Leonard Peltier, the activist imprisoned for murdering two FBI agents in South Dakota (see entry for APRIL 18, 1977). Other demands include returning the Black Hills to the Lakota Sioux; ending U.S. government interference in land disputes between the Navajo (Dineh) and the Hopi; and halting the construction of the James Bay Project, which has destroyed Cree and Inuit lands in Quebec, Canada.

April 29

Indian leaders meet with President Bill Clinton at the White House.

To announce that he intends to follow a more benevolent Indian policy than his Republican predecessor, President Bill Clinton invites leaders from all federally recognized tribes to the White House, the first such meeting since 1822. Representatives of more than 300 tribes convene at the White House, where they are asked to discuss the issues of most concern to their peoples. Among the topics broached are the inadequacy of health care and housing available to many Indians, the need for more tribal control over natural resources on Indian lands, the eroding respect for the sovereignty of Indian governments, and the desire for increased protection of sacred sites on and off reservations.

As a result of the meeting, Clinton circulates two memos to every executive department. One directs employees to try to accommodate Indians who need eagle feathers to perform traditional ceremonies (see entry for 1986). The second makes a more general request that government officials consult with Indian governments before making decisions that affect them, particularly when the use of Indians' natural resources is at issue.

August

A white buffalo calf is identified as an incarnation of the White Buffalo Calf Woman.

Indians throughout the United States gather at a farm in Jamesville, Wisconsin, where a white female buffalo calf has been born. Named Miracle by the farm owner, the calf is seen as the embodiment of White Buffalo Calf Woman, a sacred figure in stories told by many Plains tribes. According to these stories, White Buffalo Calf Woman gave Indians the pipe, then turned into a white buffalo calf and ran away, promising one day to return.

August

The Nez Perce fend off a neo-Nazi group.

Indians and non-Indians come together at the "A Gathering of Culture and Unity," a powwow to organize resistance to a neo-Nazi group that intends to develop 440 acres of land near Kamiah, Idaho, in the center of Nez Perce territory. The plan was announced by James "Bo" Gritz, who in 1988 was the Populist Party vice-presidential candidate, sharing the ticket with David Duke, then the Grand Dragon of the Ku Klux Klan.

August

Joanne Shenandoah performs at Woodstock '94.

Oneida singer Joanne Shenandoah is the opening act at Woodstock '94—a concert held at Saugerties, New York, to commemorate the 25th anniversary of the 1969 Woodstock music festival. Performed before the crowd of more than 250,000, Shenandoah's folk songs display her penetrating voice and unique blending of native and contemporary instrumentation.

August 1

Minnesota bans Indian names as liquor brands.

A Minnesota state law goes into effect that revokes state approval of any beer brand that "states or implies in a false or misleading manner a connection with an actual living or dead American Indian leader." The law effectively bans the sale of the Original Crazy Horse Malt Liquor and Chief Oshkosh Beer. It is passed in response to criticism of these products by many Indians who claim they defame the name of the Lakota Sioux warrior Crazy Horse and the Menominee leader Oshkosh. Crazy Horse's descendants are particularly offended. They point out that their famous ancestor had been a teetotaler who warned his people of the destructive effects of alcohol. (See also entry for SEPTEMBER 17, 1996.)

"Black Hills of Dakota . . . home of Proud Indian Nations. A land where imagination conjures up images of blue clad Pony Soldiers and magnificent Native American Warriors . . . where wailful winds whisper of Sitting Bull, Crazy Horse and Custer."
—from the label of the original Crazy Horse Malt Liquor

1995

Massachusetts Indian inmates fight for their freedom of religion.

Calling themselves the Native American Spiritual Awareness Council, a group of Indian inmates in a

Massachusetts state prison meet to share their spiritual beliefs and strengthen their Indian identity. Prison administrators, however, interfere with the religious group by restricting it to Indians enrolled in a tribe and by forbidding it to use pipes, drums, and other items the council regards as sacred. In the lawsuit *Trapp et al. v. DuBois et al.*, the Massachusetts Superior Court agrees with the prisoners that their right to freedom of religion is being violated. It orders the prison to allow all Indian inmates to participate in the council and to permit the group access to its religious paraphernalia.

Income from Arctic refuge leases is included in the federal budget.

Due to the efforts of the congressional delegation from Alaska, $1.4 billion from leases to oil companies for the use of land in the Arctic National Wildlife Refuge is included in the federal budget bill. The measure is meant to pressure the government to open up the refuge to oil drilling so this money can be raised (see entry for 1987). Opponents to allowing drilling in the refuge include environmentalists, who maintain the companies will destroy the delicate wilderness area, and the Gwich'in Indians, who fear drilling will decimate the refuge's caribou herd on which they, as subsistence hunters, depend for their survival. The Alaskan delegation's agenda is thwarted only when President Bill Clinton vetoes the budget bill in its entirety.

March 9

The Mescalero Apache approve a nuclear waste storage facility.

On January 31, the Mescalero Apache vote down a referendum allowing a consortium of nuclear energy companies to store waste on their reservation. Immediately, the tribal government, which supports the building of the waste storage facility (see entry for FEBRUARY 15, 1994), launches a massive campaign to persuade tribe members to sign a petition calling for a second referendum on the issue. Under great pressure from their leaders,

30 percent of the tribe signs the petition, which by the tribal constitution allows the government to hold another vote. On this second round of voting, the referendum passes.

June

A Native sentencing circle banishes a rapist.

Billy Taylor, a 28-year-old man of the La Rouge Indian Band in La Rouge, Saskatchewan, requests that the band's sentencing circle administer his sentence after he is convicted of rape. At the band's office, friends and family of Taylor and the victim discuss the case for six hours before deciding to banish Taylor to an uninhabited island near La Rouge for one year. Food will be delivered to the island once a month, but otherwise Taylor will have no human contact during his banishment. The unusual punishment emerges from a growing movement among Canadian Natives appalled by the high number of Natives serving time in prison. They hold that, following their traditions, Native lawbreakers should receive alternative sentences determined by the people of their communities.

June

Disney's *Pocahontas* premieres.

Walt Disney Studios releases *Pocahontas*, an animated theatrical feature film about the life of the daughter of Chief Powhatan and her contact with the Virginia colonists in the early 17th century (see entry for DECEMBER 1607). Although well received by the general public and critics, many Indians take exception with the film's disregard for the known historical facts about Pocahontas. In the movie, she meets the English as a beautiful woman, whereas the actual Pocahontas was no older than twelve at the time. The plot also resurrects the legend of Pocahontas as an eroticized helpmate of the colonists—a popular 19th-century representation used to imply that "good" Indians encouraged whites to overrun their lands.

June 24

The Jemez Pueblo field criticism over the gallo.

The annual St. John the Baptist Day celebration at Jemez Pueblo is closed to the public following a campaign of animal-rights groups against the gallo, or rooster pull. During this ritual, which probably originated with the Spanish conquistadores, men named John or Juan honor their patron saint by sacrificing a rooster. The rooster is buried up to its neck in the ground of the pueblo square. On horseback, gallo participants compete to be the first rider to grab the rooster's head, which is often torn off from its body. The Pueblo believe that the blood from the rooster fertilizes and renews the earth.

June 30 to September 17

Native activists take over Gustafsen Lake.

A group of Natives began occupying a site sacred to the Shuswap on Gustafsen Lake, in British Columbia. The activists came to the sacred grounds to protect Percy Rosette, a Shuswap spiritual leader. The legal owner of the site, Lyle James, a non-Indian rancher, had given Rosette his permission to hold a Sun Dance at Gustafsen Lake in early June. When Rosette later refused to leave the area, however, he was harassed and threatened by James's ranch hands. The activists are also angered by the Canadian government's delay in settling the land claims of British Columbian Natives.

On September 11, two and a half months into the tense standoff, a pickup truck carrying several activists is blown up by a device planted by the Royal Canadian Mounted Police. The incident leads to a 45-minute gunfight between the Natives and 400 heavily armed officers. The activists surrender six days later.

September 4 to 12

The Chippewa occupy Ipperwash Park.

Claiming that the land belongs to them, about 30 Chippewa activists take over the Ipperwash Provin-

cial Park on the shore of Lake Huron in southwestern Ontario. Two days later, one of the occupiers, 38-year old Anthony "Dudley" George, is shot to death by police. The protest ends after the Canadian government on September 12 agrees to return the disputed area to the tribe and to fund an environmental cleanup of the site. (See also entry for MAY 1997.)

November 11

The Navajo Nation dedicates a memorial park to Navajo (Dineh) war casualties.

At the Navajo (Dineh) capital of Window Rock, Arizona, a ceremony is held to dedicate the Navajo Nation Veterans Memorial Park. The memorial is meant to honor all Navajo warriors who have given their lives to protect the Navajo way of life, including the soldiers who have died fighting in American wars.

> "[This day is] dedicated to memorialize those who have given the ultimate sacrifice in the services of our country, our land and the Diné [Navajo] way of life, those who gave of themselves in blood; those who bravely fought and have since deceased; those who stood ready in times of peace and those who are still holding vigilance for peace and democracy."
>
> —Navajo Nation president Albert Hale, during the dedication of the Navajo Nation Veterans Memorial Park

1996

The Coeur d'Alene launch a $1 billion suit against mining companies.

The Coeur d'Alene tribe files suit against several mining companies for $1 billion to fund a cleanup of the Coeur d'Alene river basin. There the companies have dumped mining waste, contaminating the waters with extremely high levels of lead. Although the extraordinary amount of money demanded by the tribe is derided by some, the U.S. Justice Department will soon join the tribe and file a companion suit against the mining firms for $600 million. (See also entry for FEBRUARY 1998.)

The Fort Belknap Indians accept a settlement from Pegasus Gold.

The Gros Ventre (Atsina) and Assiniboine Indians of Montana's Fort Belknap Reservation file a notice of their intent to sue Pegasus Gold, the mining company that operates the nearby Zortman mine. The mine is located on land sold by the tribes in 1896 after the U.S. government threatened to withhold food rations if they refused. Rather than risk a trial, Pegasus offers a settlement to end the suit, which alleges that the Zortman mine had contaminated reservation drinking water. The $37 million settlement includes $1 million for the tribes and a $30 million bond to insure against future damages.

Buffy Sainte-Marie founds the Cradleboard Teaching Project.

As part of her Nihewan Foundation, which provides scholarships for law students, Cree singer-activist Buffy Sainte-Marie (see also entry for 1964) creates the Cradleboard Teaching Project. The enterprise offers lesson plans and curriculum advice to aid teachers in discussing Native American culture and history in their classrooms. The project also uses e-mail and live computer chats to allow Indian and non-Indian children to communicate with one another and learn about each other's way of life.

Vine Deloria's *Red Earth, White Lies* is published.

In *Red Earth, White Lies,* Dakota lawyer and journalist Vine Deloria Jr. examines the racism inherent in much of the research conducted by non-Indians into the origins of Indian people. The book questions the need for further archaeological examination of Indian remains and challenges the Bering Strait theory, which holds that Indians' ancestors were Asians who migrated to North America during the Ice Age (see entry for CA. 25,000 TO 12,000 B.C.). Drawing on ancient creation stories, Deloria instead makes the case that Indians originated in the Americas.

March 27

Seminole Tribe v. Florida addresses the role of states in Indian gaming.

In accordance with the Indian Gaming Regulatory Act (see entry for OCTOBER 17, 1988), the Seminole sue Florida to force the state to negotiate with the tribe concerning a gambling parlor it intends to open. The state counters the suit by claiming that, as a sovereign entity, it cannot be sued without its consent, according to the Eleventh Amendment.

In a five-to-four vote, the Supreme Court rules in favor of Florida. The decision is seen as an important precedent and a controversial victory for states' rights: By declaring states immune to prosecution for violating federal law, it opens the door for states to ignore congressional edicts, such as environmental legislation, that they do not want to follow.

Ironically, the Seminole's defeat is perceived by many Indians (including some Seminole) as a boon to tribal gambling. The ruling effectively strikes down the Regulatory Act's requirement that tribes negotiate with states, many of which are highly resistant to reservation gaming.

Spring

The Taos Indians defy a court order to shut down their casino.

The U.S. attorney general orders the Taos Indians to close the doors of their casino when New Mexico, pressured by non-Indian business interests, refuses to give it the state's approval. The Taos rely on the casino's income to pay a mortgage on land worth $10 million surrounding the sacred Blue Lake (see entry for DECEMBER 15, 1970), which the Indians purchased to keep the area clear of non-Indian vacationers. Rather than risk foreclosure, the Taos continue to operate the casino and file suit against the state.

April

The Human Genome Diversity Project is announced.

At the Pan American Health Conference on Indigenous Peoples in Winnipeg, Canada, researchers announce plans for the Human Genome Diversity Project. The project is an effort by anthropologists, geneticists, and other scholars to document the genes of humans around the world. The organization intends to collect DNA specimens from 722 indigenous peoples it deems in danger of extinction.

The project is immediately condemned by indigenous groups across North America, who have not been consulted about its implementation. Many peoples speak out, warning of the potential for corporations and governments for using these DNA samples for profit or for the extermination of indigenous peoples. Other groups are also angered by the suggestion that they are a "vanishing race," an idea that they feel non-Indians will use to deny them political power and dismiss their societies and cultures.

June 8

A federal court rejects the rock climbing ban at Devils Tower.

In response to requests by area Indians, the National Park Service asks vacationers to respect a voluntary ban on rock climbing at Devils Tower, Wyoming, in June. During that month, Indians from 20 tribes who consider Devils Tower a sacred site gather to perform religious ceremonies. Days after the ban has gone into effect, a federal court in Casper rules that the measure violates the First Amendment rights of a commercial rock-climbing guide service that objects to the ban.

"Suppose a group of American Indians decided to use St. Peter's Cathedral as a place to climb. They used ropes and ladders to scale the church, but they only chose Sunday to resort to this sport. Or suppose they decided to go to Israel and use the Wailing Wall as a climbing site? What if they decided to scale some of the mosques in the Muslim countries? How long do you suppose they could enjoy this sport before all hell broke loose?"

—Oglala Lakota journalist
Tim Giago on the Devils Tower
controversy

June 10

Indians launch a class-action suit against the United States.

In a lawsuit brought by the Native American Rights Fund (NARF) (see entry for 1970), 300,000 Indians allege that the Bureau of Indian Affairs (BIA) has mismanaged funds held in trust for them in Individual Indian Money (IIM) accounts. The money in these accounts—which ranges from 35¢ to more than $1 million—came from oil, gas, grazing, and timber leases negotiated by the bureau for non-Indian use of Indian-owned land.

The largest class action ever initiated against the U.S. government for financial incompetence, the suit holds that billions of dollars owed to individual Indians has been misplaced due to poor record keeping. According to the NARF, the BIA neglected to stay in contact with many account holders, and the funds due some accounts were illegally placed directly into the U.S. Treasury.

July 19

Kennewick Man is discovered.

On the bank of the Columbia River in Washington State, a college student stumbles upon a human skull. Archaeologists rush to the site and excavate the most complete human skeleton ever found in the Pacific Northwest. Named Kennewick Man after a nearby town, the skeleton is estimated to be 9,300 years old.

In October, a massive legal battle will erupt between five tribal groups in the region, who want to bury the remains, and scientists, who seek to study and test the bones. The Indians maintain that the Native American Graves Protection and Repatriation Act (see entry for NOVEMBER 16, 1990) gives them the right to the skeleton, which they call the Ancient One and consider an ancestor. The scientists, who maintain the skull has Caucasoid features, hold that a skeleton as old as Kennewick man cannot be traced back to a modern tribe as the act requires. Complicating the debate is the Asatru Folk Assembly, a group of white Americans devoted to reviving Norse pagan traditions. The Asatru members also claim Kennewick Man as an ancestor and seek legal control over the skeleton.

August 29

Activist Winona LaDuke becomes a vice-presidential candidate.

At a press conference, the Green Party announces that Winona LaDuke, a 37-year-old Ojibway activist, will run as its candidate for vice president. The founder of the White Earth Land Recovery Project, which purchases land to regain the Ojibway's original homeland for tribal use, LaDuke shares the Green Party ticket with renowned consumer advocate Ralph Nader. Running largely to raise the profile of the Green Party in the United States, LaDuke and Nader will win 0.6 percent of the popular vote in the November election. (See also entry for JUNE 25, 2000.)

"I am interested in . . . the debate on issues of this society, the distribution of power and wealth, abuse of power, the rights of the natural world, the environment, and need to consider an amendment to the U.S. Constitution in which all decisions made today would be considered in light of the impact on the seventh generation from now. Now that, I believe, is what sustainability is all about. These are vital subjects which are all too often neglected by the rhetoric of 'major party' candidates and media."

—Winona LaDuke, accepting the Green Party nomination for vice president

September 17

An appeals court overturns the ban on the Crazy Horse brand.

The Minnesota Court of Appeals rules that a state law banning the sale of the Original Crazy Horse Malt Liquor (see entry for AUGUST 1, 1994) violates the freedom of speech of the Brooklyn-based Hormell Company, which distributes the product. The lawsuit was brought on behalf of Hormell and of the G. Heileman Brewing Co., which makes the malt liquor, by the Minnesota Civil Liberties Union.

September 26

Navajo-Hopi Land Dispute Settlement Act is passed.

By the terms of the Navajo-Hopi Land Dispute Settlement Act, the 3,000 Navajo (Dineh) living on the Hopi Indian Reservation are required to lease their land from the Hopi or move from the area by the end of the year. After December 31, Navajo who have neither signed a lease nor vacated the reservation can be forcibly evicted by the Hopi Rangers.

December

Maria Tallchief is honored by the Kennedy Center.

At a gala presentation attended by President Bill Clinton, Osage ballerina Maria Tallchief (see entry for OCTOBER 11, 1954) is named as one of the five recipients of the 1996 Kennedy Center Honors at the John F. Kennedy Center for the Performing Arts in Washington, D.C. The awards honor the lifetime achievements of Americans who have made significant contributions to the performing arts.

1997

February

A design is chosen for the Indian monument at the Little Bighorn battlefield.

Established in 1994, the Little Bighorn Battlefield National Monument Advisory Committee announces that it has selected a design by John R. Collins and Alison J. Towers of Philadelphia, Pennsylvania, for a memorial to the Indian warriors who fought at the Battle of Little Bighorn (see entry for JUNE 24 TO 25, 1876). The design was one of 551 submitted as part of a nationwide competition held by the committee.

Intended as a place where American Indians can celebrate and honor the memory of ancestors lost in the battle, the design includes a circular mound of earth on which a platform supporting bronze sculptures of Indian warriors will rest. Described by the designers as a "weeping wound," a gap in the mound will lead toward an existing memorial to the Seventh Cavalry, which was defeated by Indian forces during the battle.

February

Canadian Natives are outraged by an Indian women's murder trial.

In April 1995, Pamela George, a Native woman, was found dead in a muddy roadside ditch outside of Regina, Saskatchewan. Two 20-year-old white male university students were charged with beating the woman to death after friends said they bragged about killing George because she was an Indian.

At the end of the subsequent trial, the judge tells the jury to keep in mind that the killers were drunk and that George sometimes worked as a prostitute. Likely because of his instructions, the accused are found guilty of manslaughter rather than murder. Native groups speak out against the judge's actions and the verdict, citing them as proof of the racism rampant in the Canadian justice system.

February 7

Indian prisoner Norma Jean Croy is released.

After being incarcerated for 19 years, Shasta Indian Norma Jean Croy is released from Chowchilla Women's Prison in California. Croy and her brother Hooty were convicted of first-degree murder in the death of a police officer, whom she maintained was shot by Hooty in self-defense during an altercation in July 1978. After Hooty Croy's conviction was reversed by the California Supreme Court in 1985, he was acquitted of murder in a second trial in 1990. Norma Croy, however, continued to serve a life sentence, although there was no evidence to show that she ever fired a weapon. Convinced that Croy was a victim of a racist and sexist justice system, an international campaign emerged in the 1980s to secure her freedom.

March

The Mohegan and Pequot return federal housing grants.

Following the publication of an investigative report by the *Seattle Times,* the Mohegan and the

Pequot—two Indian groups that operate successful casinos (see entry for FEBRUARY 12, 1992)—return grant funds totalling nearly $3 million to the Department of Housing and Urban Development (HUD), with the request that the money be spent on poorer tribes. The *Times* article criticized HUD's tribal housing program for directing funds for low-cost housing to Indian groups with sizable incomes from gambling operations.

April 10

Modoc author Michael Dorris commits suicide.

The Native American literary community is stunned by the suicide of Michael Dorris in a motel room in Concord, New Hampshire. Dorris was the founder of the Native American Studies Program at Dartmouth College and the author of *The Broken Cord,* in which he described his struggles raising an adopted Indian son suffering from fetal alcohol syndrome (see entry for 1989). He was perhaps best known as the literary collaborator and husband of Louise Erdrich, the best-selling Ojibway (Anishinabe) novelist and short-story writer (see entry for 1984). At the time of his death, Dorris was being investigated on charges that he sexually abused one of his daughters.

April 10

Lac du Flambeau Chippewa sign a fishing agreement with Wisconsin.

Resolving the tense relationship between the Lac du Flambeau Chippewa and non-Indian fishermen, the tribe agrees to allow each fisherman to catch three walleye trout a day in the waters it controls. In exchange, Wisconsin grants the tribe the right to sell fishing and snowmobile licenses on their reservation. These licenses are good throughout the state of Wisconsin, but the tribe is to retain all income from their sale. These profits will be used to finance the managing and replenishing of reservation fisheries.

May

A Canadian policeman is found guilty of killing activist Dudley George.

Kenneth Deane, a member of the Ontario Provincial Police, is found guilty of criminal negligence in the shooting death of Chippewa Anthony "Dudley" George, one of the activists who occupied Ipperwash two years earlier (see entry for SEPTEMBER 4 TO 12, 1995). Deane claims that he shot George to prevent him from firing at fellow officers, but others testify that George was armed with only a stick. Native supporters of George are first gratified by the verdict but will express anger in June when Deane is sentenced to 180 hours community service rather than jail time.

May 24

The first Native American Music Awards ceremony is held.

In a ceremony at the Pequot tribe's Foxwoods resort in Connecticut, the Native American Music Awards, or "Nammies," recognize excellence in the growing Native American music movement. Among those honored are Oneida singer Joanne Shenandoah ("Best Female Artist"), Navajo (Dineh) fluist R. Carlos Nakai ("Best Male Artist"), and the Black Lodge Singers ("Artist/Group of the Year"). Hosted by singer Wayne Newton, who is of Cherokee descent, the program features performances by many artists, including Joy Harjo and Robbie Robertson.

May 30

Voters reject equal gender representation in Nunavut legislature.

In the area that will become the new Canadian territory of Nunavut in 1999 (see entry for DECEMBER 16, 1991), voters decide not to require that an equal number of women and men serve in the Inuit-governed territory's legislature. The commission overseeing the creation of Nunavut had proposed that the legislature be composed of 22 representatives, one man and one woman from each district. The plan was intended to guarantee that women would have a substantial role in governing, as they had in traditional Inuit society.

June

A tax on Indian business revenue is proposed.

Chair of the House Ways and Means Commission, Representative Bill Archer proposes a 34 percent tax on revenues of Indian-owned businesses, particularly lucrative casinos. He argues that the untaxable status of these enterprises gives them an unfair advantage over neighboring non-Indian businesses. Opponents of the measure—including Ben Nighthorse Campbell, the Northern Cheyenne senator from Colorado (see entry for 1992)—successfully argue that such a tax would violate the sovereign status of Indian tribes.

August 17

Inuit whaling is resumed in the eastern Arctic.

Funded by the Keewatin Wildlife Federation, hunters from across the eastern arctic region of Canada use rifles and traditional harpoons to land a bowhead whale off the coast of Repulse Bay. The whale is the first legally hunted by the Inuit since the Canadian government began regulating their bowhead hunting in 1976. The hunt is made possible because of the expansion of Inuit hunting rights following the announcement of the creation of the Inuit-governed territory of Nunavut (see entry for DECEMBER 16, 1991). Gifts of *muktuk* (blubber) are sent to Inuit communities throughout Canada to celebrate the event.

October

The Makah are given permission to hunt whales.

The International Whaling Commission approves a 1996 application from the Makah Indians of Wash-

ington State to hunt whales off the coast of Neah Bay. The tribe's 1855 treaty with the United States gave them the right to continue their traditional whale hunts, but in 1926 a ban on whaling in the region was imposed by the commission due to overhunting by whites. News that the commission is permitting the Makah to take five California gray whales a year for five years immediately comes under harsh criticism by animal-rights groups and whale-watching organizations. (See also entry for MAY 17, 1999.)

"They want us in a museum. They'd rather we just said, 'Oh, the Makah were great whalers,' and leave it at that. They want us to have a dead culture. But it's been our way of life. We look to the ocean and we feel we not only have a legal right but a moral right to whale."
—tribal elder George Bowechop on animal-rights groups' opposition to Makah whaling

1998

February

The Environment Protection Agency plans a pollution study of Coeur d'Alene lands.

The Environment Protection Agency (EPA) announces that it will investigate the extent of the pollution of northern Idaho caused by silver mining. The area to be studied includes the reservation of the Coeur d'Alene Indians, who are attempting to sue several mining companies for $1 billion to fund an extensive cleanup (see entry for 1996).

The EPA project will access the damage done to the people and wildlife of the region and determine whether it will need Superfund monies beyond the $150 million allocation already made to clean up a small area near Kellogg, Idaho (see entry for 1992). The investigation will cover an area of 1,500 square miles, extending across Idaho's borders into Washington State and Montana. The project's scope is unprecedented and could cost as much as $1 billion.

February 11

Interior Secretary Bruce Babbitt is investigated in Indian casino scandal.

Attorney General Janet Reno announces that she will appoint a special prosecutor to investigate allegations that Secretary of the Interior Bruce Babbitt perjured himself before Congress in testimony about the department's rejection of an Indian casino project in Hudson, Wisconsin. In 1994, three Wisconsin Chippewa tribes proposed establishing an off-reservation gambling casino on the site of a dog track. The project was opposed by a group of Indians in Minnesota, who feared it would compete with their own casino. After the department decided to reject the Chippewa application, Babbitt allegedly told a pro-casino lobbyist that the Minnesota Indians were favored in the dispute because they were large contributors to the Democratic Party.

March

Coyote Tales premieres.

Coyote Tales has its world premiere in Kansas City, Missouri. An original work commissioned by the city's Lyric Opera, the opera recounts five traditional Indian stories featuring the character of Coyote, a trickster whose foibles comment on human behavior. With noted Acoma poet Simon Ortiz serving as an adviser, the work is produced in collaboration with the Haskell Indian Nations University (see entry for SEPTEMBER 1, 1884). Ortiz calls the opera "a wonderful way for people who do not know enough about our Indian heritage to learn about a rich and vibrant culture."

June

Archaeologists discover a Native skeleton in Alaska.

Archaeologists from the Forestry Service and Smithsonian Institution excavate a cave on Prince of Whales Island in Alaska and come upon a 9,800-year-old skeleton. With the Kennewick Man controversy in mind (see entry for JULY 19, 1996), the scientists stop digging when they determine the bones are human and consult with the Klawock and Craig, two Native groups in the area. After meeting with scientists, the councils of the two groups reach an agreement with the Forestry Service to allow the bones to be carbon dated and analyzed, on the condition that further excavations at the discovery site be monitored to protect its sanctity.

June

California tribes speak out against state regulation on gambling.

In meetings with Congress and Attorney General Janet Reno, Indian leaders from California seek support for their right to operate casinos without interference of the state's governor, Pete Wilson. By the Indian Gaming Regulatory Act (see entry for OCTOBER 17, 1988), tribes are required to negotiate an agreement, or compact, with a state before opening a gambling operation within its borders. The compacts offered by Wilson, however, are so restrictive that many California tribes have opened gaming houses without state approval. Wilson has further infuriated these tribes by enlisting the aid of federal prosecutors to shut down illegal gambling operations by confiscating valuable slot machines.

August 11

The Mashantucket Pequot Museum opens.

Using profits from the Foxwoods casino and resort (see entry for FEBRUARY 12, 1992), the Mashantucket Pequot open a $193 million museum and research center on their reservation in Connecticut. The museum features state-of-the-art interactive films and videos, a re-creation of a complete Pequot village, and permanent exhibits on the history of the Pequot, who were nearly decimated in a brutal conflict with British colonists (see entry for 1637). At 308,000 square feet, the lavish museum complex is 20 percent larger than the proposed National Museum of the American Indian, due to open in Washington, D.C., in 2002.

Autumn

Kareem Abdul-Jabbar coaches Apache basketball players.

Retired professional basketball star Kareem Abdul-Jabbar comes to Whiteriver, Arizona, on the White Mountain Apache Reservation, to help coach the Alchesay High School basketball team. Abdul-Jabbar was invited to teach at the school by the Whiteriver school superintendent after the athlete, a Native American–history enthusiast, attended the dedication of Alchesay's new activities center and participated in Apache ceremonies on the nearby San Carlos Reservation.

October 29

Kennewick Man is moved to a Seattle museum.

The bones of Kennewick Man—the nearly 10,000-year-old skeleton found on the banks of the Columbia River (see entry for JULY 19, 1996)—are transported from the Pacific Northwest National Laboratory to the Burke Museum of the University of Washington, where they can be examined by scientists under the supervision of the Department of the Interior.

The move is ordered by Judge John Jelderks, who is presiding over the legal battle involving the skeleton. His ruling is a disappointment to the five Northwest tribes who have been fighting for the right to bury the remains of Kennewick Man, whom they consider to be their ancestor. Before the bones are removed from the laboratory, representatives of these tribes and of the Asatru, a group committed to reviving ancient Norse religion that also claims the skeleton, are permitted to perform farewell rituals.

"Native remains are not objects for scientific curiosity. They are relatives. . . . They are grandmothers and grandfathers. When these relatives are put away . . . they're not to be disturbed by anyone . . . and the place that they rest is sacred ground."

—Debra Harry of the Indigenous Peoples Coalition against Biopiracy on the Kennewick Man controversy

December

U.S. government joins the Oneida land claims suit.

In 1970, the Oneida Indians of New York initiated a lawsuit claiming that local and state governments had illegally seized 270,000 acres of their land in the late 18th and early 19th centuries. Although the Supreme Court found in the Oneida's favor 15 years later, the tribe and New York have been unable to negotiate a settlement. To spur on the state to reach an agreement, the U.S. government files an amended complaint that names the 20,000 landowners living in the disputed area as defendants. The suit outrages many non-Indians in the area, some of whom already resent the Oneida's growing nontaxable income from their recently opened Turning Stone Casino.

1999

The U.S. Justice Department addresses concerns over offensive sports team names.

The Justice Department's Office of Civil Rights addresses the complaint of an adoptive mother of several Lakota Sioux children regarding the sports team names—the "Warriors" for a boys' team and the "Squaws" for a girls' team—used at Erwin High School near Asheville, North Carolina. The investigation focuses on whether the names violate the civil rights of Indian students. In response to the department's queries, the local school board agrees to ban the "Squaws" as a team name, while leaders of the Eastern Cherokee agree to allow the continued use of the name "Warriors."

April 1

Nunavut Day celebrates the creation of a new Canadian territory.

A day of festivities in the territorial capital of Iqualuit marks the creation of Nunavut, a new Canadian territory carved from the eastern half of the Northwest Territories. Encompassing one-fifth of Canada, Nunavut covers an area roughly the size of Mexico. At one celebration, the newly elected prime minister Jean Chrétien says, "What we affirm today, with the stroke of a pen, is the end of a very long road," referring to the 30 years of negotiation that led to Nunavut's formation. With 15 Inuit in the territory's first 19-member parliament, Nunavut promises to give Canadian Inuit—who make up 85 percent of the territory's population—their first opportunity for self-government in centuries.

An Inuit man aboard a snowmobile watches fireworks shot off at midnight on April 1, 1999, to celebrate the formation of the Inuit territory of Nunavut. *(CORBIS/AFP)*

"Native children have good names and they suffer from this hateful, hurtful one. It helps them to know that their elders are doing something about it, that our views are validated in the justice system and by myriad fair-minded people."

—Suzan Shown Harjo, on her successful lawsuit to extinguish the trademark on "Washington Redskins"

April 2

"Washington Redskins" loses its trademarked status.

After a seven-year legal battle, a coalition of prominent American Indians—including Suzan Shown Harjo and Vine Deloria Jr. (see entry for 1969 and 1996)—convinces a panel of federal judges to cancel the trademarks protecting the use of the name "Washington Redskins" for the professional football team. Although National Football League spokespeople maintain the name "honors" American Indians, the judges determine that it "may disparage Native Americans and may bring them into contempt or disrepute" and therefore cannot be trademarked under a law that bans the licensing of offensive material. The Indian litigants hope that, out of fear of losing lucrative licensing contracts, the team will change its name.

May

The National Park Service surveys the site of the Sand Creek Massacre.

An archaeological survey ordered by the National Park Service to assess adding the site of the Sand Creek Massacre to the park system is completed. On this location in southeastern Colorado, on November 29, 1864, Lt. Col. John Chivington of the First and Third Regiments of the Colorado Cavalry and 700 troops slaughtered about 200 Cheyenne men, women, and children in the camp of Black Kettle (see entry for NOVEMBER 29, 1864). Legislation introduced by Northern Cheyenne senator Ben Nighthorse Campbell, and passed into law in October 1998, called for this survey to determine the feasibility for inclusion in the park system. The survey found personal ornaments, camp equipment, ammunition, hide scrapers, arrowheads, and other items that lead to the identification of Black Kettle's camp.

May 4

The Sacagawea (Sacajawea) coin is unveiled.

Leaders from 250 tribes gather at the White House for a ceremony to unveil the design of a new one-dollar coin featuring the faces of Sacagawea (Sacajawea) (see entry for APRIL 1805) and her baby Jean-Baptiste (see entry for 1823). With her husband, Sacagawea was hired to serve as an interpreter for the Lewis and Clark Expedition. Hosting the event, First Lady Hillary Clinton tells the crowd, "Sacagawea played an unforgettable role in the history of our nation. We are here to celebrate her . . . and the even greater role that Native American women will play in the future."

May 17

Makah Indians hunt a gray whale.

A Makah whaling crew, traveling in a hand-carved cedar canoe, harpoons a gray whale off the coast of Neah Bay, Washington. The whale hunt is the first held by the Makah since the 1920s, when gray whales were declared endangered due to overhunting by commercial whalers. Although the Makah were given permission to hunt five whales a year by the International Whaling Commission (see entry for OCTOBER 1997), the event is protested by several animal-rights groups, who maintain that the hunt does not represent a revival of tribal ways because nontraditional hunting methods are employed. The protesters are particularly incensed by the teams of Makah in motorboats who accompany the hunters and shoot at the wounded whale after it is hit by the first harpoon.

May 23

Museums at Harvard and Phillips Academy at Andover, Massachusetts, return human remains to Pecos and Jemez Pueblos.

In response to the Native American Graves Protection and Reparation Act (see entry for NOVEMBER 16, 1990), Harvard University and Phillips Academy at Andover, both in Massachusetts, have their museums return Pueblo Indian human remains dating from the 12th to the 19th centuries. The event marks the largest repatriation of American Indian remains to date. Harvard alone gives the Jemez Pueblo the bones of 2,000 humans found at an abandoned village in New Mexico's Pecos Valley. The excavation was conducted by anthropologist Alfred V. Kidder between 1915 and 1929. Since the 1930s, the collection has been used by scientists to study early southwestern cultures and a variety of medical conditions, including osteoporosis, head injuries, and tooth decay. The Jemez plan to conduct a private reburial of the bones at the Pecos National Monument Historical Park, 30 miles south of Santa Fe, New Mexico.

June 16

Thirty-four Indian tribes file a tobacco suit.

Leaders of 34 tribes, most from the West and Midwest, file a suit against more than a dozen tobacco companies to recover billions of dollars the tribes have spent treating smoking-related illnesses. The legal action comes on the heels of a court ruling ordering tobacco companies to pay 46 states more than $200 billion in compensation. Although Indians have much higher smoking rates than the general population, Indian tribes are to receive no benefit from the settlement.

July 7

President Bill Clinton visits the Pine Ridge Reservation.

On a four-day tour of the poorest communities of the United States, President Bill Clinton, accompanied by the Reverend Jesse Jackson, visits the Oglala Sioux's Pine Ridge Reservation in South Dakota. The event marks the first time a U.S. president has made an appearance on an Indian reservation since the Roosevelt administration. Acknowledging that a nationwide economic boom has made little change in the standard of living of Pine Ridge residents, Clinton promises that the federal government will investigate new ways to alleviate reservation poverty, particularly by working with the private sector. In a speech, Clinton states, "We're coming from Washington to ask you what you want to do and tell you we will give you the tools and support to get done what you want to do for your children and their future." While the Oglala stage no formal demonstrations, several activists greet the president with signs demanding the release of Leonard Peltier (see entry for APRIL 18, 1977) and the return of the Black Hills (see entry for JUNE 30, 1980).

July

Tohono O'odham linguist Ofelia Zepeda receives a "genius grant."

University of Arizona professor Ofelia Zepeda is given a MacArthur Foundation fellowship—popularly known as a "genius grant"—for her pioneering work in the preservation of Indian languages. The foremost scholar of the Tohono O'odham (formerly known as Papago) language, she is the author of *A Papago Grammar*, which since its publication in 1983 has served as a model for other Indian language dictionaries. She is also active in the American Indian Language Development Institute, an organization dedicated to training teachers and instructing Indian children in Indian languages spoken by so few that they are in danger of becoming extinct.

July 4

Lakota Sioux protest alcohol sales in Whiteclay, Nebraska.

Nine people, including American Indian Movement (AIM) activist Russell Means, are arrested during a protest march in Whiteclay, Nebraska. The town, located two miles from the border of the Lakota Sioux's Pine Ridge Reservation, has long been criticized by tribe members for selling alcohol to reservation residents. By tribal law alcohol is forbidden on the reservation, but Pine Ridge nevertheless has an extraordinarily high rate of alcohol-related deaths. The protest was inspired in part by the recent murders of two Lakota men, whose bodies were found outside of Whiteclay. Although unsolved, alcohol is believed to have played a role in the crimes.

July 24

The Cherokee elect a new principal chief amidst a financial scandal.

Following a tumultuous campaign, Chad Smith is elected principal chief of the Cherokee. The tenure of the defeated incumbent Joe Byrd has been marred by charges of financial improprieties. The Department of the Interior began investigating Byrd's financial records after the principal chief fired tribal marshals executing a search warrant for financial records from his office. During the campaign, Byrd promised to provide "responsible leadership," while Smith asked voters to remove Byrd from office "while there's still time to save our nation."

July 27

Crayola abandons "Indian red" as a crayon name.

After a national contest, Binney & Smith, Inc., the maker of Crayola crayons, changes the crayon name "Indian red" to the contest winner "chestnut." The name change is made in response to complaints from teachers, who said students assumed the name referred to the skin color of American Indians. In fact, "Indian red" is a common designation for a color of oil paint originally derived from a pigment found near India.

September 1

The Aboriginal Peoples Television Network (APTN) begins broadcasting.

To give a voice to Natives in Canada, the Aboriginal Peoples Television Network (APTN) begins airing documentaries, educational programs, dramas, and children's series. Licensed as a mandatory cable channel, the APTN reaches 8 million homes throughout Canada. It offers programs on Canada's Native peoples and aboriginal cultures from around the world in English, French, and numerous Native languages.

September 17

The Gates Millennium Scholars Program announces scholarships for Indian students.

Microsoft Corporation chairman Bill Gates launches a program through his private charity that will provide $1 billion in scholarships for minority students, including American Indians. The announcement is made following a challenge by activist Jesse Jackson to the computer industry to improve its record in hiring minority workers. Over the next 20 years, the Gates Millennium Scholars Program will offer scholarships to undergraduates as well as students seeking graduate degrees in math, science, engineering, education, and library science.

September 28

The American Indian College Fund receives a $30 million donation.

The Lilly Endowment announces that it has given $30 million to the American Indian College Fund, the largest private donation ever received by an American Indian organization. The grant, which nearly equals the total amount of money the charity has raised in its 10-year history, will be spent on constructing new buildings to replace crumbling facilities at 30 tribal colleges.

November 25

The Leonard Peltier Defense Committee ends a month-long demonstration.

Several Indian organizations requesting clemency for Leonard Peltier end 25 days of rallies and demonstrations in Washington, D.C. Convicted of the murder of two FBI agents, (see entry for APRIL 18, 1977), Peltier has been imprisoned for 23 years, though many activists maintain he is innocent. Demonstrators estimate that worldwide more than 25 million signatures have been gathered on petitions demanding Peltier's release. (See also entry for DECEMBER 15, 2000 and for JANUARY 20, 2001.)

December 21

A federal judge orders an overhaul of the Indian trust fund system.

Maintaining that "it would be difficult to find a more historically mismanaged federal program," U.S. District Judge Royce Lamberth orders the U.S. government to make quarterly reports to the court and to the Native American Rights Fund, an organization that has brought suit against the government for its mishandling of Indian trust funds (see entry for JUNE 10, 1996). Although the ruling is considered a victory for the Indian plaintiffs, Lamberth does not follow the Indians' recommendation that the trust funds be taken out of the hands of the government and placed under the jurisdiction of a special receiver, who would report directly to the court. The judge, however, does threaten that if adequate changes are not made in the trust fund system, he will find the officials responsible in contempt of court.

Lamberth's ruling is delivered only weeks after an investigation found that the Treasury Department had shredded 162 boxes of documents relevant to the case. Although the government's attorneys maintain the destruction of the evidence was accidental, they neglected to tell the court about it for three months.

2000

January 14

The United States proposes the return of land to the Northern Ute.

After seven years of negotiation, the Department of Energy announces its intention to return 84,000 acres of land in northern Utah to the Northern Ute tribe. The land return is the largest made to any American Indians in the continental United States in more than a century. The land, which borders the Uintah and Ouray Reservation, was taken from the Ute in 1916 because it contained oil reserves that the U.S. government had believed might be needed by the navy during World War I. The United States, however, never tapped the oil supply or settled the area. As part of the agreement, the Ute promise to give the government royalties from any oil income they make from the land. The money is targeted to help fund the cleanup of a radioactive waste site near Utah's Arches National Park.

January 16

Lakota Sioux activists occupy their tribal headquarters.

On the Pine Ridge Reservation in South Dakota, about 100 Lakota led by tribal elders peacefully stage a takeover of the tribe's headquarters. The protesters demand that the tribal council, created

by guidelines set by the U.S. government, step down and allow a traditionally organized government to take its place. The sit-in participants also accuse the council of mismanagement of tribal funds and call for an audit.

February

A Navajo (Dineh) Code Talker G.I. Joe doll is introduced by Hasbro.

The toy maker Hasbro creates a G.I. Joe doll who is a Navajo (Dineh) Code Talker. The dolls speaks; his voice was recorded by one of the actual Navajo Code Talkers. (See entry for APRIL 1942.)

The toy maker Hasbro begins shipping the Navajo Code Talker G.I. Joe as part of a 22-figure line of classic military figures. The doll represents a member of the Navajo Code Talkers, an elite group of marines who during World War II communicated messages using an unbreakable code based on the Navajo language (see entry for APRIL 1942). When the doll's arm is lifted, one of seven phrases in Navajo can be heard. The phrases were recorded by Sam Billison, a member of the Navajo Tribal Council and former Code Talker. Hasbro agrees to donate $5,000 to the Navajo Code Talkers Association, an organization founded by the surviving Code Talkers in 1969.

February 3

An Indian media organization wins concessions from two television networks.

The CBS and Fox television networks announce plans to increase minority hiring in response to demands made by a coalition of activist groups, including American Indians in Film and Television. The announcements come after six months of negotiation, during which the coalition threatened to sponsor a "brown-out"—a minority boycott of all network programming. ABC and NBC previously agreed to some of the coalition's requests, although they resisted demands for creating an executive position for a vice president of diversity.

March

The Osage Nation sues the federal government for oil and gas royalties.

The Osage Nation files a second lawsuit against the federal government over the issue of oil and gas royalties. They already have a $100 million lawsuit against the government for nonpayment of royalties and now request that the court consolidate the two cases. The Bureau of Indian Affairs (BIA) is entrusted with handling the royalties in much the same way as it does the trust accounts for tribes and individual tribal members who receive lease, royalty, and other payments for land. A class-action lawsuit that involves some 300,000 Individual Indian Money account holders has already been filed against the federal government (see entry for JUNE 10, 1996). That suit claims that possibly billions of dollars cannot be accounted for. In that case the BIA admits years of improper management of the accounts but argues that the money is not missing.

March

Artifacts for the new National Museum of the American Indian are transported from the Heye Collection to the Smithsonian.

Trucks carry load after load of the 800,000 objects left by Indian art collector George Gustav Heye when he died in 1957. The Heye Collection also contains an 86,000-image photo collection. Ground has been broken the previous fall for the 10th and final Smithsonian museum on the Capitol Mall—the National Museum of the American Indian (see entry for NOVEMBER 28, 1989). The original concept for the museum building design—which will have a huge copper dome and be built of clifflike limestone—came from Canadian Blackfoot architect Douglas Cardinal (see entry for 1993).

March 7

California voters approve proposition allowing the expansion of tribal gaming.

By a landslide, Californians vote nearly two to one to approve Proposition 1A, which amends the state's constitution to permit Las Vegas–style gambling on Indian land. Gaming tribes have spent more than $21 million in their campaign for the proposition, while a mere $44,000 was spent by gambling opponents. Experts estimate that the expansion of California Indian casinos could raise revenues from $1 billion to more than $4 billion annually. Although only a fraction of California Indians will profit directly from the measure, gambling tribes agree to share a portion of their profits with other recognized tribes in the state.

April 7

Notah Begay III competes in the Masters Tournament.

Professional golfer Notah Begay III shoots 74 at the Masters Tournament, thereby becoming the first Indian to compete in the event. A Navajo raised on the Iseta Pueblo Reservation in New Mexico, Begay began playing golf at age six. After high school, he was recruited by Stanford University, where he established himself as a leading player while earning a degree in economics. At Stanford, he also became friends with fellow teammates Tiger Woods and Casey Martin, who later joined him on the professional circuit.

April 17

President Clinton announces a plan to provide low-cost phone service on Indian reservations to help bring the information revolution to Native Americans.

As part of a $17 million initiative to help low-income communities access the Internet and keep them from being left behind in the information revolution, President Bill Clinton announces a plan to offer dollar-a-month phone service to up to 300,000 Indians across the country. He traveled to Shiprock, New Mexico, on the Navajo (Dineh) reservation to make his speech after a letter was written to him by Myra Jodie, a 13-year-old Navajo girl who won a computer but was unable to use the Internet because her home did not have a phone.

Only about 22 percent of Navajo on the reservation have phone service; many also lack electricity.

May

The Grammy Awards add a Native American music category.

The National Academy of Recording Arts and Sciences votes to create a new Grammy Awards to honor each year's best Native American music album. Previously, Native American artists were included under award categories for new age and folk music. Although news of the award is embraced by the Native American music industry, it raises questions about what criteria the academy will use to define who is and is not a Native American artist.

Summer

Wildfires across the West threaten ancient Anasazi ruins at Mesa Verde National Park near Cortez, Colorado.

Wildfires raging across the western United States move into Mesa Verde National Park. By July 27, 23,000 acres in and near the park are burned. Mesa Verde, known for its Anasazi cliff dwellings, is likely to have other as-yet-undiscovered but significant archaeological finds. Park personnel and archaeologists work quickly to identify undiscovered sites ahead of the flames, hoping to create firebreaks around them or help firefighters steer the fires away from them. At least a dozen new sites are found.

June 22

Grand Ronde Indians agree to the display of a sacred meteorite

To avert a court battle, the Grand Ronde Tribal Council makes an agreement with New York City's Museum of Natural History regarding the 10,000-year-old Willamette meteorite. Called Tomanowas by the Indians, the meteorite, the largest ever found in the United States, is considered sacred by the tribe. The Grand Ronde Indians of Oregon will allow the museum to exhibit the 16-ton rock at its new planetarium in exchange for access to the meteorite for a religious ceremony once a year. The museum, in turn, promises to place a permanent plaque by the object to explain its religious significance to museum visitors.

June 25

Activist Winona LaDuke accepts her second Green Party nomination for the vice presidency.

At the Green Party convention in Denver, Colorado, Ojibway environmentalist Winona LaDuke agrees to run for vice president on a ticket with presidential nominee Ralph Nader. LaDuke and Nader had also been nominated by the party four yeasr earlier (see entry for AUGUST 29, 1996). The Green Party platform calls for the release of Leonard Peltier (see entry for APRIL 18, 1977 and entry for JANUARY 20, 2001), a halt to the exploitation of natural resources on Indian land, and the creation of "reservation economic zones" to improve employment opportunities for Indians.

July

Indian leaders lobby for trademark protection for tribal symbols.

In meetings with representatives of the U.S. Patent and Trademark Office, Indian leaders ask that tribal symbols be given the same legal protections applied the symbols of nations and states. While these symbols can be used by business concerns, they cannot be trademarked by them, thus discouraging their commercial use.

The issue emerged two years earlier in a dispute between the trademark office and the Pueblo Indians of Zia. The Zia Pueblo were outraged when, over their objections, the office permitted a tour company to trademark a logo incorporating the Zia sun symbol. This sacred design, which features a red circle with sixteen lines radiating from it, has been in use at Zia since 1200. To draw attention to their cause, Zia leaders demanded that New Mexico legislators pay the tribe $74 million for the state's use of the Zia sun symbol—$1 million for each year it has appeared on the flag of New Mexico.

July

Leaders of Zuni Pueblo and the Navajo Nation celebrate the return of ancestral lands near Fort Wingate, New Mexico.

Zuni Pueblo governor Malcolm Bowekaty, Navajo president Kelsey Begaye, and Zuni Pueblo head councilman Eldred Bowekaty attend a ceremony at which the first parcel of the Fort Wingate (New Mexico) Depot Activity Property is officially transferred to the Department of the Interior on behalf of the Navajo and Zuni Nations. Members of the Navajo Nation and the Zuni Pueblo in New Mexico worked together to bring about this transfer of land from the Department of Defense to the Department of the Interior, which will now hold it in trust for use by the tribes.

August

Canadian officials square off with the Micmac in Burnt Church, New Brunswick, over fishing rights.

Royal Canadian Mounted Police and Coast Guard seize about 2,000 lobster traps and arrest four Micmac in Burnt Church, New Brunswick, for violating restrictions on off-season trapping. The Indians maintain that these restrictions do not apply to them, citing a September 1999 ruling of the Supreme Court of Canada. The court upheld a 1760 treaty between the English and the Indians of Canada's Atlantic coast that granted these tribes the right to make a "moderate livelihood" through year-round hunting and fishing.

August 7

Ishi's brain is repatriated.

A group of elders from the Pit River tribe travel to Washington, D.C., to take possession of the brain of Ishi, the last Indian of the Yahi tribe (see entry for AUGUST 1911). Ishi spent his final years at the museum of the University of California in San Francisco,

where he developed a relationship with anthropologist Alfred Kroeber. Against Ishi's wishes, Kroeber had Ishi's body autopsied after his death in 1914 and sent his brain to the Smithsonian for study. As distant relatives of the Yahi, the Pit River Indians lobbied for the repatriation of the brain, which they plan to bury at a secret location at the foothills of Mount Lassen near Redding, California.

> "This may be one of the most egregious cases of violating a Native American. He was a real friend to the white man. He spent virtually all his waking hours telling us about his culture, and he was anxious to return to the land of dead when he passed away."
>
> —University of California historian Nancy Rockafeller, on the treatment of Ishi's remains

September 8

The Bureau of Indian Affairs (BIA) apologizes to American Indians.

As assistant secretary of the Bureau of Indian Affairs, Pawnee tribe member Kevin Glover issues a formal apology to American Indians on behalf of the Bureau of Indian Affairs (BIA). The apology is part of a ceremony commemorating the 175th anniversary of the BIA's formation (see entry for 1824). Glover admits that "this agency participated in the ethnic cleansing that befell the Western tribes." In addition to faulting the BIA for forcing Indians from their land and undermining their cultures, he cites the agency's recent failures to alleviate alcoholism, violence, and other problems plaguing American Indian communities. Also speaking at the event is Interior Secretary Bruce Babbitt, who tells the BIA's Indian employees, "May you prosper, grow, advocate, get under people's skins."

September 16

The Native Sun Symphony Orchestra makes its premiere performance.

Conceived four years earlier by Mescalero Apache José Cordero, the Native Sun Symphony Orchestra performs its first concert at Connecticut College in New London. The concert presents original works by four American Indian composers—Louis Ballard, Brent Michael Davids, Jerod Tate, and David Yeagley. Orchestra members include more than 70 musicians and composers from 65 tribes.

September 25

The U.S. government gives Kennewick Man to five northwestern tribes.

After four years of dispute, the Department of the Interior agrees to turn over Kennewick Man, a 9,300-year-old skeleton, to five tribes in the Northwest. The Indians claim Kennewick Man as an ancestor and wish to bury him by tribal rites. Since the skeleton was discovered (see entry for JULY 19, 1996), the tribes have been embroiled in a battle with scientists intent on studying it. The government's decision prompts eight anthropologists to file a lawsuit in federal court seeking continued access to the bones.

October

The Mescalero Apache and Comanche go to court for "Geronimo's headdress."

Two tribes—the Mescalero Apache and the Comanche—file suit to obtain a 19th-century headdress that, according to legend, was last worn by the Apache war chief Geronimo (see entry for OCTOBER 1881). In 1999, the FBI confiscated the headdress and arrested its non-Indian owner for illegally trafficking in eagle feathers after he tried to sell the artifact over the Internet. The Mescalero claim that, as one of Geronimo's possessions, the headdress belongs in their museum. The Comanche counter that they should have the headdress because its style marks it as a Comanche, not an Apache, war bonnet. The Department of the Interior plans to display the headdress in one of its museums until either the Mescalero or the Comanche can prove their claims of ownership.

The Yakama's alcohol ban is challenged in court.

The state of Washington files suit against the Yakama Nation to force the tribe to lift a recent ban on alcohol sales. The ban was instituted by tribal leaders alarmed at the high rates of alcohol-related accidents and fetal alcohol syndrome on the Yakama's reservation in eastern Washington. The state maintains that, despite the Yakama's sovereignty, the tribe does not have the right to impose the ban on the 20,000 nontribal members living within reservation borders. The lawsuit is supported by owners of taverns and liquor stores on the reservation, most of whom are non-Indians.

October 7

Indians protest Denver's Columbus Day parade.

More than 140 Indian and Hispanic activists are arrested in Denver, Colorado, during a parade to honor Italian explorer Christopher Columbus (see entry for OCTOBER 12, 1492). As part of their nonviolent protest, they pour a line of red paint across the parade path to symbolize the blood shed by Indians at the hands of the first Europeans in North America. To placate the activists, the city had agreed to publicize the event only as a celebration of Italian pride, but at the last minute the city reneged on its promise by designating it a Columbus Day parade.

October 10

Spokane school puts an end to a dramatization of George Custer's death.

Following discussions with Indian leaders, officials at Lewis and Clark High School in Spokane, Washington, agree to abandon a show dramatizing the death of Lieutenant Colonel George Custer at the Battle of Little Bighorn (see entry for JUNE 25 TO 26, 1876). The six-minute program was performed during halftime at football games by the school's marching band and dancers dressed as soldiers and Indians. The show fell under scrutiny after 16-year-old student Dylan Lodge, a Gros Ventre (Atsina) tribal member, complained that its depiction of Indian history was "cartoonish."

October 11

The Mashantucket Pequot are accused of misusing a government drug subsidy.

An audit conducted by the Department of Health and Human Services holds that the Mashantucket Pequot have illegally distributed $5.8 million worth of prescription drugs to non-Indian employees of the tribe's Foxwoods casino (see entry for FEBRUARY 12, 1992). The government maintains the drugs were obtained through a federal discount program intended for Indians only. Tribal leaders question the audits' findings in a statement reading in part, "The tribal government considers tribal employees and their families to be members of the tribal community for purposes of health care."

October 23

The Sand Creek Massacre National Historic Site is established.

Congress passes as bill to establish the location of the Sand Creek Massacre as a national historic site. At Sand Creek, the Third Colorado Cavalry murdered nearly 200 Southern Cheyenne and Arapaho, who were camping peacefully in the area (see entry for NOVEMBER 29, 1864). As a national historic site, graves at Sand Creek will be protected from artifact poachers. The designation also will allow the Cheyenne and Arapaho tribes to claim the remains of those killed. The bill was introduced to Congress by Colorado Senator Ben Nighthorse Campbell, a member of the Northern Cheyenne tribe. The second wife of Campbell's great-grandfather was a survivor of the massacre.

October 29

The Hopi are given permission to use eagle hatchlings in a religious ceremony.

The Department of the Interior announces that it will permit the Hopi to collect golden eagle hatchlings from nests at Arizona's Wupatki National Monument. Traditionally, Hopi men gathered the hatchlings in the spring and smothered them during a July ceremony to release their spirits. Environmental organizations criticize the Interior Department's decision, maintaining that only Congress has the right to determine whether animals can be hunted on federal lands.

November

The Environmental Protection Agency (EPA) covers a mural depicting attacking Indians.

Responding to complaints by employees, including several American Indians, the Environmental Protection Agency (EPA) agrees to set up temporary displays to cover "Dangers of the Mail," a 13-foot-long mural in the agency's new headquarters in the Ariel Rios Building in Washington, D.C. The mural, painted by Colorado artist Frank Albert Mechau in the 1930s, depicts Indian warriors attacking and scalping white settlers. Although the EPA asks that the mural be removed from public view, the General Services Administration, which owns the building, announces that instead it will post signs to help viewers put the mural's images in historical context.

December 11

A band of Cahuilla receives a $14 million settlement.

After eighteen years of litigation, Congress grants the Torres-Martinez Band of Desert Cahuilla Indians $14 million in compensation for reservation lands flooded by the Colorado River in 1906. The 659 band members plan to use the settlement to purchase 11,000 acres of land and build a casino in Riverside County, California.

December 15

FBI agents protest possible clemency for Indian activist Leonard Peltier.

About 500 FBI agents march outside the White House to protest President Bill Clinton's statement that he is considering commuting the life sentence Leonard Peltier, an American Indian Movement activist convicted of the shooting deaths of two FBI agents (see entries for JUNE 16, 1975, and APRIL 18, 1977). In front of the group, several agents hold a sign reading "Never Forget." The protesters also carry a petition signed by 8,000 FBI employees opposing any reduction in Peltier's sentence. Expressing the views of many Peltier supporters, one of his attorneys, Jennifer Harbury, speaks out against the protest: "We think it's a sad day for democracy when our armed forces march through the streets to influence a decision for mercy and justice by a civilian president." (See also entry for JANUARY 20, 2001.)

"Leonard Peltier has paid a terrible price for all that the American Indian Movement was blamed for during the late 1970s.... He has paid for our nation's savagery at Wounded Knee in 1890 and 1973, and for the shame of the FBI's treatment of Pine Ridge people. He has paid for the violence of the AIM "warriors" who trashed government offices, strutted, mugged, brandished weapons and used them.... He has paid enough. It is time to let him go home."

—Chippewa novelist Louise Erdrich, on commuting Leonard Peltier's life sentence

2001

January 20

President Clinton does not pardon Leonard Peltier.

On his last day in office, President Bill Clinton grants pardons to 140 people; Leonard Peltier is not among them.

GLOSSARY

agency The complex of buildings that served as a reservation's administrative center (and that usually included the agent's living quarters). Indians often gathered at agencies to receive annuities or rations due to them by treaty.

agent An employee hired by the Bureau of Indian Affairs to manage affairs on an Indian reservation. In 1908, the position was renamed superintendent.

Aleut The native people of the 1,400-mile Aleutian island chain off of Alaska's southwestern coast. In this isolated setting, the Aleut developed a unique culture based on hunting sea otters and other water animals.

Allotment Federal Indian policy, initiated by the General Allotment Act of 1887 (also known as the Dawes Act), that called for the division of communally owned Indian land into 160-acre plots called allotments. Allotments were to be assigned to individual Indians who would hold them as private property. Opposed by most Indians, the act was supported by a majority of non-Indian politicians and reformers as a way of ending tribalism and encouraging Assimilation. The law also allowed any land left over after all eligible allottees received their plots to be sold to non-Indians. Largely through this provision, the Allotment policy allowed control over 90 million acres of land to pass from Indians to non-Indians before the policy was abandoned in 1934.

American Indian Movement (AIM) An Indian activist organization founded in Minneapolis, Minnesota, in 1968. AIM members organized many of the most successful Indian protests of the 1970s, including the Trail of Broken Treaties (1972), the Wounded Knee Occupation (1973), and the Longest Walk (1978).

annuity An annual payment due to an Indian group according to the terms of a treaty with the U.S. government. Annuities were spent by the tribe as a whole or divided among tribe members in per capita payments.

Black Hills   An area of forested mountains in southwestern South Dakota and northeastern Wyoming that is sacred to several Plains Indian tribes, including the Lakota Sioux, who consider it their people's birthplace. In the 1868 Treaty of Fort Laramie, the United States recognized the Black Hills as Lakota territory but moved to take control over the area when gold was discovered there six years later. Throughout most of the 20th century, the Lakota have battled in the courts for the return of the Black Hills.

Bureau of American Ethnology   An organization established by the U.S. government in 1879 to gather information about American Indian peoples and cultures. The bureau's annual reports exerted an enormous influence over the study of Indian history and anthropology.

Bureau of Indian Affairs (BIA)   The federal agency charged with overseeing the U.S. government's dealings with Indian groups. Established in 1824 under the War Department, the BIA was transferred to the Department of the Interior in 1849.

Code Talkers   Indian soldiers in the U.S. military who used codes based on their native languages to transmit sensitive messages. The most distinguished Code Talkers were Choctaw troops serving in World War I and Navajo (Dineh) soldiers serving in World War II.

commissioner of Indian affairs   The head administrator of the Bureau of Indian Affairs, the agency responsible for handling all of the United States's dealings with Indians. In 1977, the position was renamed assistant secretary of Indian affairs.

encomienda   A land grant in North America given to a Spanish colonist by the Spanish Crown. *Encomienda* owners routinely enslaved the natives on their lands and forced them to perform hard labor, often working them to death. Instituted in 1512, the *encomienda* system stayed in effect for more than 200 years.

federal recognition   Formal acknowledgment from the U.S. government that a group is an Indian tribe, thus entitled to the services and benefits reserved for that group. For instance, membership in a federally recognized tribe may entitle a person to special health or education benefits, the right to hunt or fish in a specific area, or a portion of land claim awards or other tribal income.

Five Civilized Tribes   The Cherokee, Seminole, Creek, Choctaw, and Chicksaw tribes. These Indian groups, whose original homelands were located in the Southeast, were considered by whites to be more "civilized" than other Indians because of their early adoption of certain non-Indian customs.

friends of the Indian   Non-Indian reformers who, in the 19th century, encouraged the U.S. government to adopt more benevolent policies toward Indians. Often wealthy easterners, the friends of the Indian generally supported the Allotment policy as a means both to help individual Indians obtain legal title to their land and to encourage assimilation into the non-Indian mainstream.

fur trade   Trade network through which Indian trappers obtained metal tools, guns, cloth, and other manufactured products from European traders in exchange for animal furs. Although Indians initially benefited from the introduction of these new goods, the fur trade soon increased Indian warfare as Indian competitors began to battle one another and as Indians were pressured to help their trading partners fight their European rivals for control over North American lands.

Indian boarding schools   Boarding schools operated by the Bureau of Indian Affairs in the late 19th and early 20th centuries where Indian children, separated from their parents, were indoctrinated in non-Indian customs while learning English and other academic subjects. Founded in 1879 by Richard Henry Pratt, the Carlisle Industrial Indian Boarding School in Carlisle, Pennsylvania, served as a model for these institutions.

Indian Claims Commission (ICC)   The commission formed by Congress in 1946 to review and resolve all outstanding land claims of Indian groups within the continental United States. Before being disbanded in 1978, the ICC heard about 300 cases and awarded Indian groups approximately $800 million in compensation for lost lands.

Indian Reorganization Act (IRA)   Law passed in 1934 that dramatically redefined the direction of federal Indian policy. The IRA formally ended the Allotment policy, which in the late 19th and early 20th centuries had dispossessed American Indians of much of their remaining landholdings. The act also renounced the government's past goal of assimilating Indians as it set forth policies intended to preserve Indian traditions and tribal life. Passed during the Roosevelt administration, the IRA is also known as the Indian New Deal, and as the Wheeler-Howard Act, after its congressional sponsors.

Indian Territory   An area west of the Mississippi River to which numerous eastern Indian groups were forced to relocate during the 19th century. Although its precise boundaries were often ill defined and were frequently changed, by 1854 Indian Territory had roughly the same borders as present-day Oklahoma. When Oklahoma was admitted into the Union in 1907, Indian Territory was dissolved.

Inuit   The native people of the arctic land stretching from central Alaska to the northern coast of Canada and onto the island of Greenland. The Inuit are better known by the name *Eskimo,* a mispronunciation of an Algonquian Indian word meaning "eaters of raw meat." Considering this term insulting, they generally prefer the term *Inuit,* which means "people" in their own language.

Iroquois Confederacy (Iroquois League, Six Nations)   A confederacy of five powerful tribes—the Cayuga, Oneida, Seneca, Mohawk, and Onondaga—native to what is now New York State. According to oral tradition, the Iroquois Confederacy was founded in about 1400 by Hiawatha, under the guidance of the Peacemaker, a Huron prophet. In 1722, a sixth tribe, the Tuscarora, was invited to join the Iroquois. The Iroquois Confederacy is also known as the Iroquois League and the Six Nations.

Long Walk   The forced relocation of the Navajo (Dineh) tribe in 1864 from their large southwestern homeland to a desolate area in what is now east-central New Mexico, known as Bosque Redondo. Large numbers of Navajo died en route, and many more starved to death or were killed by disease after their arrival. After four years of misery, the Navajo were allowed to return to a small portion of their ancestral lands in 1868.

Meriam Report   An 872-page report issued in 1928 by the Meriam Commission, a team of social scientists commissioned by the secretary of the interior to study the living conditions of Indians in the United States. Officially titled *The Problem of Indian Administration,* the document found that by all measures—including housing, health, diet, and education—Indians suffered a far lower standard of living than any other American group. The Meriam Report placed the blame for Indian poverty on past federal Indian policies, particularly Allotment. Its findings contributed to the reforms outlined in the Indian Reorganization Act of 1934.

Métis   A people in Canada of Indian and European (mostly French) ancestry. A culturally distinct group, the Métis have historically been discriminated against by both Canadian Indians and non-Indians.

Native   Term used in Canada to refer collectively to Indians, the Inuit, and the Aleut.

Native American   Term for Indians that gained popularity during the 1960s and 1970s. Although still commonly used, the term "American Indian" is now generally preferred.

Native American Church   An Indian religion, developed in the late 19th century, that blends traditional Indian beliefs with elements of Christianity. Also known as peyotism, the religion centers around lengthy ceremonies during which buttons of the peyote cactus are ingested sacramentally. Incorporated in Oklahoma in 1918, the Native American Church has long fought against efforts to ban peyote as an illegal hallucinogenic.

pan-Indianism   The phenomenon of Indians of different tribal groups banding together to work toward common goals. In the 19th century, pan-Indianism generally took the form of military alliances, such as those led by Tecumseh and Pontiac, dedicated to protecting Indian land from white encroachment. In the 20th century, Indians of varied backgrounds formed lobbying organizations (e.g., the Society of American Indians and the National Congress of American Indians) and activist groups (e.g., the Indians of All Tribes and the American Indian Movement).

Peace Policy   A policy developed by President Ulysses S. Grant designed to end violence between Indians and whites in the West. By employing clergymen and lay people active in Protestant churches, the Peace Policy sought to assimilate Indians by teaching them Christian values and encouraging them to live as settled farmers. It failed in its objectives, because most Indians refused to give up hunting as a way of life and because the government provided those few who did with such poor land that they could not survive by farming.

potlatch   A ceremony held by the Kwakiutl, Haida, and other tribes of the Pacific Northwest and British Columbia. A host family sponsors a feast during which valuable gifts are distributed to the guests. The more lavish the gift-giving, the higher the hosts are esteemed by others in the village. Deemed as a threat to non-Indian concepts of private property, the ceremony was outlawed by Canada in the late 19th century and by the United States in the early 20th.

Proclamation Line   A boundary along the crest of the Appalachian Mountains established by George III in 1763 to separate lands open to settlement by English colonists from those reserved for Indian use. The Proclamation Line was meant to assure Indians to the west of the English colonies that their lands would remain undisturbed by whites, but the colonists freely ignored the edict, leading to a series of white-Indian conflicts on the frontier.

Red Power Movement   The burst of Indian activism during the late 1960s and early 1970s. The slogan Red Power evoked Black Power, a term employed by the militant wing of the African-American civil rights movement. Using similarly aggressive tactics, Red Power groups such as the American Indian Movement used dramatic protests, covered heavily in the media, to draw attention to Indian issues.

Relocation   Federal Indian policy of the late 1940s and 1950s intended to encourage Indians on rural reservations to move to urban areas. Relocation officials lured Indians to cities with promises of better jobs and housing, but many relocatees, with little education or job training, were unable to find either. Many young urban Indians, disgruntled with their situation and eager to reestablish their roots to their tribes, later became active in the Red Power Movement.

Removal   Federal Indian policy, inaugurated by the Indian Removal Act of 1830, that sought to extinguish Indian claims to lands in the East (particularly the Southeast) by treaty and then compel eastern groups to relocate to lands west of the Mississippi River.

repatriation   The return of Indian remains and Indian-made objects in the collections of museums and individuals to their tribes of origin. Long a goal of Indian activists, repatriation became national policy with the passage of the Native American Graves Protection and Repatriation Act in 1990. This act required all federal agencies to repatriate Indian bones and artifacts and added legal protection to Indian burial sites.

reservation   A tract of land set aside by the U.S. government for the exclusive use of a specific Indian group. In Canada, reservations are known as reserves.

Self-determination   Federal Indian policy inaugurated in the 1970s that sought to give Indians more control over their political and economic affairs and promoted increased Indian involvement in government-operated programs intended to improve their standard of living. Most fully articulated in the 1975 Indian Self-Determination and Education Assistance Act, the policy was a departure from the Termination and Relocation programs, which had sought to end tribalism and eliminate Indians' special status under the law.

Sun Dance   A religious ceremony traditionally performed by Indians throughout the Great Plains. Although its rites varied from tribe to tribe, the Sun Dance often featured purification in a sweat lodge, fasting, and dancing before a sacred pole. Often sensationalized by non-Indians, missionaries and reservation agents attempted to suppress the Sun Dance in the late 19th and early 20th centuries.

Termination   Federal Indian policy, implemented by House Concurrent Resolution 108 in 1953, that sought to dissolve the tribal status of Indian groups deemed affluent enough to withstand the loss of their special protections as wards of the U.S. government. For most terminated tribes, the policy proved to be an economic disaster. The federal government formally repealed the Termination policy in 1988.

Trail of Tears   The grueling journey from the Cherokee's southeastern homeland to Indian Territory (now Oklahoma) that was made by some

14,000 Cherokee in late 1838 and early 1839. During the forced removal, approximately one-quarter of the Cherokee died from disease and starvation. The tribe referred to the tragedy as *Nunna Daul Tsunyi* ("the trail where they cried"), which whites translated as the Trail of Tears—a term sometimes used generically to refer to any removal of an Indian group from its ancestral lands.

wampum   Cylindrical white and purple beads made from quahog clam shells that northeastern Indians strung on sinew to create beaded strings and belts. Traditionally, wampum was used primarily in rituals and ceremonies. After contact, it was also used as a medium of exchange in the fur trade in the Northeast.

Wounded Knee   An area on the Pine Ridge Reservation in South Dakota that was the site of the massacre of approximately 300 Lakota Sioux women, men, and children by the U.S. Army in 1890. As a symbolic act, activists of the American Indian Movement occupied Wounded Knee for 71 days in 1973 and used the protest to attract worldwide attention to contemporary Indian issues.

Works Discussed in Entries

Adair, James. *History of the American Indians.* 1775. Reprint, New York: Promotory Press, 1974.

Allen, Paula Gunn. *The Sacred Hoop: Recovering the Feminine in American Indian Traditions.* Boston: Beacon Press, 1986.

Anderson, Owanah. *Ohoyo One Thousand: A Resource Guide of American Indian/Alaskan Native Women.* Wichita Falls, Tex.: Ohoyo Resource Center, 1982.

Annals of the Cakchiquels. Translated by Daniel G. Brinton. New York: AMS Press, 1969.

Beauchamp, W. M. *The Iroquois Trail; or, Footprints of the Six Nations in Customs, Traditions, and History; in Which Are Included David Cusick's Sketches of Ancient History of the Six Nations.* 1892. Reprint, New York: AMS Press, 1976.

Black Elk. *Black Elk Speaks: Being the Life Story of a Holy Man of the Oglala Sioux.* Edited by John G. Neihardt. 1932. Reprint, with an introduction by Vine Deloria Jr. Lincoln: University of Nebraska Press, 1988.

Blowsnake, Sam. *Crashing Thunder: The Autobiography of an American Indian.* Edited by Paul Radin. 1926. Reprint, Ann Arbor: University of Michigan Press, 1999.

Boas, Frans, and Ella Deloria. *Dakota Grammar.* 1941. Reprint, Vermillion, S.Dak.: Dakota Press, 1979.

The Book of Chilam Balam of Chumayel. Translated by Ralph L. Roys. 1933. Reprint, Norman: University of Oklahoma Press, 1967.

Brave Bird, Mary, and Richard Erdoes. *Ohitika Woman.* New York: Grove Press, 1993.

Brookings Institute. *The Problem of Indian Administration.* Baltimore: Johns Hopkins University Press, 1928.

Brown, Dee. *Bury My Heart at Wounded Knee.* New York: Bantam Books, 1971.

Cahn, Edgar S., ed. *Our Brother's Keeper: The Indian in White America.* Washington, D.C.: New Community Press, 1969.

Callahan, Sophia Alice. *Wynema: A Child of the Forest.* 1891. Reprint, edited and with an introduction by A. Lavonne Brown Ruoff, Lincoln: University of Nebraska Press, 1997.

Carter, Forrest. *The Education of Little Tree.* New York: Delacorte Press, 1976.

Castillo, Bernal Diaz del. *The Discovery and Conquest of Mexico, 1517–1521.* Edited by Genaro Garcia. Translated by A. P. Maudsley. New York: Da Capo Press, 1996.

Catlin, George. *Letters and Notes on the Manners, Customs, and Conditions of the North American Indians.* 1841. Reprint, New York: Gramercy Books, 1995.

Chief Seattle. *Brother Eagle, Sister Sky: A Message from Chief Seattle.* New York: Dial Books, 1991.

Cohen, Felix S. *Felix S. Cohen's Handbook of Federal Indian Law.* 1942. Reprint of *Handbook of Federal Indian Law,* Charlottesville, Va.: Michie, 1982.

Cooper, James Fenimore. *The Last of the Mohicans.* 1826. Reprint, with a historical introduction by James Franklin Beard, Albany: State University of New York Press, 1983.

Crow Dog, Mary, and Richard Erdoes. *Lakota Woman.* New York: G. Weidenfeld, 1990.

Deloria, Ella. *Dakota Texts.* 1932. Reprint, Vermillion, S.Dak.: Dakota Press, 1978.

Deloria, Vine, Jr. *Custer Died for Your Sins: An Indian Manifesto.* 1969. Reprint, with a new preface, Norman: University of Oklahoma Press, 1988.

———. *Red Earth, White Lies.* New York: Scribner, 1995.

———. *We Talk, You Listen.* New York: Macmillan, 1970.

Dixon, Joseph. *The Vanishing Race: The Last Great Indian Council.* 1913. Reprint, Glorieta: N.Mex.: Rio Grande Press, 1973.

Dorris, Michael. *The Broken Cord.* New York: Harper & Row, 1989.

Dye, Eva Emery. *The Conquest: The True Story of Lewis and Clark.* Chicago: A. C. McClurg & Co., 1902.

Eastman, Charles A. *Indian Boyhood.* 1902. Reprint, Lincoln: University of Nebraska Press, 1991.

Erdrich, Louise. *Love Medicine.* Expanded edition. New York: Henry Holt, 1993.

Fewkes, Jesse Walter. *Hopi Katchinas.* 1900. Reprint of *Twenty-First Annual Report of the Bureau of American Ethnology to the Secretary of the Smithsonian Institution, 1899–1900,* New York: Dover Publications, 1985.

Geronimo. *Geronimo: His Own Story.* Edited by S. M. Barrett. 1906. Reprint of *Geronimo's Story of His Life,* New York: Plume, 1996.

Glancy, Diane. *Claiming Breath.* Lincoln: University of Nebraska Press, 1992.

Grey, Zane. *The Vanishing American.* New York: Harper & Bros., 1925.

Hariot, Thomas. *Briefe and True Report of the New Found Land of Virginia.* 1590. Reprint, New York: Da Capo Press, 1971.

Hawthorne, H. B., ed. *The Survey of the Contemporary Indians of Canada.* Ottawa: Indian Affairs Branch, 1966.

Hodge, Frederick Webb. *Handbook of American Indians North of Mexico.* 2 vols. 1907–10. Reprint, New York: Greenwood Press, 1969.

Jackson, Helen Hunt. *A Century of Dishonor.* 1885. Reprint, Norman: University of Oklahoma Press, 1995.

———. *Ramona.* 1884. Reprint, New York: New American Library, 1988.

Jacobsen, Oscar Brousse. *Kiowa Indian Art.* Nice, France: C. Szwedzicki, 1929.

La Farge, Oliver. *Laughing Boy.* Boston: Houghton Mifflin, 1929.

Las Casas, Bartolomé de. *A Short Account of the Destruction of the Indies.* Edited and translated by Nigel Griffin. New York: Penguin Books, 1992.

The Lenape and Their Legends: With Complete Text and Symbols of the Walam Olum. Translated by Daniel G. Briton. Lewisburg, Pa.: Wennawoods Publishers, 1999.

Lomawaima, K. Tsianina. *They Called It Prairie Light: The Story of Chilocco Indian School.* Lincoln: University of Nebraska Press, 1994.

Longfellow, Henry Wadsworth. *The Song of Hiawatha.* 1855. Reprint, New York: Bounty Books, 1982.

Mackenzie Valley Pipeline Inquiry. *Northern Frontier, Northern Homeland.* Ottawa: Minister of Supply and Services, 1977.

Mather, Cotton. *Humiliations Followed with Deliverances.* 1697. Reprint, New York: Garland, 1977.

Mathews, John Joseph. *Wah'Kon-Tah: The Osage and the White Man's Road.* Norman: University of Oklahoma Press, 1932.

Matthews, Washington. *Navaho Legends.* 1897. Reprint, Salt Lake City: University of Utah Press, 1994.

———. *The Night Chant, a Navaho Ceremony.* 1902. Reprint, Salt Lake City: University of Utah Press, 1995.

Matthiessen, Peter. *In the Spirit of Crazy Horse.* 1983. Reprint, with a new epilogue and afterword by Martin Garbus, New York: Viking Press, 1992.

McNickle, D'Arcy. *The Surrounded.* 1936. Reprint, Albuquerque: University of New Mexico Press, 1978.

Meachem, A. B. *Wi-Ne-Ma (The Woman-Chief) and Her People.* 1876. Reprint, New York: AMS Press, 1980.

Mealing, S. R., ed. *The Jesuit Relations and Allied Documents.* Toronto: McClelland and Steward, 1963.

Momaday, N. Scott. *House Made of Dawn.* 1968. Reprint, Tucson: University of Arizona Press, 1996.

Morgan, Lewis Henry. *League of the Ho-de-no-sau-nee.* 2 vols. 1901. Reprint, edited and annotated by Herbert M. Lloyd, New York: B. Franklin, 1966.

Mountain Wolf Woman. *Mountain Wolf Woman, Sister of Crashing Thunder.* Edited by Nancy Lurie. Ann Arbor: University of Michigan Press, 1961.

Mourning Dove. *Cogewea: The Half-Blood.* 1927. Reprint, Lincoln: University of Nebraska Press, 1981.

———. *Coyote Stories.* 1933. Reprint, Lincoln: University of Nebraska Press, 1990.

Núñez Cabeza de Vaca, Alvar. *Cabeza de Vaca's Adventures in the Unknown Interior of America.* Translated by Cyclone Covey. Albuquerque: University of New Mexico Press, 1961.

O'Connell, Barry, ed. *On Our Own Ground: The Complete Writings of William Apess, a Pequot.* Amherst: University of Massachusetts Press, 1992.

O'Dell, Scott. *Island of the Blue Dolphins.* Boston: Houghton Mifflin, 1960.

Parker, Arthur C. *The Code of Handsome Lake, the Seneca Prophet.* Albany: University of the State of New York, 1913.

Pokagon, Simon. *O-Gi-Maw-Kwe Mit-I-Gwa-Ki.* Hartford, Mich.: C. H. Engle, 1899.

Popul Vuh: The Mayan Book of the Dawn of Life. Translated by Ted Tedlock. New York: Simon & Schuster, 1996.

Powell, Peter J. *Sweet Medicine.* 2 vols. Norman: University of Oklahoma Press, 1988.

Ridge, John Rollin. *The Life and Adventures of Joaquin Murieta.* 1854. Reprint, Norman: University of Oklahoma Press, 1955.

Riggs, Lynn. *Green Grow the Lilacs.* New York: S. French, 1931.

Rousseau, Jean-Jacques. *Discourse upon the Origin of Inequality.* Translated by Franklin Philip. Edited and with an introduction by Patrick Coleman. New York: Oxford University Press, 1994.

Rowlandson, Mary. *A True History of the Captivity and Restauration of Mrs. Mary Rowlandson.* 1697. Reprint, New York: Garland, 1977.

Sahagun, Bernardino de. *General History of the Things of New Mexico.* 13 vols. Translated by Arthur J. O. Anderson and Charles E. Dibble. Santa Fe, N.Mex.: School of American Research, 1953–1982.

Scholder, Fritz, T. C. Cannon, and Adelyn Breeskin. *Two American Painters: Fritz Scholder and T. C. Cannon.* Washington, D.C.: Smithsonian Institution Press, 1972.

Schoolcraft, Henry Rowe. *Indian Tribes of the United States.* 6 vols. 1851. Reprint, New York: Paladin Press, 1969.

Seaver, James E. *A Narrative of the Life of Mrs. Mary Jemison.* 1824. Reprint, Norman: University of Oklahoma Press, 1992.

Silko, Leslie Marmon. *Ceremony.* New York: Viking Press, 1977.

Smith, John. *The Complete Works of Captain John Smith.* Edited by Philip L. Barbour. Chapel Hill: University of North Carolina Press, 1986.

Spicer, Edward. *Cycles of Conquest: The Impact of Spain, Mexico, and the United States on the Indians of the Southwest, 1533–1960.* Tucson: University of Arizona Press, 1962.

Squier, Ephraim G., and Edwin H. Davis. *Ancient Monuments of the Mississippi Valley.* 1848. Reprint, edited and with an introduction by David J. Meltzer, Washington, D.C.: Smithsonian Institution Press, 1998.

Starr, Emmet. *History of the Cherokee Indians.* 1921. Reprint, Tulsa: Oklahoma Yesterday, 1979.

Swift, Jonathan. *Gulliver's Travels.* 1726. Reprint, New York: Alfred A. Knopf, 1991.

Tanner, John. *The Falcon: Narrative of the Captivity and Adventures of John Tanner.* 1830. Reprint, with an introduction by Louise Erdrich, New York: Penguin Books, 1994.

Tocqueville, Alexis de. *Democracy in America.* Translated by Henry Reeves. New York: Alfred A. Knopf, 1994.

Underhill, Ruth. *Papago Woman.* 1936. Reprint of *An Autobiography of a Papago Woman,* New York: Holt, Rinehart and Winston, 1979.

Vespucci, Amerigo. *Letters from a New World: Amerigo Vespucci's Discovery of America.* Translated by David Jacobson. Edited and with an introduction by Luciano Formisano. New York: Marsilio, 1992.

Vestal, Stanley. *Warpath: The True Story of the Fighting Sioux Told in a Biography of Chief White Bull.* 1934. Reprint, Lincoln: University of Nebraska Press, 1984.

Warren, William W. *History of the Ojibway People.* 1885. Reprint of *History of the Ojibways,* St. Paul: Minnesota Historical Society Press, 1984.

Williams, Roger. *A Key into the Language of America.* 1643. Reprint, edited by John J. Teunissen and Evelyn J. Hinz, Detroit: Wayne State University Press, 1973.

Winnemucca, Sarah. *Life among the Piutes: Their Wrongs and Claims.* 1883. Reprint, Reno: University of Nevada Press, 1994.

Wuttunee, William I. C. *Ruffled Feathers: Indians in Canadian Society.* Calgary: Alberta Bell Books, 1972.

Zepeda, Ofelia. *A Papago Grammar.* Tucson: University of Arizona Press, 1983.

Selected Bibliography

General

Albers, Patricia, and Beatrice Medicine. *The Hidden Half: Studies in Plains Indian Women.* Washington, D.C.: University Press of America, 1983.

Berkhofer, Robert F., Jr. *The White Man's Indian: Images of the American Indian from Columbus to the Present.* New York: Alfred A. Knopf, 1978.

Bruchac, Joseph, ed. *Smoke Rising: The Native American Literary Companion.* Detroit: Visible Ink Press, 1995.

Calloway, Colin G., ed. *New Directions in American Indian History.* Norman: University of Oklahoma Press, 1988.

Champagne, Duane. *Native America: Portrait of the Peoples.* Detroit: Visible Ink Press, 1994.

Debo, Angie. *A History of the Indians of the United States.* Norman: University of Oklahoma Press, 1970.

Dickason, Olive Patricia. *Canada's First Nations: A History of Founding Peoples from Earliest Times.* Norman: University of Oklahoma Press, 1992.

Dockstader, Frederick J. *Indian Art in America: The Arts and Crafts of the North American Indian.* Greenwood, Conn.: New York Graphic Society, 1961.

Editors of Time-Life Books. *The American Indians.* 10 vols. Alexandria, Va.: Time-Life Books, 1992–94.

Erdoes, Richard, and Alfonso Ortiz, eds. *American Indian Myths and Legends.* New York: Pantheon Books, 1984.

Feest, Christian F. *Native Arts of North America.* New York: Oxford University Press, 1980.

Hagan, William T. *American Indians.* 3d edition. Chicago: University of Chicago Press, 1993.

Hoxie, Frederick E., ed. *Indians in American History: An Introduction.* Arlington Heights, Ill.: Harlan Davidson, 1988.

Iverson, Peter. *"We Are Still Here": American Indians in the Twentieth Century.* Wheeling, Ill.: Harlan Davidson, 1998.

Josephy, Alvin M. *500 Nations: An Illustrated History of North American Indians.* New York: Alfred A. Knopf, 1994.

Leacock, Eleanor Burke, and Nancy O. Lurie, eds. *North American Indians in Historical Perspective.* New York: Random House, 1971.

Miller, J. R. *Skyscrapers Hide the Heavens: A History of Indian-White Relations in Canada.* Toronto: University of Toronto Press, 1989.

Miller, Mary Ellen. *The Art of Mesoamerica.* London: Thames and Hudson, 1986.

Nabokov, Peter, and Robert Easton. *Native American Architecture.* New York: Oxford University Press, 1989.

Olson, James S., and Raymond Wilson. *Native Americans in the Twentieth Century.* Provo, Utah: Brigham Young University Press, 1984.

Prucha, Francis Paul. *The Great Father: The United States Government and the American Indians.* Lincoln: University of Nebraska Press, 1986.

Sturtevant, William C., ed. *Handbook of North American Indians.* 11 vols. Washington, D.C.: Smithsonian Institution, 1978–98.

Trigger, Bruce G., and Wilcomb E. Washburn, eds. *North America,* Parts 1 and 2. Vol. 1 of *The Cambridge History of Native American Peoples of the Americas.* New York: Cambridge University Press, 1996.

Utley, Robert M., and Wilcomb E. Washburn. *The American Heritage History of the Indian Wars.* Boston: Houghton Mifflin, 1977.

Viola, Herman J. *After Columbus: The Smithsonian Chronicle of the North American Indian.* Washington, D.C.: Smithsonian Books, 1990.

Waldman, Carl. *Atlas of the North American Indian.* Revised edition. New York: Facts On File, 2000.

Weatherford, Jack. *Indian Givers: How the Indians of the Americas Transformed the World.* New York: Crown Publishers, 1988.

Weeks, Philip. *Farewell, My Nation: The American Indian and the United States, 1820–1890.* Wheeling, Ill.: Harlan Davidson, 1990.

Wilkinson, Charles F. *American Indians, Time, and the Law: Historical Rights at the Bar of the Supreme Court.* New Haven, Conn.: Yale University Press, 1987.

Wilson, James. *The Earth Shall Weep: A History of Native America.* New York: Atlantic Monthly Press, 1996.

Bibliographies

Bataille, Gretchen M., and Charles L. P. Silet. *Images of American Indians on Film: An Annotated Bibliography.* New York: Garland Publishing, 1985.

Brumble, H. David, III. *An Annotated Bibliography of American Indian and Eskimo Autobiographies.* Lincoln: University of Nebraska Press, 1981.

Green, Rayna. *Native American Women: A Contextual Bibliography.* Bloomington: Indiana University Press, 1983.

Hoxie, Frederick, and Harvey Markowitz. *Native Americans: An Annotated Bibliography.* Pasadena, Calif.: Salem Press, 1991.

Prucha, Francis Paul. *A Bibliographical Guide to the History of Indian-White Relations in the United States.* Chicago: University of Chicago Press, 1977.

———. *Indian-White Relations in the United States: A Bibliography of Works Published, 1975–1980.* Lincoln: University of Nebraska Press, 1982.

Ruoff, A. Lavonne Brown. *American Indian Literatures: An Introduction, Bibliographic Review, and Selected Bibliography.* New York: Modern Language Association of America, 1990.

Biographical Sketches and Dictionaries

Bataille, Gretchen M., ed. *Native American Women.* New York: Garland Publishing, 1993.

Clifton, James A., ed. *Being and Becoming Indian: Biographical Studies of North American Frontiers.* Belmont, Calif.: Wadsworth, 1989.

Dockstader, Frederick J. *Great North American Leaders: Profiles in Life and Leadership.* New York: Van Nostrand Reinhold, 1977.

Grumet, Robert S., ed. *Northeastern Indian Lives, 1632–1816.* Amherst: University of Massachusetts Press, 1996.

Edmunds, R. David, ed. *American Indian Leaders.* Lincoln: University of Nebraska Press, 1980.

Johansen, Bruce E., and Donald A. Grinde, Jr. *The Encyclopedia of Native American Biography.* New York: Henry Holt, 1997.

Josephy, Alvin M. *The Patriot Chiefs: A Chronicle of American Indian Leadership.* New York: Viking Press, 1961.

Malinowski, Sharon, ed. *Notable Native Americans.* Detroit: Gale Research, 1995.

Matuz, Roger, ed. *The St. James Guide to Native North American Artists.* Detroit: St. James Press, 1998.

Moses, L. G., and Raymond Wilson, eds. *Indian Lives: Essays on Nineteenth- and Twentieth-Century Native American Leaders.* Albuquerque: University of New Mexico Press, 1985.

Sonneborn, Liz. *A to Z of Native American Women.* New York: Facts On File, 1998.

Waldman, Carl. *Who Was Who in Native American History.* New York: Facts On File, 1990.

Chronologies

Champagne, Duane, ed. *Chronology of Native North American History.* Detroit: Gale Research, 1994.

Dennis, Henry C., ed. *The American Indian, 1492–1976: A Chronology and Fact Book.* Dobbs Ferry, N.Y.: Oceana, 1977.

Francis, Lee. *Native Time: A Historical Time Line of Native America.* New York: St. Martin's Press, 1998.

Hazen-Hammond, Susan. *Timelines of Native American History.* New York: Perigee, 1997.

Nies, Judith. *Native American History.* New York: Ballantine Books, 1996.

Document and Quotation Collections

Armstrong, Virginia Irving, ed. *I Have Spoken: American History through the Voices of the Indians.* Chicago: Sage Books, 1971.

Deloria, Vine, Jr., ed. *Of Utmost Good Faith.* San Francisco: Straight Arrow Books, 1971.

Josephy, Alvin M., ed. *Red Power: The American Indians' Fight for Freedom.* New York: American Heritage Press, 1971.

Langer, Howard J., ed. *American Indian Quotations.* Westport, Conn.: Greenwood Press, 1996.

Miller, Lee, ed. *From the Heart: Voices of the American Indian.* New York: Alfred A. Knopf, 1995.

Moquin, Walter, and Charles Van Doren, eds. *Great Documents in American Indian History.* New York: Praeger Publishers, 1973.

Nabokov, Peter, ed. *Native American Testimony: A Chronicle of Indian-White Relations from Prophecy to the Present, 1492–1992.* New York: Viking Press, 1991.

Prucha, Francis Paul, ed. *Documents of United States Indian Policy.* 2d ed. Lincoln: University of Nebraska Press, 1990.

Rosenstiel, Annette. *Red & White: Indian Views of the White Man, 1492–1982.* New York: Universe Books, 1983.

Straub, Deborah Gillan, ed. *Native North American Voices.* Detroit: UXL, 1997.

Vogel, Virgil J. *This Country Was Ours: A Documentary History of the American Indian.* New York: Harper & Row, 1972.

Encyclopedias

Champagne, Duane. *Native America: Portrait of the Peoples.* Detroit: Visible Ink Press, 1994.

Davis, Mary B., ed. *Native America in the Twentieth Century: An Encyclopedia.* New York: Garland Publishing, 1996.

Gill, Sam D., and Irene F. Sullivan. *Dictionary of Native American Mythology.* Santa Barbara, Calif.: ABC-CLIO, 1992.

Grossman, Mark. *The ABC-CLIO Companion to the Native American Rights Movement.* Santa Barbara, Calif.: ABC-CLIO, 1996.

Hirschfelder, Arlene, and Paulette Molin. *Encyclopedia of Native American Religions.* Updated edition. New York: Facts On File, 2000.

Hoxie, Frederick E., ed. *Encyclopedia of North American Indians.* Boston: Houghton Mifflin, 1996.

Keenan, Jerry. *Encyclopedia of Indian Wars, 1492–1890.* Santa Barbara, Calif.: ABC-CLIO, 1997.

Olson, James S., ed. *Encyclopedia of American Indian Civil Rights.* Westport, Conn.: Greenwood Press, 1997.

Pritzker, Barry M. *Native Americans: An Encyclopedia of History, Culture, and Peoples.* 2 vols. Santa Barbara, Calif.: ABC-CLIO, 1998.

Waldman, Carl. *Encyclopedia of Native American Tribes.* Revised edition. New York: Facts On File, 1999.

Works Specific to Chapters

CHAPTER 1: BEFORE 1492

Coe, Michael D., et al. *Atlas of Ancient America.* New York: Facts On File, 1986.

Fagan, Brian M. *Ancient North America.* New York: Thames and Hudson, 1991.

———. *The Great Journey: The Peopling of Ancient America.* New York: Thames and Hudson, 1987.

Josephy, Alvin M., ed. *America in 1492: The World of the Indian Peoples before the Arrival of Columbus.* New York: Alfred A. Knopf, 1992.

Snow, Dean. *The American Indians: Their Archaeology and Prehistory.* New York: Thames and Hudson, 1976.

CHAPTER 2: 1492 TO 1606

Crosby, Alfred W. *The Columbian Exchange: Biological and Cultural Consequences of 1492.* Westport, Conn.: Greenwood Press, 1972.

Kupperman, Karen O. *Settling with the Indians: The Meeting of English and Indian Cultures in America, 1580–1640.* Totowa, N.J.: Rowman & Littlefield, 1980.

Morrison, Samuel Eliot. *The European Discovery of America.* 2 vols. New York: Oxford University Press, 1974.

Salisbury, Neal. *Manitou and Providence: Indians, Europeans, and the Making of New England, 1500–1643.* New York: Oxford University Press, 1982.

Tyler, S. Lyman. *Two Worlds: The Indian Encounter with the European, 1942–1509.* Salt Lake City: University of Utah Press, 1987.

Viola, Herman J., and Carolyn Margolis, eds. *Seeds of Change: A Quincentennial Commemoration.* Washington, D.C.: Smithsonian Institution Press, 1991.

CHAPTER 3: 1607 TO 1775

Jacobs, Wilbur R. *Dispossessing the American Indian: Indians and Whites on the Colonial Frontier.* Norman: University of Oklahoma Press, 1972.

Jennings, Francis. *The Invasion of America: Indians, Colonialism, and the Cant of Conquest.* Chapel Hill: University of North Carolina, 1975.

Lepore, Jill. *The Name of War: King Philip's War and the Origins of American Identity.* New York: Alfred A. Knopf, 1998.

Nash, Gary B. *Red, White, and Black: The Peoples of Early America.* Englewood Cliffs, N.J.: Prentice-Hall, 1974.

Steele, Ian K. *Warpaths: Invasions of North America.* New York: Oxford University Press, 1994.

Szasz, Margaret C. *Indian Education in the American Colonies, 1607–1783.* Albuquerque: University of New Mexico Press, 1988.

CHAPTER 4: 1776 TO 1829

Berkhofer, Robert F., Jr. *Salvation and His Savage: An Analysis of Protestant Missions and American Indian Response, 1787–1862.* New York: Atheneum, 1972.

Calloway, Colin G. *Crown and Calumet: British-Indian Relations, 1783–1815.* Norman: University of Oklahoma Press, 1987.

Graymont, Barbara. *The Iroquois in the American Revolution.* Syracuse, N.Y.: Syracuse University Press, 1972.

Harsman, Reginald. *Expansion and American Indian Policy, 1783–1812.* East Lansing: Michigan State University Press, 1967.

Prucha, Francis Paul. *American Indian Policy in the Formative Years, 1790–1834.* Cambridge, Mass.: Harvard University Press, 1962.

Sheehan, Bernard W. *Seeds of Extinction: Jeffersonian Philanthropy and the American Indian.* Chapel Hill: University of North Carolina Press, 1973.

CHAPTER 5: 1830 TO 1865

Ehle, John. *Trail of Tears: The Rise and Fall of the Cherokee Nation.* New York: Anchor Books, 1988.

Foreman, Grant. *Indian Removal: The Emigration of the Five Civilized Tribes of Indians.* 1932. Reprint, Norman: University of Oklahoma Press, 1986.

Hoig, Stan. *The Sand Creek Massacre.* Norman: University of Oklahoma Press, 1961.

Satz, Ronald N. *American Indian Policy in the Jacksonian Era.* Lincoln: University of Nebraska Press, 1975.

Trennert, Robert A., Jr., *Alternative to Extinction: Federal Indian Policy and the Beginnings of the Reservation System, 1846–51.* Philadelphia: Temple University Press, 1975.

CHAPTER 6: 1866 TO 1890

Brown, Dee. *Bury My Heart at Wounded Knee.* New York: Bantam Books, 1971.

Dunlay, Thomas W. *Wolves for the Blue Soldiers: Indian Scouts and Auxiliaries with the United States Army, 1860–1890.* Lincoln: University of Nebraska Press, 1982.

Fritz, Henry E. *The Movement for Indian Assimilation, 1860–1890.* Philadelphia: University of Pennsylvania Press, 1963.

Mooney, James. *The Ghost Dance Religion and the Sioux Outbreak of 1890.* 1896. Reprint, Lincoln: University of Nebraska Press, 1991.

Prucha, Francis Paul. *American Indian Policy in Crisis: Christian Reformers and the Indian, 1865–1900.* Cambridge, Mass.: Harvard University Press, 1962.

Roberts, David. *Once They Moved Like the Wind: Cochise, Geronimo, and the Apache Wars.* New York: Simon & Schuster, 1993.

Utley, Robert M. *The Indian Frontier of the American West, 1846–1890.* Albuquerque: University of New Mexico Press, 1984.

CHAPTER 7: 1891 TO 1933

Hertzberg, Hazel W. *The Search for an American Indian Identity: Modern Pan-Indian Movements.* Syracuse, N.Y.: Syracuse University Press, 1971.

Hoxie, Frederick. *A Final Promise: The Campaign to Assimilate the Indians, 1880–1920.* Lincoln: University of Nebraska Press, 1984.

Iverson, Peter. *Carlos Montezuma and the Changing World of American Indians.* Albuquerque: University of New Mexico Press, 1982.

Meriam, Lewis. *The Problems of Indian Administration.* 1928. Reprint, New York: Johnson Reprint, 1971.

Philip, Kenneth R. *John Collier's Crusade for Indian Reform: 1920–1954.* Tucson: University of Arizona Press, 1977.

Taylor, Graham D. *The New Deal and American Indian Tribalism: The Administration of the Indian Reorganization Act, 1934–1945.* Lincoln: University of Nebraska Press, 1980.

CHAPTER 8: 1934 TO 1968

Burt, Larry W. *Tribalism in Crisis: Federal Indian Policy, 1953–61.* Albuquerque: University of New Mexico Press, 1982.

Drinnon, Richard. *Keeper of Concentration Camps: Dillon S. Myer and American Racism.* Berkeley: University of California Press, 1987.

Fixico, Donald L. *Termination and Relocation: Federal Indian Policy, 1945–1966.* Albuquerque: University of New Mexico Press, 1986.

Steiner, Stan. *The New Indians.* New York: Harper & Row, 1967.

Szasz, Margaret C. *Education and the American Indian: The Road to Self-Determination, 1928–1973.* 2d ed. Albuquerque: University of New Mexico Press, 1977.

CHAPTER 9: 1969 TO 1979

Deloria, Vine, Jr. *Custer Died for Your Sins: An Indian Manifesto.* 1969. Reprint, with a new preface, Norman: University of Oklahoma Press, 1988.

Johnson, Troy, Joane Nagel, and Duane Champaign, eds. *American Indian Activism.* Urbana: University of Illinois Press, 1997.

Josephy, Alvin M. *Now That the Buffalo's Gone: A Study of Today's American Indians.* New York: Alfred A. Knopf, 1982.

Matthiessen, Peter. *In the Spirit of Crazy Horse.* New York: Viking Penguin, 1991.

Smith, Paul Chaat, and Robert Allen Warrior. *Like a Hurricane: The Indian Movement from Alcatraz to Wounded Knee.* New York: New Press, 1996.

CHAPTER 10: 1980 TO THE PRESENT

Cornell, Stephen. *The Return of the Native: American Indian Political Resurgence.* New York: Oxford University Press, 1988.

Frantz, Klaus. *Indian Reservations in the United States: Territory, Sovereignty, and Socioeconomic Change.* Chicago: University of Chicago Press, 1999.

Hirschfelder, Arlene B., and Martha Kreipe DeMonaño. *The Native American Almanac: A Portrait of Native America Today.* New York: Prentice-Hall, 1993.

Mason, W. Dale. *Indian Gaming: Tribal Sovereignty and American Politics.* Norman: University of Oklahoma Press, 2000.

McMaster, Gerald, ed. *Reservation X.* Seattle: University of Washington Press, 1999.

Index

Page numbers set in italics indicate photographs or *illustrations*.
Page numbers followed by *m* indicate maps.